NEONATE COGNITION:

Beyond the Blooming Buzzing Confusion

NEONATE COGNITION:

Beyond the Blooming Buzzing Confusion

Edited by

JACQUES MEHLER

École des Hautes Études en Sciences Sociales

Centre National de la Recherche Scientifique

Paris

ROBIN FOX

Rutgers University

LAWRENCE ERLBAUM ASSOCIATES, PUBLISHERS
1985   Hillsdale, New Jersey   London

Lawrence Erlbaum Associates, Inc., Publishers
365 Broadway
Hillsdale, New Jersey 07642

Library of Congress Cataloging in Publication Data
Main entry under title:

Neonate cognition.

Includes bibliographies and indexes.
1. Cognition in children. 2. Infant psychology.
I. Mehler, Jacques. II. Fox, Robin, 1934-   .
BF723.C5N45 1985   155.4'22   84-18664
ISBN 0-89859-345-X

Printed in the United States of America
10 9 8 7 6 5 4 3 2 1

Contents

Preface

Although the editors of this book are responsible jointly for the text, I would like to take this opportunity to thank Robin Fox for his friendly encouragement and ceaseless support and Lionel Tiger for his interest and enthusiasm. I have special thanks for the Harry Frank Guggenheim Foundation, who financed the Conference on Neonate Cognition and therefore made this book possible, and I would also like to say that I am particularly grateful to them for having funded much of the work reported in my chapter. My thanks also go to Karen Colvard, a perfect organizer who helped bring this project to fruition.

Some of my friends—namely, Tom Bever and John Morton—have taught me many of the ideas that go unannotated in my chapter. So have many of the authors of other chapters. I am most grateful to all of them. In addition, I would like to thank Josiane Bertoncini, Peter Eimas, Peter Jusczyk, Andrea Levitt, Joanna Miller and Virginia Valian for many helpful suggestions and careful corrections. Betsy Carpenter fought with the style of a first draft of my chapter, trying to undo all sorts of romance language influences. I would like to thank her and Laura Becker for their help.

I am grateful to the MIT Center for Cognitive Science for extending me their hospitality, support, and facilities during the preparation of this book.

Finally, my ceaseless gratitude to Susana Franck for her assistance on an unenumerable list of things.

Jacques Mehler

Introduction:
Some Reflections on
Initial State Research

Jacques Mehler
C.N.R.S.

> *Que cette théorie fut génial j'en avais jamais douté, mais ce qui*
> *me plongeait dans le désespoir, c'était son application à la pratique.*
> —Mikhail Bulgakov
> *Roman Théatrale*

Before the 1960s, by and large, psychologists turned their backs on the study
of the psychological capacities of the neonate. Recent investigations, some of
which appear in this book, point to a new chapter in psychology: Neonate
cognition. This research has benefitted from methodological advances in the
study of neonates, and also from the development of models in cognitive psychology, biology, and computer science. Specifically, information processing
models help to describe the stable structures that underlie the infant's representation of the world, and biological mechanisms may provide a means of explaining the changes in structure during the growth of the mind. In other words, the
information processing approach helps to describe what is represented in the
infant and at what levels. This approach is in some respects ill-suited to the
work, however, because the infant changes so rapidly; information processing
models deal with stable structures while those of the infant change continually.
Explanations of change in the infant's mind are often obscure. The nervous
system and the mind evolve very rapidly; but how changes in the brain affect
changes in the mind is not well understood, given the great difficulty of assessing
the maturational and environmental determinants. It would be equally wrong to
claim that grammars are learned and skiing (for example) innate. Grammars
result from specific mechanisms operating on universal grammar, and skiing

from practice on snowy slopes. But even skiing can be viewed as a recombination of preexisting sensorimotor capacities into a new action program.

Neonate cognition also offers a promising paradigm for neuropsychological studies. Neuropsychologists attempt to relate mental faculties and behaviors to neurological structures and mechanisms; most of the data are obtained by the careful study of patients with brain lesions. The study of lesions, however, has limitations in that brain damage probably disrupts uninjured as well as injured areas of the brain. Furthermore, the brain is an amazingly complex structure: 10^{11} neurons, each with as many as 10^6 synaptic connections. It is almost impossible to establish meaningful correlations between lesions and behavior in a system as complex as this. In this volume, it is argued that findings from developmental studies of the brain will increase our understanding of the relation between brain and behavior.

Neonate cognition has an added interest for psychology in that it can help illuminate the irreducible properties of the higher mental faculties, such as language, mathematics, and logic. Linguists, for example, have tried to infer universal properties of mind—specifically, properties of the language faculty—from the structure of language. Many mathematicians and logicians have engaged in a similar search. From these investigations we have inherited some of the richest and most productive models in cognitive psychology (see Chomsky, 1982). Nonetheless, psychologists have never agreed on the universals that formalists have proposed. Studies of the neonate may provide critical evidence for some of these universals. When a proposed universal meets with a positive test in the neonate, it can be confidently included in a list of basic properties of the human mind. Studies of the neonate, however, will not be useful in the negative cases. For instance, questions regarding inherent properties of the lexicon seem untestable in the neonate, because neonates have not yet acquired any lexical items. In contrast, if we can show that at birth an infant is able to imitate facial gestures, it seems legitimate to infer that a baby comes equipped with an internal representation of faces, including his or her own.

In the last 10 years, psychologists concerned with infancy have carried out explorations of deeper mental representations in conjunction with the more traditional study of psychophysical interaction. Indeed, the infant's representation of knowledge is becoming the main concern of neonatal studies. My own laboratory has studied the representation of phonology and the cerebral organization that allows infants to process speech.

An issue that touches all of neonate cognition is the specific nature of psychological abilities. Is language mediated by a language module, music by a music module, and so forth? Or is there, alternatively, a general device that underlies all mental faculties? Psychologists who believe in a modular account of the mind individuate faculties by reference to their typical effects; for instance, Fodor (1983) associates the language faculty with "whatever piece of machinery that functions to mediate the assimilation and employment of verbal capacities" (p. 10). Psychologists who espouse empiricism—an equally influential position—

believe that there is a homogeneity of process across domains, and that the mind functions as an undifferentiated whole. Neonate cognition explores whether faculties exist autonomously of each other and tries to identify the effects of environmental stimulation on different faculties. Neonate cognition also establishes whether modules that are individuated in adult behaviors appear and emerge independently of each other.

What Learning Will Not Do

Psychologists, having discovered that the human mind is not solely the product of learning, study the neonate to understand the determinants of the mind's structure. If the mind were the product of the physical regularities in the environment, nobody would study the capacities of the unexposed mind. Conversely, if the unexposed mind were structured to organize sensory and perceptual events into representations, then initial state research would uncover basic cognitive universals. In this view, the human mind is endowed with cognitive capacities as well as sensory and behavioral capacities. For example, Chomsky argues that the child must be born with *Universal Grammar*, i.e., a number of computational competencies that are used only in language processing. Theoretical linguistics formulates hypotheses about the initial state, compatible with the ability to learn any and all natural languages. Psychologists are interested in the same problem and are also interested in the device that makes language acquisition possible. Linguistic and psychological interests are complementary to each other, because in order to understand the nature of the language acquisition device, it is necessary to understand both the structure of natural languages and the information-processing abilities typical of the human mind. It is possible that similar collaborations will develop in the study of other cognitive domains, such as logic, mathematics, and knowledge of the physical world. In the latter cases, psychologists may rely on infant studies to determine the properties of the initial acquisition devices.

At birth, however, all abilities characteristic of the adult are not yet in their initial state. Infants, at a given age, can be precompetent regarding some ability, while being fully competent regarding another one. The initial state, for some abilities, is not obtained at birth, but only after all necessary neurological structures have matured. Chomsky has often stated a very similar view. Likewise, in her chapter in this volume, Carey gives a similar definition of the initial state. This way of conceiving of initial-state studies invites a close collaboration with colleagues working on developmental neuroanatomy and related disciplines.

Maturation and Development

The study of representations from infancy onward could make it possible to found neuropsychology on a broader grounding than it currently has. Neuropsychology has two major motivations: One, purely theoretical, is to gain a better understanding of the relation of mind and underlying biological mechanisms;

the other, pragmatical, is to try to relate observed syndromes of the mind to the putative neurological accidents that might have caused them.

Language disorders have been the object of numerous studies since Dax and Broca first observed that injuries to the left hemisphere (LH) often result in loss of speech production or comprehension. Neurologists having to treat patients use the symptoms to make diagnostic and prognostic statements. A major problem with neuropsychology stems from the correlational basis for all its propositions (i.e., if such an area is damaged, such a symptom will be observed). However, lesions do not necessarily constitute an equivalence class. Some lesions have instantaneous onsets, while others grow over time (CVAs and tumors are good examples). Certain kinds of injuries result in rearrangements of the cortical architecture, with age at time of injury determining the extent of possible rearrangements.

Gathering reliable neuropsychological evidence only from cerebral injury seems an unnecessary limitation. This approach can be complemented by correlating psychological changes during growth with the change and maturation of the central nervous system. Studies of brain maturation are instrumental to understanding physiological mechanisms controlling neuronal growth. These mechanisms will clarify the determinants of changes in the neuronal networks. However, the functional significance of these changes will remain obscure until a description of the corresponding psychological changes becomes available. Only when the development of cognitive functions and of cortical organization is achieved will it be possible to understand the nature of the correlations, thereby making further predictions possible on the basis of a better understanding of the interrelation of brain and psychological function.

Given the obvious potential for developmental neuropsychology, as discussed previously, experimental studies of infant cognition are bound to witness substantial expansion in the years to come. This is only one of the reasons why it seems desirable to keep the field of infant cognition fairly well connected with the biological disciplines. Mehler et al. (1983) have argued that psychological accounts alone will never explain the growth of the mind. Psychological studies may, at best, give a complete description of the structure of the mind's processes, the nature of the information handling devices that comprise it, and so forth. However, the biological sciences seem currently best equipped to explain both the causes for growth and the nature of the growing itself.

Finally, it is interesting to relate neonate neuropsychology to the disciplines related to Artificial Intelligence (AI). Insofar as AI sticks to its aim of giving actual programs for the behaviors studied by psychologists, the collaboration will be of limited interest. But, with the emergence of a number of AI investigators who are more interested in the general computational approach to the study of mind rather than its particular embodiment in a realistic program, more and more interesting and profitable exchanges seem to be taking place. Both Osherson and Pylyshyn (in this volume) agree that the AI approach provides psychology with an explanatory model of the mind. What remains to be done is to relate the AI and the biological perspectives, to get more rigorous and more realistic models for the growth of the mind.

Learning accounts do not provide explanations for the deterministic changes in psychological processing observed during development. This point has been made quite convincingly by Fodor (1975) and by Chomsky (1982). Mehler (1974) has argued that the only kind of change that psychologists seem capable of explaining is learning by the impoverishment of very rich initial states. Learning by enrichment remains as much a mystery today as it always has been, and the biological processes currently provide the best causal model by which changes in behavior can be explained. In the years to come, it is hoped that more attempts will be made to explain development in reference to biological processes. Changeux, in his chapter, explores some interesting models that deserve to be considered in the psychological sciences.

Studies of Representation

As this book attests, most research in infant psychology has dwelled on sensory-perceptual capacities. These studies have resulted in a better understanding of what the infant can see, hear, or smell. Other studies have focused on sensorimotor abilities, and some progress has been made in that domain as well. Central domains, related to the representation of knowledge, and in general to the computational potential of the organism, remain by and large unexplored.[1] Thus, very little can be said at this time about memory, imagery, linguistic dispositions, and other central faculties of the infant's mind. Recently, psychologists have shown signs of renewed interest in studying neonate cognition. After successfully developing methods for exploring peripheral systems, experimenters are now studying methods suitable for the study of central faculties. Some have tried using delayed responses, others memory traces, and yet others cross-modal tests. Imitation is also being used as a method to explore the nature of representation. Be this as it may, more psychologists seem confident studying central processing abilities in the infant, and projects are emerging simultaneously in many different laboratories. In the years to come, our understanding of central processes in infant cognition ought to occupy a more important place.

---

[1]Fodor (1983) has argued that the intrinsic opaqueness of the central faculties is likely to be an insurmountable limitation in cognitive studies rather than a temporary neglect. His argument can be paraphrased by saying that experimentalists at best are capable of doing serious psychophysics. If Fodor turns out to be right, studies with infants ought to suffer from the same intrinsic limitation as studies with adults. However, it is possible that limitations of the kind that make Fodor unhappy with cognitive studies are always voiced by practitioners who are exploring new ground, irrespective of the discipline they are investigating.

Some Shortcomings of Neonatal Cognition

The domains included in this book are partial and to some extent unfairly so. No attention is paid to studies of mother-infant interaction, or cognitive representation of emotion, states of activation, memory formation, attentional abilities, among many other aspects, all very much part of the cognitive psychology of the very young infant. These domains are excluded because few reliable findings have as yet emerged in those areas.

The psychoanalytic writings have often been attentive to infant cognition. Both Freud and Klein, but also Winnicott, have shown great interest in the working of the infant's mind. The Freudians and post-Freudians did not, however, engage in impartial experimental studies of infancy. Rather, all too often very metaphorical descriptions of infancy and the motivations of infants are given.

In this book our concern is with the infant's mind and the means, methods, and procedures used to study it. We have chosen to include areas where studies are carried out with utmost attention being paid to procedures and controls to ensure the reliability of the findings. Furthermore, only studies of very young infants are included, rather than studies that analyze what the young child and/or adult believes about his or her own infancy and that infer, from such an analysis, what the structure of infancy itself must be like. However, even if it is granted that legitimate inferences about infancy may be drawn from adult behavior, it is far from obvious that the methods of doing so are currently available within the realm of the natural sciences.

Be all this as it may, I want to stress that the absence from this volume of certain areas of infancy research does not mean that these areas may not turn out to be central. Rather, given the highly empirical nature of this particular venture, I have chosen to include only those topics in the study of infants that have a solid empirical grounding.

REFERENCES

Chomsky, N. (1982) On the representation of form and function. In J. Mehler, E. Walker, & M. Garrett (Eds.), *Perspectives on mental representation*. Hillsdale, NJ: Lawrence Erlbaum Associates.

Fodor, J. (1983) *The modularity of mind*. Montogomery, VT: Bradford.

Fodor, J., Garrett, M. F., & Brill, S. L. (1975) Pi ka pu: The perception of speech sounds by prelinguistic infants. *Perception and Psychophysics, 18*, 74–78.

Mehler, J. (1974) Connaitre par desapprentissage. In M. Piatelli & E. Morin (Eds.), *L'unité de l'homme*. Paris: Le Seuil.

Mehler, J., Morton, J., & Jusczyk, P. (1984) On reducing language to biology. *Cognitive Neuropsychology, 1*, 83–116.

1 Language Related Dispositions in Early Infancy

Jacques Mehler
C.N.R.S.

> *I did not comment or question, particularly not question, as I
> feared they would bawl at his left ear and strain their vocal chords,
> though if they approached his right ear he could guess what they
> might be saying.*
>
> —R. K. Narayan
> *Old and New*

This chapter raises some issues related to natural language acquisition and dispositions that are present at birth. In the first section, we explore notions of space in very young infants. The ability to locate sources, segregate messages coming from different sources, or preserve the identity of a source that has an input while it is moving in space, are all necessary if infants are ever to be capable of handling speech-like stimuli in naturalistic conditions.

In the second section we explain some of the neuropsychological studies that can be cited in an effort to relate psychological capacity to underlying brain structures.

In the last section, we describe some recent investigations that address how infants represent speech-like stimuli and study how these representations are preserved over time.

NOTIONS OF SPACE IN INFANCY

In this section, two contrasting viewpoints about space perception in infants are reviewed. One claims that space perception results from the maturation of modality specific cerebral structures. The other claims that perception of space develops

7

independently of modality using a single structure for all computations regardless of modality. Failures to compute space can be explained by claiming that the component cannot use certain cues (e.g., stereopsis) to compute spatial configurations but succeeds when different cues (e.g., parallax) are available.

In order to perceive speech the infant must be able to structure acoustic space and locate the acoustic sources in it. Indeed, to process speech, sounds must be kept apart from each other when they co-occur in time but originate at different sources. Likewise, it is necessary to distinguish speech from the background against which it is heard (or produced) if perception is to become possible. Otherwise, infants would be entangled in a fabulous confusion incompatible with perception and reminiscent of the Jamesian state of blooming, buzzing confusion from which it seems they could never escape.

The human ability to construct space is a classic issue in philosophy and psychology. Psychologists have studied the mechanisms that can be used to compute spatial arrangements for each of the perceptual modalities. In this volume, Spelke's, Held's, and Yonas' chapters, all of which are concerned with the visual modality, deal specifically with notions of visual space in infancy. Other investigators attempt to study how very young infants evaluate space through auditory cues. It is of interest to compare the performances across modalities, to decide whether space perception is the result of a number of modality-specific spatial computations, rather than the output of a more abstract device that organizes incoming percepts in terms of a three-dimensional framework irrespective of modality. In other words, is there a space hypothesis, or is three-dimensional space the result of modality-specific computations and procedures all of which converge with similar metrics on a spatial construction?

In a series of very elegant experiments, Held and his collaborators (see Held, this volume, for references) failed to find stereopsis in infants younger than 20 weeks. Very young infants consistently failed to use binocular cues to compute depth. Held's findings are compatible with neurological evidence showing that layer 4c of the visual cortex becomes columnarly organized some weeks after birth. In both cats and monkeys, layer 4c becomes organized in a columnar fashion 6 weeks after birth. In his chapter, Held argues that stereopsis becomes possible only after layer 4c is fully segregated into columnar structures. Before this segregation, the information regarding which eye delivers what signal is lost in a layer 4c that cannot keep track of that information. After the columnar segregation is established, it becomes possible to compute depth by means of the binocularity cues.

Is the initial incapacity to use stereopsis just a perceptual limitation, or is that limitation also accompanied by conceptual shortcomings? The infant might be unable to use stereo cues but believe nonetheless that he or she is surrounded by a three-dimensional environment. In particular, the infant might perceive space through other cues, as for instance, motion cues. In his chapter, Yonas presents evidence showing that babies are sensitive to motion cues and use them to compute depth. Of course, whether other cues can also be used is an empirical issue.

Some results suggest that the conceptual structures underlying notions of depth and space are part of the cognitive endowment of the neonate. For instance, Spelke, in this volume, suggests that the notion of *object* is the basis on which much of visual perception is built. Her experiments suggest, nonetheless, that infants use the notion of object as a primary one in conjunction with a notion of three-dimensionality and with some naïve notions about the physics of the world. Of course, it is difficult to conceive of how an organism might imagine three-dimensional objects without a notion of three-dimensional space.

My own work is concerned with infants' representations of speech. Consequently, I am interested in the way infants organize auditory percepts in space. Psychophysical research reviewed in Eisenberg (1976) and in Aslin, Pisoni, and Jusczyk (1983) indicates that human audition is quite advanced at birth. Lenard, von Bernuth, and Hutt (1969) established that infants are particularly sensitive to frequencies that are most characteristic of speech. Moreover, Aslin et al. suggest that the mechanisms underlying frequency and intensity discrimination, masking, etc., are very similar in the infant and the adult. Auditory space perception in infants is less well understood.

Since the pioneering work of Andre-Thomas (1952), it is known that neonates orient toward sources of sound shortly after birth. Peiper (1952) cites observations carried out before World War II, indicating that very young infants orient to sounds. However, many of these early, interesting investigations failed to incorporate elementary controls on which to rest the case. Recently, Wertheimer (1961) observed that neonates orient away from midline toward laterally presented clicks. Turkewitz, Birch, and Cooper (1972) showed that newborn infants tend to shift their gaze toward a sound. Muir and Field (1979) also claim that infants tend to orient their head toward a sound source. However, failures of head or sight orientation toward sounds have also been reported. For instance, Butterworth and Castillo (1976) and McGurk, Turnure, and Creigthon (1977) did not observe orienting responses to a sound stimulus. Nonetheless, Muir, Campbell, Low, Killen, Galbraith, and Karchmar (1978) found that orienting responses have very long latencies. This observation suggests that failures to observe orienting responses may be a function of the span of time, after stimulus presentation, during which the experimenter will record or accept a response as being correct. Aslin et al. have claimed that: "Past failures to observed reliable orientation towards sounds in newborns may have resulted from expectations of shorter response latencies." They may be right, because recently a number of experimenters reported having observed orienting responses to sounds in newborns. Alegria and Noirot (1982) have claimed that infants react to a sound by twisting their mouths into an asymmetrical posture a few hours after birth. Apparently, only sounds made by the human vocal tract elicit asymmetrical mouthing. But the authors claim that breast- and bottle-fed infants differ in their organization of space. As they have written (Algeria & Noirot, 1982): "experiences related to the feeding situation brings babies to integrate in their spatial framework a new object that seems to occupy a place defined by the voice location . . . The relative facility with which environmental pressures modify the behavior has been considered as an indication of the organism's "preparedness" to integrate information." [p. 396]

The aforementioned results suggest that infants can represent space in some input modalities. Spelke also has argued in favor of the infant's representing space and depth precociously, but she has not addressed the modality issue. Held, as noted, has shown that very young infants are unable to use stereopsis to compute depth. Yonas' studies, some of them reported in this volume, support the view that infants cannot use pictorial cues to perceive depth. Only further investigations will clarify whether infants can rely on other cues before they can rely upon pictorial cues and stereopsis to compute depth. Future evidence may clarify whether notions of depth appear in conjunction with the development of the neuronal tissue responsible for the computation of stereopsis. Nevertheless, there is some evidence that infants position sound stimuli in a three-dimensional space. Therefore, unless notions of space are themselves modular, in Fodor's sense, notions of depth ought to be expected in the visual domain even before the infant can use stereopsis.

The following working hypothesis may bring into focus many research issues that are currently under scrutiny: Neonates place acoustic stimuli into a spatial framework (or scaffolding). Pointers specify the locus where the acoustic events originate. These sounds are attributed to more or less compact or diffuse sources. Furthermore, differently directed pointers indicate different acoustic events and/or sources. Sequential pointers may be interpreted as due to a moving source. One source can generate more than one acoustic event, provided the structure of each event is internally coherent and different from the other. Studies of infant perception try to determine the metric and the structure that infants attribute to space. The foregoing hypothesis, as well as some of the results already mentioned, suggest that infants do, indeed, locate sources in three-dimensional space.

Even though young infants localize acoustic stimuli in space, they do so only when the sounds emanate from a single source. If two sounds, each from a different loudspeaker, are delivered, infants react differently than adults. Indeed, adults claim they hear a single sound located at the loudspeaker that delivered the temporally leading sound (for broad regions of SOA). This phenomenon is generally known as the *precedence effect*. Clifton, Morrongiello, Kulig, and Dowd (1981) claim that young infants do not show a precedence effect. They interpret this failure as a result of incomplete maturation of the auditory cortex.

If we compare the results reported by Clifton et al. with those of Held and his collaborators for the emergence of stereopsis, the ages seem to correspond. This correspondence is probably due to the infant's incapacity to use acoustic or visual disparity cues to compute spatial organization. Notice, however, that in vision differences between the right- and left-retinal images cannot be used to locate the distal stimulus in space. In audition, the sequential messages arriving to both ears but at different times cannot be fused into one single distal source located at the side of the leading message. Nonetheless, infants are able to localize and orient to sources from a very young age onward. Therefore, infants must be using ear differences in volume or phase, or both, to compute the location of acoustic sources. Clifton et al. have speculated that orienting toward sounds involves subcortical mechanisms, whereas the precedence effect requires the involvement of cortical structures. The studies of Field, Muir, Pilon, Sinclair, and Dodwell (1980), as well as those of Clifton et al. (1981) and Morrongiello (1982), have found that very young infants are capable of orienting toward a sound; however, a temporary decrement in that ability emerges at about 3 months of age.[1]

The properties of spatial representation in the visual mode have also been studied by Bower (1974) and more recently by Spelke. Both have considered the ways in which infants structure visual space and the objects that exist within it. Spelke (this volume) states that: "we nearly always perceive each object as unitary, as separate from the surfaces around it and as persisting over time." Some of Spelke's results contradict earlier findings. Because the experimental work of Spelke incorporates more extensive controls, we accept her results in what follows.

Spelke's description of objects provides a framework to predict when boundaries denote the separation of two objects rather than some aspect of one physical object. She argues that whether one or several objects have to be construed is influenced by experience and is dependent on perceptual principles. However, she argues that the Gestalt principle of good form is not operational in the neonate. Rather, Spelke invokes other principles to account for the behavior of the very young infant. These principles, she argues, are essentially involved in object perception for adults. (See her chapter in this volume.)

As with vision, acoustic events are organized very similarly by infants and adults. However, acoustic stimuli are organized in accordance with the principles of Gestalt psychology. Several examples can be advanced to illustrate this assertion. Consider, for instance, the perception of two events with different onset time, but of roughly equal overall duration. Miller, Weir, Pastore, Kelly, and Dooling (1976) showed that a noise and a buzz are perceived differently according to the noise-buzz asynchrony. Percepts fall into one of the following three categories: Noise preceding the buzz; buzz preceding the noise; or simultaneity. Indeed, the boundaries separating these three categories seem to fall in the range of those in speech perception. Furthermore, neonates categorize these buzz-noise sequences using the same 3 categories that adults use (Jusczyk et al., 1980).

Mehler and Bertoncini (1979) explored the nature of infants' perception of three sounds. They used three identical beats; the first and third beat span a 600 msec interval, and the second beat occurs somewhere between them. By moving

---

[1]The precedence effect is certainly related to the maturation of the auditory cortex, and it may be interesting to relate this to the temporary inability that 3-month-old infants have in orienting to acoustic stimuli. This drop in performance may be due to changes in processing. Mehler (1982a) claims that drops in performance often indicate changes in strategies and in representations of knowledge.

the second beat, it was found that infants organize their percepts in terms of three categories: A pair of beats plus a singleton; a series of regular beats; and lastly, a singleton followed by a pair of beats. Infants organize these sounds the same way adults do, at least in the experiments carried out so far. The boundaries between categories for the infant and the adult seem to correspond to the same temporal values.

Demany, McKenzie, and Vurpillot (1977) showed that very young infants can discriminate sequences of sounds that differ from each other only in their rhythm. These authors claim, explicitly, that their results are the consequence of the Gestalt principles of temporal proximity. Other experimenters have reached similar conclusions (Allen, Walker, Symonds, & Marcell, 1977; Chang & Trehub, 1977.)

A striking demonstration that infants organize sounds according to the principles used by adults is found in Demany's (1982) experiments. Musicians have always known, and psychologists have recently discovered, that sequences of sounds are organized into *streams* according to quality, periodicity, and so forth (Bregman, 1978a). In fact, Bregman has shown that sequences of sounds occurring within a time interval are organized according to the laws of Gestalt psychology. Bregman coined the term auditory streaming to describe the principles explaining the structural and spatial segregation of sounds. For instance, one of the principles, *spectral proximity,* states that spectrally similar sounds are grouped together, even though other sounds may periodically interrupt the stream. Demany asked whether spectral proximity is as powerful a cue for perceptual segregation in infants as it was shown to be for adults. Consider the three displays in Fig. 1.1. In test sequence A, adults report hearing two separate streams, one, *abc, abc, abc,* and the other as *d, d, d.* In B, adults claim they hear two streams, *ac, ac, ac,* and *bd, bd, bd.* Finally, for C, adults hear the same as they do in A. If the sounds are inversed (i.e., figuratively, played from right to left rather than from left to right), the outcomes are for A, *cba, cba, cba,* and *d, d, d,* which is easily distinguished from its forward presentation (one stream sounds like repetitions of *abc's* before inversion and like repetitions of *cba's* after). For C, inversion has the same consequence it has for A. However, for B, the two streams remain invariant under inversion. Since each stream has a pair of sounds, after some time, hearing repetitions of *ab* is indistinguishable from hearing repetitions of *ba.* Demany discovered that adults and infants discriminate the A and C stimuli from their inversions but not the B stimuli. These results suggest that very young infants organize sequences of sounds into streams on the basis of the same principles used by adults.

The ability of infants to stream sequences of sound is compatible with Bregman's (Bregman & Steiger, 1980) claim that: "There have to be auditory processes that 'parse' the mixture so that the correct features are assigned to each source of sound. The feature 'location' would be easy to assign if each incoming signal were a pure tone. . . . In deciding upon 'what' and 'where' we also must decide on 'how many' " [p. 539].

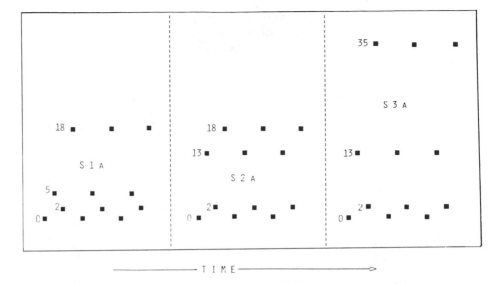

FIG. 1.1.   Three test sequences: *S1a, S2a,* and *S3a.* The component tones of the sequences are represented by squares. The squares are vertically spaced in proportion to the musical intervals formed by the tones. Numbers express in semitones the distances of the tones from E_4: $0 = E_4 = 330$ Hz; $2 = F\#_4 = 370$ Hz; $5 = A_4 = 440$ Hz; $13 = F_5 = 698$ Hz; $18 = A\#_5 = 932$ Hz; $35 = D\#_7 = 2489$ Hz. If its ordinate is reversed, the figure represents instead the test sequences *S1b, S2b,* and *S3b.* In this case, the numbers should be decoded in the following way: $0 = A\#_5$; $2 = G\#_5 = 831$ Hz; $5 = F_5$; $13 = A_4$; $18 = E_4$; $35 = B_2 = 123$ Hz. ($A\#_5$ becomes the reference note; the musical intervals remain the same size, but their directions are reversed.)

A number of observations suggest that infants track, parse, and point to sources when listening to speech. Infants recognize human voices irrespective of what they say. This ability rests on the infant's capacity to stream and track the human voice away from the background noise against which it is heard. Recognition of a voice regardless of the utterance, intonation, intensity, and spatial location, must rest on the ability of infants to extract a physical parameter characteristic of that voice, albeit one that is difficult to define. A source with the mentioned physical invariant is a prerequisite. The infant also has to ignore many other qualities that are allowed to vary as part of the normal range of productions of any vocal tract. The ability can be best described by saying that, in recognizing a human voice irrespective of volume, locus, content of speech, etc., the infant behaves as if he or she believed that the vocal tract can whisper or can shout, the person can move around while talking, and so on. If an infant were incapable of streaming and incapable of locating sources in space, it seems difficult to conceive that he or she could recognize voices as invariants.

Infants are known to track, distinguish, and recognize the voice of their mother from that of another woman. Miles and Meluish (1974) showed this by using a non-nutritive sucking procedure. In a similar experiment, Mehler et al. (1978) showed that infants respond differently to their own mother's voice than to that of another infant's mother. All the previously mentioned experiments tested infants who were over a month old. In a more recent experiment, DeCasper and Fifer (1980) showed that even 12-hour-old infants change their sucking rates to reinforce themselves with the voice of their biological mothers. This observation can be interpreted by invoking two possible mechanisms: Either very rapid bonding with the mother after birth, or effective transmission of the mother's voice *in utero*. For the latter mechanism to operate, infants must have the capacity of perceiving their mother's voice *in utero*, at least during a part of gestation. The physiological evidence shows that the receptors are ready to allow infants to perceive sounds during the last few months of gestation (Yakovlev & Lecours, 1967). Querleau and Renard (1981) implanted pregnant mothers with hydrophones and recorded all auditory phenomena reaching the infant. The reported results confirm that the mother's voice can be heard fairly free of distortions under such conditions. Similar investigations were carried out by Armitage, Baldwin, and Vince (1980) on sheep.

NEUROPSYCHOLOGICAL EVIDENCE FOR SPEECH DISPOSITIONS

When relating brain function to speech processing, two main questions can be asked. First, is all nervous tissue allotted to speech and language, or is there only some part that underlies that function? Second, how early is brain function involved in speech processing? Another question that might have to be raised is whether the tissue allotted to speech and language changes during development.

Since Broca's pioneering discoveries relating "articulated speech" to the left hemisphere, students have been taught that the left hemisphere is the locus of grammatical abilities.[2] Patients with lesions in the left hemisphere will have significantly greater language impairment than patients with equivalent lesions in the right hemisphere. The cortical tissue normally labeled as the anterior *speech area* comprises the pars opercularis and the pars triangularis of the frontal lobe, as Broca himself proposed. Subsequently, additional language areas were added by Wernicke, Dejerine, and many others. In this volume, Lecours describes the language areas as they are generally accepted today. As Lecours and also Rosen and Galaburda (see their chapters in this volume) argue, most investigations suggest

---

[2]Broca, who himself carried out the autopsy of the famous patient Leborgne, concluded that: "confirme l'opinion de M. Bouillaud qui place dans les lobes anterieurs du cerveau la faculte du langage articule." Broca proposes for the first time localizations of psychological functions in cerebral convolutions. Recently, Castaigne, Lhermitte, Signoret, and Abelanet (1980) found Leborgne's brain and submitted it to a CT-scan. They confirmed some of Broca's assertions, in particular, that the third frontal lobe was severely damaged. The study by Castaigne et al. supports Broca's description rather than that of P. Marie, who argued that the damaged area was larger than Broca had claimed.

that language is represented primarily in the left hemisphere, at least in right-handers. Furthermore, Rosen and Galaburda present several hypothetical mechanisms to explain how this asymmetry might emerge. Geschwind and Behan (1982) have suggested that the growth of the hemispheres during gestation is paced by testosterone effects that are responsible for the manifestations of handedness, learning disabilities, and certain immune disorders. From these studies, a better understanding of the relation of a function to a locus is emerging. Thus, they postulate that right-handers (and language lateralization to the left) are genetically determined, although the expression of the gene(s) may be modified by intrauterine events that produce deviations away from the norm. These, they argue, are likely to stem from hormonal and/or metabolic irregularities.

Galaburda and his collaborators have found abnormal cortical development in the language areas of the left hemisphere in the brains of dyslexics. Their finding supports the notion that the normal processes of cerebral lateralization can be interrupted by similar hormonal effects.

The case for an exclusive association of the left hemisphere with grammatical functions rests mainly on findings about brain lesions in the adult literate western adults. It is thus difficult to evaluate whether the privileged association of the left hemisphere with grammatical function is innate or emerges after some years of language use. After an extensive review of the literature, Lenneberg (1967) concluded that, in children, the two hemispheres are equipotential regarding their ability to sustain language. Of course, equipotentiality is logically compatible with lateralized functions. Yet, Lenneberg reached this conclusion after careful evaluation of aphasia in young children and of the effects of hemidecortication on language behavior. Lenneberg concluded that the Left Hemisphere (LH) does not become irreversibly and exclusively associated with language behavior until a number of years after the child has begun to speak.

For several decades Lenneberg's conclusion was accepted as an accurate description of the facts. Of course, even if equipotentiality is logically compatible with lateralization of function, other facts must be raised at this juncture. For instance, Wada, Clarke, and Hamm (1975) found that the left planum temporale is consistently bigger than the right one. This finding corroborates a similar one reported by Geschwind and Levitsky (1968), and also by Witelson and Pallie (1973). Both Wada et al. and Witelson and Pallie reported that the difference found in adult brains is already present in the infants' brains after 29 weeks of gestation. There is extensive evidence that infants have a more developed left than right planum temporale. As we saw earlier, there is an ever-growing consensus among neurologists that asymmetries are genetically determined. Likewise, many investigators tend to espouse the view that the association of the left hemisphere with language is innate. Likewise, as we see later, behavioral data favors the view that the very young infant is functionally lateralized, and also that its cortical organization is much more flexible than that of adults.

Recently, Dennis (1980) reviewed work she and her collaborators carried out with children who had surgically lost one of their hemispheres. They concluded that left hemidecorticates have a permanent diminution of linguistic skills, whereas right hemidecorticates are unaffected in their linguistic skills. Nonetheless, the children are distinguishable only on the basis of their chronometric performance and not on the basis of their general language performance. Indeed, the patients cannot be distinguished by conversation only. In addition, it is far from obvious why left and right hemidecorticates differ on some tests and not others. A possible solution to this puzzle was recently suggested by Bishop (1983), who argued that Dennis' results are due to a methodological problem. Indeed, very few hemidecorticates were studied, and no unlesioned control children, matched for age, were tested. Because patients were not compared to normals controls, it is possible that both the right and the left hemidecorticates score within the range of variability of normals. In this case, Dennis' results could be due to sampling artifacts. In fact, Bishop tested normal children in the age bracket of Dennis' patients and found that the variability on these tests of the normals encompasses all of that of Dennis' groups of patients.

Bishop's finding confirms Lenneberg's claim that, if surgery is performed early enough, children are equally proficient language users, regardless of which hemisphere is removed. Eimas (personal communication) argues that two independent issues are often compounded, namely: 1) Is the brain lateralized, for instance, for language function, and if so at what age does such a lateralization of function emerge? and 2) Is each hemisphere equipotential for language? Of course, treating these issues as interdependent leads to confusion. Most of the results presented seem to be congruent with the view that the hemispheres are equipotential during the first few years of life although lateral differences are present from birth onward.

Behavioral and physiological measures of functional lateralization may give disparate results. Therefore, it seems reasonable to secure results using both measures.

Molfese and his colleagues explore asymmetrical cortical responses using evoked potentials. They claim that the left hemisphere specializes in the processing of speech, whereas the right hemisphere is better at processing other acoustic stimuli. Barnet, Vincentini, and Campos (1974) found a similar result. These investigations, however, must be interpreted with caution. First, as Nuñez (1981) has shown, Auditory Evoked Potentials (AEPs), given the physics of dipoles, are ill-suited for localizing electrical activity, and little about the asymmetrical functioning of the lobes can be grounded on that method alone. Even if records are taken only as indicators of asymmetries to be validated through other methods, this is rarely done. Neville, in her chapter, presents a thorough review of the results obtained by means of evoked potentials.

Dichotic listening is frequently used to assess functional asymmetries in adult speakers. However, a growing number of investigators are concerned that unwarranted inferences are drawn from ear-superiority effects to cortical architecture. For instance, Bertelson (1982) has warned that: "it is necessary to take account of all the processes that mediate performance, and that some of them may be remotely related only, or not related at all, to brain asymmetry [pp. 202–203]." Yet, since Kimura's (1961) findings that there is a right ear advantage (REA) for speech stimuli and not for other acoustic stimuli, dichotic listening results are usually interpreted in terms of hemispheric differences. Dichotic listening may correlate with hard-wired asymmetries of the brain; however, many unknown facts will have to be resolved before accepting such an explanation. In fact, the REA in the right-hander is not as general as would be expected from other tests of cortical organization in such subjects. Furthermore, the REA is not very stable from test to retest trials. All these facts indicate that, irrespective of the structural causes underlying the ear differences, many other factors also determine the results. Thus, although this method is the most broadly used in ascertaining functional asymmetries, its results have to be taken as suggestive of and not as demonstrative of underlying structural causation.

Although the dichotic listening technique has often been used with children (see Gilbert & Climan, 1974; Piazza, 1977, among others), it is only in the last few years that the method has been adapted to study infants. Entus (1977) used a pair of dichotically presented syllables to infants tested with the non-nutritive sucking procedure (i.e., the same pair of syllables were presented to the infant until two consecutive drops in sucking rate were observed). Thereafter, subjects were tested with a new pair of syllables, that is, a new syllable and one of the syllables already used during habituation. She observed that 1- to 3-month-old infants show significantly greater recovery of sucking to changes in the right ear (RE) syllable as compared with changes in the left ear (LE) syllable. Entus also reported a left ear advantage (LEA) for music pairs of stimuli. Entus interpreted her results in terms of an asymmetrical cerebral organization in infants as young as 3 months of age. Nevertheless, shortly after Entus reported her findings, Vargha-Khadem and Corballis (1979) failed to replicate Entus's results, although they used her stimuli and the same procedure. Infants in both studies were, roughly speaking, the same age. However, Vargha-Khadem and Corballis incorporate a number of controls that were absent from the Entus study. These controls included a coaxial arm to hold the nipple in place and avoid possible experimenter bias. Furthermore, the experimenters were never aware of the ear being tested at any one time. Despite the improvements introduced in Vargha-Khadem and Corballis's replication, both studies are subject to the same potential sources of variability. First, the age range of the infants was too large, because it included infants varying from 1 to 3 months. Such a dispersion insures that the sample will include infants in very different maturational stages. In many studies, clear discontinuities in behavior are observed within that age range (Clifton et al., 1981, and also Maratos, 1982). Second, the changes in stimulus are not comparable (in terms of the number of phonetic features) in both parts of the experiment. Finally, two syllables spoken by the same speaker, one presented to each ear, have a tendency to fuse in the center of the head.

Given the importance of knowing whether infants, at birth or shortly there-after, are functionally lateralized, Bertoncini, Lokker, Morais, and Mehler (in press) attempted another replication of Entus' experiment. Their procedure was essentially identical to Vargha-Khadem and Corballis, but all infants were 3-to-5-days old and the stimulus changes were equated in terms of number of phonetic features.

Bertoncini et al. ran a control group to validate the index of discrimination. All infants in the experimental and control groups were tested in two stages, each including a habituation phase and a test phase. In the first and second habituation phases, experimental and control S's were treated alike. In the test phases, control S's continued to receive the same pair of syllables as during habituation. In contrast, infants in the experimental groups received another pair of syllables, one unchanged syllable in one ear and a new one that incorporated a consonant change in the other. One experimental group received a right ear (RE) change in the first test phase and a left ear (LE) change in the second test phase. The infants in the other experimental group heard the changes in the reverse order. Consequently, two recovery scores were obtained for each infant.

The results reported by Bertoncini et al. show that neonates discriminate changes in a single syllable of a dichotically presented pair, irrespective of ear. Furthermore, no overall ear advantage for speech stimuli is observed. Our results fall somewhere between those of the two previously reported experiments. How-ever, both Entus and Vargha-Khadem and Corballis classified S's as having a REA or a LEA without distinguishing those infants who discriminate from those who do not. In order to evaluate the discriminative performance of the infants, Bertoncini et al. calculated dishabituation rates (DR) for each subject in each experimental session. If we include only the experimental infants who had a DR superior to 80% of the control subjects, the distribution of DRs differs signifi-cantly (p < .001) between control and experimental groups. Consequently, this value has been chosen to select within experimental groups those infants who had at least one DR that exceeded 50%. Clearly, those are the infants who actively participated in the experiment. With this criterion, of the 40 experimental infants, only 29 were preserved. Of those infants, 62% show a REA and 28% a LEA. This significant difference (p. 05) suggests that attentive 4-day old infants show a REA for dichotically presented syllables.

In summary, Bertoncini et al. have found a REA for speech much as Entus has claimed, if a threshold criterion is used to categorize an infant as having successfully discriminated the change or not. Using this criterion, we showed that two thirds of the S's who have an ear asymmetry show a REA. That is exactly what should be expected in a population unselected for handedness. This result, if corroborated, suggests that the very young infant has lateral differences (LDs) much as the adult has. However, because Bertoncini et al. only use speech stimuli, it is impossible to decide whether the observed LD is specific to speech or general for any acoustic stimuli. Other experiments shed some light on this issue.

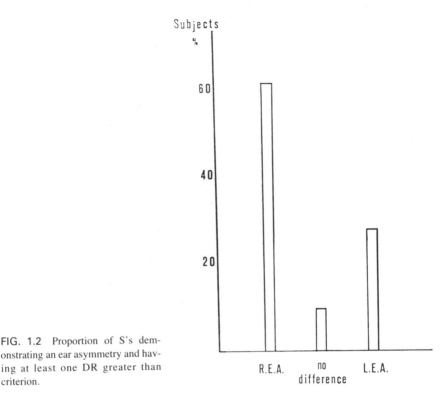

FIG. 1.2 Proportion of S's demonstrating an ear asymmetry and having at least one DR greater than criterion.

Best, Hoffman, and Glanville (1982) investigated ear advantages in 2-, 3-, and 4-month-old infants using both speech and musical stimuli. They measured the cardiac-orienting response (OR) in a habituation-dishabituation experimental paradigm. Two-month-old infants show a LEA for music but no ear advantage for speech. Three-, and 4-month-old infants have a LEA for music, but they also have a significant REA for speech stimuli. Best et al. corroborate the precocious nature of functional asymmetries. They also lend some behavioral support to the neuroanatomical observation that the R hemisphere is advanced in development compared to the L hemisphere. However, these results contrast with those reported by Bertoncini et al., who found that 4-day olds have a REA for speech. Best et al. found no REA for speech in 2-month-old infants. If bothresults stand up under replication, the discrepancy might be due to a performance dip.[4]

_____

[4]As was mentioned in the section on spatial notions in infancy, Clifton et al. showed a strong developmental tendency in infants with the precedence effect. Clifton et al. replicated findings by Field et al., according to which infants turn their heads toward a sound source at both 1 and 3 months of age, but not at 2 months. Furthermore, the precedence effect does not elicit an orienting response in the very young infants, which led Clifton et al. to claim that the younger infants have

To summarize, very young infants have a right-ear advantage for speech, much as Entus claimed. Although the results by Bertoncini et al. suggest that the same is true for infants just a few days old, other results, with 1-month-old infants, fail to find ear asymmetries at that age. It is difficult to evaluate whether we are facing a developmental trend, because not all infants were tested with the same technique at all ages. It would seem desirable to test 1-month-old infants with the same method and procedure employed by Bertoncini et al. before accepting these results at face value.

Research based on different techniques also uncovered lateral differences (LDs) in very young infants. A fairly exhaustive review is provided by Segalowitz (1983). For instance, Segalowitz and Chapman (1980) measured differential lower-limb tremors in infants who were being exposed either to speech or music. Their results suggest that even a few hours after birth the LH is more active when the infants are listening to speech stimuli and the RH is more active when they listen to music.

Recently, Segalowitz (1980) has presented a fairly comprehensive discussion of the models that can explain how and why lateralization changes with age. The author argues in support of the view that functional asymmetries are present at birth. Three models try to explain how functional asymmetry may arise: (1) Prewired perceptual differences exist for processing by the R and the L hemispheres; (2) these same prewired differences occur, and in addition cognitive abilities become lateralized because of a usual association with a sensory mode that is itself lateralized (i.e., language with audition, wine rating with olfaction); (3) cognitive abilities are themselves lateralized regardless of the usual mode of functioning. Each of these models is relevant to the developmental psychologist who is trying to understand the origin of an observed asymmetry.

SPEECH PERCEPTION AND REPRESENTATION

Eimas and his colleagues claim that speech is processed by a specialized transduction system, and that categorical perception is one of its characteristic properties. This transduction system is supposedly made up of specialized analyzers corresponding to the distinctive features of the language. If grammatical behavior (speech being only the tip of the iceberg), is found in humans but not in other

---

an immature cortex. At 5 months of age, infants turn equally to a source that is localized in space or to a location suggested by the precedence effect, as was shown by Clifton, Morrongiello, Kulig, and Dowd (1980). The authors suggest that simple orienting to a source in space is a subcortical competence. (Heffner, [1978] and Heffner and Masterson, [1975] showed that head turns toward sources persist in animals whose auditory cortex was previously ablated, although their ability to locomote toward the acoustic source in a room is lost.) In contrast, the precedence effect requires the acoustic cortex to function.

vertebrates, interesting differences between humans and other vertebrates ought to be observed as far as linguistic skills are concerned. In contrast, the work of Kuhl and her colleagues (see her chapter in this volume) suggests that sensory-perceptual functioning is quite similar in humans and other vertebrates, even for speech-like stimuli.

Recently, a number of investigators have paid more attention to the representation of speech than to the psychophysical processes that mediate speech perception. Kuhl and her collaborators in particular (see her chapter in this volume) address the problem of perceptual constancy, that is, how is invariance preserved, despite changes in the basic parameters? What makes a vowel have its character, despite changes in speaker or in volume or in both? Perceptual constancy, invariance extraction, categorization, etc., are concepts invoked to explain how perceptual processing succeeds in stabilizing percepts in an ever-changing world. Kuhl distinguishes studies on categorical perception from studies on speech-sound categorization. The former try to determine how a syllable or a word is heard as the same speech object under many different acoustical realizations. The latter explore how speech sounds that can be heard as different from one another are, nonetheless, mapped onto the same category. Kuhl claims that only the latter studies try to understand how infants select similarities to construct categories, despite their capacity for perceiving differences among stimuli. Kuhl's results suggest that by 6 months infants are quite effective hypothesis-testing operators. Kuhl's subjects have excellent inductive abilities, which they use to determine environmental regularities.

Kuhl reports results showing that infants have the ability to establish categories to classify linguistic segments. They use phonetic features to define the properties of the categories. Kuhl claims that infants hear speech in terms of segments that are bundles of phonetic features. All her results suggest that infants treat speech stimuli as analyzable bundles of features rather than as unanalyzable compounds. In one of her head-turning experiments, Kuhl shows that infants orient toward a syllable containing a consonant) (e.g., /d/), regardless of the position of the consonant in that syllable (i.e., initial, medial, or terminal position). After some training these infants will consistently orient toward syllables containing a /d/ consonant and never to syllables with a /g/ consonant, irrespective of the vocalic context. In a similar experiment, Hillenbrand (1980) showed that infants sort stop consonants from nasals even with novel tokens that were not used during training. Hillenbrand's results contrast with many other results in adult and infant psycholinguistics (see Mehler, 1982). Findings from my laboratory in Paris suggest that the syllable is the primary output of the segmenting device. The device operates equally with both words and legal-pseudowords (see Segui et al., 1981). Although languages may differ in the nature of the sublexical unit that the segmenting device exploits (Cutler et al., 1983), all speakers access distinctive features after having processed some larger unit. The model proposed by Mehler (1981), Fraunfelder (1982), and Segui et al. (1982) claims that the first stage in speech processing is the extraction of a global unit from the speech continuum. This global unit—let's say the syllable—is immediately analyzed into its basic features or phonemes. Whenever it is possible to access the lexicon, the syllable is used to do so. The important feature of the model is that the syllable is processed before its constituents. This model accounts for results of mental chronometry experiments and, apparently, for facts in development. Kuhl's view, however, is that even in the very young baby, features are available to make classes, formulate hypotheses, and confirm or reject the hypotheses.

Recently gathered results, however, clarify the facts considerably. First, both Liberman et al. (1967) and Morais (1982) have found that preliterate children, and also illiterate adults, are incapable of monitoring a consonant through a range of vocalic contexts. The same children have no difficulty whatsoever with a similar syllable-monitoring task. Of course, these S's are looking for a consonant and respond in consequence. Kuhl's task is different from that of the children and adults tested in the aforementioned experiments. Nevertheless, it is surprising that 6-month olds succeed at a task not so different from that at which young children and illiterate adults fail. This paradoxical situation requires a better understanding of the task demands facing the infants and children.

Bertoncini, Jusczyk, and Mehler used a non-nutritive sucking paradigm to explore whether the syllable is represented by the 4-day-old infant as bundles of phonemes and features or as a global, unanalyzed whole. In the first experiment, infants heard four different syllables during the habituation phase (i.e., /bi/, /si/, /li/, and /mi/). When infants were reinforced they heard one of the four syllables, all presented in random order but equally often. Four experimental groups were tested. One group heard the four syllables during the habituation phase. During the test, infants still received the same four training syllables plus a new one, say, /da/. The remaining three experimental groups were identical to the former one, except for the new syllable added during the test phase. For one group that syllable was /ma/, for another /di/, and for the last one /dI/. Two control groups were run; one received the same syllables before and after reaching criterion. The other control also received the same syllables before and after reaching criterion, but a change in the frequency distribution between the syllables intervened after criterion. As can be seen in Fig. 1.3, recovery of sucking is observed only in infants who hear the new syllable that differs from the other four in the vowel. Whenever the newly introduced syllable shares a vowel with one of the training syllables, infants do not respond to the change.

This result can be interpreted in several ways. If infants process syllables as unanalyzed wholes, changes in the vowel are more noticeable, because these weigh more heavily than consonant changes along the similarity dimension for syllables. Alternatively, infants make inferences and continuously test hypotheses. This latter view is supported by Hillenbrand and by Kuhl. Infants hearing the /bi/, /si/, /li/, and /mi/ syllables may infer that different CVs are presented provided they share /i/ as a common vowel. For them, the introduction of a new syllable

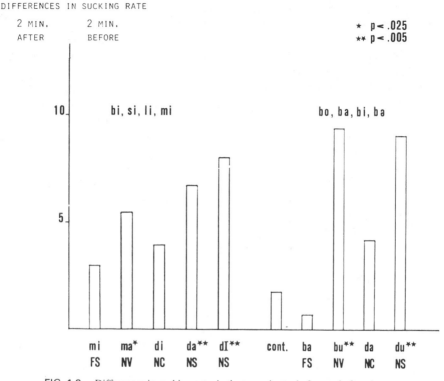

FIG. 1.3. Differences in sucking rates in the two minutes before and after change for the five groups reinforced during habituation with bi, si, li, mi (left half of figure) and the five groups reinforced during habituation with bo, ba, bi, be (right half of the figure). FS: change in frequency distribution; NV: new vowel; NC: new consonant; NS: new syllable.

that also has /i/ in final position is either unnoticed or ignored. In contrast, irrespective of the consonant, if the new syllable ends with a vowel that is not /i/, the infant will react because the inference he or she made is now disproved. In order to pull apart these two interpretations, another study had to be carried out.

Infants were trained on a procedure identical to that described previously, and the four training syllables were /bo/, /ba/, /bi/, and /bae/. Several groups were distinguished from each other by the new syllable (i.e., /du/, or /bu/, or /da/) that was added to the four training ones during the test. Interestingly enough, as seen in Fig. 1.3, only the groups for which the new syllable contains a new vowel, namely, groups /du/ and /bu/, show a significant sucking recovery. When the new syllable differs from the training ones by, at most, a consonant (i.e., /da/), no sucking recovery is observed. If the explanation of the preceding experiments requires that infants construct hypotheses during the training phases of the experiment, it will be necessary to explain why infants formulate vowel-based hypotheses but fail to formulate consonant-based hypotheses.

These experiments cannot be readily accounted for according to the view that infants classify habituation syllables by means of a logical proposition (i.e., "anything with /i/ final"). Rather, infants seem to operate with a syllabic prototype model. When the infant hears a syllable or a group of syllables, the token or tokens are rated along a similarity continuum, with the vowel being the principal attribute for judging similarity. One prediction, derivable from the prototype hypothesis is that the infant tested sometime after hearing a syllable will remember the vowel and the structure of the syllable—namely, whether it has a consonant, and if so, whether it is in the initial or final position, etc. This hypothesis suggests that infants spontaneously represent their knowledge in terms of compounds rather than as bundles of features. More research will indicate the extent to which infants' knowledge of syllabic frames is necessary to explain the preceding results. Infants are currently being tested after exposure to a sequence (e.g., /bi/), among the four training syllables with its inversion (namely, /ib/) figuring among the five test items. If sucking recovers, infants store information about order of phonetic segments in the syllable. Even though the vowel is the critical item in infants' representation of speech sounds, information about the distribution of other phonetic segments is probably also present in the representation. More empirical work is needed to determine exactly how speech is represented in the very young infant. This work is currently being carried out by Eimas, Jusczyk, Miller, and Mehler.

The results just reported are at odds with those reported by Kuhl and her collaborators. An important difference between the two sets of experiments is the age of the subjects. Kuhl's infants were 4- to 6-months old, whereas Bertoncini et al.'s infants were only a few days old. Differences in method and procedure could also partially account for the reported differences. Bertoncini et al. use the nonnutritive sucking technique, whereas Kuhl et al. use head turning. Consider also the demands made on the infant in both sets of experiments. In one case, the infant has to compare, gradually, a new token to the one presented just before. In the other case, after hearing many syllables, infants have to judge whether the new syllable is different from any of those previously presented. This comparison must be performed in a buffer where the syllables are represented. Because many minutes elapse between training and testing, it is unlikely that this task can be completed on the basis of unrecoded sensory traces only. Rather, it would seem that the judgment must be made against traces of the training syllables in their recoded form. A single habituation syllable is easily discriminated from another even when they differ only by a single feature (e.g., Eimas et al., Jusczyk et al., Mehler et al.); the same change may very well go undetected when four training syllables are used. Conceivably, some experimental procedures are better for exploring abstract representations of speech, others for studying discrimination in very young infants.

Miller and Eimas (1979) presented some infants with two habituation syllables, /ba/ and /da/, and /bae/ and /dae/ as test syllables, or vice versa. Another
group of infants heard /ba/ and /bae/ during habituation and /da/ and /dae/ during
testing, or vice versa. Eimas and Miller (1979) concluded, on the basis of their
results, that the infants had: "provided clear evidence of discriminating not only
a change in a single phonetic segment, but also a recombination of consonant
and vowel to form new syllables [p. 359]." Unfortunately, the syllables during
habituation were always presented in the same order. Hence, S's might have
combined the two syllables into a single word, in which case it would be unnecessary to invoke recombination of consonant and vowel to account for the behavior of infants. The two syllables were separated by about 500 msec, which makes
this particular interpretation speculative.

Investigations of the representation of speech in the very young infant are
only beginning, but have already provided a number of interesting findings.
Future studies will clarify the manner in which the child acquires phonological
rules, stores them, and organizes them into programs of production and comprehension. Although dealing with behavior that is quite peripheral to the grammatical component, these studies may, in the end, help us understand the manner
in which the performance system is acquired.

ACKNOWLEDGMENTS

The work reported here was carried out with the support of the Harry Frank Guggenheim
Foundation, The MIT Center for Cognitive Science, INSERM Contrat N. 133026. All
the experiments were carried out in collaboration with Josiane Bertoncini.

REFERENCES

Alegria, & Noirot, (1982) Oriented mouthing activity in neonates: Early development of differences
    related to feeding experiences. In J. Mehler, E. Walker, & M. Garrett (Eds.), *Perspectives on
    mental representation*. Hillsdale, NJ: Lawrence Erlbaum Associates.
Allen, T. W., Walker, K., Symonds, L. & Marcell, M. (1977) Intrasensory and intersensory
    perception of temporal sequences during infancy, *Developmental Psychology*, 13, 225–229.
Andre-Thomas, A. & St. Anne Dargassies, S. (1952) *Etudes neurologigues sur le nouveau-né et
    jeune nourrisson*. Paris: Masson.
Armitage, S. E., Baldwin, B. A., & Vince, M. A. (1980) The fetal sound environment of sheep.
    Science, 208, 1173–1174.
Aslin, R. N., Pisoni, D. B., & Jusczyk, P. (1983) Auditory development and speech perception
    in infancy. Technical Report, No. 4, Psychology Department, Indiana University.
Barnet, A. B., Vincentini, M., & Campos, S. (1974) EEG Sensory evoked responses (ERS) in
    early infancy malnutrition. Paper presented to Society for Neuroscience, St. Louis, Missouri.
Bertelson, P. (1982) Lateral differences in normal man and lateralization of brain function. *Inter-
    national Journal of Psychology, 17*, 173–210.
Bertoncini, J., Jusczyk, P., & Mehler, J. (Manuscript in preparation).

Bertoncini, J., Lokker, R., Morais, J., & Mehler, J. (Manuscript in preparation).

Best, C., Hoffman, H., & Glanville, B. (1982) Development of infant ear asymmetries for speech and music. *Perception and Psychophysics, 31,* 75–85.

Bishop, D. V. M. (1983) Linguistic impairment after left-hemidecortication for infantile hemiplegia? A reappraisal. *Quarterly Journal of Experimental Psychology, 35A,* 199–207.

Bower, T. G. R. (1974) *Development in infancy.* San Francisco: Freeman.

Bregman, A. S. (1978a) Auditory streaming: Competition among alternative organizations. *Perception and Psychophysics,* 23, 391–398.

Bregman, A. S. (1978b) The formation of auditory streams. In J. Requin (Ed.), *Attention and performance VII.* Hillsdale, NJ: Lawrence Erlbaum Associates.

Bregman, A., & Steiger, S. (1980) Auditory system and cortical localization: Interdependence of "what" and 'where" decisions in audition. *Perception and Psychophysics, 28,* 539–546.

Butterworth, G., & Castillo, M. (1976) Coordination of auditory and visual space in newborn human infants. *Perception,* 5, 155–160.

Castaigne, P., L'Hermitte, F., Signoret, J. L., & Albelanet, D. (1980) Description et etude scanographique du cerveau de Leborgne. *Revue Neurologique* (Paris), *13,* 563–583.

Chang, H. W., & Trehub, S. E. (1977) Auditory processing of relational information by young infants. *Journal of Experimental Child Psychology, 24,* 331.

Chomsky, N. (1982) On the representation of form and function. In J. Mehler, E. Walker, & M. Garrett (Eds.), *Perspectives on mental representation.* Hillsdale, NJ: Lawrence Erlbaum Associates.

Clifton, R. K., Morrongiello, B. A., Kulig, J. W., & Dowd, J. M. (1981a) Developmental changes in auditory localization in infancy. In R. N. Aslin, J. R. Albert, & M. R. Peterson (Eds.), *Development of perception: Psychobiological perspectives* (Vol. 1). New York: Academic Press.

Clifton, R. K., Morrongiello, B. A., Kulig, J. W. and Dowd, J. M. (1981b) Newborns' orientation toward sound: Possible implications for cortical development. *Child Development, 53,* 833–838.

Cutler, A., Mehler, J., Norris, D., & Segui, J. (1983) A language specific comprehension strategy. *Nature, 304,* 159–160.

Decasper, A. J., & Fifer, W. P. (1980) Of human bonding: Newborns prefer their mother's voices. *Science, 208,* 1174–1176.

Demany, L. (1982) Auditory stream segregation in infancy. *Infant Behavior and Development, 5,* 261–276.

Demany, L. McKenzie, B., & Vurpillot, E. (1977) Rhythm perception in early infancy. *Nature,* 266, 718–719.

Dennis, M. (1980) Capacity and strategy for syntactic comprehension after left to right hemidecortication. *Brain and Language.*

Eimas, P. D., Siqueland, E., Jusczyk, P., & Vigorito, J. (1971) Speech perception in infants. *Science, 171,* 303–306.

Eisenberg, R. B. (1976) *Auditory competence in early life.* Baltimore: University Park Press.

Entus, A. K. (1977) Hemispheric asymmetry in processing of dichotically presented speech and nonspeech stimuli in infants. In S. Segalowitz & F. A. Gruber (Eds.), *Language development and neurological theory.* New York: Academic Press.

Field, J., Muir, D., Pilon, R., Sinclair, M., & Dodwell, P. (1980) Infants' orientation to lateral sounds from birth to three months. *Child Development, 50,* 295–298.

Fodor, J. (1983) *The modularity of mind,* Montgomery, VT: Bradford.

Fodor, J., Garrett, M. F., and Brill, S. L. (1975) Pi ka pu: The perception of speech sounds by prelinguistic infants. *Perception and Psychophysics, 18,* 74–78.

Geschwind, N., & Levitsky, W. (1968) Human brain: Left-right asymmetries in temporal speech region. *Science, 161,* 186–187.

Geschwind, N., & Behan, P. (1982) Left-handedness: Association with immune disease, migraine and developmental learning disorder. *Proceedings of the National Academy of Sciences, U.S.A.,* 79, 5097–5100.

Gilbert, J. H. V., & Climan, I. (1974) Dichotic studies in 2–3 year olds: A preliminary report. Speech Communication Seminar, Stockholm.

Heffner, H. (1978) Effect of auditory cortex ablation or localization and discrimination of brief sounds. *Journal of Neuropsychology, 41,* 963–976.

Heffner, H., & Masterson, B. (1975) Contribution of auditory context to sound localization in the monkey (*macaca mulatta*). *Journal of Neuropsychology, 38,* 1340–1358.

Hillenbrand, J. M. (1980) Perceptual organization of speech sounds by young infants. Unpublished doctoral dissertation, University of Washington.

Jusczyk, P., Pisoni, D. B., Walley, A., & Murray (1980) Discrimination of relative onset time of two-component tones by infants. *Journal of the Acoustical Society of America, 67,* 262–270.

Kimura, D. (1961) Cerebral dominance and the perception of verbal stimuli, *Canadian Journal of Psychology, 15,* 106–171.

Lenard, H. G., Von Bernuth, H., & Hutt, S. J. (1969) Acoustic evoked responses in newborn infants: The influence of pitch and complexity of the stimulus. *Electroencephalography and Clinical Neuropsychology, 27,* 121–127.

Lenneberg, E. (1967) *Biological foundations of language.* New York: Wiley.

Lieberman, A. M., Cooper, F. S., Shankweiler, D. P., & Studdert-Kennedy (1967) Perception of the speech code. *Psychological Review, 74,* 431–461.

McGurk, H., Turnure, C., & Creighton, S. J. (1977) Auditory-visual coordination in neonates. *Child Development, 48,* 138–143.

Mehler, J. (1974) Connaitre par desapprentissage. In M. Piattelli & E. Morin (Eds.), *L'unité de l'homme.* Paris: Le Seuil.

Mehler, J. (1981) The role of syllables in speech processing: Infant and adult data. *Philosophical Transactions of the Royal Society, B,295,* 333–352.

Mehler, J. (1982a) Dips and drops—A theory of cognitive development. In T. G. Bever (Ed.), *Regressions in mental development: Basic phenomena and theories.* Hillsdale, NJ: Lawrence Erlbaum Associates.

Mehler, J. (1982b) Studies in the development of cognitive processes. In S. Strauss (Ed.), *Shaped behavioral growth.* New York: Academic Press.

Mehler, J. M., Barriere, D., & Jassik-Gerschenfeld (1976) Reconnaissance de la voix maternelle par le nourrisson. *La Recherche, 7,* 786–788.

Mehler, J., Bertoncini, J., & Barriere, M. (1978) Infant perception of mother's voice. *Perception, 7,* 5.

Mehler, J., & Bertoncini, J. (1979) Infants' perception of speech and other acoustic stimuli. In J. Morton & J. Marshall (Eds.), *Psycholinguistics Series II.* London: Elek Books.

Mehler, J., Morton, J., & Jusczyk, P. (1984) On reducing language to biology. *Cognitive Neuropsychology, 1,* 83–116.

Miles, M., & Melhuish, E. (1974) Recognition of mother's voice in early infancy. *Nature, 252,* 123–124.

Miller, J. (1983) *State of Mind.* New York: Pantheon Books.

Miller, J., & Eimas, P. (1979) Organization in infant speech perception. *Canadian Journal of Psychology, 33,* 353–367.

Miller, J. D., Weir, C. C., Pastore, R. E., Kelly, W. U. & Dooling, R. J. 91976) Discrimination and labeling of noise and buzz sequences with varying noise-lead times: An example of categorical perception. *Journal of the Acoustical Society of America, 60,* 410–417.

Molfese, D. (1977) Infant cerebral asymmetry. In S. J. Segalowitz & F. A. Gruber (Eds.), *Language, development and neurological theory.* New York: Academic Press.

Morais, J. (1982) The two sides of cognition. In J. Mehler, E. Walker, & M. Garrett (Eds.), *Perspectives on mental representation.* Hillsdale, NJ: Lawrence Erlbaum Associates.

Morrongiello, B. A., Kulig, J. W., & Clifton, R. K. (1982) Newborn cardiac and behavioral orienting responses to sound under varying precedence effect conditions. *Infant Behavior and Development, 5,* 249–259.

Muir, D., Campbell, D., Low, J., Killen, H., Galbraith, R., Karchmar, J. (1978) Neonatal assessments of intrauterine growth in retarded premature and asphyxiated infants: Group differences and predictive value. Paper presented to the Canadian Psychological Association.

Muir, D., & Field, J. (1979) Newborn infants orient to sounds. *Child Development, 50,* 431–436.

Nuñez, P. L., & Katznelson, R. (1981) *Electric fields of the brain.* Oxford: Oxford University Press.

Peiper, A. (1963) *Cerebral function in infancy and childhood.* New York: Consultants Bureau.

Piazza, D. M. (1977) Cerebral lateralization in young children as measured by dichotic listening and finger tapping tasks. *Neuropsychologia, 15,* 417–425.

Querleu, D., & Renard, K. (1981) Les perceptions auditives du foetus humain. *Medicine et Hygiène, 39,* 2102–2110.

Segalowitz, S. J. (1980) Cerebral asymmetries for speech in infancy. *Language function and brain organization.* New York: Academic Press.

Segalowitz, S. J., & Chapman, J. S. (1980) Cerebral asymmetry for speech in neonates: A behavioral measure. *Brain and Language, 9,* 281–288.

Segui, J., Frauenfelder, U., and Mehler, J. (1981) Phoneme monitoring; Syllable monitoring and lexical access. *British Journal of Psychology, 72,* 471–477.

Segui, J., Dommergues, J. Y., Frauenfelder, U., & Mehler, J. (1982) Perceptual integration of sentences: Syllabic and semantic aspects. In J. F. Le Ny and W. Kintsch (Eds.), *Language and comprehension.* Amsterdam: North-Holland.

Segui, J., Mehler, J., Frauenfelder, U., & Morton, J. (1982) The word frequency effect in lexical access. *Neuropsychologia, 20,* 615–627.

Studdert-Kennedy, M., & Shankweiler, D. (1981) Hemispheric specialization for language processes. *Science, 211,* 960–961.

Turkewitz, G., Birch, H. G., & Cooper, K. (1972) Responsiveness to simple and complex auditory stimuli in the human newborn. *Developmental Psychology, 5,* 7–19.

Vargha-Khadem, F., & Corballis, M. (1979) Cerebral asymmetry in infants. *Brain and Language, 8,* 1–9.

Wada, J. A., Clarke, R., & Hamm, A. (1975) Cerebral hemispheric asymmetry in humans, *Archives of Neurology, 32,* 239–246.

Wertheimer, M. (1961) Psychomotor coordination of auditory and visual space at birth. *Science, 134,* 1692.

Witelson, S. F., & Pallie, W. (1973) Left hemisphere specialization for language in the newborn: Neuroanatomical evidence of asymmetry. *Brain, 96,* 641–646.

Yakovlev, P., & Lecours, A. R. (1967) The myelogenetic cycles of regional maturation of the brain. In A. Minkowski (Ed.), *Regional development of the brain in early life.* Oxford: Blackwell.

2 Sumus Ergo Cogitamus: Cognitive Science and the Western Intellectual Tradition

Robin Fox
Rutgers University

The Harry Frank Guggenheim Foundation was instructed by its founder to pursue the scientific investigation of the relations among violence, aggression, and dominance—or "man's tendency to wish to dominate his fellows," as he put it. He saw this tendency, rather than more parochial causes, as lying behind man's proneness to violence, although he recognized that "dominance can serve many masters," and urged the examination of ideology—particularly religious ideology—in relation to man's violent tendencies.

In carrying out this mandate the Foundation has not focused narrowly on studies of violence and dominance per se, but has sought to place these in their wider context. In examining human aggression and violence, for example, one cannot ignore the cognitive dimension. Animal studies can tell us a great deal about some of the mechanisms of aggression, for example, but in the case of human aggression it is the specifically human cognitive apparatus that is called into play to monitor and channel these mechanisms. Insofar as this apparatus has certain species-specific peculiarities, these must be examined. And it most surely has. If nothing else, language and self-awareness, the use of symbols, and the possibility of conscious reflection all affect the etiology and manifestation of violence. *Perceptions* and definitions of dominance also can be crucial variables. We have, therefore, encouraged studies of these interactions, but also studies of fundamental cognitive and neurobiological factors in themselves, insofar as we felt these were necessary to a general understanding of the role of cognition in behavior, and in particular to its role in understanding violence.

In doing this, we do not see ourselves as deviating from our view of man as the end product of evolution. On the contrary, the cognitive apparatus of man, although more complex than that of other animals, evolved by the same mechanisms of mutation and selection. Man's conscious and cultural abilities, the flexibility of his learning mechanisms, are ultimately all products of the same evolutionary process, the physical traces of which are the brain and central nervous system. The organism is the living memory of its evolution.

Investigation of these cognitive processes as evolutionary products has been hampered by a number of factors, not least the lack of information about the evolution of the body's soft parts. But it has also been retarded because of the intellectual hostility to the whole idea of the innate. In our work at the Foundation, we have tried to operationalize some of the issues raised by the question of innate abilities or propensities, but we are aware that this runs counter to intellectual fashion. The intellectual establishment does not want the issues operationalized; it does not even want them raised! Thus, this book, rather than being what it should be—a straightforward contribution to the examination of the cognitive abilities of newborns and infants—will be seen as a challenge to established "truth." No doubt in 10 years this will be different, but in the meantime it deserves some examination, because it goes to the heart of the current debate on the future of the behavioral sciences.

The issue can be traced back, as can most things, to Greek philosophy, but it starts effectively at the Renaissance with the general claims of humanism versus religious dogma. By the time Bacon came to formulate the scientific method (essentially simply induction), the opposing parties were in place. On one side stood religion with its doctrine of original sin, and on the other stood science with its doctrine of the *tabula rasa*. It should be immediately noted that this was *not* a necessary opposition. One could oppose the doctrine of original sin by a doctrine of original-something-else, as Rousseau eventually did with his doctrine of innate goodness. But in the late seventeenth century, the battle lines became thus drawn, because the inductive scientists wished to oppose not only sin as innate, but *ideas* as innate. And their reasons were not simply scientific. Locke, for example, insisted that the doctrine of innate ideas was grist for the tyrant's mill, because he could always claim that, for example, deference to rulers was "innate" and so ineradicable. A tyrant could "claim for an innate principle that which would serve his purpose." The church could use "innate" or original sin in the same way: Inevitable sinners must be subject to church discipline. So it was that "science" became equated with induction and the opposition to "innate ideas," on the one hand, and with a liberal and democratic stance politically in opposition to monarchy and church.

As we have seen, it would have been just as possible to oppose one set of claimed innate ideas with another set, based on "scientific" investigation. But at the time this was not seen as an alternative. The church and reaction had claimed "the innate," so science, democracy, and progress had to embrace a rugged empiricism. Particularly in British thought, these three were considered coterminous, and empiricism dominated to the point of obliterating "subjectivism" as scientifically unthinkable. "There is nothing in the mind that was not first in the senses" became the first premise of science *and* politics, and the connection was seen as a necessary one.

It is perhaps unusual to link Kant and Rousseau, but both represented a protest against this extreme position. Rousseau, as we have seen, certainly believed in innate features—namely goodness and equality—that society had corrupted. Thus he showed how a *revolutionary* position could be derived from a doctrine of the innate. Kant, more subtly, showed that, whereas the *content* of ideas might be learned, the "categories of the understanding"—the mental schema that ordered these ideas—was not. Kant was thus the true beginning of the "interactionist" position that most sensible scientists now embrace. They ask not whether ideas or behavior are *either* innate *or* learned, but how the two aspects interact.

We have slipped in "behavior" here, but it should be noted that this came later. The original debate was about ideas. Even proponents of the *tabula rasa* had some, albeit hazy, notions of "human nature"—but these did not matter. Even if men were "by nature" lazy and greedy—as J. S. Mill believed, for example—as long as their *ideas* could be changed, then a radical reform of society was possible. Indeed, Mill most eloquently argued for the absolute necessity for "practical reformers" to embrace empiricism and combat "intuitionism"— the doctrine of innate ideas. The stubbornness with which this connection is insisted upon persists to this day and for the same reasons, although latter-day proponents of the *tabula rasa* are rarely aware of their philosophical ancestry.

That it is not a necessary connection can be seen if we examine the arch-conservative Edmund Burke. Burke's conservatism was derived, in effect, from a violent *opposition* to doctrines of "human nature." In fact, Burke saw the proponents of human rights based on human nature (such as Rousseau) as truly dangerous revolutionaries, with the French Revolution as the awful outcome of their doctrines. For Burke, there was no human nature to appeal to; there were only social institutions developed by history that are *learned*, and that were our bastion *against* the vagaries of human nature. For this reason we could only ever overturn established social institutions at our peril. Thus it made sense for Burke to attack the French Revolution, but to defend the American Revolution. The Americans, Burke argued, were defending liberties established by precedent against a ministry that was challenging these. The French, on the other hand, were arguing from abstract "human rights." Thus, the most famous advocate of conservatism was, logically, a convinced empiricist: Indeed, his conservatism derived logically *from* his empiricism!

The notion, however, that a radical reformist position *required* an adherence to empiricist doctrine persisted into the nineteenth century. Its most eloquent exponent was John Stuart Mill, who as we have seen insisted that a "practical reformer" *must* embrace an empiricist position in epistemology. Whatever men's natures, "practical reform" for the Utilitarians could be achieved as long as men's *ideas* could be changed. With the decline of the enlightenment insistence on the primacy of ideas and reason under the impact of the Romantic movement, "emotions" came to be seen as ranking with reason or even superior to it. Thus, it was not only innate *ideas* that were seen as inimical to reform, but innate *feelings*.

This was the setting for the Darwinian revolution and its peculiar effect on the debate. But before that impact could be fully felt, Herbert Spencer had in fact offered an "evolutionary" solution to the epistemological problem that Kant had theoretically solved. For Spencer, the "environment" acting on organisms did indeed implant information, but this was, during the process of evolution, "accumulated by heredity," thus becoming part of the organism's innate endowment. What Darwin added to this was the argument that such accumulation would result from natural selection rather than the inheritance of acquired characteristics (although he vacillated on this point). The interest of this is that many scholars since Spencer have adopted this position, which reconciles empiricism and a priorism in a phylogenetic framework, but it has never crystallized into a dominant "school." The reasons for this are a complex problem for intellectual history but can be simply summed up under two headings:

1. The internal failures of Darwinism to produce a satisfactory theory.
2. The eventual complete dominance of environmentalism and empiricism.

Darwinism initially was something of an ideological problem. At first it was seen as firmly in the "materialist" camp, and thus a threat to faith and establishment. On the other hand, it was clearly a doctrine of the "innate." Its materialism attracted socialists and revolutionaries, but at the same time, laissez-faire capitalist ideology seized upon some of its elements to produce so-called "Social Darwinism" stressing struggle and individualism. (This was in fact more a product of Spencer than Darwin.) Combined with the rise of eugenics and its stress on "racial health," Darwinism slid to the right, where, at least according to the epistemological myth, doctrines of the innate belonged. There was a relatively brief flourishing of "instinct psychology" under McDougall and others, but this too failed to produce much more than a thesaurus of human attributes.

The possibilities of a true "interactionist" epistemology were there. William James, for example, was brilliant on the subject of instinct. He wrote of instincts waxing and waning in strength. When an instinct was at its strongest, he said, then certain specific *learning* could take place. He quoted the experiments of the Englishman Spaulding, who placed hoods on chicks, as evidence. In essence, he had discovered "imprinting"—later to be the mainstay of the ethologists' theory of "instinctual learning."

Despite these possibilities, however, the battle lines we have been following became strongly redrawn after World War I. "Instinct" declined as an explanatory principle and no Darwinian psychology emerged until much later. The more "scientific" Behaviorism came quickly to dominate. It had the virtue of experimentation, and hence true "scientific" status, and its robust empiricism enshrined in the very terms *conditioning* and *reinforcement* put it firmly in the "progressive" mainstream. Intellectual historians again will have to puzzle over how it came to be so firmly established in both capitalist USA and socialist USSR. But both were rapidly industrializing countries, so they had a lot in common. Each wanted to make man over in its own image, and environmentalist doctrines stressing human malleability were bound to gain a foothold.

In the USA, certainly, also, there must have been relief in the "progressive radical" camp—usually referred to here as "liberal." True to the tradition of Locke and Mill and the "practical reformers," they saw in instinct psychology and eugenics the old bête noir of "innatism" and reaction. Combined with quite explicit racism this was too much. Boas in anthropology made the simple equation "genetic = race" and expanded the formula to "genetic = race ≠ culture." Thus the genetic (reactionary) versus culture (reformist) tradition was reasserted. Durkheim in Europe had similarly (in his ongoing intellectual quarrel with Spencer) equated the genetic with the individual, thus producing "genetic = individual ≠ society." This set up the same opposition and restored the ancient battle lines.

Freudian psychology was potentially an instinct psychology with the promise of an interesting interactionist position. But Freud's own vacillations on the one hand, and the persistent attempts, particularly in America, to redefine it in "operational" behaviorist terms (e.g., in the Culture and Personality school of anthropology) blocked that possible development. It has found recent expression in the work of Bowlby—but that is to jump ahead. It is interesting, though, because at least toward the end of Freud's life ethology was making some impact, and he would surely have recognized its importance. However, because the ethological tradition was locked away in "naturalist" studies, or in Nazi Germany, not much could have emerged.

In the meantime, through the 1950s Behaviorism, Environmentalism, and Culturalism dominated in all fields including linguistics (under Bloomfield), and in the USSR even agronomy (under Lysenko). Cognitive psychology, as such, is better dealt with by Mehler, but it was not at center stage, even in the discipline of psychology. Here the greatest hope lay in Piaget's work, which with all its problems was essentially an interactionist psychology. Even so, Lévi-Strauss felt it necessary to disavow Piaget because of the danger of reviving the notion of a specific "primitive mentality." He preferred to rest his psychology on the social learning theories of Susan Isaacs, now virtually forgotten.

But Lévi-Strauss had reintroduced (in 1949) the importance of the human "mind," which had, according to him, basic, built-in, irreducible "structures"— in fact, ideas or categories. He did not specify these as "innate"; indeed, his avoidance of Piaget was part of his adherence to the Durkheimian orthodoxy. On the other hand, "the mind" and its structures were returned to the center of discussion, and these were allowed to depend, ultimately, on structures of the brain. Thus a "cognitive" theory of behavior, resting on neurological foundations, found its way to the center of a lively discussion embracing anthropology, psychology, and—being French—literature and politics.

The 1950s saw a burst of activity that challenged the prevailing orthodoxy, producing a whirlwind of confusion, denunciation, and excitement that can only really be understood against the background of this long, deep-seated set of antagonisms we have been exploring. The discovery of the structure of DNA provided the greatest single breakthrough in genetics since Mendel (and possibly the discovery of mutations). Chomsky, in 1957, started a revolution in linguistics that totally reversed the behaviorist dominance and argued for an innate "Language Acquisition Device." The work of the ethologists, which had been quietly going on this whole time, at last received widespread recognition, and a burst of activity in neuroscience and endocrinology put "brain and hormones" firmly back into the debate. Behavior genetics weighed in with experimental proof of quite specific gene effects. All this was aided and abetted by an upsurge of fossil finds confirming the antiquity of the human lineage, and a new wealth of data from Primatology on the remarkable social lives and abilities of our nearest relatives, culminating in the "chimpanzee language" experiments. In the 1960s the original papers of Hamilton appeared, and eventually the brilliant work on population genetics of Fisher, Haldane, Sewall Wright, and Huxley, pioneered in the 1930s, was rediscovered, married to ethology, and transformed into the avowedly Darwinian "sociobiology." What this did was to provide the basis for a science of the evolution of social behavior—social behavior that was "species-specific" and so ultimately shaped by the gene-pool of the species—always, of course, in interaction with the environment. This coincided with the brilliant negative criticism of behaviorist "laws" by John Garcia and colleagues—demonstrations that were at first rejected out of hand by the "official" psychological journals.

The cumulative effect of these developments was to shake the citadel of environmentalism-behaviorism-empiricism. It no longer seemed self-evident that "scientific method" and "empiricist epistemology" were synonymous. An empirical science of the innate was clearly a possibility. There were many false starts and much nonsense—to be expected given the confusion of ideas and relative suddenness of their rise—but the possibility was there.

However, as it has been the purpose of this short chapter to show, so entrenched in "liberal" thinking is the dichotomy "innate = reaction/learned = progressive" that a virtually unthinking and hysterical opposition has been manifested to this cumulative onslaught on the progressivist ideology (in the marvelous colloquial American phrase, a "knee-jerk" reaction). The dust will have to clear and with calmness of hindsight, intellectual historians will have to sort out the genuine intellectual objections to specific claims from the ideological outrage. But at least with this perspective, we can understand the depth and nature of the outrage and seriousness of the challenge. For what is being challenged is an orthodoxy so entrenched that it embraces the very notion of science itself, and the very foundations of liberal progressive democracy. We can see now that these deep-rooted associations were not logically *necessary* connections; they arose out of historical circumstances. But they have been sufficiently periodically reinforced by racists and IQ fanatics to maintain, in the minds of decent liberal democratic scientists, at the very least an uneasy suspicion of innatist "science," even in its operationalized "interactive" version. No matter. The data continue to force our hand. In the field of sex difference, for example, a simpleminded cultural determinism is no longer even respectable given the facts. We need not expand, however, on the nature of the ideological opposition to such a conclusion and the desperate attempts to avoid it. (All unnecessary. "Equal rights for women" has *never* depended on proving women are the same as men, but rather on insisting that they not be penalized because of differences!) That the rise of the "new innatism" coinded with a ferment of "radical" protest against militarism and racism, and with the rise of the latest version of feminism, did not help in giving it a dispassionate hearing.

Part and parcel of the demise of behaviorism has been the rise of "cognitive science"—previously scorned as "subjective." And an essential component of this rise has been the study of neonate and infant cognition. James may have been right about instinct, but in characterizing the mind of the infant as a "blooming, buzzing confusion," he turns out to be way off the mark. To the behaviorists, the infant was a little learning machine, and it was not until the work of Fantz and Bower that this view was effectively challenged. Married to the Chomskian view of language as acquired by an innate "device," the new view of infant cognition sees the newborn as equipped with a large repertoire of "outputs" and demands on the environment. As I wrote elsewhere, "instinct," in this context, can be seen as the organism's demand for appropriate environmental input. This is the essence of the interactionist position, and the importance of neonate studies is that emphasis is shifted from the emotional system beloved of the ethologists to the cognitive system, so central to an understanding of human behavior.

Much of this revolution depends on innovations in technique, and much of this book is taken up with elaborate discussions of same. But, interestingly, few of the scientists here are concerned with technique for its own sake, which is a mercy for those of us who have undergone a lifetime of trial by methodology. The technique, however, is absolutely central. To those of us concerned with the "innate," one obvious source of information is the baby. What does it bring into the world? When I used to raise this question with students, they would usually counter with, "Why not ask the baby?" And of course the standard answer was: We can't. How wrong we were! How wrong was William James, and even Piaget in the late dates he set for the development of cognitive competencies. I do not want to preempt anything from the book that follows—merely to place it in its intellectual and ideological setting. But its genesis was a conversation on a park bench in Paris, when I casually, and foolishly, suggested to Jacques Mehler that we, unfortunately, could not ask the baby. Several hours later, considerably dazed, I agreed that the world should know about what the baby knows. I emphasize "knows" because it is *knowledge* that is explored here—cognition, knowing, understanding, awareness, competence. We are in the truly human realm—and should we have ever been surprised that this is built into the human organism? Perhaps not, and this all too brief history is a sad record of how our very human combination of knowledge and passion gets in the way of its own search for truth. But no one coming out from the other end of this book is ever likely to fall into that same trap. Despite all the internal debates (and the neuroscientists seem to be at odds with the psychologists who seem equally to be unaware of the importance of evolution), the guidelines of the new cognitive science are there: *sumus ergo cogitamus.*

3

Binocular Vision—Behavioral and Neuronal Development

Richard Held
Massachusetts Institute of Technology

In the course of the last decade or so, interest in the developing vision of infants has proceeded apace. Methods of testing infants for visual resolution including grating, stereo, and vernier acuities, contrast sensitivity, refraction, oculomotor control, and other functions have been evolved. At least one compendium of the new knowledge has appeared quite recently (Aslin, 1981). A principal source of interest in this work has been the advances in understanding of the function and structure of the visual nervous system and of their developmental courses. This research has of necessity been largely performed on animals, chiefly cats and monkeys, but its implications for the study of human vision have had profound effects, of which the burgeoning interest in infant vision is one facet.

In this chapter I review briefly some of the relevant results concerning neuronal systems and their development. I also review some of the behavioral and psychophysical findings on young animals and human infants concerning binocular vision. From these results I draw a speculative interpretation in terms of the development and modifiability of these neuronal mechanisms. My excuse for doing this exercise is an effort to draw together some of the ideas expressed by different participants in this volume.

The questions that I address deal largely with the development of binocularity. Obviously the two eyes work together insofar as the normally sighted person sees one world despite using two eyes and consequently having slightly different images on the retinas. This phenomenon, called fusion, is the most elementary form of binocularity. The condition under which fusion occurs requires that the two images be aligned on the retinas in corresponding positions. The maintenance of correspondence depends of course on maintaining proper convergence of the eyes so that both look at the same object. But assuming proper convergence, images may very well not correspond in retinal positions. For example, if two objects differ in distance from the eyes, their images will not fall on corresponding retinal loci for obvious geometric reasons (Foley, 1978). When the lack of correspondence involves distances across the retinas of more than a degree or two, doubling of the nonfixated object will be seen. Parenthetically, one may note that in a reasonably crowded environment most objects should in fact be seen double. The curious fact is that such doubling is rarely seen in normal circumstances. When the noncorrespondences are of the order of a degree or less, fusion is maintained and a new phenomenon emerges, that of stereopsis.

Stereopsis

The small noncorrespondences between the images of objects at different distances from the eyes are interpreted by the visual system as actual depth differences, and the scene gains the three-dimensional appearance that characterizes stereopsis. Because stereopsis involves a comparison of small differences between the images in the two eyes, and because the neuronal substrate for such comparison doesn't occur below the level of the visual cortex as seems to be the case, stereopsis gives us direct access to cortical visual processing. This implication is examined in great detail by Bela Julesz (1971).

In recent years, investigators working in a number of laboratories have developed techniques for testing stereopsis in very young infants. The results have shown a very satisfying agreement (Teller, 1983). Stereopsis appears to emerge on the average toward the end of the fourth postnatal month, based on full-term gestational age, with a range such that 20% appear to have it by 2 months and 80% before 5 months. More striking from a developmental point of view is the finding that the fineness of stereopsis, called stereoacuity, increases very rapidly from the onset of stereopsis, such that within a few weeks it approaches adult levels (Birch, Gwiazda, & Held, 1982; Held, Birch, & Gwiazda, 1980). This result contrasts strikingly with the rate of development of grating acuity, which increases rapidly over the first 6 months after birth and then more slowly over the first few years (Birch, Gwiazda, Bauer, Naegele, & Held, 1983; Teller, 1981). Grating acuity barely changes during the period in which stereoacuity changes rapidly. The sharpness of the change in stereoacuity implies that some radical change in the neuronal substrate is occurring, and that substrate is very probably cortical. Before considering the possibilities for modeling this underlying process, I want to consider three other developmental findings that confirm and amplify the importance of the timing of the changes under discussion.

Binocular Function

When part or all of the visual field before an observer moves in one direction, the eyes will follow up to some limiting displacement and then saccade back to their former positions. This process then repeats itself in a periodic manner that is called optokinetic nystagmus. In normally sighted adults the following response is equally well elicited by motion in either rightward or leftward directions. If only one eye is used, the same equivalence is observed. However, in observers who suffer from anomalies of binocular vision such as strabismus (crossed eyes), the following response of an eye to both directions of motion is not equivalent. The following tends to be better for motion running from the side toward the midline, called the temporonasal direction, than it is for motion in the opposite direction called nasotemporal. In this regard the optokinetic response of those who suffer from these binocular anomalies resembles that of many animals who have lateralized eyes (Tauber & Atkin, 1968). In the former case it appears that the neuronal substrate for symmetrical OKN has a cortical component related to binocularity, whereas in the latter the animal with predominantly lateral eyes has little binocular overlap and accordingly limited central convergence of the inputs from the two eyes. The goodness of the following response can be quantified in terms of the measure called gain. Gain is the ratio of the velocity of the eye to that of the moving field, where the ratio one to one is the optimal.

In recent experiments we have managed to measure the gain of the nasotemporal relative to that of temporonasal response in infants ranging in age from 1 month to 6 months (Naegele & Held, 1982). The results show that very young infants behave like strabismics and show little or no following to nasotemporal motion but relatively normal following to temporonasal motion. However, the gain of the response to nasotemporal motion increases steadily through the first 4 months, until it reaches equivalence between the two directions. In summary, the equalization of the gains of the optokinetic responses to the two directions occurs on the average toward the end of the fourth month, just as does the achievement of stereopsis.

A process similar to the aforementioned occurs in the case of binocular summation of the pupillary response. When one eye of a normally sighted adult views a large illuminated field, the other eye being closed, its pupil constricts to some steady state diameter. If the other eye is now opened, the pupil of the first eye will further constrict by a small but significant increment. One of the investigators of this phenomenon, Matthew Alpern (1970), has observed no such summation in his own pupillary responses, but he has strabismus. The lack of summation has since been observed in many observers suffering from binocular imbalance, implying that binocular convergence at the cortex may be involved in this summation. Eileen Birch in our laboratory decided to test infants for this form of binocularity. She soon found that very young infants did not show the effect, but that it appeared on the average toward the end of the fourth month of life (Birch & Held, 1983). Once again, this age emerges as a transition point in the evolution of binocular function.

Thus far I have described three types of evidence that binocular function is perfected sometime during the fourth month on average. The evidence is drawn from sources that show enhanced capabilities resulting from either direct or implied interaction between inputs to the two eyes. A fourth form of evidence comes from a source in which reduced function actually occurs. This source is the evidence for what appears to be the onset of amblyopia, resulting from congenital esotropia (crossed-eyes) with strong fixation preference by one eye. This condition is well known to be frequently accompanied by low acuity in the habitually deviated eye, a condition known as amblyopia (lazy eye).

Amblyopia

We have asked the question, what is the time course of development of this abnormally low acuity? The answer to this question could help decide between the two possibilities that either amblyopia is a consequence of esotropia, or esotropia is the consequence of poor vision in one eye. Of course, both could be true, and probably are, but the developmental sequence of the two events might distinguish cause from effect.

Using measures of grating acuity derived from a two-choice preference procedure (Gwiazda, Brill, Mohindra, & Held, 1980), we have made serial measurements on four congenital esotropes and found the following result in all cases. When first measured, the two eyes were found to be equal in acuity and at a level normal for the age tested. However, in all four cases, measurement at a later age showed significant differences in acuity, with the acuity of the deviating eye found to be less than that of the straight eye (Jacobson, Mohindra, & Held, 1981). Moreover, in every case the deviating eye showed a lesser acuity; it had actually decreased from the previous test. The average age at which the transition from equal to unequal acuities occurred turned out once again to be toward the end of the fourth month of life.

Thus it appears that at some point during development when binocularity becomes perfected, not only is the visual system capable of enhanced performance in at least three ways, it also becomes subject to the deleterious effects of binocular imbalance resulting from esotropia.

Neuronal Mechanism

The abrupt onset of binocular function suggests the sudden availability of an underlying neuronal mechanism for processing information combined from the two eyes. Do we have any candidates for such a process? So far we have discussed only data drawn from the study of human infants. The search for a neuronal mechanism must draw information from the study of animals in which the development of the visual nervous system has been delineated. Several indices of binocularity have been examined in both cat and monkey. Consider the cat first.

Timney has studied the development of depth discrimination in the kitten. He finds a rapid rise in such discrimination specific to the use of both eyes during the fifth and subsequent weeks of life (1981). He argues that this ability depends on stereopsis. Recording from single cells in the visual cortex of kittens, Pettigrew claims that sensitivity to disparity matures at this time (1974). Thus the times of onset are the same for both physiological and behavioral evidence for stereopsis in the cat.

Other evidence indicates that the sensitive period for loss of stereopsis resulting from monocular occlusion begins in the fifth week after birth, peaks during the next few weeks, and falls off over the next several weeks (Timney, in press). Moreover, results coming from surgically induced squint imply that the deviating eye becomes amblyopic if surgery is performed before 12 weeks of age and not after that time (Jacobson & Ikeda, 1979). This result is again consistent with a sensitive period for the development of amblyopia immediately following the development of stereopsis. Finally, van Hof-van Duin (1978) reports that optokinetic nystagmus becomes symmetrical in the kitten between 5 and 8 weeks of age.

Only two of these indices of the onset of binocularity in the monkey are currently to be found. Kiorpes and Boothe report that the onset of amblyopia in animals made esotropic by surgery occurs between 5 and 6 weeks of age (1980). Atkinson reports that the symmetrization of optokinetic nystagmus is achieved during the fifth week of age (1979).

According to these indices, binocularity in both cat and monkey appears to have its onset during the fifth week of life. What neural developments in cat and monkey could account for this behavioral development? Elsewhere (Held, in press) we have cited the evidence for completion of segregation of the ocular dominance columns in layer IV in the cat (LeVay, Stryker, & Shatz, 1978) and layer IV C in the monkey (LeVay, Wiesel, & Hubel, 1980). Prior to such segregation, it appears that the geniculocortical afferents from the two eyes are mixed so that they synapse on common cortical neurons in those layers (see Fig. 3.1A). Unless one assumes that the disparity selective neurons responsible for stereopsis are to be found in these layers, which appears most doubtful, one must look to the extragranular layers (outside layer IV) for such cells. In these layers axons from the cells of layer IV carrying information from noncorresponding (disparate) retinal loci may be expected to synapse so as to yield disparity selective neurons in the mature system (Poggio & Fisher, 1977) (Fig. 3.1B). However, in the immature system, prior to segregation of the columns, the output from cells of layer IV may be so mixed as to eye of origin, as to preclude the formation of disparity selective cells (Fig. 3.1A). Whereas the process that is responsible for the segregation of the columns is not yet well understood, it appears that the geniculate axons originating from one eye withdraw (atrophy?) from the region to be occupied only by axons originating from the other eye. This process may correspond to that of selective stabilization discussed in detail by Changeux and Danchin (1976).

Although this explanation of the onset of binocular function may be plausible, it is not complete. Study of the development of vernier acuity has shown that

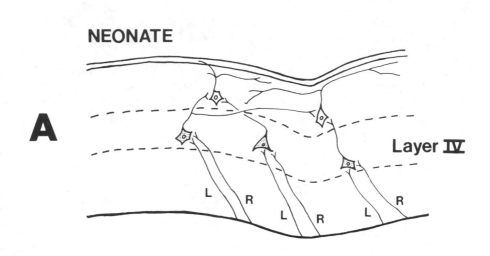

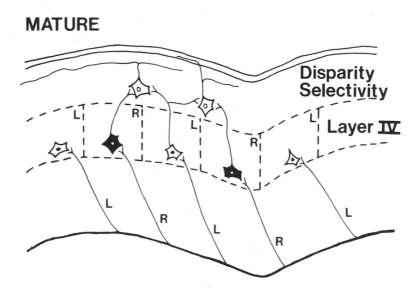

FIG. 3.1.   A. Geniculostriate afferents from both eyes (R and L) synapse on the
same cells in layer IV, thereby losing information about the eye of origin.
B. Geniculostriate afferents are segregated on the basis of eye origin (R and L),
and consequently recipient cells in layer IV may send their axons to cells outside
of that layer so as to synapse on cells that may be disparity selective.

its onset and increase occur in the human infant over a time course much like that of stereopsis (Shimojo, Birch, & Held, 1983). However, vernier acuity does not depend on having two eyes with binocular combination of their information. It can equally well be observed with the use of one eye only. Consequently, it appears that, whereas segregation of the ocular dominance columns is a necessary condition for binocular function, it is not sufficient. In addition, during this early period the cortex develops the capacity to compute the positions of edges with the precision necessary to account for both stereopsis and vernier acuities.

REFERENCES

Alpern, M. The pupillary light reflex and binocular interaction. In F. Young and D. Lindsley (Eds.), Early experience and visual information processing in perceptual and reading disorders. *National Academy of Science*, 1970.

Aslin, R. N., Alberts, J. R., & Petersen, M. R. (Eds.). *Development of perception* (Vol. 2). New York: Academic Press, 1981.

Atkinson, J. Development of optokinetic nystagmus in the human infant and monkey infant: An analogue to development in kittens. In R. D. Freeman (Ed.), *Developmental neurobiology of vision*. New York: Plenum Press, 1979.

Birch, E., Gwiazda, J., Bauer, J. A., Jr., Naegele, J., & Held, R. Visual acuity and its meridional variations in children aged 7 to 60 months. *Vision Research*, 1983, *23*, 10, 1019–1024.

Birch, E. Gwiazda, J., & Held, R. Stereoacuity development for crossed and uncrossed disparities in human infants. *Vision Research*, 1982, *22*, 507–513.

Birch, E., & Held, R. The development of binocular summation in human infants. *Investigative Ophthalmology and Visual Science*, 1983, *24*, 1103–1107.

Changeux, J. P., & Danchin, A. Selective stablization of developing synapses as a mechanism for the specification of neuronal networks. *Nature*, 1976, *264*, 705 712.

Foley, J. M. Primary distance perception. In R. Held, H. W. Leibowitz, & H.-L. Teuber (Eds.), *Handbook of sensory physiology* (Vol. 8). New York: Springer, 1978.

Gwiazda, J., Brill, S., Mohindra, I., & Held, R. Preferential looking acuity in infants from 2 to 58 weeks of age. *American Journal of Optometry and Physiological Optics*, 1980, *57*, 428 432.

Held, R. The development of binocularity. *Trends in Neuroscience*, in press.

Held, R., Birch, E., & Gwiazda, J. Stereoacuity of human infants. *Proceedings of the National Academy of Sciences, USA*, 1980, *77*, 5572–5574.

Jacobson, S. G., & Ikeda, H. Behavioral studies of spatial vision in cats reared with convergent squint: Is amblyopia due to arrest of development? *Experimental Brain Research*, 1979, *34*, 11–26.

Jacobson, S. G., Mohindra, I., & Held, R. Age of onset of amblyopia in infants with esotropia. *Documenta Ophthalmologica*, Proceedings Series, 1981, *30*, 210–216.

Julesz, B. *Foundations of cyclopean perception*. University of Chicago Press, 1971.

Kiorpes, L., & Boothe, R. G. Strabismic amblyopia development in infant monkeys. *Investigative Ophthalmology and Visual Science*, 1980, *19*, 841–845.

LeVay, S., Stryker, M. P., & Shatz, C. J. Ocular dominance columns and their development in layer IV of the cat's visual cortex: A quantitative study. *Journal of Comparative Neurology*, 1978, *179*, 223–244.

LeVay, S., Wiesel, T. N., & Hubel, D. H. The development of ocular dominance columns in normal and visually deprived monkeys. *J. Comp. Neurol.*, 1980, *191*, 1–51.

Naegele, J. R., & Held, R. The postnatal development of monocular optokinetic nystagmus in infants. *Vision Research*, 1982, *22*, 341–346.

Pettigrew, J. D. The effect of visual experience on the development of stimulus specificity by kitten cortical neurons. *Journal of Physiology*, 1974, *237*, 49.

Poggio, G. F., & Fischer, B. *Journal of Neurophysiology*, 1977, *40*, 1392–1405.

Shimojo, S., Birch, E., & Held, R. Development of vernier acuity assessed by preferential looking. *Supplement: Investigative Ophthalmology & Visual Science*, 1983, *24*, 93.

Tauber, E., & Atkin, A. Optomotor responses to monocular stimulation: Relation to visual system organization. *Science*, 1968, *160*, 1365–1367.

Teller, D. Y. The development of visual acuity in human and monkey infants. *Trends in Neuroscience*, 1981, *4*, 22–24.

Teller, D. Y. Scotopic vision, color vision, and stereopsis in infants. *Current Eye Research*, 1983, *2*, 199–210.

Timney, B. Development of bincular depth perception in kittens. *Investigative Ophthalmology and Visual Sci.*, 1981, *21*, 493–496.

Timney, B. The effects of early and late monocular deprivation on binocular depth perception in cats. *Developmental Brain Research*, in press.

Van-Hof-Van Duin, J. Direction preference of optokinetic responses in monocularly tested normal kittens and light deprived cats. *Arch. Ital. Biol.*, 1978, *116*, 471–477.

4 Development of Visual Space Perception in Young Infants

Albert Yonas
Carl E. Granrud
Institute of Child Development
University of Minnesota

INTRODUCTION

From an evolutionary perspective, perception of the three-dimensional layout of the environment is one of the most useful abilities that an animal can possess. The fact that humans possess sensitivity to so many redundant depth cues is significant, suggesting that even a small improvement in the ability to perceive the layout of objects and surfaces in the environment must have provided a significant evolutionary advantage. For those of a creationist bent, one could note that God must have loved depth cues, for He made so many of them. Our research group at Minnesota is currently studying the development of sensitivity to many of the depth cues that provide information for spatial layout. We have been trying to replace speculations about the development of spatial perception with experimental data from studies of responsiveness to the many types of potential depth information. Our first step toward this goal was to break down spatial information into three classes: kinetic, binocular, and static monocular (pictorial) information. Within each class we have attempted to isolate single depth cues and to test for the emergence of sensitivity and responsiveness to each cue. We hope that knowing when sensitivity to a particular source of depth information first appears will be useful in understanding the development of the mechanisms that accomplish the detection of that information.

In this chapter we discuss recent studies of sensitivity to kinetic, binocular, and pictorial information for spatial layout, the cumulative results of which suggest a hypothesis about the sequence in which sensitivity to these three types of stimulus information appears. Sensitivity to kinetic information may be present at birth or very soon thereafter; sensitivity to binocular information appears during the fourth month; and sensitivity to static pictorial information appears at about 5½ months. If future evidence agrees that this description is generally correct for human infants, we can then ask about the underlying mechanisms responsible for this sequence. For example, we might explore the relative importance of experience and physiological maturation in the appearance of responsiveness to various types of visual information, or we might examine the constraints employed by the visual system in detecting spatial information.

KINETIC INFORMATION

Almost without exception, the traditional lists of depth cues found in perception textbooks exclude motion-carried information. The traditional cues include the so-called "primary" cues of binocular disparity, convergence, and accommodation, and the "secondary" cues of linear perspective, familiar size, and shading (Braunstein, 1976; Gibson, 1950). The only commonly accepted depth cue based on motion-carried information is motion parallax.

Motion parallax (the relative retinal displacements of objects at different distances as an observer moves through a static environment; Helmholtz, 1925), however, is only one of a number of transformations of the proximal stimulus that occur when the observer or external objects move (Gibson, 1966). Other transformations that have been explored include the optical expansion pattern produced by movement through the visual world (Lee, 1980), the approach of an object to a viewer (Gibson, 1958), the pattern of retinal change produced by object rotation, and the accretion and deletion of texture at the edges of objects when an observer moves or when an object moves relative to an observer (Kaplan, 1969).

Research on infant perception has viewed motion primarily as a variable that is important for controlling attention, rather than as a source of invariant information for the three-dimensional structure of the environment. Very little is known about the development of sensitivity to kinetic information for the layout of the environment or for spatial events. In order to fill this gap in our knowledge of infants' perception, we have begun to study the development of sensitivity to several types of motion-carried, or kinetic, information for spatial layout. The first of these studies involved information for impending collision.

Kinetic Information for Impending Collision

Gibson's (1958) theoretical analysis of symmetrical optic expansion patterns as information for approaching objects was the basis for early studies of sensitivity to impending collision with various nonhuman species (Schiff, 1965). Whereas an expanding pattern (i.e., collision display) elicited defensive locomotions in newborn dark-reared chicks, contraction of the image did not. Studies by Pettersen, Yonas, & Fisch (1980) suggest that defensive responses develop more slowly in human infants. They found a substantial increase in the likelihood of a blink response to an approaching object from the sixth to the tenth week in full-term infants. Furthermore, 6-week-old infants who were born postterm (3 to 4 weeks after due date) blinked to an approaching object more consistantly than did full-term 6-week olds. Although this result indicates that maturation plays an important role in increased sensitivity to collision information, it does not rule out the possibility that learning the tactual consequences of an optical symmetrically expanding contour that fills the visual field may also contribute to sensitivity.

Recently, Yonas, Pettersen, Lockman, & Eisenberg (1980) have explored the properties of the kinetic event that is needed to evoke defensive blinking and backward head movement in 3-month-old infants. In this study the extent of the visual field filled by an expanding textured object was varied, as was the type of transformation. Displays expanded to fill either 30° or 100° of the visual field, and the expansion pattern specified either a small object that would collide with the subject's face or a larger object that would stop 10 inches from the face. In the collision transformation the expansion included the "explosive" portion of a hyperbolic expansion, whereas the other condition did not (see Fig. 4.1). The results of the study were quite clear. Three-month-old infants responded consistently only in the condition in which explosive expansion filled a 100° visual field. In this condition they blinked on 66% of the trials and frequently moved their heads backward. In the other approach conditions they responded much as they did on withdrawal trials, blinking on 20 to 36% of the trials. This pattern of results suggests that the blinking and backward head movements evoked by displays that specify imminent collision are not simply reflex responses to nonspatial characteristics of the display. Rather, the 3-month-old infant appears to respond to the particular spatiotemporal transformation that specifies imminent collision. This argues that depth perception based on kinetic information is present in the 3-month old. (For a detailed review of this research see Yonas, 1981.)

A series of recent unpublished experiments, utilizing the same technique of varying properties of the kinetic event, has been carried out with 4-week-old infants. In contrast to the differential response rate observed with 3-month-old infants, younger infants do not respond differently to "dangerous" and "non-dangerous" approach conditions. They do blink more frequently to expansion (approach) than to contraction (withdrawal) of an object (Yonas, Pettersen, & Lockman, 1979), but they do not discriminate an object that approaches at a constant velocity from an object that slows as it approaches. In addition, the likelihood that the 1-month-old infant will blink to an approaching object is only 30%. Unlike the 3-month-old, the young infant stares unblinking most of the time as a large object approaches the eye. This must have been one reason that

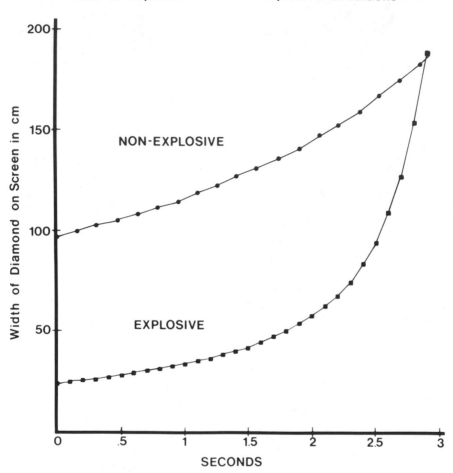

Diameter of Expanding Diamond over 3 Second
Trial in Explosive and Non-Explosive Conditions

NON-EXPLOSIVE

EXPLOSIVE

Width of Diamond on Screen in cm

SECONDS

FIG. 4.1.   Change in display size on the 3-second trial period in collision and
in noncollision conditions. Note the very rapid explosive expansion rate during
the final half second of the collision condition and the almost linear, nonexplosive
expansion in the control condition.

so many psychologists and pediatricians of the past concluded that the newborn
was blind. However, if one presents many trials in which an object is moved
toward and away from an infant's eyes, approach will evoke significantly more
frequent blinking than withdrawal. Thus, some sensitivity is present, but one
cannot feel very secure in concluding that depth perception is present in the 1-
month old on the basis of a small, but reliable, difference in blink rate.

Accretion and Deletion of Texture

Because environments are filled with opaque objects and surfaces, the visual world is divided into visible and occluded surfaces at each possible observation point. When an observer moves through an environment, or when an object moves relative to an observer, some surfaces are occluded and others are revealed (Gibson, 1966). At the level of the proximal stimulus, movement produces accretion and deletion of visible texture. Gibson (1966, 1979) has argued that, because this transformation in the proximal stimulus is lawfully determined by the spatial layout of objects and surfaces in the environment, accretion and deletion of texture in the proximal stimulus unambiguously specifies an edge, and thus one surface in front of another at that edge. Gibson's hypothesis has been supported by Kaplan (1969), who found that for adults accretion and deletion of texture provides effective information for depth at an edge.

In a recent study, Yonas, Granrud, & Smith (1982) found that 7-month-old infants can also use this information to perceive the spatial layout of surfaces. Seven-month-old infants viewed computer-generated random-dot displays in which accretion and deletion of texture provided the only information for contours or for depth at an edge (see Fig. 4.2). When adults viewed these displays, they reported seeing a textured rectangular surface moving horizontally in front of a moving textured background. Because by 20 weeks of age infants have a strong tendency to reach to the closer of two surfaces (Granrud, Yonas, & Pettersen, in press), we used reaching as an index of depth sensitivity. It was hypothesized that infants would reach more often for the apparently nearer surface than for

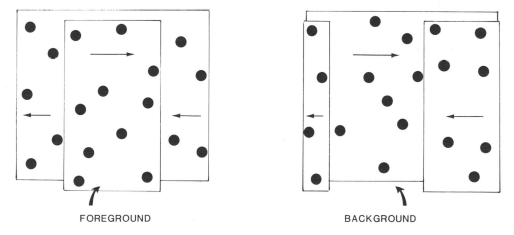

FOREGROUND   BACKGROUND

FIG. 4.2.   Schematic drawing of display in which accretion and deletion of texture provide the only information for an edge and depth. Foreground and background moved in opposite directions at equal velocity.

the apparent background surface, if they were sensitive to accretion and deletion of texture as information for depth at an edge.

It was found that 48% of the infants' reaches were for the "foreground," whereas 35% were for the "background." The remainder of the reaches were for the edges between the "foreground" and "background." The difference between the percentage of reaches to the "foreground" and the "background" was statistically significant, indicating that 7-month olds are sensitive to accretion and deletion of visual texture as information for depth at an edge. A group of 5-month-old infants is currently being studied in the same experiment.

Motion Parallax

Although it has often been suggested that motion parallax is an important, or perhaps even primary, source of information used by infants for perceiving spatial layout (Bower, 1966; E. J. Gibson, 1969), no empirical study has yet demonstrated infants' sensitivity to motion parallax. Only recently, Rogers and Graham (1979) developed a technique for isolationg motion parallax from other sources of spatial information. They found, with adults as subjects, that displays varying only the velocity of horizontally moving random dots can provide a compelling impression of three dimensionality not unlike that provided by stereopsis. In these experiments, each movement of the observer or the display oscilloscope transformed the random-dot patterns to simulate the relative movement information produced by a three-dimensional surface. We are currently planning a study in which this type of display will be shown to infants in an attempt to determine when sensitivity to motion parallax first emerges in development.

Kinetic Information: Conclusion

Although many important questions remain unanswered, some progress has been made in understanding the development of sensitivity to motion-carried information. Our research suggests that very young infants may be sensitive to kinetic information for the event of impending collision with an approaching object, and that by 7 months of age infants perceive the spatial layout of surfaces from purely kinetic information (accretion and deletion). In addition, recent work by Bertenthal and Proffitt (1982) and Fox and McDaniel (1982) suggests that 4-month-old infants may perceive three-dimensional shape from kinetic information.

These studies, taken together, demonstrate that infants can perceive spatial layout on the basis of kinetic transformations in the optic array. In addition, they support James Gibson's (1966) hypothesis that the pickup of motion-carried information is a fundamental, not secondary, aspect of the visual system, even early in life.

BINOCULAR INFORMATION

In the first of our studies on infants' sensitivity to binocular depth information, Gordon and Yonas (1976) reasoned that if reaches terminated at locations that varied systematically with the location of a stereoscopically projected virtual object, the evidence for binocular depth perception would be convincing. The virtual object was presented by using a stereoscopic shadow caster. Polarized filters were placed over the infant's eyes, and a real object was positioned between the lamps and a rear projection screen. In such a situation, an observer with binocular depth perception sees not a pair of shadows on the screen, but a single object at a precise location in space. Using this method of presentation, a virtual object was positioned within and beyond the reach of 5-month-old infants. During the study, it seemed to the experimenters that the infants were reached for the virtual object. However, an analysis of the reaches revealed that the endpoints of the reaches did not vary reliably with the location of the virtual object. However, three other measures indicated that 5-month olds were responsive to the virtual object's apparent location. When the virtual object was located beyond rather than within reach, the infants tended to lean forward so that their heads were closer to the screen. In addition, the infants reached and grasped more frequently when the virtual object was within reach. Considered together, the leaning behavior and the frequency of reaching and of grasping provide clear evidence that by 5 months infants respond to binocular stimulation. These results show that infants can distinguish an object that is within reach from one that is not.

It seems that precisely localized reaching provides an ideal index of the development of more fine-grained binocular spatial sensitivity. To investigate the development of such behavior, Gordon, Lamson, and Yonas (unpublished) tested infants of three ages in an experiment based on Gordon and Yonas' (1976) study. Infants aged 5½, 7½, and 9½ months were presented a virtual object at three distances. All three age groups reached least often to the virtual object when it was most distant. In addition, infants leaned farthest forward when the virtual object was at its most distant position, and they leaned least when the object was in the position closest to them. It seems, then, that on the basis of binocular information, infants at 5½ months may be able to make spatial distinctions finer than "within" versus "beyond" reach.

The accuracy of the reaches increased reliably with age. The 5½-month olds tended to place their hands a constant distance from their bodies, whereas the 7½- and 9½-month olds reached out farther when the object was at a greater distance. Apparently, at 5½ months, the trunk responds with more precision to binocular depth information than do the arms.

In order to investigate further the onset of sensitivity to binocular depth information, Yonas, Oberg, and Norcia (1978) presented 14- and 20-week-old infants with binocular information for a slowly approaching object. The stereoscopic shadow caster created a small virtual object that appeared to a binocular viewer as if it would collide with the bridge of the viewer's nose. To create a nonstereoscopic control condition, the polarized filters were removed from the point-source lamps. In this condition, instead of the approaching object, the viewer saw two shadows expanding and separating on the rear projection screen. The two objects appeared to be approaching on paths that would diverge and miss the viewer. This display provided the same visual experience as the stereoscopic condition would provide to a diplopic viewer.

The responses of the 20-week olds were quite different in the two conditions. In the stereoscopic condition, they reached toward the screen more frequently than in the control condition. They also blinked and withdrew their heads more often in the stereoscopic condition; this suggests that the 20-week olds were trying to avoid collision with the approaching virtual object. In contrast, the 14-week olds provided little evidence of responsiveness to binocular depth information. The frequency of forward arm movements, head withdrawal, and blinking did not differ in the two conditions for the younger infants. However, the conditions did differ on one measure for both age groups: There was a more sustained visual orientation to the center of the display in the stereoscopic condition. This behavior indicates that the viewer's eyes are converging on the approaching object (without binocular depth perception, one would see two diverging shadows and would probably look from side to side). Although convergence is not a clear indication of the presence of binocular depth sensitivity, it is a prerequisite to its appearance.

It would be a mistake to conclude, on the basis of the present evidence, that binocular depth sensitivity is absent in infants under 20 weeks of age. In a preliminary study carried out by Rezba (unpublished), the latency of swiping arm movements was recorded for a group of 15-week-old infants. In this study, a stereoscopic virtual object elicited arm movements sooner when it was located close to the infant than when it was positioned out of reach. Although the arm movements of 3½-month olds have little of the character of object-directed reaching, these infants do detect systematic variation in the stimulation. If the arm movements are actual attempts to contact the object, then the more frequent movements to the close virtual object imply that binocular depth sensitivity is present at 15 weeks.

Recently, it has been pointed out that experiments using a stereo shadowcaster display may not provide clear evidence that infants are sensitive to binocular disparity, because this apparatus does not eliminate monocular cues that could result in the availability of convergence as a source of information for the location of the virtual object (Aslin & Dumais, 1980). Fox, Aslin, Shea, and Dumais (1980), therefore, tested infants' stereopsis using random-dot stereograms that eliminate all monocular cues. They found that infants as young as 3½ months of age tracked a virtual object that was specified by binocular disparity alone. This result indicates sensitivity to binocular disparity. However, in order to conclude that infants perceive depth in a random-dot stereogram, it would be desirable to observe a spatially appropriate response to the display (Yonas & Pick, 1975). Granrud and Yonas are planning an experiment, using reaching as the dependent measure and random-dot stereograms as experimental displays, in which infants view anaglyphs with crossed and uncrossed disparity. If infants perceive the depth in these displays, they should reach more frequently for the slides with crossed disparity, because the virtual object in these slides will appear much nearer to them than the virtual object in the slides with uncrossed disparity. With this experiment we hope to discover whether infants actually perceive depth from disparity alone.

Comparison of Monocular and Binocular Depth Perception

Although there are now data suggesting that young infants are sensitive to binocular depth information, it has been suggested that infants' depth perception is based primarily on detection of monocular information. Bower (1966), for example, reported that in his experiments on infants' discrimination of object size and distance: "motion parallax was the most effective cue to depth, followed by binocular parallax [p. 88]." In a recent study, Granrud, Yonas, and Pettersen (in press) compared monocular and binocular depth perception in 5- and 7-month olds. Reaching was used as an index of depth perception. A small disc was presented within reach for the infants and a larger disc was positioned beyond reach. The visual angles of the discs were matched. Viewing the display binocularly, infants in both age groups reached for the closer object on approximately 90% of the trials; with monocular presentation, they reached to the closer object on about 60% of the trials. The high degree of consistency in reaching for the near object in the binocular condition indicated the effectiveness of binocular vision for discriminating relative distance. Furthermore, the preference to reach for the nearer object was significantly greater in the binocular than in the monocular condition.

Therefore, whereas the results from the monocular condition demonstrated infants' sensitivity to monocular depth information, the results from the binocular condition indicated that binocular information greatly facilitates perception of objects' spatial locations. Although monocular perception is sufficient for making some spatial discriminations (such as avoiding the deep side of a visual cliff, Walk, 1968), binocular perception seems to be more effective than monocular perception for guiding fine spatial behavior, such as reaching for a nearby object. These results are clearly inconsistent with Bower's claim that infants' depth perception is based primarily on monocular information. Evidently, infants as young as 5 months of age not only use binocular information for perceiving spatial layout, but binocular information combined with monocular information provides the infant with more veridical perception of distance than does monocular information alone.

Finally, the results of this study have a methodological implication. The finding that infants direct nearly all their reaches to the nearer of two objects when sufficient information is available for the objects' relative distances shows that preferential reaching is a highly sensitive measure of infants' depth perception. The studies reported in the following section all exploited infants' tendency to reach preferentially for the nearer of two objects or for the nearer side of a surface, by using reaching as the dependent measure for investigating infants' sensitivity to pictorial depth information.

PICTORIAL DEPTH INFORMATION

Until recently, little research had been done concerning infants' sensitivity to pictorial depth information. The first such studies (Bower, 1966; Day & McKenzie, 1973) suggested that young infants are not responsive to this information. However, in both these studies, kinetic and binocular information for the actual flatness of the experimental displays was available to the infants. This conflicting information may have overridden the effectiveness of pictorial information.

Trapezoidal Window Studies

More recently, Yonas, Cleaves, and Pettersen (1978) examined infants' sensitivity to pictorial depth when conflicting information for the flat surface of the experimental display was minimized. The display was based on an Ames trapezoidal window (Ames, 1951), created by photographing a rectangular window rotated 45° about the vertical axis. The resulting trapezoidal form and "window spaces" were cut from the photograph so that the infant could see through the internal spaces of the display, thereby minimizing the pictorial surface texture (see Fig. 4.3). When viewed monocularly by adults, this display creates a powerful illusion of a slanted rectangular window with one side several inches closer than the other. It was hypothesized that if infants were sensitive to the depth information in the display, their reaches would be directed to the apparently nearer side.

In the first experiment, 6-month-old infants were presented with a real rectangular window rotated to bring the left or right side of the object nearer the infant. It was established that they directed their reaching with sufficient accuracy to demonstrate sensitivity to the differential distances of the two sides of a slanted object and would do so while wearing an eyepatch. Although no binocular information was available, the infants reached to the closer side of the object

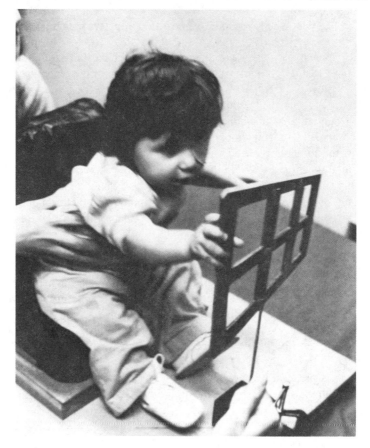

FIG. 4.3.   Six-month-old infant wearing eye patch, grasping frontal trapezoidal window.

on 75% of the trials, indicating sensitivity to accommodation, kinetic, and/or pictorial information.

In a second experiment, the trapezoidal window photograph was presented frontally without motion to 6-month-old infants. In order to control for the possibility that infants prefer to reach for the larger side of the display without regard to depth information, a size-control display was created with one side smaller than the other, but with no information that the sides were at different distances. The infants presented with the trapezoidal window reached to the larger side of the display twice as often as they reached to the smaller side. The infants presented with the size-control display, in contrast, reached for the two sides with equal frequency.

The next experiment was an attempt to replicate the finding that infants reach to the larger side of the trapezoidal window and to determine whether this is attributable to a preference to reach for some other property, such as acute angles, rather than to the apparently nearer side of the display. Infants were randomly assigned to either binocular or monocular viewing of the trapezoidal window. It was reasoned that if depth information were the basis for the tendency to reach for the larger side of the trapezoidal window, it should be possible to minimize the effectiveness of pictorial depth by providing binocular depth information for the actual orientation of the object. The results for the group of infants who viewed the trapezoidal display monocularly replicated the results of the previous experiment; the infants preferred to reach for the larger and pictorially nearer side. The infants who viewed the display binocularly showed significantly less directionality in their reaching. It is clear, then, that when conflicting binocular information is absent, 6-month-old infants are responsive to pictorial depth information. The study also demonstrates indirectly that 6-month-old infants are responsive to binocular depth information.

The final goal of these studies was to establish the age at which sensitivity to the pictorial depth information present in the trapezoidal window first appears. The display was presented to a group of 5-month olds. Although fewer of the younger infants reached frequently to the display, the infants provided us with enough responses to judge the direction of their reaching. Although these infants wore an eye patch that excluded conflicting binocular information, they showed no evidence of sensitivity to the depth information available in the window. They reached as frequently to the smaller (pictorially farther) side of the display as to the larger (pictorially nearer) side. The possibility that these infants were too inaccurate in their reaching behavior to indicate depth sensitivity was refuted when a second group of 20- to 22-week-old infants, also wearing eye patches, consistently directed their reaches toward the near side of a slanted, rectangular window. Accommodation, motion parallax, and pictorial information all provide consistent information for the difference in the distances of the two sides of an actually slanted object. The trapezoidal window makes pictorial information available, but accommodation and motion parallax specify that the window is in the frontal plane. We reasoned that some pictorial sensitivity may be present in these young infants but is perhaps so weak that conflicting information overrides its effects.

In a later study, Kaufmann, Maland, and Yonas (1981) presented the trapezoidal window to 5-month-old infants, with the smaller side slanted 30° toward the subject. When adults view this display monocularly, they report that the farther side of the window (the larger side) appears to be nearer than the side that is actually closer. The 20- to 22-week olds reached to the actually closer, but pictorially farther, side of the trapezoidal window with the same high consistency as they had to the closer side of the rectangular window. Thus it appears that at 5 months infants are not sensitive to the depth information present in the trapezoidal window. Furthermore, although pictorial information seems to be ineffective as an indicator of depth, accommodation and/or motion parallax appear to be informative for 5-month-old infants.

It is clear from these studies that 6-month-old infants do respond spatially to a trapezoidal window display. It is not clear, however, what pictorial information guides these responses. The trapezoidal window combines several different sources of spatial information (e.g., relative size, linear perspective, angular perspective, and shading). Recently, we conducted several studies to explore infants' sensitivity to various depth cues isolated from other spatial information. The first of these studies examined the development of sensitivity to the cue of relative size.

Relative Size

When two objects that are equal in size are at different distances from an observer, the nearer object subtends a larger visual angle than the farther. If the two objects are taken to be approximately equal in distal size, the relationship between the objects' visual angles can be a source of information for the objects' relative distances. This source of information, or depth cue, is called relative size.

Although there is substantial evidence that adults can employ relative size information to perceive relative distance (Epstein & Baratz, 1964), no research on the development of this ability in infants had been carried out until recently. Yonas, Granrud, and Pettersen (in press) explored sensitivity to relative size in infants from 5 to 7 months of age. In these experiments, infants viewed two different-sized objects of various shapes (squares, circles, and triangles) presented side by side suspended in front of a dark vertical surface. The two objects were always at equal distances from the infant.

To establish the effectiveness of the illusion produced by the displays, they were first presented to adults both monocularly and binocularly. Pairs of triangles, squares, and diamonds were presented; the larger object was approximately twice the size of the smaller shape. When adults viewed the displays monocularly, the depth effect was striking. They reported that the larger object appeared closer than the smaller one on approximately 80% of the trials, and that the objects appeared equidistant on 20% of the trials. When the displays were viewed with two eyes, the larger object was judged closer much less often—on only about 30% of the trials. However, some depth effect remained, because the smaller object was judged closer only 7% of the time (the objects were judged to be equidistant on the remaining trials). Furthermore, when the pair of objects differed in shape and in orientation of contours, adults viewing them monocularly perceived the larger one as closer just as frequently as they did when the objects did not differ in shape. Apparently, dissimilarity in shape does not diminish the relative size effect for adults.

In the relative size experiments with infants, reaching was used as an index of depth perception. Granrud, Yonas, and Pettersen (in press) found that infants as young as 5 months of age will reach for the nearer of two objects with great consistency if sufficient information for relative distance is available. The goal of this study was to determine whether relative size information for depth could influence reaching in the same way when binocular information for the objects' equal distance was eliminated. Seven-month-old infants were presented with pairs of discs and triangles both monocularly and binocularly. They showed a significantly greater tendency to reach for the larger object in the monocular condition than in the binocular condition.

This same pattern of reaching preferences was observed when a group of 5½-month olds (22 to 24 weeks) was presented with a pair of discs. They reached for the larger disc on 65% of the trials with monocular presentation, but on only 50% of the binocular trials. For the youngest infants studied (20-to-22-week olds), behavior in the monocular and binocular conditions did not differ. In both conditions, they reached more frequently to the larger object.

The results indicate that for 7- and 5½-month-old infants the relationship between angular sizes of objects is an effective source of information for those objects' relative distances. Results from the binocular viewing conditions eliminate the possibility that infants preferred to reach for the larger objects without regard to their apparent distances. If this were the case, infants should have reached more frequently for the larger objects under both binocular and monocular viewing conditions, but no such preference was observed in these older infants. Thus, the most plausible explanation for the results is that infants perceived the larger objects as closer than the smaller objects in the monocular conditions and detected stereoscopic information that specified the objects as equidistant in the binocular conditions. In contrast, the 20-to 22-week-old infants did not provide evidence of sensitivity to relative size.

A preliminary study of the effect of the similarity of objects on relative size as information for depth was also conducted with 7-month-old infants, who monocularly viewed pairs of objects that differed in shape and color as well as in size. The infants reached for the larger object on 60% of the trials. This percentage was significantly greater than chance, suggesting that the infants perceived the larger object as being closer than the smaller object, despite the objects' dissimilarity. Although there may be dimensions of difference that would modulate, or even cancel, the relative size depth effect, we have not yet found any. These results suggest that visual processing of relative size information for distance occurs prior to the evaluation of the similarity of objects.

Familiar Size

Another source of distance information based on visual angle is familiar size. If the distal size of an object were known, its visual angle could be a source of information for the object's distance. Yonas, Pettersen, and Granrud (1982) studied infants' sensitivity to familiar size as information for distance. Again, a preliminary experiment tested adults in order to establish the effectiveness of the experimental displays. Adults judged the apparent distances of two sets of monocularly viewed photographs of faces (a familiar class of objects). One set was larger than life-size, the other was smaller. Another group judged the distances of monocularly viewed checkerboard patterns (a class of objects with no familiar size) that were the same sizes as the faces.

Adults gave clear evidence that familiar size influenced perceived distance. These results corroborate earlier research on familiar size (Ittelson, 1951). Whereas the small face was judged to be more than twice as far from the viewer as the large face, distances judged for small and large checkerboards were not significantly different. Furthermore, adults judged the large faces to be at a distance within, and the small faces to be a distance well beyond, reach for 5- to 7-month-old infants. Therefore, if infants viewing these displays monocularly perceive them as adults do, we would expect them to reach more often to the large than to the small faces. Moreover, from the adult data we would expect no differential reaching for the large and small checkerboards when viewed monocularly, or for the faces when viewed binocularly, because stereoscopic information would specify the large and small faces as equidistant. These hypotheses were tested with 5- and 7-month-old infants, using the same displays.

For the 7-month olds under monocular viewing conditions, the large face elicited more seconds of reaching than the small face. This difference was significantly larger than the analogous differences observed in the binocularly viewed face condition or in the monocularly viewed checkerboard condition. For the 5-month olds there were no significant differences in reaching duration among the three conditions.

The results indicate that in the monocular condition the 7-month olds perceived the large faces as within reach and the small faces as out of reach. As in the relative size experiments, the control conditions rule out the possibility that the infants exhibited reaching preferences without regard to the displays' perceived distances. If the infants simply preferred to reach for large objects, we would also expect more reaching for the large checkerboard than for the small one, but no preference was observed. Furthermore, the infants were not simply showing a preference to reach for large faces, because binocular viewing eliminated the reaching preference observed in the monocular condition. Presumably, the infants detected binocular information that specified the faces as equidistant, and therefore they reached equally for the large and small faces.

We cannot draw firm conclusions from the 5-month-olds' performance. The duration-of-reaching results were similar for both age groups, but the experimental effects for the 5-month olds were smaller. Although this suggests that 5-month olds may use familiar size as distance information, the results are not clear. It is evident, however, that for infants as young as 7 months of age the visual angle of an object, in conjunction with knowledge about the object's distal size, can be a source of information for the perception of distance. This finding may be theoretically important, because it indicates that experience can influence spatial perception.

Pictorially Specified Interposition

Results from Yonas, Cleaves, and Pettersen (1978) suggest that pictorial interposition may be another source of information for spatial layout to which infants
are sensitive. Recent research in computer vision exploring the information
available in visual scenes has suggested that in two-dimensional images, line
intersection features provide information for interposition and relative distance.
Clowes (1971), Huffman (1971), and Waltz (1972) made exhaustive studies of
the ways edges of polyhedrons may intersect in two-dimensional images (for a
review of this work, see Winston, 1977). They found that given certain constraints (such as excluding special frozen viewpoints), when a "T" vertex occurs
it is always true that the crossbar of the T is the edge of an occluding surface
and that the stem of the T is the edge of an occluded surface. Thus, T-intersections
at the edges of objects could provide a moving perceiver with invariant information for the spatial layout of objects. Although intersection features could be
ambiguous from certain frozen station points (as in some of Ames' well-known
demonstrations; Ittelson, 1952). For a freely moving observer, the assumption
that stationary viewpoints are not allowed is unnecessary, because it is very
unlikely that one's eye would ever be located at the exact station point from
which a T-intersection would be ambiguous, given the infinity of possible viewpoints. Moreover, even if one found this particular station point, any movement
would eliminate the ambiguity. Finally, whereas a given retinal image at a fixed
station point could be produced by an infinite number of distal layouts, a T-
intersection that remains a T-intersection through a change in viewpoints can be
produced by only one distal layout for a moving observer: interposition of surfaces. Therefore, for a moving observer, T-shaped intersections seem to be a
source of specific information for distal interposition.

A study by Granrud and Yonas (in press) was conducted to test the hypothesis,
based on the work of Clowes, Huffman, and Waltz, that the human visual system
detects T-shaped intersections as specifying overlapping surfaces. Five- and 7-
month-old infants were used as subjects. Reaching was observed as an index of
the perceived relative distances of sections of the test displays. In each experiment, infants viewed test displays monocularly, because binocular information
might attenuate the effectiveness of pictorial interposition. Figure 4.4 shows the
test displays for the experiments. The outer contour and the dot patterns were
identical in the "T" and "Y" displays. These two displays differed only in their
interior lines. The interior lines formed T-shaped intersections in one condition
and formed Y-shaped intersections in the other condition. It was hypothesized
that T intersections should specify overlapping surfaces and that infants should
reach more frequently for the apparently nearer surface. It was also predicted
that Y-shaped intersections should specify no differential distance, and therefore
infants should show no reaching preference when viewing the Y-intersection
display.

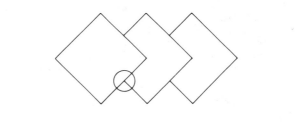

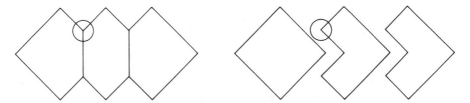

FIG. 4.4.   Schematic drawing of interposition displays. Note T-, Y-, and L-shaped intersections, circled in drawing.

The 7-month olds showed a significant preference to reach for the apparently nearer area in the "T" condition and showed no reaching preference in the "Y" condition. The reaching preference in the T condition suggests that the display was perceived as consisting of interposed surfaces. In the Y condition, the lack of a reaching preference suggests that no section of this display was seen as nearer than the others. The 5-month olds showed no reaching preferences.

It could be argued that the 7-month olds preferred to reach for the diamond-shaped region of the display rather than for the arrowhead-shaped sections, and that this preference, rather than the perception of differential distance, was responsible for the results in the T condition. A second experiment tested this hypothesis by separating the sections of the display. If infants preferred to reach for diamond-shaped sections, we would expect to observe this preference even when information for overlap is removed from the display. Seven- and 5-month olds were presented with the T and separation ("L") displays pictured in Fig. 4.4. Again, the 7-month olds showed a preference to reach for the side of the display that the T intersections specify as nearer and showed no significant preference in the separation condition. Thus, it seems that the 7-month olds were not simply reaching for the diamond-shaped area. This result supports the hypothesis that the 7-month olds' reaching preference in the first experiment was a result of the perceived relative distances of the test displays' sections and was not due to a simple preference to reach for a section of the display with a particular shape. The 5-month olds showed no significant reaching preference in either condition of the second experiment. Thus, we found no evidence that 5-month olds perceive spatial layout on the basis of pictorial interposition.

Although these results demonstrate 7-month olds' sensitivity to pictorially specified interposition, we cannot conclude with certainty that intersection features constitute the proximal stimulus variables responsible for perceived interposition. Whereas infants' reaching preferences could be predicted from the displays' intersection features, they could also have been predicted on the basis of gestalt organization principles such as completeness or simplicity (Chapanis & McCleary, 1953; Dinnerstein & Wertheimer, 1957; Hochberg, 1971). It could be argued that three squares at different distances would constitute a simpler or more complete precept than the alternative of one square and two equidistant interlocking arrowheads, because three squares might entail fewer lines and angles than the alternative (Hochberg & McAlister, 1953).

It is not clear, however, how the visual system could employ simplicity or completeness in perceiving interposition. The completeness of unfamiliar or irregular shapes, for example, would be difficult, if not impossible, to determine. Moreover, a system that used simplicity to determine interposition could supply an observer with perceptions that were probabilistic at best, because the actual spatial arrangement of surfaces does not necessarily correspond to the most economical description of the retinal image. Conversely, T intersections are specific, invariant information for distal interposition. Therefore, although in most cases intersections and simplicity are probably correlated in the retinal image, it seems likely that intersection features, not simplicity and completeness, are the proximal stimulus variables detected by infants in perceiving interposition.

Development of Sensitivity to Pictorial Information

A consistent trend has emerged from the results of our studies on pictorial depth information. In each study (trapezoidal window, relative size, familiar size, interposition), 7-month olds have shown sensitivity to pictorial information, whereas 5-month olds have not. In addition, in the relative size study, 5½-month olds were found to be sensitive to pictorial information. Thus, it seems that sensitivity to pictorial depth information first appears sometime after 20-22 weeks and before 30 weeks. This hypothesis is consistent with results from Bertenthal, Campos, and Haith (1980) and Kellman and Spelke (1981), which suggest that infants under 5 months of age are not sensitive to configurational information, such as subjective contours or the gestalt principles of similarity and good continuation.

CONCLUSIONS

In pulling together the various threads of research described previously, the first conclusion one can draw is that spatial behavior is guided by visual information early in development. We have observed responsiveness to all three classes of depth information (kinetic, binocular, and pictorial) by 24 weeks of age.

A second conclusion is that sensitivity to the three classes of spatial information seems to develop in a sequence: Sensitivity to kinetic information appears first, then sensitivity to binocular information, and finally sensitivity to pictorial information. Responsiveness to kinetic flow-field information for collision is present in 14-week olds and may be present as early as 4 weeks of age. Detection of binocular disparity develops between the fourth and fifth months (Fox et al., 1980; Held, Birch, & Gwiazda, 1980; Petrig, Julesz, Kropfl, Baumgartner, & Anliker, 1981), although there is currently no conclusive evidence that infants younger than 20 weeks of age perceive the spatial information carried by binocular disparity. Sensitivity to static monocular depth information has not yet been demonstrated in infants younger than 23 weeks of age. Moreover, we have failed to find such sensitivity in 20- to 22-week olds in several experiments where older infants did show sensitivity to pictorial information. The next study, of course, may contradict this hypothesis, but at present it appears that sensitivity to pictorial depth information does not develop until about 23 weeks, after infants are already sensitive to kinetic and binocular information for depth.

Now that we have determined when sensitivity to various types of information for depth first emerges, the next step will be to explore the mechanisms responsible for spatial perception, and how their development results in the sequence of emerging sensitivity that we have observed. Our knowledge of these mechanisms is uneven. Theoretical work on perceptual mechanisms sensitive to binocular information for depth is clearly more advanced than the work on kinetic or pictorial cues (see Marr, 1982). Unfortunately, theory building and research on perception of pictorial depth cues is suffering from neglect. It seems that the field, so popular in psychology for so long, is going through a period of unpopularity. Current theoretical work on the pictorial depth cues is sparse. Without well-worked out hypotheses concerning both the stimulus information available for static monocular perception and the mechanisms that detect pictorial cues, developmental studies of those mechanisms must remain primitive. Fortunately, recent work in computer vision has begun to deal with static monocular spatial perception in a formal, explicit way (see Yonas, Thompson, & Granrud, in press; Marr, 1982). Some of this work specifies not only the stimulus information available for spatial perception, but also the constraints that are required for its detection.

Describing the constraints embodied in the functioning of the visual system is one possible approach to the problem of discovering the underlying mechanisms of spatial perception. Computer vision researchers have found it necessary to incorporate knowledge about the nature of vision and the environment into their programs in order to make the extraction of information from the optic array possible (see Yonas, Thompson, & Granrud, in press). The properties of light (e.g., that waves or photons travel in straight lines) and of surface reflectance (e.g., that some of the light striking a surface is absorbed, whereas some is reflected), which are responsible for the structure of the ambient light at a given observation point, can be referred to as natural constraints on how light is structured. Knowledge about these natural constraints incorporated into the computer program or visual system, is the basis of reflective constraints. The notion that constraints that reflect the physics of image formation are incorporated in human visual processing is not new. Johansson (1970) and Rock (1977) have argued that decoding principles (i.e., reflective constraints) are necessary for perception. For example, an assumption or constraint of rigidity may be necessary for perceiving object shape from motion (Johansson, 1975). Similarly, even Gibson (1950) has pointed out that the perception of texture gradient information for the slant of a surface requires the constraint that texture elements are stochastically regular in size. More recent work by Barrow and Tenenbaum (1978), Marr (1982), and Ullman (1979) represents attempts to explicate the constraints required for spatial perception. Marr's work has emphasized the importance of a continuity assumption (i.e., the continuity of surfaces in space). Barrow and Tenenbaum have pointed out that incident illumination varies smoothly, and that objects often have approximately uniform reflectance. Ullman has emphasized the importance of rigidity of objects. With these constraints incorporated into computer vision systems, contours, shading, and motion in images can be used for perceiving the shapes and spatial locations of objects and surfaces in the environment. This research has already begun to provide us with explicit theories of the constraints required for the pickup of spatial information. By applying these theories to our research, we may be able to explain why the development of spatial perception occurs as it does by describing the emergence of various reflective constraints in the functioning of the visual system.

A second direction toward which research should proceed is developmental neurophysiology. Undoubtedly, poor acuity and sensitivity to visual contrast during the first months of life place limits on sensitivity to spatial information. It is clear that maturation of neurological structures (including the retina and visual cortex) plays a major role in the rapid improvement of acuity in early life. As we come to understand better the growth of the optic pathway and projection areas, we may begin to understand why contrast sensitivity improves, and perhaps the role of experience in that growth. Unfortunately for those studying space perception, we know little about the physiological processes that make spatial functioning possible, even in adults. One type of depth perception that has been the focus of much effort is binocular functioning. Here we can begin to isolate aspects of the process that generate developmental changes, because we have theories of how the process must work. For example, binocular depth perception may depend on the fine coordination of vergence movements that allows differences in horizontal disparity to be detected. Thus, the development of the oculo-motor system may be a limiting factor in the development of stereopsis; this system may require months for neural growth to take place. On the other hand, the appearance of binocular depth perception may be limited by the development of cortical processes that detect the correspondence of structure in the retinal inputs. As developmental neuroanatomy and physiology advance, we will understand better what anatomical changes are occurring coincident with behavioral shifts. It is even possible that knowledge of behavioral development may contribute to our understanding of physiological processes.

REFERENCES

Ames, A. Visual perception and the rotating trapezoidal window. *Psychological Monographs*, 1951, *65* (1, Whole No. 324).

Aslin, R. N., & Dumais, S. T. Binocular vision in infants: A review and a theoretical framework. In H. Reese & L. P. Lipsitt (Eds.), *Advances in child development and behavior* (Vol. 15). New York: Academic Press, 1980.

Barrow, H. G., & Tenenbaum, J. M. Recovering intrinsic scene characteristics from images. In A. R. Hanson & E. M. Riseman (Eds.), *Computer vision systems*. New York: Academic Press, 1978.

Bertenthal, B. I., Campos, J. J., & Haith, M. M. Development of visual organization: The perception of subjective contours. *Child Development*, 1980, *51*, 1072–1080.

Bertenthal, B. I., & Proffitt, D. R. *Development of infant sensitivity to biomechanical motion*. Paper presented at Third International Conference on Infant Studies, Austin, Texas, March 1982.

Bower, T. G. R. The visual world of infants. *Scientific American*, 1966, *215*, 80–92.

Braunstein, M. L. *Depth perception through motion*. New York: Academic Press, 1976.

Chapanis, A., & McCleary, R. A. Interposition as a cue for the perception of relative distance. *The Journal of General Psychology*, 1953, *48*, 113–132.

Clowes, M. B. On seeing things. *Artificial Intelligence*, 1971, *2*(1), 79–112.

Day, R. H., & McKenzie, B. E. Perceptual shape constancy in early infancy. *Perception*, 1973, *2*, 315–320.

Dinnerstein, A., & Wertheimer, M. Some determinants of phenomenal overlapping. *American Journal of Psychology*, 1957, *70*, 21–37.

Epstein, W., & Baratz, S. S. Relative size in isolation as a stimulus for relative perceived distance. *Journal of Experimental Psychology*, 1964, *67*, 507–513.

Fox, R., Aslin, R. N., Shea, S. L., & Dumais, S. T. Stereopsis in human infants. *Science*, 1980, *207*, 323–324.

Fox, R., & McDaniel, C. *Perception of biological motion in human infants*. Paper presented at Third International Conference on Infant Studies, Austin, Texas, March 1982.

Gibson, E. J. *Principles of perceptual learning and development*. New York: Appleton, 1969.

Gibson, J. J. *The perception of the visual world*. Boston: Houghton Mifflin, 1950.

Gibson, J. J. Visually controlled locomotion and visual orientation in animals. *British Journal of Psychology*, 1958, *49*(3), 182–194.

Gibson, J. J. *The senses considered as perceptual systems*. Boston: Houghton Mifflin, 1966.

Gibson, J. J. *The ecological approach to visual perception*. Boston: Houghton Mifflin, 1979.

Gordon, F. R., Lamson, G., & Yonas, A. *Reaching to a virtual object*. Unpublished manuscript, University of Minnesota, 1978.

Gordon, R. F., & Yonas, A. Sensitivity to binocular depth information in infants. *Journal of Experimental Psychology*, 1976, *22*, 413–422.

Granrud, C. E., & Yonas, A. Infants' perception of pictorially specified interposition. *Journal of Experimental Child Psychology*, in press.

Granrud, C. E., Yonas, A., & Pettersen, L. A comparison of monocular and binocular depth perception in 5- and 7-month-old infants. *Journal of Experimental Child Psychology*, in press.

Held, R., Birch, E. E., & Gwiazda, J. Stereoacuity of human infants. *Proceedings of the National Academy of Sciences*, 1980, *77*, 5572–5574.

Helmholtz, H. V. *Handbook of physiological optics* (translated by J. P. C. Southall). New York: Optical Society of America, 1925.

Hochberg, J. Perception: Space and movement. In J. W. Kling & L. A. Riggs (Eds.), *Woodworth and Schlosberg's experimental psychology*. New York: Holt, Rhinehart, & Winston, 1971.

Hochberg, J., & McAlister, E. A quantitative approach to figural "goodness." *Journal of Experimental Psychology*, 1953, *46*, 361–364.

Huffman, D. A. Impossible objects as nonsense sentences. In R. Meltzer & D. Michie (Eds.), *Machine intelligence* (Vol. 6). Edinburgh: The Edinburgh University Press, 1971.

Ittelson, W. H. Size as a cue to distance: Static localization. *American Journal of Psychology*, 1951, *64*, 54–67.

Ittelson, W. H. *The Ames demonstrations in perception*. Princeton, N. J.: Princeton University Press, 1952.

Johansson, G. On theories for visual space perception. *Scandinavian Journal of Psychology*, 1970, *11*, 67–74.

Johansson, G. Visual motion perception. *Scientific American*, 1975, *232* (6), 76–88.

Kaplan, F. A. Kinetic disruption of optical texture: The perception of depth at an edge. *Perception and Psychophysics*, 1969 6(4), 193–198.

Kaufmann, R., Maland, J., & Yonas, A. Sensitivity of 5- and 7-month-old infants to pictorial depth information. *Journal of Experimental Child Psychology*, 1981, *32*, 162–168.

Kellman, P. J., & Spelke, E. *Infant perception of partly occluded objects: Sensitivity to movement and configurations*. Paper presented to Society for Research in Child Development, Boston, Mass., April 1981.

Lee, D. N. The optic flow field: The foundation of vision. *Philosophical Transactions of the Royal Society of London, B*, 1980, *290*, Issue 1038, 169–179.

Marr, D. *Vision*. San Francisco: W. H. Freeman, 1982.

Petrig, B., Julesz, B., Kropfl, W., Baumgartner, G., & Anliker, M. Development of stereopsis and cortical binocularity in human infants: Electrophysiological evidence. *Science*, 1981, *213*, 1402–1405.

Pettersen, L., Yonas, A., & Fisch, R. O. The development of blinking in response to impending collision in preterm, full-term, and postterm infants. *Infant Behavior and Development*, 1980, *3*, 155–165.

Rezba, C. *A study of infant binocular depth perception*. Unpublished undergraduate honors thesis, University of Minnesota, 1977.

Rock, I. In defense of unconscious inference. In W. Epstein (Ed.), *Stability and constancy in perception*. New York: Wiley-Interscience, 1977.

Rogers, B. J., & Graham, M. Motion parallax as an independent cue for depth perception. *Perception*, 1979, *8*, 125–134.

Schiff, W. The perception of impending collision: A study of visually directed avoidant behavior. *Psychological Monographs*, 1965, 79(11, Whole No. 604).

Ullman, S. *The interpretation of visual motion*. Cambridge, Mass.: MIT Press, 1979.

Walk, R. D. Monocular compared to binocular depth perception in human infants. *Science*, 1968, *162*, 473–475.

Waltz, D. L. *Generating semantic descriptions from drawings of scenes with shadows* (Tech. Rep. AI-TR-271). Cambridge, Mass.: MIT Artificial Intelligence Laboratory, November 1972.

Winston, P. H. *Artificial intelligence*. Reading, Mass.: Addison-Wesley, 1977.

Yonas, A. Infants' responses to optical information for collision. In R. N. Aslin, J. Alberts, & M. Petersen (Eds.), *Development of perception: Psychobiological perspectives: The visual system* (Vol. 2). New York: Academic Press, 1981.

Yonas, A., Cleaves, W., & Pettersen, L. Development of sensitivity to pictorial depth. *Science*, 1978, *200*, 77–79.

Yonas, A., Granrud, C. E., & Pettersen, L. Infants' sensitivity to relative size information for distance. *Developmental Psychology,* in press.

Yonas, A., Granrud, C. E., & Smith, I. M. Infants perceive accretion/deletion information for depth. *Investigative Opthalmology and Visual Science,* 1982, *22*(3, Supplement), 124.

Yonas, A., Oberg, C., & Norcia, A. Development of sensitivity to binocular information for the approach of an object. *Developmental Psychology,* 1978, *14*(2), 147–152.

Yonas, A., Pettersen, L., & Granrud, C. E. Infants' sensitivity to familiar size as information for distance. *Child Development,* 1982, *53,* 1285–1290.

Yonas, A., Pettersen, L., & Lockman, J. J. Sensitivity in 3- and 4-week-old infants to optical information for collision. *Canadian Journal of Psychology,* 1979, *33*(4), 268–276.

Yonas, A., Pettersen, L., Lockman, J. J., & Eisenberg, P. *The perception of impending collision in 3-month-old infants.* Paper presented at the International Conference on Infant Studies, New Haven, Connecticut, April 1980.

Yonas, A., & Pick, H. L., Jr. An approach to the study of infant space perception. In L. B. Cohen & P. Salapatek (Eds.), *Infant perception: From sensation to cognition* (Vol. 2). New York: Academic Press, 1975.

Yonas, A., Thompson, W., & Granrud, C. E. Computer vision: Implications for the psychology of human vision. In R. Wu & S. Chipman (Ed.), *Learning by eye.* New York: Academic Press, in press.

5 Physiological Underpinnings of Perceptual Development

Michel Imbert
Laboratoire de Neurobiologie du Developpement
Université de Paris-Sud, Orsay, France

Much time is needed after birth for a brain to reach its full development. This period of time is relatively long when compared to the prenatal period. In the child, for example, it lasts a minimum of 10 years. During this time the emergence of the organization of the adult nervous system, remarkable for its structural complexity, for the very rigorous precision of its internal connections, and for the functional specificity of its different components, depends not only on the processes of growth but also on the interaction between those processes and the effects incurred by behavior and learning. This means that the brain is not inexorably forged according to the immanent rules of the laws of development, oblivious to external conditions. On the contrary, a remarkable plasticity manifests itself during the first years of postnatal growth, allowing the immature nervous system to remedy certain cerebral lesions and environmental deficits which in the adult would produce insurmountable deficiencies.

A fundamental problem for developmental neurobiology resides in knowing whether or not the functioning itself of a neuronal network contributes to its establishment or maintenance. Put in terms of psychobiology, the question is whether and in what way individual experience participates in the structuring of the brain, and whether it thereby conditions the realization of the ulterior perceptive performances. Dealing with such questions leads us to identify what in the development of the nervous system is brought about by the expression of the genetic program, and what is acquired by the interaction with the environment. Since its original formulation at the end of the nineteenth century by the father of experimental embryology, W. Roux, it has been generally accepted that the brain is formed during two successive periods in the development of the organism. During the first period, events pertinent to neuroembryology take place, as for example, cellular multiplication, migration, neuronal differentiation, cell death, and the setting up of the first interneuronal contacts. These events follow very rigid rules, dictated primarily by genetic factors (Sidman, 1972).

Three arguments speak for the preceding statement. The first one is that during this period an important number of different mutations affect certain aspects of the organization of the CNS (Sidman, Green, & Appel, 1965). These mutations can alter the development of a particular type of neuron or a particular type of synaptic connection. They can also interfere with the migration of newly formed neurons.

The second argument arises from the fact that the CNS develops according to a strict sequential plan. The development of the visual system in a crustacean, the Daphnia, is a good example of such a mechanism. Indeed, there the connections between the axons that originate from *omatidia* and the cells of the optic ganglia are established in a sequential manner. The recognition by each bundle of axons of a specific target among a group of five ganglionic neurons is dependent on the precise moment at which the axons arrive in the optic ganglia (F. Levinthal, Macagno, & C. Levinthal, 1976; Macagno, Lopresti, & C. Levinthal, 1973).

Finally, the third argument to put forth is that the striking precision that characterizes the normal neuronal network may be modified by the "tendency" of the axons, either in the process of growth or when fully developed, to establish synaptic contacts, even incorrect ones. For instance, many experimental results show that the denervation of target neurons occurring after lesions is followed in certain cases by reinnervation by foreign axons. This can occur in a NS either during the process of growth and differentiation or when fully developed. Generally, three types of such contacts can be established, by new axonic collaterals, preterminal axonic branches, or by synaptic contacts along the pathway of an axon (Cotman & Nadler, 1978).

During the second period, mainly postnatal, in the development of the organism, a stabilization of the synaptic contacts takes place. This phase includes the elimination of certain connections. The role of epigenetic factors, such as a physiological functioning of the brain itself, is generally considered to be essential. A very instructive example in this regard is the development of binocular connections in the mammalian visual system. There, the segregation of the afferents coming from each eye into the lateral geniculate body takes place before all visual functioning of the system. For example, in the monkey it takes place in the embryo (Rakic, 1976), and in hamsters and mice before the opening of the eyelid (Godement, Salaun, Saillour, & Imbert, 1981; So, Schneider, & Frost, 1978). However, in layer IV of the visual cortex of the monkey, the segregation in the columns of the geniculate afferents, corresponding to one or the other eye, although it seems to be underway already at birth (Rakic, 1976), necessitates that in fact normal postnatal binocular visual experience set itself up. It is not observed in the adult animal that has been submitted to only a monocular experience starting at birth (Hubel, Wiesel, & Stryker, 1978). The mechanism by which either prenatal or postnatal segregation takes place is unknown; there could be displacement of incorrect synpatic terminals or elimination of the terminals coming from one or the other eye.

A spectacular example of selection of synaptic contacts in a neuronal network is to be found in the stabilization of the trigger characteristics of neurons in the visual cortex of the newborn cat, or in their modification due to certain restricted conditions in rearing. In this chapter I describe a certain number of experiences that show that normal structural and functional maturation of the brain during the postnatal period depends in large part on early experience. The study of the development of the visual system is particularly well suited to approaching this question. And this is so for two complementary reasons. First, the morphology and physiology of this system have been well studied. Second, it is relatively easy to manipulate the visual environment in which the animal is reared: This environment can range from complete deprivation—rearing the animal in total darkness—to selective visual deprivation, during which a characteristic normally present and specifically coded by the visual system has been removed from the space/object.

Coding by Visual Neurons

> Le plus subtil de tous les sens est celui de la vue.
>
> Descartes

Interest in the visual system has recently developed due to the progress that has been made in the electrophysiological exploration of the NS. In fact, neurophysiological research in the past two decades has shown that sensorial neurons, because of the specific connections between them, are able to extract from the environment distinctive features that define objects and events with the least ambiguity. Thus, these features reduce the considerable redundancy found in the objects and events of the external world.

It is relatively easy to question directly in "perceptive" terms, by means of appropriate stimulations, isolated neurons on different levels of the visual pathway, and to gather electrophysiological responses. One must pose the question of what is "seen" by a given visual cell and, by looking for the particular characteristics of the stimulus object capable of activating it in a specific fashion, study the processes that the cell must go through in order to "see."

This heuristic has proven to be very fruitful. Barlow (1953),while studying the ganglionic cells of the retina of the frog, showed that certain neurons were very specifically activated by a small object, such as a small black disc that was rapidly moved back and forth within a limited region of the animal's visual field. When presented to a normally behaving frog, this type of stimulus triggers the stereotype response of capture. This selectivity in neuronal response and behavioral reaction suggests that there exists a class of retinal neurons operating a primitive form of biologically adapted recognition. In order to label these retina cells for illustrative purposes, Barlow coined the term "bug detectors." Thereafter, the idea according to which a given sensorial cell only discharges when stimulated by particular characteristics (key patterns) of the stimulus dominated the realm of neurophysiological research in sensorial coding (Barlow, 1972).

Moreover, it has been shown that these key patterns, or "trigger features" as they were labeled by Barlow, Hill, and Levick in 1964, continue to activate ganglionary cells selectively in spite of a large variation in the luminous intensity of the stimulus (Maturana, Lettvin, McCulloch & Pitts, 1960).

As of 1959, Hubel and Wiesel demonstrated that neurons in the primary visual cortex of the cat responded specifically to precise visual patterns. These neurons are activated when small spots of light of fine contrasting lines are shed onto a small region of the animal's retina called the *receptive field*. Following the experimental strategy just described, we know what it is that is seen by a given neuron when it vigorously emits action potentials or spikes. The more precise spatial configuration the stimulus, as presented, has, the more the response will be important in terms of the number of action potentials emitted. These forms are generally linear edges, slits of light, or fine bars, whose orientation within the receptive field is relatively precise. Such a stimulus is generally more efficient if it moves across the receptive field following an orthogonal direction in a preferred orientation. Different cortical cells prefer different orientations, but on the whole no particular orientation—vertical or horizontal for example—is privileged.

Another element to consider, besides orientation selectivity, is that the visual cortical cells are for the most part activated binocularly. Yet, if the parameters of the effective stimulus, especially its orientation, are analogous for both retinas, the visual cortical neurons are generally influenced differently on a quantitative level by the two eyes (Hubel & Wiesel, 1962; Nikara, Bishop, & Pettigrew, 1969). Moreover, for there to be binocular activation, the stimulus must be presented in such a way that the two retinal images are situated in relation to each other in a precise relationship of disparity (Barlow, Blakemore,& Pettigrew, 1967; Nikara et al., 1968). This relationship varies from one neuron to another and could serve for the stereoscopic vision of the third dimension (Barlow, Blakemore, & Pettigrew, 1967; Bishop, 1970; Pettigrew, Nikara, & Bishop, 1968).

Properties as remarkable as those described previously—orientation selectivity, binocularity, retinal disparity—do not exhaust the repertory of specific responses of the cortical cells. One may add a simple enumeration: Speed and movement detection, directional selectivity, spatial filtering, the relative complexity of the receptive field itself, as well as the tonic or phasic character of the activation, etc.

The complex interneuronal connections that, from the retina to the cerebral cortex, endow the cortical cells with such properties, are susceptible to modification. If the visual experience of an immature kitten is altered by eliminating certain characteristics in the object environment, certain activation characteristics of the cortical visual neurons will be modified in such a way as to be limited to the parameters present in the first months of postnatal life.

Monocular Deprivation

A first demonstration of the important role of visual experience in the development of the visual cortex is that of Hubel and Wiesel (1963). These authors show that the proportion of binocular neurons can be considerably reduced and pass from about 85% in the normally reared animal to less than 10% if one prevents the immature kitten (between 1 and 4 months) from coherently using its two eyes (normal binocular usage). For example, if one eye is kept closed by the suturing of the eyelids, thus producing a monocular deprivation of forms, if not of total light, one observes a considerable decline in responses obtained by subsequent visual stimulation of the previously closed eye. The cortical cells are then only influenced in a monocular fashion by the unimpeded eye. Given the fact that almost all the cortical cells are active, one can suppose that the impeded eye has yielded its territory to the one that has been subject to visual experience. Similar results were obtained with the monkey (Hubel, Wiesel, & Levay, 1977).

The Critical Period

The susceptibility of the visual system to monocular privation is limited in time. It is possible to determine this period by suturing the eyelids at different age levels and for different lengths of time, estimating the degree of functional modification in the resulting distribution of ocular dominance, for example. Thus, it can be noted that monocular privation in the adult animal, no matter how long in duration, is without effect on the physiological as well as morphological levels. The same absence of effect is observed in the kitten when deprivation takes place within the first 3 weeks of age. The susceptibility of the visual system to visual deprivation starts at 3 weeks, goes through a maximum at about 6 weeks, and thereafter progressively diminishes till the end of 3 months. The existence of such a critical period has also been demonstrated in the monkey's visual system. From birth to the sixth or eighth week, visual deprivation has an effect on all the layers of the visual cortex; beyond that time and up to the end of the first year, only the neurons located in the supragranular and in the infra-granular layer are modified.

Two explanations can be suggested for the lack of activation of neurons when stimulated by the previously closed eye. The first one is that there are anatomical modifications of the cortical connections of the closed eye. Such an explanation has been put forth by Hubel et al. (1977). In layer IVc of the monkey's striate cortex, there is a clearly physiologically and anatomically demonstrable reor-ganization of the geniculate afferents subserving one or the other eye.

According to the second hypothesis, the connections between the deprived eye and the cortex are functionally "suppressed," silenced, and rendered incap-able of activating the cortical neurons, albeit still present and ready to function. Indeed, under certain conditions, one assists to a rapid restoration. In a cat deprived of vision in one eye during the critical period, Kratz, Spear, and Smith (1976) have shown that during the hours following an enucleation of the other, experienced eye—an enucleation done after the end of the critical period—the percentage of neurons in the striate cortex activated by the deprived eye rapidly increases. However, different results have been reported by others (see Movshon & van Sluyters, 1981). The reactivation of the cortical neurons by stimulation of the deprived eye is equally "unmasked" by the intravenous injection of bicu-culline, which is an antagonist of GABA, a putative inhibitory transmitter in the visual cortex (Duffy, Snodgrass, Burdhfiel, & Conway, 1976). Finally, Tsumoto and Suda (1978), using intracellular recordings, have shown the presence of excitatory geniculostriate connections coming from the deprived afferents.

Binocular Deprivation

The morphological and physiological consequences of binocular deprivation by the neonatal suturing of both eyelids are much less striking than those observed after monocular suture (Wiesel & Hubel, 1965a). One can, however, observe a certain number of abnormalities. About 30% of the cortical neurons are no longer activated by visual stimulation. Among the visually activated neurons, 10% to 50%, according to various authors, exhibit true orientation selectivity. However, the ocular dominance distribution is abnormal, because 50% of these neurons are monocularly driven. Such a loss of binocularity is particularly striking in the superficial and the deep layers of the monkey's striate cortex.

Binocular deprivation obtained by rearing kittens in complete darkness has become less utilized, probably because of the difficulties involved in rearing animals in the dark. The results obtained by various groups using this method vary greatly, and a thorough description of the reasons as to why these results could differ is not within the scope of this chapter. One can, however, underline two main points on which, for the most part, there is agreement.

First, after 6 weeks of dark rearing, the ocular dominance distribution is normal: About 80 to 85% of the cells are binocularly activated. This figure significantly differs from the one found in animals deprived by the suture of both eyes.

The second point is that orientation selectivity is profoundly altered, and I describe this later in more detail.

Deprivation or Competition

Noticing the striking difference in deleterious effects between monocular deprivation and binocular deprivation, Hubel and Wiesel (1965) suggested that the integrity of the visual system depended not only on the global afferent activity but also, and more importantly, on the interaction between afferents coming from both eyes. If this competition between both eyes has a more important role to play than simple disuse, one would expect to observe fewer morphological and physiological abnormalities in the regions of the visual system where there are no binocular projections. Such a hypothesis concerning competition has been firmly established by numerous experiments (see Guillery [1972], and Sherman, Guillery, Kaas, & Sanderson [1974], in particular), and there are good reasons to think that the site where competitive effects do occur is cortical (see Cynader & Mitchell, 1977).

Binocular Synergy

By preventing the simultaneous or coherent use of both eyes, Hubel and Wiesel were able to dissociate the respective roles of competition and disuse.

They performed an alternating monocular deprivation by closing one eye one day and the other the next day—and did this over a period of 3 months. They also rendered animals strabismic by cutting one of the extraocular muscles of one eye. In these strabismic kittens, both eyes function simultaneously but never see the same thing at the same time. Each eye has a normal visual experience, but the retinogeniculate pathways have never been activated in a coherent binocular manner. The main result of these experiments is the following: The cortical neurons, even though exhibiting normal orientational properties, were in the great majority monocularly driven.

Disruption of ocular dominance distribution was also obtained in binocularly deprived strabismic kittens by Maffei (1978) and Maffei and Bisti (1976).

The most intriguing element in these results (but see van Sluyters & Levitt, 1980) is that the change in ocular dominance distribution of cortical neurons appears even when the animal is maintained in the dark during the period extending from the time of surgery to the time of electrophysiological exploration. Because in these animals visual deprivation is ineffective, we are led to attribute this breakdown of binocular connections to the absence of symmetry of ocular motility. This idea is supported by the fact that following the immobilization of both eyes the proportion of binocular neurons remains unaffected. We see later that during development, ocular mobility plays a determining role in the manifestation of the specific visual properties of the primary visual cortical neurons.

The Initial Functional State

If one wants to understand the role played by experience in the maturation of the visual system, it is necessary to define its initial functional state. In 1963, Hubel and Wiesel described cortical neurons recorded in 8-day-old kittens, that is to say before the opening of the eyelids, and thus in a kitten without any visual experience. Their characteristics of binocularity and of orientation selectivity were very similar to those recorded in a normal adult cat. This led the authors to conclude that "highly complex neuronal connections are possible without the benefit of visual experience." In contrast, Barlow and Pettigrew (1971) and Pettigrew (1974) uphold that the development of orientation selectivity necessitates an appropriate visual experience. Blakemore and van Sluyters (1975) describe, for their part, a higher degree of specific organization in very young kittens with or without visual experience.

Orientation Selectivity Development

Following this brief reminder of the related literature, I now summarize the main results obtained in my laboratory during the last few years.

While carefully studying the evolution of response properties of visual cortical neurons during the first weeks in kittens either normally reared or reared in complete darkness, we have brought forth a number of significant points to be presented here. I must first emphasize, however, that the microelectrode recording of neuronal activities in very young kittens poses particular methodological problems. These activities are very often weak, erratic, and sluggish, and it requires special precautions in order to be able to define the triggering characteristics of the isolated neuron under study. Although I do not go further into these difficulties here, it is important to keep them in mind. In doing so, we classified visual cortical neurons into three groups, according to their response properties:

1. *The aspecific cells* (A), activated by a circular stimulus, moving across the receptive field in any direction.
2. *The immature cells* (I), preferentially driven by a linear stimulus whose orientation is rather imprecise. Yet, there exists an orientation, orthogonal to the preferred one, along which the stimulus is ineffective.
3. *The specific cells* (S), which have all the functional properties of specific cortical neurons already described in the normal adult cat.

I want to stress an aspect that takes on its importance when one compares our results with those of other groups. As far as orientation selectivity is concerned, the preceding classification can be reduced into two categories. The first category—non-oriented neurons—is composed of the aspecific neurons (A). The organization of their receptive field prevents even an imprecise detection of the orientation of a linear edge. However, very often a receptive field is not perfectly isotropic and manifests strong directional asymmetries, and could give the false impression that a neuron that prefers a certain range of orientation is being studied. The second category—oriented neurons—includes the class of immature cells (I) and the class of specific neurons (S). Here, the organization of the receptive field, especially the existence of an orientation along which a given stimulus is totally ineffective, allows true orientation detection.

Another important aspect that should be underlined is the great temporal variability of the responses. The rate of responses as a function of the orientations of the stimulus varies from moment to moment during the time course of the experimentation. Such a variability is all the more important the younger the animal and the less selective the neuron. In contrast, the orientation coded by a selective neuron is remarkably stable (Fregnac & Bienenstock, 1981).

These considerations impose a goodly amount of caution when assigning a given neuron to one of the three classes defined previously.

While studying the repartition of the three functional classes of neurons A, I, and S, as defined earlier, during the first 6 weeks of postnatal life in kittens either normally reared or totally deprived of visual experience, we were able to put forth the following results:

1. As soon as visual response can be quantitatively studied, that is to say around the end of the second postnatal week, a rather significant proportion of these neurons (about 50%) exhibit a true orientation selectivity. For about half of these, this selectivity is as precise as the one shown by cortical neurons recorded in adult animals.

2. The relative proportion of oriented (I + S) and non-oriented (A) cells is not different until the end of the third week in animals reared in whatever conditions.

3. As of the turn of the third week, the properties of the neurons develop differently: in normally reared kittens, the number of oriented cells increases rapidly; on the other hand, in dark-reared kittens, the number of oriented cells decreases in favor of the non-oriented cells (A), which will be the only ones to remain after 6 weeks spent in total darkness.

These results clearly demonstrate that orientation selectivity is present as of the first stages of postnatal life, at the age of eye opening, and independently of any visual experience. However, the latter is necessary from the end of the third week on, in order to maintain orientation selectivity and for it to develop further.

The Special Properties of Specific Cells in Very Young Kittens

In a kitten less than 3 weeks of age, normally as well as dark reared, the oriented neurons show two remarkable characteristics: 1) They are preferentially monocularly activated by the contralateral eye; 2) They present a bias in the distribution of orientation preferences favoring the vertical or the horizontal meridian. In a normally reared kitten older than 28 days, no such meridional preference can be observed, and the neurons are in the majority binocularly driven.

Thus, during the first 3 weeks of postnatal life—the period during which visual experience does not yet influence the functional development of the visual cortex—ocular dominance and orientation preference seem to be linked parameters, resulting from the intrinsic organization of the visual cortex.

One might think that there exist two populations of specific neurons with distinctive functional characteristics and developing at different stages during ontogenesis. The early population of selective neurons that appears at the time of eye opening is composed of cells mainly activated by the contralateral eye, and whose receptive fields are aligned on vertical and horizontal orientations. The aspecific neurons observed after 6 weeks of dark rearing could potentially come from the increase with age of the number of binocularly driven cells, an increase independent of visual experience. One might hypothesize that the early specific neurons, monocularly activated by vertical or horizontal stimuli, remain stable as long as they remain monocularly driven. On the other hand, the early binocular neurons, mainly aspecific or immature, can be specified or despecified under the control of visual experience (Fregnac & Imbert, 1978).

Binocular Competition and Evolution of Orientation Selectivity

In order to verify the preceding hypothesis, binocular interaction can be suppressed by unilateral enucleation at birth, followed by dark rearing during the first 6 weeks. We thereby demonstrate that a certain population of selective-to-orientation cells resists visual deprivation. These neurons are mainly located in the hemisphere contralateral to the remaining eye. They respond preferentially to vertical or horizontal stimuli. Thus it appears that binocular competition plays an active role in the process of despecification, which adds itself to the effect of sensory deprivations "per se."

We have also studied the effects of neonatal enucleation followed by normal rearing. Two important points arising from these experiences must be stressed:

1. The neonatal unilateral enucleation does not interrupt the process of maturation of orientation selectivity.

2. Nevertheless, the proportion of neurons selectivity activated by vertical and horizontal stimuli is significantly more important in the enucleated kittens, as compared to the normally reared kittens of the same age. Thus, the coding of new orientations, the obliques, appears to be related to normal binocular visual interaction.

The fact that the same orientational bias is to be found in the enucleated kittens, whatever their rearing conditions are, suggests that binocular competition between retinal and extraretinal afferents coming from each eye intervenes in the maintenance and the development of orientational selectivity (Fregnac, Trotter, Bienenstock, Buisseret, Gary-Bobo, & Imbert, 1981).

One could infer that a unilateral suppression of extraretinal information, as is performed by enucleation and dark rearing, could be sufficient to give the other eye a competitive advantage. The projections coming from the eye left could thereby be stabilized, which would protect the target neurons from a functional degradation due to lack of visual experience and would prevent the development of other orientation selectivity.

Variability of the Visual Response and Visual Experience

I have already mentioned that in very young kittens (or in 6-week-old dark-reared kittens) oriented neurons showed important temporal variability. This probably indicates a great instability of the synaptic transmission. In all the kittens, the orientation coded by a selective neuron remains stable. The statistical analysis of the visual response fluctuations of specific neurons shows a linear dependency between variance and the mean value of the discharge. This suggests that there exist two independent sources of fluctuations: One is related to the orientation of the stimulus, and the other is nonspecific and variable in time.

Comparing the results obtained in 3-week-old kittens and those obtained in 6-week-old kittens, there appears a decrease of the variability as there is an increase in age. This seems to indicate an increase of synaptic security with visual experience. Thus, although it has been clearly demonstrated that orientation selectivity develops according to an intrinsic program, the role played by visual experience could be to stabilize some specific connections while reducing the variability of the synaptic transmission (Fregnac & Bienenstock, 1981).

Effects of Delayed Visual Experience and Recovery of Orientation Selectivity

The question I raise now can be formulated in the following way: Is it possible to transform a nonspecific cortex, which characterizes a 6-week-old dark-reared kitten, into a specific one, which characterizes a normally reared kitten of the same age, just by letting the kitten have a few hours of visual experience? In other words, does the complete absence of visual experience during the first weeks of postnatal life prevent in a definite way the organization of orientation selectivity? In order to answer that question, we performed a two-stage acute experiment. Both hemispheres of a 6-week-old dark-reared kitten were studied during two successive periods. During the first period the non-specificity of cortical neurons is verified in one of the hemispheres. At the end of this first acute experiment, the kitten is left to recover in darkness. Then, when it has completely reawakened, it is taken out of the dark room and allowed to roam freely around the lab. After 5 to 6 hours of thus roaming about, it seems entirely to recover its visually guided behavior. After this session of active visual experience, it is put back into the dark room for the night, until we perform the second acute experiment under the same experimental conditions as the first one, but now exploring the other hemisphere. The neurons then show in their great majority true orientation selectivity (Imbert & Buisseret, 1975).

Several factors could intervene in this spectacular recovery of orientation selectivity: The visual stimulation itself, or the period of consolidation, or the active visuomotor exploration. The period of "consolidation," which is the time spent between the end of the session of active visual experience and the time of the second electrophysiological exploration, does not seem necessary. When the second acute experiment is performed immediately after the session of active visual experience, an important proportion of oriented neurons still appears. If visual experience is limited to a purely passive visual stimulation obtained, for example, by immobilizing the kitten with a muscular relaxant, there is no recovery of orientation selectivity. In contrast, when motor activity is limited to ocular motor activation, orientation selectivity recovery is almost complete.

These observations demonstrate that it is ocular motility that plays an essential role in the recovery of the orientation selectivity of the visual cortical neurons (Buisseret, Gary-Bobo, & Imbert, 1978). One is therefore led to make the hypothesis that the extraocular muscle afferents could activate in the process of specification.

We were able to verify this hypothesis thanks to an anatomical particularity. Indeed, in the cat the extraocular proprioceptive afferents can be almost completely suppressed by the sectioning of the ophthalmic branches of the trigeminal nerve, and this without lesioning the ocular motor nerves (Batini, Buisseret, & Buisseret-Delmas, 1975). Under these conditions a 6-hour session of active visual experience with dark-reared kittens does not provoke the full recovery of orientation selectivity. Orientation selectivity develops when the duration of the session of active visual-motor exploration is prolonged without ever reaching, however, even after 5 weeks of visual exploration, the level observed in non-operated kittens having experienced only a 6-hour session.

The ophthalmic branch of the trigeminal nerve innervates various other receptors besides the stretch receptors located in the extraocular muscles—that is, the cutaneous receptor and the numerous orbital noci-ceptors. When sectioning the maxillary branches of the trigeminal nerves, one eliminates a contingent of cutaneous and noci-ceptive fibers that can be considered equivalent to those contained in the ophthalmic branch, and this without hindering the extraocular proprioceptive fibers that only run in the ophthalmic branch. Under these conditions, 6 hours of active visual experience promotes a degree of orientation selectivity of about the same order as that obtained in control kittens.

These results confirm the hypothesis according to which the factor, related to ocular motility, indispensable for the recovery of orientation selectivity, would be of extraocular proprioceptive origin (Trotter, Gary-Bobo, & Buisseret, 1979).

In order to study this further, Trotter et al. (1981) in our laboratory have studied the effects of partial muscular deafferentation. They performed unilateral sections of the ophthalmic branch of the trigeminal nerve in kittens at different postnatal ages and exposed to various visual experiences. When the section is performed between the fourth and the seventh week, a significant decrease in the number of binocularity activated neurons is found. This effect is observed only when a postsurgical delay of about a month is permitted. On the other hand, this effect does not seem to come from a kind of imbalance of the visual experience of the two eyes, which could have eventually resulted from some uncoordination of ocular movements incurred by the muscular deafferentation, because the same result is obtained when the kitten is reared in complete darkness. Therefore, this striking disorganization of binocular integration of visual cortical cells, observed in the aforementioned conditions, seems to occur totally independently of retinal factors, because it appears in kittens deprived of visual experience. More important is the fact that the proprioceptive "manipulation" affects visual neurons only if it is practiced within a limited period of time that coincides with the acme of the critical period for monocular deprivation.

The laboratory is now following up the same kind of questions by combining the proprioceptive deafferentation of one eye with the active monocular visual experience of 6 hours, and this in 6-week-old dark-reared kittens. In intact 6-week-old dark-reared kittens monocularly exposed to 6 hours of visual experience, one can observe two phenomena. On the one hand, a modification in the distribution of ocular dominance. The neurons are in their majority driven by the experienced eye. On the other hand, the orientation selectivity is recovered in a proportion not far removed from that of the one obtained after 6 hours of binocular visual experience. When the monocular active visual experiences are given to kittens previously having undergone a unilateral sectioning of the ophthalmic branch of the trigeminal nerve, these two aspects are affected: Fewer neurons are "captured" by the experienced eye, and very few neurons recover their orientation selectivity.

These effects are more or less independent of the relative laterality of the proprioceptive and retinal informations. Although, when the visually deprived eye is also deprived of its muscular afferents, one can observe an orientational bias favoring the horizontal and the vertical. This reminds one of the bias described previously concerning the effect of neonatal unilateral enucleation.

Extraocular proprioception is indeed an important factor in the development of the functional properties of the visual cortex. This is because it supplies, during the critical period, "gating" signals, allowing the validation or modifications induced by some specific retinal signals.

Conclusion

In my conclusion I retain from the work I have just briefly reviewed two main aspects, which seem to me particularly relevant to a chapter of this type.

One is the demonstration that the remarkable performance of orientation detection precedes the complete formation of the cortical neuropile. It should be pointed out that as soon as we are able to record visual cortical neurons that are visually activated, about half of them already are truly oriented. That is to say, we have not observed any initial period during which there were only non-oriented neurons to be recorded. It seems that specific selective neurons develop immediately at the time of eye opening. And these neurons, as I have previously indicated, present the particularities of monocularity and of meridional preference. It is important to note now that at the age when these neurons start functioning, less than 2% of cortical synaptic contacts are established (Cragg, 1972). These neurons could be considered part of a phylogenetically old system (Pettigrew, 1979). Indeed, in my laboratory recent experiments have demonstrated that these neurons are rather stable and quite resistant to visual deprivations (Buisseret, Gary-Bobo, & Imbert, 1982; Fregnac & Bienenstock, 1981).

The second main aspect I emphasize concerns the role played by the proprioceptive afferents ensuing from ocular movements, within the processes of maintenance and development of the visual properties of the cortical neurons. Numerous experiments using visual deprivation imply that there is not only a selective bias of the visual *input* but also a significant alteration of the normal motor *output* of the organism that does the perceiving (Held, 1961; Teuber, 1961). The fact that there exist visual and proprioceptive interactions, which we have demonstrated to occur at a relatively low level of visual information processing, gives a physiological content to some theories concerning perception, upholding that early experience may unite the visual system and the control systems of the visually initiated motor responses.

I have indicated that the early functioning of the visual system is essential to the maintenance and progressive adjustment of the connectivity in the visual neuronal networks, thereby rendering them capable of recognizing certain classes of attributes of the visual scenes. Several hypotheses have been proposed in order to understand more clearly these developmental phenomena.

I adopt those hypotheses that, though admitting that on a larger scale the system is intrinsically determined, also concede an important role to the progressive adjustment of the network by its own activity. According to a theory formalized by Changeux, Courrège, and Danchin (1973) under the name of *selective stabilization*, an exuberant early synaptic growth appears during the neurogenesis of the nerve connections. Presynaptic terminals occupy a number of synaptic spaces superior in number to the final contacts. This process is contained in "genetic envelopes" whose limits are rather large. When the system begins to function, the activity of the network provokes the selection of some synaptic contacts, which are then stabilized, whereas other contacts degenerate. Therefore the activity of the network introduces supplementary order from such a genetic envelope that is already somewhat selective, although including initial labile connections.

In a few instances, certain modifications of the connectivity depending on the functioning itself have been clearly demonstrated. Examples are that of neuromuscular junctions (Benoit & Changeux, 1975; Redfern, 1970), and that of the innervation of the Purkyne cells of the cerebellum by the climbing fibers (Changeux, 1979; Crepel, Mariani, & Delhaye-Bouchaud, 1976). The regression from the multi- to mono-innervated stage, mono-innervation that characterizes the final state of these systems, seems to depend on competitive mechanisms, as for example that involved in the occupation of the synaptic sites, in order to take place (Mariani & Changeux, 1981).

In systems in which the neurons are normally multi-innervated in the final stage—as it is the case, for example, with the neurons of the visual cortex—it is more difficult to demonstrate such a reduction of innervation. Moreover, the morphological studies indicate but a very small decrease in the mean number of synapses by neuron toward the end of the critical period.

In fact, some rearrangements of the cortical connectivity depending on activity have recently been described. Axon terminals issuing from lateral geniculate neurons extend over larger cortical fields in an immature cortex than in an adult one (Ferster & Levay, 1978; Levay & Stryker, 1979). Total dark-rearing delays the segregation of the afferent terminals in layer IV of the cat's visual cortex (Swindale, 1981). The blockage of impulses along the fibers of the optic nerve (by intraocular injection of TTX) inhibits the establishment of ocular dominance columns (Stryker, 1981).

Therefore, as a sign of the evolution toward a greater specialization, perhaps one should look for possible functional modifications as, for example, the following:

The effectiveness of synaptic transmission.
The capacity to generate action potentials,
The integration of various excitatory or inhibitory influences impinging on various sites of growing and changing neurons.

Now I cannot put a final point to my chapter without first venturing into the general question of the relationship between sensory coding and perception, which should be present in any developmental approach.

What often is taken to characterize the working brain is the temporal stucture of the circulating signals within the neural networks and that, at each moment, the distribution of these signals represents a special structure. This spatial-temporal order is embodied in a code whose mission it is to, more or less faithfully, mirror the external (or internal) events that give it structure. These codes are then transferred, multiplied, recast, distributed, and finally registered in the intimacy of the nervous structure. Unless—and perhaps more simply—these codes just trigger an act whose form is already engraved elsewhere within schemes of action that ensue from the hereditary nervous constitution or from the engrams stored in the remembering brain. Bergson (1970) has stated: "Percevoir finit par n'être plus qu'une occasion de se souvenir [p. 213]."

The main task for neurobiologists is to decipher these codes, that is to say, to arrive at an understanding of their meaning. As of the end of the 1920s, Adrian with his students established a simple relationship between the frequency of impulses emitted by sensory receptors and the intensity of the stimulation. This relationship holds, with just a few modifications, for brain neurons. Mountcastle described the power function for the deep sensibility impulses recorded in neurons located at the level of the thalamic relay. In that particularly well-documented case, such a relationship could be considered as a *neurophysiological explanation* of the psychophysical power law established by S. S. Stevens.

Trying to uncover the meaning of a sensory code comes to the question of how the brain handles the different fundamental aspects that characterizes the reference frame of our perceptions: Quality, position, duration, and intensity.

Very often invoked in the list of possibilities are the anatomic devices of specific projections, the selective activities of neurons, and the temporal properties of impulses.

The neurobiologist brings, moreover, to bear local mechanisms (lateral inhibition, centrifugal control, antorhythmicity, convergence, etc.) or global mechanisms (activation, motivation, attention, etc.) in order to make explicit the processes of codification.

However, in order to understand a brain code it is not sufficient to have physiological indicators, which the more and more refined techniques allow us to pick up, correspond to the characteristic features of objects and events as they are defined by the observer in his "objective language"—language that is in fact another form of cerebral code, bringing a collectively elaborated reference to bear on an out-of-reach realm of reality.

Nervous signals are not to be reduced to the structural information contained in electrophysiological recordings or in various morphological markers. These signals have meaning only when they are fully utilized by the central nervous system of the animal under study. And for this utilization to take place, there must be some adequate reading device in the brain. Recent technical advances allow us to combine the recordings of the various physiological indicators in animals (and even in man) engaged in a precise task. It is therefore possible to trace in the neural space the perceptive elaboration—an active construction of the brain whose order prefigures those of adapted action.

One must still adapt such methods to developmental studies, in order to understand how these reading devices work to select and to refine the features analyzers capable of extracting out of the external world classes of pertinent attributes.

Following this idea, one could be tempted to think that each species is equipped with repertories of action hereditarily inscribed in its brain. The interaction with the external (or internal) environment would improve the efficiency of these repertories by sharpening the sensory system in its capacity to detect more and more precise circumstances.

ACKNOWLEDGMENTS

Part of the work described in this chapter has been supported by grants from the CNRS, the INSERM, the DGRST, and the College de France. I wish to thank Y. Fregnac for his comments on the manuscript.

REFERENCES

Barlow, H. B. Summation and inhibition in the frog's retina. *J. Physiol.*, 1953, *119*, 69–88.

Barlow, H. B. Retinal ganglion cells responding selectively to direction and speed of image motion in the rabbit. *J. Physiol.*, 1964, *173*, 377–407.

Barlow, H. B. Single units and sensation: A neuron doctrine for perceptual psychology? *Perception*, 1972, *1*, 371–394.

Barlow, H. B., Blakemore, C., & Pettigrew, J. D. The neural mechanism of binocular depth discrimination. *J. Physiol.*, 1967, *193*, 327–342.

Barlow, H. B., & Pettigrew, J. D. Lack of specificity of neurones in the visual cortex of young kittens. *J. Physiol.*, 1971, *218*, 98–100.

Batini, C., Buisseret, P., & Buisseret-Delmas, C. Trigeminal pathway of the extrinsic eye afferents in cat. *Brain Res.*, 1975, *86*, 74–78.

Benoit, P., & Changeux, J. P. Consequences of tenotomy on the evolution of multiinnervation in developing rat soleus muscle. *Brain Res.*, 1975, *99*, 354–358.

Bergson, H. *Matière et mémoire*. In *Oeuvres*. Edition du Centenaire. Paris: Presses Universitaires de France, 1970.

Bishop, P. O. Neurophysiology of binocular single vision and stereopsis. In R. Jung (Ed.), *Handbook of Sensory Physiology*, New York: Springer Verlag, 1970.

Blakemore, C., & Van Sluyters, R. C. Innate and environmental factors in the development of the kitten's visual cortex. *J. Physiol.*, 1975, *248*, 663–716.

Buisseret, P., Gary-Bobo, E., & Imbert, M. Ocular motility may be involved in recovery of orientational properties of visual cortical neurones in dark-reared kittens. *Nature*, 1978, *278*, 816–817.

Buisseret, P., Gary-Bobo, E., & Imbert, M. Plasticity in the kitten's visual cortex: Effects of the suppression of visual experience upon the orientational properties of visual cortical cells. *Dev. Brain Res.*, 1982, *4*, 417–426.

Changeux, J. P. Déterminisme génétique et épigénèse des réseaux de neurones: Existe-t-il un compromis biologique possible entre Chomsky et Piaget? In M. Piatelli-Palmerini (Ed.), *Théories du langage. Théories de l'apprentissage*. Editions du seuil, p. 276–289. 1979.

Changeux, J. P., Courrege, Ph., & Danchin, A. A theory of the epigenesis of neuronal networks by selective stabilization of synapses. *Proc. Nat. Acad. Sci.*, USA, 1973, *70*, 2974–2978.

Cotman, C. W., & Nadler, J. V. Reactive synaptogenesis in the hippocampus. In Cotman, C. W. (Ed.), Neuronal plasticity. New York: Raven Press, 1978, pp. 227–271.

Cragg, B. G. The development of synapses in cat visual cortex. *Invest. Ophthalmol.*, 1972, *11*, 377–385.

Crepel, F., Mariani, J., & Delhaye-Bouchaud, N. Evidence for a multiple innervation of Purkinje cells by climbing fibers in the immature rat cerebellum, *J. Neurobiol.*, 1976, *7*, 567–578.

Cynader, M., & Mitchell, D. E. Monocular astigmatism effects on kitten visual cortex development. *Nature*, 1977, *270*, 177–178.

Duffy, F. H., Snodgrass, S. R., Burdhfiel, J. L. & Conway, J. L. Bicuculline reversal of deprivation amblyopia in the cat. *Nature*, 1976, *260*, 256–257.

Ferster, D., & Levay, S. The axonal arborizations of lateral geniculate neurons in the striate cortex of the cat. *J. Comp. Neurol.*, 1978, *182*, 925–944.

Fregnac, Y., & Bienenstock, E. Specific functional modifications of individual cortical neurones triggered by vision and passive eye movement, in immobilized kittens. In L. Maffei (Ed.), *Physiopathology of the visual system*. Doc. Ophthalmol. Proc. Series *30*, 100–108, Dr. Jank Publish., 1981.

Fregnac, Y., & Imbert, M. Early development of visual cortical cells in normal and dark-reared kittens. Relationship between orientation selectivity and ocular dominance. *J. Physiol.*, 1978, *278*, 27–44.

Fregnac, Y., Trotter, Y., Bienenstock, E., Buisseret, P., Gary-Bobo, E., & Imbert, M. Effect of neonatal unilateral enucleation on the development of orientation selectivity in the primary visual cortex of normally and dark-reared kittens. *Exp. Brain Res.*, 1981, *42*, 453–466.

Godement, P., Salaun, J., Saillour, P., & Imbert, M. Development of the retinofugal pathways in the mouse in physiopathology of the visual system, L. Maffei (Ed.), *Doc. Ophthal. Proc.* (series, *30*), 1981, Dr. W. Jank, Publish.

Guillery, R. W. Binocular competition in the control of geniculate cell growth. *J. Comp. Neur.*, 1972, *144*, 117–129.

Held, R. Exposure history as a factor in maintaining stability of perception and coordination. *J. Nerv. Ment. Dis.*, 1961, *132*, 26–32.

Hubel, D. H., & Wiesel, T. N. Receptive fields, binocular interaction and functional architecture in the cat's visual cortex. *J. Physiol.*, 1962, *160*, 106–154.

Hubel, D. H., & Wiesel, T. N. Receptive fields of cells in striate cortex of very young, visually inexperienced kittens. *J. Neurophysiol.*, 1963, *26*, 994–1002.

Hubel, D. H., & Wiesel, T. N. Binocular interaction in striate cortex of kittens reared with artificial squint. *J. Neurophysiol.*, 1965, *28*, 1041–1059.

Hubel, D. H., Wiesel, T. N., & Levay, S. Plasticity of ocular dominance columns in monkey striate cortex. *Phil. Trans. Roy. Soc.*, B, 1977, *278*, 377–409.

Hubel, D. H., Wiesel, T. N., & Stryker, M. P. Anatomical demonstration of orientation columns in macaque monkey. *J. Comp. Neurol.*, 1978, *177*, 361.

Imbert, M., & Buisseret, P. Receptive field characteristics and plastic properties of visual cortical cells in kittens reared with or without visual experience. *Exp. Brain Res.*, 1975, *22*, 25–36.

Kratz, K. E., Spear, P. D., & Smith, D. L. Postcritical period reversal of effects of monocular deprivation on striate cortex cells in the cat. *J. Neurophysiol.*, 1976, *39*, 501–511.

Levay, S., & Stryker, M. P. The development of ocular dominance in the cats. In J. Ferrendelli (Ed.), *Aspects of developmental neurobiology. Soc. Neurosc. Symp.*, 1979, *4*, 83–98.

Levinthal, F., Macagno, E. R., & Levinthal, C. Anatomy and development of identified cells in isogenic organisms. *Cold Spring Harbor Symp. Quant. Biol.*, 1976, *40*, 321–331.

Macagno, E. R., Lopresti, V., & Levinthal, C. Structure and development of neuronal connections in isogenic organisms: Variations and similarities in the optic system of *Daphnia magna. Proc. Nat. Acad. Sci.*, USA, 1973, *70*, 57–61.

Maffei, L. Binocular interaction in strabismic kittens and adult cats deprived of vision. *Arch. Ital. Biol.*, 1978, *116*, 390–392.

Maffei, L., & Bisti, S. Binocular interaction in strabismic kittens deprived of vision. *Science*, 1976, *191*, 579–580.

Mariani, J., & Changeux, J. P. Ontogenesis of olivocerebellar relationship, I. Studies by intracellular recordings of the multiple innervation of Purkinje cells by climbing fibers in the developing rat cerebellum. *J. Neurosc.*, 1981, *1*, 690–702.

Maturana, H. R., Lettvin, J. Y., McCulloch, W. S., & Pitts, W. H. Anatomy and physiology of vision in the frog *(Rana pipiens). J. Gen. Physiol.*, 1960. *43* (suppl. 2), Mechanisms of vision, 129–171.

Movshon, J. A., & Van Sluyters, A. C. Visual neural development. *Ann. Rev. Psychol.*, 1981, *32*, 477–522.

Nikara, T., Bishop, P. O., & Pettigrew, I. D. Analysis of retinal correspondence by studying receptive fields of binocular single units in cat striate cortex. *Exp. Brain Res.*, 1968, *6*, 353–372.

Pettigrew, J. D. The effect of visual experience on the development of stimulus specificity by kittens cortical neurones. *J. Physiol.*, 1974, *237*, 49–74.

Pettigrew, J. D. The paradox of the critical period for striate cortex. In C. W. Cotman (Ed.), *Neuronal plasticity.* New York: Raven Press, pp. 311–330.

Pettigrew, J. D., Nikara, T., & Bishop, P. O. Responses to moving slits by single units in cat striate cortex. *Brain Res.*, 1968, *6*, 373–390.

Rakic, P. Prenatal genesis of connections subserving ocular dominance in the rhesus monkey. *Nature*, 1976, *261*, 467–471.

Redfern, P. A. Neuromuscular transmission in newborn rats. *J. Physiol.*, 1970, *209*, 701–709.

Sherman, S. M., Guillery, R. W., Kaas, J. H., & Sanderson, K. J. Behavioral electrophysiological and morphological studies of binocular competition in the development of the geniculocortical pathways of cats. *J. Comp. Neur.*, 1974, *158*, 1–18.

Sidman, R. L. Cell interactions in developing mammalian central nervous system. In L. G. Silvestri (Ed.), *Cell Interactions, Proc. of the third Lepetit Colloquium*, Amsterdam, 1972, pp. 1–13.

Sidman, R. L., Green, M. C., & Appel, S. H. *Catalog of the neurological mutants of the mouse.* Cambridge, Mass.: Harvard University Press, 1965.

So, K. F., Schneider, G. E., & Frost, D. O. Postnatal development of retinal projections to the lateral geniculate body in Syrian hamsters. *Brain Res.*, 1978, *142*, 343–352.

Stryker, M. P. Late segregation of geniculate afferents to the cat's visual cortex after recovery from binocular impulse blockade. *Soc. for Neuroscience*, 1981, *7*, 842.

Swindale, N. V. Absence of ocular dominance patches in dark-reared cats. *Nature*, 1981, *290*, 332–333.

Teuber, H. L. Perception. In J. Field, H. W. Magoun, & V. E. Hall (Eds.), *Handbook of Physiology—Neurophysiology* (III). American Physiological Soc., Washington, 1961, pp. 1595–1668.

Trotter, Y., Gary-Bobo, E., & Buisseret, P. Restoration of orientation specificity of the visual cells in kittens after section of the ophthalmic branches of the Vth nerve. *Neurosc. Letters*, 1979, 53–296.

Trotter, Y., Gary-Bobo, E., & Buisseret, P. Recovery of orientation selectivity in kitten primary visual cortex is slowed down by bilateral section of ophthalmic trigeminal afferents. *Dev. Brain Res.*, 1981, *1*, 450–454.

Tsumodo, T., & Suda, K. Evidence for excitatory connections from the deprived eye to the visual cortex in monocularly deprived kittens. *Brain Res.*, 1978, *153*, 150–156.

Van Sluyters, R. C., & Levitt, F. B. Experimental strabismus in the kitten. *J. Neurophysiol.*, 1980, *43*, 686–699.

Wiesel, T. N., & Hubel, D. H. Comparison of the effects of unilateral and bilateral eye closure on cortical units responses in kittens. *J. Neurophysiol.*, 1965, *28*, 1029–1040. (a)

Wiesel, T. N., & Hubel, D. H. Extent of recovery from the effects of visual deprivation in kittens. *J. Neurophysiol.*, 1965, *28*, 1060–1072.

6

Perception of Unity, Persistence, and Identity: Thoughts on Infants' Conceptions of Objects

Elizabeth S. Spelke
University of Pennsylvania

In this chapter, I propose that humans begin life with a conception of material objects. That conception leads infants to perceive certain objects as unitary and bounded. That conception also leads infants to perceive an object as persisting when it moves and changes in certain ways, and to predict whether it will persist over future transformations. Finally, that conception sometimes allows infants to decide whether an object seen now is identical to, or distinct from, one seen in the past.

The conception is this: In the world are things that are wholly interconnected and separate from each other; these things can move through any place not occupied by other things, provided that they move continuously over space and time; and these things persist, maintaining their internal unity and external boundaries, during their unimpeded movements. This conception may underlie not only infants' first perceptions of objects but also their earliest learning. Despite all that humans learn about objects, this conception may continue to stand at the center of our thinking about material objects and physical causality.

This chapter focuses on research of several kinds. It begins with experiments on infants' perception of visible objects as unitary and bounded, for these experiments first led to the view that infants conceive of objects as movable and enduring. Then it turns to experiments on infants' notion that an object persists as it moves, in or out of sight. Although such studies are few in number, they too suggest that young infants conceive of objects as movable and persisting. Finally, the chapter considers infants' knowledge of the identity of an object over successive encounters. The findings of many experiments have been taken to indicate that infants have a different notion of identity (and hence a different conception of objects) than adults. I will suggest, however, that these findings are consistent with the hypothesis that infants and adults have a common notion of physical identity. Since no existing experiment appears to distinguish between these interpretations, some experiments will be proposed.

The chapter closes with a brief discussion of the development of knowledge of objects. In that context, I consider some of the puzzles that surround our intuitions as adults about object unity, persistence, and identity.

UNITY

When we as adults encounter any visual scene, we perceive a layout of persisting objects: Things like rocks, cats, and typewriters. We effortlessly break the scene into stable entities with internal unity and external boundaries. Perceiving objects is no simple accomplishment, however, for the boundaries of things are not reflected straightforwardly in the structure of light at the eye. Any natural scene consists of a three-dimensional arrangement of surfaces. Most of these surfaces are partly hidden behind other surfaces, and almost all of them are adjacent to other surfaces. To perceive objects, we need to decide whether and how adjacent surfaces are connected, and whether and how partly hidden surfaces continue in the places where we cannot see them.

Adults appear to solve these problems in a variety of ways. We sometimes group surfaces into objects in accordance with our knowledge of particular kinds of objects and their characteristic properties. After identifying an object on a table as a telephone, for example, we may judge that the dial and the receiver are parts of it whereas the table surface is not. We also group surfaces into objects in accord with certain general principles of organization, as described by the Gestalt psychologists (Koffka, 1935; Wertheimer, 1923/1958). For example, we may group together surfaces that have aligned edges (principle of good continuation), surfaces that are homogeneous in color and texture (principle of similarity), and surfaces that combine to form objects of simple shapes (principle of good form). Finally, we group surfaces into objects by detecting the spatial arrangement and movements of surfaces in the layout. Surfaces are perceived to lie on a single object if they are connected, directly or via other object surfaces, and if their movements preserve the connections between them.

With a number of colleagues, I have attempted to investigate the origins of these abilities in human infancy. We began by studying infants' perception of partly occluded objects. In these studies, 4-month-old infants were presented with a three-dimensional object whose center was hidden: For example, a tall, thin rod positioned behind a shorter block (Fig. 6.1). We have asked whether, and under what conditions, infants perceive the top and bottom of such an object as connected behind the occluder.

Some of the experiments used a habituation procedure, developed in collaboration with Phillip Kellman (Kellman & Spelke, 1983). Infants were presented

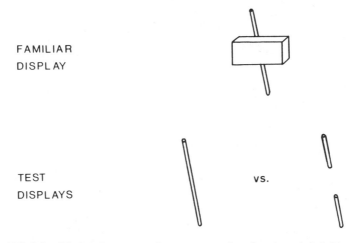

FAMILIAR
DISPLAY

TEST   vs.
DISPLAYS

FIG. 6.1.   Displays for one experiment on perception of partly occluded objects, using the habituation method (Kellman & Spelke, 1983).

with the partly hidden object repeatedly until their looking time declined, and then they were presented with two fully visible displays in alternation. One test display consisted of a single connected object; the other display consisted of two smaller objects separated by a gap where the occluder had been (Fig. 6.1). Infants were expected to look longer at the test display they perceived as more different from the original, partly hidden object. If they perceived the original object to continue behind the occluder, for example, they should have looked longer at the display with the gap.

Other experiments used a briefer procedure, developed with Hilary Schmidt and Timothy Hrynick, which we call the "disocclusion method" (Schmidt & Spelke, 1984; Termine, Hrynick, Gleitman, & Spelke, 1984). Infants were allowed to look at a partly hidden object for a few seconds, and then the occluder was removed before their eyes to reveal either a complete object or two smaller objects with the gap (see Fig. 6.2). If infants had perceived a connected object behind the occluder, they were again expected to look longer at the display with a gap, because this display was novel and possibly surprising.

With either method, it is necessary to conduct a variety of experiments to ensure that infants will look at the complete and broken objects about equally in the absence of any occlusion, that infants discriminate among all the displays, and that infants attend to the visible surfaces of the partly hidden objects. With the habituation experiments, it is also necessary to ensure that infants will generalize habituation from a display of two objects to a display containing one of those objects, and will dishabituate—increase their looking—when a display containing a different object is presented. Since all these assumptions were found to be correct (see Kellman & Spelke, 1983; Schmidt & Spelke, 1984), I will focus on the findings of the principal experiments.

FAMILIAR
DISPLAY

TEST
DISPLAYS

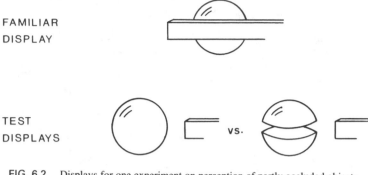

FIG. 6.2.   Displays for one experiment on perception of partly occluded objects, using the disocclusion method (Schmidt & Spelke, 1984).

When a partly hidden object is stationary, infants of 4 months do not appear to perceive it either as a single, complete object or as two separate objects. This is so regardless of the object's properties (Fig. 6.3). For example, infants do not perceive three rods arranged in the shape of a triangle as continuing behind an occluder. Adults perceive a compelling connection in this case, in accordance with the principles of similarity, good continuation, and good form (Kellman & Spelke, 1983; Michotte, Thines, & Crabbe, 1964).[1] Moreover, infants do not perceive a solid, regular sphere or cube as continuing behind an occluder, again in contrast to adults (Schmidt & Spelke, 1984). Finally, infants of 4 months do not perceive a photograph of a face as connected behind a block that occludes the ears and nose. Five-month-old infants, in contrast, perceive a unitary face (Schwartz, 1982).

When a partly hidden object moves in certain ways, however, 4-month-old infants perceive the object as a single unit behind its occluder (see Fig. 6.4). Infants perceive the unity of a rod that moves back and forth in a linear translation behind a stationary block, its center never coming into view. They also perceive the unity of a rod that moves in depth; translation in depth appears to be as effective as translation in the frontal plane. The unity of an object is not perceived if it is stationary against a stationary background and only the occluder moves, or if the object and the occluder move together. The experiments suggest that infants perceive partly hidden objects in accordance with a common movement principle (Spelke, 1982; see also Wertheimer, 1923/1958), and that the critical conditions for common movement are that an object change position in the three-dimensional layout, relative to its occluder and relative to the background.

Studies of perception of moving objects provide further evidence that infants do not perceive in accordance with the principles of similarity, good continuation,

_____

[1]The findings of the experiment with infants do not accord with the findings of an experiment by Bower, 1967a, using a similar display.

OCCLUSION DISPLAY: METHODS: FINDINGS:

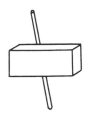

                            Habituation   No Completion[a]

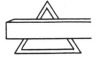

                            Habituation   No Completion[a]

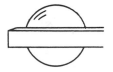

                            Habituation   No Completion[b]
                            Disocclusion   No Completion[b]

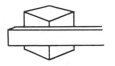

                            Habituation   No Completion[b]
                            Disocclusion   No Completion[b]

                            Habituation   No Completion[c]

FIG. 6.3.   Displays, methods, and findings of experiments on perception of partly occluded stationary objects by 4-month-old infants. **a.** Reported in Kellman and Spelke (1983). **b.** Reported in Schmidt and Spelke (1984). **c.** This experiment used a slide photograph of a face, rear-projected on a translucent screen behind a three-dimensional occluder. Reported in Schwartz (1982).

OCCLUSION DISPLAY:	METHOD:	FINDING:

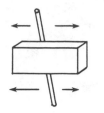 Habituation Completion [a]

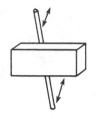 Habituation Completion [b]

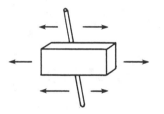 Habituation No Completion [a]

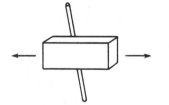 Habituation No Completion [a]

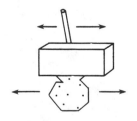 Habituation Completion [a]

FIG. 6.4. Displays, methods, and findings of experiments on perception of partly occluded moving objects by 4-month-old infants. Arrows indicate the extent and the direction of motion. **a.** Reported in Kellman and Spelke (1983). **b.** In this experiment, the motion is in depth. Reported in Kellman and Spelke (1984).

and good form. Perception of the unity of a moving object is not affected by
the similarity of its visible surfaces in color and texture, the alignment of its
edges, or the simplicity of its overall shape. In contrast, adults perceive the ends
of a moving object as more strongly or definitely connected if they are aligned
and similar (Kellman & Spelke, 1983). Infants of four months appear to perceive
partly hidden objects by detecting the movements of visible surfaces but not by
analyzing the colors or forms of surfaces.

The next experiments focused on infants' perception of stationary objects that
are adjacent or separated in depth. A number of experiments using looking time
and reaching methods have investigated whether 3-month-old infants perceive
two objects as distinct when they are touching and/or when one stands in front
of the other (von Hofsten & Spelke, 1984; Kestenbaum, Termine & Spelke,
1984; Prather & Spelke, 1982). One experiment conducted with Penny Prather
(Prather & Spelke, 1982) will serve to illustrate our findings. In this experiment,
we made use of the finding that infants can be habituated to the number of objects
or forms in a visual display (Starkey, Spelke, & Gelman, 1980; Strauss & Curtis,
1981). If infants are presented with a succession of different displays of three
objects, they will subsequently look less at new displays of three objects than
at new displays of two or four objects. Accordingly, Prather and I attempted to
induce habituation to displays of one or two objects—solid, rectangular blocks
of various sizes and shapes—and then we presented displays of one block, of
two blocks that were separated in the frontal plane, of two adjacent blocks, and
of two blocks separated in depth (Fig. 6.5). Looking times to the first two test
displays should have indicated whether the infants detected, and dishabituated
to, a change in number. If they did, looking times to the adjacent objects and
to the overlapping objects should have indicated whether each of these displays
was perceived as one unit or two.

Only a minority of the infants appeared to dishabituate to a change in number.
Among this minority, most of the infants who were habituated to one-object
displays looked longer at the blocks separated in depth than at the adjacent
blocks; most of the infants who were habituated to the two-object displays looked
longer at the adjacent blocks. These findings suggest that the adjacent blocks
were perceived as one object and that the blocks separated in depth were perceived
as two objects. Observations of infants' reaching for objects (von Hofsten &
Spelke, 1984) and of infants' habituation and dishabituation to objects that change
position (Kestenbaum et al., 1984) support the same conclusions. Infants evidently do not perceive adjacent objects by analyzing the alignment of their edges
or the simplicity of their shapes, in accordance with the principles of good
continuation and good form. Infants do appear to perceive objects by detecting
the spatial connections and separations of surfaces in a three-dimensional scene.
Two objects separated in depth are two objects, whether or not their images
overlap at the eye.

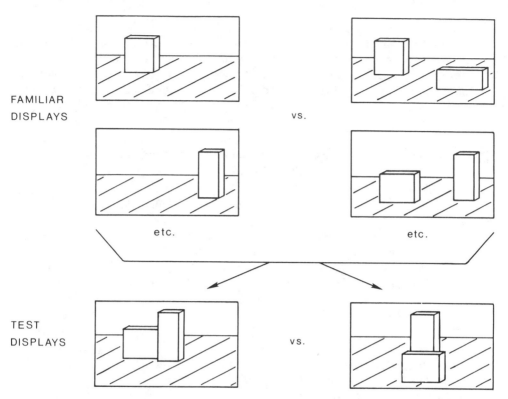

FIG. 6.5.   Displays used in an experiment on perception of adjacent objects and of objects separated in depth (Prather & Spelke, 1982).

I discuss further studies of object perception in the next section, but those described already suggest a general account of infants' perception of visible objects (Spelke, 1982). In brief, infants appear to perceive objects by analyzing the spatial arrangements and the movements of surfaces, in accord with two principles. According to the "connected surface principle," any two surfaces lie on the same object if they are touching in the three-dimensional layout, either directly or indirectly through other object surfaces. Two surfaces lie on separate objects if they are separated by empty space. According to the "common movement principle," two surfaces lie on the same object if they undergo the same three-dimensional translation relative to the other surfaces in the scene. Two surfaces lie on separate objects if one moves independently of the other. No other principles are needed to account for the abilities described thus far.

This account is still quite vague, because the existing experiments on object perception leave many questions unanswered. For example, we do not know how extensively surfaces must touch for infants to perceive them as connected. Would an infant perceive a collection of objects as one unit if they touched at isolated points, as do beads on a string? We also do not know how uniformly two surfaces must move for infants to perceive them as a unit. Would an infant perceive different surfaces as parts of one object if they underwent separate jointed motions, as do the limbs of a walking person? Finally, it is not clear what infants would perceive if the connected surface and the common movement principles were placed in conflict. Is a flock of geese one object for an infant, when its spatially distinct members move in harmony? Is a bicycle one object, with its spatially connected but separately moving parts? In these cases, human adults are prey to conflicting impressions. We can see a necklace either as a unitary object or as a collection of distinct beads; we can see a bicycle either as one object or as an arrangement of separate wheels, pedals, and gears. These problematic cases are especially interesting, and I will return to them.

What capacities give rise to the connected surface and the common movement principles? It is possible that the principles arise from the activity of specifically sensory mechanisms, attuned to certain relationships in a visual array. But I am intrigued by a different possibility, that the infant's perception is guided by a conception of physical objects. Infants may group together surfaces that touch and move together because they conceive of the world as consisting of units that are internally cohesive and separately movable. Infants may fail to group together surfaces that form units with smooth contours and a homogeneous color because they do not conceive of the world as consisting of units that are regular in shape and coloring.

On this view, developmental changes in object perception could result from the growth of conceptions of objects. Adults, unlike infants, may perceive a blue cup and a red plate as two distinct objects when one sits on the other, and as complete objects when each is stationary and partly hidden, because of what we know about plates and cups, and because we know that many objects, particularly artifacts, tend to be homogeneously colored and textured, smoothly contoured, and simply shaped. Children may attain this knowledge as they begin to categorize objects and to learn about their characteristic properties.

PERSISTENCE

Objects often move and change: Matches are struck, balls are bounced, paper is cut, bread is toasted and eaten. As adults, we can often predict whether a given object will persist over a given transformation by using knowledge of particular kinds of objects and events. Knowledge of the properties of particular sorts of objects allows us to predict, for example, that a nail will survive a long fall onto a rock, whereas a crystal vase will not. Knowledge of the effects of particular sorts of transformations allows us to predict that a teacup that will break if it is struck by a hammer but not if it is filled with tea. Some of our predictions about objects, however, may depend on more general notions. We know that all objects persist when they move freely through unoccupied spaces: No unimpeded movement, by itself, will destroy an object's integrity.

If infants conceive of objects as unitary and persisting over displacements, they too should predict that an object will retain its unity and its boundaries as it moves from place to place, provided that no other events occur during these movements. Infants should even expect an object to persist when it travels completely out of view.

Several experiments have probed these expectations by following the logic of an early study by Bower (1965). Bower had investigated whether infants expect a two-dimensional visual form to cohere as it moves. Infants of 1 to 9 months were presented with pictorial displays in which adults perceive a certain organization. Two of the displays consisted of stationary dots or lines; adults group together elements in these displays in accordance with the principles of proximity, good continuation, closure, or good form. The third pattern consisted of two lines moving in a uniform translation; adults perceive the lines as a unit in accordance with the principle of common fate. After the infant subjects viewed a display for 20 seconds while sucking spontaneously on a nipple, there began a new movement that either preserved or broke apart the configurations that adults perceive. If infants perceived the original grouping, and if they expected a group of elements to persist as a unit, they were expected to be surprised by the movement that broke this grouping. A decrease in spontaneous sucking served as the index of surprise. By this measure, infants as young as 2 months were more surprised by the movement that broke the organization in the common fate display than by the movement that preserved this organization. Not until 9 months did the infants appear more surprised by movements that broke the other con- figurations. Bower's experiment provides additional evidence that young infants organize visual scenes into units in accordance with the principle of common fate and not in accordance with the other gestalt principles. The experiment suggested, moreover, that infants expect a perceived group of elements to retain its unity when it is displaced.

Wendy Smith Born and I used a variant of this method to investigate whether infants expect a three-dimensional object to persist, maintaining its unity and boundaries, over its movements (Spelke & Born, 1984). In the first experiment, 3-month-old infants were presented with a large cylindrical object suspended in front of a uniform background surface. The object and the background differed in color and texture and were well separated in depth (Fig. 6.6). By the connected surface principle, infants should have perceived the object as unitary and separate from the background. Did they expect the object to retain its unity and its distinctness as it moved?

To address this question, the display was presented without movement for 30 seconds, and was then moved in one of two ways. In one condition, the object moved forward as a whole. In the other condition, half the object and an adjacent piece of the background moved forward, leaving the rest of the object

ORIGINAL
DISPLAY

TEST
DISPLAY

VS.

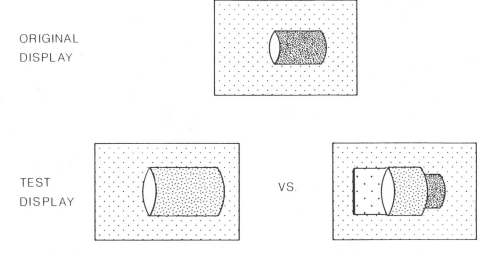

FIG. 6.6. Displays used in an experiment on perception of the unity and persistence of suspended objects (Spelke & Born, 1984). The object and background
surface were in the position depicted in the upper drawing during the stationary
periods. During the object movement and the broken movement periods, the
surfaces moved from that position to one of the two positions depicted in the
lower drawings.

and background behind (Fig. 6.6). Infants were presented with both kinds of
movement in a counterbalanced order; they were videotaped, and an observer
judged when the babies looked most surprised or puzzled (see Spelke & Born,
1984, for details). Infants were judged to be more surprised or puzzled during
the movement that broke up the object than during the movement of the object
as a whole. This experiment provides evidence that the infants perceived the
object as unitary and distinct from the background, and that they expected the
object to retain its unity as it moved.

This interpretation was supported by our next experiments. The second experiment differed from the first only in one respect: Infants were presented with the
cylindrical object in front of a background of the same color and texture. If
infants perceive objects by analyzing the spatial arrangements of surfaces and
not by analyzing surface colors and textures, then the infants in this study should
have been as surprised by the breakup of the object as were those in the first
study. The results of the two experiments were indeed the same.

The findings of the third experiment complemented those of the second.
Infants were presented with a single planar surface consisting of two regions: a
region of the same two-dimensional shape, size, color, and texture as the object
in the first study, and a surrounding region of the same shape, size, color, and
texture as the background. The object region either moved as a whole or split
in two, half of it moving with a piece of the background region. The infants

were judged to respond equally to the two types of movement. They evidently did not organize this surface into areas of homogeneous color and texture.

A second series of experiments, with 6-month-old infants, focused on perception of adjacent objects (Spelke, Born, Mangelsdorf, Richter, & Termine, 1984). Infants were presented with two adjacent objects that differed in color, texture, size, and shape, and that were arranged so that no surfaces or edges of one object were aligned with those of the other (Fig. 6.7). In one condition, the two objects moved forward together. In a second condition, one object moved forward while the other remained at rest. Most of the infants were judged to be more surprised when one object moved alone than when the two objects moved together. They apparently perceived the two adjacent objects as one unit, for they seemed to expect this unit to move coherently.

Despite these findings, a final experiment suggests that the boundary between two adjacent objects has some privileged status for a 6-month-old. Infants were presented with two different breakings of the same configuration of adjacent objects. Either one object moved relative to the other, or half of one object moved together with the other object (Fig. 6.8). The infants were judged to be more surprised by the latter movement. Six-month-old infants may perceive two adjacent objects as one unit, but they are less surprised if this unit breaks in two at the objects' boundary than if it breaks at some other place. Their perception of the object is affected by the colors, textures, and shapes of surfaces. This

ORIGINAL
DISPLAY

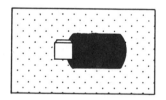

TEST
DISPLAYS

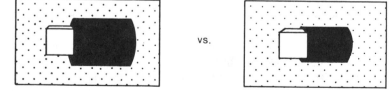

VS.

FIG. 6.7.   Displays used in an experiment on perception of the persistence of adjacent objects (Spelke, Born, Mangelsdorf, Richter, & Termine, 1984). The objects were in the position depicted in the upper drawing during the stationary periods. During the movement periods, the object(s) moved from that position to one of the two positions depicted in the lower drawings.

ORIGINAL
DISPLAY

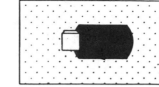

TEST
DISPLAYS

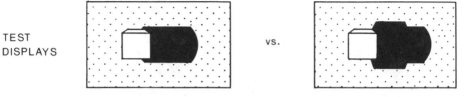

vs.

FIG. 6.8.   Displays used in an experiment on perception of the boundary between two adjacent objects. (Spelke, Born, Mangelsdorf, Richter, & Termine, 1984). The objects were in the position depicted in the upper drawing during the stationary periods. During the movement periods, the object(s) moved from that position to one of the two positions depicted in the lower drawings.

experiment, like other recent experiments (Bertenthal, Campos, & Haith, 1980; Bresson & de Schonen, 1976–1977; Piaget, 1954; Wishart, 1979), suggests that adherence to the static gestalt principles begins to emerge near 6 months of age.

In summary, infants appear to organize visual scenes into units by detecting the spatial separation of surfaces. They are less apt to organize scenes into units by analyzing the colors or textures of surfaces, the alignments of surfaces and edges, and the shapes of objects. Most importantly, infants appear to expect the units they perceive to retain their coherence and their boundaries as they move. These experiments provide evidence that infants conceive of objects as unitary, as separately movable, and as persisting over their movements.

Experiments have not investigated whether infants expect objects to cohere over other visible transformations: for example, whether infants would be surprised if an object shattered, or failed to shatter, when hit. We also do not know whether infants expect objects to retain other properties through time: for example, whether infants would be surprised if an object suddenly changed its shape or color. As adults, we are sometimes surprised by these events and sometimes not, depending on the particular object and transformation that are involved. The breaking of a doll is less surprising if it is kicked than if it is kissed; a gradual, spontaneous change in shape is more remarkable in a dish than in a dog. It is possible that humans begin life with knowledge of certain kinds of objects and transformations. Infants may distinguish rigid from nonrigid objects, for example, and expect only the latter to deform when squeezed (Gibson, 1982). Nevertheless, it is likely that most expectations about objects and their transformations develop through learning. Infants may learn about particular kinds of object transformations as they perceive objects and follow them through time.

Let us turn to objects that move fully out of view. Do infants expect an object to persist over this change? Most psychologists believe that they do not. According to Piaget (1954), a young infant has no notion that objects endure when out of sight. When an object is occluded and disoccluded, a young infant's experience is of a tableau that is destroyed and created anew. Infants slowly construct a conception of persisting objects over the first 18 months, as they develop the capacity to act on objects in a coordinated manner.

Piaget's proposal is supported by observations of infants' search for hidden objects. A very young infant does not search visually for an object that moves behind a screen (Nelson, 1971; Piaget, 1954), and an infant under about 8 months of age will not remove a cover in order to retrieve an object that is hidden beneath it (Piaget, 1954). The ability to find hidden objects seems to emerge in a succession of stages over the course of infancy (Harris, 1975; Piaget, 1954).

Nevertheless, it is not clear that the development of search for objects results from changes in the child's conception of objects. Reaching and visual following may improve with age, because children become increasingly capable of organizing different actions together in means-ends sequences (Piaget, 1952), and increasingly adept at keeping track of objects and their displacements (Harris, 1975; see also Cornell, 1979; Harris, 1983; Ninio, 1979). It would be desirable, therefore, to investigate infants' knowledge of hidden objects using methods that do not involve visual or manual searching. Two such studies have been conducted, to my knowledge, and both suggest that infants do expect objects to persist when they are fully occluded.

Bower (1967b) trained infants of 2 months to suck for reinforcement in the presence of an object, and then he made the object disappear either by gradual occlusion or by a magical, gradual or sudden dissolving. The infants were expected to continue sucking only if they perceived that the object was still present. Infants continued sucking after a gradual occlusion, but not after one of the other modes of disappearance. Bower concluded that infants perceived the object as persisting when it was occluded but not when it was dissolved.

How did the infants react to the magical events: Were they surprised to see an object dissolve, like Alice's cheshire cat? This question has not been answered. In a further experiment (Bower, 1967b), infants exhibited no drop in spontaneous sucking—one possible index of surprise or interest—during the magical disappearances. No other observations of surprise reactions have been reported.

The second experiment was conducted in collaboration with Renée Baillargéon (Baillargéon & Spelke, in preparation). Baillargéon asked whether infants will make an inference about the possibility or impossibility of an event by drawing on knowledge about a hidden object. If infants could be shown to make this inference, it would follow that they knew the hidden object continued to exist in the place where it was hidden. Five-month-old infants were presented with a bright yellow block standing on a table, fully in view behind a screen that lay flat on the table. The screen then began to rotate about its far edge, moving upward and toward the block. The screen began to occlude the block as it rotated upward, and the block was fully occluded when the screen had rotated about 70°. By the time the screen had rotated about 120°, it should have made contact with the hidden object. On half the trials it did this, and it stopped moving. On the other trials it continued its rotation through the space that the hidden block should have occupied (Fig. 6.9). If the infants knew that the block continued to exist out of view behind the screen, and if they knew that two physically distinct objects cannot occupy the same place at the same time, then they should have been surprised by the complete rotation but not by the arrested rotation.

Baillargéon assessed infants' surprise by embedding these events in a habituation study. Infants were habituated to a succession of events in which the screen rotated through the full 180° with no block present. After habituation, infants in one group were presented with the same screen with a block behind it, as described. The screen rotated either 120° or 180° on alternating trials. Infants in a second group were presented with the block beside the screen, out of the path of the screen's rotation. The screen moved 120° or 180° on alternating trials, but it never occluded the block or made contact with it. Infants who saw the block next to the screen looked equally long at the display during the equally possible 120° and 180° rotations. The infants who saw the block behind the screen, however, looked longer during the impossible 180° rotation. Although the 180° rotation was superficially the same as the original, familiar event, the infants responded as if this event was novel and/or surprising. It apeared that the infants knew that the block was behind the screen, constraining the screen's movement.

These experiments suggest that infants perceive an object to persist when it moves behind another object. It is not clear whether infants, like adults, expect an object to persist when it disappears in other ways: for example, when it is placed inside a box. It seems possible that infants do not have this expectation,

FIG. 6.9. Display used in an experiment on perception of the persistence of a hidden object (Baillargéon & Spelke, in preparation). The screen moved from the first position to the fourth position and back again (normal movement) or from the first position to the fifth position and back again (impossible movement).

for objects sometimes persist when they enter other objects and sometimes do not. Our ability, as adults, to predict the fate of objects that enter caves, mailboxes, incinerators, and mouths probably depends on what we learn about particular kinds of objects and events.

To summarize this section, young infants appear to expect objects to persist under certain conditions. When an object moves within the visual field, infants expect it to move as a whole; they seem to be surprised if a movement changes its boundaries. When an object moves out of sight behind another object, infants expect it to continue to occupy some place; they seem to be surprised if something else moves through the space that the object should occupy. These reactions could stem from an underlying conception of objects as coherent, as separately movable through unoccupied space, and as persisting over their movements.

IDENTITY

When infants encounter an object, do they ever have the notion that the very same object has been encountered in the past? If so, under what conditions does an infant perceive that objects, seen at different times, are identical or distinct?

As adults, our attributions of identity are as commonplace as they are difficult to understand. Sometimes we decide questions of object identity by drawing on knowledge of the stable and variable characteristics of particular kinds of objects. Such knowledge informs us, for example, that a sparkling blue Volkswagen seen today can be the same car as one seen last week if the old car was colored green, but not, most likely, if it was in the shape of a Cadillac. Sometimes we are guided by knowledge about the characteristic life spans of different kinds of objects. We know that an elderly gentleman might be the same individual as a young man encountered many decades ago, but that his bulldog and his lit cigarette almost certainly were not present at that first encounter. Sometimes we bring to bear knowledge about the similarities and distinctions among objects of a given kind. We know that we can identify most people on separate occasions by detecting their unique physical characteristics, but that we can identify few ballpoint pens in this way. Finally, we sometimes decide if an object seen now is identical to one seen in the past by tracing the path of the object in the interval between our encounters with it. If there is a path, continuous in space and time, between "that object then" and "this object now," and if a unitary object moved continuously through every point on that path, then the objects are one and the same. This decision depends on the notion that objects move separately, coherently, and continuously.

Many problems are raised by the view that identity judgments rest on judgments about the continuity of an object through space and time (see Wiggins, 1980). Nevertheless, such continuity seems central to our thinking. If there is a continuous path connecting a bulldog living now with a bulldog that lived in

1930, we would probably conclude that this is the same, extraordinarily old, dog. If there is no continuous path connecting a man seen today with a man seen yesterday, then we would probably conclude that they are distinct people, however, similar they appear. Dramatists sometimes mystify or amuse us by playing with these notions. Two people are presented at different times in the guise of one character, and then they are introduced at times and in places that tax our ability to connect these appearances by a single path. At some point, our imagination gives way, our perceptions shift, and we realize we have been watching two distinct characters all along (e.g., Bernard & Sullivan, 1867).

Young infants also have a basis for deciding questions of object identity if they conceive of objects as separately movable on continuous paths and as persisting over their movements. Infants should consider an object seen now as identical to one seen in the past whenever they perceive that some unitary, persisting thing has followed a continuous path from the first encounter to the second. Infants should consider the objects as distinct whenever they perceive that no such path unites them. On this hypothesis, the core of the adult's conception of object identity traces back to infancy.

No psychologist, to my knowledge, would agree with this conjecture. It is widely believed that humans begin life either with no notion of object identity or with a notion very different from that of adults. According to Piaget (1954), infants do not initially conceive of objects as persisting, external things, and so they could not found a notion of object identity on spatiotemporal continuity. Piaget asserts, in fact, that young infants have no notion of identity for physical objects. According to Bower (1974) and Moore and Meltzoff (1978), young infants have a notion of identity, but it is virtually opposite to the adult notion: An object is identified with a particular position or movement. If a car moved out of a garage and stopped at the end of a driveway, these authors propose infants would perceive at least three distinct objects: the car at rest in the garage, the car moving down the driveway, and the car at rest by the street (see Moore & Meltzoff, 1978). On this view, infants revise their identity concepts a number of times before embracing the notion that an object retains its identity as it moves.

A large number of experiments seem to support one or the other of these views, providing evidence for a radical developmental change in conceptions of object identity. I believe, however, that the findings of this research have been misunderstood. The research is fully consistent with the view that infants resolve questions of object identity by tracing the paths of objects through space and time.

In these experiments, infants are presented with one or two objects on two separate occasions. Reactions to the object(s) are observed, in an effort to determine whether, and under what conditions, infants treat the separate encounters as encounters with a single object. For example, infants have been presented with an object that moved smoothly behind a screen so that it disappeared at one edge of the screen and reappeared at the opposite edge. After infants observed this event repeatedly, a change was introduced: One object moved smoothly out of sight behind the screen, and a second object, of a different shape and color, reappeared at the appropriate time and place. If infants perceived these events as do adults, they were expected to react to the change in some way. Either of two kinds of reaction might be expected. First, adults perceive the first event as involving one object and the second event as involving two objects. Thus infants might perceive the event involving two objects as novel, and they should attend to it. Second, adults perceive the second event as surprising, because an object of one color and shape usually does not appear on the same path, moving at the same speed, as an object of a different color and shape. Infants might respond to the two-object event with signs of surprise.

Infants younger than 5 months show no signs of special interest or surprise when they watch these events. When a single object disappears and reappears, for example, infants are reported to follow the object smoothly. Until 5 or 6 months, infants follow events in the same manner when one object disappears and an object of a different shape and color reappears (Muller & Aslin, 1978; see also Bower, Broughton, & Moore, 1971). Infants also show no distinctive changes in heartrate while viewing events in which one object is substituted for another while the objects are out of sight (Goldberg, 1976), unless the objects are occluded for a very brief time (von Hofsten & Lindhagen, 1983).

In an ingenious experiment, Moore, Borton, and Darby (1978) investigated infants' reactions to a different kind of change in the original one-object event. After infants had viewed one object moving behind a wide screen on repeated trials, they were presented with two narrow screens separated by a gap. The object again disappeared behind the first screen and reappeared from behind the second screen on a series of trials. On half the trials, the object passed between the screens at the appropriate time; on the other trials, it did not. To an adult, the latter event seems to involve two objects and is surprising, because the objects look alike and their movements are coordinated. In contrast, infants of 5 months did not differentiate between the two events. They followed the dis- appearing and reappearing objects quite smoothly, whether or not an object appeared between the two screens.

These experiments all suggest that infants perceive objects moving in and out of view differently from adults. Infants do not appear to be surprised by events that adults find surprising, and they react similarly to events that adults see as different. It does not follow, however, that infants lack a notion of identity based on spatiotemporal continuity, for the infants in these experiments were presented with events in which it is impossible to determine whether one object has moved continuously. When a white sphere disappears behind a screen and a red cube emerges, adults think it likely that two distinct objects are involved: one that came to a halt behind the screen, and a second that originally stood at rest behind the screen and moved into view. It is possible, however, that a single object moved continuously behind the screen, changing its size and shape as it moved. When a white sphere disappears behind a screen and a white sphere emerges, we think it likely that only one object is present, but it is possible, again, that there are two distinct spheres. All of these possibilities are consistent with the notion that objects move continuously through space and time. If some of these events surprise us, it is because they violate other notions, such as the notion that inanimate objects tend to move on straight paths at uniform speeds, and the notion that inanimate objects do not often change color or shape. Infants may fail to be surprised when objects are substituted or move strangely, because they lack our knowledge of the ways in which these objects are likely to behave. Like adults, however, infants may conceive of objects as moving continuously through space and time and as persisting over these movements.

How reasonable is the hypothesis that infants judge object identity by tracing an object's continuous movement but not by noting its shape and color? I think it is highly plausible. Consider the quandary of an infant who encounters an object on two separate occasions, and who seeks to decide whether she is encountering one object or two. One cannot make this decision in any general way by analyzing an object's physical attributes. For example, the infant's breakfast plate this morning may look indistinguishable from her dinner plate last night, and yet it is not necessarily the same object. Moreover, her groggy, bed-clothed father may look very different this morning than during the previous evening, yet he is one object all the same. To determine the identity of objects in these cases, one must bring to bear knowledge about particular kinds of objects, their constant and variable attributes, and their unique distinguishing characteristics. Infants seem quite likely to lack this knowledge. If so, they would only be able to decide questions of identity by tracing an object's path of movement.

I suggest, therefore, that there has been no test of the hypothesis that infants attribute identity to an object by tracing its movements through space and time. It should be possible, nevertheless, to test this hypothesis with experiments quite similar to those just described. For example, one could present infants with a variety of object-screen events and investigate linkages between perception of the number of objects in a display and perception of the patterns of movement of those objects. Infants should perceive the object that reappears at one side of an occluder as identical to the object that had disappeared at the other side if, and only if, they also perceive that something moved continuously behind the occluder from one side to the other.

As a second example, one could present infants with an event that is truly inconsistent with the notion that objects move continuously. Infants could be shown that only one object is present in a display. Then a barrier could be introduced and positioned so that the object could not move continuously across the display. Finally, a screen could be lowered in front of the barrier and the standard event could be presented. If infants expect objects to move continuously, they should be surprised when the object disappears at one side of the screen and reappears at the other side. To my knowledge, no such studies have been reported (but see Baillargéon, forthcoming).

To summarize this section, I have presented a hypothesis concerning infants' notions of object identity. Infants perceive an object to maintain its identity if it is displaced as a unit and if its displacement is continuous in space and time. Spatiotemporal continuity may provide infants with their only notion of identity for physical objects. With growth, children will acquire more specific knowledge about particular sorts of objects and transformations, and will thus extend their ability to decide whether an object seen now is identical to one seen in the past. Nevertheless, infants begin with a conception of identity that is shared by us as adults.

THE GROWTH OF CONCEPTIONS OF OBJECTS

This chapter has focused on infants' conceptions of objects, and on the ways in which these conceptions might serve as a basis for perceiving objects, for predicting their future states, and for tracing their identity through time. In closing, I consider how our first notions of objects might figure in the conceptions of unity, persistence, and identity that we hold as adults.

Our conceptions of objects are puzzling. In some circumstances, we have strong and clear intuitions about the boundaries of objects and about the conditions under which objects persist. When we see a car cross a field, we have no doubt that the car is a unitary object, whereas the collection consisting of the wheels of the car and all the grass that touches them is not. We strongly suspect that this car will continue to persist as it moves, provided no other events intervene. As the car advances, we perceive one car that retains its identity over the displacement and not, for example, a succession of different cars, each replacing the one that came before.

Our intuitions falter, however, when they are pursued further. Would we say that the car is one object or many: Is each wheel, for example, a separate object? Would we say that the car persisted if it was burned to a point at which it became undrivable? unrecognizable? Would we say that the car persisted while it was disassembled for repairs or after the mechanic had replaced its tires? its body? every one of its parts? Pressed with such questions, our thinking seems neither clear nor consistent. We are not certain how to answer these questions about cars, and we might answer similar questions quite differently if we were asked about cats or kings. In view of these complexities, some philosophers have concluded that humans have no underlying notions of the persistence and identity of objects (e.g., Hume, 1738/1962). Other philosophers have concluded that we have different notions of persistence and identity for each sort of object in the world, one notion for cups and a different notion for carrots (e.g., Wiggins,

1980). These arguments may apply to our conceptions of the unity of objects as well.

Although I can offer no serious analysis of human notions of unity and identity, I suggest that the preceding conclusions are partly wrong. Human adults have a notion of the unity, persistence, and identity of physical objects that is clear and general. The usefulness of this notion is limited, however: It only serves to single out certain kinds of things in certain kinds of situations. Adults overcome its limitations by calling on special notions about objects of particular kinds. Most, and perhaps all, of these special notions are acquired over the course of development. The general notion, in contrast, is given to humans at the beginning of life. Guided by the general notion, humans formulate their clearest and most certain intuitions about objects. Guided by the special notions, humans extend these intuitions beyond their original limits, at the cost of some certainty and perhaps some coherence.

To see how this mixture of general and specific conceptions might come about, let us return to human infants. Infants, I have suggested, are born with the conception that the world consists of unitary, bounded things that maintain their unity and boundaries over displacements. This conception provides them with a basis for perceiving unitary objects in certain visual scenes, for predicting that such objects will persist under certain conditions, and for determining in certain cases whether an object encountered now is identical to one encountered before. The usefulness of this conception is limited, however, in two general respects.

First, most visual arrays do not provide sufficient information for an infant to decide where an object's boundaries are, whether the object will survive a particular kind of transformation, and whether it is identical to an object seen in the past. If infants are guided only by the conception I have described, they will not perceive the boundaries of stationary, partly hidden objects, and they will perceive the wrong object boundaries when two objects are adjacent, either if the objects are stationary or if they move together. Infants also will not be able to predict whether an object will persist when it enters another object or when it is hit. Finally, infants will not be able to decide questions of object identity, unless they can trace an object's path while it is out of view.

Children could overcome these limitations by learning about the likely characteristics of particular kinds of objects and events. They may learn that any artifact is likely to have uniform coloring and a regular shape (see Brunswik, 1956), and that it is not likely to change color and shape as it moves. They also may learn that a particular sort of object—a car—is likely to have attached wheels and bumpers (see Hirsch, 1976), and that a particular kind of event— an explosion of a certain force and proximity—is likely to blow the car to bits. This learning will allow children to apply their original conception more effectively to the world (Spelke, 1982).

The second limitation of the infant's conception is more serious: That conception does not apply to all things that human adults consider objects. Attached objects, for example, would not qualify as objects if an object must be separately movable. An infant would have no basis for singling out a tree as distinct from the ground, or a mountain as distinct from its neighboring valleys. Unstable or unconnected configurations would also not qualify as objects if an object must be unitary and coherent. An infant could not treat a pile of leaves, a teardrop, or a cloud as one unit.

Similar problems are raised by the notion that an object persists and retains its identity if, and only if, it moves continuously and coherently. There are events that might lead an adult to say that an object has lost its identity even though it remains unitary: for example, the death of a man, the burning of a car, or the melting of a vase into a lump of glass. There are also cases in which an adult might say that an object retained its identity while losing its unity. A pipe is not said to go out of existence, for example, when it is taken apart for cleaning. Finally, there are events in which objects are transformed more radically and yet are considered to persist in some sense. A branch may fall from a tree, or a ship's planks may be replaced one by one, without ending the existence of the tree or ship (see Hobbes, 1650/1839; Hume, 1738/1962).

Because the original conception does not cover these cases, humans may overcome its limitations by enriching that conception with specific notions about objects of particular sorts. How children develop these specific notions, and come to consider an object as "a cat" or "a vase' as well as "an object," is a question fraught with problems (see Armstrong, Gleitman, & Gleitman, 1983). The development of such concepts, however, allows children to extend their notions of unity, persistence, and identity. Children may learn to identify trees in the ground and to perceive their persistence as trees over transformations such as the removal of branches. They may also learn that a pipe continues to exist as a pipe when it loses its integrity as a spatially connected object. But children extend their conceptions, I believe, at a price. The adults' notions of the unity, persistence, and identity of particular sorts of objects do not seem as certain, as clear, or as consistent as the infant's original, more general conception.

In brief, I suggest that we as humans have a general, unlearned conception of objects. Throughout life, we conceive of objects as spatially coherent, as separately movable, and as persisting over their unimpeded movements. But human adults also have many specific, acquired conceptions of particular kinds of objects. Our general and specific conceptions sometimes conflict, and when they do, our judgments about objects become uncertain and confused. This confusion does not reflect the absence of general notions of unity, persistence, and identity. It reflects, instead, our imperfect attempts to extend our general conception beyond its natural bounds.

If these speculations are correct, they would seem to reverse one standard description of cognitive development. On the standard view, humans begin life with highly sketchy and unstructured notions of the world. As we encounter the regularities of the environment and come to act on the world in increasingly systematic ways, we construct representations that are more complete and balanced. On the view I have suggested, humans begin life with at least one notion that is already as coherent as it will ever be: the notion of a physical object. As we attempt to use this notion in order to find objects in particular scenes, however, we discover that we can perceive objects more quickly and effectively by acquiring and using more specific knowledge: knowledge of the likely characteristics of objects of particular kinds. As we confront the complexities of the environment and come to act in increasingly diverse ways, we also develop a need to consider new kinds of things as objects, and to follow new and more specific principles for singling them out and tracing them through time.

These enriched conceptions seem to suit the concerns of human adults rather well. I am not certain, however, that human notions of unity, persistence, and identity ever again attain the coherence of the conception with which we began.

ACKNOWLEDGMENTS

This work owes its existence, in large part, to Lila Gleitman. She has brought to my twisted thinking whatever clarity it has, and she returned me to the problem of identity when I yearned to retreat to easier matters. Preparation of this chapter was supported by a grant from the National Institutes of Health (HD–13248).

REFERENCES

Armstrong, S. L., Gleitman, L. R., & Gleitman, H. What some concepts might not be. *Cognition*, 1983, *13*, 263–308.

Baillargéon, R., & Spelke, E. S. Object permanence in the 5-month-old infant. Manuscript in preparation.

Bernard, F. C., & Sullivan, A. *Cox and box: A triumviretta*, 1867.

Bertenthal, B. I., Campos, J. J., & Haith, M. M. Development of visual organization: The perception of subjective contours. *Child Development*, 1980, *51*, 1072–1080.

Bower, T. G. R. The determinants of perceptual unity in infancy. *Psychonomic Science*, 1965, *3*, 323–324.

Bower, T. G. R. Phenomenal identity and form perception in an infant. *Perception and Psychophysics*, 1967, *2*, 74–76. (a)

Bower, T. G. R. The development of object-permanence: Some studies of existence constancy. *Perception and Psychophysics*, 1967, *2*, 411–418. (b)

Bower, T. G. R. *Development in infancy*. San Francisco: W. H. Freeman, 1974.

Bower, T. G. R., Broughton, J., & Moore, M. K. Development of the object concept as manifested in tracking behavior of infants between 7 and 20 weeks of age. *Journal of Experimental Child Psychology*, 1971, *11*, 182–193.

Bresson, F., & de Schonen, S. A propos de la construction de l'espace et de l'objet: La prise d'un objet sur un support. *Bulletin de Psychologie*, 1976–1977, *30*, 3–9.

Brunswik, E. *Perception and the representative design of psychological experiments.* Berkeley: University of California Press, 1956.

Cornell, E. H. Learning to find things. A reinterpretation of object permanence studies. In L. S. Siegel & C. J. Brainerd (Eds.), *Alternatives to Piaget.* New York: Academic Press, 1979.

Gibson, E. J. The concept of affordances in development. The renascence of functionalism. In W. A. Collins (Ed.), *Minnesota Symposia on Child Psychology* (Vol 15). *The concept of development.* Hillsdale, N.J.: Lawrence Erlbaum Associates, 1982.

Goldberg, S. Visual tracking and existence constancy in 5-month-infants. *Journal of Experimental Child Psychology,* 1976, *22,* 479–491.

Harris, P. L. The development of search and object permanence during infancy. *Psychological Bulletin,* 1975, *82,* 332–344.

Harris, P. L. Infant cognition. In M. M. Haith & J. J. Campos (Eds.), *Infancy and developmental psychobiology.* In P. Mussen (Ed.), *Handbook of child psychology, Vol. II.* New York: Wiley, 1983.

Hirsch, E. Physical identity. *The Philosophical Review,* 1976, *85* 357–389.

Hobbes, T. De corpore (Pt. 11, Ch. 11). In W. Molesworth (Ed.), *The English Works of Thomas Hobbes* (Vol. 1). London: John Bohr, 1839 (originally published 1650).

Hofsten, C. von, & Lindhagen, K. Perception of occlusion in 4½-month-old infants. *Infant Behavior and Development,* 1982, *5,* 215–226.

Hofsten, C. von, & Spelke, E. S. *Object perception and object-directed reaching in infancy.* Paper presented at the meeting of the International Conference on Infant Studies, New York, 1984.

Hume, D. *A treatise of human nature, Book 1: Of the understanding.* Cleveland, Ohio: World Publishing Co., 1962 (originally published 1738).

Kellman, P. J., & Spelke, E. S. Perception of partly occluded objects in infancy. *Cognitive Psychology,* 1983, *15,* 483–524.

Kellman, P. J., & Spelke, E. S. Perception of partly hidden objects undergoing different types of motion. Unpublished manuscript, 1984.

Kestenbaum, R., Termine, N. & Spelke, E. S. Perception of objects and object boundaries by three-month-old infants. Unpublished manuscript, 1984.

Koffka, K. *Principles of gestalt psychology.* New York: Harcourt, Brace & World, 1935.

Michotte, A., Thines, G., & Crabbe, G. *Less complements amodaux des structures perceptives.* Louvain, Belgium: Publications U. Louvain, 1964.

Moore, M. K., Borton, R., & Darby, B. L. Visual tracking in young infants: Evidence for object identity or object permanence? *Journal of Experimental Child Psychology,* 1978, *25,* 183–198.

Moore, M. K., & Meltzoff, A. N. Object permanence, imitation, and language development in infancy. Toward a neo-Piagetian perspective on communicative and cognitive development. In F. D. Minifie & L. L. Lloyd (Eds.), *Communicative & cognitive abilities: Early behavioral assessment.* Baltimore: University Park, 1978.

Muller, A. A., & Aslin, R. N. Visual tracking as an index of the object concept. *Infant Behavior and Development,* 1978, *1,* 309–319.

Nelson, K. E. Accommodation of visual tracking patterns in human infants to object movement patterns. *Journal of Experimental Child Psychology,* 1971, *12,* 182–196.

Ninio, A. Piaget's theory of space perception in infancy. *Cognition,* 1979, *7,* 125–144.

Piaget, J. *The origins of intelligence in children.* New York: International Universities Press, 1952.

Piaget, J. *The construction of reality in the child.* New York: Basic Books, 1954.

Prather, P., & Spelke, E. S. *Three-month-old infants' perception of adjacent and partly occluded objects.* Paper presented at the meeting of the International Conference on Infant Studies, Austin, Texas, 1982.

Schmidt, H., & Spelke, E. S. *Gestalt relations and object perception in infancy.* Paper presented at the meeting of the International Conference on Infant Studies, New York, 1984.

Schwartz, K. *Perceptual knowledge of the human face in infancy.* Unpublished doctoral dissertation, University of Pennsylvania, 1982.

Spelke, E. S. Perceptual knowledge of objects in infancy. In J. Mehler, E. Walker, & M. Garrett (Eds.), *Perspectives on mental representation.* Hillsdale, N.J.: Lawrence Erlbaum Associates, 1982.

Spelke, E. S., & Born, W. S. *Visual perception of objects by 3-month-old infants.* Unpublished manuscript, 1984.

Spelke, E. S., Born, W. S., Mangelsdorf, S., Richter, E., & Termine, N. *Infant perception of adjacent objects.* Unpublished manuscript, 1984.

Starkey, D. P., Spelke, E. S., & Gelman, R. *Number competence in infants: Sensitivity to numeric invariance and numeric change.* Paper presented at the meeting of the International Conference on Infant Studies, New Haven, Conn., April, 1980.

Strauss, M. S., & Curtis, L. E. Infant perception of numerosity. *Child Development, 1981, 52,* 1146–1152.

Termine, N., Hrynick, T., Gleitman, H., & Spelke, E. S. *Perceptual completion of partly occluded extended surfaces by four-month-old infants.* In preparation, 1984.

Wertheimer, M. Principles of perceptual organization (M. Wertheimer, Trans.). In D. C. Beardslee & M. Wertheimer (Eds.), *Readings in perception.* Princeton, N.J.: Van Nostrand, 1958 (originally published in German, 1923).

Wiggins, D. *Sameness and substance.* Cambridge, Mass.: Harvard University Press, 1980.

Wishart, J. G. *The development of the object concept in infancy.* Unpublished doctoral dissertation, University of Edinburgh, 1979.

Infant Into Adult: Unity to Diversity in the Development of Visual Categorization

Marc H. Bornstein
New York University

INTRODUCTION

This chapter takes color categorization as a representative domain in which to explore "neonate cognition." To do so, I first introduce pertinent background facts about color, categorization, and color categorization. These include prominently the observations that colors are perceived categorically and that certain colors are exemplary of color categories. I then present data on cultural diversity in color categorization, and I review anthropological, linguistic, philosophical, and psychological opinion about the nature and origins of color categorizations. I next turn to discuss psychophysical, developmental, and comparative findings that support a universalist position on basic color categories and exemplars, and I also consider the biological substrates of these processes. Finally, I attempt to reconcile the unity of native categorization processes with the diversity of cultural manifestation through a consideration of different developmental pathways between the two and the interplay of Nature and Nuture. Color categorization proves to be an impressively rich arena in which to examine variegated contributions to mental life in the infant and in the adult.

COLOR, CATEGORIZATION, AND COLOR CATEGORIZATION

In the broad range of electromagnetic energy, only a small sliver of the radiant spectrum—between 400 and 700 nanometers—is visible (see Fig. 7.1.). This radiation we call "light." One impressive quality of visible light is, as Sir Isaac Newton (1671–1672) observed long ago, its chromaticity; and, looking at the spectrum today, we are impressed (as was Newton) with two salient aspects of

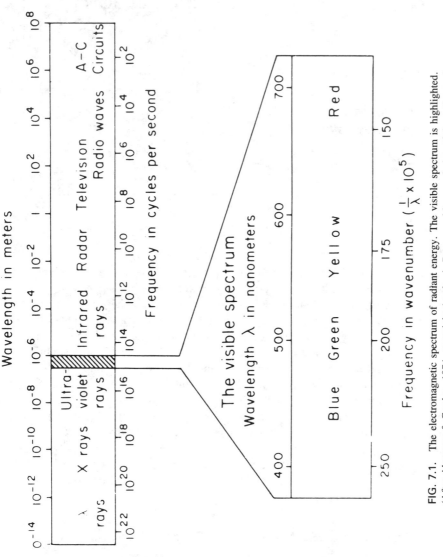

FIG. 7.1.   The electromagnetic spectrum of radiant energy. The visible spectrum is highlighted. (After Abramov & Gordon, 1974, copyright Academic Press, used by permission of the author and publisher.)

that chromaticity. The first is that broad ranges of the spectrum are character-istically dominated by different colors, or more properly *categories of hue*. The second is that, though it is apparent that most such categories contain mixtures of two (or more) hues (e.g., the short-wave end of the green category has blue in it, whereas the long-wave end has yellow in it), there exist much smaller bands within each category that are purer instances of the hue, in the sense of having little or no mixture with other hues; these are *hue foci* or *exemplars*. These two psychological characteristics are typical of "natural" categorizations (Rosch, 1981).

Both these major aspects of visual perception of the chromatic spectrum are evident in the data of a classic color-scaling experiment conducted by Boynton and Gordon (1965). These two investigators asked observers to apply four basic color terms—blue, green, yellow, and red—singly or in pairs, to describe single wavelengths presented to them. The results of this color-naming experiment are shown in Fig. 7.2, and the data lend quantitative support to the two phenomenal observations made earlier about the appearance of the chromatic spectrum. First, on categories: Boynton and Gordon's observers were satisfied to name all the visible wavelengths they were shown using one or limited combinations (pairs) of the four basic color terms the experiment permitted; further, there was a high degree of interobserver reliability in this judgment task; and, finally, Boynton has shown in other experiments (Boynton, Schaefer, & Nuen, 1964; Sternheim & Boynton, 1966) that when other, secondary color terms are permitted—such as orange or violet—observers use these terms less reliably, and all the wave-lengths that they describe can be easily analyzed into the four basic category

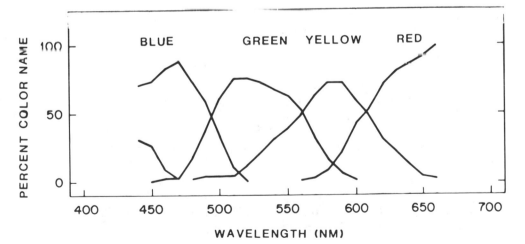

FIG. 7.2.   Adult color naming, using the basic terms blue, green, yellow, and red, as a function of wavelength. (The rising curve at very short wavelengths is for red.) The data derive from Boynton and Gordon (1965).

terms. Second, on exemplars: There are evident in the color-naming functions of Boynton and Gordon nonmonotonicities that indicate that certain wavelengths are exemplary of hue categories (i.e., purer, focal, or better representative of a category than are other instances or examples of the category).

Intriguingly, the physics and the psychology of color naming are not isomorphic. Physically, the spectrum is *continuous* with regard to wavelength— one point in the spectrum differs from another only by amount of wavelength difference. Psychologically, however, hue is *categorical*—hues jump more or less discretely from one wavelength region to another, and some wavelengths possess a higher psychological status than do others.

These data on the regularity of human categorization of the photic or visible spectrum fly in the face of nearly two centuries of ethnographic reports that numerous cultures around the world partition the visible spectrum in irregular and diverse ways. Figure 7.3 shows the world distribution of major types of color-naming systems. On this map, the color-naming systems of 126 non-European and 19 European societies are displayed in terms of "semantic identities" among the four basic color qualities: blue, green, yellow, and red (Bornstein, 1973). As we survey the world, the impressive and remarkable finding is that a minority of world societies, only about 25%, semantically distinguishes among the four basic hues, whereas the majority, about 75%, does not.[1] As can be seen, the majority of societies and languages collapses among basic categories. The most common collapsed systems are the following: (1) red, yellow, and green = blue; (2) red, yellow, and green = blue = black; (3) red, yellow = green, and blue; and (4) red = yellow, green, and blue. Figure 7.3 also shows that the distribution of color-naming systems wherein such semantic identities are common is nonrandom: Most Indo-European languages (*read:* Western societies) distinguish the four basic categories, whereas most non-European languages do not.

ON CULTURAL VARIATION IN COLOR NAMING AND CATEGORIZATION SYSTEMS

What accounts for the wide cultural variation in basic color categorization? Historically, anthropologists, linguists, philosophers, and psychologists, who have all proffered explanations, have assumed three major and different perspectives in answering this question. An assumption underlying one perspective is that language and perception are married; therefore, differences in language directly reflect differences in perception. Other perspectives divorce language

---

[1]If one only considers non-European cultures, the percentages are 15% and 85%, respectively.

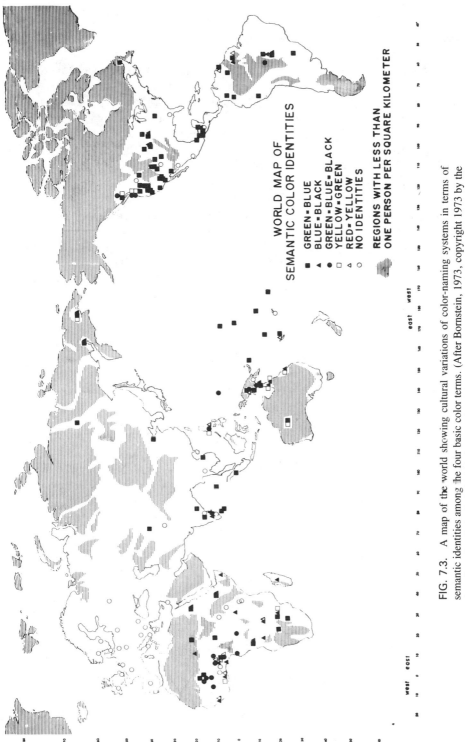

FIG. 7.3. A map of the world showing cultural variations of color-naming systems in terms of semantic identities among the four basic color terms. (After Bornstein, 1973, copyright 1973 by the American Psychological Association, reprinted by permission of the publisher and author.)

from perception; thus, differences in language can be independent of differences in perception.

Probably the oldest view is an *evolutionary* one, proposed successively in two distinct forms: In one, it was thought that in the course of human history color vision itself (and, attendant to it, color naming) evolved, and, in the other, it was thought that color-naming systems alone evolved. The earlier evolutionary view is principally associated with William Gladstone, the nineteenth-century English statesman. Avocationally, Gladstone was a Greek scholar, and, in his studies of *Homer and the Homeric Age,* Gladstone (1858) discussed the paucity of color terminology in Homer and in classical Greek from which he concluded that: "the organ of color and its impressions were but partially developed among the Greeks in the heroic age [p 488]." In short, Gladstone proposed a systematic integration of three views: that color language reflects color perception, that humans in the third century B.C. were marginally color deficient, and that between third-century B.C. Greece and nineteenth-century A.D. England human beings evolved from color deficiency to color normalcy and from incomplete, undifferentiated color vocabularies to complete, differentiated ones.

The second later evolutionary position is cultural rather than biological in nature and is principally associated with W. H. R. Rivers, an English anthropologist who accompanied the expeditions of the Royal Anthropological Institute of London to Australasia, Africa, and India at the turn of the century. In studying the color vision and color vocabulary of various peoples around the world, Rivers (1901) concluded that people were (mostly) color normal, but from a sociotechnological perspective that: "the order in which [peoples] are thus placed on the grounds of the development of their color languages corresponds with the order with which they would be placed on the grounds of their general intellectual and cultural development [p. 47]." Rivers's position strictly cleaves vision and vocabulary though it maintains a developmental attitude.

These evolutionary views were both replaced early in the twentieth century by the predominance of *cultural relativism* that also derived from linguistics and anthropology. First associated with the German polymath Humboldt and the American anthropologist Boas, relativism in language and perception is perhaps most widely identified with the anthropologist-linguist, Benjamin Lee Whorf (1950, 1964). The Whorfian hypothesis states, often baldly, that languages organize properties of the world pragmatically and, further, that that organization may in turn influence perception. Whorf himself commented on color specifically but only infrequently; another anthropologist of the Whorfian school, however, Verne Ray (1953), crystallized the Whorfian hypothesis on color in the following words: "Each culture has taken the spectral continuum and divided it upon a basis which is quite arbitrary except for pragmatic considerations [p. 102]." So, for example, in a 1955 report of color naming among the Hanunóo of the Philippines, the anthropologist Conklin suggested that four categories of color predominated in this Stone Age culture: dark colors, light colors, "dry" colors (red, orange, yellow), and "wet" colors (green, green-yellow, brown). These four categories, Conklin further observed, are strongly related to categories of vegetation and food stuffs that are important to the Hanunóo.

Cultural relativism dominated anthropological, linguistic, philosophical, and even psychological thought on color (as well as related cognitive issues) for the better part of this century. In the last decade, however, a third, *universalist* view has begun to supplant relativism. Four separate lines of argument converge to clarify, highlight, and embolden this new perspective: They include psychophysical and perceptual studies with adults from our own and from different cultures, infancy studies, studies of diverse infrahuman species, and studies of the physiological makeup and sensitivity of the visual system. Such cross-cultural, developmental, and animal comparisons are at the heart of psychological inquiry (Bornstein, 1980). In the next section, I summarize different comparative data that support the universalist view of *basic color categorization*.

ON THE UNIFORMITY OF BASIC COLOR CATEGORIZATION

The first major line of evidence that supports the universalist position draws on psychophysical and perceptual findings from studies with adults from diverse language and cultural communities. Results like those of Boynton and Gordon (1965) reviewed earlier show clearly the uniformity that may obtain in basic color naming. Other psychophysical studies of color naming among speakers of English (Beare, 1963; Boynton, 1975; Smith, 1971) and of Swedish (Ekman, 1954) have confirmed the reliability and (limited) cross-cultural generality of Boynton's findings. The major cross-cultural perceptual study contributing to the universalist position was that of Berlin and Kay (1969). They asked bilingual observers from 20 different language communities to point out on an array of 320 colors (40 hues by eight brightness levels) the best examples of a small set of basic color terms. Despite vast language and gloss differences, the different observers selected exemplars from relatively small and distinct areas of the color field (Fig. 7.4). In brief, perceptual studies that actually use colors as stimuli, rather than rely on reports of color naming, show uniformity and regularity in basic categorization, even when widely different languages and cultures are sampled.

The second and third lines of evidence that support a universalist view of basic color categorization derive from developmental and comparative studies, respectively: Human infants, long before the acquisition of language or inculcation of the rudiments of culture, and various infrahuman species, without language and culture, partition the spectral continuum into regular categories of hue. Experiments that have contributed to these two lines are summarized presently.

The infant data derive principally from a study of hue categorization conducted by Bornstein, Kessen, and Weiskopf (1976). In this study, the experimenters

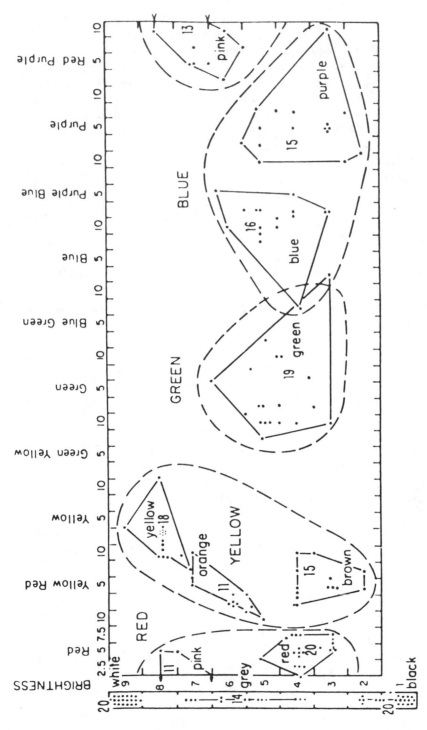

FIG. 7.4. Locations on a Munsell color array of best examples of basic color terms as indicated by informants from 20 different language communities. The original data derive from Berlin and Kay (1969). (After Lumsden & Wilson, 1981, copyright Harvard University Press, used by permission.)

used a habituation-test design and employed two classes of infant groups. The babies were 4 months of age on average. The left graph in Fig. 7.5 shows habituation and test data in one class of infant group, a "boundary group." Boundary groups explored in infants where interhue transitions fell and whether they were the same as in adult color-naming functions. As shown in Fig. 7.5, the example boundary group was habituated (over 15 successive 15-second trials) with a stimulus wavelength of 480 nm, a wavelength adults agree is mostly blue. From the beginning to the end of habituation, these infants showed (on average) a steady decline in looking from about 60% of the time the wavelength was available to about 20%. Following habituation, the babies in boundary groups saw three test wavelengths successively; the three were shown randomly three times in three triads. The three test wavelengths in the example in Fig. 7.5 included the original 480 nm stimulus (blue), 450 nm (another blue), and 510 nm (green). Note that for each group the two new test stimuli were each equally distant (in physical terms of nanometers) from the habituation wavelength. In the test, babies looked at 450 nm and 480 nm equally, that is they treated the new blue as familiar; but, they recovered looking (dishabituated) significantly to 510 nm, that is they treated the green as novel. The right graph in Fig. 7.5 provides an example of the second class of infant groups, a "category group." These babies were habituated to 450 nm, and they were then tested with 450 nm, as well as with 430 nm and 470 nm. For category groups, all three test wavelengths were selected from the same adult category, in the example case blue. As can be seen, in this test babies treated all three stimulus wavelengths (blues) similarly.

Several boundary and category groups were seen by Bornstein et al. (1976). Figure 7.6 summarizes ranges of wavelengths that infants in this study treated as similar as against those they distinguished. For comparison, Fig. 7.6 also plots ranges of wavelengths adult observers predominantly name blue, green, yellow, and red, respectively; these data derive from Boynton and Gordon (1965). As is clear, adults and infants partition the spectral continuum into very similar visual categories of hue, and they position boundaries between hue categories in similar locations. In brief, the results of this infant study revealed that the visible spectrum is organized into basic psychological categories of hue long before experience, language training, or formal tuition operate extensively on cognition.

Infrahuman species that see color have likewise been found to partition the spectral continuum into categories of hue. One study of color categorization in the monkey conducted by Sandell, Gross, and Bornstein (1979) exemplifies such a finding. These experimenters trained monkeys to press a key illuminated with a particular wavelength; following this training period and in extinction, the experimenters showed the monkeys the original training wavelength as well as four others surrounding it. The left graph in Fig. 7.7 shows responding in extinction for one monkey trained on 582 nm and tested with 559, 579, 582,

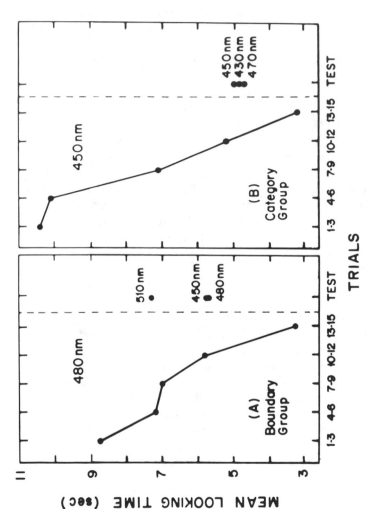

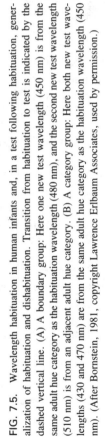

FIG. 7.5. Wavelength habituation in human infants and, in a test following habituation, generalization of habituation and dishabituation. Transition from habituation to test is indicated by the dashed vertical line. (A) A boundary group: Here one new test wavelength (450 nm) is from the same adult hue category as the habituation wavelength (480 nm), and the second new test wavelength (510 nm) is from an adjacent adult hue category. (B) A category group: Here both new test wavelengths (430 and 470 nm) are from the same adult hue category as the habituation wavelength (450 nm). (After Bornstein, 1981, copyright Lawrence Erlbaum Associates, used by permission.)

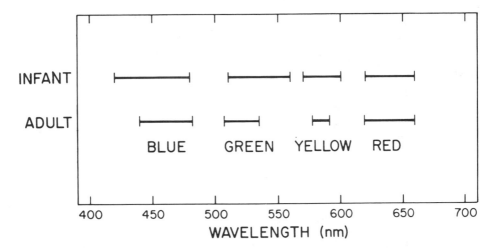

FIG. 7.6.   Hue categories in the infant and in the adult. The infant data summarize the results of Bornstein, Kessen, and Weiskopf (1976). The adult data are from Boynton and Gordon (1965); they represent regions of the wavelength spectrum that adults name as predominantly blue, green, yellow, or red 70% or more of the time. (After Bornstein, 1981, copyright Lawrence Erlbaum Associates, used by permission.)

609, and 623 nm. This monkey showed a high level of responding to the training wavelength and a symmetrically decreasing number of responses to wavelengths increasingly distant from the training wavelength. The right graph in Fig. 7.7 shows results for a second monkey trained at a different point in the spectrum (497 nm). This monkey generalized responding to two new test wavelengths (505 and 513 nm) but discriminated two others (476 and 486.5 nm). Shown also in Fig. 7.7 (as dashed vertical lines) are boundaries between basic human color categories. In these terms, as can be seen, monkeys generalize within but not between hue categories. (We know from other psychophysical studies that monkeys and humans possess highly similar color vision; DeValois & DeValois, 1975.)

Figure 7.8 shows data from one invertebrate and two vertebrate species (other than humans) whose basic hue categorizations have been studied. Data on the European honeybee from Von Frisch (1950), on the pigeon from Wright and Cumming (1971), and on the monkey from Sandell et al. (1979) converge to suggest that visual categorization of color is common phylogenetically. Although the ranges of the radiant spectrum that are visible to these different species differ (e.g., the bee sees ultraviolet but not red like humans), although different species partition the spectrum in different locations (e.g., the interhue boundary positions for the pigeon differ from those of the monkey), and although the number of categories differs across species (e.g., the pigeon has three and the human four), Fig. 7.8 clearly shows that, for all species studied, to see color is to categorize the spectrum.

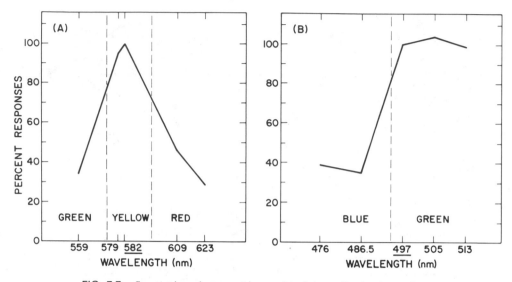

FIG. 7.7.   Symmetric and asymmetric wavelength generalization in monkeys. Generalization is expressed as a percentage of responses to the training stimulus (underlined). Boundaries between human color names are indicated by dashed vertical lines. (A) Green to yellow (573 nm) and yellow to red (596 nm). (B) Blue to green (494 nm). (After Bornstein, 1981, copyright Lawrence Erlbaum Associates, used by permission.)

In summary, data from young human infants and from various species of lower phylogenetic status indicate that language, culture, and experience are not prerequisites of visual categorization of color as once widely believed. Cumulatively, these data lend strong support to an alternative, universalist view of basic color categorization.

ON THE PSYCHOLOGICAL SALIENCE OF COLOR EXEMPLARS IN CATEGORIZATION

In the cross-cultural study of color designation by Berlin and Kay (1969) reviewed earlier, observers from a number of different language communities were found to agree remarkably when judging best examples of basic color categories. Likewise, psychophysical studies by Boynton (and others) have shown that very narrow regions of each color category represent purer, better, or focal examples of the category. Research with young infants (which is stressed here) also suggests that these exemplar colors possess distinguishing psychological properties that differentiate them from other colors in the spectrum; intriguingly, these properties are in large measure developmentally stable.

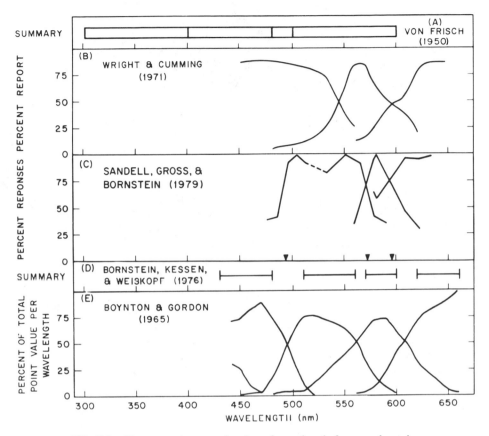

FIG. 7.8. Hue categories as a function of wavelength for several species. (A) Categorization by landings on novel-color sugar dishes in the *honeybee*. (B) Categorization by matching probe wavelengths to training wavelengths in the *pigeon*. (C) Categorization by generalization to novel wavelengths in extinction in the *monkey*. (The dashed line is an interpolation. Arrows indicate cross-over points of adult human color-naming functions from the same study.) (D) Categorization by generalization of habituation to new wavelengths in the *human infant*. (E) Categorization by color naming in the *human adult*. (Left to right: blue, green, yellow, and red. The increasing function at very short wavelengths is for red.) (After Bornstein, 1981, copyright Lawrence Erlbaum Associates, used by permission.)

First, exemplar colors tend to be preferred to other colors. When infants are shown exemplars and nonexemplars either singly or in pairs, they look significantly longer at exemplars (as a group) than at nonexemplars (Bornstein, 1975). Likewise, young children pick out exemplar colors as opposed to nonexemplars to "show the experimenter," and they attend to exemplar colors more and match them more accurately (Heider, 1971). Finally, when young adults are asked to rate the pleasantness of different colors, they rate exemplar colors as more pleasant (as a group) than nonexemplars (Bornstein, 1975; Guilford, 1940).

Second, exemplar colors are processed faster than nonexemplars in infancy as they are later in life. Heider and Olivier (1972) found that both Americans and Dugum Dani (a Stone Age people from New Guinea) learned paired associates involving exemplar colors faster than associates involving nonexemplar colors; and Bornstein and Monroe (1980) found that adults identify and classify exemplar colors as a group faster than nonexemplars. In an infant study that is a partial analogue of these adult encoding experiments, Bornstein (1981) found that infants habituate faster to re-presentations of exemplar colors than to re-presentations of nonexemplar colors.

Third, infants and adults alike appear to remember exemplar colors better than they do nonexemplars. In cross-cultural studies comparing Americans and Dugum Dani, Rosch (1978) found that exemplar colors were remembered better than nonexemplar colors in tasks that tapped both short-term and long-term memory. Likewise, Bornstein (1981) found that babies who were habituated to exemplar colors recognized them after a delay (and interference), whereas babies who were habituated to nonexemplars seemed to forget.

Finally, infants apparently see differences among exemplary colors as qualitative as opposed to quantitative. Many psychological studies of discrimination show a positive correlation between the amount of stimulus change and the amount of response change; that is, along most dimensions of sensation the degree of stimulus distance is regularly related to the degree of psychological difference. However, discrimination among colors may be qualitatively, as opposed to quantitatively, motivated. If babies were habituated to a short-wavelength blue, they might recover (or dishabituate) some to a middle-wavelength green but more to a long-wavelength red; this result would give evidence of quantitative discrimination. Alternatively, infants might show equivalent discrimination of green and red from blue. A study that directly pitted the quantitative and qualitative outcomes against one another with infants provided strong evidence for the qualitative result (Bornstein, 1981).

In summary, several studies of the infant's perception of color exemplars support the idea that near the beginning of life humans see and perceive select colors in the spectrum as affectively and cognitively special. Moreover, perceptual studies with children and psychophysical studies with adults (even from different cultures) support the developmental continuity of the specialty of these perceptions.

COLOR THEORY, BIOLOGY, AND COLOR CATEGORIZATION

When experimental studies with human infants and diverse infrahuman species result in such regularity and systematicity of perceptual response, it suggests that "Nature" is making a substantial contribution to processes involved. In such cases, it is reasonable to search for and to analyze the contribution of underlying neural substrates to perception. In this section, I review briefly classic color theory and our current understanding of the physiological sensitivity of the visual system as both relate to basic color categorization.

In the nineteenth century, two major theories of color vision rivaled one another. One theory, deriving from Thomas Young and Hermann von Helmholtz, postulated trichromasy. Helmholtz argued that three retinal receptors, one sensitive in the violet region of the spectrum, one in the green, and one in the red, combined their mechanisms of action to give rise to the gamut of color sensations. In a second theory, Ewald Hering proposed that an opponent-process system underlies color vision. Hering argued that black-and-white, red-and-green, and yellow-and-blue sensitive processes that are thus mutually antagonistic combined (we now know subtractively) to give rise to the gamut of chromatic sensations. Neurophysiological studies of the operation of the primate visual system have now reconciled Helmholtz and Hering in a "zone theory," which suggests that three retinal receptors filter their outputs in a complex fashion that eventuates in antagonistic opponent processes by the level of the horizontal and bipolar cells of the retina. Opponency is then continued through the lateral geniculate nuclei, perhaps into the cortex.

More specifically, neurophysiological investigations by DeValois and his associates (DeValois & DeValois, 1975) have identified four classes of chromatic-sensitive cells at the level of the geniculate bodies in primates, e.g., *Macaca irus*. These cells show maximal sensitivity (and maximal excitation) in the blue-, green-, yellow-, and red-appearing regions of the spectrum and show complementary reductions from spontaneous levels of activity when excited by yellow-, red-, blue-, and green-appearing stimuli, respectively. Intriguingly, the mechanism of action of these cells can account in large measure both for color categorizations and for the specialty of color exemplars in perception. The top graph in Fig. 7.9 plots the relative contribution of each of the four cell types to the total activity in the opponent system in monkeys shown various wavelengths; the bottom graph in Fig. 7.9 replots, for comparison, Boynton and Gordon's (1965) color-categorization data for human adults. The match is admirable: It would appear from this comparison that, for example, the hue quality "green" is signaled by excitation of +G–R cells, the hue quality "green-yellow" is signaled by the activity levels of +G–R and +Y–B cells, etc. Accordingly, DeValois, Abramov, and Jacobs (1966) proposed the existence of a simple "isomorphic relationship between the relative activity rates of the various cell types and the hue of a given light [p. 976]."

A similar analysis can be brought to bear to explain the specialty of focal colors. The right graph in Fig. 7.10 compares distributions of "best examples" of colors (in terms of dominant wavelengths) from the cross-cultural study by Berlin and Kay (1969) against wavelength positions of maximal physiological sensitivity of chromatic-sensitive cells in the monkey lateral geniculate nuclei (DeValois & DeValois, 1975). (The left graph shows the frequency with which

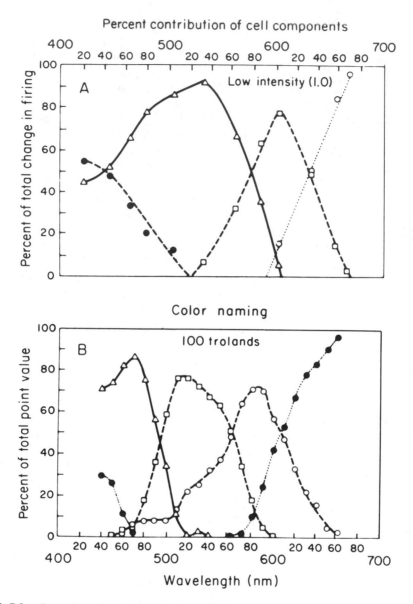

Percent contribution of cell components

Color naming

FIG. 7.9. Comparison of physiological and psychophysical data on hue categories. (A) Relative contributions of each of four components underlying the responses of opponent cells in the lateral geniculate nuclei of the macaque monkey. (From left to right, the curves are, respectively, for +B and −B (closed circles), +G and −G (open triangles), +Y and −Y (open squares), and +R and −R (open circles). The data derive from DeValois, Abramov, & Jacobs, 1966. Ambramov & Gordon, 1974, supply further information about the derivation of components and the method of computation.) (B) Human color naming as a function of wavelength. (From left to right, the curves are, respectively, for blue, green, yellow, and red. The data derive from Boynton & Gordon, 1965.) (After Abramov & Gordon, 1974, copyright Academic Press, used by permission of the author and publisher.)

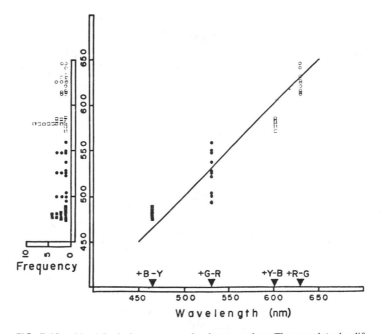

FIG. 7.10.   Physiological response and color exemplars: The wavelengths different language speakers choose as best examples of basic color names for red, yellow, green, and blue as predicted from biological sensitivities. Right: Exemplar colors in terms of dominant wavelengths chosen from a discrete array of Munsell chips as the best examples of color names for several different languages (Berlin & Kay, 1969) plotted as a function of wavelength of maximum physiological sensitivity taken from the mean response curves of opponent cells in the monkey lateral geniculate nucleus (DeValois, Abramov, & Jacobs, 1966). The goodness of fit to the solid function indicates the degree of physiological predictability. Left: The frequency with which each color chip or dominant wavelength was chosen as exemplary. (After Bornstein, 1973, copyright 1973 by the American Psychological Association, reprinted by permission of the publisher and author.)

different wavelengths were chosen as exemplars; from Bornstein, 1973.) The diagonal line on the main graph shows perfect predictability based on physiological sensitivity. As can be seen, there is again a remarkably good match between wavelengths that mark maxima of cell sensitivities on the one hand and on the other wavelengths that are the most frequent behavioral designations of color exemplars. Indeed, 95% of the overall variability in colors chosen by Berlin and Kay's respondents can be accounted for by the separation of cluster means of exemplar colors, only a 5% remainder sum of squares being attributable to language differences and/or individual subject differences. If wavelength values that express the sensitivity maxima from the four chromatic types of macaque LGN cells are substituted for those wavelength values that express cluster means, and the same variability analysis on the behavioral cluster distributions is performed, the remainder sum of squares is only 11% of the total. This indicates a high correspondence between the mean wavelengths of the exemplar color clusters and the mean wavelengths for peak sensitivities of neural cells; it also strongly suggests that the human behavioral data and monkey physiological data are interchangeably related.

A RECONCILIATION OF UNITY AND DIVERSITY IN COLOR CATEGORIZATION

In the heyday of cultural relativism, the anthropologist Ray (1952) wrote that: "the color patterning of man's world is not psychological, anatomical or physiological; there exist no natural divisions of the spectrum. Cultures divide it arbitrarily [p. 43]." On the basis of more recent human infant, infrahuman, and physiological data, we now know that the first parts of this relativist pronouncement are wholly incorrect. Psychology, anatomy, and physiology contribute integrally and critically to patterning basic categorizations of the color world, and there certainly do exist natural divisions of the spectrum.

In the face of these data, a central developmental question arises: How do humans proceed from infantile uniformity to the extraordinary diversity of categorizations that characterizes adult cultures. Until recently, diversity of categorization (documented at the beginning of this chapter) has represented the dominant fact of our response to color. New data now suggest that that diversity develops out of an original, basic, shared uniformity.

In what possible ways could development proceed to overlay heterogeneity of categorization on homogeneity? What roles do "Nature" and "Nurture" play in this development? In this section, I explore some principles by which neonatal and infant cognitions could be transformed during development into the plethora of adult modes of categorizing.

Some developmental changes that take place naturally, that is those that mature, may alter the structure of visual categorizations. For other alterations in the structuring or restructuring of visual categories of color, experience may play a more significant role. In his chapter in this volume, "Effects of Experience on Sensory and Perceptual Development: Implications for Infant Cognition," Aslin discusses various possible developmental courses of sensory and perceptual maturation and, after the onset of experience, the possible roles of experience in interaction with the biological status of the developing organism. In general, ordinary experience will either "maintain" or "attune" structures or behaviors that are partially or fully developed, such as the visual categorization of colors seems to be. Alternatively, extraordinary experience may result in the "loss" of structure(s) or behavior(s). I first discuss maintenance and attunement as applied to the categorization of hue.

Figure 7.11A shows the simplest case, that of developmental continuity in the context of normative experience—maintenance. The basic categories of hue in infancy are maintained during development and are the same as those of adults. This continuity seems adequately to describe the development of humans born into Indo-European-speaking language communities (see Fig. 7.3).

A closer analysis of the structure of visual categories of color shows, however, that categorization processes may change in the course of development in identifiable ways. Two prominant ways in which perceptual features such as hues (Bornstein, 1979) may alter in the normal course of development entail perceptual "sharpening" and "broadening." In color categorization, perceptual sharpening manifests itself in the narrowing of boundary regions between hues, and perceptual broadening manifests itself complementarily in the expansion of category plateaus. Figure 7.12 shows results from a color-naming study conducted on four age groups: younger and older children, and younger and aged adults. The data in Fig. 7.12 are actually those of individual observers whose boundary widths in color naming are representative of their age group means. As can be seen, between 3 and 4 years of age the boundary region between color categories narrows, and, complementarily, the plateau region of color naming broadens; after 4 years of age, both categories and boundaries remain stable through the balance of the life-span (Raskin, Maital, & Bornstein, 1983). Whether this early change is attributable to maturation or to experience cannot be determined from the present data.

Finally, I come full circle to confront the fact of broad cultural diversity among adult color-naming systems from the perspective of strict biological uniformity in visual color categorizations at or near birth. If color categories are present near birth (which they apparently are), and if they have an identifiable neurological substrate (which they appear to have) that is itself "hard wired" (which is apparently true), then all human infants ought to partition the spectrum regularly and in the same ways before the onset of linguistic and cultural experience. Later development may follow different courses. In Western societies it is likely, because of the infant-adult match, that developmental continuity is maintained in categorization through the period of language acquisition. However, in most non-Western societies where it is common for color-naming systems to differ fundamentally from the basic four-fold categorization (Fig. 7.3), language (and culture) must manipulate basic categorization processes in particular ways during development. As depicted in Fig. 7.11B, it may occur that categories extant in infancy are lost; or, as depicted in Fig. 7.11C, it may occur that new categories are tuned or induced. How these experiential changes are effected requires further research into cognitive and linguistic developmental processes, research that will be self-evidently rewarding. Potentially, divining these developmental connections and linkages in visual categorization of color will provide a model realm for understanding the roles of experience in infant cognitive growth and development.

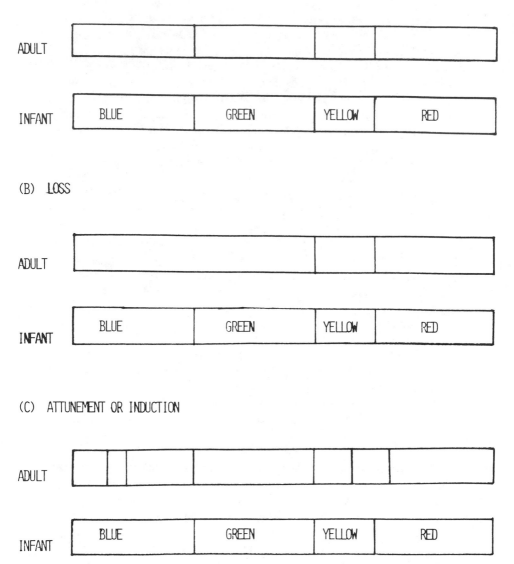

FIG. 7.11.   Various courses by which the infant structure or behavior develops into the adult form. (A) Maintenance: The infant form is maintained during development so that the adult form is essentially the same as the infant. (B) Loss: Between infancy and adulthood, form changes in a manner such that part of the infant form is eliminated. (C) Attunement or Induction: Between infancy and adulthood, form changes in a manner such that the infant form differentiates to produce new parts from old (attunement), or wholly new parts are introduced and added onto the infant form (induction).

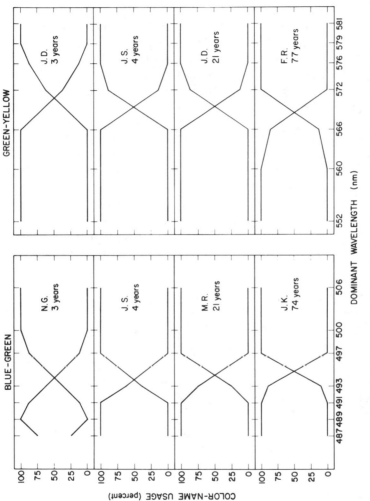

FIG. 7.12. Color naming as a function of wavelength at two points in the spectrum for four developmental levels. Three-year-old children show less regular color-name usage than children of 4 years, adults, and elderly, whose usages are quite similar to one another. Notably, color-name categories broaden and boundaries between color-name categories narrow. Each plot represents one individual's data, but the width of the boundary (at 75%) between color-naming functions for that individual is representative of the age group mean.

CONCLUSIONS ABOUT CATEGORIZATION

Physical attributes and properties of the world are complex and constantly in flux. Perception, however, is in large measure organized so that psychological unity and coherence replace physical variety and instability. In this chapter, I have discussed perceptual structures in color categorization. Many organisms that see color, whether they are adult humans or human infants near the beginning of life or infrahumans, perceive such structures in perceiving colors. All physical stimuli in the color domain are not perceived as equally different from one another psychologically; rather, some are categorized together and treated as equivalent (but not necessarily as identical) based on their perceptual similarity. Moreover, not all stimuli in a category hold the same psychological status; rather, some are exemplary in that they tend to be preferred, processed faster, remembered better, and used qualitatively in distinguishing among categories.

The psychological structures that characterize color perception have been revealed in a series of modern psychophysical studies with adults, with infants, and with various infrahuman species, and they show that basic categorizations possess an identifiable physiological substrate. The data that these studies have yielded supplant an older psycholinguistic and anthropological literature that posited that language and culture *alone* influence or direct perceptual processes and thought even at the most basic level. Indeed, these modern studies invert the traditional view and point to the basic influence of perceptual and cognitive forces on language. Thus, modern data help to resolve an anthropological-linguistic question of direct and manifest importance to the study of neonate and infant cognition: Does perception influence language, or does language influence perception? Color is a model domain. The existence in infancy of basic hue categories that are firmly rooted in physiology strongly favors a primacy of perception. Indeed, it would appear that in many ways humans, as other species, are congenitally endowed with sufficient mental capability to organize attributes and properties in the world and to begin to assay salient from nonsalient information in the environment. These are neonate cognitions worthy of our attention.

REFERENCES

Abramov, I., & Gordon, J. Seeing. In E. C. Carterette & M. P. Friedman (Eds.), *Handbook of perception* (Vol. 3). New York: Academic Press, 1974.

Beare, A. C. Color-name as a function of wave-length. *American Journal of Psychology,* 1963, 76, 248–256.

Berlin, B., & Kay, P. *Basic color terms: Their universality and evolution.* Berkeley, Cal.: University of California Press, 1969.

Bornstein, M. H. Color vision and color naming: A psychophysiological hypothesis of cultural difference. *Psychological Bulletin,* 1973, 80, 257–285.

Bornstein, M. H. Qualities of color vision in infancy. *Journal of Experimental Child Psychology,* 1975, *19,* 401–419.

Bornstein, M. H. Perceptual development: Stability and change in feature perception. In M. H. Bornstein & W. Kessen (Eds.), *Psychological development from infancy.* Hillsdale, N.J.: Lawrence Erlbaum Associates, 1979.

Bornstein, M. H. (Ed.). *Comparative methods in psychology.* Hillsdale, N.J.: Lawrence Erlbaum Associates, 1980.

Bornstein, M. H. Psychological studies of color perception in human infants: Habituation, discrimination and categorization, recognition, and conceptualization. In L. P. Lipsitt (Ed.), *Advances in infancy research* (Vol. 1). Norwood, N.J.: Ablex, 1981.

Bornstein, M. H., Kessen, W., & Weiskopf, S. Color vision and hue categorization in young human infants. *Journal of Experimental Psychology: Human Perception and Performance,* 1976, *2,* 115–129.

Bornstein, M. H., & Monroe, M. D. Chromatic information processing: Rate depends on stimulus location in the category and psychological complexity. *Psychological Research,* 1980, *42,* 213–225.

Boynton, R. M. Color, hue, and wavelength. In E. C. Carterette & M. P. Friedman (Eds.), *Handbook of perception* (Vol. 5). New York: Academic Press, 1975.

Boynton, R. M., & Gordon, J. Bezold-Brücke hue shift measured by color-naming technique. *Journal of the Optical Society of America,* 1965, *55,* 78–86.

Boynton, R. M., Schaefer, W., & Nuen, M. E. Hue-wavelength relation measured by color-naming method for three retinal locations. *Science,* 1964, *146,* 666–668.

De Valois, R. L., Abramov, I., & Jacobs, G. H. Analysis of response patterns in LGN cells. *Journal of the Optical Society of America,* 1966, *56,* 966–977.

DeValois, R. L., & DeValois, K. K. Neural coding of color. In E. C. Carterette & M. P. Friedman (Eds.), *Handbook of perception* (Vol. 5). New York: Academic Press, 1975.

Ekman, G. Dimensions of color vision. *Journal of Psychology,* 1954, *38,* 467–474.

von Frisch, K. *Bees: Their vision, chemical senses, and language.* Ithaca, N.Y.: Cornell University Press, 1950.

Gladstone, W. E. *Homer and the Homeric age* (Vol. 3). Oxford: Oxford University Press, 1858.

Guilford, J. P. There is a system of color preferences. *Journal of the Optical Society of America,* 1940, *30,* 455–459.

Heider, E. R. "Focal" color areas and the development of color names. *Developmental Psychology,* 1971, *4,* 447–455.

Heider, E. R., & Olivier, D. C. The structure of the color space in naming and memory for two languages. *Cognitive Psychology,* 1972, *3,* 337–354.

Lumsden, C. J., & Wilson, E. O. *Genes, mind and culture: The coevolutionary process.* Cambridge, Mass.: Harvard University Press, 1981.

Newton, I. New theory about light and colors. *Philosophical Transactions of the Royal Society,* 1671–1672, *80,* 3075–3087.

Raskin, L., Maital, S., & Bornstein, M. H. Perceptual categorization of color: A life-span study. *Psychological Research,* 1983, *45,* 135–145.

Ray, V. F. Techniques and problems in the study of human color perception. *Southwestern Journal of Anthropology,* 1952, *8,* 251–259.

Ray, V. F. Human color perception and behavioral response. *Transactions of the New York Academy of Sciences,* 1953, *16,* 98–104.

Rivers, W. H. R. Introduction. In A. C. Haddon (Ed.), *Reports on the Cambridge anthropological expedition to the Torres Straits.* Cambridge: Cambridge University Press, 1901.

Rosch, E. Human categorization. In N. Warren (Ed.), *Studies in cross-cultural psychology* (Vol. 1). London: Academic Press, 1978.

Rosch, E. *Prototype classification and logical classification: The two systems.* Paper presented at the Eleventh Meeting of the Jean Piaget Society, Philadelphia, May 1981.

Sandell, J. H., Gross, C. G., & Bornstein, M. H. Color categories in Macaques. *Journal of Comparative and Physiological Psychology,* 1979, *93,* 626–635.

Smith, D. P. Derivation of wavelength discrimination from colour-naming data. *Vision Research,* 1971, *11,* 739–742.

Sternheim, C. E., & Boynton, R. M. Uniqueness of perceived hues investigated with a continuous judgmental technique. *Journal of Experimental Psychology,* 1966, *72,* 770–776.

Whorf, B. L. *Four articles on metalinguistics.* Washington, D. C.: Foreign Service Institute, 1950.

Whorf, B. L. *Language, thought and reality.* Cambridge, Mass.: Massachusetts Institute of Technology Press, 1964.

Wright, A. A., & Cumming, W. W. Color-naming functions for the pigeon. *Journal of the Experimental Analysis of Behavior,* 1971, *15,* 7–17.

8 Cognitive Foundations and Social Functions of Imitation and Intermodal Representation in Infancy

Andrew N. Meltzoff
M. Keith Moore
*Department of Psychology
and Child Development and Mental Retardation Center
University of Washington*

INTRODUCTION

A distinction may be drawn between two different types of evolutionary change that operate in man. On the one hand, there is evolution mediated by genetic transmission; and on the other, evolution mediated by cultural transmission. The former is often called evolution in the Darwinian mode and the latter cultural or psychosocial evolution. Perhaps the best labels for differentiating between them were provided by Medawar (1957), who referred to them respectively as "endosomatic" and "exosomatic" evolution.

Homo sapiens profit from and rely on exosomatic evolution to a greater degree than any other species. Our everyday life and social organization have been radically altered as compared with 15th-century man's, not because of endosomatic evolution, but because of the more rapid, yet still profound process of exosomatic evolution. Most of the knowledge, traditions, and behavioral skills that we call "culture" are passed from one generation to the next not by DNA molecules, but through nongenetic channels.

By what process(es) could nongenetic information be transferred from one generation to the next? Could imitation be one means of fulfilling such a function? Dawkins (1976), an evolutionary biologist, recently developed a detailed analogy between the role of DNA in endosomatic evolution and imitation in exosomatic evolution. He argued that just as biological information is replicated and passed on through genes, cultural information is replicated and transferred through imitation. If one accepts Dawkins' analogy, one could go on to argue that imitation provides man with a kind of Lamarckian evolutionary potential: It provides a means for passing *acquired* characteristics and behavior patterns to succeeding generations. Of course, large portions of our behavior patterns, skills, and conceptual apparatus are not gained through interaction with conspecifics at all. But some portions are; and among this subset, imitative processes may play a significant role (Bandura, 1969; Bruner, 1972; Piaget, 1962).

The importance of imitation to human development and the continuance of culture has been noted by anthropologists as well as by biologists and psychologists. Reichard (1938) pointed out that in many languages the word for "teach" is the same as the word for "show," because for these cultures imitative learning and teaching by example are the main pedagogical style. Vilakazi (1962) summarized the central role of imitation in the Zulu society as follows:

> The Zulu traditional system of education was mainly informal and non-institutional in the sense that there were no regular school buildings or any particular places and specific times where and when teaching took place. . . . A child learned about its culture in the home by the methods of observation, imitation and play. . . . Most of the time, Zulu life was lived in and around the kraal and it is in this setting that the child learned many items of its cultural tradition by actual participation in or direct observance of what the old people did [p. 124].

Among the Tallensi natives in Africa, imitation is regarded as an especially efficient means of transmitting skills to the young. Fortes (1938) made the following observation about this group:

> That skill comes with practice is realized by all. When adults are asked about children's mimetic play they reply: 'That is how they learn. . . .' Rapid learning or the acquisition of a new skill is explained by *u mar nini pam,* 'he has eyes remarkably. . . .' This conception of cleverness is intelligible in a society where learning by looking and copying is the commonest manner of achieving dexterity both in crafts and in the everyday manual activities [p. 13].

In some cultures children are shown adult models in situations where we might think that such exposure would be totally ineffective. Among the Navaho Indians, the power of imitative learning is exploited in ways that would surprise many of us. For example, Leighton and Kluckhohn (1947) reported that imitation is used by the Navaho to foster toilet training: "The mother or an older sister takes the child out when she herself goes to defecate and tells the little one to imitate her position and her actions [p. 35]." In other cultures, learning by imitation is used in situations that we might consider too dangerous for such a strategy. A vivid example from Puerto Rican village life was provided by Steward, Manners, Wolf, Seda, Mintz, and Scheele (1956): "A little girl of two sat next to her mother, who was peeling vegetables, and helped her peel, using an enormous machete as her tool. She copied her mother's manner of holding the knife very closely and used the machete with a great deal of skill [p. 220]."

Elsewhere the author adds, "Consequently a child develops manual skills and mastery at a comparatively early age. A three-year-old can peel a mango with a carving knife [p. 145]."

There has thus been little disagreement among biologists, psychologists, and anthropologists about the adaptive significance and universality of imitation in human development. In contrast, there is profound disagreement among developmentalists as to *origins* and early development of imitation in infancy. Perhaps this is to be expected. Behavior that can be lumped together into a broad category of "imitation" in discussions of evolutionary biology or cultural anthropology begins to look more complicated when it is scrutinized and experimentally manipulated. Developmental psychologists must ask: How do we know a child is "really" imitating rather than performing a behavior by chance? Is the capacity to imitate conspecifics part of our innate endowment, or is imitation a skill that must itself be learned? What mechanisms underlie imitation and how do they change with age? Broad arguments outlining the adaptive value of imitation do not move developmental psychologists much closer to understanding the origins and development of this ability itself.

In our laboratory we have recently completed a new series of studies investigating the origins of imitation in infancy. The results are surprising from the viewpoint of current developmental theory, if not from the more biologically oriented positions discussed above. They indicate that *Homo sapiens* have an innate capacity to imitate adult members of their species, at least in the sense that human infants are capable of imitating adult actions from the moment of birth. In this chapter we discuss our work on infant imitation, consider alternative accounts of these findings, and investigate some of the implications of these results for our theories about the beginnings of social and cognitive development in infancy.

WHAT CONSTITUTES IMITATION IN INFANCY?

There has been some debate among developmental psychologists about what kind of behavior qualifies as "imitative" in infancy. Our own working definition of imitation is: Any infant behavior (gestural or vocal) that is produced on the basis of perceiving modeled behavior, is structurally similar to the behavior that elicits it, and is not attributable to a chance match between the modeled behavior and the response.

Such a broad definition allows that imitative behavior may be based on a variety of different mechanisms. This distinction between imitation as a behavioral event and the mechanism(s) that underlie imitative performances is a crucial one. It is often blurred in the literature by introducing terms such as "pseudo-imitation," "simple matching behavior," and "genuine imitation." The approach we advocate is to use "imitation" to label the broad class of behavioral events meeting the above definition, and then to focus on individual cases to determine the *mechanism* underlying a particular behavioral performance.

The best example of the difficulty that can arise by glossing over the distinction between the behavioral event and the underlying mechanism is a long-standing debate between Piagetians and learning theorists. Piaget outlined six stages in the development of imitation, and is often interpreted as saying that the imitation of facial gestures is impossible until 8 to 12 months of age. A simple disproof of Piaget's theory is then raised by learning theorists, who point out that 6-month-old infants will open their mouths in response to maternal mouth opening during spoon-feeding episodes. The mother holds the spoon in front of the infant's mouth and then opens her mouth to show the infant what to do. When the infant does the same, the mother pops in a spoonful of food. After some time, the infant will systematically open his mouth when shown the maternal mouth-opening cue. In other words, after sufficient experience (training) with spoon-feeding, infants appear able to imitate adult mouth opening, even before the standard Piagetian age of 8 to 12 months.

This phenomenon is not a disproof, say the Piagetians. It is merely a case of "pseudo-imitation"; true imitation does not involve such training. In response, learning theorists answer: All imitation is based to some extent on prior learning. Aren't 1-year-olds imitating when they clap their hands in imitation of a pat-a-cake gesture, or when they bang blocks together after an adult does so? Weren't adults involved in shaping these responses? Surely it is of no value, learning theorists argue, to dismiss all of this activity as pseudo-imitation, especially because there is no evidence that infants can imitate anything without prior training on the task (or components of it).

Both sides, of course, have a legitimate point, but it is not whether activity "x" should be called true imitation or pseudo-imitation. The questions they are both interested in concern the age at which infants first imitate various behaviors and the mechanisms that underlie such imitation. Perhaps certain imitative acts are shaped during early interactions, and others are mediated by infants' general skill in transforming externally perceived stimuli into motor acts of their own, whether or not there has been training in the particular task. Both of these possibilities have been referred to as "imitation" by one group or another, and this label seems legitimate as long as authors also discuss the different mechanisms and developmental histories that lie behind the behavioral performance they are studying.

We suggest that the psychology of imitation would be well served by adopting a working definition such as that offered here and moving on to examine six basic questions. The key questions are these:

1. *Existence*—Can infants imitate behavior "x" at a given age?
2. *Mechanism*—If so, what is the basis for this activity?
3. *Motivation*—Why do infants imitate in certain circumstances and not in others?

4. *Function*—What role do imitative exchanges serve in the interactions between adults and infants?

5. *Meaning*—What significance do infants attribute to imitative interactions; how do infants interpret them?

6. *Development*—Do the types of behaviors imitated, the underlying mechanisms, the motivation, the function, or the meaning of imitative exchanges change with age?

Much of the current confusion surrounding imitation in infancy can be readily clarified if we bypass the debate about labels and concentrate instead on how particular experimental results address the fundamental questions of existence, mechanism, motivation, function, meaning, and development just outlined (Meltzoff & Moore, 1983b).

ON DIFFERENTIATING IMITATIVE PHENOMENA

Of all the various acts that infants can imitate, the duplication of facial gestures is perhaps the most fascinating and difficult to explain by current development theories. Certainly facial imitation allows the sharpest empirical test of the existing theories of imitative development.

Consider the imitation of a simple facial movement, such as mouth opening and closing. Even if we focus on the simplest situation by assuming the following three things: (1) that infants can visually resolve the adult's action, (2) that this motor movement is well within their motor capabilities, and (3) that infants are fully motivated to duplicate the adult's gesture—how is it possible for the infant to imitate this gesture?

Whereas infants can see the adult's mouth-opening display, they cannot see their own mouths. The theoretical problem is to explain how the adult's act can become "linked" to the appropriate infant response. There seems to be no direct comparison that infants can make between the target gesture and their own behaviors. The target is picked up through visual perception, but the behavioral response cannot be visually monitored by the infant. Facial imitation thus seems to involve a kind of *cross-modal* matching in which one perceptual system (vision) provides the model against which information from a different system (proprioception) is compared. This presents a unique set of circumstances, both for the infant and for the adult theorist. In order to see just how unique facial imitation is, it is useful to compare it to manual and vocal imitation.

In both manual and vocal imitation, infants can perceive the adult model and their own behavior within the same perceptual modality and therefore should be able to compare the two. Infants can see both the adult's hand and their own hands. In principle they can visually guide their hand movements until they match the target. The same is true of vocal imitation. Infants can hear both the adult's voice and their own productions. In principle, they can use audition to monitor their vocal productions until they match the adult's. In both cases an *intramodal* matching process can be used.[1]

Explanations for manual and vocal imitation cannot be allowed to rest at this simple level, of course. One must go on to ask how it is possible for infants to imitate on first try, as it were, without missing the target and correcting their errors through intramodal comparisons. One interesting possibility is that infants may already have learned what movements result in the target through past experience in watching their own hand movements or listening to their own vocal productions. Thus, it may be that infants can imitate hand opening/closing on their initial attempt if and only if they have watched themselves generate this behavior in the past. The same applies to vocal productions: Accurate imitation without successive approximations may occur only with vocalizations that have been practiced beforehand.

In manual and vocal imitation, the most difficult case to explain thus becomes the immediately accurate imitation of novel behavior. Even this, however, does not present an intractable problem, at least at the broad theoretical level. Extending the current line of argument, one could propose that such imitation should be possible after infants have used the experience of watching their hands or hearing their own vocal productions to develop more generalized mapping rules. We know that young infants are, in fact, fascinated by the sight of their own hand movements (Piaget, 1962; White, Castle, & Held, 1964) and engage in vocal play or babbling during the early stages of infancy. These activities may well function to help the infant map out a general "act space" that then serves as the basis of manual and vocal imitation, even in cases of novel behaviors that they have not themselves produced many times in the past.

The point of considering manual and vocal imitation is to illustrate the differences between these activities and facial imitation. The complexities of manual and vocal imitation pale in comparison to the complexities of facial imitation. In facial imitation, the infant can use neither vision nor audition to monitor his own movements. Even if we take the easiest situation outlined previously (the imitation of familiar behaviors), there is still no ready explanation for how the infant could "link up" the model's facial gesture with a matching one of his own.

The infant may be quite familiar with feeling himself perform the act, but he can never feel the adult's act. Conversely, he may be familiar with seeing the adult's gesture, but he cannot see his own facial movements. Even when a facial

---

[1]Of course there are differences in the size of the infants' and adults' hands, and differences in the absolute frequencies composing the vocalizations of the adults and infants; but despite these differences in the signal, the relevant information can at least be perceived within the same perceptual modality (vision or audition), thus allowing intramodal comparisons between the stimulus and response in manual and vocal imitation.

gesture is both familiar to the infant and also within his motor repertoire, a profound theoretical problem still remains. *When the perception of the target and the results of production cannot be compared within the same modality, what type of experience could, even in principle, allow the infant to learn the correspondence?* This is the problem that has fascinated those of us who study facial imitation.

SOME ACCOUNTS OF FACIAL IMITATION

What are some plausible accounts for the origins of facial imitation in infancy? Three possibilities immediately suggest themselves.

First, it might be argued that the earliest instances of facial imitation are simply the result of instrumental learning. We know that young infants can be conditioned to respond to a bell or buzzer with particular head movements (Lipsitt, 1969). This shows that infants can learn to link specific motor movements to a given external stimulus. There is every reason to believe that they could be shaped to treat adult mouth opening as a discriminative stimulus for mouth opening movements of their own. The spoon-feeding episodes described earlier, in which mothers open their mouths just before popping in a spoonful of food, can be thought of in terms of instrumental learning—with maternal mouth opening as the discriminative stimulus, infant mouth opening as the response, and a spoonful of food as the reinforcer. After sufficient training, the discriminative stimulus systematically elicits the response. It thus appears plausible to argue that some instances of facial imitation may be based on instrumental learning. The question that remains is whether instrumental learning can account for all the instances of facial imitation in infancy, whether it is a *necessary* condition for the earliest imitations.

Second, it might be argued that associative learning within the context of parent-infant interaction accounts for the origins of facial imitation in infancy. This position would need to assume that parents systematically mimic their infants' behaviors. Starting with this assumption, it could be argued that infants learn to pair their behavior with the mother's matching response during these early interactions. An "association" would be formed on the basis of the regular temporal contiguity between the infant's actions and the adult's. For example, if a mother raised her eyebrows whenever the infant raised his, then these two behaviors would purportedly become associated, and thereafter maternal eyebrow raising will elicit infant eyebrow raising. By this account, then, imitation is best thought of in terms of associative learning through temporal contiguity.

Finally, one might adopt the Piagetian position (Piaget, 1962) that instrumental and associative learning are not sufficient to account for all instances of facial imitation, and moreover that they do not account for the interesting cases. Piagetians define the interesting cases as those behaviors that can be imitated even without being part of any previous adult-infant interaction. These behaviors need not be novel in the sense that the infant has never performed them before, but only novel in the sense that the stimulus-response linkage has not been shaped up or part of any associative pairing.

In order to study such cases, Piaget carefully monitored his own children's experiences and then tested for imitation of those behaviors that had not played any special role in adult-infant interactions. It is amusing to quote Piaget's answer to the objection that even after this daily observation he could not be sure of everything his infants had been trained to duplicate, and therefore still could not *prove* that infants could imitate facial gestures without specific training on this task (the latter being defined as uninteresting by Piaget, and relegated to pseudo-imitation). In answer to this extreme objection by learning theorists, Piaget (1962) replies:

> Later on we shall come to other cases, of which we have made a special study, of this acquired pseudo-imitation (obs. 17 and 18). For the present, all that need be said is that in view of Guillaume's findings we took great care from the outset to eliminate as far as possible the influence of training when making our observations. It was for this reason that our three subjects showed much slower but more regular progress in imitation than babies who are continually subjected to adult influence, and more especially to the pedagogical mania of nurses [p. 18].

As is well known, Piaget's findings were that facial imitation did not emerge before about 8 to 12 months as long as adult training, what he called "pedagogical mania," was not involved. His interpretation was that infants lacked the perceptual-cognitive ability to recognize correspondences between visually and proprioceptively perceived events before this age. The onset of facial imitation, or more precisely those acts of facial imitation that were not themselves reducible to adult training, became a classic development milestone in Piagetian theory, one that indicated a fundamental reorganization of the infant's cognitive abilities (Piaget, 1962).

THE EXISTENCE OF FACIAL IMITATION IN NEONATES: AN ANOMALY FOR CURRENT THEORIES

In 1977 we reported laboratory experiments showing that 12- to 21-day-old infants could imitate one manual and three facial gestures (Meltzoff & Moore, 1977). More recently these effects were replicated using a different design with newborn infants, the youngest of whom was 42 minutes old at the time of testing (Meltzoff & Moore, 1983a). If neonates in the first hours of postnatal life can already imitate facial gestures, then none of the accounts considered thus far—instrumental learning, associative learning, or Piagetian cognitive development—

are *necessary* conditions for the existence of this behavior. In short, the demonstration of facial imitation in neonates presents existing accounts of imitative development with a genuine anomaly that they cannot easily incorporate.

At a theoretical level, the findings force either: (1) a reconsideration of the psychological prerequisites of facial imitation (they might be simpler than anything traditionally proposed); or (2) a reconsideration of the cognitive and social capacities of neonates (they might be more sophisticated than traditionally assumed). Before examining which if either of these two resolutions is the more appropriate (see next section), it is worth reviewing some key elements in the empirical studies themselves, for the experiments were specifically designed to provide a critical test of theories of infant imitation.

Our 1977 report contained two experiments. In Experiment I, each infant was shown four gestures in a randomized order using a repeated-measures design. The gestures were lip protrusion, mouth opening, tongue protrusion, and sequential finger movements. The experiment was videotaped for subsequent analysis, and scored by observers who were kept uninformed about which adult gesture had been demonstrated in any given trial.

The observer's task was to watch the infant's response and to make a judgment as to which adult gesture the infant had been shown. This "perceptual judgment" scoring system (Meltzoff & Moore, 1983b) was utilized because we were not able to predict on a priori grounds what a neonate's imitative response would look like, if it existed. Would neonates match the form of the adult's mouth-opening gesture exactly, or would they only approximate the model and open their mouths halfway? How should we operationalize the difference between "one" mouth opening and "two"—should lip closure be used, or do neonates never fully seal their lips before starting their second effort? Because we did not know the answers to these and other questions about the imitative response when we began the experiment, it seemed judicious not to adopt arbitrary behavioral criteria that then might lead us to miss the effect. Our perceptual judgment system enabled unbiased observers to use the whole pattern of the response to evaluate imitation (while remaining blind to the actual experimental condition). Using this scoring system, imitation was demonstrated. (See Meltzoff & Moore, 1983b, for a fuller discussion of the advantages and disadvantages of the "perceptual judgment" technique for scoring imitative responses.)

The second experiment in the 1977 paper was designed to meet three primary goals. First, because we had difficulty ensuring that all the infants in Experiment I fixated the experimenter's display, and yet the problem of imitation cannot be properly posed without fulfilling this precondition, we realized that the experiment might have underestimated the neonates' true imitative competence. We thus wanted to conduct a study that would improve our control of the infants' attention. Our idea was to equate all the infants at a given level of visual fixation before beginning the imitation test per se.

Second, because Experiment I used a perceptual judgment scoring system, we could not specify the accuracy of the imitative matches. Evidently, the infants' responses were precise enough for observers to discriminate the infants' reactions to several different types of movements within the same body region (the mouth). The results showed that the infants' imitative reactions to the lip-protrusion display were discriminably different from those to the tongue-protrusion and mouth-opening displays. Nevertheless, we could not specify exactly how far infants were protruding their lips, how often they did so, and other particulars of the nature of the imitative response. We therefore interviewed the judges and conducted further pilot testing to provide more precise operational definitions of the infants' imitative movements and then used these definitions to score the frequencies of specific behaviors in Experiment II.

Third, it was of theoretical interest to go beyond the first experiment to test whether neonates could imitate even if the target gesture had disappeared. If they could, it might imply that infants were capable of imitating on the basis of some stored model or "representation" of the perceptually absent display (Meltzoff, 1981).

We used a nonnutritive sucking technique to accomplish the goals of delaying the response and increasing our control of the infant's visual experience. The pacifier technique is depicted in Fig. 8.1. As shown, each infant was given a baseline period. Next, a pacifier was inserted into the infant's mouth and then the facial gesture was demonstrated until the infant fixated it for 15 seconds. The experimenter then stopped gesturing, assumed a passive face pose, and *only then* removed the pacifier to allow the infant to respond. The passive face pose was maintained throughout the 2½-minute response period. At the end of this period, the pacifier was reinserted and a second gesture was administered, following an identical procedure.

Because the criterion for removing the pacifier was that the infant had fixated the gesture, we could be sure that any failure to imitate was not due to inattention to the model. Because the infants in our experiment actively sucked on the pacifier while it was in their mouths—the reflexive sucking response pattern apparently taking precedence over imitative responses (Meltzoff & Moore, 1977)—

Condition	Baseline exposure	Baseline period (150 seconds)	Experimental exposure 1	Response period 1 (150 seconds)	Experimental exposure 2	Response period 2 (150 seconds)
Experimenter	Passive face	Passive face	Gesture 1	Passive face	Gesture 2	Passive face
Infant	Pacifier	No pacifier	Pacifier	No pacifier	Pacifier	No pacifier

FIG. 8.1.   The pacifier technique used to assess facial imitation in 2- to 3-week-old infants (Meltzoff & Moore, 1977). Each infant was given a baseline period and then exposed to two adult facial gestures (mouth opening and tongue protrusion). The gestures were demonstrated to the infants while they sucked on the pacifier. The pacifier was then removed and the infants were allowed to respond during the subsequent 150-second period. The experimenter presented a passive face pose during the entire response period.

the procedure served to delay imitative responding until after the adult display ended.

The gestures used as models were full mouth openings and full tongue protrusions. The infant movements counted as responses were stringently defined to be isomorphic with the adult display. Infant tongue protrusion was scored only if the tongue was thrust clearly beyond the lips; and infant mouth opening was scored only if the infant fully opened his mouth. Small tongue movements or lip separations were not scored as imitative, because they did not exactly match the adult's display.

The experiment was scored from videotape by an observer who was kept uninformed about the gesture shown to the infant in any given trial. The results showed that these large tongue protrusions and full mouth openings did not occur very frequently as part of the infant's spontaneous movements during the control conditions (thus these large behaviors might not themselves be classified as "familiar" acts, depending on one's criterion for familiar versus novel acts). More importantly, the results showed significantly more infant mouth openings after the mouth-opening demonstration than during the baseline period or after the adult tongue-protrusion demonstration. Similarly, the infants responded with significantly more tongue protrusions after the tongue-protrusion demonstration than during the baseline period or after the mouth demonstration.

In sum, the results of Experiment II showed that infants could imitate both displays even under the conditions imposed by the pacifier technique. It also went beyond the perceptual judgment system used in the first experiment and showed that the imitative pattern could be documented using the frequency of the very high-fidelity behavioral matches.

At the end of these two studies, the possibility remained that the infants had somehow learned to imitate the particular gestures shown to them during earlier interactions with their caretakers. This seemed an unlikely possibility, given the age of the subjects and the ethological description of naturally occurring interactions in home settings during the first 3 weeks of life (Whiten, 1975). Nevertheless, the potential anomaly presented by these findings could easily be explained away if one chose to argue that these early imitations were based on adult training in the first 2 to 3 weeks of life.

In order to address this issue, we conducted a new study using newborn infants. All the subjects were less than 72 hours old, and the youngest was only 42 minutes old at the time of test (Meltzoff & Moore, 1983a). In pilot studies we found it difficult to ensure that infants this young would visually inspect the experimenter's face. Infants cannot imitate if they do not perceive the model. Therefore, certain experimental procedures were instituted to focus the infant's attention on the adult's display. Three points are especially noteworthy and they are briefly outlined below.

First, because newborns are sensitive to ambient lighting, the room lights were extinguished. The only source of visible illumination was a small spotlight that shone on the experimenter's face. The experimenter's torso was covered by a black gown to reduce reflectance, and testing took place within a black-lined test chamber (Fig. 8.2). Second, because normal cinematic or videotape recording was impossible in such low illumination, we used an infrared-sensitive video camera to record a close-up image of the infant's face. Third, the experimenter's face was placed 25 ± 2 cm from the infant's eyes, a distance previously found effective in tests of newborn vision (Fantz, 1963). Given these three procedures, the experimenter's face was the brightest object in an otherwise dark field, and the newborns seemed to stay "on task" over the course of the 8-minute test.

We tested 40 newborns. Each infant was presented with both a mouth-opening and a tongue-protrusion gesture in a repeated-measures design, counterbalanced for order of presentation. Two 4-minute modeling periods were used (one for the mouth-opening demonstration and the other for the tongue-protrusion demonstration), and the experiment was electronically timed. There were no breaks between modeling periods or anywhere during the test. The experimenter's behavior was thus fixed from the beginning of the test to the end, and not contingent upon the infant's activity. (See Meltzoff & Moore, 1983a, for details).

The experimental design allowed us to distinguish between random oral movements, arousal responses, and imitation. Each infant acted as his own control. The two successive modeling periods utilized the same face, presented at the same distance, and moving at the same rate. These periods differed only with respect to the type of facial gesture presented. Within this design, imitation was demonstrated if infants responded with: (1) significantly more mouth openings to the adult mouth-opening gesture than to the tongue-protrusion gesture, and conversely (2) significantly more tongue protrusions to the tongue gesture than

FIG. 8.2. Schematic of the experimental room used to assess imitation in newborn infants under 72 hours old (Meltzoff & Moore, 1983a). The test chamber was lined with a black homogeneous background. The only source of visible illumination came from the spotlight directed toward the experimenter's face (E) from behind the infant (S). This arrangement helped to direct the infant's attention toward the experimenter's face. The camera used to videotape the closeup picture of the infant's face (left) was infrared-sensitive, thus ensuring a high-resolution record of the infant's behavior for subsequent behavioral scoring. Two videodecks were housed in a sound-dampening chamber to reduce auditory distractions as much as possible.

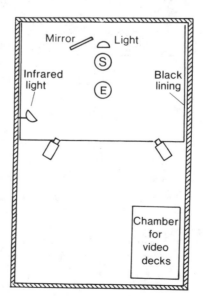

the mouth gesture. Such a pattern of *differential* response could not arise from a global arousal of oral movements in the presence of a moving human face, because the moving face was present in both periods.

The results provided strong support for the imitation hypothesis. The infants produced significantly more mouth openings in response to adult mouth-opening gesture than to the tongue-protrusion gesture ($p < .05$, Wilcoxon test). Similarly, they produced more tongue protrusions to the tongue-protrusion gesture than to the mouth-opening gesture ($p < .001$).

Beyond these statistical findings, there are several interesting aspects of the morphology and temporal organization of the imitative response that deserve mention, because they help fill in the picture of what the imitative reactions are like in these very young infants. As mentioned earlier, the infants imitate with reasonable accuracy. Our results are not based on lip quiverings or small tonguing movements inside the oral cavity. The criteria used in our behavioral scoring system (Meltzoff & Moore, 1977; 1983a) insured that only behaviors that were structurally similar to the model's were scored, and consequently the significant effects reflect a pattern in high-fidelity matches.

It is also interesting that these accurate imitative matches were not typically elicited the moment the adult presented his display. In the 1977 study, for example, we found that infants actively sucked on the pacifier while the gesture was demonstrated, and moreover that the imitative responses did not burst forth the moment the pacifier was removed. Some infants paused after pacifier removal and stared intently at the experimenter (who was now presenting the passive face pose) before beginning their imitative responding (Meltzoff, 1981; Meltzoff & Moore, 1977). In the newborn study too, we observed that the response was not suddenly triggered by the adult display (Meltzoff & Moore, 1983a).

Finally, when the infants began to respond, they often commenced by producing small approximations of the model and then gradually homing in on the target gesture. Their acts became more and more like the adult's act over successive efforts. We have coined the term *convergence* as a descriptor for this effect (Meltzoff & Moore, 1983b). Evidently this is not a necessary aspect of the response organization, because accurate imitative responses were sometimes observed after a period of rapt attention and virtually no preliminary oral movements. Nonetheless, it is of theoretical interest (discussed later) that a progressive homing in on the target—convergence—was one of the imitative patterns that presented itself.

A RESOLUTION OF THE ANOMALY: THE ROLE OF INTERMODAL REPRESENTATION IN FACIAL IMITATION

The finding that young infants, indeed newborns as young as 42 minutes old, can imitate certain simple facial gestures forces us to consider alternatives to the traditional accounts of facial imitation. Because this behavior can be elicited at birth, neither instrumental or associative learning nor the cognitive-developmental processes suggested by Piaget can be necessary conditions for such behavior.

In the 1977 paper we introduced two new alternatives that might explain this anomalous infant competence. We suggested that neonatal facial imitation might be accomplished by either: (1) innate releasing mechanism of the type outlined by Lorenz and Tinbergen (Tinbergen, 1951); or (2) a more active intermodal matching process. The critical distinction between the releasing mechanism and active mapping views is whether the neonate does or does not use the similarity between the act seen and the act done in the course of organizing his actions. Although there are certain resemblances between these accounts (e.g., that adult tuition is not involved), the distinctions between them are also important, as elaborated below.

Innate Releasing Mechanisms (IRM)

On the releasing mechanism account, the infant's response is a preprogrammed motor packet that is called up by a particular visual pattern (the sign stimulus). The similarity between the stimulus and the response does not enter into the equation. There is, after all, no requirement within ethological theory that a sign stimulus must be isomorphic with the fixed action pattern (FAP) it releases. In most examples of the classic sign stimulus → IRM → FAP system, the sign stimulus and the FAP do not match (Tinbergen, 1951). The egg-rolling behavior of Greylag geese is released by the sight of an egg, the food-begging response in newly hatched herring gull chicks is released by the mandible patch of the adult, and so forth. In these and other cases, the sign stimulus and the action pattern that are released are not isomorphic. The innate releasing mechanism is a central device that links an innately determined motor packet with a particular stimulus display. It does not require a stimulus-response isomorphism.

In fact, releasing mechanisms could just as well have accounted for the present findings if the results had been the direct opposite of what was actually found. IRMs could be invoked if it had turned out that the adult mouth-opening display elicited infant tonguing, and conversely that the tongue display elicited infant mouthing. Infants would not have to imitate but could produce any systematic motor response, and the IRM view would still be a potential explanatory concept.

The attraction of importing the IRM concept from ethology to account for infant imitation is not that it predicts, or is uniquely suited to, explaining stimulus-response isomorphisms. Rather it is that IRMs do not demand any more sophisticated perceptual-cognitive functioning that the traditional developmental theories, such as Piaget's, have already attributed to neonates. If neonatal imitation can be reduced to IRMs, then the anomaly we reported can be assimilated into existing theories simply by admitting that Piaget missed the fact that newborns imitate, but that this has no real implications for our theories of the newborn's mind. Newborn imitation may present an empirical surprise, but it is no challenge to existing theories of infant psychology.

Active Intermodal Mapping (AIM)

We favor a very different interpretation of the findings of early imitation. *In our view, this early imitation reflects a process of active intermodal mapping in which infants use the equivalences between visually and proprioceptively perceived body transformations as a basis for organizing their responses.* We also posit that imitation, even this early imitation, is mediated by an internal representation of the adult's act. The next question concerns the nature of this representation. There are several possibilities. Our working hypothesis is that the newborn could not be using a mental image of the adult's display in the sense of a visual picture or iconic copy, because then again we would be left with the problem of how infants could ever link up the "visual image" of the adult's act with the "motor image" of their own movements.

We therefore have suggested that neonates are capable of picking up "supramodal" information about the adult's movements that is then used directly as the basis for the infant's own motor plans. Thus conceived, the neonate's representation of the adult's act is neither exclusively visual nor exclusively motor but rather is a non-modality specific description of the event. Such an internal representation constitutes the "model" that directs the infant's actions and against which he matches his motor performance.

At this juncture, then, the fundamental theoretical point is whether early imitative responses ought to be conceived of as reflecting hard-wired stimulus-response linkages, or as a more active mapping procedure in which the infant uses the equivalence between his own body transformations and those of the adult as the basis for organizing the response. These two alternative conceptions, referred to here as "innate releasing mechanism" (IRM) and "active intermodal mapping" (AIM), are very different. A given behavioral pattern may reflect any one of several different levels of organization within the organism (Bower, 1979, 1982; Bruner, 1973; Kagan, 1967; Piaget, 1954). The distinction we have drawn between the IRM and AIM accounts specifies two different types of psychological organization that might underlie early imitation. To phrase this point in terms of the questions posed at the outset of this chapter, these accounts provide two different *mechanisms* that may mediate imitative behavior during the newborn period.

We think that most of the data and observations in hand favor the AIM account. The fact that some infants converge toward more accurate imitative matches over successive efforts is especially relevant to this theoretical issue. Such convergence can be viewed as ongoing correction by the infants, and as such suggests that they are engaged in an active matching process in which they compare the "obtained" behavior against their representation of the "target." If convergence does indicate a true correction process, this would certainly be more compatible with the AIM than with the IRM account. In the classic IRM account, the sequence of motor commands would be expected to "run off" in the absence of feedback about the status of the ongoing movements and their relation to the target (Lorenz & Tinbergen, 1938).

NOTES TOWARD THE FUTURE

Intermodal Representation, Imitation, and the Roots of Social Development

We are now attempting to distinguish between interesting IRM and AIM accounts experimentally. In the AIM account there is the possibility that infants could reverse the imitation effect and detect whether an adult was matching or mismatching their behavior. That is, if infants use the equivalences between their own acts and the adult's to produce imitation, they might also *recognize* when their own behavior is being imitated. This is being tested in an experiment in which the adult either performs: (1) tongue protrusions contingent on infant tongue protrusions (the case of adult matching), or (2) mouth openings contingent on infant tongue protrusions (the case of adult mismatching). The AIM view suggests that infants should react differentially to these two instances, because they can detect an intermodal equivalence in one case and not in the other. The preliminary results from this experiment are in accord with this suggestion. Infants who are being mismatched show more avoidance behaviors than do those who are being matched.

The preliminary findings are thus compatible with the idea that at some level of processing, infants can indeed compare information picked up by two different modalities (vision and proprioception). This is precisely the role of the internal representations postulated by the AIM account. There seems to be a reciprocal relationship between acts seen and acts done, and not merely simple triggering of innately organized motor patterns.

Put at a more theoretical level, what we are suggesting is that the same representational capacities that underlie the infant's imitation of adults may also allow the infant to "run the system in reverse," as it were, and appreciate the adult's imitation of the infant. In short, the mechanisms of production can also direct perception.

There are some interesting implications of the AIM model for theories of social development. Take the problem of how infants differentiate the people from the inanimate world, how they become interested in, identify with, and become attached to tokens from the former and not the latter. If our model is correct, it raises the idea that young humans may be especially attracted to other human beings (as opposed to inanimate objects) just because it is other humans who imitate their behavior. Because neonates can recognize the equivalences between the acts they themselves perform and those performed by the adults, they have a means by which to identify with other human beings. Thus our model opens the possibility that imitation and intermodal representation, even from the earliest postnatal periods, serves an important social function in the development of the infant's self-other relations.

Summary and Conclusions

It is traditionally assumed that facial imitation is a sophisticated cognitive achievement because the model and the infant's response cannot be compared within the same perceptual modality. Our demonstration of facial imitation in newborn humans under 72 hours old shows that the capacity is available at birth, and does not develop out of repeated experience in face-to-face interaction. Our working hypothesis is that human newborns have an innate ability to appreciate equivalences between their own acts and the acts they see. In our view neonates imitate by actively directing their movements to match the target gesture.

Our position can be tested in the future by (1) assessing the range of gestures that can be imitated, (2) evaluating the organization/morphology of the responses, and (3) conducting converging experiments on intermodal perception in neonates. It is our prediction that infants can imitate a variety of gestures beyond the oral movements we have tested to date; that infants' imitative responses are not rigidly fixed, stereotypic action patterns; and finally, that converging experiments will demonstrate a rich set of intermodal mappings in early infancy. Some support for the latter proposition at least has already been reported (Bower, 1982; Kuhl & Meltzoff, 1982; Meltzoff & Borton, 1979). Pending the results of future studies, we suggest that the capacity for intermodal representation is not a late-emerging skill, but rather a basic starting point for infant psychological development. Armed with an innate capacity for intermodal representation and imitation, the human newborn is provided with a firm foundation and powerful tools for subsequent cognitive and social development.

ACKNOWLEDGMENTS

The preparation of this chapter and much of the experimental work reported here were supported by the National Science Foundation (BNS 8309224), the Harry Frank Guggenheim Foundation, and the Spencer Foundation. We thank Alison Gopnik and Patricia Kuhl for helpful comments on an earlier draft of this chapter. We also thank Calle Fisher and Craig Harris for assistance on all phases of the research.

REFERENCES

Bandura, A. Social-learning theory of identificatory processes. In D. A. Goslin (Ed.), *Handbook of socialization theory and research*. Chicago: Rand McNally, 1969.

Bower, T. G. R. *Human development*. San Francisco: W. H. Freeman, 1979.

Bower, T. G. R. *Development in infancy* (2nd ed.). San Francisco: W. H. Freeman, 1982.

Bruner, J. S. Nature and uses of immaturity. *American Psychologist*, 1972, *27*, 1–22.

Bruner, J. S. Organization of early skilled action. *Child Development*, 1973, *44*, 1–11.

Dawkins, R. *The selfish gene*. New York: Oxford University Press, 1976.

Fantz, R. L. Pattern vision in newborn infants. *Science*, 1963, *140*, 296–297.

Fortes, M. Social and psychological aspects of education in Taleland. Memorandum XVII of the International Institute of African Languages and Cultures. Oxford: Oxford University Press, 1938.

Kagan, J. On the need for relativism. *American Psychologist*, 1967, *22*, 131–142.

Kuhl, P. K., & Meltzoff, A. N. The bimodal perception of speech in infancy. *Science*, 1982, *218*, 1138–1141.

Leighton, D., & Kluckhohn, C. *Children of the people*. Cambridge: Harvard University Press, 1947.

Lipsitt, L. P. Learning capacities of the human infant. In R. J. Robinson (Ed.), *Brain and early behavior development in the fetus and infant*. New York: Academic Press, 1969.

Lorenz, K., & Tinbergen, N. Taxis and instinctive behavior pattern in egg-rolling by the Greylag goose (1938). In K. Lorenz (Ed.), *Studies in animal and human behavior* (Vol. 1), trans. R. Martin. Cambridge: Harvard University Press, 1970.

Medawar, P. B. *The uniqueness of the individual*. London: Methuen, 1957.

Meltzoff, A. N. Imitation, intermodal coordination, and representation in early infancy. In G. Butterworth (Ed.), *Infancy and epistemology*. Brighton, England: Harvester Press, 1981.

Meltzoff, A. N., & Borton, R. W. Intermodal matching by human neonates. *Nature*, 1979, *282*, 403–404.

Meltzoff, A. N., & Moore, M. K. Imitation of facial and manual gestures by human neonates. *Science*, 1977, *198*, 75–78.

Meltzoff, A. N., & Moore, M. K. Newborn infants imitate adult facial gestures. *Child Development*, 1983, *54*, 702–709. (a)

Meltzoff, A. N., & Moore, M. K. The origins of imitation in infancy: Paradigm, phenomena, and theories. In L. P. Lipsitt (Ed.), *Advances in infancy research* (Vol. 2). Norwood, N.J.: Ablex, 1983. (b)

Piaget, J. *The construction of reality in the child*. New York: Basic Books, 1954.

Piaget, J. *Play, dreams, and imitation in childhood*. New York: Norton, 1962.

Reichard, G. Social life. In F. Boas (Ed.), *General anthropology*. Boston: D.C. Heath, 1938.

Steward, J. H., Manners, R., Wolf, E., Seda, E., Mintz, S., & Scheele, R. *The people of Puerto Rico*. Urbana, Ill.: University of Illinois Press, 1956.

Tinbergen, N. *The study of instinct*. New York: Oxford University Press, 1951.

Vilakazi, A. *Zulu transformations: A study of the dynamics of social change*. Pietermaritzburg: University of Natal Press, 1962.

White, B. L., Castle, P., & Held, R. Observations on the development of visually directed reaching. *Child Development*, 1964, *35*, 349–364.

Whiten, A. *Neonatal separation and mother-infant interaction*. Paper presented at the meeting of the International Society for the Study of Behavioral Development, Guildford, July, 1975.

9 Effects of Experience on Sensory and Perceptual Development: Implications for Infant Cognition

Richard N. Aslin
Indiana University

Perhaps the most pervasive issue in the study of behavioral development is the relative contribution of genetic and experiential factors to the ontogeny of individual members of a species. Concern with this issue stems in part from basic scientific questions about developmental processes, and in part from the practical implications of an individual who either can or cannot be provided with postnatal experiences that exert a significant influence on the subsequent course of development. During the many decades of controversy surrounding this issue, no systematic model of development has reconciled the dichotomy between genes and environment. Recently, however, studies of sensory and perceptual development in several nonhuman species have uncovered seemingly unique instances of experiential processes. In this chapter, I examine the generality of these roles of experience as they are applied to a variety of topical areas in human development. To this end, I hope to accomplish four things. First, I briefly describe examples of the different roles of early experience, based in large part on research in visual neurophysiology. Second, I offer a metaphor for describing the processes by which early experience may influence the course of sensory and perceptual development. Third, I provide three concrete instances of developmental change in the human infant to show how the metaphor of experiential influence can assist in illustrating gene-environment interactions. And fourth, I offer some speculations on the applicability of the metaphor to issues in cognitive development. My overall goal is to foster discussions of the role that early experience plays in modifying or determining the course of development within particular topical areas.

EXPERIENTIAL INFLUENCES IN VISUAL NEUROPHYSIOLOGY

The pioneering research by Hubel and Wiesel (1965, 1970) on the response properties of single neurons in the cat visual cortex provided investigators of development with a number of interesting findings. First, binocular neurons (those that are responsive to stimulation delivered to either eye) are present in newborn kittens prior to the onset of visual input (eye opening). Second, the absence of balanced binocular input during the first few postnatal weeks, either through monocular occlusion or eye misalignment, results in a loss of the binocular property of cortical neurons. And third, this loss of binocularity does not occur in similarly deprived adult cats. Thus, there is a relatively restricted sensitive period during which anomalous binocular experience leads to a permanent loss of binocular functioning at the cortical level. Subsequent research (Blake & Hirsch, 1975; Packwood & Gordon, 1975) has documented the fact that these neural deficits are accompanied by perceptual deficits; that is, behavioral assessments of binocularly deprived cats indicate degradations in binocular depth perception.

A second property of cortical neurons is their responsiveness to a restricted range of line orientations. Blakemore and Cooper (1970) and Hirsch and Spinelli (1970) demonstrated that all line orientations are represented in the responding of cortical neurons in the adult cat, that newborn kittens have this same distribution of orientation responsiveness, and that kittens who receive a restricted range of line orientations during the early postnatal period lose responsiveness to nonexperienced orientations. Although all line orientations are represented in the newborn visual cortex, each neuron's tuning curve is relatively broad compared to the adult cat. Thus, experience during the sensitive period appears to sharpen the tuning characteristics of orientation responsiveness (see also Sherk & Stryker, 1976). Behavioral measures of orientation selectivity have not as yet been conducted with cats, but measures of visual resolution, such as acuity, indicate that large improvements in spatial vision occur during the early postnatal period in both cats (Berkley, 1981; Smith, 1981) and monkeys (Boothe, 1981; Teller, Regal, Videen, & Pulos, 1978).

A third property of cortical neurons is their responsiveness to differences in retinal disparity. Each binocular neuron responds most vigorously when a stimulus is presented simultaneously to each eye's receptive field. These corresponding receptive fields intersect at different locations in space with respect to the current fixation position. Thus, a population of binocular neurons, which are each responsive to a different amount of retinal disparity, can provide an index of relative depth. Several investigators have shown that disparity sensitive binocular neurons are present in adult cats (e.g., Barlow, Blakemore, & Pettigrew, 1967) and monkeys (e.g., Hubel & Wiesel, 1974). Furthermore, Pettigrew (1974) has shown in newborn kittens that cortical responsiveness to disparity, although present, is very broadly tuned. In other words, binocular neurons are initially responsive to a wide range of disparities, indicating that depth resolution is quite poor. During the early postnatal period, disparity tuning becomes more narrow and approaches an adult-like level near the end of the sensitive period for binocularity (approximately 10–14 weeks).

These three examples of neural response properties in the cat visual cortex illustrate the relatively complex interaction between genetic constraints and experiential influences in neural development. A useful scheme for categorizing the various roles of experience in development has been proposed by Gottlieb (1976a, b, 1981) and expanded upon by myself in a recent chapter (Aslin, 1981). Figure 9.1 illustrates Gottlieb's modified scheme for describing the effects of early experience. The top panel depicts a case of developmental change in which the presence or absence of a specific experiential input exerts little or no influence on the course of development. Although some minimal level of experiential input is clearly required to *support* the functioning of the entire organism (e.g., nutrients), no specific experiential input related to the perceptual ability in question is required for development to proceed normally. I have termed this absence of a specific experiential effect a *maturational* role for early experience. This maturational role does not provide a good description of the three types of neural response properties discussed earlier (binocularity, orientation, disparity), because the absence of specific visual inputs does in fact significantly affect neural development.

The second panel depicts what Gottlieb has called a *maintenance* role for early experience. The maintenance role refers to a perceptual ability that is already fully developed prior to the onset of specific experiences. In the absence of these specific experiences the perceptual ability declines, and it may exhibit a permanent loss if the experiences are absent during the entire sensitive period. This maintenance role appears to provide a reasonable description of the neural property of binocularity, because this property is present at the time of experiential onset (eye opening), remains present if balanced binocular experience is provided, and is eliminated permanently if binocular deprivation occurs during an extended postnatal period.

The third panel depicts what Gottlieb has called a *facilitation* role for early experience. I know of no clear examples of this facilitation effect in sensory systems, because Gottlieb has limited its applicability to changes in the rate but not the endpoint of development. There may in fact be facilitation effects in sensory development, but as yet most researchers have studied only relatively severe deprivation regimens. Thus, it is possible that variations in subtle qualities of experience, or perhaps the concentration of experiential inputs, may modulate the rate of development, even though the presence or absence of such facilitating experiences does not alter the eventual level of sensory functioning.

The fourth panel depicts an addition to Gottlieb's scheme that was made by myself and David Pisoni in the context of phonetic development (Aslin & Pisoni, 1980). In this case of *attunement,* the perceptual ability is already present in

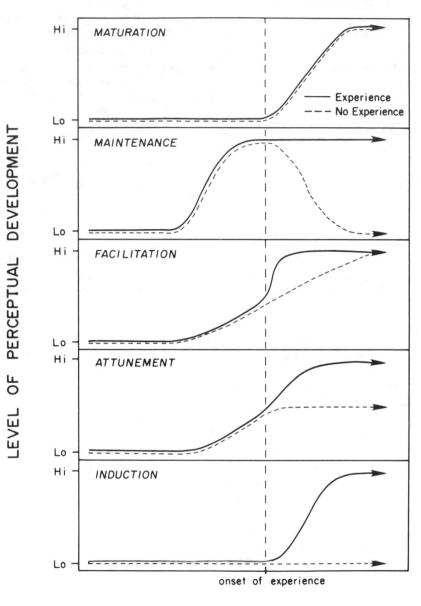

FIG. 9.1.   Five roles of experience in the development of a perceptual ability (reprinted from Aslin, 1981).

rudimentary form prior to the onset of specific experiences. The ability will remain only partially developed, however, unless specific experiences are presented during the sensitive period. In addition, there clearly are restrictions on the variety of specific experiences to which the ability will become finely tuned. For example, in the case of orientation selectivity there are limits to the shift in responsiveness that can be obtained from early experience with a restricted set of line orientations. All neurons in a vertically stripe-reared kitten do not shift responsiveness to vertical lines. Rather, some neurons that were already responsive to near-vertical orientations shift their responsiveness slightly, whereas neurons initially responsive to nonvertical orientations become dormant.[1] Another example of orientation tuning comes from a study by Shinkman and Bruce (1977). They showed that the preferred orientation of binocular neurons, which is normally identical in the two receptive fields, can be shifted by a limited amount during the sensitive period if the kitten wears goggle-mounted rotating prisms. And finally, Shlaer (1971) has shown that the distribution of disparity responsiveness can be shifted slightly during the sensitive period, if the kitten wears prisms that induce a vertical displacement.

Finally, the bottom panel depicts what Gottlieb has called an *induction* role for early experience. In this case, specific experiences are necessary for the onset and continued improvement of the perceptual ability. If the experiences are present, the ability will emerge and eventually reach an adult endpoint. If the experiences are absent, the ability will not emerge. Moreover, if the experiences are absent during the sensitive period, then subsequent experiential inputs, even though sufficient to induce development during early periods of ontogeny, may not act as an effective inducer. In other words, if there is in fact a highly constrained sensitive period, the induction process may be rendered ineffective at later periods during development.

As in the case of facilitation, there are few if any clear examples of induction in sensory development. In fact, it seems implausible that a sensory system could be so open-ended that drastically different developmental outcomes could result from specific experiential inputs. However, it should be noted that inductive processes are very common at the neurochemical level during embryonic development. Moreover, at the cognitive level inductive processes are also quite likely. Thus, it is possible that induction may occur for some aspects of sensory systems, but as yet no good examples are readily apparent.

---

[1]The use of the term *dormant* rather than *atrophied* is based on the results of several studies that have shown remarkable recovery of function in neural and behavioral responding, even though the animal was deprived during the entire sensitive period (see Mitchell, 1981, and Smith, 1981, for recent reviews). Apparently, many neural functions are suppressed as a result of unbalanced early visual input, but this suppression can be released if the animal is subjected to rather severe forms of postdeprivation recovery (e.g., removal of the nondeprived eye).

A final comment on the five roles of experience outlined in Fig. 9.1 is the progressive ordering of experiential influence from low to high as one goes from maturation to induction. Complementing this increase in experiential influence is a progressive decrease in genetic constraints. Thus, maturation occurs with little or no experiential influence; maintenance simply stabilizes an already mature endpoint; facilitation enhances the acquisition rate but not the final level of the ability; attunement enhances the final level and/or the characteristics of an ability that is already partially developed; and induction actually determines the presence and final level of the ability. The task of empirical research in a given topical area of development is to specify which of these five roles of experience best describes the mechanism underlying developmental change. Unfortunately, this task is particularly difficult in research with humans, because the timing and quality of specific experiential inputs can rarely be manipulated, either for practical or ethical reasons. For example, without manipulating experiential inputs, all five developmental functions would be nearly identical, as long as the specific inputs required for normal development were not missing from the organism's species-typical environment. The use of animal models of human sensory and perceptual development has been particularly useful in generating hypotheses about analogous developmental processes in humans. In fact, it could be argued that these animal models have been a direct catalyst for the generation of new approaches to developmental research with humans (see, for example, Banks, Aslin, & Letson, 1975).

To summarize this background section on visual neurophysiology, it should be apparent that there are several ways in which early visual experience influences the course of both neural and perceptual development. At least five descriptions of experiential influence have been proposed, and each generates a set of empirically testable predictions about developmental change. However, the applicability to human development of these roles of experience remains incomplete without a further set of characteristics to account for the vast array of genetic and experiential interactions that are potentially present. Next, I discuss one way in which such interactions could be viewed.

FILTERING AS A METAPHOR FOR GENETIC CONSTRAINTS

The puzzle that emerges from the foregoing discussion of the roles of experience is why certain specific experiential inputs are so influential to the course of development, whereas other inputs are not. Clearly, one must conclude that there are selective pressures placed upon the underlying mechanisms that employ experiential inputs in guiding the process of development. In a previous chapter (Aslin, 1981), I argued that a useful way to think about this notion of experiential selectivity is by analogy to the properties of a filter. In essence, a filter is a device that passes or transmits only certain aspects of stimulation or information, while blocking or filtering all other aspects. For example, in optics and acoustics, filters can be constructed to pass only certain wavelengths of light or frequencies of sound, and the bandpass characteristics of the filter can be specified by a mathematical function.

By analogy, we could consider specific perceptual experiences as lying along a dimension of environmental input (e.g., the orientation of lines or the relative balance between binocular inputs). Only inputs at specific locations along this dimension will exert a significant influence on the course of perceptual development. A trivial example of this selectivity for experiential inputs is the fact that humans are insensitive to acoustic and electromagnetic wavelengths that are either very low or very high. A more intriguing example of this selectivity occurs when a broad range of experiential inputs is available, particularly when each of these inputs can affect the organism if presented individually. In most cases of this multiple availability of suprathreshold stimuli, the organism is affected by only a limited range of these inputs and may develop a heightened sensitivity or behavioral preference to those specific experiences. Clearly, this selectivity must be species-specific and determined, at least in part, by genetic factors.

In Fig. 9.2, I have illustrated a specific narrowband filter lying along a hypothetical dimension of experience, as well as several examples of different experiential inputs and their effects on the course of development. For those who need a concrete anchor, consider this dimension of experience to be retinal disparity and the perceptual ability to be stereoacuity. First, consider experiential input A, which covers the entire disparity filter for the development of stereoacuity. All the experience relevant to the development of stereoacuity is transmitted by the filter, and the endpoint of development is one of very good stereoacuity tuned to the peak of the filter. Notice that in the bottom panel I have illustrated three possible developmental functions for the ontogeny of stereoacuity by placing the preexperiential status of stereoacuity at three different levels. Second, consider input B, which matches the mean of the filter but is reduced in bandwidth and intensity (or concentration). The lower panel shows that in this case one would expect an attenuation of the developmental function. Finally, consider input C, which does not overlap at all with the filter. In this case, the developmental function shown in the lower panel will decline or fail to emerge, and the species-typical endpoint for the development of stereoacuity will not be reached.

The foregoing examples have considered the filtering of experiential inputs to be constant during development. In fact, what has been illustrated is only one slice in time during the sensitive period. Figure 9.3 shows a more complete example of the filtering process, which for many aspects of sensory development is likely to be different at different times during development. The height of the filter represents the *sensitivity* of the perceptual system to experiential inputs at different ages. If sensitivity to experiential inputs shows a peak during the course of development, as shown in Fig. 9.3, then the duration of the peak defines the

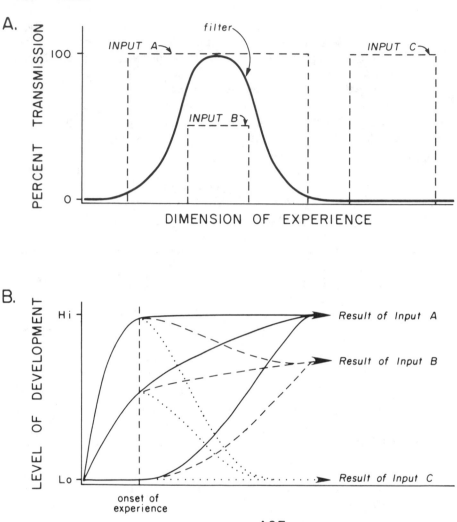

FIG. 9.2.   (A) Scheme for illustrating a hypothetical experiential filter and three
different experiential inputs (B) Illustration of the result of the transmission of the
three experiential inputs by the filter (reprinted from Aslin, 1981).

sensitive period (the projection onto the left side of Fig. 9.3). The width and
relative location of the filter along the dimension of experiential input defines
the *selectivity* of the perceptual system. This schematic diagram, then, provides
a metaphor for the operation of different experiential inputs at different times
during development. In cases of experiential deprivation, or biased experiential
input that fails to match the bandpass characteristics of the filter, the developmental function will deviate from the species-typical norm.

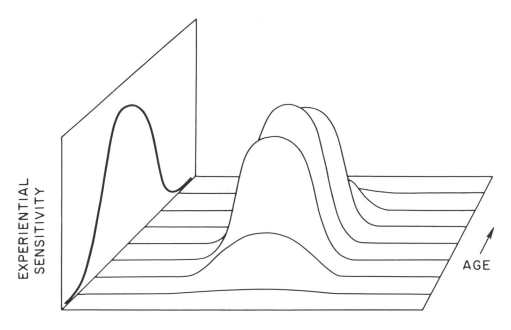

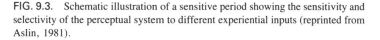

EXPERIENTIAL   SELECTIVITY

FIG. 9.3.   Schematic illustration of a sensitive period showing the sensitivity and selectivity of the perceptual system to different experiential inputs (reprinted from Aslin, 1981).

Figure 9.4 illustrates the filtering process as it affects the development of a perceptual ability when a biased experiential input is presented during the sensitive period. Note that the filter is centered at a particular location, M, along the dimension of experience. In this figure, I have introduced two types of filtering: broad and narrow. For a broad filter there are several different types of experience that are transmitted by the filter, even though the biased experiential input shown in the figure does not match the species-typical norm. Thus, if the maintenance role for experience were applicable to the present case of broad filtering, the perceptual ability that was already present prior to the onset of the sensitive period would shift its characteristics from location M to location M'. If, however, the attunement or induction roles for experience were applicable, the perceptual ability would either become attuned to location M' or emerge to become aligned with location M'. In contrast to the case of broad filtering, a narrow filter that transmitted none of the biased experiential input would result in a more drastic change in the species-typical perceptual ability. An ability already present at the onset of the sensitive period (maintenance) would be lost, and an ability that would have been induced by experience that matched the filter (induction) would fail to emerge. Finally, it should be noted that the

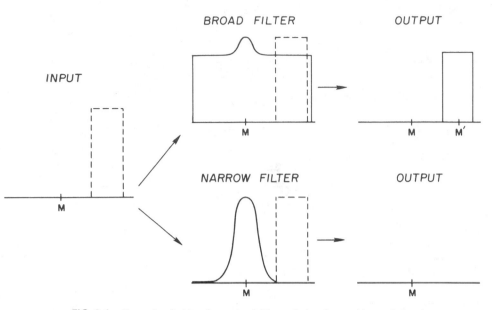

FIG. 9.4. Example of a biased experiential input during the sensitive period and its attenuation by either a broad or narrow filter (reprinted from Aslin, 1981).

magnitude of these deprivation effects will depend not only on the mismatch between the filter and the particular experiential inputs, but also on the duration of the mismatch during the sensitive period. Partial deprivation or a biased input will result in only a partial attenuation or shift in the species-typical characteristics of the perceptual ability.

In summary, this filtering metaphor provides an easily illustrated description of the way in which different levels of genetic constraints or filtering properties interact with different types of experiential inputs. I have made the critical assumption that the shape and timing of the filtering process is relatively fixed by the genotype. In a later section, I detail my rationale for this assumption, as well as its applicability to topical areas other than sensory development. At this point, however, I offer two cautionary notes. First, the filtering process is proposed as a metaphor for illustrating the properties of the gene-environment interaction. There may not be structural properties of the perceptual system that are filter like, but a filter-like process seems to capture what the underlying mechanism is doing *in some fashion*. Second, one must be wary of the common assumption that a species-specific perceptual ability is the result of genetic factors. For example, it is possible for a species-typical environment to restrict the range of possible experiential inputs, such that all members of the species possess seemingly unique perceptual abilities. However, the abilities may be induced or attuned by early inputs that are either experienced only by members of that species, or only at times when the perceptual system of that species happens to be sensitive to such inputs. Thus, two different species may follow identical paths of neural and physical development, but one species may be introduced to visual inputs earlier than another via different birth processes. Identical sensitive periods for the two species may result in quite different perceptual abilities. Only the precise control of the timing and quality of experiential inputs during a broad age range can determine the genetic constraints placed upon species-specific development. A novel experiential input delivered to a particular species, followed by the emergence of a species-*atypical* perceptual ability, does *not* necessarily imply a change in the filter underlying the ability. Rather, it need only be assumed that prior to that demonstration the characteristics of the filter had been poorly specified.

EXAMPLES OF EXPERIENTIAL EFFECTS IN HUMAN VISUAL DEVELOPMENT

The foregoing descriptions and speculations may appear somewhat open-ended without specific empirical examples. I now provide several examples from the literature on visual development in humans to bolster my claims for the usefulness of the filtering metaphor. Unfortunately, as in many areas of developmental psychology, the data on infant vision are far from definitive. Thus, I take some liberties with my interpretations of data (in part to guarantee a good fit with my theorizing). I should emphasize at this point, however, that my intent is not to be precise or even correct. Sometimes it is more beneficial to be clearly wrong than only 90% correct. I can only hope that, as our data base becomes more robust in the years ahead, the issues raised here will generate new approaches to the investigation of questions in sensory and perceptual development.

Fusion, Stereopsis, and Strabismus

The first example I consider is the perceptual side of the neural properties of binocularity and disparity responsiveness discussed earlier. Before proceeding to the empirical evidence from human infants, it might prove beneficial to discuss the application of the filtering metaphor to neural responding. Figure 9.5 illustrates the hypothesized filters for binocularity and disparity at the peak of the sensitive period. Note that these two filters are quite different in shape. Both have a peak along different dimensions of experiential input, but the binocularity filter is much broader than the disparity filter.

It is now clear from a number of studies (e.g., Blakemore, 1976) that the relative balance of visual inputs to the two eyes during the sensitive period can drastically alter the percentage of binocular neurons in the cat visual cortex. The traditional measure of binocularity is called an ocular dominance distribution, and in normal adult cats and kittens it is normally distributed for a sample of

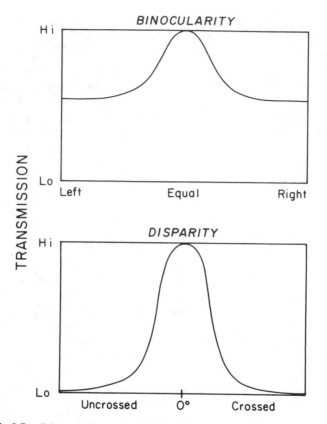

FIG. 9.5.   Schematized experiential filters for cortical binocularity (top) and disparity (bottom) (reprinted from Aslin, 1981).

cortical neurons. Thus, the majority of neurons are binocular, and only a small percentage of neurons are responsive to inputs delivered to the left or right eye alone. If the kitten is presented with unbalanced inputs during the sensitive period, the ocular dominance distribution becomes skewed, indicating a much larger representation of monocular neurons (i.e., those sensitive only to inputs from one eye). In terms of the binocularity filter, there is a bias to transmit balanced inputs. However, even unbalanced inputs are transmitted, as indicated by the resultant shift in the ocular dominance distribution.

In contrast to the binocularity filter, the filter for disparity is much more narrow. First, it should be noted that only binocular neurons can show evidence of disparity responsiveness, because disparity is defined as the relative alignment of binocular receptive fields. Second, there are several studies of artificially induced strabismus (i.e., a deviation in eye alignment) that indicate binocularity is lost if the deviation is larger than approximately 4° of visual angle (Baker, Grigg, & vonNoorden, 1974; Crawford & vonNoorden, 1980; Hubel & Wiesel,

1965; Smith, Bennett, Harwerth, & Crawford, 1979; Van Sluyters & Levitt, 1980; Yinon, 1976). Shlaer (1971) provided evidence of a shift in the disparity distribution for a 2° prism-rearing experiment. And, Van Sluyters and Levitt (1980) showed that only large prisms induce a loss of binocularity. Thus, it would appear that disparity experience during the early postnatal period is limited to a relatively restricted range. Experience during the sensitive period that is biased beyond approximately a plus or minus 4° bandwidth of disparities is not passed by the filter and results in a loss of binocularity and disparity responsiveness.

Behavioral evidence of binocularity and disparity responsiveness in humans comes from several lines of evidence, some of it direct and some inferential. The inferential evidence is from two studies of older children and adults who have received unbalanced binocular inputs resulting from crossed eyes (Banks, Aslin, & Letson, 1975; Hohmann & Creutzfeldt, 1975). A behavioral measure of binocularity was taken from samples of patients who had each had crossed eyes during a different period of development. This retrospective view of the amount of functional binocularity remaining after a period of binocular deprivation indicated that there is a sensitive period for binocularity in humans, and a mathematical model of these results provided the function shown in Fig. 9.6.

SENSITIVE   PERIOD   FOR   BINOCULARITY   IN   HUMANS

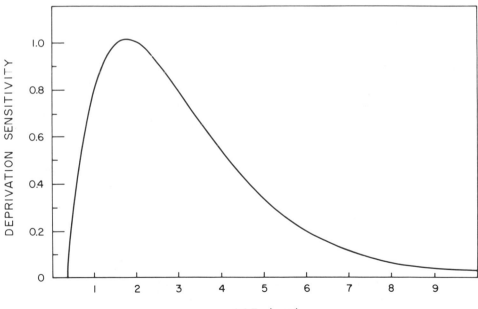

FIG. 9.6.   Representation of the sensitive period for human binocular vision (adapted from Banks, Aslin, & Letson, 1975).

This function represents the relative sensitivity of the visual system to binocular deprivation at different postnatal ages. Note that the function does not begin until several months after birth, peaks at approximately 2 years of age, and shows a gradual drop in deprivation sensitivity beyond 4 years of age.

The foregoing description of a sensitive period for human binocularity does not answer many questions related to the interaction of genetic constraints and experiential influences, other than the fact that the property of binocularity can be influenced by certain types of anomalous early experiences. To characterize the filtering process for binocularity, it is necessary to assess binocular function at different postnatal ages. It may be that infants have binocularity at birth and lose it if maintaining experience is absent, or it may be that binocularity is absent at birth and emerges if the appropriate types of early experience are present. Moreover, the shape of the filter could not be determined from these retrospective studies, because experimental control of the quality of binocular experience during the sensitive period was impossible.

To assess binocular function in human infants, several behavioral measures have been used. The first measure, called fusion, refers to the fact that the images received by the two eyes when fixating a stimulus are combined at the perceptual level into a single phenomenal percept. Unfortunately, because fusion is a subjective phenomenon, it is impossible given present techniques to unambiguously document its presence in preverbal infants. However, indirect evidence of fusion in infants comes from a study I completed several years ago (Aslin, 1977). A small wedge prism was placed in front of one eye while the infant fixated a stimulus. In adults, this prism induces a refixation movement of the eyes that indicates an attempt to re-fuse the stimulus. As shown in Fig. 9.7, infants did not show this refixation response until the fourth postnatal month. Although we have not collected additional data, we would predict that as the infant matures, smaller and smaller prisms would be required to induce the refixation response. In other words, the tuning of the sensory information that triggers the refixation response improves with age.

Figure 9.8 shows group data from several studies of stereopsis in human infants. Stereopsis refers to the appreciation of relative depth based on retinal disparity. As discussed earlier, animals who are deprived of balanced binocular inputs during the sensitive period lose binocularity and the finely tuned disparity responsiveness required for good stereoacuity. Two different types of stereogram displays have been used with infants: random-dot displays that assess what is called global stereopsis and contour displays that assess what is called local stereopsis. In both displays, the key stimulus variable involved in the detection of relative depth is retinal disparity. Based on the results of two studies conducted by Fox and his associates (Fox, Aslin, Shea, & Dumais, 1980; Shea, Fox, Aslin, & Dumais, 1980), global stereopsis appears to emerge during the fourth postnatal month. Similar findings have been reported recently using visual-evoked potentials (Petrig, Julesz, Kropfl, Baumgartner, & Anliker, 1981). Finally, the rapid

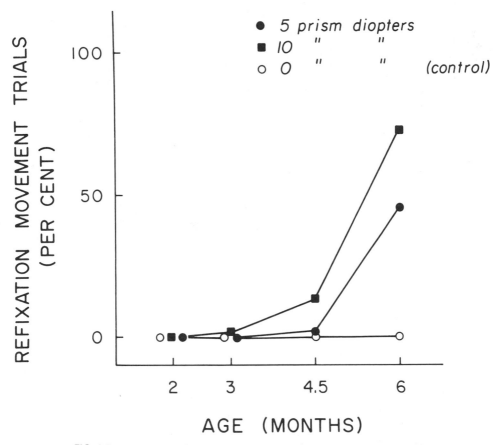

FIG. 9.7.   Refixation response probabilities from infants whose binocular alignment was altered with base-out wedge prisms (replotted from Aslin, 1977).

emergence of stereopsis and improvements in stereoacuity have been demonstrated by Held, Birch, and Gwiazda (1980) and Birch, Gwiazda, and Held
(1982). These three sets of results on fusion, global stereopsis, and local stereoacuity all converge on the same conclusion; namely, that disparity processing
is initially very poor and emerges during the postnatal period from 3 to 6 months.

    These results from normal infants have recently been extended to a sample
of infants and young children who have had strabismus. We have tested both
infants from families with a history of eye disorders and children who have been
surgically treated for crossed eyes (Shea & Aslin, 1982). In general, our results
confirm previous retrospective studies in that the presence of strabismus during
the sensitive period leads to the absence of stereopsis even after the eyes have
been realigned. Data from infants who received early surgery (i.e., before the
end of the sensitive period) are somewhat mixed. Some infants appear to have

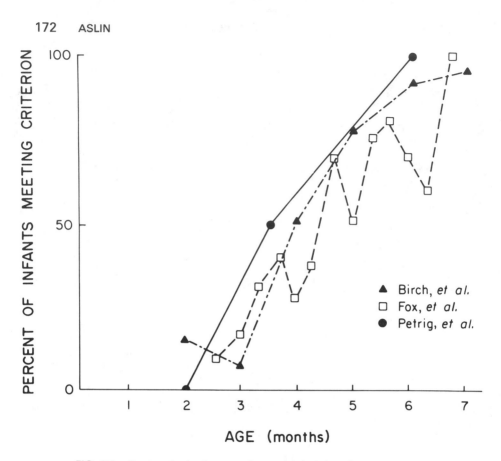

FIG. 9.8.   Data on the development of stereopsis in infants from three studies that used different stimulus displays and different measurement techniques. Birch et al. used a polarized line stereogram and preferential looking, Fox et al. used a dynamic random-element stereogram and preferential looking, and Petrig et al. used a random-element stereogram and visual-evoked potentials (redrawn from Teller, 1982).

stereopsis, whereas others do not. Those infants who fail to show evidence of stereopsis postoperatively may in fact have had no stereopsis prior to the onset of strabismus. Unfortunately, we have been unable to test a large sample of infants preoperatively. Moreover, those preoperative infants who already have strabismus would not be expected to show stereopsis because the eyes are mis-aligned. What is needed is a test of binocular function that does not require correctly aligned eyes. In this way one could assess the integrity of the binocular system to determine if the neural mechanism underlying stereopsis is intact. Corrective surgery for those patients who do not have the neural mechanism for stereopsis will not result in a restoration of an ability that is absent for genetic reasons.

To summarize this section on binocular function in infants, it seems clear that there are fairly narrow constraints placed upon the binocular aspects of visual development. If unbalanced inputs, or slightly misaligned eyes, are present during the sensitive period, the infant will fail to develop normal stereopsis. Nevertheless, there is some plasticity in the system to allow for slight differences in ocular alignment or dominance. In fact, a slight misalignment, if left uncorrected during the entire sensitive period, can lead to a permanent shift in disparity processing. For these subjects who develop what is called anomalous retinal correspondence, the surgical correction of their misalignment in later life can lead to the constant presence of double images. Finally, the prognosis for infants who have received anomalous binocular input as a result of strabismus is somewhat confounded by the possibility that a subset of strabismic infants does not have the neural substrate required for normal binocular function. For these infants, the ocular misalignment is secondary to the neural deficit, and rapid elimination of the unbalanced binocular input during the sensitive period is irrelevant to the restoration of binocular function.

Acuity, Accommodation, and Astigmatism

The second example of visual development I consider involves the ability of the infant to resolve fine details of a visual stimulus. Acuity refers to the smallest resolvable visual detail, and several studies in the past 5 years (see Dobson & Teller, 1978 and Salapatek & Banks, 1978 for recent reviews) have documented the rapid improvement in acuity from birth to the end of the first 6 postnatal months. Acuity itself appears to undergo this rapid course of development as long as patterned visual input is provided to the two eyes, and as long as the balance of visual resolution in the two eyes is relatively equal. If an interocular refractive error is allowed to continue during the early postnatal period (primarily due to the absence of spectacle corrections), then a permanent amblyopia may develop (see chapter by Held). However, I describe a more elementary aspect of the development of visual resolution, one that is concerned with the mechanism underlying improvements in acuity.

The previous discussion of orientation tuning among neurons in the cat visual cortex described the fact that each neuron is optimally responsive to lines of a particular orientation, plus or minus several degrees of tilt. Although all orientations are represented in the population of neurons at birth, kittens deprived of all but a single line orientation during the sensitive period lose responsiveness to those orientations that were not experienced (see recent replication studies by Gordon, Presson, Packwood, & Scheer, 1979; Stryker, Sherk, Leventhal, & Hirsch, 1978). A similar type of orientation deprivation has been proposed for humans who are prevented from receiving clearly focused lines of certain orientations during the early postnatal period. Mitchell, Freeman, Millodot, and Haegerstrom (1973) demonstrated that adults who had a history of optically uncorrected astigmatism during early childhood showed poorer acuity for line orientations that had been defocused. In astigmatism, the aspherical corneal surface differentially refracts different line orientations. Thus, the accommodative or focusing mechanism cannot bring all line orientations into sharp focus at the same time. Either a compromise accommodative position is used, so that orthogonal orientations are equally defocused, or one line orientation is focused accurately and all other orientations are defocused by some variable amount. Presumably, the subjects in the Mitchell et al. study were of the latter type, because their astigmatism resulted in a permanent loss of acuity for the optically defocused orientation.

Mitchell et al. also showed that in subjects without astigmatism there is a bias toward better acuity for horizontal and vertical orientations than for oblique orientations. This phenomenon, called the oblique effect, indicates that the human visual system may be biased toward vertical and horizontal inputs during an early sensitive period. Data from kittens (Fregnac & Imbert, 1978; Leventhal & Hirsch, 1975) have shown that vertical and horizontal lines maintain orientation responsiveness only to vertical and horizontal orientations, whereas oblique lines maintain orientation responsiveness to all orientations, including verticals and horizontals. Thus, there appears to be a bias for vertical and horizontal orientations to be transmitted during the sensitive period. Given these findings from cats and humans, it seems reasonable to conclude that the filter for orientation responsiveness is similar to the illustration shown in Fig. 9.9. All line orientations

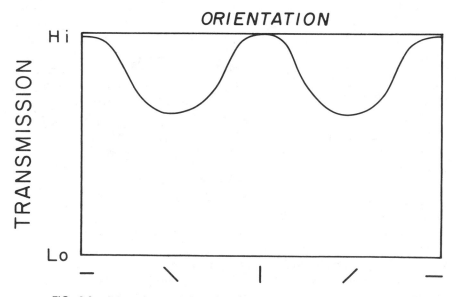

FIG. 9.9.   Schematized experiential filter for cortical orientation selectivity (reprinted from Aslin, 1981).

are transmitted, but verticals and horizontals have a selective advantage over obliques.

The data from infants on the question of orientation biases are mixed. Teller and her colleagues (Teller, Morse, Borton, & Regal, 1974) have found no evidence in support of early orientation biases, at least in terms of acuity values, whereas Held and his colleagues (Gwiazda, Brill, Mohindra, & Held, 1978; Leehey, Moskowitz-Cook, Brill, & Held, 1975) have found some evidence for an oblique effect. Perhaps a more interesting aspect of this controversy, however, involves the mechanism by which acuity for different line orientations develops. If, as assumed by Mitchell et al. in their study of adults, differential acuity for different orientations is the result of selective early deprivation via defocus, then how does the infant's visual system show improvements in acuity when accommodative accuracy is initially so poor? In other words, the accommodative system utilizes stimulus blur to trigger a focusing response. At birth, acuity is poor, as is blur detection. If improvements in acuity depend on the presence of clearly focused images, then the infant will experience blurred images and acuity should never improve (see Banks, 1980, for a more extensive discussion of this issue). One possible explanation of this puzzle is to assume that some minimal level of acuity development is controlled by maturational factors independent of experience. Thus, if the accommodative system can function fairly well with medium levels of acuity, perhaps the almost-in-focus images will be sufficient to allow further improvements in acuity via experiential factors. If this explanation holds, then it must be the case that subtle variations in experiential input during the initial postnatal period should have little effect on acuity development. Such seems to be the case. However, once acuity has reached a mid-level at approximately 4 to 6 months of age, the effects of experience become apparent (see Jacobson, Mohindra, & Held, 1981).

A final aspect of acuity development in human infants involves astigmatism. Several reports have shown that astigmatism is quite common in early infancy (Howland, Atkinson, Braddick, & French, 1978; Mohindra, Held, Gwiazda, & Brill, 1978). However, there appears to be a considerable decline over the course of the first postnatal year in the magnitude of astigmatism. Most infants with astigmatism appear to balance the amount of defocus between the two orthogonal orientations that are most different in refractive state (Dobson, Howland, Moss, & Banks, 1983). Because the majority of astigmatism involves vertical and horizontal orientations rather than obliques, these two primary orientations would be equally out of focus. For infants with a large amount of astigmatism (or perhaps a low amplitude of accommodation and/or a biased resting point of accommodation), only one orientation is selected for optimal focus via the accommodative system. Thus, the orthogonal orientation is always quite defocused. These infants do not appear to reduce ocular astigmatism during the first postnatal year. It may be that the biased input provided to these infants who have large amounts of astigmatism acts to prevent the corrective mechanism that alters the growth pattern of the corneal surface and eliminates the aspherical corneal curvature. Infants who split their focus between the orthogonal orientations, however, do not experience a biased input of a single focused orientation, and presumably their compensatory growth mechanism rebalances the curvature of the corneal surface during the period of rapid eyeball growth in the first postnatal year.

In summary, the orientation filter appears to be double peaked, with a selective advantage given to vertical and horizontal orientations (explaining the oblique effect). In addition, it appears that the accommodative system, even though poorly controlled by blur detection shortly after birth, is capable of focusing all orientations sufficiently to allow for rapid improvements in acuity. However, if refractive errors go uncorrected during the second half of the first postnatal year, permanent losses of acuity may result. Finally, if differential refractive errors are present for different orientations (i.e., astigmatism), there may be no deprivation effect unless the accommodative system selects only one orientation for clear focus, thereby sacrificing clear focus for all other orientations.

Convergence and Accommodation

The third and final example I consider involves a sensory-motor relation that is at least a candidate for an induction effect via early experience. This sensory-motor relation is between accommodation and convergence. Convergence refers to the turning inward of the two lines of sight to fixate a near object. Under normal binocular viewing conditions, there is a close correspondence between accommodation and convergence angle. As an object approaches, accommodation is increased to maintain focus and convergence angle is increased to maintain fusion. In adults, this linkage between accommodation and convergence is so stable that convergence occurs even under *monocular* viewing conditions. In this case, the approach of the object only requires a change in accommodation, because any change in the alignment of the occluded eye is irrelevant to the maintenance of fusion when both eyes are not viewing the object. Nevertheless, the occluded eye turns inward as the monocularly viewed object approaches.

The intriguing aspect of accommodative-convergence in infants is whether the linkage is specified innately, acquired via associative processes during the postnatal period, or determined by both genetic and experiential factors. All three alternatives have received some theoretical support, yet no empirical data on infants had previously been collected. Recently, we (Aslin & Jackson, 1979) demonstrated that accommodative-convergence is present in infants as young as 2 months of age. Because this is the age at which convergence under binocular viewing conditions becomes clearly evident (Aslin, 1977), as well as the age at which accommodative responses begin to approach an adult-like form (Banks, 1980), it seems likely that the basic linkage is already established prior to experiential inputs. However, there must be an experiential tuning of the linkage during the later postnatal period. The large increase in interocular separation between birth and adulthood indicates that the same accommodative stimulus must signal a much larger convergence response in adults than in 2-month-olds. Our data support this argument in that the adults showed a greater angular change in convergence to the same accommodative stimulus than the infants. Thus, a strictly nativist linkage between accommodation and convergence seems untenable.

An associative model of the accommodative-convergence linkage also seems implausible. Nearly all adults have a condition called a phoria. Phorias are misalignments of the two eyes that only become evident under monocular viewing conditions. When viewing an object with both eyes, the fusional mechanism keeps the object fixated accurately. However, when one eye is occluded, it may deviate either inward (esophoria) or outward (exophoria). If the accommodative-convergence relation were established via an associative process during early development, one would certainly not expect phorias to be very common. Rather, one would expect a convergence position under monocular conditions that was nearly identical to convergence under binocular conditions. Thus, the high incidence of phorias argues against a strict associative basis for the accommodative-convergence linkage.

The most plausible theory for accommodative-convergence is that the linkage is already present in rudimentary form prior to the onset of visual experience. During the early postnatal period, the linkage is susceptible to the effects of experience, either in the form of refractive errors or changes in interocular separation. These experiential factors influence the specific relation between the two responses, and after some as yet unknown postnatal period the linkage becomes relatively permanent (the so-called accommodative-convergence/ accommodation or AC/A ratio). At present, a precise description of the filter for the effects of experience on the accommodative-convergence linkage is unavailable. However, it seems likely that large refractive errors, although transmitted by the accommodative-convergence filter, may constrain the accommodation system itself and in turn disrupt accommodative-convergence.

To summarize this section on examples of experiential filtering in visual development, it would appear that the majority of sensory and perceptual abilities in human infants are influenced according to what we have termed an attunement role for early experience. Most abilities are partially specified at the time when visual inputs become available to the infant (birth). In addition, most abilities seem to be susceptible to some effects of early experience. However, there appear to be rather severe constraints placed upon the characteristics of the experiential filter. Binocular functions, including fusion and stereopsis, require a restricted range of ocular alignment and balanced inputs. Orientation responsiveness, as assessed by differential acuity, requires a relatively in-focus retinal image without large amounts of astigmatism. And the sensory-motor linkage between accommodation and convergence requires the absence of large interocular refractive differences. Future research in the area of sensory and perceptual development in human infants should be directed to the precise specification of those aspects of early experience that are essential to a normative course of development, as well as the timing of these inputs during the postnatal period.

SPECULATIONS ON COGNITIVE DEVELOPMENT

I now grapple with several basic issues in cognitive development, speaking largely as an outsider, but one who is well aware of the qualitative differences in levels of analysis between sensation and cognition. I do not have high hopes that the ideas I have raised from sensory development will transfer directly to cognitive phenomena, but I do hope that some of the basic issues will provide a slightly different perspective from which cognitive development may be viewed.

First, let us confront what is surely the single most frustrating issue in applying the notion of an experiential filter to cognitive development: What is a dimension of experience in the cognitive domain? It seems quite straightforward to speak of a dimension of binocular imbalance or line orientation. But where does one begin to describe the types of experiential inputs that may be essential to the normative course of cognitive development? Unfortunately, I do not have an answer to this question, other than to suggest that investigators might select a smaller slice of the cognitive pie. It seems that many researchers either choose a neo-Piagetian or anti-Piagetian stance on cognitive development, with the application of traditional global theoretical approaches and tried and true methods of assessment. Fortunately, recent investigations in the area of infant cognition have begun to buck this trend (Fischer, 1980). It may be that no single overriding theory of cognitive development is either possible or desirable. Certainly in the case of perceptual development, there is no omnibus metatheory. Rather, individual research programs have arisen to investigate relatively restricted questions. As long as investigators do not lose sight of theoretical issues, as well as the benefits of continual interchange with researchers in related areas, problem areas will be confronted and definitive answers will be forthcoming.

Second, can we assume a genetically fixed experiential filter when dealing with cognitive phenomena? In fact, one might question this assumption of a fixed filter in the case of sensory development. Here is my rationale for making this assumption. If it is possible for the filter to be modified during the course of sensory development, then consistent species-specific abilities and a relatively fixed sensitive period would be very unlikely. Although I assume that the filter can change over generations via processes of natural selection, the highly consistent endpoints of development in sensory and perceptual systems argue against an easily modifiable filtering process during ontogeny. To assume, in contrast to the present model, that the filter can undergo modifications during a given organism's lifetime not only implies that a well-defined sensitive period does not exist, but it also raises a problem of reductionism. A modifiable filter would allow the possibility of many different paths of development, resulting from selective pressures operating at the level of the individual organism rather than at the level of the species. The fact that individual organisms progress through a relatively constrained course of sensory development would require some additional process to constrain the "changeability" of the filter. But this constraint on the filtering process (a constraint on a constraint) is in essence another filter. Why posit a series of filters to account for one aspect of development, particularly when this series of filters has the logical force of a homunculus guiding developmental processes? The assumption of the present model is simply that the filtering process is fixed during ontogeny, and the expression of particular sensory and perceptual abilities is dependent on the interaction of the filter and the potential diversity of experiential inputs.

One might counter the foregoing argument with evidence that individual organisms are capable of remarkable examples of recovery of sensory and perceptual function after lengthy periods of deprivation or gross neural lesions. Under extreme conditions that deviate greatly from the species-typical norm, it is likely that redundant or back-up systems are triggered. In such cases, the original filter that was applicable to the ability undergoing development may become irrelevant as a new structural mechanism begins to function. Presumably, this new system carries with it a new set of filtering characteristics.

An issue related to this notion of multiple levels of filtering is the fact that most abilities, whether sensory, perceptual, or cognitive, depend on underlying abilities that emerged during earlier periods of development. If the earlier abilities do not emerge, the higher level ability may be prevented. One could interpret this absence of the later developing ability as an instance of a change in the filter for that higher level ability. However, the present model assumes that the filter for the higher level ability remains intact. It is the *input* to that higher level filter that has been altered as a result of the failure of the earlier ability to emerge. For example, in human infants visual preferences for specific faces typically emerge after several months of postnatal development. This higher level preferential behavior is dependent on lower level abilities such as attention to and fixation of contours. If contour deprivation occurs during the early postnatal period, a deficit in contour processing may prevent the normal development of facial preferences. Thus, the deficit in the higher level ability is assumed to be the result of an inability of the lower level to transmit inputs to the filter for the higher level ability.

From this discussion, it should be clear that for many abilities the process of development is characterized by the serial application of a set of experiential filters. There are, however, some aspects of development that involve competitive experiential effects. In other words, the filter may be broad enough to transmit a variety of experiential inputs, but these inputs may be mutually exclusive. For example, different line orientations can be experienced simultaneously, whereas different binocular imbalances cannot. Similarly, perceptual abilities that involve preferential behaviors are often mutually exclusive. Certainly, some of this distinction between serial and parallel inputs is largely methodological, because standard two-choice preference techniques could be expanded to include multiple choices. However, in higher level cognitive and linguistic abilities, it is quite likely that the load on processing is so high that only one of several inputs can be operated upon, not only in short-term processing such as memory and lexical access, but also in long-term processing such as the formation of cognitive structures and grammatical categories. Thus, an issue that would have to be incorporated into the present filtering model, if it were applied to cognitive phenomena, is the distinction between serial and parallel filtering processes.

Given this notion that a set of filtering processes is operative during the course of development, either in a true serial fashion or via multiple parallel inputs, one might ask whether this hierarchical filtering process proceeds in only one direction. In other words, we tend to think of cognitive operations and their underlying structures as increasing in complexity and organizational properties during development. Moreover, we tend to view the process of increasing structural complexity in a generative sense, such that small increments in structure can lead to new reorganizations of the entire cognitive processing network. If one views cognitive development according to the present model (i.e., as a series of genetically fixed filters), then how can we account for the apparent diversity of cognitive outcomes and the ability of cognitive operations to generate new structures? Pushing the filtering metaphor to its limit, the apparent diversity and generativity of cognitive development may simply be a manifestation of mechanisms that were already present but suppressed by more robust or less-filtered mechanisms. If so, then what appears to be a novel solution to a cognitive problem is just the natural process of working through the path of least resistance in a complex filtering network.

Note that I am not claiming that a characterization of all low-level filters will provide a good prediction of the characteristics of higher level abilities. It is clear from many areas of science that predicting the organizational principles of a system from the characteristics of its components is nearly always impossible. If, however, one has an accurate description of the constraints placed upon the higher level abilities by the low-level filtering processes, then one can at least eliminate alternatives at the higher level that violate the logical principles of the low-level filtering process. Moreover, one can, with the aid of statistical descriptions of developmental endpoints, make good predictions about specific developmental outcomes when low-level filtering processes are accurately specified. This is not a true point prediction about developmental outcomes, but rather a prediction that places boundary conditions on what must occur, given knowledge about genetic constraints, experiential processes, and past developmental outcomes.

I realize that what I have just outlined is a view of development that is blatantly nativist, both in tone and mechanism. However, I am struck by the fact that many commonalities exist among different members of a species even in the face of highly variable environments. This intraspecies consistency implies a set of narrowly tuned constraints on development. Clearly, these constraints operate in a complex network of subtle experiential inputs that modulate the initial tendencies of neural structure and function. It may prove to be an utterly absurd model of developmental processes, but I think the notion of filtering, along with the assumptions I have made in the present model, offer a clear alternative to traditional views of development. Moreover, the properties of the filter can be inferred and submitted to empirical test, thereby confirming or refuting the specific model of development. The usefulness of the filtering metaphor in sensory development seems clear, but its applicability to cognitive development remains for others to judge.

ACKNOWLEDGMENTS

Preparation of this chapter was supported in part by a Research Career Development Award (HD-00309) from NICHHD and research grants from NSF (BNS 80-13075) and the March of Dimes Birth Defects Foundation (12-2). The helpful comments provided by Linda Smith are gratefully acknowledged.

REFERENCES

Aslin, R. N. Development of binocular fixation in human infants. *Journal of Experimental Child Psychology*, 1977, *23*, 133–150.

Aslin, R. N. Experiential influences and sensitive periods in perceptual development: A unified model. In R. N. Aslin, J. R. Alberts, & M. R. Petersen (Eds.), *Development of perception: Psychobiological perspectives* (Vol. II): *The visual system*. New York: Academic Press, 1981.

Aslin, R. N., & Jackson, R. W. Accommodative-convergence in young infants: Development of a synergistic sensory-motor system. *Canadian Journal of Psychology*, 1979, *33*, 222–231.

Aslin, R. N., & Pisoni, D. B. Some developmental processes in speech perception. In G. H. Yeni-Komshian, J. Kavanagh, & C. A. Ferguson (Eds.), *Child phonology* (Vol. 2): *Perception*. New York: Academic Press, 1980.

Baker, F. H., Grigg, P., & vonNoorden, G. K. Effects of visual deprivation on the response of neurons in the visual cortex of the monkey: Including studies on the striate and prestriate cortex in the normal animal. *Brain Research*, 1974, *66*, 185–208.

Banks, M. S. The development of visual accommodation during early infancy. *Child Development*, 1980, *51*, 646–666.

Banks, M. S., Aslin, R. N., & Letson, R. D. Sensitive period for the development of human binocular vision. *Science*, 1975, *190*, 675–677.

Barlow, H. B., Blakemore, C., & Pettigrew, J. D. The neural basis of binocular depth discrimination. *Journal of Physiology*, 1967, *193*, 327–342.

Berkley, M. Animal models of visual development: Behavioral evaluation of some physiological findings in cat visual development. In R. N. Aslin, J. R. Alberts, & M. R. Petersen (Eds.), *Development of perception: Psychobiological perspectives* (Vol. II): *The visual system*. New York: Academic Press, 1981.

Birch, E. E., Gwiazda, J., & Held, R. Stereoacuity development for crossed and uncrossed disparities in human infants. *Vision Research*, 1982, *22*, 507–514.

Blake, R., & Hirsch, H. V. B. Deficits in binocular depth perception in cats after alternating monocular deprivation. *Science*, 1975, *190*, 1114–1116.

Blakemore, C. The conditions required for the maintenance of binocularity in the kitten's visual cortex. *Journal of Physiology*, 1976, *261*, 423–444.

Blakemore, C., & Cooper, G. F. Development of the brain depends on the visual environment. *Nature*, 1970, *228*, 477–478.

Boothe, R. G. Development of spatial vision in infant macaque monkeys under conditions of normal and abnormal visual experience. In R. N. Aslin, J. R. Alberts, & M. R. Petersen (Eds.), *Development of perception: Psychobiological perspectives* (Vol. II): *The visual system*. New York: Academic Press, 1981.

Crawford, M. L. J., & vonNoorden, G. K. Optically induced concomitant strabismus in monkey. *Investigative Ophthalmology and Visual Science*, 1980, *19*, 1105–1109.

Dobson, V., Howland, H. C., Moss, C., & Banks, M. S. Photorefraction of normal and astigmatic infants during viewing of patterned stimuli. *Vision Research*, 1983, *23*, 1043–1052.

Dobson, V., & Teller, D. Y. Visual acuity in human infants: A review and comparison of behavioral and electrophysiological studies. *Vision Research*, 1978, *18*, 1469–1483.

Fischer, K. W. A theory of cognitive development: The control and construction of hierarchies of skills. *Psychological Review*, 1980, *87*, 477–531.

Fox, R., Aslin, R. N., Shea, S. L., & Dumais, S. T. Stereopsis in human infants. *Science*, 1980, *207*, 323–324.

Fregnac, Y., & Imbert, M. Early development of visual cortical cells in normal and dark-reared kittens: Relationship between orientation selectivity and ocular dominance. *Journal of Physiology*, 1978, *278*, 27–44.

Gordon, B., Presson, J., Packwood, J., & Scheer, R. Alteration of cortical orientation selectivity: Importance of asymmetric input. *Science*, 1979, *204*, 1109–1111.

Gottlieb, G. Conceptions of prenatal development: Behavioral embryology. *Psychological Review*, 1976, *83*, 215–234. (a)

Gottlieb, G. The roles of experience in the development of behavior and the nervous system. In G. Gottlieb (Ed.), *Neural and behavioral specificity*. New York: Academic Press, 1976. (b)

Gottlieb, G. Roles of early experience in species-specific perceptual development. In R. N. Aslin, J. R. Alberts, & M. R. Petersen (Eds.), *Development of perception: Psychobiological perspectives* (Vol.) I: *Audition, somatic perception and the chemical senses*. New York: Academic Press, 1981.

Gwiazda, J., Brill, S., Mohindra, I., & Held, R. Infant visual acuity and its meridional variation. *Vision Research*, 1978, *18*, 1557–1564.

Held, R., Birch, E., & Gwiazda, J. Stereoacuity of human infants. *Proceedings of the National Academy of Science, U.S.A.*, 1980, *77*, 5572–5574.

Hirsch, H. V. B., & Spinelli, D. N. Visual experience modifies distribution of horizontally and vertically oriented receptive fields in cats. *Science*, 1970, *168*, 869–871.

Hohmann, A., & Creutzfeldt, O. D. Squint and the development of binocularity in humans. *Nature*, 1975, *254*, 613–614.

Howland, H. C., Atkinson, J., Braddick, O., & French, J. Infant astigmatism measured by photorefraction. *Science*, 1978, *202*, 331–333.

Hubel, D. H., & Wiesel, T. N. Binocular interaction in striate cortex of kittens reared with artificial squint. *Journal of Neurophysiology*, 1965, *28*, 1041–1059.

Hubel, D. H., & Wiesel, T. N. The period of susceptibility to the physiological effects of unilateral eye closure in kittens. *Journal of Physiology*, 1970, *206*, 419–436.

Hubel, D. H., & Wiesel, T. N. Stereoscopic vision in macaque monkey. *Nature*, 1974, *225*, 41–42.

Jacobson, S. G., Mohindra, I., & Held, R. Age of onset of amblyopia in infants with esotropia. *Documenta Ophthalmologica*, 1981, *30*, 210–216.

Leehey, S. C., Moskowitz-Cook, A., Brill, S., & Held, R. Orientational anisotropy in infant vision. *Science*, 1975, *190*, 900–902.

Leventhal, A. G., & Hirsch, H. V. B. Cortical effect of early selective exposure to diagonal lines. *Science*, 1975, *190*, 902–904.

Mitchell, D. E. Sensitive periods in visual development. In R. N. Aslin, J. R. Alberts, & M. R. Petersen (Eds.), *Development of perception: Psychobiological perspectives* (Vol. II): *The visual system*. New York: Academic Press, 1981.

Mitchell, D. E., Freeman, R. D., Millodot, M., & Haegerstrom, G. Meridional amblyopia: Evidence for modification of the human visual system by early visual experience. *Vision Research*, 1973, *13*, 535–558.

Mohindra, I., Held, R., Gwiazda, J., & Brill, S. Astigmatism in infants. *Science*, 1978, *202*, 329–331.

Packwood, J., & Gordon, B. Stereopsis in normal domestic cat, Siamese cat, and cat raised with alternating monocular occlusion. *Journal of Neurophysiology*, 1975, *38*, 1485–1499.

Petrig, B., Julesz, B., Kropfl, W., Baumgartner, G., & Anliker, M. Development of stereopsis and cortical binocularity in human infants: Electrophysiological evidence. *Science*, 1981, *213*, 1402–1405.

Pettigrew, J. D. The effect of visual experience on the development of stimulus specificity by kitten cortical neurons. *Journal of Physiology*, 1974, *237*, 49–75.

Salapatek, P., & Banks, M. S. Infant sensory assessment: Vision. In F. D. Minifie & L. L. Lloyd (Eds.), *Communicative and cognitive abilities: Early behavioral assessment*. Baltimore: University Park Press, 1978.

Shea, S. L., & Aslin, R. N. *Stereopsis in strabismic and potentially strabismic children*. Paper presented at the biennial meeting of the International Conference on Infant Studies, Austin, Texas, March, 1982.

Shea, S. L., Fox, R., Aslin, R. N., & Dumais, S. T. Assessment of stereopsis in human infants. *Investigative Ophthalmology and Visual Science*, 1980, *19*, 1400–1404.

Sherk, H., & Stryker, M. P. Quantitative study of cortical orientation selectivity in visually inexperienced kittens. *Journal of Neurophysiology*, 1976, *39*, 63–70.

Shinkman, P. G., & Bruce, C. J. Binocular differences in cortical receptive fields of kittens after rotationally disparate binocular experience. *Science*, 1977, *197*, 285–287.

Shlaer, R. Shift in binocular disparity causes compensating change in the cortical structure of kittens. *Science*, 1971, *173*, 638–641.

Smith, D. Functional restoration of vision in the cat after long-term monocular deprivation. *Science*, 1981, *213*, 1137–1139.

Smith, E. L., Bennett, M. J., Harwerth, R. S., & Crawford, M. L. J. Binocularity in kittens reared with optically induced squint. *Science*, 1979, *204*, 875–877.

Stryker, M. P., Sherk, H., Leventhal, A. G., & Hirsch, H. V. B. Physiological consequences for the cat's visual cortex of effectively restricting visual experience with oriented contours. *Journal of Neurophysiology*, 1978, *41*, 896–909.

Teller, D. Y. Scotopic vision, color vision, and stereopsis in infants. *Current Eye Research*, 1982, *2*, 199–210.

Teller, D. Y., Morse, R., Borton, R., & Regal, D. Visual acuity for vertical and diagonal gratings in human infants. *Vision Research*, 1974, *14*, 1433–1439.

Teller, D. Y., Regal, D., Videen, T., & Pulos, E. Development of visual acuity in infant monkeys (*Macaca nemestrina*) during the early postnatal weeks. *Vision Research*, 1978, *18*, 561–566.

Van Sluyters, R. C., & Levitt, F. B. Experimental strabismus in the kitten. *Journal of Neurophysiology*, 1980, *43*, 686–699.

Yinon, U. Age dependence of the effect of squint on cells in kittens' visual cortex. *Experimental Brain Research*, 1976, *26*, 151–157.

10

Constraints on a Model of Infant Speech Perception

Peter D. Eimas
Brown University

In the past two decades, the experimental study of perception and cognitive functioning in the human infant has yielded a number of findings that have dramatically altered our conception of the earliest capabilities of human beings. We have begun to appreciate, for example, the highly developed nature of the infant's information-processing system and the extent to which this system provides an encoded, categorical representation of the environment. As a result of these and other findings, we have come to realize the extent to which our biology and, perhaps, our specific human biology have shaped these initial abilities and in so doing have made possible acquisition of our mature forms of cognitive and linguistic competence.

Although we are far from being able to write a comprehensive description of infant perception and cognition, it is, I believe, not premature to consider theoretical descriptions of the infant's information-processing systems. In the discussion that follows, I attempt to describe the requirements for one such processing system—that which underlies the perception of speech at what would correspond roughly to the phonetic level of language in adult listeners. In essence, what I attempt to describe are some of the necessary capabilities and operating characteristics of the system; speculations on the actual nature of the mechanisms and their manner of operation I leave for the future. It is my hope that by detailing the known requirements of the system and at least noting those aspects that remain open to question, progress toward the goal of a formal model of speech processing in the human infant will be possible.

In constructing a model for the perception of speech in prelinguistic infants, there are a number of sources of constraint on the nature and form of the model. First, as is true for all theoretical descriptions, the proposed system must be capable of explaining existing empirical findings, and as parsimoniously as possible. Second, a theoretical description of speech perception is constrained in terms of the nature of the processing mechanisms, in that these mechanisms must be acutely atuned to those critical acoustic characteristics resulting from the processes of speech production.[1] Thus, for example, at some point in the processing system it must be assumed that the means exist for detecting and timing such products of articulation as rapidly changing formant transitions, onset bursts, frication, and even silence. A third form of constraint is that which is imposed by the structure of language, and the fact that human languages are learned and indeed learned, at least in the early years of life, rapidly and effortlessly by virtually all members of a linguistic community. As a consequence of the latter, the perceptual system for processing speech, at least up to a level at which higher order linguistic rules can be extracted from the signal, must be highly developed before the end of the second year of life.

In the discussion to follow, I consider many of the empirical findings on infant speech perception that have begun to shape our assumptions regarding the capabilities of the infant's perceptual system for speech, capabilities, which interestingly appear to be strongly determined by our biological inheritance. In addition, consideration is given to some of the constraints imposed on the operating characteristics of this system by the processes of production and by the conditions of language acquisition.

THE CATEGORIZATION OF SPEECH

As in the visual world, where a particular pattern or object may be experienced in a myriad of sizes, orientations, locations, and motions, so too do we experience the segmental units of human languages in virtually an infinite variety of acoustic forms. Many of the acoustic characteristics of speech that signal vocalic and consonantal distinctions are dramatically altered by the age and sex of the speaker, the rate of speech, the surrounding phonetic environment, and the inherent variation in the processes of production. Despite this variation in the signal, of which we are often aware as our abilities to describe the speaker or rate of speech well evidence, we perceive the many instantiations of a segmental unit as being perceptually identical or constant. We have, in effect, the capability to form categories, such that under many circumstances the members of these categories are perceptually indistinguishable.

---

[1]The information for the perception of speech is not unique in being constrained by action, in this instance, the operation of the articulatory apparatus. As Gibson (1979) has contended, visual perception can only be understood in terms of information provided by an organism's environment that is determined to considerable degree by the action of the organism.

Of course, perceptual constancy must exist in all modalities. There is no other way in which human or nonhuman beings could adapt to an environment, which characteristically presents the members of natural categories in a range of variation that is virtually infinite. We must be capable of perceiving through this variation. If this were not true, then each and every encounter with some aspect of the environment would be a novel experience and would define a category onto itself. Such a state of affairs would seem to preclude survival, let alone development of abilities to acquire language and the extensive knowledge that is characteristic of human beings.

We do not as yet know how constancy is achieved in the domain of speech. It may be the case that there exists some as yet unspecified set of acoustic invariants in the signal that are readily detected by the mechanisms of perception, and that by definition provide the basis for perceptual identity. Discovery of this set of invariants has been the motivation and focus of a number of researchers, including most recently Searle, Jacobson, and Rayment (1979) and Stevens and Blumstein (1981). Of course, even if invariants were found, it would still be necessary to explain how listeners are able to ignore, even if only momentarily, other acoustic differences that are discriminable. Alternatively, the perceptual system may in some unknown manner transform the incoming signal such that the necessary isomorphism between antecedent events and the perceptual experience is achieved. The motor theories of speech perception are based on assumptions of this nature (Liberman, Cooper, Shankweiler, & Studdert-Kennedy, 1967; Stevens & House, 1972), as are some versions of feature detector theories of speech perception (Cooper, 1974; Eimas & Corbit, 1973).

Despite our ignorance about the means by which perceptual constancy is achieved within the domain of speech, a number of investigators have begun to examine the origin of this phenomenon in infants. This line of study should provide, at minimum, theoretically interesting information regarding the role of experience and the extent to which this achievement is a result of relatively lower level sensory mechanisms or higher level cognitive processing routines and inferences. Of course, it is not possible to investigate perceptual constancy per se in young infants; there is simply no means by which we can determine whether an infant perceives two different events as perceptually identical. What can be investigated, however, is whether infants can form equivalence classes so that the members of the natural categories of speech can be responded to as equivalent elements, despite discriminable differences along any of a number of nondefining acoustic features. This ability is obviously a necessary prerequisite for perceptual constancy, regardless of modality.

That infants by the age of 6 months are able to form equivalence classes or categories based on the segmental units of speech is well documented by the recent studies of Kuhl and her associates (Kuhl, 1980). In brief, she has shown that infants are able to treat as functionally equivalent the members of a number of vocalic and consonantal categories that are acoustically quite different as a result of variation in speaker, intonation, or phonetic context. Kuhl has also shown that these classes are probably not solely a result of the training procedures or of an inability to discriminate at least some of the acoustic variation.

There is a second line of evidence that strongly supports the contention that infants, even very young infants, are able to categorize the sounds of speech. This evidence comes from a series of investigations that are similar in principle to earlier studies that showed categorical perception, or very nearly this form of perception, in adult listeners (Liberman et al., 1967, and Pisoni, 1978, provide reviews of this literature).

It is well known that the production of a particular phonetic segment will vary in its defining acoustic characteristics within a single speaker from one moment to another, despite attempts to limit such variation (Lisker & Abramson, 1964, 1967; Miller & Baer, 1983; Peterson & Barney, 1952). For example, Lisker and Abramson (1964, 1967) have shown that the production of the three major categories of voicing in syllable-initial stop consonants is marked by considerable variation in voice onset time (VOT), a complex acoustic continuum that provides an adequate metric for defining the categories of voicing in many human languages. There is, in effect, a distribution of VOT values for each voicing category in a given language. However, in normal conversation we are not aware of this variation; each instance of a voicing category, all other factors being equal, is perceived as being identical to any other instance. Further and more rigorous evidence for this categorization process comes from studies in which listeners are asked to identify and discriminate computer-generated speech that varies systematically in VOT alone. Listeners typically assign members of the VOT continuum to the voicing categories of their language with great consistency, and of greater importance is the fact that the discriminability functions are discontinuous; that is to say, a given difference in VOT in much more discriminable when the stimuli are from different phonetic categories than when they are instances of the same category (Abramson & Lisker, 1970, 1973; Lisker & Abramson, 1970). The greater discriminability across categories as opposed to within categories is a major criterion for concluding that perception is categorical.[2]

---

[2]The categorical perception of speech is by no means absolute (Pisoni, 1978, for a review of this literature). Some aspects of the defining acoustic information for the categories of speech, that is, the within-category variations, can be discriminated, and to greater extents in some situations than others. That this is true does not invalidate the findings that there are other conditions under which speech is perceived in a nearly categorical manner, just as the fact that we perceive speaker differences does not undermine the fact that we can form equivalence classes based on the consonantal and vocalic categories of speech that extend across speakers. What it does indicate is that the phenomenon of categorical perception of speech is not simply a result of an inability to discriminate some, within-category acoustic differences.

This form of perception, as evidenced by discontinuous discriminability functions, is also characteristic of the perception of voice onset time by infants as young as 1 month of age, an age well before that when the linguistic significance of the sounds could have been recognized (Eimas, Siqueland, Jusczyk, & Vigorito, 1971; Lasky, Syrdal-Lasky, & Klein, 1975; Streeter, 1976). Moreover, infants divide the VOT continuum into three categories that presumably underlie the formation of the three major categories of voicing that are found in human languages, although all three categories frequently do not occur in a particular language. Discontinuous discriminability functions have also been found in studies of the infant's ability to process the acoustic information underlying adult phonetic distinctions based on place of articulation (Eimas, 1974) and manner of articulation (Eimas & Miller, 1980a,b), as well as for the distinction among the glides [r] and [l] (Eimas, 1975) and the vowels [i] and [I], provided the vowels are quite brief (Swoboda, Kass, Morse, & Leavitt, 1978).

Although these processing capabilities are impressive in that they can reasonably be assumed to provide the infant with rudimentary perceptual categories that will come to have linguistic significance during the acquisition of language, there is in fact more to the story of the categorization of speech by infants. It has been well established recently that not only does a single value along some complex acoustic continuum not signal a phonetic segment, but the range of values defining a phonetic category is likewise not invariant. Rather, the range of values changes with such contextual factors as rate of articulation (Miller & Baer, 1983; Miller & Liberman, 1979) and the phonetic environment (Miller, 1977). Furthermore, it is influenced by the fact that many, and perhaps most, phonetic distinctions are signaled by more than one form of acoustic information, and these multiple sources of information enter into trading relations. The value along one dimension determines the range of values along a second dimension that signal a particular phonetic segment and conversely (Best, Morrongiello, & Robson, 1981; Fitch, Halwes, Erickson, & Liberman, 1980; Repp, Liberman, Eccardt, & Pesetsky, 1978).

As an example of the influence of contextual factors on the categorization of speech, I consider the perception of the acoustic information for the manner distinction between the stop consonant [b] and the semivowel [w]. A sufficient source of information for this distinction is the duration of the formant transitions; shorter transitions tend to be perceived as [b], whereas longer transitions tend to be perceived as [w]. However, Miller and Liberman (1979) have shown that the phonetic boundary separating [b] from [w] is systematically altered by varying the duration of the vocalic portion of the syllables in which these consonants were the initial segments. Presumably, these changes in syllabic duration are a consequence of changes in rates of articulation (Miller, 1981a). With short syllables that are perceived as rapid speech, adult listeners require reliably shorter transitions before their percepts change from [b] to [w]. Consequently, the phonetic boundary shifts from high to low values of transition duration as syllabic duration varies from long to short, with the result that some values of transition duration signal both [b] and [w]. Obviously, the categorization of at least some transition durations cannot occur without information concerning syllabic duration, if perception is also to reflect the intentions of the speaker.

For those who wish ultimately to construct a model of infant speech perception, it is particularly notable that infants also use syllabic duration in the categorization of transition duration (Eimas & Miller, 1980a; Miller & Eimas, 1983). Moreover, the manner in which this contextual information is used is exactly the same as was found for adult listeners; the category boundary is situated at higher values of transition duration when the syllables are long in duration than when they are short.

With respect to the interaction among the several sources of information signaling a phonetic distinction, the perception of voicing information presents a classic instance. Voice onset time, as noted previously, is a complex acoustic continuum that has both temporal and spectral components, of which several, when appropriately varied, arc capable of signaling changes in voicing (Lisker, Liberman, Erickson, Dechovitz, & Mandler, 1977; Summerfield & Haggard, 1977). Two particularly relevant sources of information for voicing are the time per se between the release burst and the onset of periodicity or voicing in the signal and the frequency of the first-formant transition at the onset of periodicity in the signal. Moreover, these two sources of voicing information can enter into a trading relation. This trading relation is evidenced by a shift in the phonetic boundary value between voiced and voiceless stops, and in the locus of the peak in the discriminability function from lower values of VOT to higher values as the onset frequency of the first formant decreases (Lisker et al., 1977). Analogous effects have recently been obtained with 3- and 4-month-old infants (Miller & Eimas, 1983). The peak in the infants' discriminability function shifted from lower VOT values to higher VOT values as the frequency of the first formant at the onset of voicing decreased. Thus, infants, like adult listeners, use both spectral and temporal information in the formation of the perceptual categories that will later form the linguistic categories of voicing, and they do so in a manner that indicates a trading relation between these two sources of information.

The evidence for the existence of categorization procedures in very young infants is, I believe, well demonstrated by the results of studies on the perception of speech. Moreover, the procedures for categorization of speech in infants have many of the properties of the speech processing systems of mature listeners. These include the capacity to utilize contextual information as well as multiple sources of information for the same categorical designation in a compensatory manner. Our models of speech processing in the infant must reflect this level of sophistication, which is, on reflection, not entirely surprising, especially given the cognitive and linguistic competence that must be developed during the first years of life.

Certainly, if an infant had to learn the principles of categorization (i.e., that environmental events require categorization and the appropriate criteria for categorization) as a basis for acquiring future knowledge, the acquisition of this form of representation of the environment would be slow in the extreme, if at all possible. And surely, without categorical representations of the environment or some very close approximation of them, much of human knowledge would not be possible, including the lexicons of human languages. What would exist instead, if anything, is the material for science fiction.

Categorization procedures also serve the purpose of information reduction. As Liberman, Mattingly, and Turvey (1972) have noted, there is of the order of a thousand-fold reduction in the amount of information in bits when an analogic representation of the speech signal is transformed into a categorical, digital representation, such as that which is assumed to occur during phonetic encoding. Regardless of the exact nature of the encoded speech signal, it is apparent that without some form of categorical representation, the initial auditory storage system would be overwhelmed during language processing. As a consequence, the nature of human languages would be very different; at the very least, utterances would necessarily be brief and grammars simple. For only in this way would we be able to extract the intended meaning of the speaker, which comes not only from the meaning of individual morphemes but from their ruled-governed relations to one another. Given that the nature of language is as it is, the difficulty with an analogic representation of speech is likewise readily apparent when we consider the child's task of acquiring the rules of phonology, syntax, and semantics during late infancy. Certainly these rules, which often involve numerous constituents and thus relatively long durations of speech, cannot be acquired even by the most sophisticated of learning routines, if the critical information in the signal cannot be stored and easily made available to the processes of rule acquisition.

THE UNIT OF PROCESSING

Further constraints on a theoretical description of the perception of speech by young infants come from investigations that have provided information on the nature of the unit of processing. There are a number of quite different sources of data indicating that the infant's perceptual system for speech, like that of the more mature listener, has the capability of processing acoustic units that correspond approximately, in terms of structure and duration, to syllabic units. Indeed, this unit of processing, albeit relatively complex, may be more effectively processed than acoustic segments that are simpler in structure or shorter in duration. The first data we should consider are those previously discussed findings demonstrating that infants use the after-occurring information regarding syllabic duration in categorizing transition durations, information, which, it will be recalled, is sufficient to signal the [b] - [w] distinction (Eimas & Miller, 1980a; Miller & Eimas, 1983). This form of processing is obviously impossible if the units of processing were restricted in duration to brief acoustic segments, or if processing only occurred in a temporally determined, linear fashion. Rather, contextual effects of this nature require a processing system that operates on syllabic-like units, unconstrained by the temporal arrangement of the critical acoustic information within the processing unit.

As to the possibility that processing may be more effective with units that are syllabic in structure, there are the recent findings of Bertoncini and Mehler (1981). They showed that the infant's ability to discriminate a consonantal distinction was enhanced when the distinction was embedded in a linguistically permissible syllabic structure as opposed to when it was embedded in a nonpermissible structure, namely, a consonant-consonant-consonant structure. In addition, Eimas (1974, 1975) has shown that the information underlying such phonetic distinctions as [b] versus [d] and [r] versus [1] is not as well discriminated when presented in isolation as when it is presented in a context that is perceived as a coherent syllable by adult informants. And, in a more recent study (Eimas, unpublished experiment), it was found that the discriminability of the burst and formant transitions, which signaled the [b]-[d] distinction, was reliably poorer when this information was separated by only 200 msec from the vocalic portion of the syllable, than when it was smoothly integrated with the final redundant portion of the syllable. In fact, the level of discriminability was no better in the separation condition than in a third condition where the burst and formant transitions were presented in isolation.[3] It would appear on the basis of these data that the infant's perceptual system for speech is not only capable of processing syllabic-like units, but that it also operates more effectively with units of this nature.

An analysis of the processes of speech production also supports the contention that the unit of perceptual processing must be very close to the syllable in structure and duration. As Liberman (1970; Liberman et al., 1967, 1972) has noted, the fact that human languages seem to require that phonetic segments be transmitted at very rapid rates demands the coarticulation of segmental units. As a consequence, there is parallel transmission of information for successive segments, in addition to the more obvious parallel transmission of the necessary information for perception of individual segments. Recovery of this information by the listener would undoubtedly be inordinately difficult, unless there was a very close correspondence between the units of production and the units of processing. That

---

[3]The infant's ability to use redundant contextual information to enhance discriminability is not a unique property of speech perception. Recently, Bomba, Eimas, Siqueland, & Miller (in press) found that the discrimination of line segments was facilitated by the presence of a noninformative, that is, redundant, contextual frame.

the parallel transmission of information for successive segments appears to be largely, although not entirely, confined to syllabic units provides a reasonable rationale for assuming a processing unit that approximates the syllable. Of interest is the fact that we apparently do not have to learn the appropriate unit of processing, just as we do not have to learn the appropriate unit of production: This knowledge is inherent in the systems of production and perception.

OTHER CONSTRAINTS AND UNRESOLVED ISSUES

In summary, a theoretical description of infant speech perception must assume a processing system that operates on syllabic-like units and is capable of generating equivalence classes and categories. In other words, it must be capable of generating the initial categorization of the speech signal, categorizations that a number of investigators believe to be the forerunners of the phonetic categories of mature users of human languages. In addition, it must be assumed that the mechanisms of categorization are flexible enough to accommodate the pervasive effects of contextual information, as well as to utilize multiple sources of acoustic information for the same categorization in what is effectively a trading relation. But these are by no means the only constraints necessitated by the available data. First, Miller and Eimas (1979) recently found that 3- and 4-month-old infants recognized rearrangments of acoustic features to form new segmental units and rearrangements of segmental units to form new syllables. One inference from these data is that the perceived speech of infants is not an unorganized collection of features of segments but is rather an organized entity, reflecting the organization in the speech signal that is imposed by the processes of production. It is this organization in the speech signal that a model of infant speech perception must preserve. In addition, the mechanisms of categorization must be modifiable as a result of experience with the parental language. The need for malleability is readily apparent when one compares, for example, the categorization of the VOT continuum by infants and adults in different language communities. There is often a difference in the number of categories, and in some cases a difference in the location of the category boundaries (Lasky et al., 1975; Lisker & Abramson, 1964; cf. Eimas, 1975; Trehub, 1976; and see MacKain, 1980, for a discussion of the effects of linguistic experience on speech perception). Finally, provision must also be made for an amodal representation of speech information, if we are to accommodate the impressive body of literature attesting to the infant's capacity to integrate information from objects and events across more than one modality, including that of speech (Dodd, 1979; Spelke, 1979).

As I hope has been evident from this discussion, our knowledge of the perception of speech by infants is considerable, and whereas it obviously determines many aspects of a theory of infant speech perception, issues of critical importance to theory construction remain unresolved. One of the most important of these is the nature of the mechanisms of perception that provide the initial categorization of the speech signal. A recent approach to this problem has been to assume, not without evidence, the existence of feature or property detectors, analogous to those that had previously been assumed to underlie the perception of such diverse phenomena as visual patterns and the mating calls of frogs (see Eimas, 1982, and Eimas & Tartter, 1979, for reviews of this approach to a theory of speech perception). However, difficulties with this view, both empirical and logical have become evident (Diehl, 1981; Miller & Eimas, 1982; Remez, 1979), resulting in alternative descriptions of the processes of perception. For example, Diehl (1981) has advocated holistic, as opposed to analytic, processing systems. However, this type of model, as well as others similar in nature, has not been systematically developed. As a consequence, we do not know whether they are capable of accommodating the many phenomena of speech perception, especially those that appear to be strongly contradictory (Miller, 1981b). Interestingly, other discussions of speech perception have avoided the issue of mechanisms, taking instead, as the major issue, delineation of the information for perception (Studdert-Kennedy, 1981). Although there are quite diverse metatheoretical positions among those who search for the appropriate description of the speech signal, it is obvious that discovery of acoustic invariants will significantly constrain the theoretical endeavors of those who search for the mechanisms of perception.

In describing the mechanisms of speech perception, it is not only necessary to describe their nature and mode of operation, but it is also necessary to determine whether they form a part of a general auditory processing system, common perhaps to all mammals, or whether they constitute a separate, species-specific system that evolved for the primary purpose of processing speech. It should be noted that at issue here is not whether there are any species-specific processes involved in the comprehension of language, obviously there are, but rather at what level of processing do these mechanisms begin to determine our unique capacity to understand language. Those readers who are familiar with the speech literature know that this issue, or really subissue, has had a long history, marked by considerable polemics and an ever-shifting data base (cf. Eimas, 1982; Liberman, 1970, 1982; Pastore, 1981). Athough my own opinion is that the weight of evidence at this time favors the existence of species-specific mechanisms at the level of the initial categorization of the speech signal, the matter is far from resolved. In terms of theory construction, it will obviously be an easier task if it were to be shown that one need posit only a single, general set of auditory processors for the perception of speech, rather than a second, specialized processing system that must be interfaced at some level with the general auditory system.

Finally, we must come to know how the processes of speech perception are altered by increasing linguistic and cognitive competence during the first few years of life. Although we know that the phonetic categories of human languages are modified by the demands of the linguistic environment, we do not know the processes that are modified or the nature of this modification. Experience could alter or retune general auditory or specialized speech mechanisms or both. Or it could be that processes, more cognitive in nature, such as attention or perceptual biases, are altered during the course of language acquisition. Resolution of these issues and others will be difficult as will be formal attempts to construct comprehensive models of infant speech perception. Nevertheless, the task of theory development has a well-developed base: The evidence from over a decade of experimental effect on the perception of speech by infants and our knowledge of speech production as well as language acquisition will markedly constrain the final form of this endeavor.

ACKNOWLEDGMENTS

The preparation of this discussion and the author's cited research were supported by Grant HD 05331 from the National Institute of Child Health and Human Development.

REFERENCES

Abramson, A. S., & Lisker, L. Discriminability along the voicing continuum: Cross-language tests. In *Proceedings of the Sixth International Congress of Phonetic Sciences,* Prague, 1967. Prague: Academic, 1970.

Abramson, A. S., & Lisker, L. Voice-timing perception in Spanish word-initial stops. *Journal of Phonetics,* 1973, *1,* 1–8.

Bertoncini, J., & Mehler, J. Syllables as units in infant speech perception. *Infant Behavior & Development,* 1981, *1,* 247–260.

Best, C. T., Morrongiello, B., & Robson, R. Perceptual equivalence of acoustic cues in speech and nonspeech perception. *Perception & Psychophysics,* 1981, *29,* 191–211.

Bomba, P. C., Eimas, P. D., Siqueland, E. R., & Miller, J. L. Contextual effects in infant visual perception. *Perception,* in press.

Cooper, W. E. Contingent feature analysis in speech perception. *Perception & Psychophysics,* 1974, *16,* 201–204.

Diehl, R. L. Feature detectors for speech: A critical reappraisal. *Psychological Bulletin,* 1981, *89,* 1–18.

Dodd, B. Lip reading in infants: Attention to speech presented in- and out-of-synchrony. *Cognitive Psychology,* 1979, *11,* 478–484.

Eimas, P. D. Auditory and linguistic processing of cues for place of articulation by infants. *Perception & Psychophysics,* 1974, *16,* 513–521.

Eimas, P. D. Auditory and phonetic coding of the cues for speech: Discrimination of the [r-l] distinction by young infants. *Perception & Psychophysics,* 1975, *18,* 341–347.

Eimas, P. D. Speech perception: A view of the initial state and perceptual mechanisms. In J. Mehler, E. Walker, & M. Garrett (Eds.), *Perspectives in mental representation.* Hillsdale, N.J.: Lawrence Erlbaum Associates, 1982.

Eimas, P. D. Effects of noninformative vowel information on the discrimination of cues for place of articulation in infants. Unpublished study.

Eimas, P. D., & Corbit, J. D. Selective adaptation of linguistic feature detectors. *Cognitive Psychology*, 1973, *4*, 99–109.

Eimas, P. D., & Miller, J. L. Contextual effects in infant speech perception. *Science*, 1980, *209*, 1140–1141. (a)

Eimas, P. D., & Miller, J. L. Discrimination of the information for manner of articulation. *Infant Behavior & Development*, 1980, *3*, 367–375. (b)

Eimas, P. D., Siqueland, E. R., Jusczyk, P., & Vigorito, J. Speech perception in infants. *Science*, 1971, *171*, 303–306.

Eimas, P. D., & Tartter, V. C. On the development of speech perception: Mechanisms and analogies. In H. W. Reese & L. P. Lipsitt (Eds.), *Advances in child development and behavior* (Vol. 13). New York: Academic Press, 1979.

Fitch, H. L., Halwes, T., Erickson, D. M., & Liberman, A. M. Perceptual equivalence of two acoustic cues for stop-consonant manner. *Perception & Psychophysics*, 1980, *27*, (4), 343–350.

Gibson, J. J. *The ecological approach to visual perception*. Boston: Houghton Mifflin, 1979.

Kuhl, P. K. Perceptual constancy for speech-sound categories in early infancy. In G. H. Yeni-Komshian, J. F. Kavanagh, & C. A. Ferguson (Eds.), *Child phonology* (Vol. 2): *Perception*. New York: Academic Press, 1980.

Lasky, R. E., Syrdal-Lasky, A., & Klein, R. E. VOT discrimination by 4-to-6½-month-old infants from Spanish environment. *Journal of Experimental Child Psychology*, 1975, *20*, 215–225.

Liberman, A. M. The grammars of speech and language. *Cognitive Psychology*, 1970, *1*, 301–323.

Liberman, A. M. On finding that speech is special. *American Psychologist*, 1982, *37*, 148–167.

Liberman, A. M., Cooper, F. S., Shankweiler, D. S., & Studdert-Kennedy, M. Perception of the speech code. *Psychological Review*, 1967, *74*, 431–461.

Liberman, A. M., Mattingly, I. G., & Turvey, M. T. Language codes and memory codes. In A. W. Melton & E. Martin (Eds.), *Coding processes in human memory*. Washington, D.C.: H. V. Winston, 1972.

Lisker, L., & Abramson, A. S. A cross-language study of voicing in initial stops: Acoustical measurements. *Word*, 1964, *20*, 384–422.

Lisker, L., & Abramson, A. S. Some effects of context on voice onset time in English stops. *Language and Speech*, 1967, *10*, 1–28.

Lisker, L., & Abramson, A. S. The voicing dimension: Some experiments in comparative phonetics. In *Proceedings of the Sixth International Congress of Phonetic Sciences*, Prague, 1967. Prague: Academic, 1970, pp. 563–567.

Lisker, L., Liberman, A. M., Erickson, D. M., Dechovitz, D., & Mandler, R. On pushing the voice-onset-time (VOT) boundary about. *Language and Speech*, 1977, *20*, 209–216.

MacKain, K. S. *On assessing the role of experience on infants' speech discrimination*. Unpublished manuscript. 1980.

Miller, J. L. Nonindependence of feature processing in initial consonants. *Journal of Speech and Hearing Research*, 1977, *20*, 519–528.

Miller, J. L. The effects of speaking rate on segmental distinctions. In P. D. Eimas & J. L. Miller (Eds.), *Perspectives on the study of speech*. Hillsdale, N.J.: Lawrence Erlbaum Associates, 1981. (a)

Miller, J. L. Phonetic perception: Evidence for context-dependent and context-independent processing. *Journal of the Acoustical Society of America*, 1981, *69*, 822–831. (b)

Miller, J. L., & Baer, T. Some effects of speaking rate on the production of /b/ and /w/. *Journal of the Acoustical Society of America*, 1983, *73*, 1751–1755.

Miller, J. L., & Eimas, P. D. Organization in infant speech perception. *Canadian Journal of Psychology*, 1979, *33*, 353–365.

Miller, J. L., & Eimas, P. D. Feature detectors and speech perception: A critical evaluation. In D. G. Albrecht (Ed.), *Recognition of pattern and form*. Berlin: Springer-Verlag, 1982.

Miller, J. L., & Eimas, P. D. Studies on the categorization of speech by infants. *Cognition*, 1983, *13*, 135–165.

Miller, J. L., & Liberman, A. M. Some effects of later-occurring information on the perception of stop consonant and semivowel. *Perception & Psychophysics*, 1979, *25*, 457–465.

Pastore, R. E. Possible psychoacoustic factors in speech. In P. D. Eimas and J. L. Miller (Eds.), *Perspectives on the study of speech*. Hillsdale, N.J.: Lawrence Erlbaum Associates, 1981.

Peterson, G. E., & Barney, H. L. Control methods used in the study of the vowels. *Journal of the Acoustical Society of America*, 1952, *24*, 175–184.

Pisoni, D. B. Speech perception. In W. K. Estes (Eds.), *Handbook of learning and cognitive processes* (Vol. 6). Hillsdale, N.J.: Lawrence Erlbaum Associates, 1978.

Remez, R. E. Adaptation of the category boundary between speech and nonspeech: A case against feature detectors. *Cognitive Psychology*, 1979, *11*, 38–57.

Repp, B. H., Liberman, A. M., Eccardt, T., & Pesetsky, D. Perceptual integration of acoustic cues for stop, fricative, and affricate manner. *Journal of Experimental Psychology: Human Perception and Performance*, 1978, *4*, 621–637.

Searle, C. L., Jacobson, J. Z., & Rayment, S. G. Stop consonant discrimination based on human audition. *Journal of the Acoustical Society of America*, 1979, *65*, 799–809.

Spelke, E. S. Perceiving bimodally specified events in infancy. *Developmental Psychology*, 1979, *15*, 626–636.

Stevens, K. N., & Blumstein, S. E. The search for invariant acoustic correlates of phonetic features. In P. D. Eimas & J. L. Miller (Eds.), *Perspectives on the study of speech*. Hillsdale, N.J.: Lawrence Erlbaum Associates, 1981.

Stevens, K. N., & House, A. S. Speech perception. In J. Tobias (Ed.), *Foundations of modern auditory theory* (Vol. 2). New York: Academic Press, 1972.

Streeter, L. A. Language perception of 2-month-old infants shows effects of both innate mechanisms and experience. *Nature*, 1976, *259*, 38–41.

Studdert-Kennedy, M. *Are utterances prepared and perceived in parts? Perhaps.* Paper presented at the First International Conference on Event Perception, Storrs, Connecticut, June 1981.

Summerfield, Q., & Haggard, M. On the dissociation of spectral and temporal cues to the voicing distinction in initial stop consonants. *Journal of the Acoustical Society of America*, 1977, *62*, 435–448.

Swoboda, P. J., Kass, J., Morse, P. A., & Leavitt, L. A. Memory factors in vowel discrimination of normal and at-risk infants. *Child Development*, 1978, *48*, 332–339.

Trehub, S. E. The discrimination of foreign speech contrasts by infants and adults. *Child Development*, 1976, *47*, 466–472.

11

On Characterizing the Development of Speech Perception

Peter W. Jusczyk
University of Oregon and
Centre National de la Recherche Scientifique
Paris, France

Speech perception has occupied a rather curious place within the field of psycholinguistics. Although no one explicitly denies its importance, speech perception often appears to be treated as a fringe area of the field. In the past there have been very few attempts to integrate findings in speech perception with those in other areas of psycholinguistics or vice versa. There are a number of possible reasons for this state of affairs. One factor may be the unique vocabulary used by investigators studying speech perception to describe their subject matter. Another factor is the background of the investigators themselves a diverse group drawn from fields such as electrical engineering, physiology, and acoustics, as well as linguistics and psychology. Still another factor may be the rather unusual experimental paradigms that workers in speech perception have had to employ in their investigations. Whatever the reasons, there have been few attempts until quite recently to integrate information about speech perception into psycholinguistic models.

With respect to developmental issues, the situation has been much the same. When the first findings from infant speech-perception studies were reported (Eimas, Siqueland, Jusczyk, & Vigorito, 1971), they were greeted with much excitement. Many developmental psycholinguists saw these findings as an indication of the existence of innate linguistic processing mechanisms. Yet, there was little effort to integrate the findings from these studies into the larger body of work on language acquisition. Again, there are a number of reasons for this situation, not the least of which is the fact that only a limited amount of information was available concerning the infant's speech perception capacities.

Today, the place of speech perception within psycholinguistics appears to be changing. As researchers grapple with the problems of developing devices to understand spoken language, they are being forced to try to integrate speech perception with the rest of psycholinguistics (Klatt, 1979; Marslen-Wilson & Tyler, 1980). Advances in technology have also made it possible for workers in speech perception to employ longer, more complex, and more natural strings of stimuli (Cole & Jakimik, 1980; Remez, Rubin, Pisoni, & Carrell, 1981). There is a heightened awareness on the part of researchers on the need to understand speech perception in more natural settings. Furthermore, in the developmental area there now exists a rather substantial body of information concerning the infant's discriminative capacities for speech. The body of knowledge that exists concerning the infant's initial state makes it possible to undertake studies of the way in which speech perception affects and is affected by the acquisition of a particular language.

In what follows, I review what we know about the basic speech-perception capacities of infants, the similarities and differences between these capacities and those of adults, factors that might influence the development of speech perception, and a possible model for the development of speech perception.

INFANT SPEECH-PERCEPTION CAPACITIES

Perhaps, the most important finding of the early studies of infant speech perception was Eimas et al.'s (1971) demonstration of the existence of categorical discrimination of VOT information. This result indicated not only that infants were capable of discriminating between certain speech sounds, but that their ability to do so was similar in a very important respect to that of adults. Prior to this time, investigators had invoked explanations based on acquired distinctiveness and learned equivalence of cues to account for the fact that adults were sensitive to subtle acoustic differences between members of different phonetic categories, but relatively insensitive to differences of the same magnitude occurring within a particular phonetic category (Liberman, Harris, Kinney, & Lane, 1961). The basic argument here was that through extensive practice in producing and perceiving speech, listeners would, in time, learn to treat variants of a particular phonetic segment as being the same and as different from variants of other phonetic segments. A key factor in this process was extensive practice in always assigning the same label to the variants of a particular phonetic segment; this presumably contributed to the difficulty that adults had in distinguishing one variant from another on standard speech discrimination tests such as ABX. However, the Eimas et al. results indicated that such categorical effects were present in the responses of infants who had not been subjected to a long period of discriminative training. Hence, many researchers began to view categorical perception as a consequence of the way in which the human perceptual system is structured right from birth (Eimas & Corbit, 1973). Moreover, because at the time categorical perception was thought to occur only for speech sounds, these findings were taken to be an indication of an innate linguistic capacity (Cutting & Eimas, 1975; Eimas et al., 1971).

Although the implications of the Eimas et al. (1971) results for the existence of speech-perception capacities in infants were widely recognized, some of the developmental implications appear to have been overlooked at the time. Previous work by Lisker and Abramson (1964, 1970) had demonstrated that both cross-language similarities *and differences* exist in the location of the VOT boundary (see Fig. 11.1). Hence, even if infants across all cultures could be assumed to have an innate predisposition toward categorical discrimination of VOT, then experience in a particular language-learning environment could be expected to exert some influence on the location of adult VOT boundaries.

On almost any account it would be expected that, if infants are innately endowed for categorically discriminating VOT differences, at some point shortly after birth infants from different language environments should display similar category boundaries (i.e., that the initial category boundaries should be language neutral). Otherwise, the claim for innate mechanisms would be equivalent to saying that some infants are endowed to learn English, others Swahili, others Thai, etc. Hence, it was important to determine whether infants from other language environments also displayed categorical discrimination for VOT in a manner similar to the infants tested by Eimas et al. Two studies with infants from non-English-speaking cultures supported the notion of an innate basis for VOT discrimination. Lasky, Syrdal-Lasky, and Klein (1975) found that infants from a Spanish-speaking environment showed sensitivity in the same region of the VOT continuum as did Eimas et al.'s subjects, despite the fact that the VOT boundary for adult speakers in the same environment differed considerably from that of English speakers. Likewise, Streeter (1976) found that the discrimination performance for infants from a Kikuyu-speaking culture corresponded well to that of infants in Eimas et al.'s study. Thus, the results of these studies served to establish the generality of Eimas et al.'s findings with respect to VOT differences between voiced and voiceless segments.

The generality of Eimas et al.'s claims concerning innate capacities for detecting VOT differences are also subject to test in another direction. English makes use of only one of two possible voicing contrasts, namely the one between voiced segments like /b/ and voiceless segments like /p/. However, other languages also employ a contrast between prevoiced and voiced segments. Given that such contrasts exist in other languages, one might expect that any innate predisposition toward categorical discrimination in the voiced/voiceless region of the VOT continuum would also extend to the prevoiced/voiced region. Eimas (1975b) examined the sensitivity of infants from English-speaking environments to contrasts from the prevoiced/voiced region. He found only weak evidence of discrimination and no conclusive evidence for categorical discrimination. More recently, Aslin, Pisoni, Hennessy, and Perey (1981) have employed a more sensitive measure and found some indication of categorical discrimination of the

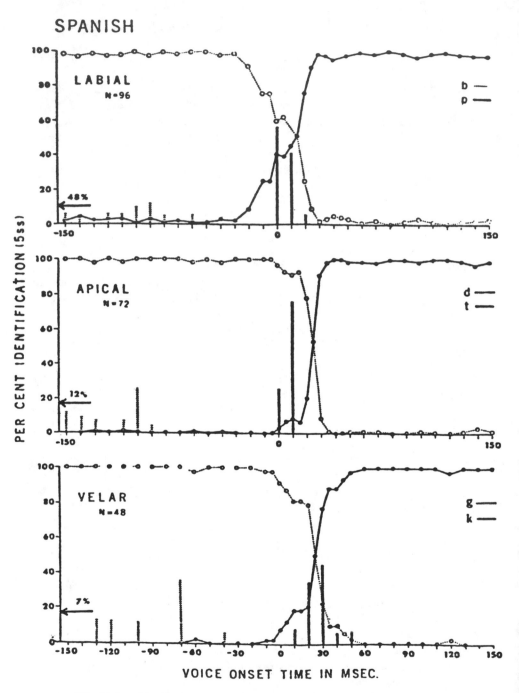

FIG. 11.1.   Identification curves displayed as functions of VOT values for Spanish (1a), English (1b), and Thai (1c) speakers for stop consonant contrasts. The vertical bars show the frequency distributions of VOT values measured in speech from each language.

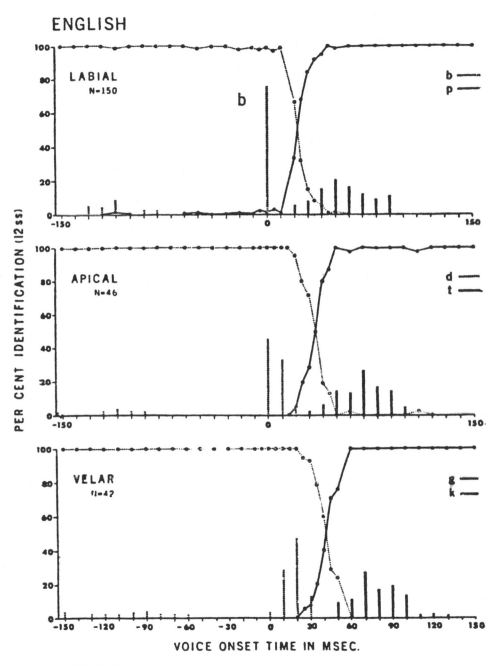

FIG. 11.1b.

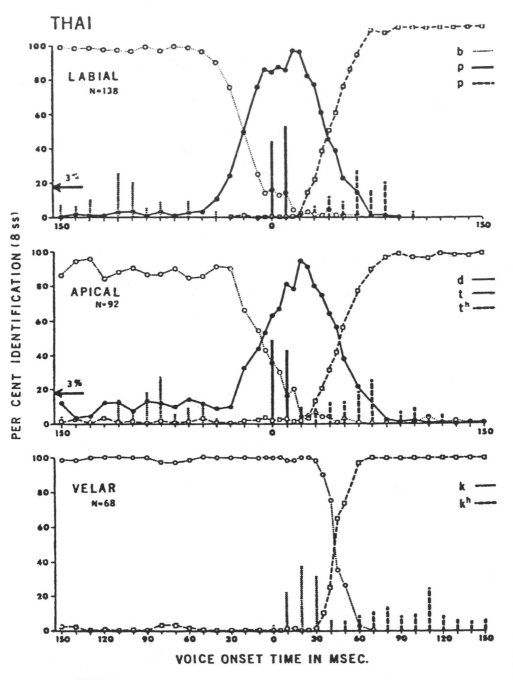

FIG. 11.1c.

prevoiced/voiced contrast. Thus, it would appear that any necessary mechanisms required for discriminating prevoiced/voiced contrasts are also in place soon after birth.

The VOT studies indicated that infants possess some underlying capacities for discriminating speech sounds. However, many questions were raised by these studies that could only be answered by extending the domain of inquiry to other kinds of speech contrasts. In particular, it was important to determine whether the infant would show a similar capacity for discriminating speech sounds differing on some other basis besides voicing. Thus, it is logically possible that, although infants might come biologically prepared to perceive some kinds of phonetic contrasts, they might have to learn how to perceive others.

A number of studies were undertaken to determine the variety of contrasts that infants are capable of perceiving. By and large, these studies indicate that infants are capable of discriminating virtually every type of phonetic contrast that they have been tested on (for a complete review, see Aslin, Pisoni, & Jusczyk, 1983; Jusczyk, 1981). For example, there is evidence that infants are sensitive to place of articulation differences between stops (Eimas, 1974; Miller, Morse, & Dorman, 1977; Moffit, 1971; Morse, 1972; Till, 1976), fricatives (Holmberg, Morgan, & Kuhl, 1977; Jusczyk, Murray, & Bayly, 1979), glides (Jusczyk, Copan, & Thompson, 1978), and nasals (Eimas & Miller, 1977). Similarly, infants have been shown to discriminate manner of articulation contrasts such as those between stops and nasals (Eimas & Miller, 1980b), stops and glides (Eimas & Miller, 1980a; Hillenbrand, Minifie & Edwards, 1979), liquids (Eimas, 1975a), and nasalized and nonnasalized vowels (Trehub, 1976). Also, infants are able to discriminate a variety of vowel contrasts including [I]-[ɪ] (Swoboda, Kass, Morse, & Leavitt, 1978, Swoboda, Morse, & Leavitt, 1976), [a]-[i] (Kuhl, 1979; Trehub, 1973), [a]-[ɔ] (Kuhl, 1977), and [i]-[u] (Trehub, 1973). Therefore, it is quite apparent that the underlying capacities that infants possess for discriminating speech sounds extend well beyond those required for the detection of voicing contrasts.

In addition to tracking the variety of contrasts that infants are capable of discriminating, a number of researchers have investigated the way in which various contextual factors affect the infant's discriminative capacities. One approach has been to look at the effect of varying the location of the phonetic contrast in an utterance. The early studies in the field had all employed contrasts between the initial segments of single syllables. Hence, there was no way of determining from these investigations if infants processed information beyond the initial segment. Jusczyk (1977) attacked this problem in a study in which he looked at the infant's ability to detect a [d]-[g] contrast occurring in either the initial or final segment of CVC syllables. His results indicated that infants are capable of processing phonetic differences beyond the initial segments of syllables (see also Williams & Bush, 1978). Moreover, there was no evidence that the syllable-final contrasts were any less discriminable for infants than syllable-initial ones. Interestingly, this latter result contrasts with findings observed for studies of phonemic perception in infants 1 year of age and older (Garnica, 1973; Shvachkin, 1973). Possible reasons for this discrepancy are considered later.

Additional studies have explored the infant's discrimination of phonetic contrasts in multisyllabic utterances. Again it was found that infants have the capacity to detect contrasts between segments occurring in other than the utterance-initial position (Jusczyk, Copan, & Thompson, 1978; Jusczyk & Thompson, 1978; Trehub, 1976b; Williams, 1977a). Another aspect of these studies with multisyllabic tokens was that it was possible to examine how discrimination was affected by the presence of information regarding syllable stress. To date, there is no indication that unstressed syllables are any less discriminable for infants than are stressed syllables (Jusczyk et al., 1978; Jusczyk & Thompson, 1978; Williams, 1977a).

Equally important as the ability to discriminate phonetic contrasts, regardless of their position in an utterance, is the ability to recognize the same phonetic segment when spoken by different speakers or with a different inflection. The acoustic characteristics of speech sounds vary greatly from speaker to speaker, yet the adult listener is able to ignore such differences in recognizing the identity of a given word. Kuhl and her coworkers have looked at the infant's capacity to ignore irrelevant differences in speaker's voice and intonation patterns in making phonetic discrimination. They first trained infants to discriminate between single tokens of two different syllables spoken by the same speaker. Then, in successive phases of the experiment they introduced new tokens of the syllables spoken by different speakers and with varying intonation contours. The infant was deemed to have achieved some degree of perceptual constancy for the phonetic segments being tested, if he or she could successfully maintain the discrimination between the two types of segments in the face of irrelevant changes, introduced by adding new tokens varying the intonation pattern and speaker's voice. Kuhl found evidence that 6-month-old infants are able to ignore changes in intonation patterns and speakers voices for both vowel (Kuhl, 1977, 1979) and fricative (Holmberg, Morgan, & Kuhl, 1977) segments.

To summarize to this point, infant speech-perception studies have revealed a number of things regarding the infant's perceptual capacities. First, categorical discrimination along certain phonetic continua is present for infants as well as adults. Second, the infant is able to successfully discriminate a wide variety of contrasts within the first 2 or 3 months of life. Third, little or no experience appears to be required for making phonetic distinctions, because the infant is able to discriminate contrasts that are not present in the native language-learning environment. Fourth, the infant is able to process information about phonetic segments in noninitial positions of utterances. Fifth, the infant is sensitive to phonetic contrasts occuring in unstressed as well as stressed syllables. Sixth, the infant displays some capacity for perceptual constancy in that he or she is able to ignore differences in speaker's voices and intonation contours in making phonetic discriminations. Therefore, the infant possesses many of the capacities required for analyzing the acoustic stream of speech into the phonetic segments employed in the native language that he or she will be trying to acquire. To be sure, other skills are also necessary. For example, little is known about the infant's ability to segment the stream of speech into discrete words. And, undoubtedly there are many other factors—cognitive, semantic, syntactic, pragmatic, and the like—that play a critical role in recovering the linguistic message from the stream of speech. However, from the point of view of speech perception, the infant appears to be well endowed with many of the most important perceptual capacities.

DOES THE INFANT HAVE PHONETIC CAPACITIES?

The preceding question can be read in two different ways. On the one hand, one can treat it as a question about the infant's ability to discriminate between various phonetic segments. In this case, the answer is most certainly yes. On the other hand, the question can be interpreted as asking whether the capacities that the infant has are exclusively devoted to speech processing. When read in this way, there is considerable disagreement about the answer. As noted earlier, when Eimas et al. (1971) conducted their study, they concluded that the infant was endowed with mechanisms specialized for processing language. However, this claim was based on an assumption, now known to be false, that categorical perception occurs only with speech sounds. Since that time, there have been numerous demonstrations of categorical perception with nonspeech stimuli (Miller, Wier, Pastore, Kelly,& Dooling, 1976; Pastore, Ahroon, Buffuto, Friedman, Puleo, & Fink, 1977; Pisoni, 1977). Moreover, there have also been indications that categorical perception for speech dimensions can be found in nonhuman species such as the chinchilla (Kuhl & Miller, 1975, 1978). Hence, the mere demonstration that infants exhibit categorical discrimination for speech would not appear to provide sufficient grounds for claiming specialized speech-perception capacities exist in infants.

Nevertheless, there are other grounds on which one might base a case in favor of the existence of specialized speech processing mechanisms. A reasonable way to support a claim for specialized speech mechanisms would be to demonstrate that infants process speech sounds differently than they do nonspeech sounds. Some evidence in favor of such a speech-nonspeech processing difference was reported in studies conducted by Eimas (1974, 1975a) and Till (1976). Eimas used nonspeech patterns called "chirps," which were truncated versions of the speech syllables that he employed. Specifically, the chirps consisted of only the second (Eimas, 1974) or third (Eimas, 1975a) formant transition portion of the speech syllables. These formant transitions, which serve to distinguish the different speech syllables, do not sound like speech sounds when heard in isolation. Instead, listeners often reported that these stimuli sound like something a bird might produce, hence the name "chirps." Because the only source of acoustic variation that occurred between the speech syllable pairs were differences in the second or third formant transitions, Eimas reasoned that the chirps served as appropriate nonspeech controls. In particular, he argued that infants had to discriminate the same acoustic differences in the speech and nonspeech test pairs. The results of his investigations indicated that infants processed the chirps and speech syllables differently. Discrimination performance for the speech contrasts tended to be categorical in that between-category contrasts (e.g., [ba] versus [da] were discriminated, but within-category contrasts (e.g., [ba$_1$] versus [ba$_2$] were not. By comparison, discrimination of the nonspeech contrasts was continuous with no differences in performance evident for between-category and within-category contrasts. Till (1976) found similar results in his study that employed a different set of nonspeech controls.[1]

The results of these studies involving speech-nonspeech comparisons would appear to provide two grounds for contending that infants possess specialized speech-processing mechanisms. First, categorical discrimination was obtained only with speech contrasts. Second, the same acoustic information was apparently processed differently in speech and nonspeech contexts. However, subsequent research has undercut both of these grounds. First, it had been demonstrated that categorical discrimination does occur with certain nonspeech contrasts (Jusczyk, Pisoni, Walley, & Murray, 1980).[2] Hence, for the infant as well as the adult, categorical discrimination is not limited to speech. Second, the assumption that the same acoustic information is available in both the chirps and speech syllables has also been challenged (Jusczyk, Smith, & Murphy, 1981; Pisoni, 1976). In particular, Jusczyk et al. have suggested that the omission of first formant transition information from chirp stimuli deprives the listener of a context against which to evaluate differences in second or third formant transition differences. Jusczyk et al. found marked differences in the way in which adults

---

[1]Specifically, Till inverted the first formant to produce his nonspeech stimuli from a speech-syllable pair. The effect of this manipulation is to change the context in which the second and third formants are heard. Consequently, his study is subject to the same criticism as the Eimas studies (see text).

[2]Previously, a demonstration of the infant's categorical discrimination of nonspeech contrasts was thought to exist in the study by Jusczyk, Rosner, Cutting, Foard, & Smith (1977). However, a recent investigation by Rosen & Howell (1981) has shown that there was an artifact in the stimuli generated for the original Cutting and Rosner (1974) study. Ruefully, all the other studies of the perception of the original sinewave stimuli, including our own, have been tarred by the same brush. Hence, pending a replication of the infant work with correctly generated stimuli, we will have to withhold judgment as to whether the infant's discrimination of rise times in sinewave stimuli is categorical.

processed chirp stimuli with and without accompanying first formant information. Hence, it cannot be assumed that infants are processing the same acoustic differences in the syllable and chirp stimuli, especially if the acoustic analysis is conducted not on the individual formants, but on the relationship between the formants. Therefore, the speech-nonspeech comparisons to date offer no strong grounds for assuming the existence of specialized speech-processing mechanisms in infants. On the contrary, the similarities observed between earlier speech studies and the nonspeech studies of Jusczyk et al. (1980) argue in favor of a common explanation for speech and nonspeech processing by infants.

Another possible candidate for basing a claim for specialized speech-processing mechanisms is the finding of perceptual constancy across differences in speakers' voices. In particular, it might be argued that the only commonality that exists in tokens of the same syllable uttered by different speakers is phonetic rather than acoustic. Though it is true that studies such as that of Peterson and Barney (1952) indicate that there is a great deal of acoustic variation in tokens produced by different speakers, it is also the case that nonhuman mammalian species such as the dog (Baru, 1975) and the chinchilla (Burdick & Miller, 1975) are apparently capable of adjusting to variations in speaker's voice and intonation contour. Hence, the mechanisms that extract constancies of this sort appear to be generally available in the mammalian auditory system, suggesting a basis in some measure of overall acoustic similarity rather than an analysis into speech-related component dimensions.

Recently, another type of finding has been offered as evidence of specialized speech processing by infants. Eimas and Miller (1980) found that the infant's discrimination of formant transition duration differences used to signal a contrast between [ba] and [wa] depended on contextual information in the form of syllable duration, even though the information for syllable duration came well after the transition information. The argument that the infants' behavior in this setting is indicative of specialized speech-processing mechanisms rests on certain assumptions drawn from a study with adults by Miller and Liberman (1979). In their study, Miller and Liberman observed a similar effect of syllable duration on the locus of the perceptual boundary between [ba] and [wa]. Whereas the [ba]-[wa] formant transition duration boundary for syllables with overall durations of 80 msec was 32 msec, it was 47 msec for syllables with durations of 296 msec. In other words, the adult listener appears to compensate for the overall duration of the utterance in the course of deciding what phonetic segment is spoken. However, the compensation is not based solely on duration, rather the specific nature of the information contained in the longer duration utterance plays a critical role. Miller and Liberman observed that increasing the duration of the steady-state portion of a vowel, as might happen when speaking rate slows down, had the effect of shifting the perceptual boundary toward longer transition duration values. On the other hand, an equivalent increase in syllable duration produced by adding a final stop consonant to the vowel (which would tend not to slow down speaking rate) actually produced shifts in the transition duration boundary toward shorter values. Thus, *it was not just the syllable duration but the nature of the syllable structure that determined the location of the perceptual boundary.* For this reason, Miller and Liberman argued that the phonetic boundary location was dependent on estimates of speaking rate. Eimas and Miller (1980) employed similar logic in arguing for phonetic processing effects in their study. However, unlike the Miller and Liberman (1979) study they were not able to assess the consequences of substituting an additional consonant in place of an increased vowel duration for their long-duration syllables. Hence, there is no way of knowing whether, for infants as well as adults, the effect was dependent on the nature of the syllable structure rather than overall duration. More importantly, Carrell, Pisoni, and Gans (1980) have demonstrated that effects similar to those observed by Miller and Liberman can be obtained with nonspeech stimuli, including the different directions of boundary shifts induced by adding either steady-state or transition-type information. In addition, Jusczyk, Pisoni, Reed, Fernald, and Myers (1983) found that infants discriminate rapid spectrum changes in nonspeech sounds in a manner analogous to that observed by Eimas and Miller (1980) with speech sounds. That is, the infants' perceptual boundary shifted with changes in the overall duration of the stimuli. Therefore, it appears that the type of compensation observed by Miller and Liberman is a general feature of human auditory processing rather than a specific response to a change of speaking rate.

In summary, an examination of the possible grounds for attributing the infant with specialized speech-processing mechanisms reveals very little support for the notion. Instead, it appears that the existing body of data from studies of infant speech perception can be explained in terms of general processes and mechanisms of the human auditory system.

EVIDENCE FOR A SPEECH MODE IN ADULTS

One of the oldest arguments in the field concerns the existence or nonexistence of a special mode of perception for speech. Having dismissed the claims for the existence of specialized speech-processing mechanisms in infants, it might seem as though a similar dismissal of a specialized speech mode is also in order. However, there currently exists a substantial body of evidence from research with adults that is very difficult to account for without assuming that speech sounds undergo some form of specialized processing. In particular, there are a number of studies that demonstrate that the same sounds can be processed in quite different ways depending on the listener's set to hear them as speech or nonspeech signals.

One experimental paradigm that has been employed in studies of speech and nonspeech processing involves the dichotic presentation of different portions of a speech syllable simultaneously (Liberman, Isenberg, & Rakerd, 1981; Rand, 1974). For example, the third formant transition may be played to one ear, while the remaining portion of the syllable is played simultaneously to the other ear. Under such testing conditions subjects report hearing the acoustic signal as both speech and nonspeech simultaneously. The so-called "duplex perception" is one of hearing both a speech syllable and a chirp. Thus, the information on the third formant transition contributes to the perception of the whole syllable as well as standing alone as a chirp. Liberman et al. (1981) showed the listeners were able to make independent judgments about the speech and nonspeech qualities of the stimuli. For example, varying the intensity of the third formant transition affected only judgments about the perceived loudness of the chirp, and not the overall syllable. The implication is that the third formant transition undergoes two modes of processing simultaneously, and that one of these modes is used in the perception of speech.

Further evidence for the view that speech sounds undergo special processing comes from studies that have employed ambiguous stimuli (Bailey, Summerfield, & Dorman, 1977; Best, Morrongiello, & Robson, 1980). Bailey et al. created a set of nonspeech stimuli by replacing the formant structure of synthetic speech syllables with frequency- and amplitude-modulated sinewaves. Of most interest was their finding that perceptual boundary shifts occurred when subjects were instructed to hear the stimuli as speech rather than nonspeech sounds. Unfortunately, Bailey et al.'s results are clouded by the fact that in a second experiment there was little evidence of a difference in the performance of subjects who heard the sounds as nonspeech. However, a more recent investigation by Best et al. (1980) upholds Bailey et al.'s original finding of differences under speech and nonspeech expectations. More specifically, Best et al, observed a trading relation between two cues—the onset value of the first formant and the duration of a silent closure interval following an initial fricative sound—only when subjects perceived the sinewaves as speech. The trading relation with the sinewaves mirrors the one that occurs with speech sounds, where less silence is needed to change "say" to "stay," when the first formant has a low onset than when it has a high onset. No subjects who interpreted the sinewaves as nonspeech stimuli gave any evidence of employing a trading relation between the first formant onset value and silent closure interval. Thus, the trading relation emerged only under conditions in which subjects analyzed the sinewaves as speech. This finding suggests that subjects are employing different criteria in evaluating speech and nonspeech signals.

To the extent that listeners do weight the information available in the acoustic signal differently when they are set to interpret it as speech, it becomes sensible to refer to a special mode of perception for speech. The studies involving duplex perception and ambiguous sinewave stimuli are suggestive of such specialized processing. There are at least two possible ways by which specialized processing of speech might come about. First, the speech signal might be processed by some specialized perceptual mechanisms (i.e., undergo some form of special sensory coding). Second, no special perceptual mechanisms may be involved; instead, the special processing may take the form of certain strategies used when treating the acoustic signal as a linguistic message (phonological categorization). At the present time, the data from the infant and animal studies would seem to favor the second sort of explanation for the existence of a special speech mode of perception.

A MODEL FOR THE DEVELOPMENT OF SPEECH PERCEPTION

It makes sense that the kinds of speech perception capacities included in the infant's innate endowment should be broad enough to permit the acquisition of the phonological structure of any human language. Given that languages do differ markedly in their phonological structure, one might expect that the analysis of the speech signal provided by the infant's capacities would constitute only an initial approximation to the phonological categories observed in adult language. The initial categorization imposed by the infant's analysis of speech would then have to be fine tuned to coincide with the phonological structure of the native language being acquired.

At the present time the precise nature of the infant's categorization of speech is unknown. The existing data on infant speech perception have been derived from discrimination studies and thus provide only indirect clues as to the way in which the infant categorizes. For example, it is possible (although improbable) that infants might put into a single category, and hence treat as equivalent, a large number of stimuli that they are able to discriminate according to current testing procedures.[3] Thus, until a suitable method can be developed that allows the infant to label stimuli judged to be the same with one response and members of an alternative stimulus class with another response, the true nature of the categories can only be speculated on.

There are certain findings in the literature that suggest that the infant's initial partitioning of speech sounds is based on well-defined psychophysical properties. First, categorical discrimination occurs for nonspeech sounds as well as for speech (Jusczyk, Pisoni, Walley, & Murray, 1980). Second, there are strong parallels between human and nonhuman species in the processing of certain speech sounds (Baru, 1975; Kuhl & Miller 1975, 1978). These results suggest

---

[3]Such a result would sharply contrast to the findings for adult speech perception, where the match between peaks in discriminability tends to match closely the category boundaries. But, this is precisely the point. Present methods do not tell us whether the match between discrimination and categorization is a close one right from the beginning or not.

that a partitioning of speech sounds according to certain psychophysical properties would also be consistent with the finding that infants from different language backgrounds exhibit similarities in the way in which they discriminate contrasts along phonetic continua, as suggested by the work of Aslin et al. (in press), Eimas et al. (1971), Lasky et al. (1975), and Streeter (1976).

The claim here is that infants are perceiving speech in terms of psychophysical properties rather than phonetic ones.[4] However, in the course of acquiring language it is clear that infants from different language environments begin to process the acoustic information contained in the speech signal differently. This is evidenced by the fact that adults from different language backgrounds often differ in where they locate major perceptual boundaries along phonetic continua (Lisker & Abramson, 1970; Williams, 1977b). Hence, at some point in the course of language acquisition, the basis for the infant's classification of speech sounds shifts from a psychophysical one to a phonological one. The same acoustic information is available to the infant as before, only now the infant has begun to process that information differently. One possible impetus for this change in processing is the infant's desire to communicate. More specifically, the operation of trying to assign a meaning to a given set of utterance tokens encourages the child to attend in a new way to similarities and differences that exist in the acoustic attributes of these tokens. The child must be able to focus on those acoustic variations that result in a change in the meaning of an utterance. Feedback with regard to the meaning of the utterances that he or she produces or perceives enables the child to pinpoint those properties of the acoustic signal that play a critical role in the language being learned. In other words, the child has an important check on the consequences that different acoustic characteristics have for conveying a particular message. Just what acoustic properties are the

---

[4]Having stated my bias, let me say that I remain open to the possibility that special speech-processing mechanisms do exist in the infant. However, the evidence to date has not convinced me of the existence of such mechanisms. In regard to this issue, it is worth considering something that is sometimes overlooked in these discussions (viz., just what are the characteristics of the speech signal that could serve to identify it as speech for the infant?). In other words, just what aspects of the speech signal serve to engage the speech processers? Whereas in the past much attention has been given to looking for possible processing differences for speech and nonspeech sounds, little if any attention has been given to the question of just what distinguishes speech from nonspeech signals. This issue is a critical one that cannot be sidestepped simply by claiming that the child picks up information in the environment that indicates an articulatory source for the signal. If there really are specialized mechanisms, then they must be triggered by something in the signal. If we knew what the boundary conditions are for speech processing, then perhaps we could manipulate them in such a way as to demonstrate whether infants process acoustic signals any differently when such conditions do or do not obtain. Recent work by Remez et al. (1981) shows just how impoverished a signal can be and still be processed as speech. One possible dimension to look for cues differentiating speech and nonspeech signals is the structure of prosodic information in the signal. It is possible that there are characteristic patterns that are present for speech but not for nonspeech signals.

most critical is presumably closely tied to phonological constraints of the particular language. Thus, as the child begins to acquire the phonological structure of the language, he or she begins to weight various aspects of the acoustic information present in the speech signal according to their salience in marking distinctive contrasts in the language.[5] Therefore, the shift from a psychophysical classification of speech to a phonological one takes the form of assigning a new set of weightings to different aspects of the acoustic information in the speech signal. The child now begins to treat speech sounds differently than nonspeech sounds.

By this view, the speech mode of perception develops as a consequence of trying to attach linguistic meaning to speech. The speech mode is not the result of a set of specialized innate perceptual mechanisms; rather, it is an interpretive schema for weighting the acoustic information gained via general auditory-processing mechanisms. In other words, the difference between speech and nonspeech modes of perception lies solely in the weightings assigned to various aspects of the acoustic signal. A similar view of the differences between speech and nonspeech processing has been expressed by Oden and Massaro (1978).

Identifying the speech mode with an interpretive schema rather than with specialized perceptual mechanisms makes it possible to account for the fact that in adults there is evidence for important processes operating at both the auditory and cognitive levels. For example, evidence from studies of selective adaptation with speech indicates that these effects appear to be directly tied to acoustic rather than phonological properties of the stimuli (Diehl, 1981; Sawusch, 1977; Sawusch & Jusczyk, 1981; Simon & Studdert-Kennedy, 1978). On the other hand, response-contrast effects such as those observed by Diehl, Elman, & McCusker (1978) appear to reside at a higher cognitive level—one at which phonological labels are assigned (Sawusch & Jusczyk, 1981). Hence, Sawusch and Jusczyk took advantage of a mismatch in the acoustical and phonological structure of English to pit cues at these levels against one another in a selective adaptation experiment. In English, stop consonants following the fricative /s/ are considered to be voiceless (i.e., /p/, /t/, or /k/). This is reflected in the orthography that represents these clusters as "sp," "st," and "sk." However, an examination of the acoustic characteristics of the stops in these clusters shows them to be much more similar to voiced than voiceless stops (Klatt, 1975). This sets up a very interesting situation for adaptation. If adaptation follows the linguistic labeling of the stimuli, then adaptation with a cluster like /spa/ should have an effect similar to that with a voiceless consonant like /pa/ (i.e., the phonetic boundary should shift toward the voiceless end of a /ba/-/pa/ continuum).

---

[5]It is likely that when one learns a second language exactly the same sort of thing probably happens (i.e., one develops a set of weightings appropriate for the phonological structure of the language).

On the other hand, if adaptation follows the acoustic characteristics of the stimuli, the shift in the boundary should occur in the opposite direction toward the voiced end (i.e., toward /ba/). In fact, Sawusch and Jusczyk found the latter result (the boundary shifted in accordance with the acoustic characteristics of the stop toward "ba.") This illustrates the auditory component in speech perception, but what about the cognitive component? Sawusch and Jusczyk conducted a second experiment utilizing a paradigm that was more likely to involve a cognitive component (response contrast). The essential idea here is that when a stimulus that normally considered to be ambiguous between two phonetic segments (i.e., one from the boundary region) is paired with a strong exemplar of either of these segments, it will be perceived as belonging to the opposing category. Thus, in their second experiment then, Sawusch and Jusczyk presented listeners with ambiguous tokens from a /ba/-/pa/ continuum and paired these sounds in an identification task with various other sounds including tokens of /spa/. The subjects' task was simply to identify the tokens that they heard. This time the results showed that the stop segment in /spa/ behaved like a /p/, in that the ambiguous tokens paired with it tended to be labeled as "ba." Hence, here is a nice example of the way in which a higher order phonological label can interact in perception. The fact that selective adaptation and response contrast effects can have opposite consequences, as Sawusch and Jusczyk found, indicates the existence of two distinct components— one consistent with psychophysical characteristics of the stimuli and the other with their phonological characteristics.

Similarly, the notion that the speech mode is an interpretive schema fits well with findings that show that some speech perception effects seem to be manipulable by changing the subject's cognitive set about the stimuli. A case in point is offered by the studies that employed ambiguous sinewave stimuli (Bailey et al., 1977; Best et al., 1980). The finding that subjects show different perceptual boundaries for the same stimuli under speech and nonspeech instruction sets is consistent with the view that different schemes for weighting the information are employed in each situation. Moreover, there is even evidence that subjects' interpretation of one speech cue can be influenced by their expectations about another cue. Carden, Levitt, Jusczyk, & Walley (1981) demonstrated that instructions regarding the manner of articulation of a syllable (i.e., whether it contained a stop or a fricative) affected their classification with respect to place of articulation (i.e., whether it was considered to be labial or dental).

Finally, the notion that an interpretive mode for speech perception develops is also consistent with some findings regarding the effects of linguistic experience on speech perception. As noted earlier, there are a variety of studies that demonstrate that young infants are capable of perceiving foreign language contrasts (Lasky et al., Streeter, 1976; Trehub, 1976a; Werker, Gilbert, Humphrey, & Tees, 1981). By the same token there are a number of studies that appear to indicate that adult speakers may lose their ability to discriminate certain foreign language contrasts (Lisker & Abramson, 1970; Miyawaki, Strange, Verbrugge,

Liberman, Jenkins, & Fujimura, 1975; Strange & Jenkins, 1978; Trehub, 1976a; Werker et al., 1981). One possible explanation for this decline in ability is that certain perceptual mechanisms atrophy as a result of nonuse in the native language environment. However, any notion that permanent damage to any underlying mechanisms occur as a result of nonuse is countered by the finding that relatively short periods of training can greatly improve the discrimination performance of nonnative listeners (Pisoni, Aslin, Perey, & Hennessy, 1982; Werker et al., 1981). In fact, the latter results suggest that poor performance on the part of nonnative listeners may be an attentional deficit brought about by many years of practice in learning to ignore or deemphasize aspects of the acoustic signal not pertinent to the phonological constraints of the listener's native language. That the poor performance of a nonnative listener is rooted in an attentional deficit rather than a sensory one follows directly from a model that equates the speech mode with an interpretive schema.

HOW THE MODEL MIGHT WORK: A FIRST PASS

As it stands, the description in the previous section provides only the barest outline of a model of the development of speech perception. Many details need to be supplied before one can arrive at a model that makes testable predictions. In this section, I want to make some preliminary steps in that direction. Although what I am about to present seems plausible to me now, I am well aware of the fact that there are probably a number of assumptions being made here that will be shown subsequently to be false. My main objective is to present a framework that I hope at least gets us started in the right direction.

   The first issue to be considered is what form might the basic units for infant speech perception take. There seems to be some agreement in the field of infant speech perception at present that the stretch of information that the infant deals with is apt to be something on the order of duration as a syllable (Aslin, Pisoni, & Jusczyk, 1983; Bertoncini & Mehler, 1981; Eimas, this volume; Jusczyk, 1982). Assuming that infants do conduct their analysis on units of this size, one can ask what the nature of the information is that they represent. One possibility is that the infant analyzes the syllable-sized unit into a series of running spectra in a manner similar to the one proposed by Klatt (1980) for his speech recognition device.[6] The spectral representations that Klatt's analysis produces are based on a number of psychophysical considerations, including such things

---

[6]I should preface my remarks here by noting that though I have chosen to try to fit the data into Klatt's framework, there are a number of alternative acoustic analyses that are similar in character to his that might do just as well or perhaps even better (Kewley-Port, 1983; Searle, Jacobson, & Rayment, 1979).

as the temporal resolution of the auditory system, the dynamic range of the critical information in speech sounds, the intelligibility of different portions of the spectrum, and auditory masking (for further details see Klatt, 1980). For a given unit of analysis, a short-term spectrum would be computed every 10 msec. A display of just what such a spectral analysis might look like, and its relation to a traditional speech spectrogram is shown in Figure 11.2. For Klatt the basic unit is the diphone, which is defined as "a transition from the middle of one phone to the midpoint of the next." However, he emphasizes that the size of the unit is not central to the model and that larger units such as triphones (Wickelgren, 1969, 1976), demisyllables (Fujimura & Lovins, 1978), or syllables (Studdert-Kennedy, 1976) might do equally as well.

Klatt's model is presented as a means of accounting for speech perception in adults; hence, he offers only a few suggestions for the way in which such a process may develop. However, before putting forth our own proposals in this regard, it is worth considering the way in which the model accounts for speech perception in the adult listener. I present here only a brief description (for further details the reader should consult Klatt, 1980). Essentially, the adult listener has at his or her disposal a dictionary of all the lawful two-phone sequences that can occur in the listener's native language. Associated with each entry is a series of prototypical spectral representations that characterize the two-phone sequence at various intervals of time. Speech identification occurs by conducting a spectral analysis on the incoming signal and finding the best match between the pattern of incoming spectra and an entry in the dictionary. Because some of the entries, such as those that include the same phone, may share similar spectral representations for some intervals, the goal is to find the path through the network that best represents the observed input spectra.[7,8]

Consider now how a system like the one described might be developed. Initially, the infant would be seen as conducting an analysis of speech sounds into a series of running spectra. Psychophysical considerations would specify the dimensions according to which any two speech sounds might be compared.

---

[7]Naturally, certain adjustments would have to be made for differences in speakers' voices and other factors that affect the characteristics of the speechwave, but all models of speech recognition face similar difficulties.

[8]Lest the reader panic and think that either Klatt or I am proposing a model that dictates that all speech recognition takes place by recovering a phoneme by phoneme, I must hasten to add that I am only dealing with that portion of the model that does permit the recovery of phonemes. In fact, the full model assumes that most speech recognition does not take place phone-by-phone, but rather as word-by-word, or in the case of highly familiar sequences even phrase-by-phrase. The model is able to capture this aspect of speech processing by representing whole words as spectral sequences and, thereby, by passing any stage of directly computing a phonemic representation on the way to on-line word recognition. However, by also including a means of phonemic representation, as outlined previously in the text, the model is also able to deal with situations that arise when one hears an unfamiliar word or a nonword.

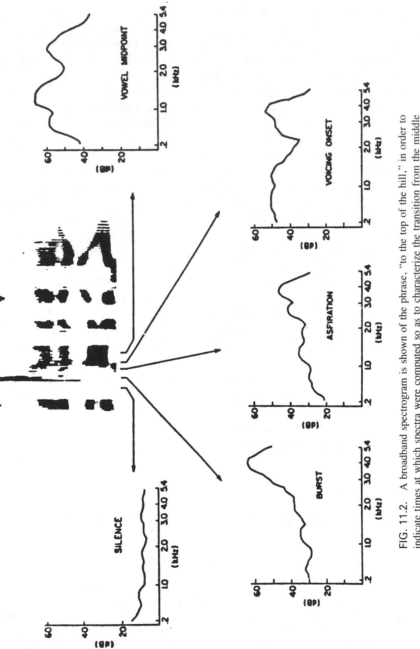

FIG. 11.2.   A broadband spectrogram is shown of the phrase, "to the top of the hill," in order to indicate times at which spectra were computed so as to characterize the transition from the middle of closure for [t] to the middle of the vowel [a] in the SCRIBER phonetic decoding network.

Constraints of this sort on the comparison process that reflect the original weightings of the acoustic cues are necessary to reflect the fact that categorical discrimination occurs for infants. Subsequently, as the infant begins to acquire meaningful lexical items in the language being learned, the process of building up a set of prototypical spectral representations commences. It is at this time that the child begins to weight the information available in the acoustic waveform so as to reflect characteristics of the phonological structure of the language being acquired. In essence, then, the achievement of an appropriate set of weightings arises in conjunction with developing a set of prototypical spectral representations to be used in word recognition. At first it is likely that the child develops prototypical spectral representations to recognize highly salient words. Thus, during the early stages there may be no connection between individual words. Later, as the number of words in the child's vocabulary increases so as to become unwieldy to conduct an exhaustive search, a reorganization into a network would take place. One expects that the network would be organized so that words having similar onset characteristics (i.e., in their spectral representations) would occupy positions relatively close to one another. An example of what a portion of such a network might look like is shown in Fig. 11.3. The advantage that such a system has is that it would be consonant with data concerning phonemic confusions (Miller & Nicely, 1955), but also it would be useful in explaining the ability that the mature listener has for breaking down words into component phones. Because words sharing common initial segments would be located relatively close to one another because of their acoustic onset characteristics, the possible set from which to draw prototypical characteristics in providing a representation to serve in recognizing an individual phoneme would be naturally narrowed.[9] When the process of extracting component phonemes from words begins is difficult to say. It seems doubtful whether this type of process is one that the infant readily engages in. There is little evidence that the infant recognizes a commonality between utterances sharing initial stop consonant segments. (For further discussion of this point see Aslin et al., 1983). Moreover, studies involving the ability to consciously access phonological identities across different words suggest that this process may not be complete until after one learns how to read (Liberman, Shankweiler, Fisher, & Carter, 1974; Morais, Cary, Alegria, & Bertelson, 1979; Walley, Smith, & Jusczyk, 1980). Whether the child might engage in some other form of phonemic analysis before this time is difficult to say. However, it is noteworthy that in a recent paper on the acquisition of phonology, Menyuk and Menn (1979) reviewed data from production and perception and suggested that the initial phonological distinctions made by the child

---

[9]This is not to say that the child might not make some mistakes in defining what the appropriate set is from which to abstract the necessary characteristics. But notice that one would predict that the kinds of mistakes made would involve phonemes having very similar acoustic properties.

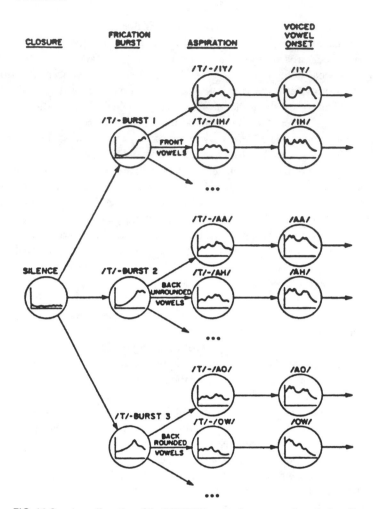

FIG. 11.3.   A small portion of the SCRIBER spectral-sequence phonetic decoding network is shown to illustrate the defining characteristics of prestressed prevocalic [t]. Each state of the network (circle) is characterized by a spectral template (dB versus frequency, as shown inside the circle). Not shown are durational constraints in the form of a feedback path to each state, indicating the expected number of input 10-msec spectra that can be associated with each state during recognition.

may involve gestalts the size of a whole word. Subsequent distinctions would be made on the basis of syllable-sized units, and only later would the child begin to engage in anything like an analysis into phonetic segments. Recently, Bever (in press) has expressed a similar view that the child may not begin by processing the smallest possible units either at the phonological or syntactic levels. Certainly, the whole notion that the child may not begin with the smallest possible units seems to be becoming quite prevalent in discussions of language acquisition. One finds versions of this view in the work of Rosch and Mervis (1981) concerning the existence of basic level categories, in the aforementioned work on the acquisition of phonology by Menyuk and Menn (1979), and in Bowerman's (1983) statements on the possibility that the child tends to deal on a case to case basis with certain syntactic constructions, before extracting more generally applicable syntactic rules.

The next issue that I want to consider is that of determining the weighting factors. I have argued that the phonological structure of the language influences the weighting of the acoustic information in the speech signal. How might this work? Consider the voicing dimension. Voicing differences are used to describe a variety of contrasts across different languages. In fact, however, there is good reason to believe that distinctly different cues may be involved in some languages. English is a case in point. Although the general tendency is to theorize about English stops being voiced and voiceless, these terms are in some sense misapplied to the language. As Ladefoged (1971) has pointed out, the real contrast in English seems to be between aspirated and unaspirated stops.[10] On the other hand, a language like Spanish could be more properly said to have a voiced-voiceless distinction. The point here is that the different languages are often using very different cues to signal a contrast between different labial stops. In other words, the two languages are selecting for different aspects of the acoustic signal. Accordingly, one might expect there to be some consequences for perception as a result of this; and there is. The phonemic boundary is in a different place for the two languages (Williams, 1977b). More important for the present purpose is a finding by Marlys Macken (1980) regarding speech production. She compared the early productions of stops by children acquiring either Spanish or English. There are two aspects of her results that are pertinent to the issues raised here. First, she found that in production, the English learners seemed to make the appropriate VOT distinctions sooner. On closer inspection she noticed that the Spanish children were contrasting the segments, but on the basis of a stop-spirant feature instead of VOT. Interestingly enough, a check of adult speech showed that in conversation adults substituted the stop-spirant feature for VOT between 30–40% of the time in the utterance initial position. A second indication that the distribution of tokens in the child's language-learning environment can have an important impact on the course of phonological development is illustrated

---

[10]This is because, given the location of the VOT boundary in English at around 25 msec., there is a sizable number of voiced stops such as /b/ in which the release from closure occurs before voicing begins. Moreover, for voiceless stops like /p/ stops in the syllable-initial position in English, there tends to be a large amount of aspiration present. By contrast, in Spanish the VOT boundary is very close to 0 msec (Williams, 1977b), so that virtually all voiced stops have some period of voicing before the release from closure. Furthermore, voiceless stops in Spanish are not heavily aspirated.

by the fact that there was a difference in the order in which the children in the different environments learned the contrasts for different places of articulation. Specifically, the Spanish children were much more prone to learn the contrast in the labial position first, whereas the English-learning children showed no order differences. Coincidentally, Spanish has many more voicing contrasts for labials than it does for other places of articulation, whereas for English the proportion of voicing contrasts appears to be about the same across the various places of articulation. Now, although these data are from production and, therefore, present some problems with respect to inferring the exact nature of the underlying representation, they certainly are suggestive of a way in which the phonological structure could influence the representation of phonetic segments. It would be very interesting to know just what the perceptual categories of the children looked like during the same period.

This leads to still another important question—just what are the salient dimensions that go into the representation that the child uses as a basis for acquiring the phonological structure of the language? And, what relationship does this *working representation* bear to the child's underlying perceptual capacities? A major problem faced by all current theories of phonological development is being able to adequately describe the underlying representations that reflect the child's knowledge of the phonological structure of the language. It is obvious why the child's knowledge of the phonological structure may exceed what he or she produces overtly. Not the least of the reasons is the fact that the child may have great difficulty in the execution of various types of articulatory gestures. Researchers in child phonology have long been aware of this problem and have sought ways of surmounting it. Thus, they have looked for evidence of systematic patterns in the words that the child produces, or as Menn (1980) has done, avoids producing.

The problem of specifying the nature of the child's working representation is a critical one for understanding phonological development, in that the kinds of phonological rules proposed to characterize the child's knowledge all rest on some assumptions as to what it is (Ingram, 1974, 1976; Menn, 1980; Stampe, 1969). The natural tendency would be to assume that the working representation is equivalent to the child's perceptual capacity. But, this assumption would be erroneous on several counts. First of all, as Locke (1979) has also noted, just because the child can discriminate a particular contrast on some comparison test does not mean that he will do so in all contexts. Second, as Garnica (1973) has pointed out, the task for the child mastering a phonemic contrast is considerably more complex than the kinds of tasks used to assess the infant's ability to distinguish between two phonetic segments. In particular, the correct mastery of a particular phoneme involves encoding it in such a way so as to simultaneously distinguish it from other possible phonemes in the language, so as to be able not only to discriminate it when contrasted with others, but also to recognize it when it occurs. Indeed, studies of phonemic perception (Garnica, 1973; Shvachkin,

1973) suggest that the 1-year-old child is often unable to make many phonemic distinctions that appear to be well within the limits of the perceptual capacities of the average 2-month-old. The point is that much work needs to be done before we are in a position to identify the nature of child's working representation. But, it is likely that it takes the child a considerable amount of time before his or her skills in the phonemic realm—perceiving speech as language—match his or her underlying perceptual capacities. Building up a dictionary of inter-related prototypical spectral representations is apt to be a long and arduous process. However, the beauty of such a system is that it is, in Klatt's (1980) words, "precompiled knowledge." Once the system is in place, on-line processing can take place automatically without the need to access rules directly a step at a time.

The final point to be made concerns the relation of the present model to theories of phonological development. In its present state any attempt to link the present model with any one model of phonological development would not be very meaningful; however, a few points are worth nothing. It might appear that the most likely partner for the present model is some form of natural phonology. After all, I have proposed that the phonological system develops from basic psychophysical capacities. Nevertheless, although I am positing some of the origins of phonological development in the infant's speech perception capacities, I also recognize that many other factors enter into the final state of the phonological knowledge attained. Some of these factors may be purely linguistic constraints on just what kinds of interactions between rules or segments are permitted in a language. Although there may have been a very close tie between psychophysical dimensions and phonological structures early on in the evolution of language, the fact is that languages have changed for many reasons, and these changes have probably destroyed any semblance of direct correspondence between these two levels. In fact, the cross-language differences in phonemic boundaries suggest as much. Furthermore, as Stephen Anderson (1981) has pointed out, there is evidence that some sound changes that have occurred in the evolution of particular languages have actually had the effect of separating a rule from its original phonetic explanation. Similar claims have been made by Hellberg (1978) and by Bach and Harms (1972). In some cases it is possible to trace a series of changes that led to the existence of some current phonological rule that is considerably removed from any direct phonetic correspondence. However, as logical as such an explanation might be to explain the historical changes in a language, it does not alter the fact that the child must master the phonological structure that exists in the language today. And, as Anderson (1981) has noted, in a number of cases there seems to be no evidence for language learners acquiring the phonological structures in question by recapitulating the historical changes. The point here is that one must take care not to extrapolate from a few cases in which there might be a direct correspondence between some psychophysical dimension and some phonological structure to the generalization that all phonological structures have the same origins.

The account that I have offered here is admittedly a preliminary one. There are many issues of considerable importance that I have not dealt with that will have to be tackled by any successful model of the development of speech perception. In the future the model will have to address such issues as the relationship between perception and production. Also, greater consideration will have to be given to the roles that the child's developing syntactic, semantic, and pragmatic knowledge plays in the development of speech perception. Another important domain to be explored is the way in which the child's sensitivity to prosodic information affects the course of speech-perception development. The latter sort of information is apt to be an important factor in accounting for another critical detail of successful speech perception—the child's ability to segment the speech stream into distinct units. We still know little about how the child is able to accomplish this task, although there are some interesting suggestions by Mehler (1981) and in the work of Demany (in press), that something like auditory streaming may be involved.

CONCLUSION

Previous work on speech perception with infants and adults has provided an indication of the nature of the initial and final states in speech perception. Knowledge of what these states are makes it possible to formulate models and testable hypotheses about the developmental course of speech perception. In the present chapter, I have presented a preliminary model regarding the way in which speech perception may develop. The focus of research efforts over the next few days will be to test this and other models of this sort about the way in which speech perception develops and the role that it plays in language acquisition.

ACKNOWLEDGMENTS

This chapter was prepared while the author was receiving support from N.I.C.H.H.D. (#1 RO1 HD15795-01) and from C.N.R.S. In addition, I would like to acknowledge the helpful comments by Dick Aslin and Jacques Mehler on previous versions of the manuscript.

REFERENCES

Anderson, S. Why phonology is not natural. *Linguistic Inquiry,* 1981, *12,* 493–539.
Aslin, R. N., Perey, A. J., Hennesy, B., & Pisoni, D. B. *Perceptual analysis of speech sounds by prelinguistic infants: A first report.* Paper presented at the 94th meeting of the Acoustical Society of America, Miami Beach, Florida, 1977.
Aslin, R. N., Pisoni, D. B., Hennessy, B. L., & Perey, A. J. Discrimination of voice-onset-time

by human infants: New findings concerning phonetic development. *Child Development,* 1981, *52,* 1135–1145.

Aslin, R. N., Pisoni, D. B., & Jusczyk, P. W. Auditory development and speech perception in infancy. In M. Haith & J. Campos, (Eds.), *Handbook of child psychology: Infant development.* New York: Wiley, 1983.

Bach, E. T., & Harms, R. T. How do languages get crazy rules? In Stockwell & Macawley (Eds.), *Linguistic change and generative theory.* Bloomington: Indiana University Press, 1972.

Bailey, P. J., Summerfield, Q., & Dorman, M. On the identification of sinewave analogues of certain speech sounds. *Haskins Laboratories: Status report on speech research* (SR-51/52), 1977.

Baru, A. V. Discrimination of synthesized vowels [a] and [i] with varying parameters in dog. In G. Fant & M. A. A. Tatham (Eds.), *Auditory analysis and the perception of speech.* London: Academic Press, 1975.

Bertoncini, J., & Mehler, J. Syllables as units in infant speech perception. *Infant Behavior & Development,* 1981, *4,* 247–260.

Best, C. T., Morrongiello, B., & Robson, R. The perceptual equivalence of two acoustic cues is specific to phonetic perception. *Perception and Psychophysics,* 1980, *29,* 191–211.

Bever, T. G. Regression in the service of development. In T. G. Bever, (Ed.), *Regressions in mental development: Basic phenomena and theories.* Hillsdale, N.J.: Lawrence Erlbaum Associates, 1982.

Bowerman, M. Reorganizational processes in lexicval and syntactic development. In E. Wanner & L. Gleitman (Eds.), *Language acquisition: State of the art.* New York: Cambridge University Press, 1983.

Burdick, C. K., & Miller, J. D. Speech perception by the chinchilla: Discrimination of the sustained /a/ and /i/. *Journal of the Acoustical Society of America,* 1975, *58,* 415–427.

Carden, G., Levitt, A., Jusczyk, P. W., & Walley, A. Evidence for phonetic processing of cues to place of articulation: Perceived manner affects perceived place. *Perception & Psychophysics,* 1981, *29,* 26–36.

Carrell, T. D., Pisoni, D. B., & Gans, S. J. *Perception of duration of rapid spectrum: Evidence for context effects with speech and nonspeech signals.* Paper presented at the 100th meeting of the Acoustical Society of America, Los Angeles, November 1980.

Cole, R. A., & Jakimik, J. A model of speech perception. In R. Cole (Ed.), *Perception and production of fluent speech.* Hillsdale, N.J.: Lawrence Erlbaum Associates, 1980.

Cutting, J. E., & Eimas, P. D. Phonetic feature analyzers and the processing of speech in infants. In J. F. Kavanaugh & J. E. Cutting (Eds.), *The role of speech in language.* Cambridge, Mass.: MIT, 1975

Cutting, J., & Rosner, B. S. Categories and boundaries in speech and music. *Perception & Psychophysics,* 1974, *16,* 564–570.

Demany, L. Auditory Stream segregation in infancy. *Infant Behavior & Development,* in press.

Diehl, R. L. Feature detectors for speech: A critical reappraisal. *Psychological Bulletin,* 1981, *82,* 1–18.

Diehl, R. L., Elman, J. L., & McCusker, S. B. Contrast effects in stop consonant identification. *Journal of Experimental Psychology: Human Perception and Performance,* 1978, *4,* 599–609.

Eimas, P. D. Auditory and linguistic processing of cues for place of articulation by infants. *Perception & Psychophysics,* 1974, *16,* 513–521.

Eimas, P. D. Auditory and phonetic coding of the cues for speech: Discrimination of the [r-l] distinction by young infants. *Perception & Psychophysics,* 1975, *18,* 341–347. (a)

Eimas, P. D. Speech perception in early infancy. In L. B. Cohen & P. Salapatek (Eds.), *Infant perception: From sensation to cognition* (Vol. 2). New York: Academic Press, 1975. (b)

Eimas, P. D., & Corbit, J. D. Selective adaptation of linguistic feature detectors. *Cognitive Psychology,* 1973, *4,* 99–109.

Eimas, P. D., & Miller, J. L. Perception of initial nasal and stop consonants by young infants. Unpublished study, 1977.

Eimas, P. D., & Miller, J. L. Contextual effects in infant speech perception. *Science,* 1980, *209,* 1140–1141. (a)

Eimas, P. D., & Miller, J. L. Discrimination of the information for manner of articulation by young infants. *Infant Behavior and Development,* 1980, *3,* 367–375. (b)

Eimas, P. D., Sigueland, E. R., Jusczyk, P., & Vigorito, J. Speech perception in infants. *Science,* 1971, *171,* 303–306.

Fujimura, O., & Lovins, J. B. Syllables as concatenative phonetic units. In A. Bell & J. B. Hooper (Eds.), *Syllables and segments.* Amsterdam: North Holland, 1978.

Garnica, O. The development of phonemic speech perception. In T. E. Moore (Ed.), *Cognitive development and the acquisition of language.* New York: Academic Press, 1973.

Hellberg, S. Unnatural phonology. *Journal of Linguistics,* 1978, *14,* 157–177.

Hillenbrand, J., Minifie, F. D., & Edwards, T. J. Tempo of spectrum change as a cue in speech sound discrimination by infants. *Journal of Speech and Hearing Research,* 1979, *22,* 147–165.

Holmberg, T. L., Morgan, K. A., & Kuhl, P. K. *Speech perception in early infancy: Discrimination of fricative consonants.* Paper presented at the 94th meeting of the Acoustical Society of America, Miami Beach, Florida, December 16, 1977.

Ingram, D. Phonological rules in young children. *Journal of Child Language,* 1974, *1,* 49–64.

Ingram, D. Current issues in child phonology. In O. Morehead & A. E. Morehead (Eds.), *Normal and deficient child language.* Baltimore: University Park Press, 1976.

Jusczyk, P. W. Perception of syllable-final stop consonants by two-month-old infants. *Perception & Psychophysics,* 1977, *21,* 450–454.

Jusczyk, P. W. Infant speech perception: A critical appraisal. In P. D. Eimas & J. L. Miller (Eds.), *Perspectives on the study of speech.* Hillsdale, N.J.: Lawrence Erlbaum Associates, 1981.

Jusczyk, P. W. Auditory versus phonetic coding of speech signals during infancy. In J. Mehler, E. Walker, & M. Garrett (Eds.), *Perspectives in mental representation: Experimental and theoretical studies of cognitive processes and capacities.* Hillsdale, N.J.: Lawrence Erlbaum Associates, 1982.

Jusczyk, P. W., Copan, H. C., & Thompson, E. J. Perception by two-month olds of glide contrasts in multisyllabic utterances. *Perception & Psychophysics,* 1978, *24,* 515–520.

Jusczyk, P. W., Murray, J., & Bayly, J. *Perception of place-of-articulation in fricatives and stops by infants.* Paper presented at the biennial meeting of the Society for Research in Child Development, San Francisco, March 1979.

Jusczyk, P. W., Pisoni, D. P., Reed, M. A., Fernald, A., & Myers, M. Infants' discrimination of the duration of a rapid spectrum change in nonspeech signals. *Science,* 1983, *222,* 175–177.

Jusczyk, P. W., Pisoni, D. B., Walley, A., & Murray, J. Discrimination of relative onset time of two-component tones by infants. *Journal of the Acoustical Society of America,* 1980, *67,* 262–270.

Jusczyk, P. W., Rosner, B. S., Cutting, J. E., Foard, C. F., & Smith, L. B. Categorical perception of nonspeech sounds by two-month-old infants. *Perception and Psychophysics,* 1977, *21,* 50–54.

Jusczyk, P., Smith, L. B., & Murphy, C. The perceptual classification of speech. *Perception & Psychophysics,* 1981, *30,* 10–23.

Jusczyk, P. W., & Thompson, E. Perception of a phonetic contrast in multisyllabic utterances by two-month-old infants. *Perception & Psychophysics,* 1978, *23,* 105–109.

Kewley-Port, D. Time-varying features as correlates of place of articulation in stop consonants. *Journal of the Acoustical Society of America,* 1983, *73,* 322–335.

Klatt, D. H. Voice onset time, friction and aspiration in word-initial consonant clusters. *Journal of Speech and Hearing Research,* 1975, *18,* 686–706.

Klatt, D. H. Speech perception: A model of acoustic-phonetic analysis and lexical access. *Journal of Phonetics,* 1979, *7,* 279–312.

Klatt, D. Speech perception: A model of acoustic-phonetic analysis and lexical access. In R. Cole (Ed.), *Perception and production of fluent speech*. Hillsdale, N.J.: Lawrence Erlbaum Associates, 1980.

Kuhl, P. K. Speech perception in early infancy: Perceptual constancy for vowel categories /a/ & /ɔ/. *Journal of the Acoustical Society of America*, 1977, *61 (Suppl. No. 1)*, 539(A).

Kuhl, P. K. Speech perception in early infancy: Perceptual constancy for spectrally dissimilar vowel categories. *Journal of the Acoustical Society of America*, 1979, *66*, 1668–1679.

Kuhl, P. K., & Miller, J. D. Speech perception by the chinchilla: Voiced-voiceless distinction in alveolar-plosive consonants. *Science*, 1975, *190*, 69–72.

Kuhl, P. K., & Miller, J. D. Speech perception by the chinchilla: Identification functions for synthetic VOT stimuli. *Journal of the Acoustical Society of America*, 1978, *63*, 905–917.

Ladefoged, P. *Preliminaries to linguistic phonetics*. Chicago: The University of Chicago Press, 1971.

Lasky, R. E., Syrdal-Lasky, A., & Klein, R. E. VOT discrimination by four- to six-and-a-half month-old infants from Spanish environments. *Journal of Experimental Child Psychology*, 1975, *20*, 213–225.

Liberman, A. M., Cooper, F. S., Shankweiler, D. P., & Studdert-Kennedy, M. Perception of the speech code. *Psychological Review*, 1967, *74*, 431–461.

Liberman, A. M., Harris, K. S., Kinney, J. A., & Lane, H. The discrimination of relative-onset time of the components of certain speech and nonspeech patterns. *Journal of Experimental Psychology*, 1961, *61*, 379–388.

Liberman, A. M., Isenberg, D., & Rakerd, B. Duplex perception of cues for stop consonants: Evidence for a phonetic mode. *Perception & Psychophysics*, 1981, *30*, 133–143.

Liberman, I. Y., Shankweiler, D., Fisher, F. W., & Carter, B. Explicit syllable and phoneme segmentation in the young child. *Journal of Experimental Child Psychology*, 1974, *18*, 201–212.

Lisker, L., & Abramson, A. A cross-language study of voicing in initial stops: Acoustical measurements. *Word*, 1964, *20*, 384–422.

Lisker, L., & Abramson, A. S. The voicing dimension: Some experiments in comparative phonetics. In *Proceedings of the Sixth International Congress of Phonetic Sciences*, Prague, 1967. Prague: Academia, 1970.

Locke, J. The child's processing of phonology. In W. A. Collins (Ed.), *The Minnesota Symposium on Child Psychology* (Vol. 12). Hillsdale, N.J.: Lawrence Erlbaum Associates, 1979.

Macken, M. A. Aspects of the acquisition of stop systems: A cross linguistic perspective. In G. Yeni Komshian, J. F. Kavanagh, & C. A. Ferguson (Eds.), *Child phonology* (Vol. I). New York: Academic Press, 1980.

Mann, V. A., & Repp, B. H. Influence of vocalic context on the perception of the [ʃ] - [s] distinction. *Perception & Psychophysics*, 1980, *28*, 213–228.

Marslen-Wilson, W., & Tyler, L. K. The temporal structure of spoken language understanding. *Cognition*, 1980, *8*, 1–71.

Mehler, J. The role of syllables in speech processing: Infant and adult data. *Philosophical Transactions of the Royal Society London*, 1981, *B295*, 333–352.

Menn, L. Phonological theory and child phonology. In G. A. Yeni-Komshian, J. F. Kavanagh & C. A. Ferguson (Eds.), *Child phonology* (Vol. I). New York: Academic Press, 1980.

Menyuk, P., & Menn, L. Early strategies for the perception and production of words. In P. Fletcher & M. Garman (Eds.), *Studies in language acquisition*. Cambridge, England: Cambridge University Press, 1979.

Miller, J. L., & Liberman, A. M. Some effects of later-occurring information on the perception of stop consonant and semivowel. *Perception & Psychophysics*, 1979, *25*, 457–465.

Miller, C. L., Morse, P. A., & Dorman, M. Cardiac indicies of infant speech perception: Orienting and burst discrimination. *Quarterly Journal of Experimental Psychology*, 1977, *29*, 533–545.

Miller, G. A., & Nicely, P. E. Analysis of perceptual confusions among some English consonants. *Journal of the Acoustical Society of America*, 1955, *27*, 338–353.

Miller, J. D., Wier, L., Pastore, R., Kelly, W., & Dooling, R. Discrimination and labeling of noise-buzz sequences with varying noise-lead times: An example of categorical perception. *Journal of the Acoustical Society of America*, 1976, *60*, 410–417.

Miyawaki, K., Strange, W., Verbrugge, R., Liberman, A. M., Jenkins, J. J., & Fujimura, O. An effect of linguistic experience: The discrimination of [r] and [l] by native speakers of Japanese and English. *Perception & Psychophysics*, 1975, *18*, 331–340.

Moffit, A. R. Consonant cue perception by twenty- to twenty-four-week-old infants. *Child Development*, 1971, *42*, 717–731.

Morais, J., Cary, L., Alegria, J., & Bertelson, P. Does awareness of speech as a sequence of phones arise spontaneously? *Cognition*, 1979, *7*, 323–331.

Morse, P. A. The discrimination of speech and nonspeech stimuli in early infancy. *Journal of Experimental Child Psychology*, 1972, *14*, 477–492.

Oden, G. C., & Massaro, D. W. Integration of featural information in speech perception. *Psychological Review*, 1978, *85*, 172–191.

Pastore, R. E., Ahroon, W. A., Buffuto, K. A., Friedman, C. J., Puleo, J. S., & Fink, E. A. Common factor model of categorical perception. *Journal of Experimental Psychology: Human Perception and Performance*, 1977, *4*, 686–696.

Peterson, G. E., & Barney, H. L. Control methods used in a study of the vowels. *Journal of the Acoustical Society of America*, 1952, *24*, 175–184.

Pisoni, D. B. Discrimination of brief frequency glissandos. *Research on Speech Perception*, 1976. Progress Report No. 3, Indiana University.

Pisoni, D. B. Identification and discrimination of the relative onset time of two-component tones: Implications for voicing perception in stops. *Journal of the Acoustical Society of America*, 1977, *61*, 1352–1361.

Pisoni, D. B., Aslin, R. N., Perey, A. J., & Hennessy, B. L. Some effects of laboratory training on identification and discrimination of voicing contrasts in stop consonants. *Journal of Experimental Psychology: Human Perception and Performance*, 1982, *8*, 297–314.

Rand, T. C. Dichotic release from masking for speech. *Journal of the Acoustical Society of America*, 1974, *55*, 678–680.

Remez, R., Rubin, P., Pisoni, D. B., & Carrell, T. Speech perception without traditional speech cues. *Science*, 1981, *212*, 947–950.

Rosch, E., & Mervis, C. B. Categorization of natural objects. *Annual Review of Psychology*, 1981, *32*, 89–115.

Rosen, S. M., & Howell, P. Plucks & Bows are not categorically perceived. *Perception & Psychophysics*, 1981, *30*, 156–168.

Sawusch, J. R. Peripheral and central processes in selective adaptation of place of articulation in stop consonants. *Journal of the Acoustical Society of America*, 1977, *62*, 738–750.

Sawusch, J. R., & Jusczyk, P. W. Adaptation and contrast in the perception of voicing. *Journal of Experimental Psychology: Human Perception and Performance*, 1981, *7*, 408–421.

Searle, C. L., Jacobson, J. Z., & Rayment, S. C. Phoneme recognition based on human audition. *Journal of the Acoustical Society of America*, 1979, *65*, 799–809.

Shvachkin, N. K. The development of phonemic speech perception in early childhood. In C. A. Ferguson & D. I. Slobin (Eds.), *Studies of child language development*. New York: Holt, Rinehart, & Winston, 1973.

Simon, H. J., & Studdert-Kennedy, M. Selective anchoring and adaptation of phonetic and nonphonetic continua. *Journal of the Acoustic Society of America*, 1978, *64*, 1338–1357.

Stampe, D. The acquisition of phonetic representation. *Papers from the Fifth Regional Meeting, Chicago Linguistic Society*, 1969.

Stevens, K. N. The quantal nature of speech. In E. E. David, Jr. & P. B. Denes (Eds.), *Human communication: A unified view*. New York: McGraw-Hill, 1972.

Strange, W., & Jenkins, J. J. Role of linguistic experience in the perception of speech. In R. D. Walk & H. L. Pick (Eds.), *Perception and experience*. New York: Plenum, 1978.

Streeter, L. A. Language perception of 2-month-old infants shows effects of both innate mechanisms and experience. *Nature,* 1976, *259,* 39–41.

Studdert-Kennedy, M. Speech perception. In N. J. Lass (Ed.), *Contemporary issues in experimental phonetics*. New York: Academic Press, 1976.

Swoboda, P., Kass, J., Morse, P., & Leavitt, L. Memory factors in infant vowel discrimination of normal and at-risk infants. *Child Development,* 1978, *49,* 332–339.

Till, J. A. *Infants' discrimination of speech and nonspeech stimuli*. Paper presented at the annual meeting of the American Speech and Hearing Association, Houston, Texas, November 1976.

Trehub, S. E. Infant's sensitivity to vowel and tonal contrasts. *Developmental Psychology,* 1973, *9,* 91–96.

Trehub, S. E. The discrimination of foreign speech contrasts by infants and adults. *Child Development,* 1976, *47,* 466–472. (a)

Trehub, S. E. *Infants discrimination of multisyllabic stimuli: The role of temporal factors*. Paper presented at the annual convention of the American Speech and Hearing Association, Houston, Texas, November 21, 1976. (b)

Walley, A. C., Smith, L. B., & Jusczyk, P. W. Classification of CV syllables by readings and prereaders. *Research on Speech Perception,* 1980, Progress Report No. 6, Indiana University.

Werker, J., Gilbert, J. H. V., Humphrey, K., & Tees, R. C. Developmental aspects of cross-language speech perception. *Child Development,* 1981, *52,* 349–355.

Wickelgren, W. A. Context-sensitive coding, associative memory, and serial order in (speech) behavior. *Psychological Review,* 1969, *76,* 1–15.

Wickelgren, W. A. Phonetic coding and serial order. In E. C. Carterette & J. Friedman (Eds.), *Handbook of perception* (Vol. VIII). New York: Academic Press, 1976.

Williams, L. *The effects of phonetic environment and stress placement on infant discrimination of place of stop consonant articulation*. Paper presented at the Second Annual Boston University Conference on Language Development, Boston, October 1, 1977. (a)

Williams, L. The perception of stop consonant by Spanish-English bilinguals. *Perception & Psychophysics,* 1977, *21,* 289–297. (b)

Williams, L., & Bush, M. The discrimination by young infants of voiced stop consonants with and without release bursts. *Journal of the Acoustical Society of America,* 1978, *63,* 1223–1225.

12 Categorization of Speech by Infants

Patricia K. Kuhl
Department of Speech and Hearing Sciences and
Child Development and Mental Retardation Center
University of Washington

> *There is nothing more basic to thought and*
> *language than our sense of similarity;*
> *our sorting of things into kinds.*
> —W. V. Quine, 1969, p. 116

INTRODUCTION

This chapter describes experiments on the perception of similarity among speech sounds by infants. The experiments examine (1) whether infants demonstrate the perception of speech categories, and (2) whether infants' perceptual categories conform to those based on a linguistic classification of the sounds. The data reviewed here suggest that infants can indeed "sort" sounds. Moreover, infants' categories correspond to linguistic categories. The perception of phonetic equivalence in early infancy is critical to the development of speech perception and speech production.

A Focus on Perceptual Similarity

The speech heard by infants does not lack diversity. It is spoken by men, women and children in varying tones of voice. It is sufficiently rich in information-bearing elements to convey (to an adult) not only the speaker's intended meaning, but information about the speaker's identity, age, and sex, as well as details about the speaker's demeanor and intent—whether he is nervous, depressed, happy, or has a cold. It is not hard to imagine that infants discriminate among these acoustically diverse events. What is of greater consequence is the infant's ability to group them together, to perceive their similarity. For if infants are to derive information about the message, and the identity and state of its bearer, they must demonstrate an ability to categorize sounds—to "render discriminably different things equivalent" (Bruner, Goodnow, & Austin, 1956, p. 1).

Categorization requires infants to map complex acoustic cues onto the perceived attributes of sound. What we know of this mapping suggests that it is not a trivial problem. The acoustic events that convey such information are not related in a one-to-one fashion to the perceived attributes of sound. The specific concern here is with the infant's recognition of similarity for phonetic events. This particular instance represents a very complex mapping between physical representation and percept.

The Study of Perceptual Organization for Speech

The acquisition of language obviously requires that infants distinguish among the smallest entities that convey meaning—the phonetic units of the language. That is, infants must have the requisite auditory acuity for frequency, intensity, and duration to perceive differences between words such as "pat" and "bat," which differ by a single phonetic unit. But the categorization of speech requires more than this. It requires that infants perceptually group sounds that are phonetically equivalent. This seemingly straightforward requirement is complicated by the fact that the phonetic structure of language is itself complex and abstract.

The earliest experiments in the field provided ample evidence that the perceived phonetic segments—the consonants and vowels in speech—are not related in a simple one-to-one fashion to acoustic segments in the sound stream (Liberman, Cooper, Shankweiler, & Studdert-Kennedy, 1967). The exact nature of the acoustic events signaling phonetic identity have been shown to depend on the phonetic context in which the sound appears, the talker who produced it, its position in a syllable, and the rate at which it was spoken. (See Liberman et al., 1967; Miller, 1981; Peterson & Barney, 1952 for examples.) Due to these factors, identical acoustic information can be perceived as different phonetic units, and different acoustic information can be perceived as the same phonetic unit. Yet, the listener must process the speech signal in such a way as to preserve the identity of the phonetic segments intended by the speaker, in spite of radical transformations in the acoustic information used to signal them.

What do we know of infants' abilities to perceive speech-sound categories? Do they hear a difference between sounds that differ by a single phonetic unit? If so, do infants demonstrate an ability to perceive similarity? Do they preserve the identity of a phonetic unit over transformations in talker, context and position?

Two Approaches to Categorization

The study of infants' perception of speech categories has focused on two different phenomena. One approach has been the extensive work on "categorical perception" (Eimas, 1974, 1975; Eimas, Siqueland, Jusczyk, & Vigorito, 1971), and the other on "categorization" (Kuhl, 1979, 1980, 1983). Both of these approaches tap the infant's proclivity to perceive categories. Categorical perception studies focus on the perception of differences among stimuli along a continuum, and the data provide evidence that infants perceive discontinuities (boundaries) between categories. Categorization studies focus on the perception of similarity among phonetically equivalent but discriminably different instances representing a category. These latter studies include an examination of the rules used to form the category, and how the category is represented. While both approaches provide valuable data concerning infants' perceptual organization for speech sounds, they contribute to our understanding of speech-sound categorization in different ways.

Categorical Perception: Studies on the Perception of Differences. Studies of categorical perception involve a highly restricted and narrowly defined set of conditions for testing the discrimination and identification of stimuli. They involve the use of computer-synthesized stimuli in which one set of acoustic cues, sufficient to distinguish between two phonetic categories, is varied in stepwise fashion to create a continuum; all other noncriterial dimensions, such as fundamental frequency, intensity, and duration, are held constant. The evidence for categorical perception derives from the fact that under these testing conditions listeners show poor discriminability among variants of the stimulus within a phoneme category, while demonstrating enhanced sensitivity to stimulus differences for variants crossing phoneme boundaries.

Discrimination tests on 1- to 4-month-old infants, involving a sucking-habituation technique, demonstrated that infants' discrimination performance mirrored that of adults (Eimas et al., 1971). Infants failed to discriminate stimuli that were given the same phonetic label by adults, while providing evidence of discrimination for stimuli separated by the same physical distance but given different phonetic labels by adults. In other words, infants responded to stimuli on the continua as though they perceptually grouped those within a single phonetic category, while discriminating between those stimuli representing different phonetic categories. Thus, infants' responses were consistent with an adult's partitioning of the physical continuum into phonetic categories. More recently, Eimas and Miller (1980) have shown that the locations of infants' perceptual boundaries are context-sensitive, just as they are for adults (Eimas, this volume).

To what extent do these kinds of categorical perception tests provide evidence of categorization—that is, to what extent do they demonstrate that infants have the ability to "render discriminably different things equivalent"? Using this test paradigm, the relevant data derive from infants' failure to discriminate within-category contrasts. The main problem with accepting this result as evidence of categorization as defined here (as opposed to "categorical perception"), is that it has two possible interpretations. Either infants fail to discriminate the stimuli because they recognize category equivalence, or they fail because they simply are not capable of discriminating the stimuli.[1] Moveover, even if the within-category stimuli were shown to be discriminable, thereby meeting the categorization criterion, these types of experiments do not involve a direct test of the perceived equivalence of stimuli across context. The most interesting tests of categorization in infants will involve ones in which either context, position, talker, or rate are varied. Under these circumstances the stimuli will undoubtedly be discriminable. What is needed, therefore, is a technique that measures infants' perception of equivalence for stimuli that are discriminably different.

Categorization: Studies on the Perception of Similarity.   When we ask whether infants can categorize we want to know if they can sort a variety of instances into "Type A" and "Type B" events, even though the various A's (or B's) are clearly differentiable. To perform such a task requires that infants recognize the similarity among discriminably different instances representing a category, while at the same time recognizing the essential difference that separates the two categories. Thus, categorization requires that the perceiver recognize equivalence, at some level, among discriminably different stimuli. Our intent, then, was to design experiments in which we could present stimuli to infants varying along many dimensions, and examine their ability to "sort" them along one of the dimensions.

The approach (Hillenbrand, 1983, in press; Kuhl, 1979, 1980, 1983) involved the use of discrimination training coupled with a transfer-of-learning design. The experiments were designed to assess the degree to which training an infant to discriminate two speech sounds, each representing a different phonetic category, would result in a transfer-of-learning to novel, discriminably different, instances from those same phonetic categories. To the degree that infants demonstrated equivalent treatment of the training stimulus and the novel stimuli in this design, one could argue that infants recognized the two stimuli as members of the same category.

Two main features distinguish this approach from the categorical-perception approach. First, the nature and the diversity of the stimuli representing the categories; second, the technique, which requires the infant to produce an equivalent response to stimuli that are perceived to be equivalent.

---

[1]In a recent paper, Miller and Eimas (1983) argue that there is a trend in the data suggesting that infants may discriminate within-category contrasts. Given that this claim is important to the categorization issue, studies should be directed at establishing it firmly.

Regarding the first, rather than differing on a single acoustic parameter, as in the studies involving discrimination of sounds drawn from a physical continuum, the stimuli varied along a number of dimensions. For example, in the first experiment using this design, Kuhl (1979) examined infants' discrimination of two vowel categories, /a/ (as in "pop") and /i/ (as in "peep"). The stimuli used in the experiment varied along three dimensions, phonetic identity (/a/ vs. /i/), pitch contour (interrogative vs. declarative), and talker identity (male, female, or child). Stimuli belonging to the same category (all /a/'s, for example) were highly discriminable.

Each of the three dimensions is physically represented in the stimulus in a complex way. In no case can the acoustic rules for sorting along any of the dimensions be stated in a simple, frequency-specific way. Furthermore, each dimension is physically represented by cues that are acoustically prominent, providing potential distraction effects when attempting to sort the stimuli along any one particular dimension. Thus, categorization along the phonetic dimension requires that the diverse acoustic events underlying phonetic identity be recognized as equivalent, while the acoustically prominent but irrelevant acoustic events associated with changes in the pitch contour and talker be ignored.

Regarding the second, infants produced an equivalent response to stimuli that, while discriminably different, were perceived as equivalent. This provided us with a measure of their ability to categorize the sounds. The test involved the modification of an operant head-turn technique (Kuhl, 1979, 1980, 1983, in press a), wherein a visual stimulus was presented when a constantly repeated vowel, such as /a/, was changed to /i/. Infants were trained to make a headturn response when the /a/ vowel, synthesized to simulate a male voice with a falling pitch contour, was changed to an /i/ vowel. The two vowels were acoustically matched in every other detail. After this initial training, infants were tested with novel stimuli representing the two categories, ones which simulated the productions of female and child talkers, with either rising or falling pitch contours. We measured the extent to which infants demonstrated the correct response to novel stimuli from both categories. If an infant had been reinforced for producing head-turns to /a/, but not to /i/, we examined responses to novel /a/'s and /i/'s, expecting to see that a novel /a/—one produced by a new talker—would result in a head-turn response, while an equally novel /i/ would not.

In summary, our experiments are distinguished from the previous ones using the "categorical perception" approach both by stimulus considerations and by response considerations. On the stimulus side our design included (1) substantial variation in the acoustic cues underlying phonetic identity, and (2) substantial variation in dimensions that were irrelevant to phonetic identity. In some cases, these irrelevant variations were concomitant with variation in the critical dimensions. For example, varying the talker alters the locations of the formant frequencies (the critical dimension), but also introduces irrelevant variation in the fundamental frequency, and in the spectral differences that help identify the voices of particular talkers.

On the response side, two factors distinguish our experiments. First, the design requires the infant to form two categories. We think infants in our experiments provide strong evidence that they are capable of categorizing a given stimulus as an "A" or a "B." These are the first experiments providing such evidence. Second, in our experiments the infant produces a response to indicate the detection of similarity, rather than to indicate the detection of a difference. We think that the perception of similarity is fundamental to the ability to categorize.

TECHNIQUES

Two techniques were adapted for the study of categorization of auditory stimuli in infants, the high-amplitude sucking (HAS) technique and the headturn (HT) technique. These procedural adaptations have been discussed in detail elsewhere (HAS: Kuhl, 1976; Kuhl & Miller, 1982. HT: Kuhl, 1979, 1980, 1983, in press a), and will be described only briefly here.

High-Amplitude Sucking

Eimas et al. (1971) used a high-amplitude sucking technique to study speech discrimination in infants. The infant sucks on a non-nutritive nipple coupled to a pressure transducer until a baseline sucking rate is obtained. A threshold defining high-amplitude responses is established. Then, a speech sound is presented contingent upon these high-amplitude sucking responses. Continued presentation of the same stimulus generally results in a decrease in high-amplitude sucking by the infant. When a criterion decrement in response is reached (habituation), one group of infants is presented with a new sound while a control group is presented with the original stimulus. Infants in the sound-change group typically show an increase in sucking when compared to the control group. A statistical analysis is made of the difference scores resulting from a comparison of pre- and post-shift scores for the two groups.

The modification employed by Kuhl (1976; Kuhl & Miller, 1982) involved the presentation of multiple exemplars during the pre- and post-shift phases of the experiment. As is typical in the HAS design, a stimulus change always occurred at the shift-point in the experiment (for the experimental group). Our modification involved examining the infant's detection of that change in the presence versus the absence of constant variation (pre- and post-shift) in an irrelevant dimension. We argued that such a design could potentially answer two kinds of questions: (1) whether infants were capable of detecting a change in a target dimension when a second dimension was constantly varied; and (2) whether infants perceived similarity along a particular dimension.

Operant Head-Turn

The development of the operant head-turn technique (HT) has been described in detail (Kuhl, in press a). Kuhl (1979) modified the procedure to study speech-sound categorization in infants. In the original design, the infant is conditioned to turn her/his head toward a loudspeaker when the repetition of a single stimulus (the "background") is changed to the repetition of a new stimulus (the "comparison"). These are called "Change" trials. If the infant produces a head-turn at the appropriate time, s/he is reinforced with a visual stimulus. On an equivalent number of "Control" trials, no change in the sound occurs, but the infant is monitored for head-turn responses. Performance is measured by comparing the number of head-turn responsess on Change versus Control trials. If the infant produces significantly more head-turn responses on Change trials, we infer that the infant can discriminate the two stimuli.

Kuhl (1979) modified the technique such that infants were initially trained on a speech-sound contrast until they met a criterion (9 out of 10 correct). Then, novel instances representing both the "background" and the "comparison" categories were introduced. The introduction of new stimuli was done in one of two ways: progressive transfer-of-learning and immediate transfer-of-learning.

In progressive transfer-of-learning, novel stimuli are introduced in a series of stages, typically five (Kuhl, 1979, Experiment I; 1983, Experiment I). Progression from stage to stage occurs when the infant reaches a preset criterion (9 out of 10 consecutive trials correct). The trials are run as previously described, but the infant has to monitor the stimuli for a change in the *category* rather than simply in the sound. Figure 12.1 shows the stimulus format on Change and Control trials. Head-turn responses to all variants in the "comparison" category are reinforced, but head-turn responses to any variant in the "background" are not reinforced. This is not an easy task because the sounds within a single category are discriminably different. The infant has to ignore these prominent differences and recognize their similarity to succeed on the task. A trials-to-criterion measure is used to assess the infant's ease of transfer. If the infant readily perceives the similarity between stimuli belonging to the same category, the trials-to-criterion measure should not increase significantly as novel instances are introduced. Parametric statistics are used to make these comparisons (Kuhl, 1983).

The immediate transfer-of-learning design is similar but provides a more sensitive measure of the infant's ability to generalize to novel members of a phonetic category. The initial stage again consists of training the infant to produce a head-turn response in the presence of one stimulus while refraining from

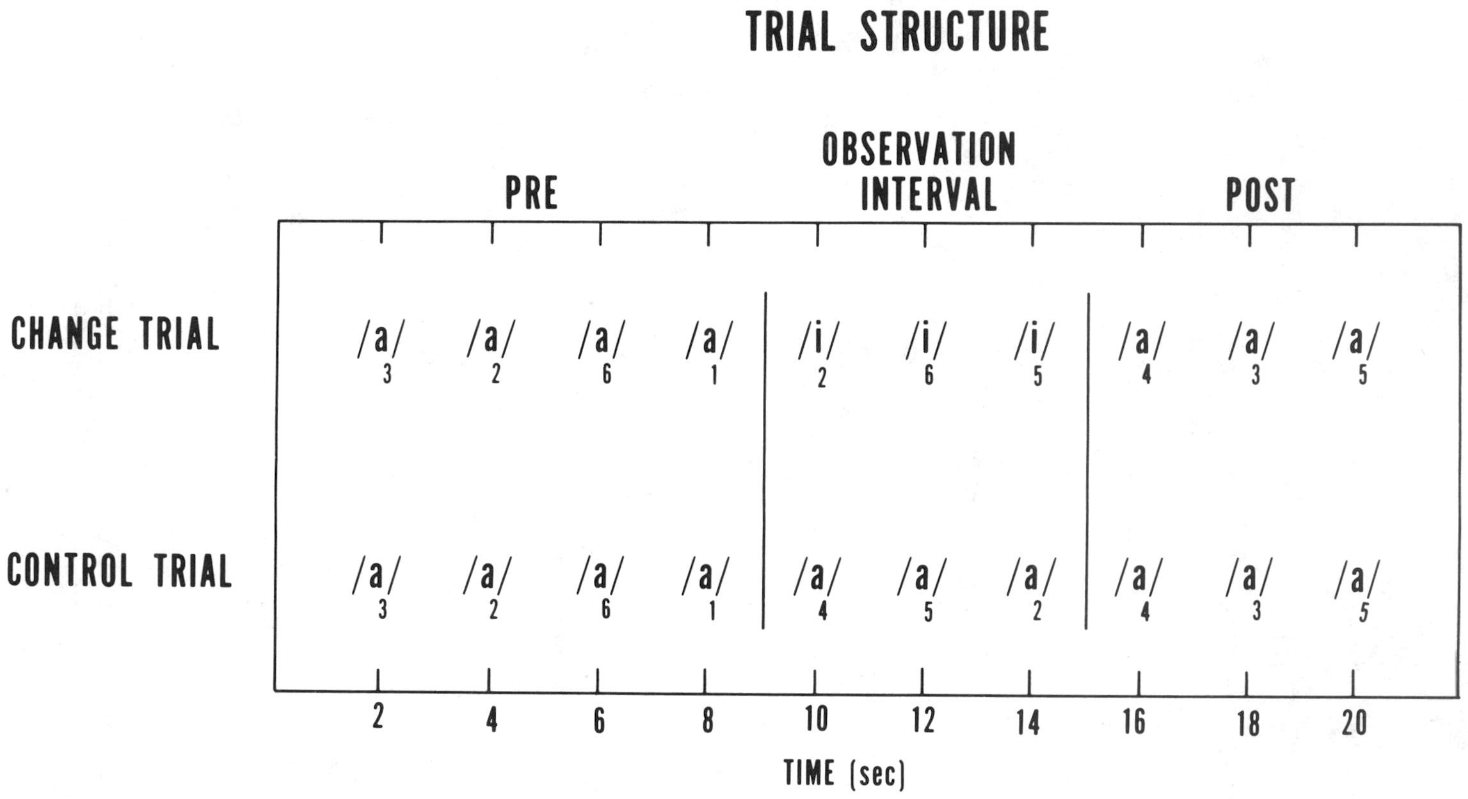

FIG. 12.1. Stimulus presentation during Change and Control trials. As shown, a random presentation of the vowels from the "background" category (subscripts indicate the different instances) occurred prior to and after each trial, as well as during Control trials. During Change trials, a random presentation of the vowels from the "comparison" category occurred (from Kuhl, 1979).

producing the response in the presence of a second stimulus. Following this training, infants are presented with all of the novel stimuli presented in the final stage of the progressive transfer-of-learning design, without the intermediate stages. A fixed number of trials are presented, and the percent correct response is measured for each novel stimulus. Analysis of first-trial data can be used to measure whether the infants produce the correct response upon first exposure to the novel stimulus. Again, parametric statistics are used to compare percent correct performance for the training stimulus and the novel stimuli.

DATA ON SPEECH-SOUND CATEGORIZATION BY INFANTS

Vowel Categories

When a talker produces different vowel sounds the overall configuration of the vocal tract is changed. This change in configuration alters the resonant frequencies of the tract, which are directly reflected in the locations of the formants (frequency regions in which the concentration of energy is greatest) on the frequency axis. Early work in the field demonstrated that (1) vowel perception is directly related to the locations of the formants, and (2) the first two formants are sufficient to distinguish all English vowels (Delattre, Liberman, & Cooper, 1951). Thus, the critical acoustic cues governing the categorization of vowels were presumed to involve either the absolute values of the formant frequencies or some measure of the relationship among the formant frequencies.

Research has shown, however, that when vowels are produced by talkers whose vocal tracts have different overall dimensions, such as when the identical vowel is produced by a male, a female, and a child, the formant frequencies are quite different (Peterson & Barney, 1952). Vowel categories adjacent in "vowel space" are not completely separable on the basis of their first two formants. This is due to the fact that the overall dimensions of the vocal tracts of men, women, and children are not proportional (Fant, 1973), so the resulting resonances (and therefore formant frequencies) are not related as ratio transforms. Thus, the perception of equivalence among vowels spoken by different talkers is difficult to explain on purely acoustic grounds.

Infants must perceive the phonetic equivalence among vowels produced by different talkers if they are to understand speech, but the phenomenon is of interest from another standpoint as well. Equivalence classification for the productions of different talkers is a prerequisite for vocal imitation. This is the case because the infant's vocal tract is not capable of producing the absolute formant frequencies represented in the speech of adult listeners (Lieberman, 1980). Attempting to imitate adult speech by a direct match of the frequencies involved would not prove possible. An infant's recognition of the equivalence among the vowels produced by men, women, and children would suggest that the infant has access to a level of representation that is not frequency-specific. If so, then infants attempting to imitate the vowels produced by adults would not have to produce a sound whose absolute formant frequencies matched those produced by the adult in order to perceive a similarity between the two.

Kuhl and Miller (1982; described in Kuhl, 1976) initiated categorization studies using vowel stimuli. In a study in which a manner of findings related to infants' processing of multidimensional stimuli were obtained, two were of particular importance to the specific issue of vowel categorization. First, we obtained data suggesting that infants are capable of detecting a change in a particular dimension in the presence of variation in a second irrelevant dimension. Second, the evidence suggested that infants perceived similarity for discriminably different vowels.

The study examined whether 4- to 16-week-old infants could detect a change in a target dimension if an irrelevant dimension was randomly varied throughout the experiment. The HAS paradigm was employed. A change in the target dimension occurred at the "shift-point"; the irrelevant dimension was randomly varied throughout both the pre- and post-shift periods. In one condition, the target dimension was a phonemic change in the vowel and the irrelevant dimension was the pitch contour of the vowel; in a second condition, the target dimension was the pitch contour of the vowel and the irrelevant dimension was the vowel's identity. The choice of pitch contour as a distracting acoustic dimension was particularly appropriate given that the literature is replete with suggestions that suprasegmental dimensions such as pitch contour, loudness, and stress pattern are more salient than segmental dimensions at this age (Crystal, 1973). The stimuli were two /a/'s and two /i/'s synthesized such that one /a/ and one /i/ had identical monotone pitch contours and one /a/ and one /i/ had identical rise-fall pitch contours. Discrimination of vowel identity and pitch contour were tested *with* and *without* irrelevant variation in the second dimension.

Figures 12.2 and 12.3 display the findings. They plot the minute-by-minute sucking responses for the vowel and pitch-target groups, respectively. The data are shown for each experimental group and its corresponding control group under two conditions, with and without variation in the second dimension. Recall that in each case the control groups do not experience a stimulus change at the shift point.

The data show that when either a change in vowel identity or in pitch contour occurs in the absence of variation in a second dimension, infants demonstrated the ability to discriminate the change. That is, sucking responses reliably increased after the shift point when compared to their control groups. On the other hand, when a change in a target dimension occurred against a background of random change in a second dimension, performance depended upon the specific dimension that served as the target. When vowel identity was the target dimension and pitch contour served as the second dimension, infants provided evidence of discrimination; however, when pitch contour was the target dimension and vowel

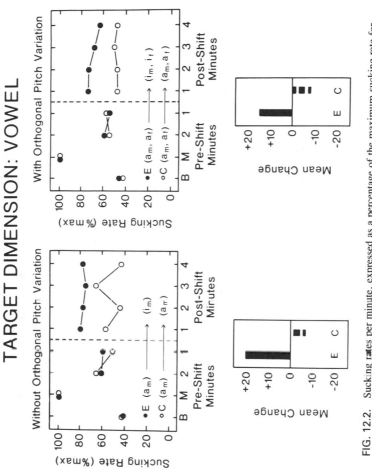

FIG. 12.2.   Sucking rates per minute, expressed as a percentage of the maximum sucking rate for base line, maximum, habituation, and the 4 postshift minutes of the experiment for infants tested in the vowel target groups, both experimental and control. Data for infants tested on the vowel target *without* pitch variation are shown on the left, whereas data for infants tested on the vowel target *with* pitch variation are shown on the right. The average difference scores for each condition are centered under the minute-by-minute data. They were obtained by subtracting the mean of the 2 habituation minutes from the mean of the first 2 postshift minutes for each infant (from Kuhl & Miller, 1982).

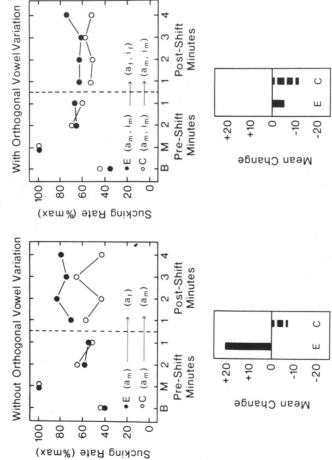

FIG. 12.3.   The minute-by-minute and difference-score data for infants tested in the pitch target groups, both experimental and control.   Data for infants tested on the pitch target *without* vowel variation are shown on the left, whereas data for infants tested on the pitch target *with* vowel variation are shown on the right (from Kuhl & Miller, 1982).

identity served as the second dimension, no evidence of discrimination was obtained.

Kuhl and Miller argued that the results supported the notion that infants are capable of making phonemic discriminations in the presence of irrelevant variation along another dimension. Regarding the asymmetric nature of the effect, the authors interpreted the data to mean that the vowel dimension was more salient than the pitch dimension, at least for these stimuli. The interpretation of a *general* precedence for the acoustic cues underlying vowel identity over the acoustic cues underlying pitch perception was rejected, given the lack of any systematic manipulation of the acoustic cues representing the two levels of each dimension.

The study also provided evidence to support the idea that infants recognize similarity along the vowel dimension. The evidence consisted of the amount of time taken to habituate across conditions. We argued that in order to demonstrate habituation, the infant must store a composite description of the original stimulus and eventually recognize that the stimulus being presented matches the stored representation. The recognition of the similarity between the stimulus being presented and the stored representation reduces the infant's interest in that stimulus and therefore results in a decrease in the response being measured (habituation).

Habituation to multiple stimuli requires the infant to remember the entire set. We argued that sets of stimuli that shared a particular dimension would be more similar perceptually than sets that did not. We argued further that the perception of similarity would serve as an aid to memory. Thus, if infants were capable of detecting that similarity, then the time it took to reach the habituation criterion should decrease.

The data are shown in Fig. 12.4. Time-to-habituation (TH) was defined as the number of minutes spent in the preshift phase of the experiment, excluding the baseline minute. The TH scores for all groups presented with a single sound during preshift are shown as well as for those groups presented with two stimuli. No significant differences were obtained among groups presented with a single stimulus, so these groups were collapsed for further analyses. Comparisons between the two-stimulus groups and the single-stimulus group taken as a whole revealed that infants took significantly longer to meet the habituation criterion when two sounds were presented during the preshift period rather than one. However, this result was also shown to be asymmetric; it was dependent on the specific dimension that the two sounds had in common. When the two sounds shared the vowel dimension, time-to-habituation was not significantly greater than it was in any condition in which a single sound was presented. In contrast, when the two sounds shared the pitch dimension or shared neither of the two dimensions, time-to-habituation was significantly longer than when a single sound was presented or when two sounds that shared the vowel dimension were presented.

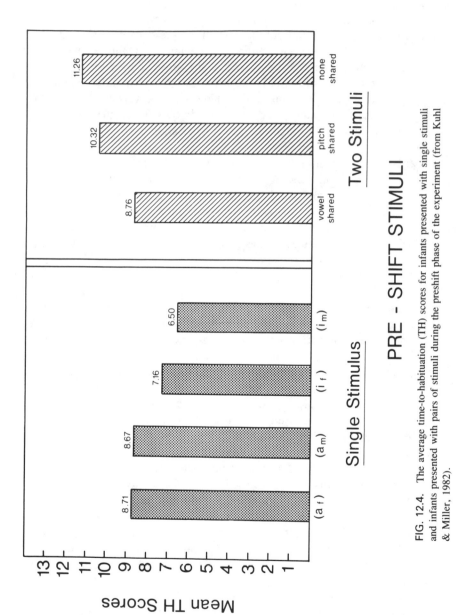

FIG. 12.4. The average time-to-habituation (TH) scores for infants presented with single stimuli and infants presented with pairs of stimuli during the preshift phase of the experiment (from Kuhl & Miller, 1982).

We interpreted the data in support of the notion that infants recognized the similarity among stimuli sharing the vowel dimension and that this reduced the memory load during the habituation phase of the experiment. We noted, though, that a shared dimension did not always make two stimuli easier to remember, since, when the two stimuli shared pitch, a significant increase in TH scores was obtained. In fact, it took almost as long to habituate when the stimuli shared pitch as it did when they had no features in common. We argued, therefore, that infants did not recognize similarity along the pitch dimension, perhaps because they were distracted by a constant change in the second dimension, vowel identity.

While the Kuhl and Miller (1982) study demonstrated the infant's ability to tolerate variation in irrelevant dimensions and perceive the similarity among vowels, it did not examine the infant's ability to recognize phonetic similarity among diverse vowel stimuli, such as those produced by different talkers. To extend these results to such a situation, Kuhl (1979) used the modification of the head-turn technique described earlier to examine the perception of the same two vowel categories, /a/ and /i/. In this experiment, infants were trained to discriminate the /a/ and /i/ vowels produced by a male talker. Then, generalization of the correct response was tested for novel stimuli produced by women and child talkers. Table 12.1 lists the stimuli presented in the "background" and "comparison" categories in each stage of the experiment.

The results of the progressive transfer-of-learning experiment on the /a-i/ contrast (Kuhl, 1979, Experiment I) demonstrated excellent performance on the novel stimuli. Most infants met the performance criterion at each stage in the experiment in the minimum number of trials necessary (10 trials). Group data showing percentage of head-turn responses to each of the novel stimuli on Change trials during the transfer-of-learning phase are shown in Fig. 12.5. As demonstrated, performance is uniformly above 85% correct. For nearly half of the infants, performance was near perfect.

More convincingly, however, in the immediate transfer-of-learning experiment on the /a–i/ contrast (Kuhl, 1979, Experiment II), performance was significantly above chance on each of the novel stimuli on the first trial during which it was presented. This is the strongest evidence for categorization, since it is unaffected by reinforcement. Thus, the data from the two experiments provided strong evidence that six-month-old infants recognize phonetic equivalence among the vowels spoken by different talkers.

In a second study (Kuhl, 1983), we extended these results to a more difficult vowel contrast, /a/ (as in "cot") versus /ɔ / (as in "caught"). The vowel /ɔ/ is acoustically very similar to /a/. They are both "compact" vowels with formants spaced closely together. In naturally produced words containing these vowels considerable overlap in the first two formant frequencies occurs, such that the two categories cannot be separated on this acoustic dimension (Peterson & Barney,

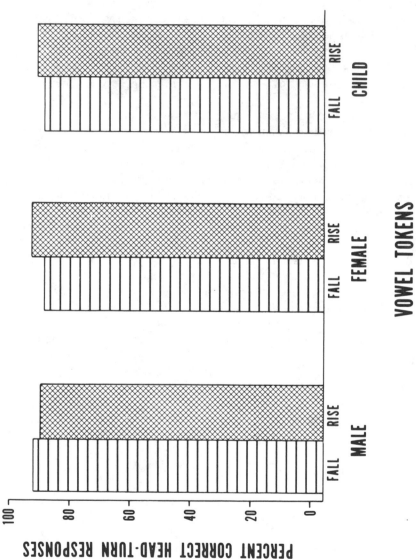

FIG. 12.5.   Group data showing correct head-turn responses to the original training stimulus (Male-fall) and to the novel stimuli in the vowel categorization experiment. These data were obtained using the immediate transfer-of-learning design (see text for details) (from Kuhl, 1979).

1952). In the speech produced by most talkers in the United States, the two vowels are not phonemically distinct.

Results of the /a–ɔ/ study using both the progressive transfer-of-learning design and the immediate transfer-of-learning design again suggested that infants perceived the phonetic equivalence among the vowel stimuli produced by different talkers (Kuhl, 1983). In this, as in the earlier study with the /a–i/ vowel contrast (Kuhl, 1979), generalization to the novel stimuli was immediate; infants demonstrate transfer-of-learning on the first trial. Thus, studies of both spectrally similar and spectrally dissimilar vowel categories strongly suggest that by six months of age infants recognize equivalence classes that conform to the vowel categories of English. Given the demonstration that infants categorize variants for an easily discriminable contrast (/a–i/), as well as for a difficult contrast (/a–ɔ/), Kuhl (1983) interpreted the data in support of the notion that infants demonstrate vowel "constancy," probably for all vowel categories in English.

Consonant Categories

Most of the early research on the acoustic cues for consonant classes (Liberman et al., 1967) emphasized the extreme context-dependency of the cues. For example, when a consonant occurs in different contexts such as the /d/ in /di/, /da/, and /du/, the accoustic cues representing the consonant are altered significantly. One question, then, is whether infants perceive the similarity among consonant-vowel (CV) syllables whose initial phonetic units (the consonants) are identical, but whose final phonetic units (the vowels) are discriminably different. Our next series of experiments (Kuhl, 1980; Hillenbrand, 1983, in press) provided an answer to this question. The studies on consonant categories can best be illustrated using data obtained as part of a dissertation recently completed in this laboratory (Hillenbrand, 1983).

The design of this experiment differed from the vowel tests just described (Kuhl, 1979, 1983) and from our early studies on consonants involving fricatives (Kuhl, 1980). First, the experiment was designed such that the performance of two groups of infants could be compared. The two groups differed with respect to the relationship among the stimuli assigned to the reinforced category. For a "phonetic" group, the stimuli were assigned to the reinforced and the unreinforced categories on the basis of their phonetic identity. For a "random" group, the stimuli were simply assigned to either the reinforced or the unreinforced group on a random basis. This new design provided an assessment of the infant's ability to perform the task based on either chance responding or some other strategy, such as "memorizing" the stimuli in the reinforced stimulus category. We could then statistically compare performance by the two groups of infants.

Hillenbrand's (1983) study was designed to examine another issue. We wanted to know whether infants would perform more accurately when reinforcement was based on a phoneme-level sorting rule as opposed to a feature-level sorting

TABLE 12.1
Stimuli in the Background and Comparison Categories for all Stages in the /a–i/ Categorization Experiment. The Talker and Pitch Contour Values for each Stimulus are Given in Parentheses (from Kuhl, 1979).

Experimental Stages	Background Category	Comparison Category
Conditioning	/a/ (Male, fall)	/i/ (Male, fall)
Initial training	/a/ (Male, fall)	/i/ (Male, fall)
Pitch variation	/a/ (Male, fall)	/i/ (Male, fall)
	/a/ (Male, rise)	/i/ (Male, rise)
Talker variation	/a/ (Male, fall)	/i/ (Male, fall)
	/a/ (Female, fall)	/i/ (Female, fall)
Talker × pitch variation	/a/ (Male, fall)	/i/ (Male, fall)
	/a/ (Male, rise)	/i/ (Male, rise)
	/a/ (Female, fall)	/i/ (Female, fall)
	/a/ (Female, rise)	/i/ (Female, rise)
All stimuli	/a/ (Male, fall)	/i/ (Male, fall)
	/a/ (Male, rise)	/i/ (Male, rise)
	/a/ (Female, fall)	/i/ (Female, fall)
	/a/ (Female, rise)	/i/ (Female, rise)
	/a/ (Child, fall)	/i/ (Child, fall)
	/a/ (Child, rise)	/i/ (Child, rise)

rule. By comparing phoneme-level versus feature-level rules, we hoped to determine the optimum level at which categorization occurs in infants. Many studies on adults can be explained by assuming that listeners have access to a feature-level representation of phonetic units. This notion argues that phonetic units such as /d/ are represented at some level as a bundle of distinctive features. These features describe its manner of articulation ("voiced," "plosive," etc.), as well as its place of articulation ("alveolar"). Speech production theorists argue that the acquisition of speech is more economically described in terms of a progressive mastery of particular distinctive features than as a gradual mastery of individual phonetic units (Blache, 1978).

Recognition of feature-level groupings requires infants to classify sounds using cues that are not specific to any one phoneme. Hillenbrand (1983) examined the perception of categories based on the plosive-nasal distinction. A set of stop-plosives (/b/, /d/, and /g/) was contrasted with a set of nasals (/m/, /n/, and /ŋ/).In order to perform in the task, infants had to recognize properties common to stops but not to nasals, while disregarding the differences among stops, and among nasals. In order to compare the efficiency with which infants categorized sounds at the feature versus phoneme level, he also examined the perception of a phoneme-level distinction using categories based on the /m/ versus /n/ contrast (Hillenbrand, in press).

Both the experiment involving the nasal contrast and the experiment involving the feature-level contrast employed the phonetic-random design. In each study, two groups, a phonetic and a random group, were initially trained to discriminate single stimuli from each of the two categories. Then, additional stimuli were progressively introduced for a set number of trials (20). Finally, when all of the stimuli had been introduced, each group was given 75 trials. The data obtained during these last 75 trials were statistically compared for the two groups.

The stimuli presented in Hillenbrand's (1983) feature-level experiment are shown in Table 12.2. The phonetic group was initially trained on the /ma–ba/ contrast. Stimuli were then gradually added until the final stage, in which the stimulus pairs (ma, na, ŋa/, each produced by a male and a female talker, were contrasted with the stimulus pairs /ba, da, ga/ produced by the same male and female talkers. Infants in the random group were initially trained on the contrast between the syllable /na/ produced by a male voice and the syllable /ba/ produced by a female voice. Stimuli were added to each category in stages analogous to those for the phonetic group, with the exception that the stimuli in each category could not be perceptually organized along a phonetic, or any other, dimension.

The stimuli presented in Hillenbrand's (in press) phoneme-level experiment are shown in Table 12.3 This study involved the nasal contrast /m/ versus /n/. The infants in the phonetic group were tested on the /m–n/ contrast with syllables varying in both talker and vowel context. The final stage of the experiment contrasted the syllables /ma, mi, mu/ produced by a male and a female with the syllables /na, ni, nu/ produced by the same two talkers. In the random version of the experiment, the same 12 stimuli were used, but they were assigned to the

TABLE 12.2

Stimuli Presented during Each Stage for Infants Tested in the Phonetic Group of the Feature-Level Categorization Experiment (from Hillenbrand, 1983).

Experimental Stages	Background Category	Comparison Category
Initial training	ba (male)	ma (male)
Place variation	ba (male)	ma (male)
	da (male)	na (male)
Talker × place variation	ba (male)	ma (male)
	da (male)	na (male)
	ba (female)	ma (female)
	da (female)	na (female)
All stimuli	ba (male)	ma (male)
	da (male)	na (male)
	ga (male)	ŋa (male)
	ba (female)	ma (female)
	da (female)	na (female)
	ga (female)	ŋa (female)

TABLE 12.3
Stimuli Presented during each Stage for Infants Tested in the Random Group of the Feature-Level Categorization Experiment (from Hillenbrand, 1983).

Experimental Stages	Background Category	Comparison Category
Stage 1	ba (female)	na (male)
Stage 2	ba (female)	na (male)
	ŋa (male)	ga (female)
Stage 3	ba (female)	na (male)
	ŋa (male)	ga (female)
	da (female)	ma (female)
	ma (male)	ba (male)
Stage 4	ba (female)	na (male)
	ŋa (male)	ga (female)
	da (female)	ma (female)
	ma (male)	ba (male)
	ga (male)	da (male)
	na (female)	ŋa (female)

reinforced and nonreinforced categories such that they could not be perceptually organized along any single dimension.

The results demonstrated that in both experiments infants in the phonetic groups performed significantly better than infants in the corresponding random groups. Percent-correct scores for the phonetic and random groups tested in the feature-level task are shown in Fig. 12.6. The main effects of Trial Type (Change vs. Control) and Group (Phonetic vs. Random) were both significant, as well as the Trial Type X Group interaction, indicating the superior performance by infants in the phonetic group.

Analysis of the scores for individual stimuli showed that infants in the phonetic group responded correctly to all of the individual stimuli in the category, while infants in the random group tended to respond primarily to the first stimulus in the reinforced category. Figure 12.7 illustrates this by providing group data for individual stimuli in Hillenbrand's (1983) feature-level experiment. As shown, infants in the phonetic group produced head-turn responses to all stimuli representing the reinforced category, and refrained from making head-turn responses to all of the stimuli in the nonreinforced category. In contrast, infants in the random group did not learn which stimuli were reinforced, presumably because they could not be perceived as a category. These infants produced head-turn responses only to the first stimulus in the reinforced category. This was the stimulus initially paired with reinforcement, and was probably remembered because of this.

The results were similar for the phoneme-level experiment. Infants in the phonetic group produced head-turn responses to all stimuli representing the

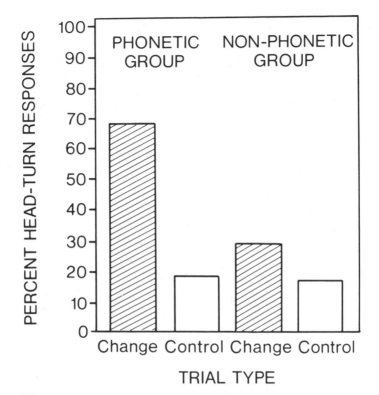

FIG. 12.6.   Percent head-turn responses on Change and Control trials for infants in the phonetic and random groups in the feature-level categorization study (from Hillenbrand, 1983).

reinforced category, while refraining from responding to all members of the nonreinforced category. In contrast, infants in the random category had difficulty learning which stimuli were reinforced. They responded reliably only to the first stimulus that was presented from the reinforced category.

Of particular interest was the fact that infants tested in the phonetic group of the feature-level experiment outperformed infants in the phonetic group of the phoneme-level experiment. The fact that feature-level categorization was easier may have implications for developmental phonology. More specifically, the recognition of feature classification could form the basis for the acquisition of phonological rule systems, most of which are specified at the level of feature values rather than at the level of individual phonetic segments. The developmental phonology literature suggests that young children acquire phonetic segments by mastering phonetic-feature systems (Blache, 1978).

It would take additional studies, however, to provide strong evidence that the order of phonological-rule acquisition as evidenced by production data is predicted by the relative difficulty of organizing perceptual categories along various

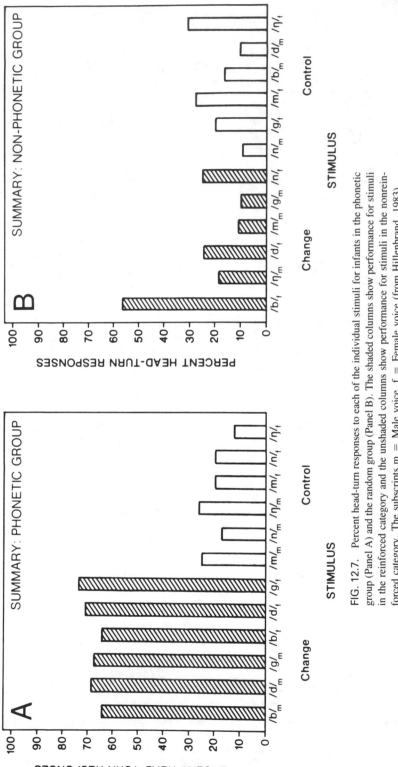

FIG. 12.7.   Percent head-turn responses to each of the individual stimuli for infants in the phonetic group (Panel A) and the random group (Panel B). The shaded columns show performance for stimuli in the reinforced category and the unshaded columns show performance for stimuli in the nonreinforced category. The subscripts m = Male voice, f = Female voice (from Hillenbrand, 1983).

feature dimensions. The feature categories tested in this particular experiment can be organized within even broader feature classes, such as /sonorant/ versus /obstruent/, or /continuant/ versus /noncontinuant/, so that quite a number of experiments would have to be completed before one could determine the optimum level at which segments can be grouped by infants and then examine the predictive value of such data.

Categories Based on Suprasegmental Distinctions

Suprasegmental cues are those acoustic elements that extend beyond a single phonetic segment. These include fundamental frequency (f_0), intonation contour, and stress, with the latter involving complex changes in frequency, duration, and intensity. Studies of the perception of categories based on suprasegmental cues in infancy are interesting because the literature on phonological development has provided examples in which children accurately reproduce the intonation contour or stress pattern of utterances while failing to reproduce the phonetic elements accurately (Oller, 1980). These data have been taken in support of the idea that suprasegmental acoustic cues are more salient to young infants than phonetic acoustic cues (Crystal, 1973).

There are very few categorization studies where the use of suprasegmental sorting rules is tested. The experiment by Kuhl and Miller (1982) tested infants' abilities to recognize the similarity among different vowel sounds produced with the same pitch contour. In that study, very young infants (4 to 16 weeks) were shown to be incapable of recognizing a pitch change in the presence of random variation in the vowel. (Recall that they could detect the change in the absence of random variation in the vowel.) Kuhl and Miller interpreted the data to mean that young infants were sufficiently distracted by the change in the vowel that they failed to attend to the pitch dimension, but predicted that young infants would find it easier to attend to pitch if either (1) the perceptual difference between the two levels of the pitch dimension was increased, or (2) the perceptual difference between the two levels of the competing dimension—vowel identity—was decreased. Speeded-classification studies on adult listeners demonstrate that reaction time when classifying stimuli on the pitch dimension decreases under both conditions listed above (Carrel, Smith, & Pisoni, 1981).

To test this, Kuhl and Hillenbrand (1979) employed the same set of vowel stimuli used in the /a–i/ and /a–ɔ/ studies, and tested older infants (six-month-olds) using the head-turn technique. Recall that the stimuli consisted of the vowells /a/, /i/, and /ɔ/, each produced by a man, a woman, and a child, and each produced with both a rising and a falling intonation contour. The set of stimuli can be organized perceptually on the basis of either vowel identity, pitch contour, or talker. Kuhl and Hillenbrand (1979) were interested in determining (1) whether infants were capable of performing on the head-turn task when reinforcement was predicted by intonation contour rather than vowel identity, and (2) whether infants were better at sorting stimuli using the pitch dimension when the perceptual difference between the two vowels was smaller. They predicted, therefore, that infants would perform more accurately when the levels of the vowel dimension were represented by /a/ and /ɔ/ than when they were represented by /a/ and /i/.

Two groups of six-month-olds were run in experiments identical to the ones previously described on vowel identity. In these tasks, reinforcement was predicted by the pitch contour of the stimulus rather than its vowel identity or the talker who produced the sound. Thus, infants were reinforced for producing head-turn responses for all stimuli with a rising (interrogative) intonation contour, and not reinforced for producing head-turn responses to any stimuli with a falling (declarative) intonation contour.

The progressive transfer-of-learning task was used, identical to that used in the /a–i/ (Kuhl, 1979, Experiment I) and /a–ɔ/ (Kuhl, 1983, Experiment I) studies. The results confirmed that the six-month-olds were capable of sorting these stimuli using the pitch dimension. The trials-to-criterion data are shown in Fig. 12.8. The data show that performance is as good as that demonstrated when infants sorted these stimuli using the vowel dimension, and also that infants performed with equal facility in the two experiments.

To summarize, two things were demonstrated by these experiments. First, at least by six months of age, infants are capable of preserving constancy for pitch. They recognize the similarity between two discriminably different vowels whose pitch contours are identical. Four- to sixteen-week-old infants, tested using a different technique, did not demonstrate the ability to do this. Second, infants were successful on the pitch task regardless of the perceptual distance between the two vowels. Sorting on the basis of pitch was no more difficult with the /a–i/ stimuli than with the /a–ɔ/ stimuli. Perhaps the more difficult task in which the novel stimuli are immediately added to the set (the immediate transfer-of-learning task) would have revealed differences in the predicted direction.

DISCUSSION

Infants Perceive Speech-Sound Categories

We have demonstrated that infants perceive similarities between speech sounds that have undergone various transformations due to the talker who produced the sound and the context in which it appeared. Thus, infants preserve a "constancy" of sorts for speech.

At the phonetic-unit level, our experiments show that infants perceive the similarity among vowels produced by different talkers, and among syllables containing the same consonant. In the latter case, infants have been shown to recognize the similarity among syllables whose consonant segments are identical,

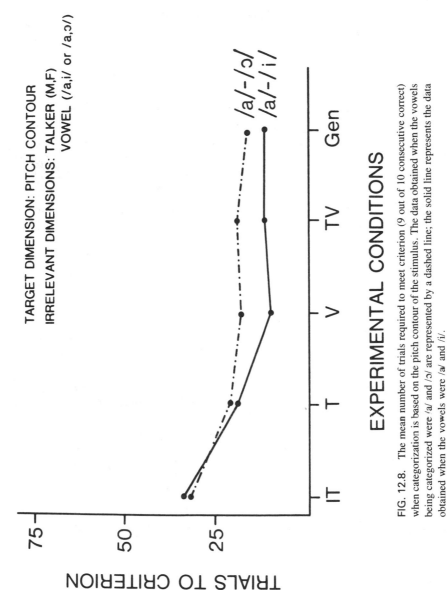

FIG. 12.8.   The mean number of trials required to meet criterion (9 out of 10 consecutive correct) when categorization is based on the pitch contour of the stimulus. The data obtained when the vowels being categorized were /a/ and /ɔ/ are represented by a dashed line; the solid line represents the data obtained when the vowels were /a/ and /i/.

regardless of the vowel context in which the consonant appears or the talker producing it. Categorization is not restricted to the phonetic-unit level. Our data show that infants perceive the equivalence among sounds at the phonetic-feature level. Moreover, we show that infants recognize similarity among sounds at the suprasegmental level as well. In each of these cases, infants treat discriminably different sounds as equivalent, while maintaining a distinction between two categories.

The existence of these perceptual categories in six-month-old infants has important implications for the development of speech. Without the ability to recognize that the sounds produced by different talkers are equivalent, infants would have to learn sound-meaning correspondences independently for each talker. Moreover, preserving a "constancy" for speech uttered by different talkers is fundamental to the infant's own production of speech. An important component of infants' learning to speak is the imitation of sounds produced by another talker, and imitation depends on the ability to equate the sounds produced by others with ones they themselves produce. That infants do indeed preserve phonetic identity, regardless of the talker producing the sound, is thus of enormous importance to the acquisition of speech.

In summary, these studies address a classic problem in speech perception—the perceived equivalence among sounds that are phonetically identical but acoustically diverse. As adults, we preserve a constancy for the phonetic units of speech. We perceive the identical consonant or vowel despite changes in talker or context, unaware that the mapping between the acoustic cues and phonetic percepts is so complex that computers cannot be programmed to perform similar feats. Our specific concern in the studies reported here was the development of this ability. We asked whether infants preserved constancies for speech. Our results showing that infants perceive similarities for phonetically identical units across talker and context serve as existence proofs for such phenomena in early infancy.

Given that this much is established, these findings raise further questions about speech perception by infants, particularly about its representation. Specifically, do infants' abilities to perceive the similarities among speech sounds reflect a rule-governed phonology wherein segments consisting of consonants and vowels are represented? The question actually has two parts. One addresses the size of the unit that the representation is based on, that is, the "unit-of-analysis." The other addresses the nature of the information involved, whether it is speech information, per se, that is specified.

The Representation of Speech: The Unit of Analysis

The first question has to do with the representation of speech. Theorists argue that an adult's representation of speech probably consists of phonetic-unit and feature-level listings (Chomsky & Halle, 1968). The question is, do data showing that infants recognize the similarities among speech sounds provide support for the notion that the infant's "speech code" contains phonetic units and features? Or is some larger unit, such as the syllable, represented as an undividable "whole"?

Our studies show that infants perceive the similarity among syllables whose initial consonants are similar, such as /sa/, /si/, and /su/, and differentiate them from the syllables /ʃa/, /ʃi/, and /ʃu/ (Kuhl, 1980). Similarly, infants perceive the similarity among the syllables /ma/, /mi/, and /mu/, and distinguish them from /na/, /ni/, and /nu/ (Hillenbrand, in press). Does this mean that infants represent these syllables as being comprised of two phonetic elements—/C/ and /V/? Furthermore, does the recognition of equivalence derive from the specification that syllables such as /sa/, /si/, and /su/ share the common consonant /s/? The data are certainly consistent with the claim that infants have access to a phonetic-unit representation. In fact, the data presented in these studies (Hillenbrand, 1983, in press; Kuhl, 1979, 1980, 1983) provide the first evidence allowing one to advance such a claim. Nevertheless, it should be pointed out that while infants' abilities can be explained by a phonetic-unit representation, the data do not necessitate this explanation.

Consider the /sa, si, su/ case. The claim that the perception of similarity is based on the recognition of a common phonetic unit (/s/) in each of the syllables depends upon a number of factors. First, we need to establish the fact that perceptual grouping is not due to a failure to discriminate. If infants cannot hear the difference between /sa/, /si/, and /su/, then we have no evidence of "categorization," much less of "segmentation."

We do, in fact, have evidence that the perception of similarity is not due to a failure to discriminate. Infants readily perceive the differences between the syllables. Yet, they perceive their similarities. We know, then, that infants' representation of these syllables allows them to break the syllables down into some kind of subunits. This in turn allows them to detect similarity at the beginnings of the syllables in spite of differences at the ends. At the very least, this ability must rely on a representation of units that allows the beginnings and endings of CV syllables to be isolated and compared across syllables. Thus, it would appear that infants "segment" CV syllables into some kind of "parts."

But the claim that the parts listed in the representation consist of phonetic units or phonetic features would require that the code contain much more specific information. It necessitates a notational system that specifies that CV syllables have exactly two segments, not one or three, and that CVC syllables contain three segments. Moreover, a phonetic-unit representation should allow a unit's recognition regardless of its position in an utterance. In other words, the syllables /ba/, /aba/, and /ab/ would be recognized as containing the same two phonetic units. (See Kuhl, 1980, for pilot data relevant to this point.)

Finally, a phonetic-level analysis requires that the sound's identity be uniquely specified. In the case of the nasal /m/, the representation would have to code it as a nasal continuant with a bilabial place of articulation, thus distinguishing it from all other phonetic units. Should the phonetic unit /m/ be distinguished from all other contrasting phonetic units, and yet be recognized as similar to other instances of /m/ regardless of the vowel context in which it appeared and its position in an utterance, then a strong claim could be made stating that phonetic units, or the information underlying phonetic units, are represented by infants.

Thus, the basis of category recognition in these experiments could be the infant's perception of a common identity at the phonetic-unit or phonetic-feature level. However, it is also possible that infants could succeed at the task without having access to a phonetic-unit or feature representation. Infants could be referencing the representation of a larger unit, such as a syllable, as long as the representation is comprised of independent parts that allow infants to compare *portions of the syllables*. On the basis of the experiments reported here, we argue that the representation includes segments or parts. However, there is no definitive evidence that the segments involve a phonetic-unit or a phonetic-feature code. A representation in which these syllables are specified as sequences of spectra no longer than the longest piece of information that has been shown to be perceptually equated (about 50–100 msec) would allow these similarities to be detected.

In summary, these experiments constrain the unit-of-analysis used by infants to represent speech. They show that infants can detect similarities for units that are smaller than syllables. Thus, syllables are not undividable "wholes" for infants; they can be broken down into parts and those parts can be independently compared across syllables. Future research must be directed toward identifying whether these "parts" are phonetic units, phonetic features, or something else.

The Basis of Infants' Perceptual Categories: Speech Information, Per Se?

We have noted in the previous section that the representation of speech necessitated by our examples is one in which temporally specified *portions of syllables* can be compared across talker and vowel context. Of interest in that discussion was the size of the unit represented. The issue addressed here is the specific nature of the information represented; that is, whether or not it is phonetic information that is represented.

When infants recognize that vowels spoken by different talkers are similar, or that plosive consonants such as /b/, /d/, and /g/ are similar, what kind of information is the recognition of equivalence based on? Can one assume that what is recognized as similar is speech information, per se? Or is some other information, wholly independent of speech, responsible? The answer depends on whether or not some property can be identified that allows one to group sounds within a category together, while at the same time serving to separate the two categories. Once the property is specified, its status as "phonetic" information can be assessed.

This is a difficult problem to pose, one that the speech literature has grappled with on numerous occasions (Kuhl, in press b). The difficulty arises in attempting to dissociate the "speech, per se" account completely from the "wholly independent of speech" account. The arguments can be made on logical grounds, but definitive proof in experimental form has infrequently been obtained.

Briefly, the arguments are as follows. Consider the vowel example. Kuhl (1979) argued that the categories /a/ and /i/ might have been distinguished on the basis of the diffuse-compact feature (Jakobson, Fant, & Halle, 1969). The vowel /a/ is "compact," with one mid-frequency peak in the spectrum, while /i/ vowels are "diffuse," with two or more widely spaced spectral peaks. This feature would be present regardless of the talker producing the vowel. Thus, infants could have sorted the vowels produced by different talkers on this basis. If we had evidence that the vowels /a/ and /i/ were separated on the basis of the diffuse-compact feature (setting aside the data on /a–ɔ/ for the moment, which suggests that vowels sharing the same compact feature can also be discriminated), could we claim that the categorization involved speech information, per se? Stating that categorization was based on a distinctive feature such as compact-diffuse suggests that it is speech information, but it does not have to be. The feature can be described in purely acoustic terms. Compact spectra have a single prominent spectral peak while diffuse spectra have more than one. Therefore, categorization could presumably have occurred without recognizing the information's status as a feature of speech.

The same argument can be made for Hillenbrand's (1983) feature-level experiments. Infants in that experiment separated consonant categories on featural grounds. Plosives were distinguished from nasals. But did categorization depend on the recognition of a common featural specification of the sounds, or on an acoustic property that underlies featural specification? Recognizing this, Hillenbrand (1983) argued that infants in his featural-level experiment may have separated the categories based on a simple property of their overall spectra—their rise-time characteristics. Plosives, as the term implies, have rapid onsets. Their amplitudes grow faster than those of nasals, whose rise-times are comparatively slow. In addition, nasals have a low-frequency resonance associated with them. Infants could have used these relatively simple properties in distinguishing the plosive category from the nasal category.

One approach to this would be to test infants' responses to nonspeech sounds whose spectral shapes mimic the formant patterns of the vowels without allowing them to be identified. Sine-wave analogs of plosives and nasals would capture their rise-time differences without being identified as speech. Would these nonspeech analogs be perceptually grouped with their speech counterparts?

We have experiments such as these underway, but even they are not definitive. Let us argue, for the moment, that nonspeech sounds are categorized with their speech-sound counterparts. What could we claim? Unfortunately, while it would indeed be an interesting finding, such results would not allow one to claim that categorization occurs "wholly independently of speech." These nonspeech analogs mimic the critical features in speech and may be perceived as similar solely because of this (Kuhl, in press b). That is, the mechanisms underlying speech perception may be designed to detect these properties, and stimuli mimicking these properties may "fool" them.

I have argued elsewhere (Kuhl, in press b; Kuhl & Meltzoff, 1984) that the only way to dissociate the "phonetic" account from the "wholly independent" account is to: (1) construct a case in which the two accounts lead to opposite predictions, that is, construct categories in which categorization using the acoustic property does not correlate with categorization by phonetic identity; or (2) show that a nonhuman species perceives the same categories. In the former, the two are effectively dissociated because the predictions are opposite one another. Depending on the outcome, infants can be argued to be using either purely acoustic or some other information to categorize. In the latter, the two are logically dissociated because animals presumably have no phonetic representation. If they succeed, they do so using a purely auditory strategy. Their success indicates that categorization can be accomplished without the recognition of the information's status as speech, per se. Since the former method of dissociating the two has been difficult to achieve, the latter method has often been adopted. (See Kuhl & Padden, 1982, 1983 for examples, and Kuhl, in press b; Kuhl & Meltzoff, 1984, for relevant discussion.) In summary, we do not know whether the information used to categorize these sounds is recognized as speech, per se. Future experiments will be necessary to determine this.

SUMMARY AND CONCLUSIONS

We have shown that infants perceive as similar phonetically identical vowels spoken by different talkers, syllables that share an initial or final consonant, and syllables whose initial consonants share a phonetic feature. Thus, infants preserve the identity of speech units over transformations in talker and context—they preserve "constancies" in speech. The importance of such abilities cannot be overestimated. Without the ability to equate speech produced by different talkers, infants would learn neither to perceive speech nor to produce it.

Infants' recognition of equivalence for consonants across vowel context is a more complex case. The finding is consistent with the notion that infants have access to a phonetic-level representation of speech. However, other possibilities cannot at present be ruled out.

Infants recognize the similarity among syllables whose initial portions are similar but whose end portions are not. Thus, the results suggest that infants have access to a representation that allows portions of syllables to be analyzed and compared. In this sense, infants' representations of syllables involve "segmenting" them into parts. But we have no evidence that the parts consist of phonetic units or phonetic features. At present, we do not even know how many parts are specified. Thus the experiments described here place some constraints on the unit-of-analysis, but they do not determine it. Nor do they specify whether the information that is represented, regardless of its size (the unit-of-analysis question), involves speech information, per se. Further experiments will be necessary to do this.

ACKNOWLEDGMENTS

The preparation of this manuscript and the experiments described were supported by a grant to the author from the National Science Foundation (BNS 8103581). The author thanks Andrew Meltzoff for helpful comments on the manuscript.

REFERENCES

Best, C. T., Morrongiello, B., & Robson, R. Perceptual equivalence of acoustic cues in speech and nonspeech perception. *Perception and Psychophysics*, 1981, *29*, 191–211.

Blache, S. E. *The acquisition of distinctive features*. Baltimore: University Park Press, 1978.

Bruner, J. S., Goodnow, J. J., & Austin, G. A. *A study of thinking*. New York: Wiley, 1956.

Carrel, T. D., Smith, L. B., & Pisoni, D. B. Some perceptual dependencies in speeded classification of vowel color and pitch. *Perception and Psychophysics*, 1981, *29*, 1–10.

Chomsky, N., & Halle, M. *The sound pattern of English*. New York: Harper & Row, 1968.

Crystal, D. Non-segmental phonology in language acquisition: A review of the issues. *Lingua*, 1973, *32*, 1–45.

Delattre, P. C., Liberman, A. M., & Cooper, F. S. Voyelles synthetiques a deux formantes et voyelles cardinales. *Maitre Phonetique*, 1951, *96*, 30–36.

Eimas, P. D. Auditory and linguistic processing of cues for place of articulation by infants. *Perception and Psychophysics*, 1974, *16*, 513–521.

Eimas, P. D. Auditory and phonetic coding of the cues for speech: Discrimination of the /r–l/ distinction by young infants. *Perception and Psychophysics*, 1975, *18*, 341–347.

Eimas, P. D., & Miller, J. L. Contextual effects in infant speech perception. *Science*, 1980, *209*, 1140–1141.

Eimas, P. D., Sigueland, E. R., Jusczyk, P., & Vigorito, J. Speech perception in infants. *Science*, 1971, *171*, 303–306.

Fant, G. *Speech sounds and features*. Cambridge: MIT Press, 1973.

Hillenbrand, J. Perceptual organization of speech sounds by infants. *Journal of Speech and Hearing Research*, 1983, *26*, 268–282.

Hillenbrand, J. Speech perception by infants: Categorization based on nasal consonant place of articulation. *Journal of the Acoustical Society of America*, in press.

Jakobson, R., Fant, G., & Halle, M. *Preliminaries to speech analysis*. Cambridge: MIT Press, 1969.

Kuhl, P. K. Speech perception in early infancy: The acquisition of speech-sound categories. In S. K. Hirsh, D. H. Eldredge, I. J. Hirsh, & S. R. Silverman (Eds.), *Hearing and Davis: Essays honoring Hallowell Davis*. St. Louis: University Press, 1976.

Kuhl, P. K. Speech perception in early infancy: Perceptual constancy for spectrally dissimilar vowel categories. *Journal of the Acoustical Society of America*, 1979, *66*, 1668–1679.

Kuhl, P. K. Perceptual constancy for speech-sound categories in early infancy. In G. Yeni-Komshian, J. Kavanagh, & C. Ferguson (Eds.), *Child phonology, (Vol. 2): Perception.* New York: Academic, 1980.

Kuhl, P. K. The perception of auditory equivalence classes for speech in early infancy. *Infant Behavior and Development,* 1983, *6,* 263–285.

Kuhl, P. K. Methods in the study of infant speech perception. In G. Gottlieb & N. Krasnegor (Eds.), *Measurement of audition and vision during the first year of life: A methodological overview.* Norwood, N.J.: Ablex, in press (a).

Kuhl, P. K. Reflections on models of infant speech perception. In J. S. Perkell (Ed.), *Invariance and variability of speech processes.* Hillsdale, N.J.: Lawrence Erlbaum Associates, in press (b).

Kuhl, P. K., & Hillenbrand, J. *Speech perception by young infants: Perceptual constancy for categories based on pitch contour.* Paper presented to the Society for Research on Child Development, San Francisco, March 1979.

Kuhl, P. K., & Meltzoff, A. N. The intermodal representation of speech in infants. *Infant Behavior and Development,* 1984, *7,* 361–380.

Kuhl, P. K., & Miller, J. D. Discrimination of auditory target dimensions in the presence or absence of variation in a second dimension by infants. *Perception and Psychophysics,* 1982, *31,* 279–292.

Kuhl, P. K., & Padden, D. M. Enhanced discriminability at the phonetic boundaries for the voicing feature in macaques. *Perception and Psychophysics,* 1982, *32,* 542–550.

Kuhl, P. K., & Padden, D. M. Enhanced discriminability at the phonetic boundaries for the place feature in macaques. *Journal of the Acoustical Society of America,* 1983, *73,* 1003–1010.

Liberman, A. M., Cooper, J. S., Shankweiler, D. P., & Studdert-Kennedy, M. Perception of the speech code. *Psychology Review,* 1967, *74,* 431–461.

Lieberman, P. On the development of vowel production in young children. In G. Yeni-Komshian, J. Kavanagh, & C. Ferguson (Eds.), *Child phonology, (vol. 1): Production.* New York: Academic, 1980.

Miller, J. L. Some effects of speaking rate on phonetic perception. *Phonetica,* 1981, *38,* 159–180.

Miller, J. L., & Eimas, P. D. Studies on the categorization of speech by infants. *Cognition,* 1983, *13,* 135–165.

Oller, D. K. The emergence of the sounds of speech in infancy. In G. Yeni-Komshian, C. A. Ferguson, & J. Kavanagh (Eds.), *Child phonology, (vol. 1): Production.* New York: Academic, 1980.

Peterson, G. E., & Barney, H. L. Control methods used in a study of the vowels. *Journal of the Acoustical Society of America,* 1952, *43,* 822–828.

Quine, W. V. Natural kinds. In W. V. Quine, *Ontological relativity and other essays.* New York: Columbia University Press, 1969.

13

Remarks on the Complexity of the Nervous System and Its Ontogenesis

Jean-Pierre Changeux
Institut Pasteur and College de France

The nervous system differentiated very early during the evolution of animal species as an organ specialized in regulation. To use an 18th-century term, it acts as a central *regulator* of the organism both with regard to itself and to its environment. It centralizes signals received from the outside world via the sensory organs, processes them, and works out orders for every action on the environment, or behavior. These actions are carried out after delays that can vary within very wide limits after reception of these signals. The existence of such delays requires that the signals be recorded in the form of a material impression. When this impression possesses a temporal stability that is greater than the duration of the signal itself, it is by definition part of a memory process.

Higher vertebrates and certain cephalopods work out strategies of action upon the environment that take into account both signals that have just been received and previously recorded signals. The processing of these signals and the calculations undertaken in these strategies are only conceivable if there exist material entities capable of being manipulated by the cerebral machine, that will be termed *mental objects* (Denis, 1979). Operations of comparison, association, combination, or choice performed with mental objects are the elements of a *simulation function* (Monod, 1970), peculiar to the central nervous system and unique to living organisms. The role of regulator organ played by the nervous system can be imagined only if it contains, within the organism to which it belongs, a *minimal representation* of the organs and hence of the organism that it commands, as well as the strategies it organizes. There is therefore a hierarchical relationship established between the nervous system and the organism, both by its function and by the organization it brings into play.

The thesis or ontological approach underlying all the facts and speculations presented in this chapter is that every operation performed by the nervous system in the framework of the relations of the organism with itself and with its environment is completely described by:

1. The *anatomical* organization of groups of neurons and of the neuronal circuits involved.
2. The *activity*, for example, all the electrical and chemical phenomena that are propagated in these circuits, spontaneously or following an interaction with the environment.
3. The sensory and motor processes that it enlists in the form of a *behavior*.

A satisfactory description of this nature, including a mathematical model that leads to the "reconstitution" of behavior from anatomical and physiological findings, has indeed been achieved in the case of the swimming of the leech (Stent, Kristan, Friesen, Ort, Poon, & Calabrese, 1978). Other analogous examples have been described (Kandel & Schwartz, 1981), and it is legitimate to think that this thesis is valid for any brain function, whatever it might be, in the same way that it is undeniable that each living cell is composed of molecules and each molecule of atoms. Every brain operation and all behaviors are therefore from a theoretical point of view determined and calculable.

However, when one considers the central nervous system of higher vertebrates and in particular of man, objections to this conception become apparent both on the theoretical and practical levels.

On the theoretical level

1. Signals received from the outside world can possess a spatiotemporal configuration that confers on them a "significance" that is apparently intrinsic. In reality, the significance or symbolic value of such an external configuration becomes apparent only after processing and "internal" analysis by the brain, which must possess a suitable functional organization.
2. Certain unitary integrated phenomena, grouped under headings such as thought, mind, or consciousness seem on first inspection not to be reducible to more elementary mechanisms. In fact, one can imagine them as operations or *second-order regulatory processes* affecting the mental objects themselves.

On the Practical Level

Every integrated function necessarily brings into play considerable numbers of neurons (millions to billions) dispersed in different regions of the brain. Every attempt at identifying them seems doomed to failure. The basic answer to all these objections is that they have to be considered in a historical perspective. The present state of our knowledge and techniques does not allow us to answer the theoretical objections irrefutably, using quantitative measures. This does not mean that they are irrefutable. On the contrary, one of the positive aspects of the ontological approach adopted is in fact that of promoting an analytical experimental approach that includes, in particular, the development of suitable techniques. The other positive aspect is that of underlining the *complexity* of the neuronal organization concerned, that includes both a *hierarchy* of levels of organization and *parallel* functional groupings. This approach leads us to try to outline and define the complexity of the central nervous system and the mechanisms responsible for its construction during embryogenesis and evolution.

COMPLEXITY OF FUNCTIONAL ORGANIZATION

The word "complexity" is frequently invoked by authors attempting either a fine analysis of the anatomy of the central nervous system of vertebrates, and of man in particular, or a causal explanation of higher brain functions. It should never become a refuge for our ignorance but on the contrary should serve as a pretext for deciphering and classifying the functional organization of the nervous system. Two ways of looking at this complexity are opposite and complementary: First there is histology, which after having investigated microscopic morphology identifies centres, nuclei, zones or layers, and characterizes them using a *number,* generally *limited,* of *morphological* types. The group considered then results from the manifold repetition of cells of the same type. Secondly, there is that of the microphysiologist, who, using juxtacellular or intracellular microelectrodes, records the activity of single nerve cells that are in some cases well identified and defines the functional patterns that distinguish each neuron from its neighbor. The apparent morphological regularity, or even redundancy, contrasts with the remarkable cellular diversity revealed by electrophysiological analysis.

Nervous tissue is composed of cells just as any other organ of the body. All these cells have a nucleus, mitochondria, and cytoplasm and are enveloped by a cell membrane. They are constituted from a series of molecules that, apart from a small number of them, are common to all the cells of the organism. These latter molecules can be used to define the differentiated state and to distinguish *biochemical* types. A biochemical type should therefore, at least in theory, be able to be defined by its repertoire or "menu" of "open" genes (i.e., those capable of being expressed as proteins). The chemistry of the nervous system is thus far insufficiently understood to allow a final list of these states to be drawn up.

The use of various cytochemical and immunochemical techniques has already permitted several biochemical types to be distinguished within one apparently homogeneous morphological type (Karten & Brecha, 1980; Chan-Palay, Nivaler, Palay, Beinfeld, Zimmerman, Wu, & O'Donohue, 1981). To avoid this ambiguity, we define as a *category* the most limited group of cells of the same morphological and biochemical type. Recent results from biochemistry and immunocytochemistry (and others to come) will certainly contribute to increasing the number of cell categories of neurons and glial cells in the vertebrate central nervous system. Our thesis is that this chemical diversity is limited. Even if it led to an increase by an order of magnitude in the number of categories identified only on the basis of morphological criteria, the resulting diversity would remain much inferior to that detected by electrophysiological methods.

The nerve cell is distinct from every other cell of the organism owing to its ability to establish material contacts via its axonal and dendritic processes with often several thousand other cells and sometimes many more. These synapses have the universal property of maintaining an intercellular *discontinuity*. There is never cytoplasmic continuity from one nerve cell to another, but rather a juxtaposition of cell membranes at distances of several nanometers (2 nm in the case of gap junctions, 20–50 nm for chemical synapses). In addition, the ultrastructure of these contacts reveals most often (chemical synapses), but not always (gap junctions), a morphological polarity.

Knowledge of the state of connection of the nerve cell has made considerable progress, thanks to the use of juxtacellular and above all intracellular recording methods. The most original concept that emerges from these studies is an extreme diversity of physiological properties at the cellular level.

Let us take as an example the case of the cerebellar cortex. In the adult cat, several million Purkinje cells can be counted, but few anatomical characteristics allow each cell to be distinguished from its neighbor. On the other hand, unitary recordings of these cells, which are identifiable by electrophysiological criteria directly related to their morphological type (e.g., antidromic stimulation of their axon or a characteristic climbing fibre response), reveal unambiguous physiological differences between one cell and its neighbor. One cell in the area of projection of the eye muscle onto the vermis will respond by a diminution of firing rate when the lateral right *rectus* muscle is stretched, whereas another will respond by an increase when the left median *rectus* muscle is extended. In other regions of the cerebellar cortex, certain Purkinje cells can be characterized by a pattern of *several* sensory modes, elsewhere just by one. As much by its precise afferences as by its efferences, practically every cell is *functionally* distinct from its neighbor. In other words, within a single *category* of cells a remarkable functional diversity exists.

It seemed useful to introduce the term *singularity* to refer to this diversity. The singularity of a given cell is evidently determined by its connectivity. This detailed map of connections will differ from one cell to another and can in practice be considered *unique* for each cell. At this degree of resolution, real redundancy seems very limited. According to this point of view, the molecular or chemical diversity of nerve cells remains poor compared to that of the immune system. Only the diversity created by connectivity, that is to say singularity, will be comparable to diversity of immunoglobulin structure.

Comparative anatomy shows that the organization of the nervous system has evolved following two different trends. Starting from a diffuse or metamerised cellular distribution, as in worms, that is very redundant, maximal specialization is achieved by increasing the number of categories without increasing the total number of cells. The number of categories is approximately equal to the number of cells: This is the case with the Aplysia nervous system, for example. The other pattern of evolution is that in which the number of categories does not change greatly, but the number of cells per category increases considerably: A diversification by "singularization" occurs. This pattern became predominant during the evolution of vertebrates and of mammals in particular, and in some invertebrates such as cephalopods.

A first attempt at resolving the complexity at the cell level thus consists in describing categories and if possible connectional singularity, but this description soon becomes insufficient. Another order of complexity results from the organization among cells, from their sequential linking up (transverse organization), or from their arrangement in a plane parallel to the surface of the tissue (tangential or laminar organization). In the first case, the convergence of afferences onto the dendritic arborizations and the divergence of the axonal arborization create hierarchical relationships and contribute to the delocalization of any "localized" group of cells. In the second case, examination of the singularity of neighboring cells reveals in general that they belong to the same functional grouping, which makes up a *"representation"* by projection or "map," often involving transformation of sensory organs, muscles, or even other nervous centers.

Examination of these transverse and tangential organizations in a vertebrate brain often reveals arrangements that at first view appear neither minimal nor functionally necessary. The most plausible interpretation of this organization is that it results from evolutionary constraints and represents, for example, the vestiges of an ancestral organization, as do certain reptilian structures in the mammalian brain. The reason for their presence only becomes apparent in a historical perspective. The existence of this constraint makes more difficult any purely formal "model" of the functional organization of the nervous system and limits any inference of this organization from the analysis of a behavior. The description of the complexity of organization of the nervous system will thus often take on an arbitrary aspect that can, to a certain degree, be compared to that of the amino-acid sequence of a protein that is nevertheless highly specific for a given function.

NERVE ACTIVITY: A SERIES OF MECHANISMS THAT CAN BE EXPLAINED IN MOLECULAR TERMS

Since Galvani it has been known that nerve activity involves measurable electrical phenomena. The nerve signal is a wave of depolarization that is propagated along the axon without attenuation at a rate that is constant, but less than the speed of sound. The energy required is drawn from the ionic gradient set up between the inside and outside of the cell by the ATPases involved in active transport.

The depolarization associated with the nerve impulse arises from the successive opening of two types of ionic channel that cross certain specialized macromolecules of the cytoplasmic membrane of the axon; these are known as *ionophores*. The opening is accompanied by a flux of Na^+ and K^+ ions down their electrochemical gradients, giving rise to an electric current across the membrane and so to a change in potential. Taken together, these ionic processes are sufficient to account quantitatively for the properties and propagation of the nerve impulse, on condition however that the opening of the ionophores be caused by the electric potential. There has been progress recently in identifying voltage-dependent ionophores that are without doubt proteins.

There are few differences among the giant squid axon, the rat sciatic nerve, or the neurons of the cerebral cortex as far as the initiation and propagation of nerve impulses are concerned. It is a mechanism that is universal but also unique, as it is responsible only for rapid signaling along nerves. At the level of the morphological discontinuities, or synapses, that exist between nerve cells, other systems of signal transfer take over. There can be either electrical coupling at "gap junctions" or chemical coupling at "chemical synapses." In the latter case, a small molecule, the neurotransmitter, is synthesized and accumulated in the nerve terminal and then liberated into the synaptic cleft as a pulse of concentration. The binding of neurotransmitter to the membrane facing the nerve terminal causes a change in electrical properties that leads to the initiation of a nerve impulse or, on the contrary, to its prevention. In the well-studied peripheral synapse between motor nerves and striated muscle, the binding of the neurotransmitter, acetylcholine, causes the opening of channels distinct from those responsible for propagating nerve impulses. The protein that carries this receptor site and also contains the ionic channel has been isolated and purified. It is composed of four distinct polypeptide chains whose primary sequence is known. When reinserted into an artificial lipid film, this molecule confers on the membrane the characteristic physiological properties of the response to acetylcholine. Therefore it contains all the structural elements required to detect the chemical signal (Changeux, 1981).

Other mechanisms of transmission of the chemical signal are known and merit a description in molecular terms. Although the nerve impulse can in theory be propagated along the axon in both directions, the asymmetry of the chemical synapse creates a *polarity* (axon → dendrite) in signal transfer from one nerve cell to another. Through its dendrites and soma, the neuron collects synaptic signals and on the basis of simple local calculations responds by an overall change in electrical properties that cause the initiation of a nerve impulse at the base of the axon. The circulation of nerve impulses, just as briefly described previously, is alone responsible for communication between nervous centers and the periphery.

Classical cybernetic schemes envisage the passage of nerve impulses in the direction sensory organs → centers → motor organs as the origin of nerve impulses. In fact, many nerve cells have high levels of intrinsic "spontaneous" activity that continues even when they are cut off from the rest of the network. This activity, most often oscillatory, takes the form, for example, of a regular series of nerve impulses, or of bursts of 10–20 impulses separated with clockwork regularity by periods of silence. Only a small number of molecular elements are required to set up the latter type of oscillation: two slow ionic channels in addition to those involved in the action potential. These two slow channels have opposite effects on the membrane potential. One is voltage sensitive and allows Ca^{++} ions to enter, depolarizing the cell. Once they are inside the cell, the Ca^{++} ions stimulate the opening of hyperoplarizing antagonist channels; then the Ca^{++} is eliminated from the cytoplasm by an active transport system, etc. This simple scheme, common to different cell types, both neuronal and non-neuronal, is sufficient to account for the initiation of nerve activity in the absence of any interaction with the environment.

Spontaneous activity can be recorded in central neurons, but sensory cells are often also active. What is more, the effect of a physical signal from the outside world in a number of well-defined systems, such as vestibular receptors, is to modulate a spontaneous activity that is clearly preexistent to the interaction with the environment. The nerve impulses sent out by a sensory organ, whichever it might be, are the same, and their nature bears no relation to that of the physical signal received. In general, there is a simple relation between the frequency of impulses recorded at the sensory organ and the intensity of the physical signal, but this rule can differ from one cell to the next of the same organ ("on" or "off" cells in the retina), or from one sensory organ to another. In no case, however, is it characteristic of a particular sensory mode. Only the connectional wiring between the sensory apparatus and the nervous centers has functional specificity. For the same reason, unitary recordings of central neurons do not allow their function to be defined if details of their connectivity are not forthcoming. In the same way, the command of skeletal muscles whose contraction gives rise to an action of the organism on its environment and thus to its behavior is also determined by the pathways followed by the nerve impulses.

The coding of propagated signals seems both rudimentary and degenerate (i.e., common to several functional modes), and so it is the connectivity that determines the functional significance of any propagated signal.

However, analysis of the phenomena of perception and *recognition* of the form or movement of an object by the visual system, for example, shows that it is necessary for the central nervous system to recognize relations of coherence and order between the nerve impulses propagated by multiple axons from the same sensory organ. It must do this both at a given moment and during the course of time. These signals taken together can lead to the construction of "representations" that are apparently analogous to the object. These can then be confronted with internal preexisting representations of the object and by this means be identified. As a general rule, these different representations will be termed *mental objects* (see Denis, 1979).

We have no knowledge at present of the neurobiology of these mental objects, although it is clear from the start that their existence and manipulation require a particularly complex organization of the nervous centers. The material nature of these mental objects is apparent from experiments of very different kinds:

1. Experimental psychology: Temporal delays have been demonstrated for the identification of the movements of an object in the visual field (Shepard & Metzler, 1971).

2. Neuropsychology: Localized brain lesions alter selectively certain mechanisms of perception.

3. Psychopharmacology: Certain hallucinogens cause mental objects to appear spontaneously and out of "context."

The interest of the as yet theoretical postulate of mental objects is that they establish a bridge between the "distal" structure of an object and its "proximal sensation" accessible by introspection. These mental objects could indeed be elements of calculation; they could be recorded in a durable form, organized with time, associated, compared, and could perhaps transform each other. The idea that they are originally "evoked" by interaction with the environment seems most plausible, but it is also probable that certain of them have a spontaneous endogenous origin, resulting from the setting up of a memory of neural organization. Their "conscious" manipulation in a temporal sequence can be considered as the result of a regulation that has to do with the mental objects themselves, which necessitates a more "integrated" connectional organization than that required by the mental objects themselves. Perhaps one day we will manage to describe in "map" form the neurons that they involve and the development of their activity with time. The interest of the postulate of mental objects is at least that it stimulates demonstration of their material nature, their identification, and their description in neurobiological terms.

More precisely, the scientific analysis of mental objects leads to a problem of coding *correlated unitary activities of groups of neurons* that are apparently both numerous and topographically dispersed. Direct access to these objects by recording methods currently available seems difficult but not impossible a priori.

It will involve the identification of the connectional organization that has been selected by evolution to receive and give rise to them.

ONTOGENESIS OF CONNECTIONAL COMPLEXITY

Invariance and Genetic Determination

Simply to envisage a description, even one that is partial, of the connectional organization of the nervous system implies that this organization is *reproducible,* from one individual to the next within the zoological species under consideration. In other terms, this organization is conserved through the generations. However, the invariance that is copiously illustrated by anatomy textbooks is not as absolute as it might seem.

With a natural species that is genetically very heterogeneous, like the human species, a significant variability of individuals is encountered in the mass and even the histology of the brain. R. Guillery has investigated quantitatively this variability in the lateral geniculate nucleus. Out of 58 human brains examined postmortem, one came from an *albino* Nigerian who had died of uremia and showed, in accordance with results obtained on other mammalian species such as cat, rat, and tiger, a major reorganization of the different layers of this center. The others showed signs of more or less extensive fusion among the eight layers of the geniculate nucleus; in certain brains, the eight-layer segment was completely missing. The causes of such a large morphological variability, hitherto unsuspected, are only known in the case of the albino, where the observed alterations unambiguously result from a hereditary genetic mutation.

Genetic analysis of this variability has only been carried out systematically for *Drosophila* and for mice. In the first case, methods of selection allow mutants of a precise function to be isolated. In the second, one has to be content with the list of variants that have arisen spontaneously during breeding (see Sidman, Green, & Appel, 1965). One group of mutations affects proteins that participate in one way or another in giving rise to or propagating "activity." These are for example voltage-sensitive ionophores, enzymes of active transport, or enzymes involved in the synthesis or degradation of neurotransmitters (review in Stent, 1981). The behavioral deficiency that results is simple to interpret.

A second group that is of more direct interest in the present context alters the morphology of the nervous system. The extent of the lesions is remarkably different from one mutation to another. Some cause entire regions of the brain to disappear (anencephaly, absence of corpus callosum in mouse and in man), others perturb the laminar organization of different "cortical" regions ("reeler" mutation in mice), and yet others affect well-defined classes of cells (such as the cerebellar Purkinje cells in "nervous" mice) or even a single class of synapse

(parallel fibre-Purkinje cell in "staggerer" mice). The prime target of these mutations is rarely known. In one very special case (albino), the target is part of a
distinct group of cells in the nervous system (pigment cells). Nevertheless, it
seems clear that whatever the mutant locus, the earlier this gene is expressed
during development, the more extensive and pleiotropic will be the effects of
the mutation. The complex organization of the adult nervous system is built up
in a progressive and sequential manner during embryonic and postnatal development, and the mechanisms of gene expression that govern this development
have the reliability necessary to assure the reproducibility of the final organization.

Complexity of the Genome and Complexity of the Nervous System

S. Brenner and other molecular biologists have proposed that the course of this
development is regulated by a "genetic program" present in the fertilized egg.
This notion of a genetic program has recently, and rightly, been questioned by
G. Stent (1981). The concept of a unitary program arose apparently from cybernetics, whose model may be correctly applied to the bacterial cell. However,
on passing from bacteria to man, one cannot simply state (Jacob, 1970) that
"the complication of organization corresponds to a lengthening of the program."
It should first be noted that DNA possesses a linear structure, whereas development occurs in three dimensions. Furthermore, a program implies a single
control center, but such a center only physically exists in the fertilized egg and
is "delocalized" during the first steps of embryonic development. At this point,
it becomes useful to replace the "organism as cybernetic machine" model by
that of an "organism as system" (see Von Bertallanffy, 1973). The system, a
group of elements interacting with each other and with the environment, is then
defined by counting the elements that compose it, describing their states and
transitions between these states, and by the relations between elements and their
rules of interaction. The abstract notion of a program on magnetic tape is replaced
by the exhaustive description of a series of spatiotemporal processes. Moving
from theoretical vocabulary to observational vocabulary, elements become
embryonic cells, whose number, position, state, etc. vary with time, rules of
interaction represent reciprocal exchanges between cells of signals that are still
poorly understood, and the state becomes the list of "open" or "closed" genes.
Abandoning the concept of "genetic program" leads to a description of reality
that is at once more precise and more complete and allows the contribution of
cellular interactions to the organism's development and to the establishment of
adult complexity to be emphasized. In these conditions, the term *genetic determinism* will apply to different processes according to whether it refers to the
primary structure of a protein or to highly integrated "faculties" such as human
language.

In the first case, there is an immutable and nonambiguous relation between
the base sequence of the structural gene and the amino-acid sequence of the

protein. In the second, we are concerned with a brain function that involves considerable numbers of cells that have been arranged progressively in the course of time, and not necessarily synchronously. It is no longer possible to ascribe one function to one gene. To understand the determinism of highly integrated functions such as cognitive processes or language then, we need first to understand the communications *among* embryonic, and later nerve cells during development and the local expression of genes directed by these communications. The task is perhaps not as unrealistic as it seems.

A crude and simplistic way of setting about it is to compare the complexity of the genome to that of the adult nervous system in different animal species. This examination leads to a now "classical" paradox. Taking the number of nerve cells as a (bad) indication of the level of complexity, one finds that *Drosophila* with $0.24 \times 10^{-6}g$ DNA per nucleus (24 times the *E.coli* chromosome) has a nervous system of about 100,000 neurons. The fertilized egg of mice contains 27 times more DNA than that of *Drosophila,* but its brain is nearly 60 times richer in nerve cells. Man, with 2 to 16.5 billion neurons has a genome that does not, in terms of DNA weight, differ much from that of mice. Lastly, the hybridization of total chimpanzee DNA with that of man discloses differences in nucleotide sequence of only about 1.1% (King & Wilson, 1975). The absolute number of average-sized genes contained in the DNA of the fertilized egg seems at first *low*: 5–6,000 in *Drosophila* and 20–100,000 in mammals. So to the paradox of nonlinearity may be added that of the limited quantity of structural information available in the genome.

One formal solution to this double paradox takes into account the observation just mentioned that no immutable relationship between gene and neuronal morphology exists. Genes can on the other hand be combined together to label each cell (J. Monod). The number of combinations obtained by choosing, say, 10 examples from tens of thousands is sufficiently great to create a repertoire of labels of the same order of magnitude as that of the neurons or the synapses in the brain. This reasoning however does not take into account the paradox of nonlinearity.

A second and more biological solution is to envisage that a combinatory mechanism of another kind, hence "epigenetic," occurs during the morphological diversification of nerve cells during development, and that its operation only requires a small number of genes. At the later stages of mammalian evolution where the "nonlinearity" is most striking, this combinatory mechanism would take on a major importance.

Limits of Genetic Determinism

The hypothesis of labeling of cells or synapses by a combination of gene products (Sperry, 1963) allows in theory for a very precise, point by point, genetic determinism of nervous organization. Detailed observation of the genetic determinism of the anatomy of the nervous system reveals a "fringe" that is free of this determinism.

The first way of defining this "fringe" is to analyze the fine details of organization modifiable by a mutation. In other words, what is the "minimal" effect associated with a gene mutation? It is difficult to answer this question experimentally, because a mutation is only detectable in a litter if it brings about a detectable change in behavior, or in microscopic anatomy. Several well-studied examples of lesions in the final setting out of the network in both *Drosophila* and mice show that they affect *all the cells* or synaptic contacts making up what was defined previously as a *category*. For example, all the Purkinje cells in the PCD mouse and all the photoreceptors of the R7 type in *Drosophila* are affected. Genetic determinism could therefore stop at the "category" of nerve cell or synapse.

If this is true, nervous systems of Type I where the number of cell categories is close to the total number of cells should be subject to a strict genetic determinism. However, even in this case a small but significant fringe of nervous system organization could escape it. This fringe has been demonstrated by comparing organization in "isogenic" invertebrates that are in principle genetically identical, coming from the same clone, as with *Draphnia magna,* a crustacean, or from inbred strains, in the case of *Cenorhabditis,* a nematode. In these organisms, the *total number* of cells is fixed: There are exactly 258 neurons in each individual *C.elegans.* Yet a significant variation in connectivity is observed. To judge the "grain" of this connectivity, complete serial sections of nervous centers from individuals of an isogenic population were observed in the electron microscope, and then identifiable neurons and their arborizations were reconstructed (Levinthal, Macagno, & Levinthal, 1976). The principal connections between neurons were not observed to vary qualitatively, but the details of axonal arborizations (i.e., the number and distribution of branches) and the absolute number of morphological synapses fluctuated significantly.

For nervous systems of type II, such as that of mice, even the variation in the total number of cells is difficult to evaluate, because the numbers involved are so great. Some partial studies carried out on the hippocampus show that this number fluctuates significantly between individuals of an inbred strain, but that the fluctuation is less than that from one strain to another. Although it is not yet measurable, one would expect type II nervous systems to display even greater variability of connectivity than that observed in nervous systems of type I. A variability of a different order is observed following experimental lesions that cause the loss of a cell category, for example, either in the adult or during development. A reorganization of the connectivity takes place, sometimes with regain of function. These phenomena of "plasticity" are especially spectacular in type II nervous systems. Once again, they demonstrate the existence of *limits* to a strict genetic determinism. It seems appropriate to introduce the term *genetic envelope* to distinguish invariant characteristics, subject to strict genetic control, from those subject to phenotypic variations determined by this envelope.

Transitory Structural Redundancy: An Oligogenic Mechanism of Amplification

The existence of a phenotypic variation within defined limits is in accord with the possibility mentioned earlier of setting up during development a new combination distinct from a combinatory mechanism strictly at the level of the gene. To be compatible with the nonlinearity paradox, its installation should only require a small number of genes. Two groups of observations from comparative anatomy and embryology provide a possible anatomical basis for this combination.

Comparative measures of the volume of different brain regions in a range of mammals from insectivores to primates and man show a differential increase in the neocortex without any essential modification of its laminar organization. The mechanisms responsible for this evolution are not known. Nevertheless, the most plausible hypothesis is that the observed surface increase results from the *prolongation* of a tangential proliferation of the neuroblasts of the telencephalic neural tube during development. Maintaining some genes "open" in the neurula for a longer period should suffice to bring about this process. They could be homologous to the recently discovered genes that determine the development of body segmentation in *Drosophila* by selectively regulating blastomere division in the young embryo (Nüsselein-Volard & Wieschaus, 1980).

The positioning of Purkinje cells in the cortex during development has been retraced by the method of chimaeras (Mullen, 1978). No simple relation is observed between the distribution of the Purkinje cells in the cortex of the adult and the sequence of cell divisions of their embryonic precursors. In the course of the migration that follows the last divisions of the Purkinje cell precursors, they distribute themselves statistically in the layer of the same name. In other terms, when they reach their final position all the Purkinje cells are equivalent. They have the same state of differentiation and probably the same repertoire of open genes. At this stage of development, structural redundancy is considerable. The more prolonged the phase of proliferation of the precursors of the category under consideration, the greater will be the redundancy.

A similar situation is observed at the following step, that of the establishment of synaptic contacts, which takes place at birth in the rat. Each Purkinje cell receives up to five functional climbing fibres, whereas in the adult only one is present (Mariani & Changeux, 1981). This is also the case for the vertebrate motor endplate, which at birth receives three to five nerve terminals, whereas only one remains in the adult (see Changeux, 1979). The phenomenon appears to be a general one. This synaptic redundancy may be interpreted simply on the basis of labeling not each synapse taken individually but the whole category of synapses, considered as the finest state of organization subject to genetic determinism. This then allows for an indiscriminate invasion of target cells by growing nerve terminals, and hence redundancy.

This structural redundancy is, however, only transitory. It is rapidly removed by the "singularization" of the neurons. This process is accompanied by regressive phenomena: cell death (Cowan, 1979) and a decrease in nerve terminal numbers toward adult values. This transitory structural redundancy does exist in type I nervous systems but only to a small degree. It takes on considerable importance in type II nervous systems, to such an extent that one can imagine that type II nervous systems might be evolutionarily derived from type I nervous systems by the introduction of this process to embryonic development.

Nervous Activity as a Vehicle for Epigenetic Combinations

The classical cybernetic models for the functioning of the nervous system take the activity of the nervous system into account from the point of view of the input-output relations or those of external stimulus-action on the environment. Here we envisage the activity of the nervous system as a mechanism of *internal* signaling for the developing organism. The term *activity* is to be taken in its broadest sense, including all processes that directly or indirectly result in a change in the electrical properties of the neuronal membrane. It includes the propagation of action potentials, electrical coupling and processes of chemical synaptic transmission and modulation, and the possible evoked liberation of "trophic" factors.

Various electrical phenomena have been recorded from the first stages of embryonic development onward and even in the unfertilized egg. Xenopus oocytes respond to acetylcholine by a depolarization and to dopamine or serotonin by a hyperpolarization (Kusano, Miledi, & Stinnakre, 1977). In axolotl, when the neural gutter forms, a difference in membrane potential between ectoderm cells (about -30 mV) and presumptive nerve cells (-44 mV) develops.

In 1885, while studying developing chick embryos, W. Preyer noticed that from $3\frac{1}{2}$ days of incubation onward they underwent spontaneous movement. The movements are at first unilateral but then spread progressively through the body of the embryo and become alternating and periodic (type I activity). From the 9th to 16th day, short, arhythmic, general movement of large amplitude develops: The embryo bends and stretches its legs, beats its wings, and opens and closes its beak (type II activity). Finally, from the 17th day till hatching, stereotyped coordinated movements appear with a regular time course. This is also true for the behavior that allows the chick to crack the shell and leave the egg (type II activity). The overall frequency of movement is highest, at 20–25 movements per minute, around the 11th day, just when the motor innervation of the skeletal muscles is differentiating; this frequency then decreases until hatching.

These spontaneous movements are blocked by curare and coincide with an electrical activity of the same frequency in the "spinal cord." Embryonic motility has without doubt neural origins. Electrophysiological recordings of embryo spinal cords reveal units with regular periodic firing and units that fire in bursts, from 5 days onward. Polyneural bursts of firing of large amplitude and with retarded activity become more and more frequent. They spread to the whole of the spinal cord and are responsible for initiating movements (Hamburger, 1970).

Spontaneous movements of neural origin have been reported in all embryos or fetuses investigated. In man, these movements start during the eighth week, when the fetus is only 4 cm long, and are accompanied by spontaneous electrical activity, as recorded in the brain stem of 70-day fetuses obtained by caesarian (Bergstrøm, 1969). This activity continues and diversifies during the following months.

In the embryo or fetus, nervous activity develops in a strictly endogenous fashion. Four types of ionic channel are sufficient for the appearance of activity, and so the genetic cost of its development in the course of development is very low.

At the periphery, the sensory organs also undergo spontaneous activity, and the molecular mechanisms could be very similar. Most often the effect of the physical signal is to modulate this activity. For example, in the rat the illumination of the retina gives rise to a change in ganglion "on" cell activity, which increases from 40 to 70 pulses per second. In the same organism, the first signs of spontaneous activity appear 8 days after birth, but *before* the response to light. To take another example, high levels of spontaneous activity may be recorded in the afferent nerve to the vestibular receptors of the adult. When the head position changes, it varies between 5 and 35 pulses per second. One can record signs of this activity as far as the neurons of the vestibular nuclei and even the cerebellar cortex. The sensory receptors therefore are "peripheral" oscillators, whose activity contributes to the spontaneous activity recorded in the nervous centers.

As the sensory organs become functional one after the other, evoked activity begins to predominate over spontaneous activity in the waking state. In man, the sense of touch appears very early. From 49 days *in utero*, the fetus responds to tactile stimulation of the lips. Between the 5th and 7th months, the sensory innervation of the fingers is practically completed. The vestibular apparatus starts to function between the 90th and 210th day, and potentials evoked by a flash of light have been recorded in premature babies whose eyes open at the 29th week after conception. However, these fetal sensory functions are far from having the same performance as those of the adult. A maturation of sensory organs that is characterized by a diminution of the threshold of sensitivity and of the period of latency continues for a long while after birth.

Man is born with a brain that weighs about 5 times less (350 g) than that of the adult. In contrast, the weight of the chimpanzee encephalon at birth is already 60% of that of the adult. In the cerebral cortex of rat and man, denditric arborizations and synapses are formed after birth. In area 17 of the visual cortex, the average number of synapses per neuron increases from a few hundred to more than 12,000 between the 10th and 35th days *after* birth; then this number decreases significantly by between 20–30% toward the adult value. It seems reasonable to think that activity evoked by interaction with the environment, which is predominant at this stage, might be able to have a regulatory effect on the development of these synapses.

The possible involvement of nerve activity as regulator of the development of the nervous system presents a number of advantages:

1. Any electrical phenomenon can lead to an integration at the cell level.

2. In the context of the "system" model, activity propagated by the network of developing neurons represents a mode of *interaction* among elements, cells, and organs, including nervous centers, sensory organs, and effectors, which assures both integration and diversification. As a result of the properties of convergence and divergence that the neural network possesses, this interaction introduces a *new means of combining* signals.

3. Spontaneous activity present very early in embryonic development can be modulated or even relayed by the evoked activity that results from the interaction of the developing organism with the outside world. The combination mechanism for endogenous signals is "enriched" by those that are evoked.

SELECTIVE STABILIZATION: AN OLIGOGENIC MECHANISM FOR DIVERSIFICATION

The theory of epigenesis by selective stabilization (Changeux, 1972; Changeux et al., 1973; Changeux & Danchin, 1976) deals with the observations presented in the preceding sections, and in particular with the existence of limits to genetic determination that might leave room for another means of combination. According to the theory, this mechanism of combination should use the signals circulating in the neuronal network at the stage where structural redundancy occurs and should lead to a limited but significant increase in the order of the system.

At the stage of development referred to as "transitory structural redundancy," functional synaptic contacts may exist in at least three states: labile (L), stable (S), and degenerate (D). Only the L and S states transmit nerve impulses and the acceptable transitions among states are L → S, L → D, and S → L. The evolution of the connective state of a given synapse is governed by all signals received (afferent message U) by the postsynaptic soma. This regulatory function is referred to as the "evolutive power," Δ, of the soma. The maximal connectivity Φ, the mechanisms of its creation, the integrative properties of the soma, and its evolutive power constitute in other terms the rules of growth and stabilization of synaptic contact. They are all determinate expressions of genes that in their totality constitute the genetic envelope.

The connectional organization of the neuronal network can be described in graphic terms (C, Σ), where the synapses are labeled by elements of Σ. If Φ

and η represent the rules of propagation and "memorization" of the multimessages by the soma, one may define a mathematical structure R $= (C, \Sigma, \Theta, \eta, \Phi, \Delta)$ or *neuronal program*. The actualization of the neuronal program R, corresponding to the multimessage having entered the neuronal network during the critical period of synaptic plasticity, results in the stabilization of a particular set of synapses from the graph C, Σ, whereas the others regress.

One consequence of the theory is that it offers a plausible mechanism for the recording of a temporal sequence of nerve impulses in the form of a stable trace that can be described in geometrical terms. This trace is established from an organization that is completely preexistent to "experience." It is before a "selective" mechanism, which requires no "induced" synthesis of new molecules or structures.

A second consequence is that the same afferent message can stabilize different connectional organizations but lead nevertheless to an identical input-output relationship. This possible "variability" of the connectivity accounts simply for the phenotypic variation noted in isogenic individuals. It also accounts for diversification by singularization of the neurons of a given cell category at the period of transitory redundancy. This means that several connective combinations can result in the same behavior. The code for behavior is thus degenerate.

Finally, the genes that compose the genetic envelope, and in particular those that determine the rules of growth and stabilization of synaptic contacts, could be shared in type II nervous systems, by all the neurons of a given category. These genes could even be common to several neuronal categories. The cost in genes of epigenesis by selective stabilization would thus be quite low. The development of an amplification mechanism by transitory redundancy associated with an epigenetic mechanism of combination could account for the paradox of nonlinearity between the genome and neuronal organization observed during the course of evolution of mammals, especially the primates.

Experimental Test of the Theory

In our laboratory two systems have been chosen to test the theory experimentally:

1. The neuromuscular junction between motor nerves and skeletal muscle in the chicken embryo and rat, because of its simplicity, accessibility, and our advanced knowledge of its molecular architecture.
2. The cerebellum of the mouse and some of its neuropathological mutants, because of its small number of neuronal categories and the very large number of cells per category.

Some of the results obtained using these two systems are briefly described here.

EFFECTS OF CHRONIC PARALYSIS OF THE CHICK EMBRYO ON THE DEVELOPMENT OF THE NEUROMUSCULAR JUNCTION

Injection of nicotinic antagonists such as curare or snake venom α-toxins into the egg causes a block of the spontaneous movements of the embryo without killing it. This essentially peripheral paralysis (these compounds have few central effects) is followed by a significant twofold diminution in the specific activity of *presynaptic* choline acetyltransferase in motor nerves and spinal cord if α-bungarotoxin is injected from the 6th to 8th day of incubation (Giacobini, Filogamo, Weber, Boquet, & Changeux, 1973). In agreement with this observation, the total number of surviving motoneurons in the spinal cord decreases (Pittman & Oppenheim, 1979). On the other hand, if embryos are paralyzed from the 4th to 6th days, the number of motoneurons remaining is higher than in controls (Pittman & Oppenheim, 1979). Paralysis interferes with neuronal death, which, as predicted by the hypothesis of selective stabilization, is thus a process regulated by the activity of the neuromuscular system.

At the *postsynaptic* level, chronic paralysis does not prevent local accumulation of receptor but slows the disappearance of extrajunctional receptor (references in Betz et al., 1980). In normal conditions, the electrical activity of the muscle switches off receptor synthesis; chronic blockage frees it. In the same conditions, acetylcholinesterase synthesis changes in the opposite sense: Its localization at the junction requires muscle activity. The experiments with chronic paralysis thus demonstrate without ambiguity the critical role played by spontaneous activity in the morphogenesis of the motor endplate.

EFFECTS OF CHRONIC STIMULATION OF THE SPINAL CORD OF CHICKEN EMBRYOS ON MOTOR ENDPLATE DISTRIBUTION

In the chicken, the *anterior latissimus dorsi* (ALD) and *posterior latissimus dorsi* (PLD) wing muscles receive two distinct types of innervation. The ALD bears a large number of equidistant endplates per muscle fibre (distributed innervation), whereas the PLD has only one junction, situated in the middle of the fibre (focal innervation).

Furthermore, the spontaneous activity of these two types of muscle differs during embryonic development. At 15 days, the ALD receives a sustained low-frequency activity of 0.2–1 Hz, whereas the activity of the PLD is made up of high-frequency bursts (8 Hz), separated by intervals of silence. In order to test the hypothesis that embryonic spontaneous activity regulates, or determines, endplate topology, chick embryos were exposed to chronic electrical stimulation at ~ 0.5 Hz from the 10th to the 15th day of incubation, at the brachial level of the spinal cord. Quantitative analysis of the aggregates of cholinergic receptor (Toutant, Bourgeois, Toutant, Renaud, Le Douarin, & Changeux, 1980) and cholinesterase (Toutant, Toutant, Renaud, Le Douarin, & Changeux, 1981) reveals a significant increase (1.8 to 2 times) in their number per PLD muscle fibre or per total PLD muscle. Nevertheless, the distribution of the multiple receptor aggregates that appear in the PLD after stimulation is not as regular as in the ALD. The parallel evolution of spots of receptor and of esterase strongly suggests that chronic stimulation at the sustained rhythm of the ALD type gives rise to a distributed topology of motor endplates.

A biochemical mechanism that is still strictly theoretical (Changeux, Courrège, Danchin, & Lasry, 1981) could qualitatively explain the epigenetic dependence of ALD and PLD topographies on the afferent multimessages. This model has as its point of departure the state of the system where exploratory nerve fibres from a given neuron contact the muscle fibre at several points. At each point, the nerve terminals liberate acetylcholine and the evoked activity of the muscle fibre shuts off receptor synthesis. The biochemical postulates of the model are limited to:

1. The transformation of the receptor from a labile L state to a diffusible A state capable of being aggregated.

2. The liberation of an "anterograde factor" of finite half-life by the nerve terminals. The quantity of factor liberated is directly related to the afferent multimessage U; once liberated it triggers the transformation $L \rightarrow A$.

3. The aggregation of A receptor that starts and continues with increasing speed as the local concentration of A crosses a threshold value.

Computer simulation confirms that the biochemical hypotheses of the model are sufficient to obtain the formation of multiple aggregates, inferior in number to the initial number of contacts, when the input multimessage is continuous, or single aggregates when it is in bursts. However, this does not prove that the hypotheses are correct.

POSTNATAL EVOLUTION OF POLYNEURONAL INNERVATION OF RAT SKELETAL MUSCLE

At birth in the rat, the cholinergic receptor and acetylcholinesterase are localized at the motor endplate, which is at this stage occupied by several nerve endings from different neurons. Twenty days after birth only one nerve terminal per muscle fibre remains. This regression leads to segregation of motor units. In the most simple situation, each motoneuron innervates the same number of muscle fibres, its motor unit, but there is no geometrical regularity in the relative distribution of the fibres constituting a given motor unit. A first attempt to demonstrate an effect of activity on the regression of multiinnervation involved sectioning the tendon of the sartorius muscle in newborn rats. This operation causes a block of the mechanical activity of the muscle and, in consequence, a considerable delay in the regression of multiinnervation (Benoit & Changeux, 1975). Paralysis of the motor nerve using a cuff of anesthetic also gives rise to a similar delay (experiments on reinnervation in the adult; Benoit & Changeux, 1978). Chronic electrical stimulation accelerates this regression.

A theoretical model that is currently being formalized (Gouzé et al., 1983) accounts at least qualitatively for this evolution if it is supposed that:

1. A *retrograde* factor, produced by muscle fibres in limited amounts, is required for the stabilization of motor nerve terminals.

2. The retrograde factor is taken up by the nerve ending when a nerve impulse arrives.

3. This factor combines with an *internal* factor in the neuron, present in limited supplies in the neuron and all its terminals. The product of this reaction would be an active complex, and only this would possess the stabilizing property.

POSTNATAL EVOLUTION OF OLIVOCEREBELLAR INNVERVATION IN RATS AND MICE

In the newborn rat, each Purkinje cell receives several climbing fibres from the olive, but only one of them remains in the adult (Crepel et al., 1976; Mariani & Changeux, 1980b; Mariani & Changeux, 1981a). High levels of spontaneous activity were recorded in the system (Mariani & Changeux, 1981a, b), but its involvement in the stabilization of adult innervation has not been demonstrated. Nevertheless, the elimination of the granule cells, experimentally or by mutation, leads to the persistence of multiinnervation of Purkinje cells by climbing fibres in the adult (Crepel & Mariani, 1976; Mariani, Crepel, Mikoshiba, Changeux, & Sotelo, 1977; Mariani & Changeux, 1980a; Mariani, 1982). Transitory multiinnervation phenomena have also been reported for other neuronal systems.

CONCLUSION

During the last 10 years, the neurosciences have developed to the point that it is becoming possible to envisage an objective analysis of higher brain functions at the most elementary levels, that is to say cellular and molecular. These capacities are associated with an organization whose structure and rules or construction we can only just perceive. Nevertheless, what we already know is sufficient to justify the ontological approach taken from the beginning of this chapter.

REFERENCES

Benoit, P., & Changeux, J. P. (1975) Consequences of tenotomy on the evolution of multiinnervation in developing rat soleus muscle. *Brain Res., 99*, 354–358.

Benoit, P., & Changeux, J. P. (1978) Consequences of blocking nerve activity on the evolution of multiinnervation at the regenerating neuromuscular junction of the rat. *Brain Res., 149*, 89–96.

Bergström, R. (1969) Electrical parameters of the brain during ontogeny. In *Brain and Early Behavior* (R. J. Robinson, Ed.), Academic Press, New York, pp. 15–42.

Betz, H., Bourgeois, J. P., & Changeux, J. P. (1980) Evolution of cholinergic proteins in developing slow and fast skeletal muscles in chick embryo. *J. Physiol.* (London), *261*, 387–422.

Changeux, J. P. (1972) Le Cerveau et l'évènement. *Communications 18*, 37–47.

Changeux, J. P., Courrège, P., & Danchin, A. (1973) A theory of the epigenesis of neural networks by selective stabilization of synapses. *Proc. Natl. Acad. Sci, USA, 70*, 2974–2978.

Changeux, J. P. (1979) Molecular interactions in adult and developing neuromuscular junction. In *The Neurosciences, Fourth Study Program*. The MIT Press, Cambridge & London, pp. 749–778.

Changeux, J. P. (1981) The acetylcholine receptor, an allosteric membrane protein. *Harvey Lectures, 75*, 85–255.

Changeux, J. P., Courrège, P., Danchin, A., & Lasry, J. M. (1981) Un mécanisme biochimique pour l'épigénèse de la jonction neuromusculaire. *C. R. Acad. Sci.*, Paris, *292*, 240–253.

Changeux, J. P., & Danchin, A. (1976) Selective stabilization of developing synapses as a mechanism for the specification of neuronal networks. *Nature, 264*, 705–712.

Chan-Palay, V., Nivaler, G., Palay, S. L., Beinfield, M., Zimmerman, E. A., Jang-Yen Wu, & O'Donohue, T. L. (1981) Chemical heterogeneity and cerebellar Purkinje cells: Existence and coexistence of glutamic acid decarboxylase-like and motiline-like immunoreactivity. *Proc. Natl. Acad. Sci, USA, 78*, 7787–7791.

Cowan, W. M. (1979) Selection and control in neurogenesis. In *The Neurosciences, Fourth Study Program*. The MIT Press, Cambridge & London, pp. 59–81.

Crepel, F., & Mariani, J. (1976) Multiple innervation of Purkinje climbing fibres in the cerebellum of the *weaver* mutant mouse. *J. Neurobiol., 7*, 579–582.

Crepel, F., Mariani, J., & Delhaye-Bouchaud, N. (1976) Evidence for a multiple innervation of Purkinje cells by climbing fibres in the immature rat cerebellum. *J. Neurobiol., 7*, 567–578.

Denis, M. (1979) *Les images mentales*. PUF, Paris.

Giacobini, G., Filogamo, G., Weber, M., Boquet, P., & Changeux, J. P. (1973) Effects of a snake α-neurotoxin on the development of innervated motor muscles in chick embryo. *Proc. Natl. Acad. Sci.*, USA, *70*, 1708–1712.

Gouzé, J. L., Lasry, J. M., & Changeux, J. P. (1983) The selective stabilization of motor unit during development of muscle innervation: A mathematical model. *Biol. Cybern., 46*, 207–215.

Hamburger, V. (1970) Embryonic mobility in vertebrates. In *The Neurosciences, Second Study Program* (F. O. Schmitt, Ed.). The Rockefeller University Press, New York, pp. 141–151.

Jacob, F. (1970) *La logique du vivant*. Gallimard, Paris.

Kandel, E., & Schwartz, J. (1981) *Principles of neural science*. Elsevier/North Holland, New York.

Karten, H. J., & Brecha, N. (1980) Localization of substance P immunoreactivity in amacrine cells of the retina. *Nature, 283*, 87–88.

King, M. C., & Wilson, A. C. (1975) Evolution at two levels in humans and chimpanzees. *Science, 188*, 107–116.

Kusano, K., Miledi, R., & Stinnakre, J. (1977) Acetylcholine receptors in the oocyte membrane. *Nature, 270*, 739–741.

Levinthal, F., Macagno, E., & Levinthal, C. (1976) Anatomy and development of identified cells in isogenic organisms. *Cold Spring Harbor Symp. Quant. Biol., 40*, 321–333.

Mariani, J., & Changeux, J. P. (1980). Etude par enregistrements intracellulaires de l'innervation multiple des cellules de Purkinje par les fibres grimpantes dans le cervelet du rat en developpement. *C.R. Acad. Sci., 291,* 97–100.(a)

Mariani, J., & Changeux, J. P. (1980). Multiple innervation of Purkinje cells by climbing fibers in the cerebellum of the adult staggerer mutant mouse. *J. Neurobiol., 11,* 41–50.(b)

Mariani, J., & Changeux, J. P. (1981). Ontogenesis of olivocerebellar relationships. I—Studies by intracellular recordings of the multiinnervation of Purkinje cells by climbing fibers in the developing rat cerebellum. *J. Neurosci., I,* 696–702; id. II—Spontaneous activity of inferior olivary neurons and climbing fiber-mediated activity of cerebellar Purkinje cells in developing rats and in adult cerebellar mutant mice. *J. Neurosci, I,* 703–709.

Mariani, J., Crepel, F., Mikoshiba, K., Changeux, J. P., & Sotelo, C. (1977). Anatomical, physiological and biochemical studies of the cerebellum from *reeler* mutant mouse. *Phil. Trans. Roy. Soc. B, 281,* 1–28.

Monod, J. (1970). *Le Hasard et la Nécessité.* Le Seuil, Paris.

Mullen, R. J. (1978) Mosaicism in the central nervous system of mouse chimeras. In *The clonal basis of development,* S. Bubtelny & I. M. Sussex (Eds.), Academic Press, New York.

Nüsslein-Volard, C., & Wieschaus, E. (1980) Mutations affecting segments member and polarity in *Drosophila. Nature, 287,* 795–801.

Pittman, R., & Oppenheim, R. W. (1979). Cell death of motoneurons in the chick embryo spinal cord. *J. Comp. Neurol., 187,* 425–446.

Shepard, R. N., & Metzler, J. (1971) Mental rotation of three-dimensional objects. *Science, 171,* 701–703.

Sidman, S. L., Green, M. C., & Appel, S. (1965). *Catalog of the neurological mutants of the mouse.* Harvard University Press, Cambridge.

Sperry, R. W. (1963) Chemoaffinity in the orderly growth of nerve fiber patterns and connections. *Proc. Natl. Acad. Sci., USA, 50,* 703–710.

Stent, G. (1981) Strength and weakness of the genetic approach to the development of the nervous system. *Ann. Rev. Neurosci, 4,* 163–194.

Stent, G., Kristan, W. B., Friesen, W. O., Ort, C. A., Poon, M., & Calabrese, R. L. (1978). Neuronal generation of the leech swimming movement. *Science, 200,* 1348–1357.

Toutant, M., Bourgeois, J. P., Toutant, J. P., Renaud, D., Le Douarin, G., & Changeux, J. P. (1980). Chronic stimulation of the spinal cord in developing chick embryo causes the differentiation of multiple clusters of acetylcholine receptor in the *Posterior latissimus dorsi* muscle. *Develop. Biol., 76,* 384–395.

Toutant, M., Toutant, J. P., Renaud, D., Le Douarin, G., & Changeux, J. P. (1981). Effet de la stimulation médullaire chronique sur le nombre total de sites d'activité acétylcholinerasique du muscle *Posterior latissimus dorsi* de l'embryon de poulet. *C.R. Acad. Sci.,* Paris, *292,* 771–775.

Von Bertallanffy (1973). *Théorie générale des systèmes.* Dunod, Paris.

14 Toward a Neurobiology of Cognitive Development

Patricia S. Goldman-Rakic
Section of Neuroanatomy
Yale University School of Medicine

INTRODUCTION

Research and observations on cognition in neonates and children have proceeded for centuries in the absence of hard biological facts about the anatomical structures and neuronal processes that must underlie these functions. Some would say that information about the brain provides little aid to those who would understand childhood competence and developmental schedules, through allowing that data on brain may be useful when considering pathological development. Such arguments have long since ceased to be made for analysis of spinal reflexes, sensory or certain motor functions, perhaps because reliable information about the anatomy and physiology of spinal cord and central structures of the sensimotor apparatus has proven of value in clinical diagnosis. In contrast the systems of the brain that are critical for maturation of higher order cognitive processes have to a large extent remained enigmatic and unapproachable. In large measure, slow progress in this field has been due to the inadequate methods available in the past. A perhaps related problem is that few neuroscientists or physiological psychologists have chosen this field because of its very real uncharted character. As I have indicated previously, however, prospects for understanding structurally and functionally complex neural systems have changed dramatically over the last decade (Goldman-Rakic, 1981a). It has become possible to understand the anatomical details of complicated circuitry at a high level of detail and to relate anatomy to biochemical, electrophysiological, and behavioral data in both the developing and mature animal. Importantly, though nonhuman primates, particularly rhesus monkeys, have become extremely scarce and costly, application of powerful methods and experimental designs have produced a high yield of information on development and plasticity of neural systems in both normal and experimentally altered animals closely related to homo sapiens. It does not have to be argued that the rhesus monkey is unexcelled as an animal model of human development, and that its brain bears a close resemblance to man's in cortical expanse, neuronal organization, parameters of development, and capacity for expressing complex behavior.

The present chapter focuses on selected studies carried out in my laboratory over the past several years on the prefrontal association cortex. The substantial advances made in elucidating the organization of major classes of connections of prefrontal cortex and remarkable plasticity of these connections in brain-damaged primates is reviewed elsewhere (Goldman-Rakic, 1981a,b). Here I have decided to focus on experiments that may be of more immediate interest to the developmental psychologist. I describe several studies that illustrate new methodological approaches to structure-function issues in cognition. The intent is to show how multidisciplinary neurobiological analysis can inform us about basic issues and possible mechanisms involved in cognition and its development. Sophisticated cognitive psychologists may find more subtle theoretical ramifications of these results that we have missed or that have escaped us. That is my hope.

REVERSIBLE CORTICAL LESIONS AND DELAYED-RESPONSE FUNCTION

A basic observation of developmental psychology is that complex cognitive and linguistic skills develop later and at a slower rate than more elementary sensory and motor skills. It is assumed with some justification that the neuroanatomical, biochemical, and physiological substrates of such capacities must also develop slowly, and that their maturation is a necessary precondition for the emergence of complex functional competence. In developmental psychobiology, we are concerned with determining the neural basis of functional maturation, the elucidation of how different subdivisions of neocortex and subcortical structures assume or take on specialized function, and how these structure-function relationships are altered by experience.

An essential requirement for demonstrating a linkage between neuroanatomical and psychological development is the availability of suitable behavioral tests that provide a sufficiently sensitive reflection of mature function in adult animals and yet are amenable to tests and probes in younger organisms. Additionally, it is critical to have a means of assessing cortical engagement in a particular function, as discussed in the following section.

The Delayed-Response Task

Under proper conditions, nonhumans and humans are able to remember the location of an object following only a single presentation and retain such information for hours and even days (Hunter, 1913; Tinklepaugh, 1928). This ability can be measured in tests of delayed reaction originally devised by Hunter (1913) for comparative psychological studies (Fig. 14.1). In the classical or widely used standard version of this test, the subject is shown the location of a food that is then hidden from view. Following a delay period, the subject is allowed to choose the correct of two or more locations. In a variation of this task, delayed alternation, the subject is required to alternate between left and right foodwells on successive trials that are separated by delay periods. In the latter task, the subject's choice on any given trial is predicated upon faithful memory of the preceding choice. Tests of spatial delayed reaction have often been maligned by psychologists, perhaps because they may seem too simple; yet, they have proven to be invaluable as experimental tools in the study of brain damage (Jacobsen, 1936), drug action (Brozoski, Brown, Rosvold, & Goldman, 1979), and most significantly for present purposes, development (Goldman, 1971; Harlow, Thompson, Blomquist, & Schiltz 1970). It should be pointed out that use of the delayed response task provided the first objective behavioral demonstration of deficits in memory function attributable to a localized region of the central nervous system—the prefrontal cortex in monkeys (Jacobson, 1936). The dependence of delayed response function upon prefrontal cortex remains one of the best and most solidly established structure-function relationships in neuropsychology.

Irreversible and Reversible Lesion Methods

Since the last century, the main experimental technique for demonstrating functional localization in the central nervous system was the lesion method, by which circumscribed areas of the brain were removed and the behavioral consequences analyzed. This method can yield extremely valuable and reliable findings, but interpretations of these findings can often be difficult and complicated (see Goldman-Rakic, Isseroff, Schwartz, & Bugbee, 1983). The problems of interpretation are exacerbated when comparing the consequences of lesions at different stages of development, particularly as it is well established that functions are spared to a greater degree following lesions in the immature cortex (Harlow et al., 1970; Goldman & Galkin, 1978). It is now possible to circumvent many of these problems by studying specific cortical functions with the method of cortical cooling, a method that allows reversible inactivation of restricted regions of cortex in normal animals. Essentially, the neuronal activity of an area (and hence, its information processing capacity) can be temporarily suppressed by lowering neuronal temperature to 20°C without injuring the tissue. Although this method

DELAYED RESPONSE

CUE

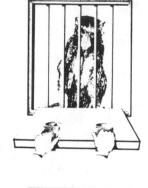

DELAY
0″–10″

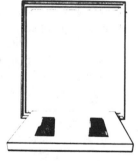

RESPONSE

FIG. 14.1.   Diagram illustrating the three components of a delayed-response trial. In the cue period, the monkey watches an experimenter bait the well. During the delay phase, the screen is lowered for 1 or more sec. In the response phase, the monkey must select the correct well for reward.

had previously been used only in research on mature animals (Bauer & Fuster, 1976; Fuster & Alexander, 1971), I thought that it would be highly suitable for analysis of functional development of cortex. Accordingly, rhesus monkeys varying in age between 9 and 36 months were trained to perform the two-choice delayed-response task. After each animal had reached a performance criterion of 90% correct on 4 consecutive days, cooling chambers were implanted over a portion of the dorsolateral prefrontal cortex in each hemisphere under pento-barbital anaesthesia. Lesions of even a small portion of prefrontal cortex (in the principal sulcus) are sufficient to produce large behavioral deficits on this task in adult rhesus monkeys (Butters et al., 1972; Goldman, Rosvold, Vest, and Galkin, 1971). The disk-shaped stainless steel cooling probes (12.5 mm diameter) were implanted over the brain, centered 4 mm above the midpoint of the principal sulcus; the dura matter which envelops the brain remained intact, except for two small openings through which insulated bead thermistors were inserted to monitor the subdural temperature. Experimental testing began 1 week after recovery from surgery and consisted of repeated sessions, in which the subject's delayed-response performance was assessed before, during, and after cooling to 20°C. Each monkey received 100–200 trials in each of the three conditions (precool, cool, postcool) over the course of 10 sessions.

Intracerebral temperature gradients measured during cooling at terminal stages of the experiment revealed that the areas cooled to 20°C in all brains was limited to tissue directly beneath the probe and included only the superficial banks of the principal sulcus. The depths of that sulcus remained within 2–3°C of the normal core temperature. In addition there was no significant hypothermia beyond the boundaries and subjacent white matter of the dorsolateral prefrontal cortex. It should be emphasized that no significant variation was found in the size or locus of the area cooled in relation to age (Goldman & Alexander, 1977; Alexander & Goldman, 1978). In contrast, the behavioral results were clearly age dependent, as shown in Fig. 14.2, where the monkeys have been grouped according to age. Dorsolateral prefrontal cooling did not impair delayed-response performance in monkeys 9–16 months of age (Group I). This group made a small number of errors during cooling, but this figure did not differ significantly from the number of errors made during postcool trials. A small but significant increment (7%) in errors due to cooling was first observed in monkeys 19–31 months of age (Group II), but cooling-induced deficits comparable in magnitude (23%) with those seen in adult monkeys did not appear until 34–36 months of age (Group III). The percentage of cooling-induced errors exhibited by Group III monkeys was on the average 2.5-fold higher than that exhibited by the monkeys in Group II.

The pattern of increasing sensitivity to dorsolateral prefrontal cooling, apparent in the comparisons among groups of monkeys at different ages, is also demonstrable in the ontogenetic history of individual monkeys. Thus, one monkey exhibited a significant but relatively small increase in errors during prefrontal

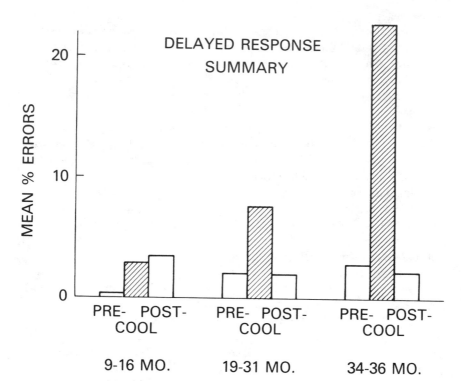

FIG. 14.2.   Delayed-response (DR) performance in relation to cryogeneic depression of the dorsolateral prefrontal cortex (DLC). Mean errors on DR trials presented before, during, and after DLC cooling for groups of monkeys in the age spans indicated. Percent of DR errors for each animal and condition were subjected to an arcsin transformation, and the transformed data underwent a 3 (age groups) × 3 (DLC cooling condition) factorial analysis of variance with repeated measures on the last-named variable. The main effect for DLC cooling condition was significant ($F(2, 10) = 28.1$, $P 0.001$) as was the age × DLC cooling condition interaction ($F(4, 10) = 8.8$, $P 0.005$). Comparisons of mean DR errors in the different DLC conditions within groups were made using Tukey's (a) test with the critical level of $P 0.01$. Both Groups II (ages 19–31 months, $n = 3$) and III (ages 34–36 months, $n = 2$) made significantly more errors during cooling than either before or after, whereas their performance under the two latter conditions did not differ significantly. In contrast, for Group I (ages 9–16 months, $n = 3$) there were no significant differences in performance among any of the three conditions (from Rakic and Goldman-Rakic, 1982).

cooling at the age of 31 months, although 3 months later this same animal exhibited a 2.5-fold increment in the percentage of errors during cooling—whereas its control performance during this same interval showed a slight improvement.

The finding that prefrontal cooling did not induce deficits in the Group I monkeys is in agreement with previous reports that even complete resections of dorsolateral prefrontal cortex in infancy do not produce impairments on delayed response (Goldman, 1971; Harlow et al., 1968). The 23% performance decrement observed in the oldest (Group III) monkeys during cooling is, however, substantially less than the nearly 50% decrement usually seen in adult monkeys with prefrontal lesions. This discrepancy is most likely due to the fact that the cortex in the depths of the principal sulcus, normally included in dorsolateral surgical ablations, was not sufficiently depressed by cooling owing to its position away from the cooling probe. But, as the magnitude of the cooling-induced impairment in the Group III monkeys is nearly identical to that reported in independent studies of adult monkeys carried out with comparable methods (Alexander & Fuster, 1973) it seems that the Group III monkeys represent the age at which the dorsolateral cortex reaches functional maturity.

Thus, the present results indicate that a considerable portion of the dorsolateral prefrontal cortex does not participate significantly in the mediation of delayed-response performance during the first 16 months of postnatal life; subsequently, this region participates only minimally until, by 36 months of age, the process of maturation seems to be essentially complete. Previous evidence from lesion studies for the protracted maturation of the dorsolateral prefrontal cortex was open to the alternative explanation that early lesions of this area had failed to result in deficits months after surgery because there had been time for recovery of function through compensatory neural reorganization. This explanation now seems improbable because prefrontal cooling did not produce delayed-response deficits in young, non-lesioned monkeys. In these animals neural reorganization should not be a factor unless it were assumed that such a process could be stimulated by cortical hypothermia within the course of a testing session.

The lack of dependence on the dorsolateral prefrontal cortex for delayed-response behavior in young monkeys, shown now both in studies of surgical and functional ablation, contrasts with the dependence for such behavior, from infancy through sexual maturity, on certain brain regions other than the dorsolateral prefrontal cortex, such as the orbital prefrontal cortex (Goldman, 1971; Miller, Goldman, & Rosvold, 1973), the anterodorsal caudate nucleus (Goldman & Rosvold 1972), and the mediodorsal nucleus (Goldman, 1974; Isseroff, Rosvold, Galkin, & Goldman-Rakic, 1982). I have previously proposed that these earlier developing components of a frontal lobe network are capable of mediating delayed-response performance before the dorsolateral cortex matures (Goldman & Rosvold, 1972). The function performed is more primitive, however, and the behavioral strategy different (Goldman-Rakic, unpublished results). The results

obtained with the reversible cooling method additionally suggest that the dorsolateral prefrontal cortex assumes its mature functions by augmenting rather than
replacing these other antecedent neural mechanisms, because there is no evidence
of disturbance in the basis ability to perform delayed-response during the transition
from minimal to maximal dependence on the dorsolateral prefrontal cortex.

Implications for Developmental Psychology

I see at least two important implications of this work for developmental psychology. One is an experimental demonstration that behavioral analysis is not
always sufficient for deductions about brain maturation. One-year-old monkeys
perform the delayed-response task as well as juvenile and adult monkeys (Goldman, 1971; Goldman & Galkin, 1978). As I have indicated, more extensive
behavioral probes and manipulations can lead eventually to a distinction in the
level and/or nature of mental processing or strategies employed at different ages.
However, had we studied only the time of emergence of delayed-response competence, we would have concluded, erroneously, that the neural substrates of
this function were basically mature within the first year of life. Actually they
seem to develop fully only in the third year of life, closer to the age of sexual
maturity. Thus, the appearance of an ability (e.g., imitation behavior, attention,
visual pursuit), however adult-like in its phenotypic expression, cannot be taken
as evidence that the neural system in question is fully differentiated.

The second point that may be emphasized about functional development is
that it involves more than a linear process of differentiation; rather, there may
be a major reallocation or shift of function from subcortical control to cortical
regulation. Although the mechanisms by which such shifts occur are at present
poorly understood, nevertheless, they provide a basis for understanding qualitative as well as quantitative differences between infants and adults in concept
formation, social sensitivity, and orientation toward future goals. I have previously suggested that functional development reflects a certain heterology of brain
organization in childhood and adulthood (for more detailed discussion of this
issue, see Goldman, 1974; Goldman-Rakic, Isserof, Schwartz, and Bugbee,
1983). Such heterology allows us to appreciate why children may outgrow certain
behavioral problems, why adults lose memories of their childhood, why certain
disturbances appear for the first time in adolescence, etc.

ELECTROPHYSIOLOGY OF COGNITION IN ADULT MONKEYS

Not long ago, electrophysiological analysis of neuronal activity in relation to
higher order behaviors would have been considered unthinkable. Only recently,
in 1971, the first pioneering studies of prefrontal cortical neurons were conducted
in behaving primates (Fuster & Alexander, 1971; Kubota & Niki, 1971). Again

an important impetus for these studies was the dependence of delayed-response functions upon prefrontal cortex, particularly the cortex lining the principal sulcus. Because this task can be decomposed into the elemental structure of cue, delay, and response periods, it has become possible to record neuronal activity in prefrontal neurons and time-lock their activity to these main components of a delayed-response trial. Perhaps the most significant finding of electrophysiological research to date has been the discovery of specific classes of neurons that fire preferentially in relation to these components of the delayed-response task. Of very particular significance is the special class of cells that code spatial information and fire during the delay period (Kojima & Goldman-Rakic, 1982; Niki, 1974a). Examples of two such neurons are shown in Fig. 14.3 Neuronal activity during the intertrial period (which serves as a control or base-line period), reflects the spontaneous discharges of the neuron being studied. At the onset of the "cue period," when a visual stimulus appears on either the left or the right side of the response panel to signal the eventual location of the food reward, the neuron continues to fire at about the same rate as during the intertrial interval. However, as soon as the delay commences, the unit shows a significant increase in firing that, in the present instance, decreases before the end of the delay and remains at base-line level during the response. Significantly, the neurons illustrated exhibit the delay-related increment in firing only when the cue is presented in one of the two positions, in this instance on the right. Thus, although we cannot say what precisely triggers the activation of this neuron, we can say that it is not simply the sensory stimulus nor the execution of the response. Rather this and many other units like it are registering a psychological event interposed between stimulus and response—in the terminology of classical psychology—a mental event.

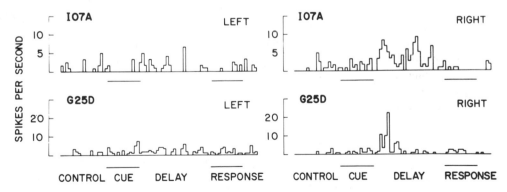

FIG. 14.3. Two examples of prefrontal neurons that exhibited delay-related spatially discriminative activity while the monkey from which they were recorded was performing a delayed-response task. In this experiment, the cue and response periods lasted 5 sec; the duration of the delay was 12 sec. (from Alexander, Witt, & Goldman-Rakic, unpublished).

Very little is yet known about this highly specialized class of prefrontal neurons. However, some evidence indicates that the differential activation of selected prefrontal neurons depends on the relative and not the absolute position of cues (Niki, 1974b). Also, there are two types of delay-related spatially discriminative units: some are more related to the position of the cue, whereas others are more related to the position of the impending response (Niki & Watanabe, 1976).

Recently, a study in my laboratory was designed to examine more precisely the prefrontal neuronal activity that occurs during the delay interval of delayed-response trials performed by rhesus monkeys (Kojima & Goldman-Rakic, 1982). Although delay length is an important variable in spatial short-term memory, only limited information concerning its relationship to prefrontal neuronal activity was available. The mnemonic character of the delayed-response task as well as its spatiality has been shown to be a critical feature of its vulnerability to prefrontal damage (Goldman & Rosvold, 1970; Goldman et al., 1971). Accordingly, attention was focused on the discharge pattern of the same neuron across trials with different delays; and the differential activity within the delay related to the spatial position of the cue of individual prefronal neurons was also of considerable interest.

Young adult rhesus monkeys served as subjects in this experiment. Before being prepared for electrophysiological recording subjects were trained to perform a delayed-response task as follows (Fig. 14.3). The monkey was required to depress a hold key for 2 or 4 sec. to start a trial. The intertrial interval was followed by the cue presentation period (C) in which either the left or the right disc on a panel in front of the subject was illuminated by a white light for .5 sec. Thereafter, the light was turned off and the delay period (D) commenced. When the delay period was over, both the left and right discs were illuminated by red light, signaling the onset of the response period (RSP) and the availability of juice reinforcer. If the monkey released the hold key and pressed the disc that had been white during cue presentation, it was rewarded with orange juice. A press on the other disc was recorded as an error and terminated the trial. The position of the cue was randomized from trial to trial. In the present study, three delay intervals were employed: 2, 4, and 8 or 12 sec.

Changes in the duration of the delay elicited two distinct patterns of activity in these neurons: Some (62%) exhibited a fixed pattern of discharge regardless of the duration of the ensuing delay; others (33%) altered their pattern of activity in relation to temporal changes (Fig. 14.4). An additional finding concerns the small subclass of neurons that fire significantly more when the cue is presented on the left (right) or right (left) or vice versa. A striking 80% of these spatially discriminative neurons exhibited peak activation in the first few seconds of the delay period.

At present we can only speculate about the functional significance of prefrontal neurons that showed a fixed latency, duration of discharge, and/or fixed position of firing peak irrespective of delay length. One possibility is that these neurons

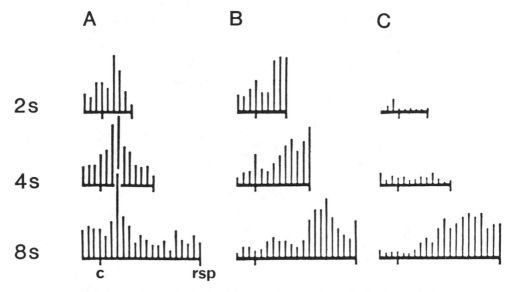

FIG. 14.4. (A) Example of a delay-related neuron that has a fixed pattern of discharge independent of whether the delay is 2, 4, or 8 sec. (B and C) Examples of delay-related neurons that exhibit a variable pattern of discharge dependent on the duration of the delay. Note that the latency of peak firing shifts to the right (occurs later in the delay) as the delay lengthens. c = cue; rsp = response (modified from Kojima & Goldman-Rakic, 1982).

have distinctive temporal "assignments," and their sequential activation may serve as the mnemonic "bridge" in the delay interval of the delayed-response task. Alternatively, it is tempting to interpret the fixed pattern of discharge as a neuronal manifestation of the encoding process. Such a process would reasonably occur at a fixed point in time after cue presentation and would not depend on the duration of the ensuing delay. It may be relevant in this regard that twice as many fixed discharge neurons fired in the early as compared with the later stages of the delay, as might be expected if these neurons were engaged in encoding or registration of the position of the stimulus. Perhaps more significant was our observation that over 80% of spatially selective neurons exhibited their peak activity in the early portion of the delay whereas only a few late-firing neurons showed spatially selective firing. The spatial information coded by this special class of neurons presumably forms the content of the encoding process.

About 33% of the delayed-related prefrontal neurons changed their latency, duration, peak position, and/or pattern of discharge as the delay lengthened. Although it is considerably more difficult to assess the role of these more time-dependent neurons, an appealing hypothesis is that they may be involved in "anticipatory" or "expectancy" processes. In this context, it is important to note that in the experiment described, the length of the delay was increased in a predictable order throughout the testing session, and that a tone indicated a change in the duration of the delay. Thus, the monkey not only had to remember the location of the reward on any given trial but could also attend to the absolute duration of the waiting period for obtaining the reward. The tuning of neuronal activity to this parameter of the task (delay length) indicates the existence of neuronal machinery that can be modified by changes in the temporal contingencies among events in the delayed-response task. This type of response at the single unit level may provide a cellular basis for the slow surface negative potentials (the so-called "expectancy waves") that have been shown to spread over the prefrontal convexity in man (Walter, 1967) and monkey (Low, Borda, & Kellaway, 1966), when a given stimulus becomes a warning signal for a second event that requires a decision or motor response. Slow wave potentials develop only after repeated pairings of the stimulus events, and in this sense the conditions of changing delays in the present study correspond to behavioral paradigms that elicit slow wave negativity. On the other hand, we cannot rule out that the monkey adopts a covert position depending on the duration of the delay or may exercise an inhibition of premature, irrelevant, or incorrect responses also in relation to the length of the delay. Only future experimentation in which behavior of the monkey is controlled in different ways can resolve these various possibilities.

As mentioned, the present findings suggest that neuronal processes that occur in the early delay may be critical for delayed-response performance, particularly as the behavior of spatially sensitive neurons fire in this period. This notion supports and is supported by several studies in which external events or brain stimulation were interpolated at various points in a delayed-response trial. Stamm (1969) has shown that electrical stimulation of the middle region of the principal sulcus severely disrupts delayed-response performance only when applied during the first few seconds of the delay period. Similarly, Kojima (1980) has shown that distraction is most efficacious in disrupting such performance in the early delay period. Recently, we observed that removal of the prefrontal cortex in monkeys impairs the response selection process in the early delay period (Kojima, Kojima, & Goldman-Rakic, 1982). Together these findings suggest that the cellular events that occur in the early delay period may be particularly critical for performance on spatial short-term memory tasks and, moreover, may be involved in the encoding process.

DEVELOPMENT OF PREFRONTAL NEURONAL ACTIVITY

Not surprisingly, the study of neuronal activity in prefrontal cortex has been confined to the adult animal. To examine the neural activity associated with behavioral maturation of delayed-response behavior, we performed an electrophysiological examination of individual neurons in the dorsolateral prefrontal cortex of imma-ture (12-month-old) and mature (36-month-old) monkeys as they performed a delayed-response task (Alexander, Witt, & Goldman-Rakic, 1980). In this devel-opmental study, 38% of the neurons in prefrontal association cortex of adult rhesus monkeys could be characterized as "delayed-activated" neurons (Figure 14.5) In contrast, in immature monkeys, only 20% of prefrontal units manifested increased rates of discharge during the delay period. The use of stringent control paradigms, such as "mock delay" (in which no cue is presented) or "action withholding" (in which the animal is allowed to visualize the cue throughout the delay period), show that these delay-related increases in firing rate are task specific and do not occur unless the animal is required to retain and eventually utilize the spatial information presented in the cue period. Other discharge param-eters, such as the magnitude and spatial selectivity of unit responses, did not differ significantly between recordings from mature and immature monkeys; nor were there any age-related differences in the number of units showing activation during the cue and response periods (Fig. 14.6).

In order to compare the functional maturation of prefrontal association cortex with that of other brain regions, analysis of unit activity during DR testing was also carried out in parietal association cortex (Brodmann's areas 5 and 7 of), in the head of the caudate nucleus, and in the mediodorsal nucleus (MD) of the thalamus. In parietal cortex, some neurons were activated during the delay phase of the DR trial, but the number of such units was very small and did not differ between infants and adults (Fig. 14.6). Cells of the caudate and MD nuclei were studied because these structures have strong anatomical connections with pre-frontal cortex (Goldman, 1979; Goldman & Nauta, 1977a), and because lesions of these structures result in DR impairment in both infants and adults (Goldman & Rosvold, 1972). In these regions, a relatively large proportion of neurons showed activity changes associated with the events of DR testing. As in parietal regions, the proportion of delay-activated units remained constant from infancy to adulthood. Thus, of the areas studied, only neurons of prefrontal cortex demonstrated postnatal maturation in terms of DR performance.

Thus, the population of delay-activated neurons of prefrontal cortex actually expands (by as much as two-fold) in the course of the first 3 years of postnatal life. Because, in primates, the number of cortical neurons remains essentially constant from birth to maturity, the age-related increase in delay-activated neu-rons indicates that some form of functional or structural recruitment must occur postnatally. In young animals, the proportion of prefrontal neurons that do not respond to any phase of the DR testing paradigm is slightly, but significantly, greater than in adults. It may be from this subpopulation of unresponsive cells that the later appearing delay-activated cells are recruited. Thus, the quantitative changes in delay-activated neurons may provide a partial explanation for the monkeys' gradually increasing dependence on prefrontal cortex for the solution of spatial problems.

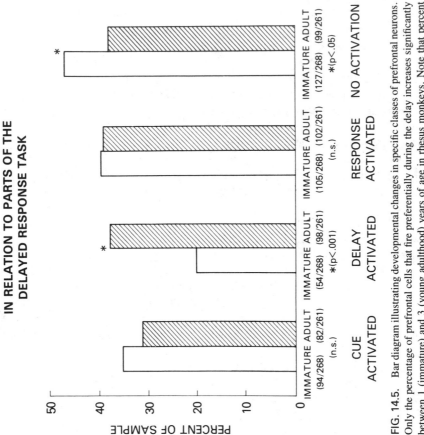

FIG. 14.5.   Bar diagram illustrating developmental changes in specific classes of prefrontal neurons. Only the percentage of prefrontal cells that fire preferentially during the delay increases significantly between 1 (immature) and 3 (young adulthood) years of age in rhesus monkeys. Note that percent of unresponsive prefrontal neurons (no activation) decreases over the same age span (from Alexander, Witt, & Goldman-Rakic, unpublished).

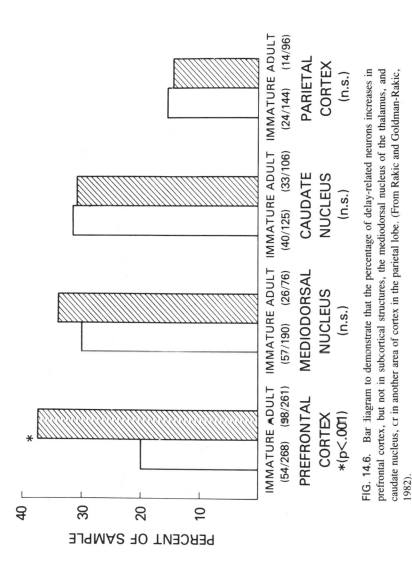

FIG. 14.6.   Bar diagram to demonstrate that the percentage of delay-related neurons increases in prefrontal cortex, but not in subcortical structures, the mediodorsal nucleus of the thalamus, and caudate nucleus, or in another area of cortex in the parietal lobe. (From Rakic and Goldman-Rakic, 1982).

FUTURE DIRECTIONS

One of the limitations of neuropsychological and neurophysiological studies today and in the past has been that they permit analysis of practically only one structure or a small sample of neurons at a time. However, we are very well aware that even an elementary behavioral act may represent the activity of an entire neural system, if not several interrelated systems. We are daily learning more about neural ensembles and interactions between and within them. Also, with the aid of new methodologies now available to neuroscientists, we have unprecedented possibilities for analysis. It would therefore be fitting to conclude this chapter by pointing to the new directions that these methods are taking us in and suggest how they may illuminate the neural bases of cognition.

Neuroanatomical Methods

Over the past 10 years, a virtual revolution has taken place in techniques and factual information about the precise anatomical organization of the central nervous system of a variety of species, including primates. Of particular significance for understanding the functions of prefrontal cortex is the discovery of a modular compartmentalization in the organization of major classes of cortical input to prefrontal cortex (Goldman & Nauta, 1977b). The spatially periodic distribution of axonal connections in the central nervous system has generally been regarded as a special adaptation of sensory systems, reflecting primarily the peripheral segregation of sensory surfaces, such as the retinae of left and right eyes. However, we now realize that modular organization is a more general feature of central nervous system organization, and describes the disposition of a wide variety of connections in all parts of the brain (Fig. 14.7A). The techniques used to demonstrate columnar organization of fiber systems in my laboratory involve the placement of radioactive isotopes or certain enzymes into circumscribed territories of the prefrontal cortex of rhesus monkeys. These substances are taken up by cell bodies in the vicinity of the localized injection, synthesized into proteins, and transported along the axons that issue from the parent cells by a process referred to as anterograde axonal transport.

Michael Schwartz and I recently injected a radioactive anterograde tracer into the principal sulcus of the right hemisphere and another distinctly different nonradioactive tracer into the parietal cortex of the left hemisphere (Goldman-Rakic & Schwartz, 1982). Both cortical inputs converge in the principal sulcal cortex of the left hemisphere, but their arrangement in this zone could take a number of different forms: The two inputs may overlap, or they may interdigitate or mutually avoid each other. The use of a double labeling strategy allowed us to provide the first evidence that columns of axons originating in one hemisphere alternate with those of the other in the principal sulcus of the rhesus monkey. This is the region of prefrontal cortex that is a cortical focus for delayed-response

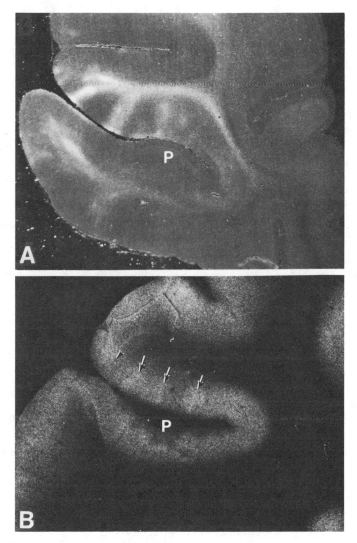

FIG. 14.7.   (A) Dark-field photomicrograph of a coronal section cut through the frontal lobe, showing the principal sulcus (P) and labeled columns of fibers that represent the terminal distribution of callosal neurons residing in the contralateral principal sulcus. These callosal columns interdigitate with spaces devoid of callosal input from the opposite hemisphere. We have recently shown that these spaces are filled by inputs from cortical regions in the same hemisphere. Thus, intra-hemisphere and interhemispheric inputs are interdigitated in the principal sulcus (photograph modified from Goldman & Nauta, 1977b). (B) Contact print of x-ray film of a comparable section through the frontal lobe of a monkey pulse labeled with ^{14}C-deoxyglucose. The photograph shows that metabolic activity in the principal sulcus is columnar. Whether metabolic columns are coincident with anatomic columns remains to be determined, but the technology is now available to answer this question.

performance and contains neurons with spatial-mnemonic processing activity, as described earlier. The interdigitation of ipsilateral and contralateral inputs in this cortical region provides a mechanism for interhemispheric integration through communication between adjacent columns of neurons. It is too early to identify these behaviorally interesting neurons as part of a particular cortico-cortical circuit, but studies combining electrophysiology and anatomical tracing methods promise to identify the neural circuits engaged in mediating a fragment or even a sequence of events necessary for processing spatial information. As we identify specific central pathways, we will also learn about their biochemical makeup and be able to alter neurotransmitter levels and syntheses pharmacologically.

2-Deoxyglucose Metabolic Labeling

The second promising approach for understanding structure-function relationships is the availability of a powerful method, the 2-deoxyglucose method, for mapping the functional activity in the central nervous system (Sokoloff, Reivich, Kennedy, Des Rosiers, Patlak, Pettigrew, Sakurada, & Shinohara, 1977). This method is based on the simple principle that there is a close relationship between neuronal activity and cerebral metabolism of glucose, which is the brain's only significant energy source. In practical terms, when ^{14}C-deoxyglucose is injected in tracer amounts into the blood stream, its uptake in the brain will be virtually identical to that of glucose. Unlike glucose, however, 2-deoxyglucose is not rapidly metabolized and instead builds up within cells, more so in neurons that are metabolically most active during the period of availability of the tracer. Thus, an experimental subject can be injected with ^{14}C-deoxyglucose, allowed to engage in a particular behavior for enough time to insure that all deoxyglucose is taken up in brain tissue (approximately 45 minutes), and then sacrificed. The brain is quickly frozen to prevent diffusion of the label and cut into thin 20 µm sections. The sections are then exposed to x-ray film, which when developed provides a radiographic image of the section. The most densely labeled areas in the image reflect the areas of the brain that were most active during the test.

Using this method, neuroscientists have already succeeded in demonstrating central correlates of sensory and motor stimulation in a variety of animals. Nellie Bugbee and I (Bugbee & Goldman-Rakic, 1981) are now using this method to reveal the contribution of several brain regions to cognitive behavior at different stages of development. To do so we again used the "work-horse" of frontal lobe function, the delayed response task, because its dependence on prefrontal cortex is so well established.

In this experiment, six monkeys were required to remember the location of a target over a 12-second delay period. Correct responses were rewarded with food. Four control (CON) animals were tested under identical circumstances, with the same number of trials and reinforcements, except that no delay was interposed; these subjects were allowed to respond as soon as the target was presented. To insure that motor activity and auditory input were similar for both groups, all subjects were restrained in primate chairs and exposed to amplified white noise. At the beginning of the final testing session, each monkey received an intravenous pulse of ^{14}C 2DG (100 μCi/kg) via a femoral catheter; arterial samples were collected throughout the session. Subjects worked steadily over the 45-minute period of 2DG administration, with DR animals performing at 90% correct.

Local cerebral glucose utilization (LCGU), quantified according to the procedures described by Sokoloff et al. (1977), was measured in eight cortical regions: prefrontal, motor, auditory, striate, extrastriate, entorhinal, and superior and inferior temporal gyrus. The great advantage of this method over other functional approaches is that it allows the assessment of the contribution to behavior of many structures simultaneously. To compensate for individual variations in absolute LCGU, data for each animal was expressed as ratios. LCGU of each of the aforementioned cortical regions was compared to that of primary auditory cortex, a region in which sensory input was constant for all subjects. Statistical comprisons demonstrated that only the prefrontal ratio differed for the DR and CON groups (p .05, t test, two-tailed). None of the other cortical areas examined could be differentiated according to behavioral task.

An important finding in these studies is that metabolic activity is itself not uniformly distributed throughout the cortex, but, like cortico-cortical connections, is distributed in a pattern of columns of high activity alternating with areas of low activity (Fig. 14.7B). This single fact opens up the possibility that metabolic activity and specific afferent inputs are coincident (i.e. that the metabolic activity of known anatomical pathways can be identified). Because we can visualize the areas of high activity in 2-DG autoradiograms, we can identify the contribution of a specific callosal, associational, or thalamo-cortical projection to delayed-response or any other behavior of interest. This can be done not only in normal subjects but also in those suffering brain injuries at different stages of development. With the latter, it would be possible to determine the neural basis of functional recovery when it takes place on the locus of dysfunction when deficits are permanent.

CONCLUSIONS

In this chapter I have tried to acquaint the developmental and cognitive psychologist with the variety of datum gathered in one laboratory that may have relevance for the study of cognition and its eventual explanation in neural terms. From the present vantage point, the possibilities for unraveling complex systems are limitless. However, these possibilities can only be realized by a joining of the efforts of a wide range of specialists with a common interest in cognition. We have demonstrated that a relatively simple cognitive test, delayed response, can serve excellently as a model system for analyzing development of cortical function. However, we have every reason to believe that the same approaches used here can be successful in unraveling neural mechanisms responsible for more complex and subtle aspects of cognition. We are limited only by the lack of communication between our disciplines.

REFERENCES

Alexander, G. E., & Fuster, J. M. Effects of cooling prefrontal cortex on cell firing in the nucleus medialis dorsalis. *Brain Research*, 1973, *61*, 93–105.

Alexander, G. E., & Goldman, P. S. Functional development of the dorsolateral prefrontal cortex: An analysis utilizing reversible cryogenic depression. *Brain Research*, 1972, *143*, 233–250.

Alexander, G. E., Witt, E., & Goldman-Rakic, P. S. Neuronal activity in the prefrontal cortex, caudate nucleus, and mediodorsal thalamic nucleus during delayed-response performance of immature and adult rhesus monkeys. *Neuroscience Abstracts*, 1980, *6*, 86.

Bauer, R. H., & Fuster, J. M. Delayed-matching and delayed-response deficit from cooling dorsolateral prefrontal cortex in monkeys. *Journal of Comparative and Physiological and Psychology*, 1976, *90*, 293–302.

Brozoski, T., Brown, R. M., Rosvold, H. E., & Goldman, P. S. Cognitive deficit caused by regional depletion of dopamine in prefrontal cortex of rhesus monkey. *Science*, 1979, *205*, 929–932.

Bugbee, N. M., & Goldman-Rakic, P. S. Functional 2-deoxyglucose mapping in association cortex: Prefrontal activation in monkeys performing a cognitive task. *Neuroscience Abstracts*, 1981, *7*, 239.

Butters, N., Pandya, D., Stein, D., & Rosen, J. A search for the spatial engram within the frontal lobes of monkeys. *Acta Neurobiol. Exp.*, 1972, *32*, 305–329.

Fuster, J. M. Unit activity in prefrontal cortex during delayed-response performance: Neuronal correlates of transient memory, *J. Neurophysiol.*, 1973, *36*, 61–78.

Fuster, J. M., & Alexander, G. E. Neuronal activity related to short-term memory. *Science*, 1971, *173*, 652–654.

Goldman, P. S. Functional development of the prefrontal cortex in early life and the problem of neuronal plasticity. *Experimental Neurology*, 1971, *32*, 366–387.

Goldman, P. S. An alternative to developmental plasticity: Heterology of CNS structures in infants and adults. In D. G. Stein, J. Rosen, and &. Butters (Eds.), *CNS Plasticity and Recovery of Function*. New York: Academic Press, 1974.

Goldman, P. S. Neuronal plasticity in primate telencephalon: Anomalous crossed cortico-caudate projections induced by prenatal removal of frontal association cortex. *Science*, 1978, *202*, 768–776.

Goldman, P. S. Contralateral projections to the dorsal thalamus from frontal association cortex in the rhesus monkey. *Brain Research*, 1979, *166*, 166–171.

Goldman, P. S., & Alexander, G. E. Maturation of prefrontal cortex in the monkey revealed by local reversible cryogeneic depression. *Nature*, 1977, *267*, 613–615.

Goldman, P. S., & Galkin, T. W. Prenatal removal of frontal association cortex in the rhesus monkey: Anatomical and functional consequences in postnatal life. *Brain Research*, 1978, *52*, 451–485.

Goldman, P. S., & Nauta, W. J. H. An intricately patterned prefronto-caudate projection in the rhesus monkey. *J.Comp. Neurol.*, 1977, *177*, 369–386. (a)

Goldman, P. S., & Nauta, W. J. H. Columnar distribution of cortico-cortical fibers in the frontal association, motor, and limbic cortex of the developing rhesus monkey. *Brain Research,* 1977, *122,* 383–386. (b)

Goldman, P. S., & Rosvold, H. E. Localization of function within the dorsolateral prefrontal cortex of the rhesus monkey. *Experimental Neurology,* 1970, *27,* 291–304.

Goldman, P. S., & Rosvold, H. E. The effects of selective caudate lesions in infant and juvenile rhesus monkeys. *Brain Research,* 1972, *43,* 53–66.

Goldman, P. S., Rosvold, H. E., Vest, B., & Galkin, T. W. Analysis of the delayed alternation deficit produced by dorsolateral prefrontal lesions in the rhesus monkey. *J. Comp. Phyiosl. Psychol.,* 1971, *77,* 212–220.

Goldman-Rakic, P. S. Development and plasticity of primate frontal association cortex. In F. O. Schmitt, F. G. Worden, S. G. Dennis, & G. Adelman (Eds.), *The organization of cerebral cortex.* Cambridge: M.I.T. Press, 1981. (a)

Goldman-Rakic, P. S. Morphological consequences of prenatal injury to the brain. *Progress in Brain Research,* 1981, *53,* 3–19. (b)

Goldman-Rakic, P. S., Isseroff, A., Schwartz, M. L., & Bugbee, N. M. Neurobiology of cognitive development in nonhuman primates. In P. H. Mussen (Ed.) *Manual of child psychology: Infancy and the developmental psychobiology.* New York: Wiley, 1983, 282–344.

Goldman-Rakic, P. S., & Schwartz, M. E. Interdigitation of contralateral and ipsilateral columnar projections to frontal association cortex in primates. *Science,* 1982, *216,* 755–757.

Harlow, H. F., Blomquist, A. J., Thompson, C. I., & Schiltz, K. A. Learning in rhesus monkeys after varying amounts of prefrontal lobe destruction during infancy and adolescence. *Brain Research,* 1970, *18,* 343–353.

Hunter, W. S. The delayed reaction in animals and children. *Behav. Monogr.,* 1913, 2.

Isseroff, A., Rosvold, H. E., Galkin, T. W., & Goldman-Rakic, P. S. Spatial impairments following lesions of the mediodorsal nucleus of the thalamus in rhesus monkeys. *Brain Research,* 1982, *232,* 97–113.

Jacobsen, C. F. Studies of cerebral function in primates: I. The functions of the frontal association areas in monkeys. *Comp. Psychol. Monogr.,* 1936, *13,* 3–60.

Kojima, S. Short-term memory in the rhesus monkey: A behavioral analysis of delayed-response performance. *J. Exp. Anal. Behav.,* 1980, *33,* 359–368.

Kojima, S., & Goldman-Rakic, P. S. *Delay-related activity of prefrontal neurons in rhesus monkeys performing delayed response. Brain Research* 248, 1982, 43–49.

Kojima, S., Kojima, M., & Goldman-Rakic, P. S. *Operant behavioral analysis of delayed-response performance in rhesus monkeys with prefrontal lesions. Brain Research, 248,* 1982, 51–59.

Kubota, K., & Niki, H. Prefrontal cortical unit activity and delayed alternation performance in monkeys. *Journal of Neurophysiology,* 1971, *34,* 337–347.

Low, M. D., Borda, R. P., & Kellaway, P. "Contingent negative variation" in rhesus monkeys: An EEG sign of a specific mental process. *Percept Mot. Skills,* 1966, *22,* 443–446.

Miller, E. A., Goldman, P. S., & Rosvold, H. E. Delayed recovery of function following orbital prefrontal lesions in infant monkeys. *Science,* 1973, *182,* 304–306.

Niki, H. Prefrontal unit activity during delayed alternation in the monkey. I. Relation to direction of response. *Brain Research,* 1974, *68,* 185–196. (a)

Niki, H. Prefrontal unit activity during delayed alternation in the monkey. II. Relation to absolute *versus* relative direction of response. *Brain Research,* 1977, *68,* 197–204. (b)

Niki, H. Differential activity of prefrontal units during right and left delayed-response trials. *Brain Research,* 1974, *70,* 346–349. (c)

Niki, H., & Watanabe, M. Prefrontal unit activity and delayed response: Relation to cue location *versus* direction of response. *Brain Research,* 1976, *105,* 78–88.

Rakic, P., & Goldman-Rakic, P. S. (Eds.) *Development and plasticity of the cerebral cortex.* Neurosciences Research Program Bulletin, v. 20, no. 4. Cambridge, Mass.: MIT Press, 429–606.

Sokoloff, L., Reivich, C., Kennedy, C., des Rosier, M., Patlak, C., Pettigrew, O., Sakurada, O., & Shinohara, M. The (^{14}C)-deoxyglucose method for the measurement of local cerebral glucose utilization. Theory, procedure, and normal values in the albino rat. *J. Neurochem.* 1977, *28*, 897–916.

Stamm, J. S. Electrical stimulation of monkeys' prefrontal cortex during delayed-response performance. *J. comp. Physiol. Psychol.*, 1969, *67*, 535–546.

Tinklepaugh, O. L. An experimental study of representational factors in monkeys. *J. Comp. Psychol.*, 1928, *8*, 197–236.

Walter, W. G. Slow potential changes in the human brain associated with expectancy, decision and intention. *Electroencephalogr. Clin. Neurophysiol.*, (Suppl.) 1967, *26*, 123–130.

15 Development of Language: A Question of Asymmetry and Deviation

Glenn D. Rosen
Albert M. Galaburda
Department of Neurology
Harvard Medical School
and
Neurological Unit and Charles A. Dana Research Laboratories
Beth Israel Hospital, Boston

INTRODUCTION

In this chapter we discuss the neuroanatomical substrates of language from a developmental perspective. In the first section we briefly review evidence illustrating the importance of cerebral asymmetry to the organization of the brain for language. Having established that asymmetry is present by the time of birth, we ask what might be the effects of alterations in the normal process of development of asymmetry on language acquisition. Specifically, we describe two cases of developmental language disturbance associated with alterations in brain development primarily affecting the language-dominant hemisphere. In order to attempt to explain the nature and origin of these alterations, a brief outline of the normal process of structural development of the brain is presented. Finally, we speculate on possible relationships between structure and function with special emphasis on the issue of laterality of language representation.

LANGUAGE AND THE LEFT HEMISPHERE

It has been known for over a century that in the adult the "language centers" of the brain are lateralized (Broca, 1865; Wernicke, 1874). In the majority of dextral individuals, lesions of Broca's area or of Wernicke's area in the left hemisphere often result in severe language disturbances, whereas lesions in homologous locations of the right hemisphere produce such aphasias much less frequently. Lateralization to the left hemisphere for language has since been confirmed in stimulation experiments during surgery (Penfield & Roberts, 1959) and spontaneously during epilepsy, in "split-brain" patients (Sperry, 1974), and in intact subjects from a variety of techniques including dichotic listening (Kimura, 1961), tachistoscopic lateralized presentation (see Springer, 1977), regional cerebral blood flow (Larsen, Skinhoj, & Lassen, 1978), evoked potential (see Anderson, 1977), and positron emission tomography (Phelps, Hoffman, & Mazziota, 1981). Thus, language in most right-handed individuals tend to be lateralized to the left hemisphere.

Consistent anatomical asymmetries in the brain were demonstrated as early as the 1880s (Eberstaller, 1884). However, these findings were largely ignored until recently when Geschwind and Levitsky (1968) demonstrated anatomical asymmetries to be present in large numbers of brains. They found that 65% of 100 brains had a longer left planum temporale,[1] whereas the right planum was longer in only 11% of the cases. The remaining 24% had symmetrical plana. They (Geschwind & Levitsky, 1968) concluded that the differences in size between the left and right planum temporale were: "easily of sufficient magnitude to be compatible with the known functional asymmetries [p. 187]."

Since that time the finding of a larger left planum temporale has been replicated by a number of other studies. Wada, Clarke, & Hamm (1975) found that the left planum was larger in 85% of the cases they examined. Witelson and Pallie (1973) found that 69% of the adult brains they studied had a larger left planum. It is important to stress that the planum temporale contains cortical auditory representations and is commonly affected by lesions that result in Wernicke's aphasia.

Additional investigators have confirmed the presence of planum asymmetry and have described asymmetries in the Sylvian fissure as well. The Sylvian fissure is the deep furrow on the lateral convexity of the brain that, on the left side, contains in its banks many of the standard language areas. Direct observations on histological material (Chi, Dooling, & Gilles, 1977; Rubens, Mahowald, & Hutton, 1976; Teszner, Tzavaras, Gruner, & Hécaen, 1972), measurements of intact brains through computerized axial tomography (LeMay & Kido, 1978) and other radiological techniques have demonstrated consistent asymmetries in the Sylvian fissures and in the cerebral ventricles (Hochberg & LeMay, 1975; LeMay & Culebras, 1972; McRae, Branch, & Milner, 1968; Rubens et al., 1976; Yeni-Komshian & Benson, 1976). Many of these asymmetries can be demonstrated in casts made of the internal surface of the brain in fossil skulls (Gundara & Zivonovic, 1968; LeMay, 1976). In general there is agreement that the left planum temporale tends to be larger and the left Sylvian fissure longer and more

---

[1]Planum temporale refers to a gross anatomical landmark, triangular in shape, located on the superior temporal surface and bound anteriorly by the auditory gyrus of Heschl. It contains cortical auditory fields.

horizontally placed, thus permitting a better development of both the temporal and parietal opercula.

We have shown that there are asymmetries in the volume of auditory cytoarchitectonic areas (Galaburda, LeMay, Kemper & Geschwind, 1978; Galaburda, Sanides, & Geschwind, 1978). We measured both the planum temporale and cytoarchitectonic area Tpt (an auditory association field likely to comprise a major component of Wernicke's area) in four serially sectioned brains. We found striking asymmetries in area Tpt, with the left up to 620% larger than the right. Moreover, the degree of cytoarchitectonic asymmetry perfectly correlated with the degree of planum asymmetry. This work, then, indicates: (1) a demonstrable asymmetry in volume in an auditory association area; and (2) a direct relationship between cytoarchitectonic and planum temporale asymmetries.

Additional asymmetries of volumes of other architectonic areas in the cortex and thalamus have been reported. Thus there is a strong left-sided preponderance of a cortical field present in the pars opercularis of the frontal lobe, an area comprising an important portion of Broca's region (Galaburda, 1980). There is also an asymmetry in the angular gyrus of the parietal lobe (Eidelberg & Galaburda, in press) and in the language relevant lateralis posterior nucleus[2] of the thalamus (Eidelberg & Galaburda, 1982).

Ontogeny of Asymmetry

The question as to whether infants exhibit lateralization of function at birth is one that has interested researchers for a number of years. One school of thought contended that the two hemispheres of the brain were equipotential for language during the first 6 years of life. This theory was based on the work of Basser (1962), who reported that lesions of the right hemisphere in early life resulted in language deficits much more often than comparable lesions in adulthood; that as the infant matured, the incidence of aphasia following right-hemisphere lesions decreased; that the aphasia seen in these children was much less severe than that of adults; and that aphasia acquired sometime after the 8th year of life approached the severity of aphasia acquired in adulthood. These findings led Lenneberg (1967) to conclude that the hemispheres were equipotential for language at birth, and that this equipotentiality diminished as the infant matured. By 6 years of age, more and more of the speech and language processes became lateralized until the individual acquired the adult pattern between 10 and 12 years of age.

There are, however, some problems with the behavioral observation in the brain-damaged children. First, conclusions derived from brain-damaged subjects must be examined in the light of knowledge of the biological characteristics of

---

[2]The lateralis posterior nucleus is a component of the pulvinar-LP complex in the posterior thalamus, where left-sided lesions often result in aphasia.

acquired disease at different ages and in different populations. For instance, when one talks about right-hemisphere lesions in childhood, the most common culprits are trauma, infection, stroke, and tumor. Discrete localization of traumatic injury has always been difficult to demonstrate, especially in closed head trauma cases where bilateral injury is more often the case (Hendrick, Harwood-Hash, & Hudson, 1963). Likewise, localized effects of infectious agents have been classically attributed to brain abscesses, but these most commonly produce bilateral mass effect. On the surface, the most interpretable of all etiologic agents is stroke in childhood. However, even here we are faced with some difficult problems. Unlike the situation in the adult where isolated deficits are the result of strokes that are most likely the result of degenerative vascular disease producing localized infarction, stroke in childhood is more often the result of hemorrhage into brain tissue. These hemorrhages arise mostly from maldeveloped blood vessels that are embedded in abnormal brain tissue. Formation of abnormal vessels of this type occurs right after midgestation, and it is safe to assume that the brain has had ample time to reorganize into unpredictable patterns of language representation. It is not possible, therefore, to arrive at any conclusions about localization of language in brains that probably do not follow the standard rules. This argument can also be extended to include brain tumors in childhood. In this situation not only do the tumors act as masses and distort the brain bilaterally, but it is also known that the tumors often arise from glial or neuronal remnants representing developmental anomalies capable of altering brain organization. The presence of these anomalies, therefore, excludes the possibility of comparing deficits in childhood to acquired deficits in the adult.

Another issue that plays a very important role in lesions in childhood as compared to similar lesions in adult life has to do with plasticity and recovery. It has been shown (see Goldman, this volume) that major reorganization of structure is possible when lesions take place during critical stages of brain development. It is possible to restructure the architecture of the cortex as well as the architecture of the connections (Goldman, 1978; Innocenti & Frost, 1980; Schneider, 1981) following early interference. It is reasonable to expect that with such a degree of structural reorganization there will be accompanying changes in function. As similar strategies are not available to the adult brain, direct comparisons should be handled cautiously.

The theory of equipotentiality of the hemispheres at birth must be viewed in the light of demonstrable functional lateralization in early life. Evidence that infants might be lateralized came directly from work involving infant speech perception. Eimas, Siqueland, Jusczyk, & Vigorito (1971) found that 1–4 month-old infants could perceive and distinguish various speech sounds—a finding that has since been replicated by Moffit (1971) and Morse (1972). Molfese, Freeman, & Palermo (1975) then recorded auditory evoked potentials over homologous areas of the left and right hemispheres of infants during the presentation of speech and musical stimuli. They appear to have found that the left hemisphere was more active during the presentation of speech stimuli, and that the right hemisphere was more active during musical stimuli.

Further evidence that infants were lateralized for speech perception came from dichotic listening procedures that demonstrated that infants had a left-ear advantage for music and nonspeech sounds and a right-ear advantage for speech sounds (Entus, 1977). This is the same pattern of ear advantage that is seen in the adult. Vargha-Khadem and Corballis (1979) failed to replicate these results; however, Mehler (in this volume) reports more recent investigations that suggest a right-ear superiority for linguistic-like stimuli. Additionally, lateralization for speech perception was reported by Segalowitz and Chapman (1980), who found that speech stimuli delivered to an infant disproportionately affected right-limb movement, thereby possibly indicating greater left-hemisphere involvement in speech processing.

Finally, there is evidence to indicate that lesions sustained in the left hemisphere early in development may have profound effects on later language abilities. Dennis (1983) examined young children who underwent either left or right hemispherectomy. She found that those children with left hemispherectomies showed deficits in the verbal section of the Illinois Test of Psycholinguistic Abilities (ITPA), whereas the right-hemispherectomized child was deficient in spatial aspects of the test. This suggested that hemispheric specialization was present at 1 year of age. Again, one must consider these data with caution, because children undergoing hemispherectomy are also likely to have dramatic reorganization of brain structure and function, as these operations are done for congenital disorders or tumors of great severity.

The main difficulty we have with accepting the theory of equipotentiality arises from the knowledge that the infant brain is structurally asymmetrical. Anatomical asymmetries present at birth have been reported in several studies. Witelson and Pallie (1973) found that the left planum temporale was larger than the right in the majority of the infants they studied. Wada et al. (1975) described similar asymmetries as early as the 29th week of gestation. If there is indeed equipotentiality of the hemispheres at birth, it would still be necessary to explain why the standard language areas are already asymmetrical at this stage of development. Thus, the infant brain may have at least one biological determinant leading to a tendency to develop control of language by the left hemisphere. The variability in response to lesions and in response to physiological tests may simply reflect issues of variability of this biological determinant.

In summary, it is clear that language and specific areas of the left hemisphere are inexorably linked—damage sustained to these areas can result in severe disturbances of language. Moreover, these areas of the left hemisphere have been shown to be larger than their homologues on the right in adults and infants.

In addition to lateralization and asymmetry found in the normal brain of the infant and child, we are aware of the existence of disordered lateralization and asymmetry. Dyslexia is a commonly occurring learning disability in which impaired performance affects predominantly functions of one hemisphere, in this case the left. In our laboratory, we have analyzed the brains of two boys who during life had that diagnosis, and the findings provide additional insight into possible mechanisms underlying the cerebral representation of language.

Developmental Dyslexia

The first case of developmental dyslexia studied at postmorten was that of Drake (1968), who reported abnormalities in cortical development that consisted chiefly of abnormal convolutional patterns and excessive neuronal remnants in ectopic[3] locations. The second case was reported by Galaburda and Kemper (1979). This was the case of a left-handed boy with a family history of dyslexia, who despite normal intelligence, educational opportunities, and emotional stability had been unable to achieve satisfactory competence in reading and writing by the time of his death at the age of 20 years; yet he had become a successful artist. The third case was that of a 14-year-old right-handed boy, also from a family in which dyslexia was prevalent, who had been severely affected for many years despite special education and normal inelligence.

The findings in the brain differed in severity between the latter two specimens but belonged to the same type of developmental alteration. There was a general disorganization of the architecture of the cortex of the left hemisphere consisting of inarticulate layering and paucity of cells. There were numerous instances in the left hemisphere of focal dysplastic[4] abnormalities. These consisted of ectopic cells located both within the cortex and in subcortical areas. There was persistence of primitive neuronal elements. In one case there was an instance of severe cortical malformation (micropolygyria[5]) involving a major portion of the left planum temporale. Both brains showed the symmetrical pattern of the Sylvian fissures and planum temporale seen in 24% of the population (vide supra).

Although the cortex of the right hemisphere was relatively uninvolved by dysplasias, there were subtle qualitative differences in the architecture of areas homologous to the affected left language areas, consisting of a general decrease in the definition of the architectonic fields. It was not possible to say whether the right cortical changes were primary or represented a response to the severe left-sided alterations. The bilateral involvement in the cortex was mild as compared with the striking bilateral changes in the thalamus, especially in its posterior

---

[3]Ectopias and heterotopias are used interchangeably to denote the presence of a tissue or portion of a tissue in a place from which it is normally absent.

[4]Dysplasia refers to any of a variety of developmental abnormalities affecting the morphology of a tissue.

[5]Micropolygyria is a severe form of cortical dysplasia in which there is incomplete lamination, abnormal folding, fusion of adjacent layers, and accompanying heterotopias.

portions. These thalamic alterations were less severe in the second case, whereas the first case showed marked distortion of the outline and cellular architecture of the lateralis posterior and medical geniculate nuclei. We have discussed elsewhere the developmental interdependence between thalamus and cortex, which might help explain the more obviously bilateral thalamic involvement (Galaburda & Eidelberg, 1982).

Inasmuch as the normal asymmetries of the human brain can be found at least during the late period of fetal brain development, likewise the origin of the abnormalities shown by the three brains thus far reported in the literature date back to the second half of gestation. It is reasonable to suggest, therefore, that the abnormalities seen in the brain in developmental dyslexia may represent an aberration of the normal process of lateralization. The finding of increased left-handedness in those affected with learning disabilities and their relatives (Geschwind & Behan, 1982) support this notion. In order to better understand this possible relationship between normal and abnormal lateralization, we briefly outline the process of normal development of the nervous system with special consideration paid to the development of the cerebral cortex.

DEVELOPMENT OF THE CORTEX

There are three major events in the development of the nervous system: determination, migration, and maturation. The cells of the nervous system originate from a portion of the embryonic ectoderm (one of the three embryonic germ layers) that is modified into the neural plate. The transformation of general ectodermal cells into neuroectoderm is completed by the end of gastrulation (passage from 2- to 3-layered stage), and, in fact, determination (the restriction of future capabilities) of the neural plate is completed by that time. Thus, by the third or fourth week of gestation, neuroectoderm can only differentiate into neural tissue.

The process of neurulation involves the infolding of the neural plate to form the neural tube that surrounds a central canal. A group of cells, the neural crest, that originally broke off the neural plate during neurulation is found dorsal to the neural tube on each side. The neural tube will eventually give rise to the white and gray matter of the central nervous system, whereas portions of the central canal will differentiate into the ventricular cavities. The cranial portion of the neural crest gives rise to numerous neural and non-neural structures, which include the soft and bony tissues of the face, the teeth, as well as many of the cranial nerves. The more caudal neural crest segments give rise to the peripheral nervous system and some components of the immune and endocrine systems.

After the closure of the neural tube, the next step of differentiation is the proliferation of specific types of neural and glial germ cells. This takes place in the subependymal and subventricular germinal zones located near the central canal. After a series of mitotic divisions, neurons begin to migrate to their final locations. Different cells are generated and migrate at different times. In general, large cells migrate before small cells, motor cells before sensory cells, glial cells after neurons, and interneurons (local-circuit neurons) differentiate last. Furthermore there is a focal differentiation within these germinal zones, such that cells arising from a given portion of the zone will be directed to given portions of the cortex, probably respecting the future architectonic differentiation. During the later stage of cortical development, the stage of maturation, dendritic processes are developed and elaborated, synapses are formed, connections are made, and cells begin expressing their neurological properties. Also during this period there is a massive amount of neuronal death, which affects primarily those neurons that were unable to establish adequate numbers and types of synaptic relationships.

In the early stages of cortical development, the cells are dispersed throughout the neural tube. These cells then move toward the central canal and aggregate to form the subependymal germinal zones previously mentioned. This aggregation of cells divides the neural tube into an inner ventricular zone containing the germinal zone and an outer marginal zone. The marginal zone contains essentially no cell bodies with the exception of the Cajal-Retzius cells,[6] which will later populate the immature cortex. The marginal zone instead contains the processes of the cells of the ventricular zone. When the cells of the ventricular zone become postmitotic, they migrate to the intermediate zone. From this intermediate zone, cells pass through to form the cortical plate from which all cells of the cortex will mature. The path and final placement of neurons is determined partly by their interaction with radial glial fibers. After the ventricular zone, a second proliferative zone, the subventricular zone, is formed between the intermediate and the ventricular zone. It is from this second proliferative center that most glial cells and small neurons are formed. The cells from the cortical plate begin to form the six layers of adult neocortex in an "inside-out" manner, so that the cells of layer VI are the first to be formed and migrate and the cells of layer II are the last and have to migrate through the other layers of cells. The beginning of the migration period in the human can be dated to approximately the 16th week gestation, and its completion is more tentatively placed between the 20th and 30th weeks.

Development of the Cortex and Anatomical Asymmetries

The asymmetries in planum temporale just described have been demonstrated in fetal brains not much younger than 29 weeks of gestation, which is well beyond the time when the bulk of migration to the cerebral cortex has taken place; visible

---

[6]Cajal-Retzius cells are bipolar horizontal neurons present in layer I that disappear by the time of birth, except in some developmental pathological states.

asymmetries, therefore, represent changes in the morphology of the cortex that are the result of postmigrational (maturational) events. The growth of the cortex at that time reflects the development of individual neurons that are then elaborating their neuropil, axonal collaterals, and myelinated fibers. In addition this is a period when there is continuing glial proliferation and migration to the cortex capable of altering volumes. Another possibility for the appearance of gross asymmetry at this time may not be growth of a given area but the remodeling of the opposite side during the process of cell death. Thus asymmetries may arise because the subordinate side loses in the competition for synapses and undergoes cell death in excess of the dominant side.

In addition to the finding of static asymmetries in the fetal brain akin to those seen in the adult (i.e., asymmetries in the planum temporale and Sylvian fissure), there are also dynamic asymmetries in the rate of the development of the two sides. It has long been known that the right hemisphere structurally matures earlier than the left hemisphere. Hervé (1888) pointed out that the gyri of Broca's area on the right side appeared earlier than those on the left. Fontes (1944) demonstrated that in general the gyri and sulci surrounding the Sylvian fissure appear earlier on the right. More recently, Chi et al. (1977) also showed that the development of convolutions around the Sylvian fissure occurs earlier on the right side and pointed out that structures surrounding the planum temporale may be recognizable on the right side as long as 2 weeks earlier than on the left. Therefore it can be said that although certain language areas of the left hemisphere are visibly larger on the left side as early as the 29th week of gestation, they develop more slowly than their mates in the nondominant hemisphere.

Thus it would appear that portions of the right hemisphere develop first *in utero*, but the left hemisphere eventually catches up and surpasses the right in size and complexity of development. These are several hypothetical reasons for this. It may be that the right hemisphere develops faster than the left, but the left grows for a longer period of time and eventually surpasses the right. Alternatively, the rate of development may be faster in the right during the early period and faster on the left during the later period of gestation, without having to implicate an arrest of the development of the right side. In either case, the observation invites the notion that the left and right hemisphere receive different instructions during development, and that this difference contributes to the formation of asymmetrical hemispheres capable of asymmetrical functions.

It is not clear at which time during development does the process of anatomical lateralization actually begin. Even though asymmetries first become visible in the later stages of gestation, particularly after the period of neuronal migration is finished, this does not necessarily mean that an asymmetry at a more subtle, (and as yet undetectable) level is not present earlier. Boklage (in press) has argued strongly for the notion that asymmetry has its origins during the first divisions of the ovum. As his major argument, he cites data that relates statistically the incidence of left-handedness and twinning in the human population. He suggests that the normal pattern of twinning involves the more symmetrical division of the egg into fertilizable halves (as opposed to the standard asymmetrical polar body division), in which the polar body is not fertilizable. The symmetrical division will then determine the presence of greater symmetry in the body, including the brain. Interestingly, he has cited data that showed that among twins, in addition to an increase in left-handedness and ambidexterity, there is more symmetry in the dentition of the two sides, another derivative of the neural ectoderm. Although it is not possible to ascertain at which point asymmetry begins, at this time it is not possible to exclude the possibility that there may be asymmetry in the rate of DNA replication, cell division, and neuronal migration. Later on, asymmetries in the rates of proliferation of the neuropil as well as aymmetries in cell death may additionally contribute to the adult pattern of side differences and render it visible for the first time in late gestation.

There are some data to suggest that process begins at least as early as the time of neuronal migration in the rat.[7] Debassio, Kemper & Galaburda (1982) showed that the growth of the frontal pole of the rat tended to differ in rate on the two sides during the time when neuronal migration to the olfactory bulb was actively taking place. Although neuronal migration to the frontal lobe is completed before that to the olfactory bulb, it is possible that differential rates of migration contribute to the frontal asymmetry. The presumed influence of the period of neuronal migration on the development of the cerebral asymmetries may be further illustrated by migrational anomalies involving only one hemisphere, such as seen in developmental dyslexia.

ABNORMAL DEVELOPMENT OF ASYMMETRY

The types of neuroanatomical abnormalities seen in the dyslexic brain are not unique to this behavioral disorder, although their localization may be. Micropolygyria, ectopic neurons in layer I, subcortical ectopias, and cortical dysplasias are found in a wide variey of "normal"[8] and abnormal brains. Micropolygyria

---

[7]Behavioral lateralization and structural asymmetries have been repeatedly demonstrated in nonhuman species (for reviews see Denenberg, 1981; Sherman, Galaburda, & Geschwind, 1982). In the absence of language systems in these species comparable to the human, it is safe to assume that asymmetries in the brain do not just underlie language processes but also other lateralized behaviors. On the other hand, it is quite likely that the same mechanisms leading to asymmetry in animals for nonlanguage behaviors play a role in human asymmetries underlying language.

[8]It should be noted, however, that what are termed normal brains at autopsy refers to a situation where little or no detailed history relating to the cognitive, perceptual, or motor abilities of the individual is available. It simply refers to subjects with no known neurological "diseases." Thus, it is possible that those individuals determined to be normal may have had deficits not well-documented in life.

and neuronal ectopias have been associated with profound psychomotor retardation (Brun, 1975; Caviness, Evrard, & Lyon, 1978; Levine, Fisher, & Caviness, 1974). What is unique to the brains of the two dyslexic individuals is the localization and lateralization of the lesions predominantly to the perisylvian regions of the left hemisphere.

The etiology of micropolygyria and associated neuronal ectopias remains uncertain, but strong evidence points toward an insult to the cerebrum during the later part of the period of neuronal migration to the cortical plate, i.e., from 20–25 weeks of gestation. (McBride & Kemper, 1982). The position of ectopic neurons in the subcortical white matter serves as evidence that the disruptions occurred before the end of the migrational period. In laboratory animals similar alterations can be produced experimentally only during the period before neuronal migration to the cortical plate is completed (Dvorak, Feit, & Jurankova, 1978). Because the cytoarchitectonic areas in which the most striking alterations are seen in the dyslexic brain are the last neocortical areas to complete neuronal migration (Chatel, 1976), we can ostensibly narrow down the time of insult to the sixth month of gestational age.

The question can be then raised as to why the left hemisphere is preferentially affected in the dyslexic brain. The knowledge about differential rates of growth of the two hemispheres provides a springboard from which to consider a number of possible mechanisms. For example, it may be that any given cerebral insult presented at random acts preferentially on the side developing more slowly, in a manner analogous to the situation of the shooting gallery, where slowly moving ducks are easier to hit. Another possibility is that the dyslexic abnormalities result from the more prolonged exposure of the left hemisphere to an etiologic agent than the right. This would be a type of window effect whereby a causative agent acts only during critical periods (windows), and the windows are open for a longer time on the left side. Still another possibility would argue that the injurious agent does not occur at random but is specifically directed at a particular biological feature present in the left but not the right hemisphere. The production of an antibody against an antigenic component of cells present only on one side would be an instance of this type of mechanism. Although not looked at from the point of lateralization, the neurological consequences of rubella in pregnancy (Cooper, 1975) illustrate the principles that rates of development and critical windows are important determinants of the pathological effects of the virus. Chemical (Oke, Keller, Mefford, & Adams, 1978) and immunological (Bizière, Burdos, Degenne, & Renoux, 1981) asymmetries argue for nonrandom mechanisms for unilateral damage.

Another group of explanations would contend that the lateralized abnormalities occur as a result of random insults to the left and right hemisphere, irrespective of their distinct biological properties. We then have a scenario whereby some random cerebral insult occurs to one of the cerebral hemispheres during development, and the behavioral consequences of the insult are dependent on the time of the insult, the hemisphere affected, and the location within the hemisphere. In the two cases described, therefore, the patients might have been dyslexic because the insult occurred in the left hemisphere late in the stage of cortical migration coincidental with the period during which areas crucial to language are at a critical period of development. In fact, similar abnormalities might have occurred in the left hemisphere of subjects who exhibited no signs of dyslexia. The abnormalities would, in this situation, be localized to areas and pinpointed to developmental periods not essential for language organization. Likewise, similar distortions in development might be seen to affect the right hemisphere. These alterations might then produce clinically recognizable right-hemisphere disturbances (akin in severity to the dyslexia of the left hemisphere), or simply subclinical manifestations. In short, a set of random insults could affect various locations in either developing hemisphere, and the presence or absence of clinical manifestations would depend entirely on whether the regions involved handle everyday functions. Thus, for example, one would not be aware of dyslexia in illiterate societies or of dysmusia among Albigensian ascetics. In fact, it is quite possible that in our society the right-hemisphere abnormalities escape notice because the associated cognitive deficits may not be as obvious as those seen in dyslexia.

ASYMMETRY AND DEVIATION

There is some preliminary evidence to suggest that the disturbances in developmental dyslexia may be traceable to an abormal locus in the 15th chromosome (Smith, Kimberling, Pennington, & Lubs, 1983). It is possible, therefore, that a genetic abnormality impairs the development of one hemisphere (in this case the left) by mechanisms similar to those outlined earlier. It is also possible that normal lateralization itself arises from a related gene or group of genes, and that the information contained within the gene(s) determines the formation of a variety of styles of asymmetrical cerebral organization (Fig. 15.1). Thus, there may be genetic control over the distribution of handedness as well as the organization of the brain for language. Let us propose for the moment that when these gene(s) are present, the common pattern of lateralization in the population (a right-handed individual with left-sided dominance for language) will occur. Any modification of the gene action capable of changing its expression would produce a deviation from this pattern. This would include modifications caused by trauma, toxic metabolic changes, and consequences of the actions of other genes. The alterations in dyslexia, then, may arise from a modification by a genetic lesion of the normal expression of asymmetry, which would be evident in the incomplete or abnormal development of the left hemisphere.

Less-striking deviations from the genetically coded pattern of asymmetry could result in a variety of anatomical and functional styles of cerebral lateralization. Using the percentage derived from studies of brain asymmetry as a benchmark, we postulate that 65% of individuals will have standard coded-for dominance pattern, whereas the remaining 35% will have (deviant) anomalous dominance. Thus, whereas the largest group of individuals would have left-hemisphere dominance for language and right-handedness, the remainder of the population, reflecting any of several intrauterine influences, would show a variable degree of shifting away from the standard pattern leading to a more bilateral language representation and greater right-hemisphere participation.

It should not be inferred that influences that deviate dominance need be unwanted or pathological. Any active influence would by necessity shift dominance. Thus, among the 35% with anomalous dominance, there would be both more individuals with diminished as well as with superior capacities.

One question that needs to be resolved by experimental observations is whether subjects with this standard pattern of cerebral dominance exhibit a demonstrably different style of language processing from the group that has anomalous dominance. Just as the anatomical organization for language is different between the standard and anomalous groups, so may be the style of language performance. This clearly appears to be the case in the situation of developmental dyslexia, where the anatomy of asymmetry and linguistic abilities are demonstrably different from normal. It is therefore possible that the interindividual differences one sees in brain-language relationships may be the result of underlying structural deviations from the normal pattern of asymmetry. Thus, for instance, we estimate that the 65% with the standard asymmetry pattern will make up the bulk of subjects who respond in a standard fashion to lesion of the left hemisphere affecting language performance. Likewise, recovery of function after aphasia-producing lesions in this group will be the least satisfactory in the population. One would also anticipate that these lesions will produce relatively more severe disturbances of language even when they occur in children, although in this group, features of plasticity and recovery will play a modifying role. On the other hand, the remaining 35% of the population, those with anomalous dominance, will make up the bulk of patients who have unusual responses after lesions, such that in the group left-hemisphere lesions will tend to be accompanied by nonstandard aphasias and better recovery (Gloning, Gloning, Haub, & Quate-member, 1969; Luria, 1970). Similarly, if those lesions occur during childhood in this group, the degree of recovery will tend to be the best of all the groups.

We would like to see future research in this area as dealing with the behavioral accompaniments of brain asymmetry, taking the form of correlations between patterns of anatomical asymmetry and normal language processing, as well as patterns of asymmetry and response to lesions. We also see the special role of developing animal models of lateralization and asymmetry in order to specify

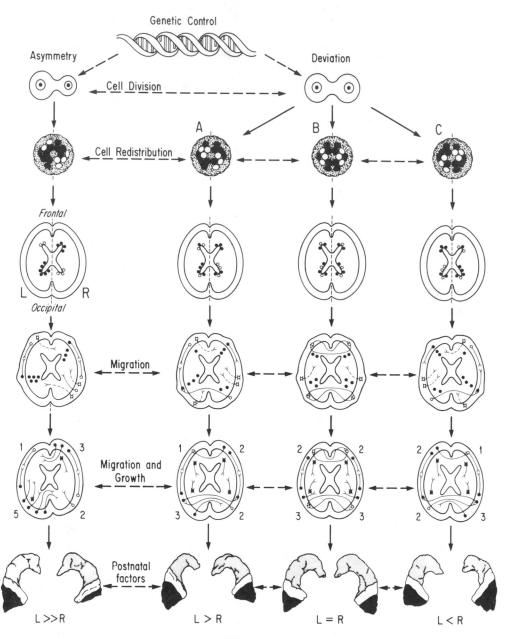

FIG. 15.1.

FIG. 15.1. *(Opposite page)* Hypothetical schema to explain the development of brain asymmetry and its deviations. Also see text.

Genetic control—A gene or genes (15th chromosome?) determine asymmetry development. Presence of gene(s) may lead to asymmetry, whereas absence may lead to random deviations. Genetic expression may take place in any of several subsequent stages.

Cell division—One early step during which genetic expression may take place. Asymmetric cell division may lead to a general state of asymmetry later, whereas symmetry at this stage may lead to deviant states (also see Boklage, cited in text). Failure of genetic expression may convert asymmetric division to deviant states.

Cell distribution and redistribution—Asymmetric distribution of cell types may occur soon after the establishment of the embryonic midline. Marked asymmetry of distribution is seen in the Asymmetry case, whereas milder asymmetries, or symmetry, is seen in the Deviant state. Redistribution of cells across the midline may convert one style to another, as early cell migrations are known to occur.

Cell replication—After formation of the neural tube, cells replicate in the periventricular germinal zones. Asymmetric distribution of cells at this stage and/or asymmetric rates of replication may result in asymmetry. In the Asymmetry state this event is exaggerated, whereas milder asymmetries, or symmetry, are seen in the Deviant states. It would be difficult to propose conversion of one state to another at this stage without implicating cell migration across the midline, a situation not known to take place until (possibly) later.

Cell migration—After cell replication there is migration to the cortex and to subcortical cellular structures. Asymmetry in migration rates alone, or as a result of earlier asymmetries, leads to asymmetric cellular enrichment of the young cortical plate. Local thickening and folding of the cortex occurs with arrival of migrating cells. Some cells arriving very early may be lost, as they are unable to establish adequate connections (cells with interrupted axons in figure). This scheme may explain the early reversed asymmetry of folding reported by Hervé (1888), Fontes (1944), and Chi et al. (1977). Migration of cells across the midline, as well as modification of migration rates by intrauterine influences, may convert the Asymmetry state to Deviant states.

Continued cell migration and growth—With arrival of late migrating cells, and with development of cell connectivity, the cortex continues to be modified. At this state the cells that migrate the slowest may run out of time and never arrive in the cortex, thus remaining in ectopic locations (crossed black cells). Factors leading to further showing of migration may exaggerate this effect, thus increasing subcortical ectopias and preventing the formation of mature patterns of asymmetry (e.g., dyslexia). The same excessive slowing may prevent loss of early-arriving cells, again modifying asymmetry patterns. The diagram shows at this stage the mature patterns of asymmetry and symmetry. In the Asymmetry state the right frontal and left posterior regions are larger than their mates. In the Deviant states asymmetry is present in both directions, albeit less pronounced, and symmetry is also possible. Numbers denote the relative cell ratios underlying the different patterns. Also note that different patterns of axons crossing the midline are possible. Comparing the Asymmetry State with the A-Deviant pattern shows a greater ratio of L to R callosal axons in the former. This asymmetry in callosal axons may further increase hemispheric dominance effects. Also note that the A-Deviant and C-Deviant States are virtual mirror images of each other and are both less asymmetrical than the Asymmetry State.

Mature state—This is shown in the final step as different patterns of asymmetry seen in the planum temporale (dark cross hatching). The Asymmetry State shows the greatest degree of asymmetry in favor of a larger left planum. The A- and C-Deviant States show milder asymmetry in favor of the left and right plana, respectively. The symmetric plana are seen in the B-Deviant State. All plana come from tracings made on real brain photographs. Also note that the Deviant States have more additive planum on the two sides. This may result from lesser cell death during early migration, and, perhaps, later as well. Finally, conversion from one pattern to another may be possible at this stage in young children, and, to a lesser extent, in adults, after brain lesions.

the genetic control and the mechanisms underlying deviations from the standard pattern of asymmetry.

ACKNOWLEDGMENTS

We thank Professor Norman Geschwind for providing the inspiration behind much of the work reported here. Supported in part by NIH grants 14018 and 07211, and grants from the Beth Israel Hospital, the Wm. Underwood Company, The Powder River Company, and the Essel Foundation.

REFERENCES

Anderson, S. W. Language-related asymmetries of eye-movement and evoked potentials. In S. Harnad, R. W. Doty, L. Goldstein, J. Jaynes, & G. Krauthamer (Eds.), *Lateralization in the nervous system.* New York: Academic Press, 1977.

Basser, L. S. Hemiplegia of early onset and faculty of speech with special reference to the effects of hemispherectomy. *Brain,* 1962, *85,* 427–460.

Bizière, K., Bardos, P., Degenne, D., & Renoux, G. Modulation of lymphoproliferative T-cell responses by the cerebral cortex. *Society for Neuroscience Abstracts,* 1981, *7,* 221.

Boklage, C. E. Twinning, handedness, and the biology of symmetry development. In N. Geschwind & A. M. Galaburda (Eds.), *Biological foundations of cerebral dominance.* Cambridge: Harvard University Press, 1984.

Broca, P. Sur la faculté de langage articulé. *Bulletin de la Société de Anthropologie, Paris,* 1865, *6,* 337–393.

Brun, A. The subpial granular layer of the foetal cerebral cortex in man. *Acta Pathologica Microbiologica Scandinavica* (Supplement), 1975, *179,* 40–47.

Caviness, V. S., Evrard, R., & Lyon, G. Radial neuronal assemblies, ectopia and necrosis of developing cortex: A case analysis. *Acta Neuropathologica,* 1978, *41,* 67–72.

Chatel, M. Développement de l'isocortex du cerveau human pendant les périodes embryonnaires et foetales jusque la 24éme semaine de gestation. *Journal für Hirnforschung,* 1976, *17,* 189–212.

Chi, J. G., Dooling, E. C., & Gilles, F. H. Gyral development of the human brain. *Annals of Neurology,* 1977, *1,* 86–93.

Cooper, L. Z. Congenital rubella in the United States. In S. Krugman & A. A. Gershon (Eds.), *Infections of the fetus and the newborn infant.* New York: Alan R. Liss, 1975.

DeBassio, W. A., Kemper, T. L., & Galaburda, A. M. Asymmetric olfactory migratory stream growth in the rat. *Society for Neuroscience Abstracts,* 1982, *8,* 326.

Denenberg, V. H. Hemispheric laterality in animals and the effect of early experience. *The Behavioral and Brain Sciences,* 1981, *4,* 1–49.

Dennis, M. The developmentally dyslexic brain and the written language skills of children with one hemisphere. In U. Kirk (Ed.), *Neuropsychology of language, reading, and spelling.* New York: Academic Press, 1983.

Drake, W. E. Clinical and pathological findings in a child with a developmental learning disability. *Journal of Learning Disorders,* 1968, *1,* 486–502.

Dvorak, K., Feit, J., & Jurankova, Z. Experimentally induced focal microgyria and status verrucosus deformis in rats—pathogenesis and interrelations histological and autoradiographical study. *Acta Neuropathologica,* 1978, *44,* 121–129.

Eberstaller, O. Zur oberflachen Anatomie des Grosslirn Hemispharen. *Wiener Medizinische Blaetr,* 1884, *7,* 479–642.

Eidelberg, D., & Galaburda, A. M. Symmetry and asymmetry in the human posterior thalamus. I. Cytoarchitectonic analysis in normal persons. *Archives of Neurology,* 1982, *39,* 325–332.

Eidelberg, D., & Galaburda, A. M. Inferior parietal lobule: Divergent architectonic asymmetries in the human brain. *Archives of Neurology,* in press.

Eimas, P. D., Siqueland, E. R., Jusczyk, P., & Vigorito, J. Speech perception in infants. *Science,* 1971, *171,* 303–306.

Entus, A. K. Hemispheric asymmetry in processing of dichotically presented speech and nonspeech stimuli by infants. In S. J. Segalowitz & F. A. Gruber (Eds.), *Language development and neurological theory.* New York: Academic Press, 1977.

Fontes, V. *Morfologia do cortex cerebral.* Lisbon: Boletim do Instituto de Antonio Aurelio da Costa Ferreira, 1944.

Galaburda, A. M. La région de Broca: Observations anatomiques faites un siècle après la mort de son découvreur. *Revue Neurologique (Paris),* 1980, *136,* 609–616.

Galaburda, A. M., & Eidelberg, D. Symmetry and asymmetry in the human posterior thalamus. II. Thalamic lesions in a case of developmental dyslexia. *Archives of Neurology,* 1982, *39,* 333–336.

Galaburda, A. M., & Kemper, T. L. Cytoarchitectonic abnormalities in developmental dyslexia: A case study. *Annals of Neurology,* 1979, *6,* 94–100.

Galaburda, A. M., LeMay, M., Kemper, T. L., & Geschwind, N. Right-left asymmetries in the brain. *Science,* 1978, *199,* 852–856.

Galaburda, A. M., Sanides, F., Geschwind, N. Human brain: Cytoarchitectonic left-right asymmetries in the temporal speech region. *Archives of Neurology,* 1978, *35,* 812–817.

Geschwind, N., & Behan, P. Left-handedness: Association with immune disease, migraine, and developmental learning disorder. *Proceedings of the National Academy of Sciences (U.S.A)* 1982, *79,* 5097–5100.

Geschwind, N., & Levitsky, W. Human brain: Left-right asymmetries in temporal speech region. *Science,* 1968, *161,* 186–187.

Gloning, I., Gloning, K., Haub, G., & Quatemember, R. Comparison of verbal behavior in right-handed and non-right-handed patients with anatomically verified lesions of one hemisphere. *Cortex,* 1969, *5,* 43–52.

Goldman, P. S. Neuronal plasticity in primate telecephalon: Anomalous crossed cortico-caudate projections induced by prenatal removal of frontal association cortex. *Science,* 1978, *202,* 768–776.

Gundara, N., & Zivonovic, S. Asymmetry in east African skulls. *American Journal of Physical Anthropology,* 1968, *28,* 331–338.

Hendrick, E. B., Harwood-Hash, D. C. F., & Hudson, A. R. Head injuries in children: A survey of 4465 consecutive cases at the Hospital for Sick Children, Toronto, Canada. *Clinical Neurosurgery,* 1963, *11,* 46.

Hervé, G. *La circonvolution de Broca.* Paris: Delahage and Lecrosnier, 1888.

Hochberg, F. H., & LeMay, M. Arteriographic correlates of handedness. *Neurology,* 1975, *25,* 218–222.

Innocenti, G. M., & Frost, D. O. The postnatal development of visual callosal connections in the absence of visual experience or of the eyes. *Experimental Brain Research,* 1980, *39,* 365–375.

Kimura, D. Cerebral dominance and the perception of verbal stimuli, *Canadian Journal of Psychology,* 1961, *15,* 166–171.

Larsen, B., Skinhoj, E., & Lassen, N. A., Variation in regional cortical blood flow in the right and left hemispheres during automatic speech. *Brain,* 1978, *101,* 193–209.

LeMay, M. Morphological cerebral asymmetries of modern man, fossil man, and nonhuman primate. *Annals of the New York Academy of Sciences,* 1976, *280,* 349–366.

LeMay, M., & Culebras, A. Human brain: Morphological differences in the hemispheres demonstrable by carotid arteriography. *New England Journal of Medicine,* 1972, *287,* 168–170.

LeMay, M., & Kido, D. K. Asymmetries of the cerebral hemispheres on computed tomograms. *Journal of Computer Assisted Tomography,* 1978, *2,* 471–476.

Lenneberg, E. *Biological foundations of language.* New York: Wiley, 1967.

Levine, D. N., Fisher, M. A., & Caviness, U. S. Porencephaly with microgyria: A pathologic study. *Acta Neuropathologica,* 1974, *29,* 99–113.

Luria, A. R. *Traumatic aphasia.* The Hague: Mouton, 1970.

McBride, M. C., & Kemper, T. L. Pathogenesis of four-layered microgyric cortex in man. *Acta Neuropathologica,* 1982, *57,* 93–98.

McRae, D., Branch, C., & Milner, B. The occipital horns and cerebral dominance. *Neurology,* 1968, *18,* 95–98.

Moffit, A. R. Consonant cue perception by 20–24-week-old infants. *Child Development,* 1971, *42,* 717–731.

Molfese, D. L., Freeman, R. B., & Palermo, D. S., The ontogeny of brain lateralization for speech and nonspeech stimuli. *Brain and Language,* 1975, *2,* 356–368.

Morse, P. A. The discrimination of speech and nonspeech stimuli in early infancy. *Journal of Experimental Child Psychology,* 1972, *14,* 447–492.

Oke, A., Keller, R., Mefford, I., & Adams, R. N. Lateralization of norepinephrine in the human thalamus. *Science,* 1978, *200,* 1411–1413.

Penfield, W., & Roberts, L. *Speech and brain mechanisms.* Princeton, N.J.: Princeton University Press, 1959.

Phelps, M. E., Hoffman, E. J., & Mazziota, J. C. A new high resolution position computed tomograph (PCT) for mapping cerebral glucose metabolism: Studies in normal and sensory stimulated subjects. *Society for Neuroscience Abstracts,* 1981, *7,* 243.

Rubens, A. B., Mahowald, M. W., & Hutton, J. T. Asymmetry of lateral (sylvian) fissures in man. *Neurology,* 1976, *26,* 320–324.

Schneider, G. E. Early lesions and abnormal neuronal connections. *Trends in Neuroscience,* 1981, *4,* 187–192.

Segalowitz, S. J., & Chapman, T. S. Cerebral asymmetry for speech in neonates: A behavioral measure. *Brain and Language,* 1980, *9,* 281–288.

Sherman, G. F., Galaburda, A. M., & Geschwind, N. Neuroanatomical asymmetries in nonhuman species. *Trends in Neuroscience,* 1982, *5,* 429–431.

Smith, S. D., Kimberling, W. J., Pennington, B. F., & Lubs, H. A. Specific reading disability: Identification of an inherited form through linkage analysis. *Science,* 1983, *219,* 1345–1347.

Sperry, R. W. Lateral specialization in the surgically separated hemispheres. In B. Milner (Ed.), *Hemispheric specialization and interaction.* Cambridge: MIT Press, 1974.

Springer, S. P. Tachistoscopic and dichotic-listening investigations of laterality in norman human subjects. In S. Harnod, R. W. Doty, L. Goldstein, J. Jaynes, & G. Krauthamer (Eds.), *Lateralization in the nervous system.* New York: Academic Press, 1977.

Teszner, D., Tzavaras, A., Gruner, J., & Hécaen, H. L'asymmétrie droite-gauche du planum temporale: A propos de l'étude anatomique de 100 cerveaux. *Revue Neurologique,* 1972, *126,* 444–449.

Vargha-Khadem, F., & Corballis, M. C. Cerebral asymmetry in infants. *Brain and Language,* 1979, *8,* 1–9.

Wada, J. A., Clarke, R., & Hamm, A. Cerebral hemispheric asymmetry in humans. *Archives of Neurology,* 1975, *32,* 239–246.

Wernicke, C. *Der aphasische Synptomenkomplex.* Poland: M. Cohn & Weigart, 1874.

Witelson, S. F., & Pallie, W. Left hemisphere specialization for language in the newborn: Neuroanatomical evidence of asymmetry. *Brain,* 1973, *96,* 641–646.

Yeni-Komshian, G. H., & Benson, D. A. Anatomical study of cerebral asymmetry in the temporal lobe of humans, chimpanzees, and rhesus monkeys. *Science,* 1976, *192,* 387–389.

16 Keeping Your Brain in Mind

André Roch Lecours
*Laboratoire Théophile Alajouanine, Centre de Recherche du Centre
Hospitalier Côte des Neiges, Montréal, and
Centre de Recherche en Sciences Neurologiques,
Université de Montréal*

Yves Joanette
*Laboratoire Théophile Alajouanine, Centre de Recherche du Centre
Hospitalier Côte des Neiges, Montréal*

Although this is usually done in the context of (friendly) conversations rather than by way of public written documents, it has of late become fashionable among experimental psychologists to state that it does not matter much whether one's language is biologically represented in one's brain or in either of one's little fingers (Mehler, 1981a). This can of course be taken as a perfectly legitimate point of view for a psychologist (Morton, 1980, 1981a,b) who has never had to consult a neurosurgeon for personal reasons. Nonetheless, we agree with the editor of this volume that it is also legitimate to include in it a chapter pertaining to certain aspects of the cerebral rather than the digital representation of language. The authors of this chapter were instructed to aim, among other things, at explaining why psychologists who are interested in the cognitive capacities of normal human babies might also be interested in anatomoclinical data on acquired disorders of speech and language, as they can be observed in the human species from infancy to senescence (Mehler, 1981b). We are not sure that we can do this unless eventual readers already agree that the disastrous effects of hepatic coma on linguistic behavior are a direct result of brain dysfunction rather than liver disease, and also that experimental psychologists working with babies are more interested in brain functions—although indirectly, of course—than in the modes of action of the orbicularis oris and masseter muscles.

Let us be candid awhile. If one is both a neuroscientist and is interested in the mutual relationships of brain and language, one is likely to have first approached this problem through the anatomoclinical method, as originally put forward by Jean-Baptiste Bouillaud (1825) (Fig. 16.1a), probably named by Jean-Martin

FIG. 16.1.   The pioneers of the anatomoclinical method: A: Jean-Baptiste Bouillaud (1796–1881); B: Jean-Martin Charcot (1825–1893); C: Joseph-Jules Dejerine
(1849–1917); D: Augusta Dejerine-Klumpke (1859–1927).

Charcot (1872–73) (Fig. 16.1b), and given its canon by the Dejerines (Klippel,
1908) (Figs. 16.1c, d), that is through the correlative study of clinical observations of deviant language behaviors, on the one hand, and, on the other hand,
of the presumably responsible brain lesions as they can be seen at postmortem.
If one is optimistic by nature, one may even have yielded to the temptation of
making up physiopathological interpretations of the disorders one has observed
(such as suggesting that the destruction of a given axonal bundle between two
cortical areas "explains" this or that anomaly in language behavior). In one's
initial approach, one has thus been interested in pathological behavior as well
as in pathological anatomy, and, conceivably, in pathological physiology. From

this, one has derived one's two basic notions on the matter, that of "aphasia" (a word coined by Armand Trousseau; Broca, 1864, Fig. 16.2), and that of "speech area." Maybe it took one some time to understand that the latter notion, that of "speech area," if obviously pertinent in discussions on language disorders, at least in a sizeable proportion of cases (Lecours, 1980a), does not really have as clear a status when it comes to the cerebral foundations of normal language function (Freud, 1891). Furthermore, having observed several different types of aphasia, clinically, it is probable that one has attributed to them different names that might tell—more or less explicitly—about one's preconceptions, conceptions, and misconceptions, or else about one's cautious lack of ideas concerning the physiopathology of speech and language disorders (one can live without ideas of this sort).

Now, if one is not in charge of neurological wards, or if one is a fast reader, one may have later found the time to gather some elementary knowledge about normal language acquisition and standard linguistic behavior, and to review a few notions concerning normal human brain maturation and functional anatomy;

FIG. 16.2.   Armand Trousseau (1801–1867). This photograph was kindly given to the authors by Doctors Max and Gérard Dordain.

one may even temporarily have had the impression that one's ideas on the physiopathology of aphasia—again if any—were somehow relevant to normal brain-language physiology. This was step two in one's approach.

Back to step one and to the "speech area." The first question about it is the following: Where is it? Well, any university student, nearly anywhere in the world and in nearly any field but theology and law, will find it easy to answer this one: The speech area is in the left cerebral hemisphere and it comprises four interconnected cortical regions (Fig. 16.3) the *pars opercularis* (foot) and *pars triangularis* (cape) of the third frontal convolution, the caudal part of the first temporal convolution, the supramarginal gyrus, and the angular gyrus (Geschwind, 1970). A number of other definitions have been proposed, some more generous and some less, and we might add some in better agreement with clinical aphasiology such as that suggested by Freud (1891). All of them have been limited to some components of the left hemisphere, but none has attained a large enough diffusion in time and space to deserve mention in the present context. We have the impression, however, that general expectation is now such that one gifted for drawing might propose a tridimensional representation that would have a fair chance to replace, within a few months if published in *Brain and Language* or *Cognition,* the classical bidimensional scheme: Speech people are getting more and more interested in various thalamic nuclei and other subcortical structures.

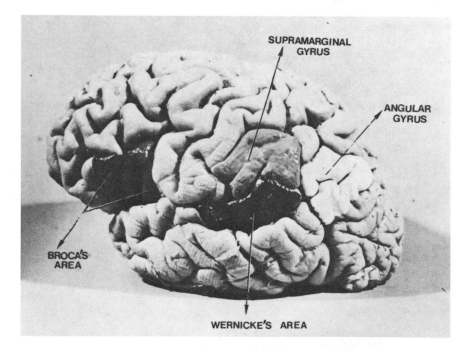

FIG. 16.3.   The cortical components of the speech area, classical conception.

Let us pretend, for a moment, that we now have a 3-D definition of the "speech area" on which everybody agrees. Let us pretend that it has been shown, through cytoarchitectonic studies, that all its components are larger or bigger than their counterparts in the right hemisphere: After all, we already have reasons to believe, through cytoarchitectonic studies, that the left *planum temporale* is usually larger than the right one (Galaburda, LeMay, Kemper, & Geschwind, 1978; Galaburda, Sanides, & Geschwind, 1978), that *pars opercularis* of the third frontal convolution is usually larger than that in the right hemisphere (Galaburda, 1980), and even that the lateral posterior nucleus is probably bigger in the left thalamus than it is in the right one (Eidelberg & Galaburda, in press). Let us also pretend that it has been shown that these anatomical asymmetries are already there to be seen at some time during embryological life: After all, Gratiolet had already documented something of this sort in 1854, and macroscopical asymmetry of the *planum temporale* has been observed at about the end of the seventh month of gestational life (Tezner, Tzavaras, Gruner, & Hécaen, 1972; Wada, Clarke, & Hamm, 1975). And let us pretend, finally, that we know for sure that there is a definite relationship between these anatomical asymmetries and left cerebral dominance for language: After all, "a possible relationship" has been suggested when it was shown that people with a larger left planum, as seen on carotid arteriograms (LeMay & Culebras, 1972), are often those with a clear left dominance for language, as assessed through Amytal testing (Ratcliff, Dila, Taylor, & Milner, 1980).

Of course, one might object that Albert Galaburda, as he is no doubt ready to admit, has not yet scrutinized enough brains to provide absolutely irrefutable evidence; and of course there are people who systematically question cytoarchitectonic data based on the use of Braak's (1978) lipofuscin method, because the amount of intraneuronal lipofuscin normally varies with age and can in certain cases be linked to pathology, which is a very weak argument in our opinion; and there are also people who doubt that it is at all possible to make exact enough volumetric measurements of thalamic nuclei, including LP (Kimura, 1981a). Whatever the method, it is a point of view that we do not share either, if only because we think that one has the privilege of putting trust in one's friends. Furthermore, one might object that *planum* measurements on carotid arteriograms are all but impossible to do with an acceptable degree of accuracy, and therefore argue that the Rattcliff et al. (1980) demonstration, which remains unique as yet, does not in fact have the weight that we would personally attribute to it until someone does better.

Well, whatever one's opinion(s) on these technicalities, "let us pretend, for a moment," as we wrote earlier. Then, one might be inclined to give some credit to Broca's (1865) teaching when he claimed, more than a century ago, that left hemisphere specialization for language depends on an innate biological predisposition; and, by the same token, discredit might—once again (Lecours & Caplan, 1984; Lecours & Joanette, 1984)—fall on Marie's (1922) claim that there is nothing innate[1] about which part of the brain should take care of language. With this in mind, even a neurologist becomes interested in knowing whether or not it is possible to show, at birth or soon after, that the left hemispheres of neonates are more interested in language than are their right hemispheres. Entus (1977) says yes, as do Segalowitz and Chapman (1980); Vargha-Khadem and Corballis (1979) say no. Now, this is not our field and we soon diverge, but if the yes proponents were right, would this necessarily mean that the newborn's innate biological predisposition is such that it can show a whiff of "functionality" without any previous experiential exposure to language whatsoever? We would find this hard to swallow and therefore try to find a way out, be it a narrow one. On the one hand, a human fetus is certainly submitted to all sorts of acoustic informations, including those generated by its mother's overt linguistic productions; on the other hand, the prethalamic acoustic fibers of the human fetus display a most precocious prenatal cycle of maturation—if myelinogenesis is to be taken as a somewhat reliable parameter—at least up to the level of the inferior colliculus (Yakovlev & Lecours, 1967). Obviously, we do not know if these two facts are linked to one another in some way, and we suspect that Jacques Mehler might object that a human adult cannot discriminate speech sounds from the noise currently generated by the rusted muffler of his Alfa Romeo if both informations are transmitted through an amniotic-like fluid. Furthermore, we do not know to what extent data on myelinogenesis are in concordance or in discordance with other ontogenetic data, evoked potentials for instance, and, if there is gross discrepancy, we do not know which parameter should be considered as more reliable for the time being. And if it turned out that myelinogenesis has nothing to do with the ontogenesis of function, we would still wonder why prethalamic acoustic fibers have a short perinatal myelinogenetic cycle, whereas thalamocortical acoustic fibers have a long postnatal cycle, which is quite different from what is observed—say—in the optic pathway, where both prethalamic and thalamocortical fibers have a relatively short postnatal cycle (Yakovlev & Lecours, 1967). Enough of that and back to our let-us-pretend argument.

If things were as we said, then could one claim that one would now hold a fairly clear and universal view of what the "speech area" is (always keeping in mind, of course, that, if functional specialization for language can be studied through a variety of methods, such as Amytal testing, dichotic listening, cerebral blood flows, and evoked potentials, anatomical definitions of the "speech area" have so far been grounded on anatomoclinical studies exclusively)? Well, we do not think so. The reason for our negative answer is that the notion of "speech area" can only be defined considering sets of factors or "clusters," some of which are conceivably but not necessarily common to all members of the species, and

---

[1]Pierre Marie (1922) indeed wrote this, but if one reads him attentively, one comes to the conclusion that he did not believe all of it all of the time. Moreover, he was well known as one who could easily allow himself to be carried away.

others certainly not. From a functional point of view, and after convincing onself that individual variations (Ojemann, 1979) of some importance are still to be considered as exceptional, one must therefore characterize a population from various points of view before one attempts to define the speech area within this population.

The way we see it, characterization of a given population in this respect is done by confronting two groups of factors, premorbid ones and morbid ones. Premorbid factors can in turn be considered under two main headings: biological (genetic) factors and environmental (social) factors.

Among the biological (genetic) factors, one obviously has to take into consideration: (1) the status of brain maturation when the brain lesion takes place, that is, the age of the subject; (2) the handedness of the subject as well as that of other members of his family; (3) the presence or absence of a past history, individual or familial, of developmental disorders involving spoken and/or written language; and (4) if McGlone (1980) and Kimura (1981b) are right, the sex of the subject.

Among the environmental (social) factors, there is now sufficient evidence for one to seriously consider: (1) the inherent characteristics of the subject's mother tongue (we still have to demonstrate that the cerebral representation of language is exactly the same in one speaking a tone language, or else an agglutinating language, rather than French or English; and it seems that Chinese scientists of the continent have never shown much interest for the study of aphasia; Geley, 1981); (2) the status of the unilingual subject as opposed to that of the bilingual and polyglot (Albert & Obler, 1978; Galloway, in press; Obler, 1981; Paradis, 1977; Vaid, 1983; Vaid & Genese, 1980); (3) the status of the illiterate subject as opposed to that of one who has learned to read and write and, for the latter, the length of her or his training; and (4) as Sasanuma and her collaborators have so elegantly shown, the status of the literate subject who writes following a pictographic code as opposed to an alphabetic or syllabical one (Sasanuma, 1975; Sasanuma & Fujimura, 1971, 1972; Sasanuma & Monoi, 1975). (As we did with individual variations [supra], we are going to leave out—in spite of their potential interest—factors eventually linked to basic premorbid "personality" [Charman, 1979], if only because we could not decide whether to file them under biological or under environmental factors.)

In defining the "speech area" of a given population, these premorbid factors are then to be studied in parallel with a group of morbid factors including: (1) side of lesion (yes, we mean left versus right hemisphere); (2) site of lesion; (3) size of lesion; (4) nature of lesion (CVAs, tumors, and so forth); and (5) duration of lesion, a factor itself to be linked to the presence or absence of various attempts at therapeutic intervention, whether it be by speech therapy (Basso, Capitani, & Vignolo, 1979) or otherwise.

By mathematically combining clusters of premorbid and morbid factors of these two groups, and although our lists of factors are certainly not exhaustive, one would get to an important number of possibilities. Actually doing such mathematical combinations would be of limited interest, however, because one already knows that certain clusters occur with a relatively high frequency within the species, whereas others occur only exceptionally; and also because one knows that several clusters would be so improbable that they never occur. For instance, sylvian left hemisphere CVAs are probably relatively frequent among adult right-handed literate unilingual males speaking a tonal language: We know of no published data about this particular population. On the other hand, males and females sharing the same characteristics but speaking a nontonal nonaggluctin-ating language have been studied in the West for more than a century, and this has led to our current conceptions of the "speech area," whether they be bidi-mensional or tridimensional; a generous estimation led us to believe that the overall validity of these conceptions has now been demonstrated for about 25% of the human population (Lecours, 1980a), and this although we do not deny that they might well be valid for a far greater proportion of the species. Among the factorial clusters with much lesser probability of apparition, one might men-tion, for instance, adult left-handed unilingual literate females speaking an agglu-tinating language and having suffered a CVA with brain softening limited to Broca's area (it remains unclear to us whether or not Lavorel, 1980, discusses a case of this sort in his doctoral dissertation). As to the nearly impossible clusters, one might try to estimate, for instance, one's chances of gathering a population of 3-year-old heptaglots with an astrocytoma limited to the right pulvinar.

Given the scope of this chapter, we now concentrate on three particular clusters. We successively discuss the problems of cerebral representation of language in children, in adult literate dextrals, and in illiterate versus literate adults. In each case, we limit our comments to data related to aphasia "and kindred disorders" (if we can borrow a syntagm from a well-known linguist; Head, 1926).

Aphasia in Children

It looks as if the early stars of aphasiology, whether they be French or German, were too busy trying to discover the one and universal speech area, pondering on the damaged brains of their adult patients, to spend much time raising ques-tions about the linguistic behavior of children with acquired brain lesions. We are told, however, that some of their contemporaries did raise such questions: Cotard (1868), for instance, in his doctoral dissertation, which was published hardly 3 years after Broca's (1865) main paper on aphasia, and Clarus (1874), in a paper published the same year as Wernicke's (1874) monograph (Woods & Teuber, 1978), and others including Freud (1897), whose influence on classical teaching about childhood aphasia should not be underestimated and whose lack of influence on classical teaching about aphasia in adults (Freud, 1891) is perhaps regrettable. These and later authors, such as Guttman (1942), Branco-Lefèvre

(1950), Basser (1962), and Alajouanine and Lhermitte (1965), have provided the empirical substratum of the now "classical" doctrine on the topic of childhood aphasia.

Here and now, one might indeed say that the history of pediatric aphasiology can be divided into two periods: before Bryan Woods and after Bryan Woods or, if you are a nationalistic Canadian spending a few days in New York, before Maureen Dennis and after Maureen Dennis.

The story as it was told to a neurology resident of the pre-Woods generation underlined three basic differences between aphasia in children and aphasia in adults: (1) Aphasia in children can result of lesions of either the left or the right hemisphere; (2) aphasia in children is of the nonfluent Broca type whatever the localization of lesions; and (3) complete recovery is the rule among aphasic children, whatever the side of the lesions. Items one and three were attributed to a critical-age specification, usually lower for item one than for item three (for instance, one of us [A.R.L.] remembers being told that it was 5 years of age for the former and up to 12—or puberty—for the latter). These were the high days of the equipotentiality theory (Lenneberg, 1967).

Now, the story as it might conceivably be told to a young M.I.T. student of the post-Woods generation taking a course in experimental psychology could be the following: (1) As in adults, it is the rule that acquired aphasia in children is the result of left hemisphere lesions; (2) jargonaphasia with severe comprehension disturbances can be observed in children as in adults; (3) recovery of children's aphasia is not so complete after all. We readily admit that these are lapidary and therefore potentially mendacious terms, but one might say that it is for a good cause; moreover, in spite of Woods' constantly cautious wording in his statements and conclusions, (Woods, 1980a,b; Woods & Carey, 1979; Woods & Teuber, 1978), the differences between the before- and the after-Woods periods are also somewhat lapidary, because none of the classical three doctrinal points has been spared the stoning.

Let us consider each of the three points in turn, but, as a preliminary pre caution, let us underline a basic fact of life: There are two ways of making a diagnosis of aphasia, whether it be at the onset of disease or years later. You make Type I diagnosis—the clinical type—while examining a patient, and you can do it without overt pencil-and-paper calculation of any sort: Basic discoveries on the mutual relationships of brain and language have been done in this manner, usually by people who had the habit of listening and looking at patients themselves rather than relying on someone else's reports; you perhaps need a big right hemisphere in order to be good at this game. On the other hand, you make Type II diagnosis—the subtle type—as the result of pondering on numerical results properly recorded on data sheet, whether it be by yourself or someone else: Interesting discoveries have been done in this manner, some of which have substantially increased our knowledge about the mutual relationships of brain and language; you perhaps need a big left hemisphere in order to be good at this game. We might add that applying Type II methodology to old Type I data is probably the trickiest game of them all.

With regard to the first point, that is, the frequency of aphasia following right-hemisphere lesions in children, all published data to this day have been gathered through Type I methodology, including those of Woods and Teuber (1978). Given that nobody ever published data about a group of patients in which aphasia by right-hemisphere lesion was as frequent as aphasia by left-hemisphere lesion, the equipotentiality theory (Lenneberg, 1967) was already vulnerable in this respect when it was first clearly formulated. Through a very clever review of the literature, Woods and Teuber (1978) discovered a massive difference in the number of cases of childhood aphasia by right-hemisphere lesions before and after the 1930s: from nearly 35% of cases of unilateral lesions to something between 5 and 10%. Their suggestion is that authors before the 1930s were often mistaken, i.e., often considered that there existed a unilateral right-hemisphere lesion in cases of bilateral lesions; they relate this to the introduction of anti-biotherapy, which is a most interesting suggestion, but then one does not see why mistakes of this sort should have been more frequent for right-than for left-hemisphere lesions. Be that as it may, a minimal figure of 5% of crossed aphasia in right-handed kids with a unilateral brain lesion is still largely 10 times more than in adults, if one compares with the minimal figure, 0.4% provided by Russell and Espir (1961). Nonetheless, the 5% figure is low enough to support Woods' (1980a) rectification of the equipotentiality theory: The rule is that both hemispheres initially have the potential for language acquisition, not that they initially play "an active role in both comprehension and production of language." In other words and so to speak, we are born with two speech areas, but the left one, because of innate properties (Broca, 1865 Clarus, 1874), is readier to take over and will do so immediately or at least after 1 year of postnatal life (Woods, 1980a), whereas the activities of the right one will remain most elementary speechwise unless pathology occurs. Obviously, these are also lapidary terms.

Unless we are grossly mistaken, the second point is easily settled: The classical doctrine remains unchanged. Woods and Teuber (1978) tell about a single "ga-ga"–"oo-oo" 5-year-old patient reported by someone else to have had comprehension disorders and a left sylvian lesion, and Maureen Dennis (1980) has a similar story about an older kid with a left thalamic tumor. In our opinion, these two cases are still more exceptional than cases of Type I diagnosed crossed aphasia in adult dextrals and should therefore be disregarded in the formulation of any general theory. Furthermore, and we know that this is a weak argument, we are not at all sure that either the Dennis or the Woods conception of jargon-aphasia corresponds to our own: Remember that we are still on Type I ground. To the best of our knowledge, childhood aphasia is characterized by reduced fluency and preserved comprehension, which means that a kid's speech area is not functionally the same as an adult's, one of the main differences being that language comprehension seems to be bilaterally represented to some extent for a fair number of years after birth.

The best summary that we can propose concerning the third point—the one dealing with a potential of right hemisphere take over in case of left-hemisphere lesion—is that it has been assessed through Type I methodology during the before-Woods era and, in line with a suggestion of Alajouanine and Lhermitte (1965), through Type II methodology since the after-Woods era has begun. In brief, it has been shown that subjects who had been considered to be aphasic at one time between age 1 and 15, and later considered to have completely recovered following Type I criteria, still presented "subtle" Type II deficits when tested through "subtle" Type II procedures (Woods, 1980b; Woods & Carey, 1979). This is not really in contradiction with classical teaching: Kids still recover much better than adults do, and this still seems to be related to a greater disponibility of the right hemisphere with regard to language cybernetics. This holds true even if Dennis and her collaborators (Dennis & Kohn, 1975; Dennis & Whitaker, 1977) are right, as they no doubt are, when they claim that you deal better with syntactic oddities following a right than following a left hemidecortication, when surgery has taken place before the (presumed) onset of the process of language acquisition.

In our opinion, and this is in line with Woods' (1980a) own suggestions, the child-adult dichotomy has given a lot but has now reached the maximum of its productivity. It should therefore be allowed to rest in peace awhile. This was already implicit in the data presented in one of Teuber's (1975) World War II—Korea—Vietnam papers (recovery from aphasia was somewhat better in younger than in older soldiers, whatever the battlefield, and no further demonstration from the Pentagon is required). Following the same thread of ideas, we are quite sure that Jason Brown (1975) is right when he says that a left-temporal lesion results in a "motor" type of aphasia in a standard 5-year-old child; perhaps he allows himself to be carried away when he asserts that the same lesion results in amnestic aphasia in a 10-year old; we would not be surprised if he were right when contending that conduction aphasia is the usual result of such a lesion later in life, and Wernicke's aphasia proper still later. And we know of a very particular form of jargonaphasia, with fluent entirely or nearly entirely neologistic discursive behavior, that perhaps occurs only in the elderlies, again as the result of a left-temporal lesion (Lecours, Travis, Osborn, & Lavallée-Huynh, 1980; Perecman & Brown, 1981). Likewise, the average age of Broca's aphasics is known to be lower than the average age of Wernicke's aphasics (Dordain, 1968). On the whole, these facts might be taken as indicative of a continuum or at least of a step by step evolution of the speech area throughout life, rather than of a binary affair in which a childhood status would at one point leave the place to an adulthood status.

One might suggest, in summary, that what Bryan Woods and others have done, essentially, is to change Eric Lenneberg's initial equipotentiality theory into an initial potential equipotentiality theory (Lenneberg, 1967; Woods, 1980a, b; Woods & Carey, 1979; Woods & Teuber, 1978). This is no doubt a significant change.

Right-Hemisphere Lesions in Adult Dextrals

If one is a Type I diagnoser dealing with human brain lesions, one knows that, as a nearly absolute rule, aphasia is the result of left-hemisphere lesions in adult dextrals; if one sees a lot of patients, one may come across a dextral adult with a focal right-hemisphere lesion and full-blown "crossed" aphasia; if one's case is well documented, clinically and anatomically (the latter meaning that one is reasonably certain that there does not exist a concomitant left-hemisphere lesion), one will know that one has observed something exceptional enough to deserve a published case report; if one has the time, one will publish the case. And if one has read Patricia Goldman's chapter in this book, one might then be tempted to raise a new question about crossed aphasia in adult dextrals, which after all represents the really exceptional exception concerning the cerebral representation of language (Joanette et al., 1982). The question might be candidly phrased in the following terms: Could it be that crossed aphasia (dextrals) sometimes represents the effect of damage to a brain that has been functionally and perhaps anatomically reprogrammed as the result of an early lesion at some moment of fetal life? If this is conceivable or taken seriously, it would follow that the anatomoclinical method itself should change its cannons in such (and perhaps other exceptional) cases (i.e., that the crucial issue might then be evidence of anatomical oddities within undamaged brain tissue rather than exact location of damaged tissue).

In the preceding section of this chapter, we opposed the minimal Russell and Espir (1961) figure of 0.4% to the minimal Woods and Teuber (1978) figure of 5% concerning the frequency of "crossed" aphasia in dextral adults versus children; other authors have given other data, and these can go as high as 35% for children (Basser, 1962), a conceivably but not necessarily misleading figure, and as high as 3% for adults (Hécaen, Mazars, Ramier, Goldblum, & Merienne, 1971) (note that the proportions remain roughly the same if one looks at it this way). On the other hand, if one determines the side of predominant cerebral representation for language by Amytal testing, one can find that as much as 7% of adult epileptic dextrals have a predominantly right-hemisphere representation of language (Milner, Branch & Rasmussen, 1966). Whatever the data considered, one remains well within the domain of exceptions.

Now, one can also decide to be a Type II diagnoser and then tackle the problem of speech-language disturbances in adult dextrals with focal right-brain lesions differently; one is then becoming "subtle." We made an attempt and our findings in this respect have been discussed elsewhere (Joanette, 1980; Joanette, Lecours, Lepage, & Lamoureux, 1983). The following is a brief summary.

The population we studied comprised 62 persons: 20 of them were neurologically healthy, although hospitalized for some reason (C-subjects), and each of the 42 remaining ones had suffered a single stroke resulting in a unilateral focal right-hemisphere lesion (E-subjects). The two groups were comparable with regard to age, schooling, sex, family history of ambidextrality and/or left-handedness, and frequency of bilingualism. All subject of both groups had scored higher than $+80$ at the *Edinburgh Handedness Inventory* (Oldfield, 1971) and were therefore considered to be "absolute" right-handers. Nobody we know, including ourselves, would have attributed a Type I diagnosis of "crossed" aphasia to any of the 42 E-subjects.

Testing was akin to that in modern aphasia test batteries, but several subtests were somewhat more complex than those generally in use with left-hemisphere patients (for instance, naming aimed more at parts of objects rather than objects themselves and word reading aimed at catch words of various types rather than more simple items), and a few more were added that do not belong with standard aphasia test batteries[2] (for instance, a modified version of the *Closure test*, a verbal reasoning test adapted from Caramazza, Gordon, Zurif, & Deluca, 1976). The protocol comprised 20 subtests that yielded 52 measures (47 continuous and 5 nominal variables). Statistically significant differences were found between the two groups for 34 of the 47 continuous variables (from $p < 0.05$ to $p < 0.0001$) and for 3 of the 5 nominal variables (from $p < 0.06$ to $p < 0.00001$), always to the disadvantage of the E-group: Although their speech-language disorders were mild to the point of remaining subclinical for a Type I diagnoser, E-subjects more frequently made phonemic paraphasias in repeating or reading aloud, took longer in textual reading, showed more difficulties in naming parts of objects or in finding lexical antonyms, produced fewer referential words in narrative discourse (Nespoulous, 1981), had difficulties managing with verbal reasoning, appreciating sentence synonymy, and so forth.

Given the non-normal distribution of the 47 continuous variables, attempts at semeiological grouping were done through the method of Chernoff (1973). Following this method, each subject was represented by a computer drawing of a human face. The features of this face—for instance, length of nose, level of mouth, and orientation of eyebrows—were determined by the subject's results at various tests in our battery. Eight sets of 62 such faces were printed on individual cardboards and given to as many judges who were asked to proceed to blind holistic groupings following particular instructions. Judges finally agreed on several families and brotherhoods (Joanette et al., 1983): For instance, one of the families thus defined comprised all the 20 C-subjects as well as 9 of the E-subjects (Fig. 16.4), and another grouped 16 E-subjects that were judged to show relatively marked overall intensity of features, disregarding the presence or absence of individual resemblances (Fig. 16.5).

In view of the previous literature on this topic, we now want to underline a particular point. In the past, authors who have dealt with the problem of

---

[2]Mainly because submitting standard aphasics to such tasks would be like submitting an hemiplegic to a running task.

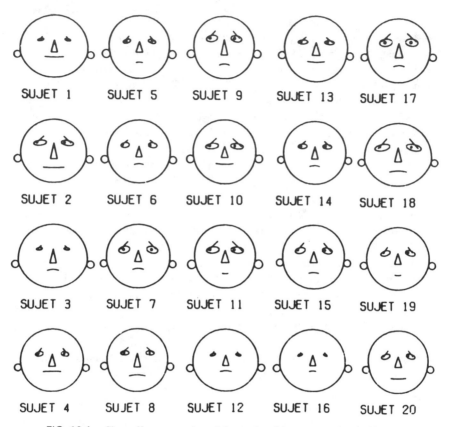

FIG. 16.4. Chernoff representation of the results of language testing in 20 subjects without brain lesions (see text).

speech-language disorders in adults with focal right-brain lesions have usually ended up insisting on either of two partially opposed conclusions: Some have contended that it is characteristic for patients of this sort to display—if anything—discreet "instrumental (or elementary) disorders," interfering for instance with articulation and writing (Dordain, Degos, & Dordain, 1971; Marcie, Hécaen, Dubois, & Angelergues, 1965; Marie & Kattwinkle, 1897); others have contended that it is characteristic for patients of this sort to display—if anything—disorders in "super-" or extra-" or "higher than ordinary" language behavior (Brodal, 1973; Critchley, 1961; Eisenson, 1962; Wepman, 1968; Zangwill, 1967); in this respect, Critchley (1970) goes as far as speaking of a disablement in "creative literary work." But for a few—very few—exceptions, both the instrumentalists and the higher-than-normalists agree and usually insist on one point: The disorders observed in these cases are "nonaphasic" in nature. We must say that we disagree on both the semeiological dichotomy and the contention about

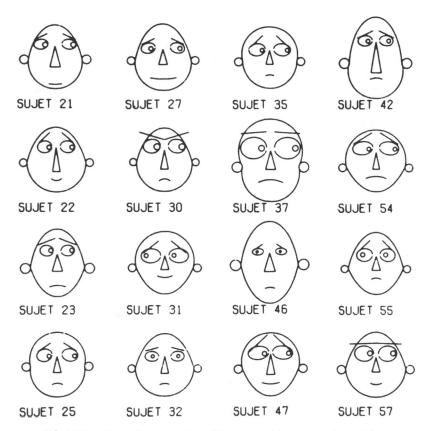

FIG. 16.5.   Chernoff representation of the results of language testing in 16 subjects with focal right-hemisphere lesions (see text).

the nature of the disorders. Besides the fact that our findings do not support the
former, it is striking that proponents of either pole of the dichotomy have usually
observed and reported on disorders of the other pole, and therefore that reasons
for insisting on one type of disorder rather than the other are never clear (unless
one considers the personality of the authors: One is not surprised, for instance,
when Critchley, 1970, mentions dysarthria sort of en passant although he attributes much importance to "higher than ordinary" disorders). On the other hand,
and with the possible exception of reading-writing anomalies, presumably linked
to visuo-spatial disorders, we see no evidence of qualitative differences between
the behavior of our patients with right-brain lesions and that of standard aphasics:
the differences are essentially qualitative. One might argue that the results observed
following right-brain lesions in particularly subtle tests, such as verbal reasoning,
point at qualitative differences: This would be like arguing that there is a qualitative difference between total hemiplegia and mild hemiparesis, because a

patient with the former can walk and one with the latter cannot. (And what can one tell about the production of phonemic paraphasias in a patient with massive phonetic disintegration?) Indeed, our impression is that we have observed, through Type II methodology, 33 adult dextrals with subclinical or, if one prefers Pichot's (1955) expression, with "latent" "crossed" aphasia. It might be that most of us do not entirely lose the little something-for-language that there is in the right hemisphere, however strong the innate predominance of the left one.

Given our data (Joanette, 1980; Joanette et al., 1983), we might tentatively define, in the following terms, the profile of the absolute dextral adult most likely to present sizeable (although "subtle") speech-language disorders as the result of a focal right-hemisphere lesion: (1) anatomopathologically, he would be one with a recent large cortical prerolandic and retrorolandic, or retrorolandic lesion; (2) genetically, he would be one with a family history of ambidextrality and/or left-handedness; and (3) socially, he would be one with a limited school education. It is also possible that he would rather be a male than a female.

We skip further comments on the sex issue because our data in this respect are not strong enough to permit siding either with those who believe that language is less strongly lateralized in men than in women (Buffery & Gray, 1972), or with those who believe the reverse (McGlone, 1977, 1980). And we save the anatomoclinical correlations data for a publication under the editorial responsibility of anybody but Jacques Mehler or John Morton. The genetic data certainly provide nice complementary information for those who have shown that the prognosis of standard aphasia is better, whether you are right-handed or left-handed, if you come from a family with stock left-handedness (Brown & Hécaen, 1976; Hécaen, 1976; Subirana, 1958, 1969). As to the socially determined factor, it is—although our results in this respect were somewhat unexpected—the one that we find the most interesting for the time being. Indeed, it provides the best possible transition to the third and last cluster that we wish to discuss here.

Aphasia in Illiterates

Ernst Weber (1904) was no doubt the first, at the turn of this century, to suggest that the acquisition of reading and writing might be one of the factors determining firm functional lateralization to the left cerebral hemisphere for language. Critchley (1956) and Eisenson (1964) also toyed with this idea. Gorlitzer von Mundy (1957), who practiced neurology in India, reported the case of his illiterate dextral butler who presented severe persistent right hemiplegia, but no aphasia, following a left-hemisphere stroke; and he took this occasion to tell, in anecdotal terms, about more than a dozen similar cases of people he had observed in the course of his hospital duties, some of whom had shown only transient aphasia, but persistent hemiplegia, following left-brain lesions. More recently, Wechsler (1976) rang the bell once again and revived the discussion with his excellent report of a case of "crossed" aphasia in an elderly illiterate dextral.

As far as we know, however, the problem of aphasia in illiterate adults has been approached only twice through systematic research. The first attempt was done by Cameron, Currier, & Haerer (1971), in Mississippi. These authors reviewed the cases of 65 adults with right hemiplegia resulting from a left-hemisphere stroke (62 right-handers and 3 left-handers). Thirty-seven subjects were considered as "literates," 14 as "semiliterates," and 14 as "illiterates." Aphasia was considered to be "present" even in cases where it had lasted "only a day or two." Twenty-nine of the 37 "literate," 9 of the 14 "semiliterate," and only 5 of the 14 "illiterate" patients presented aphasia. Cameron et al.'s (1971) conclusion was that aphasia following focal left-hemisphere lesions is significantly less frequent in illiterates than it is in those who have learned to read and write, and, consequently, that the acquisition of written language plays a role of some sort in left-brain specialization for language.

The second study was done a few years later, in Portugal, by Damasio, Castro-Caldas, Grosso, & Ferro (1976). These authors considered "a random series of 247 adults" with unilateral focal brain lesions of various etiologies (including CVAs and tumors). Thirty-eight of these subjects were illiterates, 24 of whom with left- and 14 with right-brain lesions. For some reason, the proportion of left- versus right-brain lesions among the remaining 209 literate subjects is not provided. Twenty-one of the 38 analphabets and 114 of the 209 literate subjects were considered to be aphasics. This and other computations of their data convinced Damasio et al. (1976) that the aphasias of literate subjects and those of illiterates differ neither as to frequency nor as to "clinical types" and "semeiological structure" (which, we presume, indicates that eventual reading-writing impairments were not considered as part of the "semeiological structure" of the aphasias observed in the 209 literate patients). The authors' conclusion (and the title that they give to their paper) is that "Brain specialization for language does not depend on literacy." (One might see potential discordance between these findings and conclusion and other findings by the same Portuguese group suggesting, this time, that lateralization of "visuo-spatial functions" to the right is enhanced, in dextrals, by the acquisition of reading-writing capacities; Ferro, Castro-Caldas, Martins, & Salgado, 1981).

Two studies, two stories. One still has to find out why a 6-year-old kid, who normally masters spoken language (nearly) as well as a standard adult (we are not referring to encyclopedic knowledge), should be better fitted—or, at least, better protected—brain wise than those of us who have already reached the age of discretion. Is it that biological senescence begins at 6, when you enter elementary school (in certain countries), or is it conceivable that redhibitory functional Type I lateralization to the left for language, that is, redhibitory renouncement of one's second (potential, minor, right-sided) "speech area," in full answer to one's innate biological predisposition, is the biological price one has to pay in order to gain the advantages—social among others—inherent to the apprenticeship leading to reading-writing skills? Clearly, the third study should be quite cautious: Experimental subjects should be not only functional illiterates but also totally unschooled people, they should belong with societies that have long invented writing, they should be unilingual, they should not be too young, the side of lesion should not be a parameter of selection, etiology might be limited to CVAs, and, above all, the natural evolution of aphasia (in illiterates) should be taken into consideration as well as its mere occurrence; furthermore, experimental subjects should be paired to controls with regard to age, sex, handedness, family history of handedness, and side, size, site, and etiology of lesions. We are not at all sure that it is feasible but it is certainly worth trying: Although it is a recognized fact that one can die of hunger, the mutual interactions of biological and social factors in the depth of human brain cybernetics are not that well known after all.

Now, we are ready to admit that we have allowed ourselves to be carried away from the daily preoccupations of experimental psychologists working with babies, and we are ready to admit that there might well be sizable differences between the speech area of a square right-handed hardly unilingual neurologist from colonial Québec and that of an imaginative ambidextral hardly literate heptaglot psychologist from sophisticated Argentina. We keep thinking, however, that even if brain is not one's trade, one should keep one's own in mind, if only because it might provide one with ideas for one's next application for a research grant.

ACKNOWLEDGMENTS

This research was supported in part by Grant MT-4210 of the Conseil de la Recherche Médicale du Canada to the senior author.

REFERENCES

Alajouanine, T., & Lhermitte, F. Acquired aphasia in children. *Brain*, 1965, *88*, 653–662.

Albert, M., & Obler, L. *The bilingual brain*, New York: Academic Press, 1978.

Basser, L. S. Hemiplegia of early onset and the faculty of speech with special reference to the effects of hemispherectomy. *Brain*, 1962, *85*, 427–460.

Basso, A., Capitani, E., & Vignolo, L. A. Influence of rehabilitation on language skills in aphasic patients. A controlled study. *Archives of Neurology*, 1979, *36*, 190–196.

Bouillaud, J. B. Recherches cliniques propres à démontrer que la perte de la parole correspond à la lésion des lobules antérieurs du cerveau et à confirmer l'opinion de M. Gall, sur le siège de l'organe du langage articulé. *Archives Générales de Médcine*, 1825, *8*, 25–45.

Braak, H. On the pigment architectonics of the human telencephalic cortex. In M. A. B. Brazier & H. Petsche (Eds.), *Architectonics of the cerebral cortex*. New York: Raven Press, 1978.

Branco-Lefevre, A. E. Contribuiçao para o estudo da psicopatologia da afasia em crianças. *Archivos Neuro-Psiquiatria*, 1950, *8*, 345–393.

Broca, P. Sur les mots aphémie, aphasie et aphrasie. Lettre à M. Le professeur Trousseau. In H. Hécaen & J. Dubois (Eds.), *La naissance de la neuropsychologie du langage,* Paris: Flammarion, 1864 (reprinted 1969).

Broca, P. Sur le siège de la Faculté du langage articulé. *Bulletin de la Sociètè d'Anthropologie,* 1865, *6,* 337–393.

Brodal, A. Self-observations and neuro-anatomical considerations after a stroke (in the right hemisphere). *Brain,* 1973, *96,* 675–694.

Brown, J. W. The neuralorganization of language: Aphasia and neuropsychiatry. In S. Arieti (Ed.) *American handbook of psychiatry* (Vol. 4). New York: Basic Books, 1975.

Brown, J. W., & Hecaen, H. Lateralization and language representation. *Neurology,* 1976, *26,* 183–189.

Buffery, A., & Gray, J. Sex differences in the development of spatial and linguistic skills. In C. Ounsted & D. Taylor (Eds.), *Gender differences, their ontogeny and signification.* Edinburgh: Churchill Livingstone, 1972.

Cameron, R. F., Currier, R. D., & Haerer, A. F. Aphasia and literacy. *British Journal of Disorders of Communication,* 1971, *6,* 161–163.

Caramazza, A., Gordon, J., Zurif, E. B., & Deluca, D. Right-hemispheric damage and verbal problem-solving behavior. *Brain and language,* 1976, *3,* 41–46.

Charcot, J. M. *Leçons sur les maladies du système nerveux faites à ls Salpêtrière.* Paris: Delahaye, 1872–73.

Charman, D. K. Do different personalities have different hemispheric asymmetries? A brief communiqué of an initial experiment. *Cortex,* 1979, *15,* 655–657.

Chernoff, H. The use of faces to represent points in k-dimensional space graphically. *Journal of the American Statistical Association,* 1973, *68,* 361–368.

Clarus, A. Uber Aphasie bei Kindern. *Jahresb Kinderheilkd,* 1874, *7,* 369–400.

Cotard, J. *Etude sur l'atrophie partielle du cerveau.* Faculté de Médecine de Paris: Thèse, 1868.

Critchley, M. Premorbid literacy and the pattern of subsequent aphasia. *Proceedings of the Society of Medicine,* 1956, *49,* 335–336.

Critchley, M. Speech and speech-loss in relation to the quality of the brain. In V. B. Mountcastle (Ed.), *Interhemispheric relations and cerebral dominance.* Baltimore: Johns Hopkins Press, 1961.

Critchley, M. *Aphasiology and other aspects of language.* Londres: Arnold, 1970.

Damasio, A. R., Castro-Caldas, A., Grosso, A., & Ferro, J. M. Brain specialization for language does not depend on literacy. *Archives of Neurology,* 1976, *33,* 300–301.

Dennis, M. *Personal communication to A.R.L.,* 1980

Dennis, M., & Kohn, B. Comprehension of syntax in infantile hemipligico after cerebral hemidecortication: Left hemisphere superiority. *Brain and language,* 1975, *2,* 475–486.

Dennis, M., & Whitaker, H. Hemispheric equipotentiality and language acquisition. In S. J. Segalowitz & F. A. Gruber (Eds.), *Language development and neurological theory.* New York: Academic Press, 1977.

Dordain, G. *Contribution à l'étude neurolinguistique de l'aphasie. Analyse comparative des performances grammaticales de 28 aphasiques dont 14 agrammatiques.* Faculté de Médecine de Paris: Thèse, 1968.

Dordain, M., Degos, J. D., & Dordain, G. Troubles de la voix dans les hémiplègies gauches. *Revue de Laryngologie,* 1971, *13,* 178–188.

Eidelberg, D., & Galaburda, A. M. Symmetry and asymmetry in the human posterior thalamus. Part II: Cytoarchitectonic analysis in normals. *Archives of Neurology,* in press.

Eisenson, J. Language and intellectual modifications associated with right cerebral damage. *Language and Speech,* 1962, *5,* 49–53.

Eisenson, J. Discussion. In A. V. S. de Reuck & M. O'Connor (Eds.), *Disorders of language.* Londres: Churchill, 1964.

Entus, A. K. Hemispheric asymmetry in processing of dichotically presented speech and non-speech stimuli by infants. In S. J. Segalowitz & F. A. Gruber (Eds.), *Language development and neurological theory*. New York: Academic Press, 1977.

Ferro, J. M., Castro-Caldas, A., Martins, I. P., & Salgado, V. Verbal and visuo-spatial disturbances: Influence of literacy. Communication to the annual meeting of the *International Neuropsychological Society*, Tronheim, 1981.

Freud, S. *Zur Auffasung der Aphasien*. Vienne: Deuticke, 1891.

Freud, S. *Infantile cerebral paralysis*. Coral Gables: University of Miami, 1897 (L. A. Russin, Trans., 1968).

Galaburda, A. Cytoarchitectonie des aires du langage. Communication to the *Commémoration du centenaire de la mort de Paul Broca* (1824–1880). Paris: Hôpital de la Salpêtrière, 1980.

Galaburda, A. M., Le May, M., Kemper, T. L., & Geschwind, N. Right-left asymmetries in the brain. *Science*, 1978, *199*, 852–856.

Galaburda, A. M., Sanides, F., & Geschwind, N. Human brain. Cytoarchitectonic left-right asymmetries in the temporal speech region. *Archives of Neurology*, 1978, *35*, 812–817.

Galloway, L. Towards a neuropsychological model of bilingualism and second language performance. In M. Long, S. Peck, & K. Bailey (Eds.), *Research in second language acquisition*. Rowley: Newbury, in press.

Geley, V. *Personal communication to A.R.L.*, 1981.

Geschwind, N. The organization of language and the brain. *Science*, 1970, *170*, 940–944.

Gorlitzer von Mundy, V. Zur Frage der paarig veranlagten Sprachzentren. *Der Nervenarzt*, 1957, *28*, 212–216.

Gratiolet, L. P. *Mémoire sur les plis cérébraux de l'homme et des primates*. Paris: Bertrand, 1854.

Guttman, E. Aphasia in children. *Brain*, 1942, *65*, 204–219.

Head, H. *Aphasia and kindred disorders of speech*. New York: Hafner, 1926.

Hecaen, H. Acquired aphasia in children and the ontogenesis of hemispheric functional specialization. Brain and Language, 1976, *3*, 114–134.

Hecaen, H., Mazars, G., Ramier, A. M., Goldblum, M. C., & Merienne, L. Aphasie croisée chez un sujet droitier bilingue. *Revue Neurologique*, 1971, *126*, 319–323.

Joanette, Y. *Contribution à l'étude anatomo-clinique des troubles du langage dans les lésions cérébrales droites du droitier*. Thèse, Faculté de Médecine, Montréal: Université de Montréal, 1980.

Joanette, Y., Lecours, A. R., Lepage, Y., & Lamoureux, M. Language in the adult right-handed with focal right hemisphere lesions. *Brain and Language*, 1983, *20*, 217–248.

Joanette, Y., Puel, M., Nespoulous, J.-L., Rascol, A., & Lecours, A. R. Aphasie croisée chez les droitiers. *Revue Neurologique*, 1982, *138*, 575–586.

Kimura, D. *Personal communication to A. Galaburda*, 1981. (a)

Kimura, D. *Sex Differences in Speech Organization within the Left Hemisphere*. Research Bulletin #548, London: Department of Psychology of the University of Western Ontario, 1981. (b)

Klippel, M. (Ed.). Deuxième discussion sur l'aphasie. *Revue Neurologique*, 1908, *16*, 974–1024.

Lavorel, P. M. *Aspects de la performance linguistique*. Dissertation Université de Lyon II, 1980.

Lecours, A. R. Corrélations anatomo-cliniques de l'aphasie. La zone du langage. *Revue Neurologique*, 1980, *136*, 591–608. (a)

Lecours, A. R. Asymétries anatomiques et asymétries fonctionnelles: L'aphasie des illettrés. *Cahiers de Psychologie*, 1980, *23*, 283–304. (b)

Lecours, A. R., & Caplan, D. Augusta Dejerine Klumpke or The lesson in anatomy. *Brain and Cognition*, 1984, *3*, 166–197.

Lecours, A. R., & Joanette, Y. François Moutier or From Folds to Folds. *Brain and Cognition*, 1984, *3*, 198–230.

Lecours, A. R., Travis, L., Osborn, E., & Lavallée-Huynh. Glossolalia as a manifestation of Wernicke's aphasia: A comparison to glossolalia in schizophasia and in possession. In M. Taylor-Sarno & O Höök (Eds.), *Aphasia: Concepts of analysis and management*. Stockholm: Almquist & Wiksell, 1980.

Le May, M., & Culebras, A. Human brain—Morphologic differences in the hemispheres demonstrable by carotid arteriography. *The New England Journal of Medicine,* 1972, *287,* 168–170.

Lenneberg, H. *Biological Foundations of Language.* New York: Wiley, 1967.

Marcie, P., Hecaen, H., Dubois, J., & Angelergues, R. Les réalisations du langage chez les malades atteints de lésions de l'hémisphère droit. *Neuropsychologia,* 1965, *3,* 217–245.

Marie, P. Existe-t-il chez l'homme des centres préformés ou innés du langage? In P. Marie, *Travaux et mémoires* (Vol. I). Paris: Masson, 1922 (reprinted 1926).

Marie, P., & Kattwinkel. Sur la fréquence des troubles du réflexe pharnygé et de la parole dans les lésions de l'hémisphère droit du cerveau. *Bulletin de la société médicale des hôpitaux de Paris,* 1897.

McGlone J. Sex differences in the cerebral organization of verbal functions in patients with unilateral brain lesions. *Brain,* 1977, *100,* 775–793.

McGlone, J. Sex differences in human brain asymmetry: A critical survey. *The Behavioral and Brain Sciences,* 1980, *3,* 215–263.

Mehler, J. *Personal communication to A. R. L.,* 1981. (a)

Mehler, J. *Personal communication to A. R. L.,* 1981. (b)

Milner, B., Branch, C., & Rasmussen, T. Evidence for bilateral speech representation in some non-right-handers. *Transactions of the American Neurological Association,* 1966.

Morton, J. *Personal communication to A. R. L.,* 1980.

Morton, J. *Personal communication to A. R. L.,* 1981. (a)

Morton, J. *Personal communication to A. R. L.,* 1981. (b)

Nespoulous, J. L. Two basic types of semiotic behavior: Their dissociation in aphasia. In P. Perron (Ed.), *The neurological basis of signs in communication processes.* Toronto: Victoria University, 1981.

Obler, L. The neuropsychology of bilingualism. Communication to the *Third Symposium of the Centre Recherches en Sciences Neurologiques de l'Université de Montréal, Montréal,* 1981.

Ojemann, G. A. Individual variability in cortical localization of language. *Journal of Neurosurgery,* 1979, *50,* 164–169.

Oldfield, R. C. The assessment and analysis of handedness: The Edinburgh inventory. *Neuropsychologia,* 1971, *9,* 97–113.

Paradis, M. Bilingualism in aphasia. In H. Whitaker & H. A. Whitaker (Eds.), *Studies in neurolinguistics* (Vol. 111). New York: Academic Press, 1977.

Perecman, E., & Brown, J. W. Phonemic jargon: A case report. In J. W. Brown (Ed.), *Jargonaphasia.* New York: Academic Press, 1981.

Pichot, P. Language disturbances in cerebral diseases. Concept of latent aphasia. *Archives of Neurology and Psychiatry,* 1955, *74,* 92–96.

Ratcliff, G., Dila, C., Taylor, L., & Milner, B. The morphological asymmetry of the hemispheres and cerebral dominance for speech: A possible relationship. *Brain and Language,* 1980, *11,* 87–98.

Russell, W. R., & Espir, M. L. E. *Traumatic aphasia. A study of aphasia in war wounds of the brain.* London: Oxford University Press, 1961.

Sasanuma, S. Kana and Kanji processing in Japanese aphasics. *Brain and Language,* 1975, *2,* 369–383.

Sasanuma, S., & Fujimura, O. Selective impairment of phonetic and nonphonetic transcription of words in Japanese aphasic patients: Kana versus Kanji visual recognition and writing. *Cortex,* 1971, *7,* 1–18.

Sasanuma, S., & Fujimura, O. An analysis of writing errors in Japanese aphasic patients: Kanji versus Kana words. *Cortex,* 1972, *8,* 265–282.

Sasanuma, S., & Monoi, H. The syndrome of Golgi (word-meaning) aphasia. *Neurology,* 1975, *25,* 627–632.

Segalowitz, S. J., & Chapman, J. S. Cerebral asymmetry for speech in neonates: A behavioral measure. *Brain and Language,* 1980, *9,* 281–288.

Subirana, A. The prognosis in aphasia in relation to cerebral dominance and handedness. *Brain,* 1958, *81,* 415–425.

Subirana, A. Handedness and cerebral dominance. In P. J. Vinken & G. W. Bruyn (Eds.), *Handbook of clinical neurology* (Vol. 4). Amsterdam: North-Holland, 1969.

Teuber, H. L. Recovery of function after brain injury in man. In Ciba Foundation (Ed.), *Outcome of severe damage to the central nervous system.* Amsterdam: North-Holland, 1975.

Tezner, D., Tzavaras, A., Gruner, J., Hecaen, H. L'asymétrie droite-gauche du planum temporale: A propos de l'étude anatomique de 100 cerveaux. *Revue Neurologique,* 1972, *126,* 444–449.

Vaid, J. Bilingualism and brain lateralization. In S. Segalowitz (Ed.), *Language function and brain organization.* New York: Academic Press, 1983.

Vaid, J., & Genese Neuropsychological approaches to bilingualism: A critical review. *Canadian Journal of Psychology,* 1980, *34,* 417–445.

Vargha-Khadem, F., & Corbalis, M. Cerebral asymmetry in infants. *Brain and Language,* 1979, *8,* 1–9.

Wada, J., Clarke, R., & Hamm, A. Cerebral hemispheric asymmetry in humans. *Archives of Neurology,* 1975, *32,* 239–246.

Weber, E. Das Schreiben als Ursache der einseitigen Lage des Sprachzentrums. *Zentralblatt für Physiologie,* 1904, *18,* 341–347.

Wechsler, A. F. Crossed aphasia in an illiterate dextral. *Brain and Language,* 1976, *3,* 164–172.

Wepman, J. *Personal communication to O. L. Zangwill,* 1966, 1967.

Wepman, J. M. Aphasia therapy: Some relative comments and some purely personal prejudices. In J. W. Black & E. G. Jancosek (Eds.), *Proceedings of the Conference on Language Retraining for Aphasics.* Ohio: Colombus University, 1968.

Wernicke, C. *Der aphasische symptomemkomplex.* Breslau: Cohn & Weigert, 1874.

Woods, B. T. Observations on the neurological basis for initial language. In D. Caplan (Ed.), *Biological studies of mental processes.* Cambridge, Mass: M.I.T. Press, 1980. (a)

Woods, B. T. The restricted effects of right-hemisphere lesions after age one; Wechsler test data. *Neuropsychologia,* 1980, *18,* 65–70. (b)

Woods, B. T., & Carey, S. Language deficits after apparent clinical recovery from childhood aphasia. *Annals of Neurology,* 1979, *6,* 405–409.

Woods, B. T., & Teuber, H. L. Changing patterns of childhood aphasia. *Annals of Neurology,* 1978, *3,* 273–280.

Yakovlev, P. I., & Lecours, A. R. The myelogenetic cycles of regional maturation of the brain. In A. Minkowski (Ed.), *Regional development of the brain in early life.* Oxford and Edinburgh: Blackwell, 1967.

Zangwill, O. L. Speech and the minor hemisphere. *Acta Neurologica et Psychiatrica Belgica,* 1967, *67,* 1012–1020.

17

Effects of Early Sensory and Language Experience on the Development of the Human Brain

Helen J. Neville
The Salk Institute

> *The nervous system of man and animals is moulded structurally according to the modes of its functional exercise.*
> —H. Maudsley
> *The Physiology of Mind*, 1876

Consideration of the codevelopment of human cognition and the human brain raises important issues concerning the relative roles of biological factors and environmental variables in that development. Does activity of developing neural systems in response to environmental variables serve to specify their ultimate organization, or does interaction with the environment serve merely to trigger the maturation of systems that are genetically determined? Evidence on this issue is of considerable theoretical interest and in the long run would be of great practical significance.

Several studies of nonhuman animals have shown that there are strong biological constraints on the development of brain organization and behavior—but that these factors interact with experience to determine the functional organization of the mature brain. These animal studies have shown that both enriched and deprived early sensory experience have marked effects on the fine structure of the nervous system, the functional properties of cortical neurons, and on behavior (Blakemore & Cooper, 1970; Greenough & Juraska, 1979, pages 295–320; Rosenzweig, 1971, pages 303–342; Spinelli & Jensen, 1979). Moreover, there are specific times, or critical periods, in development when experience exerts its major effects on brain development (Fiala, Joyce, & Greenough, 1978; Freeman, 1979; Hubel & Wiesel, 1970).

Most of these studies have investigated changes in the anatomy and physiology of single neurons following abnormal experience. However, a few investigators have compared such changes with alterations in evoked potentials that reflect the pooled activity of large numbers of neurons. For example, Glass (1977) reported that the response to light from single neurons in area 17 was brisk and the simultaneously recorded evoked potentials displayed a sharp peak after stimulation of the normal eye, but when the deprived eye was stimulated the unit response was exceptionally prolonged and the evoked potential peak was absent. This, Glass suggests, may reflect an aberration of cortical inhibitory processes following visual deprivation. Snyder and Shapley (1979) reported that the imbalance in the cortical representation of the two eyes following monocular deprivation (Hubel & Wiesel, 1970) is apparent in evoked responses recorded from the visual cortex. Stimulation of the experienced eye elicited a response that was normal in morphology and depended on spatial frequency of the stimulus, whereas stimulation of the deprived eye elicited a smaller response that was abnormal both in morphology and in its relation to spatial frequency. These results and others (Parnavelus, 1978; Rebillard, Carlier, & Pujol, 1977; Rebillard, Rebillard, & Pujol, 1980) suggest that the evoked response may be a sensitive measure of both structural and functional neural changes after altered early experience. The existence of a noninvasive analogue of the evoked potential or event-related potential (ERP) technique makes it possible to study the intact human brain. In fact, ERPs recorded from electrodes on the scalp have been shown to reliably assess both the structural integrity of sensory pathways and the activity of neural systems associated with several cognitive processes (see Starr, Sohmer, & Celesia, 1978, pages 155–196; Hillyard, Picton, & Regan, 1978; Donchin, Ritter, & McCallum, 1978, pages 349–411; and Desmedt, 1981 for reviews). Thus ERPs can be valuable tools with which to assess the possibility that altered early experience affects the organization of the human brain.

Comparatively little is known about the development of the human brain and the extent to which deviations in environmental variables might modulate the course of neural and behavioral maturation. However, relevant to this issue is the fact that the human brain has a very protracted postnatal development during which it displays considerable recovery of function after damage. Lenneberg (1967) assembled evidence to show that several parameters of brain development including neurodensity and dendritic arborization do not reach adult values of maturation until at least 15 years after birth. Results from a recent study (Huttenlocher, 1979) suggest the development of synaptic density in human cortex has a similarly protracted, though more complex, postnatal course. The density of synapses in layer three of human frontal cortex increases rapidly to a maximum value around age 2 years and then declines to 50% of this level by 16 years when density is at adult values. These important results suggest that human cerebral cortex is similar to other neuronal systems (reported in Cowan, 1973, pages 19–41; Oppenheim, 1981, pages 74–133), in which loss of synapses and neurons occurs rather late in development. Huttenlocher (1979) and others (Purves & Lichtman, 1980) suggest that early neuronal and synaptic redundancy may underlie the functional recovery often observed following damage to the immature brain. Dramatic evidence of developmental neural plasticity has come from the study of individuals with congenital hydrocephalus, in which the flow of CSF is blocked causing the ventricles to expand and fill up to 90% of the cranium, pressing the brain against the skull. The brain must be organized rather abnormally in these individuals; nonetheless, more than 50% of these individuals function apparently normally (i.e., they have normal sensory and motor skills and their language and nonlanguage skills are intact as well; Lorber, 1980). This example and others emphasize the potential for functional reorganization of the developing human brain. Thus it is further conceivable that early experience may play a role in determining the course of specialization of human cortex.

We have approached this issue by using ERPs to study adults with an extreme (though naturally occurring) form of altered early experience—unimodal deprivation since birth (Neville, Schmidt, & Kutas, 1983). These subjects (S's) are bilaterally and profoundly deaf due to an inherited condition in which the cochlea does not differentiate normally. The central nervous system is probably not directly affected in these individuals, and indeed they are otherwise neurologically normal. We investigated the possibility that following auditory deprivation ERPs might provide evidence for reorganization of the classical auditory cortical areas, and/or of the remaining sensory systems, specifically the visual system. Theoretically, two types of compensatory change might occur after unimodal deprivation: (1) Brain regions that are normally allocated to subserve function in the deprived modality—in this case auditory areas of the brain—might become organized to process information from other, remaining modalities (e.g., vision); and (2) there might be compensatory hypertrophy or increased capacity in the brain regions subserving the remaining modalities. The few studies of other animals that have investigated cross-modal organization after unimodal deprivation suggest both types of change may occur (Bonaventure & Karli, 1968, Gyllensten, Malmfors, & Norrlin, 1965; Rebillard et al., 1977; Ryugo, Ryugo, Globus, & Killackey, 1975).

In our study 8 congenitally deaf and 132 normal-hearing S's foveated the center of a monitor on which small (1° visual angle) white squares were randomly presented, either to the fovea or 8° visual angle in the left or right visual field. The interstimulus interval (ISI) ranged from 0.5 to 3.0 seconds, so that we could compare the refractory period of visual ERPs over several different brain regions. A major result, shown in Fig. 17.1, was that in hearing subjects the amplitude of the N1 (150 msec) of the visual ERP recorded over the temporal and frontal regions was small and refractory. However, in deaf subjects N1 amplitude recovered more rapidly. Following the longest ISI, the N1 was two to three times larger from these regions in the deaf than in the hearing S's. This group difference was found for peripheral stimuli only. Fig. 17.2 compares the N1

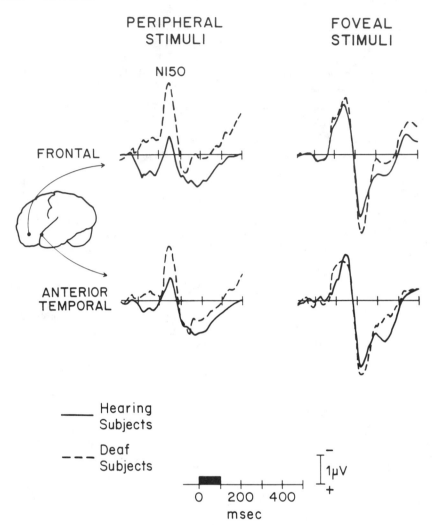

FIG. 17.1   Visual-evoked potentials (VEPs) from left frontal and anterior temporal electrodes to peripheral and foveal stimuli after the 3.0 second interstimulus
interval. VEPs averaged over 13 normal-hearing (solid line) and 8 congenitally
deaf (dashed line) adults are superimposed.

amplitude recorded from temporal, anterior temporal, and frontal electrode locations of the deaf and hearing subjects. In hearing subjects, peripheral stimuli
evoked smaller responses than did foveal stimuli. In contrast, in deaf subjects,
the peripheral and foveal stimuli evoked large and equal responses over these
anterior brain regions. These data suggest that, when deprived of auditory input,
cortical areas that normally subserve audition may become organized to process

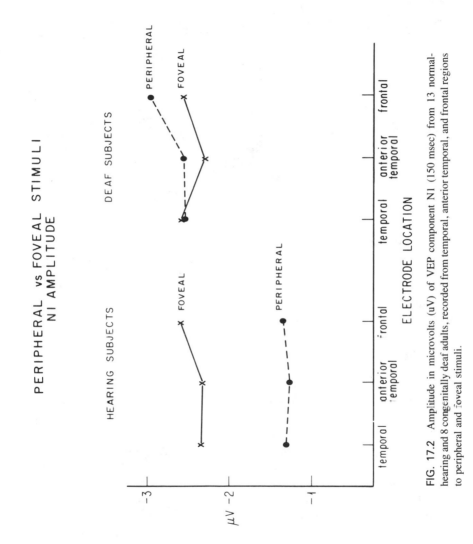

FIG. 17.2 Amplitude in microvolts (uV) of VEP component N1 (150 msec) from 13 normal-hearing and 8 congenitally deaf adults, recorded from temporal, anterior temporal, and frontal regions to peripheral and foveal stimuli.

visual information. These results also suggest that in the deaf *peripheral* visual information receives special compensation—perhaps because, whereas normally hearing subjects can rely on audition to provide information about important events in the periphery, deaf people must rely on peripheral vision.

What neural mechanisms might underlie such intermodal reorganization following auditory deprivation? Studies of cats by Marty (1962) suggest that early in development there may be multimodal afferentation of several cortical areas. Perhaps in the normal course of development there is competition for synaptic space, and this multimodal afferentation is replaced by selective responding only to stimuli within the appropriate modality. Perhaps with early auditory deprivation, the elimination of visual afferents and selective stabilization of auditory afferents does not occur in auditory cortex, so that visual information continues to be processed in those regions (see Changeux & Danchin, 1976, and Changeux, this volume, for discussion of selective stabilization of synapses).

We have studied a few individuals in whom the degeneration of the cochlea was delayed until 4 years after birth. In these individuals, who have had considerable auditory experience, we did not observe the large visual potentials over auditory regions. Further research along these lines may enable us to determine whether there are restricted times in human development when neural reorganization occurs in response to altered sensory input.

Most congenitally deaf individuals have also had extremely abnormal early language experience. The individuals we have studied have not learned to speak, nor have they acquired any language through the auditory modality. Instead, these deaf subjects have acquired American Sign Language (ASL). We investigated the possibility that this very different language experience might lead to altered functional specialization of regions within and between the cerebral hemispheres (Neville, Kutas, & Schmidt, 1982a and 1982b). Specifically, we reasoned that if language experience plays a role in determining neural functioning, aspects of cerebral organization ought to be different in deaf and hearing subjects when they read English, because these groups have had markedly different experience in learning to read English. Hearing subjects first learn English through the auditory modality, and by several indications when they read they convert the written symbols (graphemes) to sounds (Conrad, 1977). On the other hand, congenitally deaf subjects learn English through the visual modality and surely do not perform the same grapheme/phoneme conversion. In 1874 Wernicke predicted that brain organization for reading would be different in deaf subjects, because visual language information would not have to pass from the occipital regions through the left angular gyrus to Wernicke's area for (auditory) decoding.

To investigate this question we first developed a paradigm that would produce reliable patterns of intrahemisphere and interhemisphere specialization during a language task in hearing subjects, because several prior attempts to record ERP manifestations of functional hemisphere specialization had produced negative or equivocal results (for discussion see Donchin, Kutas, & McCarthy, 1977, pages 339–384; Galambos, Benson, Smith, Schulman–Galambos, & Osier, 1975; Hillyard & Woods, 1979, pages 345–378; and Neville, 1980). We incorporated a number of methodological features to maximize the appearance of language-related patterns of cerebral specialization (see Neville et al., 1982a). One important factor was to require subjects to perform a difficult task that itself provided evidence of lateral hemispheric specialization in the differential accuracy of reporting words presented to the two visual fields. Subjects foveated a central point on a video monitor where a fixation symbol occurred simultaneously with a vertically oriented word 2° out in the left or right visual field; on some trials two different words were presented to the two visual fields. After 2 seconds (to allow ERP recording) S's indicated what the fixation symbol was and then they wrote the word(s). Every one of 10 hearing subjects showed behavioral evidence of left hemisphere specialization (i.e., they correctly identified more words after right than left visual field presentations; see Fig. 17.3a).

The simultaneously recorded ERPs also displayed significant lateral asymmetries. The amplitude of several components in ERPs from the *occipital* electrodes seemed to be determined by the anatomy of the visual system. For example, a prominent negative wave at 200 msec was largest over the hemisphere contralateral to the visual field in which a word was presented and was symmetrical after bilateral word presentations. On the other hand, ERPs from more anterior electrodes showed large asymmetries that occurred in the same direction, regardless of position of the word in the visual field. The region from 300–500 msec (shaded in Fig. 17.3b) was more negative from the left than from the right hemisphere, whether words were presented to the right visual field, bilaterally, or to the left visual field. Every subject showed this asymmetry (see Fig. 17.3c). From Fig. 17.3b and 17.3c it is also apparent that the largest asymmetries occurred when words were presented directly to the left hemisphere (i.e., after right visual field presentations). We propose that this asymmetric negativity is a sign of some aspect of the left hemisphere's specialized role in this reading task, because every subject also displayed behavioral evidence of left hemisphere specialization on the task. Also, in a nonlanguage version of this paradigm (see Neville et al., 1982a) we did not observe these asymmetries.

The behavioral and electrophysiological results from deaf subjects in this task were indeed different from those of hearing subjects. Although the deaf S's were as accurate in identifying the words, they did not demonstrate any behavioral asymmetries (i.e., their accuracy was the same for left and right visual field presentations, see Fig. 17.4a). ERPs to the words did display asymmetries, however. At the occipital electrodes, ERPs displayed a similar morphology to that of the hearing subjects; however, N200 tended to be larger from the right hemisphere after both left and bilateral visual field presentations, and symmetrical following right visual field presentations. As in the hearing subjects, very marked asymmetries appeared in ERPs from the anterior temporal electrodes of the deaf S's; however, the pattern of the asymmetries was different. As shown in Fig. 17.4b,

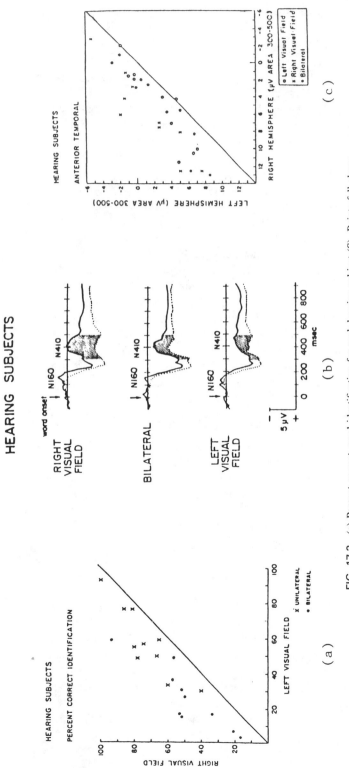

FIG. 17.3 (a) Percent correct word identification for each hearing subject (S). Points fall above the diagonal if accuracy was better after right visual field (left hemisphere) presentations. (b) ERPs averaged over all 10 hearing S's from left (solid line) and right (dotted line) anterior temporal electrodes during right, bilateral, and left visual field word presentations. (c) Amplitude of N410 for each S after words were presented to the left, right, or bilateral visual fields. Points fall above the diagonal if the amplitude was greater from the left than from the right anterior temporal region.

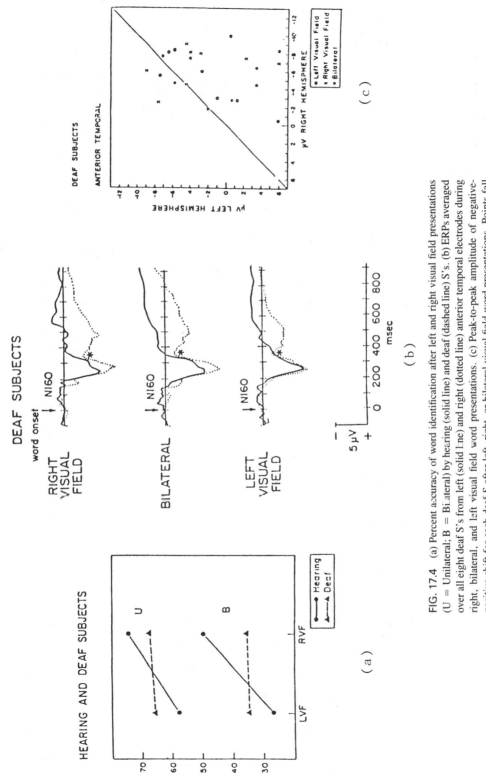

FIG. 17.4   (a) Percent accuracy of word identification after left and right visual field presentations (U = Unilateral; B = Bilateral) by hearing (solid line) and deaf (dashed line) S's. (b) ERPs averaged over all eight deaf S's from left (solid line) and right (dotted line) anterior temporal electrodes during right, bilateral, and left visual field word presentations. (c) Peak-to-peak amplitude of negative-positive shift for each deaf S after left, right, or bilateral visual field word presentations. Points fall below the diagonal if the right anterior temporal amplitude was greater than the left.

after 250 msec the left hemisphere returned to baseline, whereas the right hemisphere displayed a negative peak around 330 msec (marked by the asterisk), which was followed by a positive component before returning to base line. This asymmetry was the same in direction and size, whether words were presented to the right visual field, left visual field, or bilaterally (see Fig. 17.4b). These results were observed fairly consistently in the deaf S's (see Fig. 17.4c). Thus a major difference between deaf and hearing subjects was that the positive shift observed in ERPs from the anterior left hemisphere in hearing subjects was not seen in the deaf S's. Additionally, the negative peak in the right hemisphere ERPs from deaf S's was less pronounced in ERPs from hearing subjects.

These results provide evidence that cerebral organization during reading is indeed different in subjects who learned to read through different modalities and using different strategies. Further studies should help to determine those specific aspects of reading that might be related to the asymmetries in the hearing subjects, and why we did not observe the same pattern in the deaf subjects. For example, it has been proposed that, in hearing subjects, the specialized role of the left hemisphere for language exists primarily to subserve acoustic processing, such as is required to decode the phonology of spoken language (Schwartz & Tallal, 1980). If the ERP asymmetry we have observed in hearing subjects is a neurophysiological manifestation of left hemisphere specialization for phonological decoding during reading, this may be why we did not observe similar evidence for left hemisphere specialization in the deaf subjects, because by all accounts they do not perform a grapheme/phoneme conversion during reading.

On the other hand, another important way in which deaf and hearing subjects differ with respect to English is in their facility with the grammar of the language. Many deaf subjects do not fully acquire the grammar of English; indeed this may be the reason why less than 3% of congenitally deaf adults read at a level that is normal for their age (Conrad, 1977, 1979). If, as has been proposed by Liberman (1974), left hemisphere specialization for language exists to subserve grammatical recoding of information, this may account for the different pattern of hemispheric specialization in deaf subjects.

If these ERP asymmetries are related to phonological (sound-based) processing, we should not observe them in ERPs recorded from deaf S's in response to American Sign Language (ASL) stimuli. On the other hand, aspects of ERPs that are related to the processing of a language that is formal (i.e., grammatical) should be recorded from deaf subjects presented with ASL, because ASL has a highly complex grammar (Klima & Bellugi, 1979). Thus similar studies of ASL may help to clarify factors in development, such as acquisition of speech, acquisition of phonology, and acquisition of grammar, that may determine the development of functional specializations within and between the cerebral hemispheres. Such studies will also bear on the issue of whether languages that are highly dissimilar in terms of the modality of perception and production, in their use of time and space, and in their grammar (i.e., ASL and English), may nonetheless develop within a similar biological framework and be subserved by common neurophysiological systems.

From the results presented previously we can propose that the very altered early sensory and language experience of our deaf S's has altered the normal developmental trajectory of sensory and language related neural processes, and moreover that these changes can be studied using the ERP technique. The ERP may likewise be a valuable tool with which to study neural processes in infants and children as they pass through different stages of language and cognitive development. Although there are several studies of the development of the early, sensory-related evoked potentials (Desmedt & Manil, 1970; Hecox, 1975, pages 151–191; Hecox & Galambos, 1974), very few investigators have studied cognitively labile ERPs in infants and children. In one such study we wondered whether congenitally deaf children who had not acquired any language (i.e., neither speech nor ASL) would display a pattern of cerebral specialization during a nonlanguage task (matching line drawings to photographs) different from that of normal-hearing children. Indeed we observed major ERP differences not only between hearing and deaf children but also between deaf children who did and did not know ASL (Neville, 1975, 1977). These results were interpreted as suggesting that the acquisition of language plays an important role in establishing aspects of cerebral specialization, and further that the particular pattern of cerebral specialization may be determined by the nature (spoken or signed) of the language acquired. In that study we also noted that ERPs from children 9–13 years old were very different in morphology from ERPs from adults, even when recorded to the same physical stimuli (line drawings) under the same task conditions. As seen in Fig. 17.5, the children's ERPs were characterized by a large negativity around 400 msec, whereas adults' ERPs were characterized by a positivity around the same time. Similar observations have been made by Courchesne (1979, pages 224–242).

Whereas little is known about the neural origins of ERPs, available studies suggest that they reflect volume conducted currents associated with synaptic activity (Goff, Allison, & Vaughan, 1978, pages 1–79). In view of Huttenlocher's (1979) work suggesting that synaptic development continues until at least 16 years of age, it is likely that developmental changes in ERPs reflect both structural and functional changes in neural systems during normal development. Moreover ERPs apparently index alterations in neural development that occur when early experiences are abnormal. Since at this time our understanding of the functional significance and the neural origins of ERPs is limited, developmental ERP studies should proceed in parallel with studies of normal adults, and with research in which homologues of ERPs in other primates are subjected to anatomical and chemical analyses not possible in humans. Such studies in conjunction with studies of development hold the promise of clarifying our

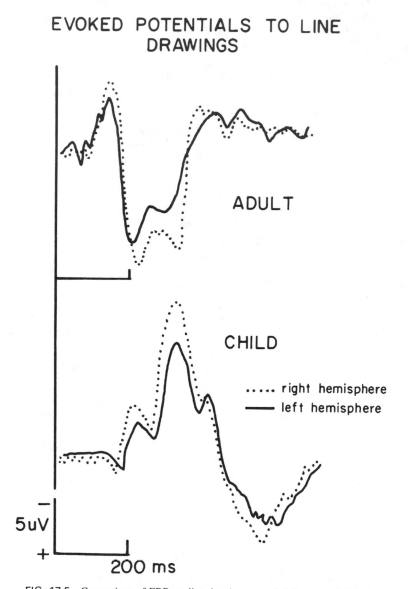

FIG. 17.5   Comparison of ERPs to line drawings recorded from an adult and a
12-year-old child (left and right temporal electrodes).

understanding of neural systems that subserve cognitive processes in normal children and adults, and the ways in which these systems might be altered by early experience.

ACKNOWLEDGMENTS

I am grateful to Drs. P. Kaushall and M. Kutas for comments on the manuscript, and to the National Institute of Health (grant NS14365), the John D. and Catherine T. MacArthur Foundation, the Axe-Houghton Foundation, and Alfred P. Sloan Foundation, for research support.

REFERENCES

Blakemore, C., & Cooper, G. F. Development of the brain depends on the visual environment. *Nature (London), 1970, 228,* 477.

Bonaventure, N., & Karli, P. Apparition au niveau du cortex visuel de potentiels évoqués d'origine auditive chez la souris privée de photorécepteurs. *Journal of Physiology (Paris),* 1968, *60,* 407.

Changeux, J. P., & Danchin, A. Selective stabilization of developing synapses as a mechanism for the specification of neuronal networks. *Nature,* 1976, *264,* 705–712.

Conrad, R. The reading ability of deaf school-leavers. *British Journal of Educational Psychology,* 1977, *47,* 138–148.

Conrad, R. *The deaf schoolchild—Language and cognitive function.* London: Harper & Row, 1979.

Courchesne, E. From infancy to adulthood: The neurophysiological correlates of cognition. In J. E. Desmedt (Ed.), *Cognitive components in cerebral event-related potentials and selective attention; Progress in clinical neurophysiology* (Vol. 6). Basel: Karger, 1979.

Cowan, W. M. Neuronal death as a regulative mechanism in the control of cell number in the nervous system. In M. Rockstein (Ed.), *Development and aging in the nervous system.* New York: Academic Press, 1973.

Desmedt, J. E. Scalp-recorded cerebral event-related potentials in man as point of entry into the analysis of cognitive processing. In F. O. Schmidt et al., *The organization of the cerebral cortex.* Cambridge, Mass.: MIT Press, 1981.

Desmedt, J. E., & Manil, J. Somatosensory evoked potentials of the normal human neonate in REM sleep, in slow wave sleep and in waking. *Electroencephalography and Clinical Neurophysiology,* 1970, *29,* 113–126.

Donchin, E., Kutas, M., & McCarthy, G. Electrocortical indices of hemispheric utilization. In S. Harnad, R. W. Doty, L. Goldstein, J. Jaynes, & G. Krauthamer (Eds.), *Lateralization in the nervous system.* New York: Academic Press, 1977.

Donchin, E., Ritter, W., & McCallum, W. C. Cognitive psychophysiology: The endogenous components of the ERP. In E. Callaway, P. Tueting, & S. H. Koslow (Eds.), *Event-related brain potentials in man.* New York: Academic Press, 1978.

Fiala, B. A., Joyce, J. N., & Greenough, W. T. Environmental complexity modulates growth of granule cell dendrites in developing but not adult hippocampus of rats. *Experimental Neurology,* 1978, *59,* 372–383.

Freeman, R. D. (Ed.). *Developmental neurobiology of vision; NATO Advanced Study Institutes Series.* New York: Plenum Press, 1979.

Galambos, R., Benson, P., Smith, T. S., Schulman–Galambos, C., & Osier, H. On hemispheric differences in evoked potentials to speech stimuli. *Electroencephalography and Clinical Neurophysiology*, 1975, *39*, 279–283.

Glass, J. D. Photic evoked activity in the visual cortex of monocularly deprived cats. *Experimental Neurology*, 1977, *55*, 211–225.

Goff, W. R., Allison, T., & Vaughan, H. G., Jr. The functional neuroanatomy of event-related potentials. In E. Callaway, P Tueting, & S. H. Koslow (Eds.), *Event-related brain potentials in man*. New York: Academic Press, 1978.

Greenough, W. T., & Juraska, J. M. Experience-induced changes in fine brain structure: Their behavioral implications. In *Development and evolution of brain size: Behavioral implications*. New York, Academic Press, 1979.

Gyllensten, L., Malmfors, T., & Norrlin, M. L. Growth alteration in the auditory cortex of visually deprived mice. *Journal of Comparative Neurology*, 1965, *126*, 463.

Hecox, K. Electrophysiological correlates of human auditory development. In Cohen & Salapatek (Eds.), *Infant perception: From sensation to cognition* (Vol. 2). New York: Academic Press, 1975.

Hecox, K., & Galambos, R. Brain stem auditory evoked responses in human infants and adults. *Archives of Otolaryngology*, 1974, *99*, 30–33.

Hillyard, S. A., Picton, T. W., & Regan, D. Sensation, perception and attention: Analysis using ERPs. In E. Callaway, P. Tueting, & S. H. Koslow (Eds.), *Event-related brain potentials in man*. New York: Academic Press, 1978.

Hillyard, S. A., & Woods, D. L. Electrophysiological analysis of human brain function. In M. S. Gazzaniga (Ed.), *Handbook of behavioral neurobiology* (Vol. 2). New York: Plenum Press, 1979.

Hubel, D. H., & Wiesel, T. N. The period of susceptibility to the physiological effects of unilateral eye closure in kittens. *Journal of Physiology (London)*, 1970, *206*, 419–436.

Huttenlocher, P. R. Synaptic density in human frontal cortex—developmental changes and effects of aging. *Brain Research*, 1979, *163*, 195–205.

Klima, E. S., & Bellugi, U. *The signs of language*. Cambridge: Harvard University Press, 1979.

Lenneberg, E. *Biological foundations of language*. New York: Wiley, 1967.

Liberman, A. M. The specialization of the language hemisphere. In F. O. Schmitt & F. G. Worden (Eds.), *The Neurosciences Third Study Program*. Cambridge, Mass.: MIT Press, 1974.

Lorber, J. Reported in R. Lewin. Is your brain really necessary? *Science*, 1980, *210*, 1232–1234.

Marty, R. Développement post-natal des réponses sensorielles du cortex cerébral chez le chat et le lapin. *Archives d'Anatomie Microscopique et de Morphologie Experimentale*, 1962, *51*, 129–264.

Neville, H. J. *Cerebral specialization in normal and congenitally deaf children: An evoked potential and behavioral study*. Unpublished doctoral dissertation, Cornell University, Ithaca, New York, 1975.

Neville, H. J. Electrographic and behavioral cerebral specialization in normal and congenitally deaf children: A preliminary report. In S. Segalowitz & F. Gruber (Eds.), *Language development and neurological theory*. New York: Academic Press, 1977.

Neville, H. J. Event-related potentials in neuropsychological studies of language. *Brain and Language*, 1980, *11*, 300–318.

Neville, H. J., Kutas, M., & Schmidt, A. Event-related potential studies of cerebral specialization during reading, I—studies of normal adults. *Brain and Language*, 1982a, *16*, 300–315.

Neville, H. J., Kutas, M, & Schmidt, A. Event-related potential studies of cerebral specialization during reading, II—studies of congenitally deaf adults. *Brain and Language*, 1982b, 16, 316–337.

Neville, H. J., Kutas, M. & Schmidt, A. Event–related potential studies of cerebral specialization during reading: A comparison of normally hearing and congenitally deaf adults. *Annals of the New York Academy of Sciences*, 1983, *667*.

Neville, H. J., Schmidt, A., & Kutas, M. Altered visual evoked potentials in congenitally deaf adults. *Brain Research*, 1983, *266*, 127–132.

Oppenheim, R. W. Neuronal cell death and some related regressive phenomena during neurogenesis: A selective historical review and progress report. In W. M. Cowan (Ed.), *Studies in developmental neurobiology—Essays in honor of Viktor Hamburger.* New York: Oxford University Press, 1981.

Parnavelas, J. G. Influence of stimulation on cortical development. In *Progress in brain research* (Vol. 48), *Maturation of the nervous system.* New York: Elsevier, 1978.

Purves, D., & Lichtman, J. W. Elimination of synapses in the developing nervous system. *Science*, 1980, *210*, 153–157.

Rebillard, G., Carlier, E., & Pujol, R. Réponses d'origine visuelle au niveau du cortex auditif primaire, chez le chat privé précocement de récepteurs cochléaires. *Revue d'Electroencephalographie et de Neurophysiologie Clinique*, 1977, *7*, 284–289.

Rebillard, G., Rebillard, M., & Pujol, R. Factors affecting the recording of visual-evoked potentials from the deaf cat primary auditory cortex (AI). *Brain Research*, 1980, *188*, 252–254.

Rosenzweig, M. R. Effects of environment on development of brain and of behavior. In E. Tobach, L. R. Aronson, & E. Shaw (Eds.), *The biopsychology of development.* New York: Academic Press, 1971.

Ryugo, D. K., Ryugo, R., Globus, A., & Killackey, H. P. Increased spine density in auditory cortex following visual or somatic deafferentation. *Brain Research*, 1975, *90*, 143–146.

Schwartz, J., & Tallal, P. Rate of acoustic change may underlie hemispheric specialization for speech perception. *Science*, 1980, *207*, 1380–1381.

Snyder, A., & Shapley, R. Deficits in the visual-evoked potentials of cats as a result of visual deprivation. *Experimental Brain Research,* 1979, *37*, 73–86.

Spinelli, D. N., & Jensen, F. E. Plasticity: The mirror of experience. *Science*, 1979, *203*, 75.

Starr, A., Sohmer, H., & Celesia, G. G. Some applications of evoked potentials to patients with neurological impairment. In E. Callaway, P. Tueting, & S. H. Koslow (Eds.), *Event-related brain potentials in man.* New York: Academic Press, 1978.

Wernicke, C. *Der aphasische Symptomencomplex.* Breslau: Frank & Weigert, 1874.

18

Pediatric Contribution to the Present Knowledge on the Neurobehavioral Status of Infants at Birth

Claudine Amiel-Tison
Department of Neonatology, Baudelocque Maternity Hospital, University of Paris V

My goal is to discuss some observations that have been gathered about the sensorimotor repertoire and behavioral competence of the newborn infant. Mine is a modest contribution given the amazing output on the subject over the last two decades and the increase in interdisciplinary communication: neurological and psychological observations, anatomoclinical correlations, neurophysiological studies, experimental work, etc.

It is now a well-established fact that normal newborn infants enter the world with all their sensory systems functioning and that learning processes are immediately demonstrable. Lipsitt (1977) has recently published a very complete overview of recent advances in the field to help pediatricians handle the more important findings in the area. I do not go over what he has already described but rather focus on a few points more particularly related to what the pediatrician in his or her role of caring for the newborn can clarify about early development.

I divide my chapter into three sections. In the first, I discuss the neurological implications of certain kinds of behaviors in the full-term newborn. Some of those behaviors suggest important "prewiring" in infants that might be qualified as *subcortical*. In other examples, precocious integrative or *cortical* behaviors are proposed. In the second section, I describe briefly neurological maturation from 28 weeks in the gestation period to the end of the first year of life. In the third, I devote a few minutes to various observations concerning pathology.

CLINICAL OBSERVATIONS ON THE NORMAL FULL-TERM NEWBORN

The debate on cortical and subcortical functions invariably underlies any observations made on the full-term newborn. In what follows I cite a few examples that should illustrate the evolution of concepts in the area over the last 20 years.

Pre-Wiring

Automatic walking   One typical example of research in this area is the work of Andre Thomas (1949, 1952, 1960, 1966) on automatic walking. Thomas was not only fascinated by the amazing precision of the mechanism underlying this behavior from the very first hours of life, but he described the adaptability of the newborn to various situations, such as walking upwards on an inclined plane or stepping over an obstacle. At the time these experiments were carried out, the tendency was to imagine that the more extraordinary forms of activity could only be attributed to the functioning of higher cortical centers. However, two kinds of observations were later made by Saint Anne Dargassies (1955) and by Thomas himself (1966), namely, that automatic walking is present in fetuses and in premature newborns and in anencephalic newborns. The dilemma posed by these observations was summarized by Thomas himself in the foreword to his last book (1966): "responses which are found both in the normal newborn and in the anencephalic are intriguing and it is embarrassingly difficult to imagine the nervous mechanisms which are involved and their localisation in the Nervous System."

Thomas (1966), in his pioneering work in experimental psychology, has also described a test called the *Christian Name* test in which he studied infant responses to the indicators he knew best (i.e., automatic walking and modifications of tone). In this test a 16-day-old baby and her mother were used. The mother had been instructed to use the baby's name often during the preceding fortnight. During the test, the mother or a stranger placed to the baby's left called the baby by her name. Thomas noted that the baby's head and body leaned to the left if and only if the mother pronounced her name (Fig. 18.1). At the same moment the baby's legs moved and the right leg crossed over the medial place in a gesture that looked as though she were taking a step to the left. Thomas (1966 p. 86) comments by remarking on the complexity of the act performed and considers the muscular synergies involved and the "mathematical and geometrical precision" of the performance.

Looking more carefully to the level of attention of the infant when performing, it appears that the attention involved helps organizing this complex act. The high level of attention seems then more important nowadays when trying to define a

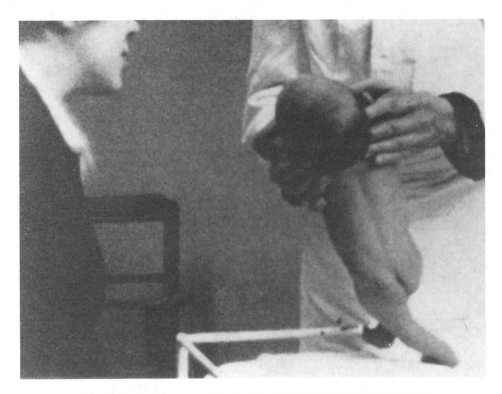

FIG. 18.1   *Christian name test.* The baby is held in the upright position and automatic walking is elicited. The mother, placed to the baby's left, calls the baby by her name: The baby's head and body lean to the left and she appears to take a step to the left when the mother pronounces her name. (In Thomas & Autgaerden, *Locomotion from pre to postnatal life.* London: Spastics Society, 1966, p. 28, with permission.)

normal cerebral function in the newborn that the automatic response itself (see below).

In looking back at the work of Thomas, it is striking that he was constantly searching for programmation in the newborn. It should further be noted that if automatic walking invariably elicits a very strong response from observers it is perhaps because it demonstrates that one of the most characteristic symbols of our species is present at birth and that, as Thomas tried to demonstrate, a high level of species specific pre-wiring is present at birth.

Learning Abilities   Another example of specific pre-wiring are the dispositions to learning that can be observed in newborns. Such dispositions are emphasized in Brazelton's Neonatal Assessment Scale (1973). His aim was to evaluate and measure precisely what he termed 'integrative behaviors' i.e., behaviors that were supposed to involve cortical processing by the infant. His approach was a reaction against the "rather stereotyped neurological examinations that assess reflex behavior with an oversimplified positive-negative approach." Moreover, the goal of this type of assessment was to test "higher brain centers" serving to modify responses through partial inhibition or facilitation in the neonate. Brazelton certainly succeeded in his aim and his scale is today used in all major neurological centers.

Recently, however, several observations have been made showing that in anencephalic (Graham, Leaviti, & Strock, 1978) or hydranencephalic (Aylward, Lazzara, & Meyer, 1978; Tuber, Berntson, Bachman, & Allen, 1980) newborns, integrative behavior can be demonstrated as well. These findings support the view that subcortical networks are capable of mediating complex behavioral processes such as learning, and so these processes therefore cannot appear to be exclusively in the domain of cortical function. Thus, it would seem very difficult to describe these behaviors as reflecting cognitive or affective responses implying cortical mediation, because habituation and quieting to the examiner's voice have been found in the absence of any appreciable quantity of cortex (Aylward, et al., 1978). As Aylward et al. note: "Perhaps behaviors such as smiling, hand-to-mouth activity, quieting to sounds and visually following a moving field suggest that, in addition to basic reflexive automatisms, the neonate also possesses socially relevant behavioral automatisms [p. 216]."

Some of the data on anencephalic infants allows us to speculate further. Graham et al. (1978), in their observation of an anencephalic infant, 3-to-6-weeks old, found responses to acoustic stimulation with cardiac deceleration typical of the response pattern seen in normal, older infants. Such precocity on the part of the anencephalic infants implies unexpected competence of the lower brain structures and moreover suggests that in the normal infant feedback from immature higher centers could even possibly interfere with, rather than modulate, the functioning of lower centers.

These observations, showing how the higher brain centers serve to modify responses through partial inhibition or facilitation in the neonate, drove to recognize the need of a more qualitative assessment to define the intact function of the CNS in the neonatal period. As Brazelton (1979) notes: "Brain damaged infants may have reflex responses available but they may be distortedly exaggerated or partially suppressed, stereotyped or obligatory; the quality of these responses is different from that of the graded ones seen in the intact baby [p. 37]."

Integrative Cortical Behaviors

State Regulation.   One of the last domains where higher cortical function remains the dominant view is that of State Regulation. Since Prechtl (Prechtl & Beintema, 1964), evaluation of states has been considered indispensable to any kind of behavioral evaluation in the newborn. Prechtl and Bientema's intention was to obtain optimal responses from newborn infants, which is only possible during the state of quiet alertness. In order to do this, they defined a five point scale in which the alertness of an infant could be described; using this scale in clinical experiments allows us comparisons of data.

Brazelton (1979) went even further than Prechtl's state description and showed how certain environments seem to exceed certain infants' capacities and make them simply "switch off." Conversely, other infants "emerge" in order to increase communication with their environments. He asserts: "State no longer needs to be treated as an error variable but serves to set a dynamic pattern to allow for full behavioral repertoire of the infant. . . . The variability of state indicates the infant's capacities for self-organization. His ability to quiet himself as well as his need for stimulations also measures this adequacy [p. 38]." Brazelton's claim concerning cortical control of the infant's capacities for self-organization would appear to be supported by the fact that the hydranencephalic infant studied by Aylward et al. (1978) demonstrated poor state regulation. In addition, very premature infants do not seem to be capable of state regulation either. Studies on ontogenesis of sleep patterns showed that before 31 weeks G.A., wakefulness is not clearly established; it is only by 36 weeks G.A. that EEG patterns differentiate during wakefulness, active sleep, and quiet sleep, as reviewed by Dreyfus–Brisac (1979). Thus, we may make the tentative hypothesis that state regulation is a high level of organization only present in normal, full-term newborns. Consequently, state regulation should be our most consistant predictor.

Role of Posture on Motor Behavior and Level of Attention   A transitory modification of motor behavior and level of attention has been demonstrated by Grenier (1980, 1981) in an experiment in which he held a baby's head firmly in the axis of its trunk in a sitting position. Grenier's hypothesis was that many obligatory responses manifested during the first weeks of life, like brisk primary reflexes in the upper extremities (more reflex, grasping reflex) and the anxiety provoked by these brisk and uncontrolled reactions, are linked to neck impotence. This aspect changes dramatically when head control is acquired at about 6 to 8 weeks. Grenier's hypothesis, therefore, was that if head control could be realized during the first weeks of life, a transformation in motor aptitude and behavior might be observed. This speculation is fully verified in his experiment (Fig. 18.2). If a baby's neck is patiently held in position for a certain time, these changes are quite apparent. Grenier's observations are of considerable theoretical interest and offer one way of demonstrating that upper structures are already functioning very early in life, but that this functioning can only be demonstrated if head control is achieved for a period of approximately half an hour. In going further in his speculation and after observing (with ultra sonography) the harmonious mobility of the fetus in utero, where the head is strongly maintained, one can imagine that the motor and behavioral characteristics of the infant from birth to

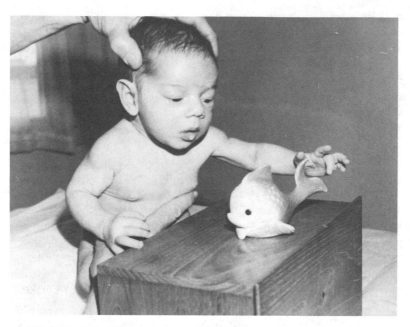

FIG. 18.2 *Role of posture on motor behavior and level of attention.*
Head control is obtained transitorily in a 17-day-old infant. A transformation of
posture and behavior is observed, with a visuo-motor coordination that is not
observed during the third week of life in ordinary circumstances. (In Amiel-Tison
& Grenier, *Evaluation neurologique du nouveau-né et du nourrisson.* Paris: Masson, 1981, with permission.)

2 months do, in fact, derive from neck impotence, and that this is merely a short
interval where certain kinds of behavior become impossible in spite of the fact
that the potential is readily available, either before birth or after 2 months
postnatal age.

   From a practical point of view, Grenier's observations make it clear that in
any experimentation on the newborn not only must the state of the infant be
determined but some kind of neck fixation must be achieved, because it improves
the level of alertness in Stage 3 and diminishes uncoordinated movements. In
all future clinical investigation and psychological research on newborn infants,
it is certain that neck fixation will have to be taken into account.

   As a conclusion, if we look back over the data on automatic walking and
learning abilities, for instance in the newborn, we find undisputable evidence of
elaborated motor programming and early ability to adapt this program to environmental modifications. Nonetheless, it would appear that these observations
will have to be repeated in experiments that take into account recent advances
on state regulation and recent observations concerning the role of active head
control on visuomotor coordination. In other words, a new approach allowing

us to draw a much more dynamic picture of the newborn appears necessary. This might help us to make far more subtle interpretations about the capacities of adaptation of the newborn and the beginning of cognitive processes.

CLINICAL OBSERVATIONS ON NEUROLOGICAL MATURATION

Neurological Maturation from 28 to 40 Weeks of Gestation

We believe that a better understanding of the newborn may be achieved through the detailed study of the maturation of the nervous system between 28 and 40 weeks of gestation. In this section, I go over some of the more salient features of the maturational studies that have already been carried out.

Saint Anne Dargassies described the stages of development that characterize maturation between 28 and 40 weeks of gestational age (1955, 1974). Her work is largely based on the methods developed by A. Thomas in the study of the full-term infant. She has adapted Thomas' work to the study of the premature infant and relies to a large extent on the evaluation of reflexes and tone reactions.

In her description, at 28 weeks G.A., the premature newborn is flaccid, lying in extension, and legs and arms are almost lacking in tone. Progressively, tone increases in a caudocephalic direction, with posture in flexion observed first in the legs (around 34 weeks G.A.) and later in the upper extremities (36 to 38 weeks G.A.) (Fig. 18.3). This pattern is so precise and individual variations so slight that we can describe landmarks at 2-week intervals. The full-term newborn, when lying on the examination table, is in full flexion in four extremities with a lot of resistance to movements of extension. During the same period, a cau docephalic reinforcement of active tone is observed in the axis (Fig. 18.4). When the infant is held in the upright position, a righting reaction first appears in lower limbs (32 weeks G.A.), later in the trunk (36 weeks G.A.), and finally in the neck, allowing him to maintain the head in the axis for a few seconds. At the same time Saint Anne Dargassies has shown that maturative pattern progresses almost identically in a prematurely born infant, and that the time as well as the ordered sequence are barely affected.

As the need to determine G.A. has increased rapidly with the development of Perinatology, the work of Saint Anne Dargassies has been adapted into a practical tool for pediatricians. The most salient items of this kind of examination have been selected with precise descriptions of each maneuver involved (Amiel-Tison, 1968, 1974).

The use of neurological evaluation to determine G.A. relies on the dogma that maturation in the fetus progresses in an unvarying pattern regardless of environmental circumstances. But further observation has shown that there are exceptions to this rule (Gould, Gluck, & Kulovich, 1972; 1977). Unfavorable intrauterine conditions may accelerate the development of the infant's central

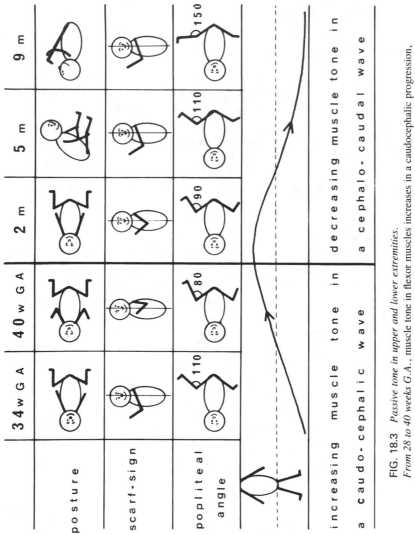

FIG. 18.3   *Passive tone in upper and lower extremities.*

From 28 to 40 weeks G.A., muscle tone in flexor muscles increases in a caudocephalic progression, as indicated by posture, scarfsign (evaluating extensibility in upper limbs), and popliteal angle (evaluating extensibility in lower limbs.) *Within the first year of life*, muscle tone in flexor muscles decreases in a cephalocaudal progression to reach a global hypotonia maximum at 8 to 10 months.

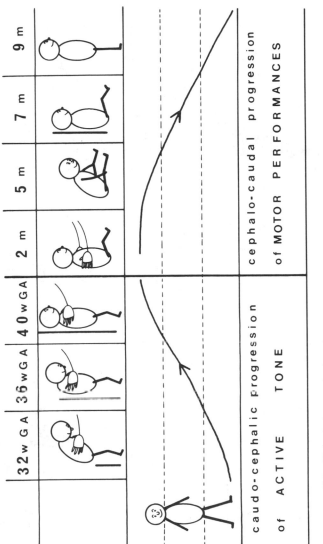

FIG. 18.4 *Active tone in the axis.*

From 28 to 40 weeks G.A., when the infant is held in the upright position, a righting reaction first appears in the legs, later in the trunk, and finally in the neck and is maintained for a few seconds. *Within the first year of life,* head control is acquired first, later the sitting position; finally, around 9 months, the infant can stand up and maintain the standing position for a while. From about 4 to 7 months, no righting reaction is observed when the infant is held in the upright position, at the time when sitting position is being acquired.

nervous system. Evidence of a 4-week or more advance in neurological maturation was detected in 16 infants with G.A. between 30 and 37 weeks (Amiel-
Tison, 1980). These infants were all from abnormal pregnancies (chronic hyper-
tensive diseases, pregnancy-induced hypertension, uterine malformation, or multiple pregnancy). It can be speculated that corticosteroid secretion by the fetus,
in response to intra-uterine stress, may play a role in the induction of these
effects. The same possibility of biochemical advance in lung maturation (Gould
et al., 1977) in unfavorable gestational circumstances, such as maternal hypertension or delay in maturation in maternal diabetes, is of theoretical interest. All
these observations show that the speed of programmed fetal maturation can be
modified by unfavorable circumstances. Recent advances in the study of neuromotor behavior of the premature infant tend to show more sensitivity to environmental influences than what was thought in the past. It is probable that new
methods of fetal investigation, particularly ultrasonography, will allow us to
further explore early patterns of motricity and fetal sleep patterns, eventually
using eye movements as an indicator (Birnholz, 1981).

Neurological Maturation within the First Year of Life

Precise analysis of tone in the full-term infant during the first year of life allows
us to recognize successive waves of decrease and increase in flexor tone in the
limbs (Amiel-Tison, 1978, 1980; Grenier, 1980; Thomas & Ajuriaguerra, 1949;
Thomas & Saint Anne Dargassis, 1952). These waves, as we indicated for the
premature, do not reach the whole body at the same time. In the first year of
life, flexor tone first decreases in the upper extremities (beginning around 2
months postnatally), then in the lower limbs (from 4 to 8 months) (Fig. 18.3).
Later on, tone slowly increases again, reaching during infancy norms already
characteristic of the adult. Individual variations are much greater in this postnatal
wave: first in timing as maximum hypotonicity is attained any time between 8
and 15 months; second in intensity. The slower the overall development of the
infant, the higher the hypotoncity observed. In extreme cases, a very hypotonic
infant will sit at a normal age but will not walk before 18 months, when the
hypotonic stage begins to decrease (Stambak & Ajuriaguerra, 1958).

   At the same time, while this change in limb tone is observed, tone of the
axis also undergoes some changes. If an infant is lifted up and held with her
feet touching the examination table, she will straighten up for a while. This
straightening reaction in the upright position follows fairly strict patterns
(Fig. 18.4). These reactions excellent at the full-term period, remain so up to 2
to 4 months postnatally, and then from about 4 to 6 months, the straightening
reaction in the upright position disappears. However, at the same time, the
beginning of the sitting position at 5 months demonstrates increasingly active
tone in the axis. Around 7 months, straightening reaction reappears. Our awareness of these normal patterns of evolution and their individual variations is

extremely helpful for the diagnosis of abnormalities. As an example, the normal pattern at 5 months of age is a tripodic sitting position and no straightening reaction in the standing position. Conversely, a child who has suffered perinatal asphyxia often shows a persistance of very strong straightening reactions in the upright position, whereas at the same time the delay in relaxation in the lower limbs makes the tripodic sitting position impossible.

The intricate relationship between tone distribution and reflex activity clearly appears as important for a harmonious motor development. The global straightening reaction being very strong at birth and in the first 2 to 4 months of life, automatic walking can easily be elicited. Later on, from 4 to 6 months, it is very difficult to elicit automatic walking in a semiflexed child with no righting reaction. This phenomenon probably explains the discrepancies in the literature concerning the normal age of disappearance of automatic walking. It is only after 7 months that the postural changes allow for the beginning of voluntary steps. Furthermore, transitory hypotonicity in the lower limbs, pelvis, and spine may be considered as protective for the immature bones and articulations. Any attempts to accelerate the acquisition of walking are dangerous from an osteoarticular point of view.

The neuromotor abilities are changing so fast during the first year that the pediatrician has to be careful to take into account the gestational age in order to detect cerebral dysfunction or abnormalities. It is important to correct for the gestational age of the premature infant throughout the first year of life.

CLINICAL OBSERVATIONS ON BRAIN DAMAGE OF PERINATAL ORIGIN

Affirmation of Functional Normalcy in the Full-Term Newborn

Normal cerebral functions can now be fairly well defined in the full-term newborn by combining physical examinations, neurological evaluations, the dynamic of state regulation, and behavioral interaction with the adult. Clinical screening in the full-term newborn therefore appears reliable. With repeated clinical evaluations, within the first week of life, it is unlikely that many cases of brain damage will go undetected. Only a few isolated cases of mental retardation are not diagnosed in the first weeks.

Apparent Fragility of the Capacities Most Recently Acquired

Observation of hypotonia in the upper part of the body (neck flexors and upper limbs) is a very common pattern in the first week of life after minimal birth trauma. Distribution of tone in such an infant looks like the normal pattern for a 36-week G.A. newborn premature. However, the infant with minimal birth trauma catches up on the normal pattern after only a few days, when circulatory trouble or mild brain edema disappear. When the insult is very mild there is regression to an immediately prior stage of maturational functioning. For cases of severe neurological insult rather than a regression, what strikes the clinician is the presence of additional symptoms. It must be stressed that, although these observations seem acceptable to most clinicians, it is very difficult to demonstrate their overall validity.

Hierarchy of Signs During the Neonatal Period

In cases of abnormalities, a precise lesional diagnosis is difficult in the neonatal period. There is obviously a hierarchy of signs and symptoms; however, at this point it is often impossible to differentiate transitory brain dysfunction due to metabolic or circulatory troubles from definitive cell damage. The kind of symptoms observed, the severity of the perinatal insult, and the duration of symptoms roughly allow us to evaluate the risk and predict the outcome. Recent advances in radiological investigation such as craniocerebral computerized axial tomographies (CAT Scan) and ultrasonography have brought more precision to anatomoclinical correlations. Unfortunately, these methods rarely reveal much more than intracranial hemorrhages, and, with the exception of massive bilateral intraventricular hemorrhages in the premature newborn, the bleeding itself is rarely life threatening. Resorbtion of clots is observed in about 10 days and hemorrhages are poorly correlated to later difficulties. There is no precise method at this time, be it radiological, bioelectrical, or biochemical, better equipped than clinical evaluation for the diagnosis of definitive cellular damage.

Short-Term Evaluation at 1 Year of Age

Twenty years' experience in the pediatric outpatient department of a Paris Maternity Hospital has gradually taught me how to make reliable guesses. I have known for a long time which of my patients would come back to see me between the ages of 8 and 10 owing to scholastic difficulties. Generally speaking, they seem to be the ones who suffered from transitory neuromotor abnormalities during their first year, appeared normal at 1 year, had a normal career in kindergarden from ages 3 to 6, and then began to encounter more or less great scholastic difficulties. If one tries to adopt an organistic point of view, the essential is to identify the link between perinatal insult and later difficulties through a clinical method based on neuromotor evaluation (Amiel–Tison, 1978; Amiel–Tison, Dube, Garel, & Jequier, 1983).

In our work at the Port Royal Maternity Hospital we selected a sample of 15 full-term newborns who presented abnormal neurological symptoms during their first week and neuromotor symptoms within the first year of life but not beyond. They all seemed normal at 1 year of age. At 5 to 6 years of age, these 15 children were again reassessed and compared to 15 controls selected on a normal neurological status in the first week of life (Table 18.1). Normalization was observed in 5 out of 15 (30%) (i.e., they manifested no overt symptoms and succeeded in all the tests). In all likelihood these 5 should not encounter any scholastic difficulties. However, 4 out of 15 had abnormal scores on the tests. These 4 will in all likelihood encounter scholastic difficulties. They all manifested some motor difficulty, had problems in fine motoric adjustments, manifested signs of dyspraxia, and their IQ scored less than 85 in the Terman–Merill test. The remaining 6 children were intermediate in their symptoms as well as in the predictions that can be made for their future. In the control group, 13 out of 15 children are normal, 1 is classified abnormal, and 1 is in the intermediate group.

It is difficult at this point to offer a definite explanation concerning these results. However, it seems possible that the symptoms observed during the tests carried out during the first week may be attributed to damage in both white matter and gray substance (Banker & Larroche, 1962). Given the kind of functioning that cannot, as yet, be explored, white matter deficit can be detected more rapidly than that of gray substance.

Because of the amount of technical difficulties encountered in prospective follow-up studies of this kind, neurological plasticity, as recently reviewed by Saint James Roberts (1979), is at the moment an area of extraordinary complexity and contradictions. An objective look at the literature may fully justify this discouraged comment by Saint James Roberts (1979): "Data linking cerebral palsy and retardation to low birth weight or anoxia, for example, are difficult to reconcile with the failure of prospective studies to isolate effective risk criteria or with the importance of social class as a determinant of trauma outcome [p. 254]." Facing the complexity and intricateness of various favorable and unfavorable processes involved in the recovery or nonrecovery from brain insult, one often reacts according to preconceived opinions and fashionable paradoxes. For instance, any pediatrician can remember a few cases of children with extensive destruction of cerebral parenchyma visible on CAT scan and a perfectly normal life and good adaptation to school. Conversely, the same pediatrician

TABLE 18.1.
Fifteen Children in the Target Group, Who had Transitory Neuromotor Abnormalities within the First Year of Life, are Compared with 15 Control and Classified at 5 to 6 Years of Age According to Three Categories

Number of Cases	Categories at 5 to 6 Years		
	Abnormal	Intermediate	Normal
Target group 15 children	4	6	5
Control group 15 children	1	1	13

can remember newborns who behaved perfectly normal but who turned out to be very poorly adapted children in school for sociofamilial reasons. Two manichean positions, one by Pasamanick and Knoblock (1961), the other by Sameroff and Chandler (1975), on the validity of exclusively organic or purely social contingencies in accounting for amount or continuity of abnormality in the child, are irreconcilable and extreme.

Conclusion

In closing, I would like to stress that every recent experiment tends to demonstrate that the infant's competence regardless of whether she is full-term or premature has been grossly underestimated (Fig. 18.5). One of the most striking examples of this is the 60-minute-old newborn infant's capacity (Meltzoff & Moore, 1977) to imitate facial gestures, when Piaget maintained that such an ability was only achieved by the end of the first year of life. Therefore, as proposed by Meltzoff and Moore (1977): ". . . we must revise our current conceptions of infancy, which hold that such a capacity is the product of many months of postnatal development. The ability to act on the basis of an abstract representation of a perceptually absent stimulus becomes the starting point for psychological development and not its culmination [p. 78]." It is now time for the fetus to claim the recognition of its competence.

FIG. 18.5   A full-term just-born infant taking a cheerful walk as he eliminates amniotic fluid from his ears. After such dazzling achievements, he has no more to claim for the recognition of his competency. (Cartoon from Annette Tison.)

REFERENCES

Amiel–Tison, C. Neurological evaluation of the maturity of newborn infants. *Archives of Diseases in Childhood*, 1968, *43*, 89–93.

Amiel–Tison, C. Neurological evaluation of the small neonate: the importance of head straightening reactions. In L. Gluck (Ed.) *Modern Perinatal Medicine*. Chicago: Year Book Medical Publishers, 1974.

Amiel–Tison, C. A method for neurological evaluation within the first year of life: experience with full-term newborn infants with birth injury. In *Major mental handicap: Methods and costs of prevention*. Ciba Foundation Symposium (No. 59). New York: Elsevier/North Holland, 1978.

Amiel–Tison, C. Possible acceleration of neurological maturation following high risk pregnancy. *American Journal of Obstetrics and Gynecology*, 1980, *138*, 303–306.

Amiel–Tison, C., Dube, R., Garel, M., & Jequier, J. C. Late outcome after transient neuromotor abnormalities within the first year of life. In Stern, Bard, & Früs-Hansen (Eds.), *Intensive Care* (IV). New York: Masson, 1983, 247–258.

Aylward, G. P., Lazzara, A., & Meyer, J. Behavioral and Neurological characteristics of a hydranencephalic infant. *Developmental Medicine and Child Neurology*, 1978, *20*, 211–217.

Banker, B. Q., & Larroche, J. C. Periventricular leukomalacia of infancy. *Archives of Neurology and Psychiatry*, 1962, *7*, 386–410.

Birnholz, J. C. The development of Human Fetal Eye Movement Patterns. *Science*, 1981, *213*, 679–681.

Brazelton, T. B. *Neonatal Behavioral Assessment Scale*. London: London National Spastics Society, 1973.

Brazelton, T. B. Behavioral competence of the newborn infant. *Seminars in Perinatology*, 1979, *3*, 35–44.

Dreyfus–Brisac, C. Ontogenesis of brain bioelectrical activity and sleep organization in neonates and infants. In F. Faulkner & J. M. Tanner (eds.), *Human Growth* (Vol. 3), New York Plenum, 1979.

Gould, J. B., Gluck, L. & Kulovich, M. V. The acceleration of neurological maturation in high stress pregnancy and its relation to fetal lung maturity. *Pediatric Research*, 1972, *6*, 276.

Gould, J. B., Gluck, L. & Kulovich, M. V. The relationship between accelerated pulmonary maturity and accelerated neurological maturity in certain chronically stressed pregnancies. *American Journal of Obstetrics and Gynecology*, 1977, *127*, 181–190.

Graham, F. K., Leaviti, L. A., & Strock, B. D. Precocious cardiac orienting in a human anencephalic infant. *Science*, 1978, *199*, 322–324.

Grenier, A. Révélation d'une expression motrice différente par fixation manuelle de la nuque. In A. Grenier & Amiel–Tison (Eds.), *Evaluation Neurologique du Nouveau-Né et du Nourrisson*. Paris: Masson, 1980.

Grenier, A. "Motricité libérée" par fixation manuelle de la nuque au cours des premiéres semaines de la vie. *Archives Françaises de Pediatrie*, 1981, *38*, 557–561.

Lipsitt, L. P. The study of sensory and learning processes of the newborn. *Clinics in Perinatology*, 1977, *4*, 163–186.

Meltzoff, A. N. & Moore, M. K. Imitation of facial and manual gestures by human neonates. *Science*, 1977, *198*, 75–78.

Pasamanick, B. & Knobloch, H. Epidemiologic studies on the complications of pregnancy and the birth process. In G. Caplan (Ed.), *Prevention of mental disorders in children*. New York: Basic Books, 1961.

Prechtl, H. F. R. & Beintema, D. H. The Neurological examination of the full-term newborn infant. *Clinics in Developmental Pediatrics* (No. 12). London: Spastics Society with Heinemann, 1964.

Saint Anne Dargassies, S. La maturation neurologique du prématuré. *Etudes Neonatales*, 1955, *4*, 71–116.

Saint Anne Dargassies, S. *Le développement neurologique du nouveau-né à terme et prématuré.* Paris: Masson, 1974.

Saint James Roberts, I. Neurological plasticy, recovery from brain insult, and child development. *Advances in child development and behavior,* 1979, *14,* 253–319.

Sameroff, A. J., & Chandler, M. J. Reproductive risk and the continuum of care-taker casualty. In F. D. Horowitz (Ed.), *Review of child development* (Vol. 4). Chicago: University of Chicago Press, 1975.

Stambak, M. & Ajuriaguerra, J. de. Evolution de l'extensibilité musculaire depuis la naissance jusquà 2 ans. *Presse Médicale,* 1958, *66,* 24–27.

Thomas, A., & Ajuriaguerra, J. de. Etude séméiologique du tonus musculaire. *Editions Médicales Flammarion,* Paris, 1949.

Thomas, A., & Autgaerden, S. *Locomotion from pre to post-natal life.* London: Spastics Society with Heinemann, 1966.

Thomas, A., Chesni, Y. & Saint Anne Dargassies, S. The Neurological Examination of the Infant. *Clinics in Developmental Medecine* (No. 1). London: National Spastics Society, 1960.

Thomas, A., & Saint Anne Dargassies, S. *Etudes Neurologiques sur le nouveau-né et le jeune nourrisson.* Paris: Masson, 1952.

Tuber, D. S., Berntson, G. G., Bachman, D. S., & Allen, J. N. Associative learning in premature hydranencephalic and normal twins. *Science,* 1980, *210,* 1035–1037.

19 Constraints on Semantic Development

Susan Carey
Massachussetts Institute of Technology

As clearly recognized at least from the time of the British Empiricists, any theory of the nature of human knowledge must come to grips with the problem of how it is acquired. This problem, in turn, decomposes into two—the problem of specifying the initial state of the child and the problem of specifying the principles by which the initial state is modified. For any given domain of knowledge one cannot say, a priori, whether the study of human infants will bear on the solution to these problems. One reason is that the initial state may not be operative until after infancy. Some maturationally determined state of the central nervous system may be required; alternatively, certain intellectual achievements, themselves attained during infancy or early childhood, may be required to trigger the initial state in that domain. In this chapter I argue that, in spite of these very real possibilities, the empirical study of infants will be crucial to the understanding of the human semantic and conceptual system.

Recently, Keil (1979) has proposed a fragment of a theory of semantic development concerning the principles by which the initial state[1] is modified. I argue in this chapter that his proposal is both importantly right and importantly wrong. A diagnosis of what went wrong implicates a greater role for the specification of the initial state in the explanation of semantic development.

---

[1] My use of the locution "initial state" in this chapter is nonstandard. I mean the state of the system when it first becomes active. More is innate than the initial state. On a parameter-setting model, for example, the entire set of allowable configurations of parameters, plus the principles by which the environment fixes parameter values, are innate. On my usage, only the first setting of the parameters would constitute the initial state.

The Problem

Learning the meaning of a new word is an inductive process. The child must infer its meaning from the uses he hears others make of the word and from their reactions to his usage. A major goal for the theorist trying to understand the process of meaning acquisition, like that for the theorist trying to understand any case of induction, is to specify the constraints on the hypotheses the child will entertain.

This point can be illustrated through Quine's (1960) well-known scenario, in which he asks us to imagine ourselves interrogating an informant who speaks an alien language. Our information about the meanings of words is to come from pointing to putative referents, saying the word, and observing assent or dissent on the part of our informant. The informant points to a rabbit and says *gavagai*. Our hypothesis is that *gavagai* means the same thing as the English word *rabbit*, and we proceed to test our hypothesis by pointing out other rabbits and other animals and querying of each one, *gavagai*? The informant assents in each case of a rabbit and demurs in each case of a nonrabbit. The problem is that there are infinitely many other hypotheses about the meaning of *gavagai* that are consistent with the data we have so far. *Gavagai* could designate a particular species of rabbit found in that glen. This is a hypothesis we might well entertain, and it is clear how we would rule it out (seek out other species of rabbits). But *gavagai* could also mean *rabbit or light bulb*. Although it is clear how we would rule out that hypothesis too (query about a light bulb), there are an infinitude of such hypotheses, such that we could spend the rest of our lives and then forever after just learning the meaning of the word *gavagai*. The problem is still worse. Quine pointed out that there are some hypotheses we might entertain that would be impossible to rule out from such information. *Gavagai* might mean, for example, *undetached rabbit part*, any part of a rabbit, its ear, tail, left leg, its body, and so on, as long as it is currently attached to a rabbit. Any pointing to a rabbit requires pointing somewhere, and so is a case of pointing to an undetached rabbit part.

Quine's example applies equally to the young child's learning the meaning of the word *rabbit*, where the hypotheses the child entertains are stated in terms of the concepts he represents in mentalese (*mentalese* is Fodor's term for the language of thought). Of course, neither we nor the child would ever entertain hypotheses like *undetached rabbit part* or *rabbit or light bulb*. The child's hypotheses are severely constrained to those that will converge on the correct meaning over a relatively short period (sometimes one-trial learning).[2]

----

[2]My use of this example is quite different from Quine's. He shows that the problem arises even if we allow information from other sources than the assent/dissent scenario imagined earlier, because of the "indeterminacy of translation." A skeptic about meaning, Quine endorses the consequences of this line of argument—that for us the meaning of *rabbit* is indeterminate between the animal, undetached parts of the animal, and a host of other possibilities. This is not the place to engage in a debate about Quine's skepticism. Here the examples serve the much simpler point that our inductive processes must be highly constrained.

The problem of induction *is* the central problem of knowledge acquisition in any domain, including the domain of word meanings. Constraints on induction are provided by the initial state—the concepts first available to the child for hypothesis testing about word meanings—and from the nature of the processes by which those concepts are combined and modified. Keil's (1979) constraint is of the latter type and would rule out a class of those unnatural concepts we considered earlier, those like *rabbit or light bulb*.

The M Constraint on Linguistic Categories

Keil's proposal is adapted from work by the philosopher, Fred Sommers (1963). Sommers' thesis is that there is a level of concepts (the ontological level) that have a special status in our conceptual system, and that there is a structural constraint on these concepts (they form a strict hierarchy). His argument depends on a subsidiary thesis concerning the relation between language and ontological types, to which we now turn.

Ontology is that branch of philosophy that concerns what exists. There are myriad issues in the literature on ontology that Sommers' theory does not touch on (for instance, the hotly debated issues of whether our ontology admits properties, or whether numbers exist). Sommers' theory concerns the categories in terms of which we conceptualize our world, categories named by terms such as *table, star, storm, woman, milk, country, Richard Nixon,* and *love*. The level of ontologically important concepts is distinguished from other concepts in terms of the contrast between category mistakes and false statements. This is equivalent to the contrast between a predicate's spanning a term and a predicate's truly applying to a term. *The idea is green* is a category mistake; an idea is not the kind of thing that can be green or any other color. *The Empire State Building is green*, in contrast, is merely false. It could be green; it has some color that just happens not to be green. Spanning is the relation between a predicate and a term when the predicate could possibly truly apply to the term, whether or not it actually does. *Green* spans *building, table, animal, grass,* etc., but not *idea, hour, war,* etc. A category mistake results when a predicate that does not span a term is predicated of it. Truly applying is the relation between a predicate and a term such that a true sentence is formed by a predication. *Green* truly applies to *grass* and *gall bladder*, but not *Empire State Building*. A falsehood results when a predicate that does not truly apply to a term is predicated of it.

Some would deny that there is a true distinction between category mistakes and falsehoods. We do not enter this debate here. For the sake of argument, let us accept both the distinction *and* its importance for understanding semantic development. My criticisms of Sommers' theory lie elsewhere. His theory contains two theses: (1) Ontological categories form a strict hierarchy; and (2) predicates in natural language do not span different ontological types, where "different" here means on different branches of the ontological hierarchy. I argue that both theses are false.

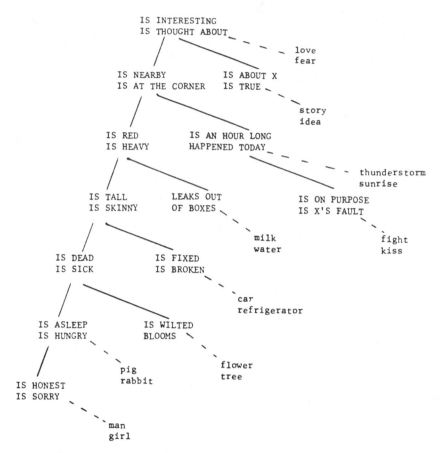

FIG. 19.1   Sample predicability tree (redrawn from Keil, 1979).

These two theses of Sommers' theory allow the production of a predicability tree, such as that in Fig. 19.1 (adapted from Keil, 1979). Keil explains the predicability tree as follows:

The general rule for interpreting a tree structure is that a predicate spans all those terms that every predicate below it spans. For example, the predicate *is sick* spans all terms spanned by *is asleep* and *is wilted*, namely, all living things. The highest node in the tree contains predicates that span all terms. Intuitively, this seems correct, since anything, physical, or nonphysical, may be interesting or not. Every nonterminal node represents an indefinitely large class of predicates, although only a few examples are shown here. Thus, the node containing *is asleep* and *is hungry* would also include *is awake* and *is frightened*, among many other predicates. Similarly, terminal nodes represent indefinitely large classes of terms, so that in addition to *man* and *girl*, the node under *is honest* and *is sorry* would contain all terms denoting conscious beings. Nonterminal nodes also represent classes of terms, namely the supersets of all sets of terms under any such node. For example, the node with the predicate *is heavy* represents the union of several classes of terms that forms a superordinate class consisting of all physical objects. Every node in the tree represents a class of terms that in turn denotes members of an ontological category. Thus, isomorphic to the predicability tree is an ontological tree with a different ontological category at each node [Keil, 1979].

The claims that ontological categories form a strict hierarchy, and that predicates in natural language do not span different ontological types, are equivalent to the structural constraints Sommers and Keil propose for the ontological commitments of natural language: the M and W constraints. The M constraint is that different predicates cannot span intersecting sets of terms. One predicate can span a subset or superset of the terms spanned by another (as in the relation between *is tall* and *is dead*), or they may have no terms in common (as in the relation between *is fixed* and *is honest*), but they can never span terms in common and also have terms that are spanned by each alone. To use Keil's example again: Fig. 19.2a shows an apparent violation of the M constraint. *The bat* is spanned by both *is made by hand* and *was dead*, but each of those predicates

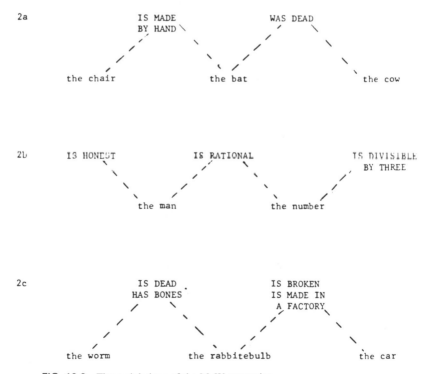

FIG. 19.2   Three violations of the M–W constraint.

spans some terms not spanned by the other. Sommers and Keil argue that this is not a true counterexample, for it depends on ambiguity: *The bat* is ambiguous.

The W constraint is the converse of the M constraint: Two terms cannot be spanned by intersecting sets of predicates. Figure 19.2b shows an apparent counterexample. *Is rational* spans both *the man* and *the number*, but there are also predicates that span one term and not the other. Again, this counterexample hangs on the ambiguity of *is rational*. Sommers' thesis is that there are no violations of the M–W constraints, except those that depend on ambiguity and metaphor.

The M–W constraint is structural in that it concerns the structure of the tree, irrespective of the particular terms and predicates on the tree. The constraint is domain independent with respect to particular fields of knowledge, such as knowledge of the physical world, the biological world, the social world. Terms and predicates from all these domains are represented on the tree and are all subject to the M–W constraint. Sommers intended the M–W constraint to provide a test for true ambiguity, as opposed to vagueness. At this point in the research program, Keil and Sommers part company. Keil goes on to suggest that the M–W constraint actually limits hypotheses during word learning. Violation of the constraint is sufficient to rule out a candidate word meaning. *Rabbit or light bulb (rabbitebulb)*, for example, is ruled out by the violation of the M constraint in Fig. 19.2c. Some of the predicates that span *the rabbitebulb* span *the car* but not *the worm*, and, conversely, some that span *the rabbitebulb* span *the worm* but not *the car*.

In his writings Keil concentrates on the role of the structural constraint, the M–W constraint, in limiting hypotheses. But, for the M constraint to work in any particular case, an equally important condition must also be met. The word learner must already represent nodes in the tree that are defined by predicate clusters like *is dead, has bones* (animate objects) and *is broken, is made in a factory* (artefacts); that is, particular spanning relations between predicates and terms must be represented such that an M violation could be generated. Let us call this source of constraint the *present state constraint*. According to Keil's theory hypotheses as to possible word meanings are limited by the present state of the semantic system, at the time of encountering the word, and by the M–W constraint.

Keil (1979) offered several forms of evidence for his thesis. He showed that adults honor the M constraint when asked to make judgments about sensible predications. He then developed a technique by which very young children can be induced to make spanning judgments. Children are asked to say whether sentences like "The table is happy" are silly or not. To check whether the child was using "silly" to indicate false statements or category mistakes, Keil probed with opposites; that is, the child would also be given "The table is unhappy." If he judged both to be silly, Keil credited him with the view that neither *happy* nor *unhappy* spans *table*. If a predicate-term combination is false, that predicate's

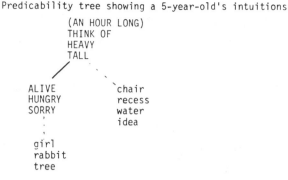

Predicability tree showing a 5-year-old's intuitions

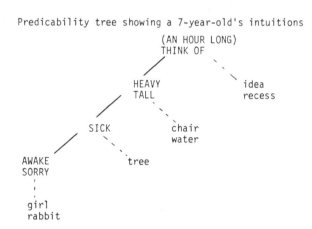

Predicability tree showing a 7-year-old's intuitions

FIG. 19.3 Sample predicability trees from children's intuitions.

opposite will be true of the term, whereas the opposite of a predicate that does not span a term also does not span that term. Keil also followed up all judgments with short interviews to clarify the child's beliefs.

Keil found that children's predicability trees were M constrained; that is, children virtually never violated the M–W constraint. Their trees differed from those of adults, however, in being collapsed versions of the adult tree. The child made many fewer distinctions than did the adult. Figure 19.3 shows a typical 5-year-old's tree and a typical 7-year-old's tree. A collapsed tree means that the child accepts predicate-term combinations an adult would not. To give just one example, Keil reports the following exchange with a 6-year-old:

E. The squirrel is fixed.
S. That's O.K.

E. How could you fix a squirrel?

S. With a screwdriver—like if his stomach was broken or something.

E. How could you fix a squirrel's stomach with a screwdriver?

S. Very carefully.

This child's entire pattern of judgments indicated that he did not distinguish between animate objects and human artefacts.

By concentrating on the structural constraint, and by ignoring the role played by the present state constraint, Keil failed to see an undesirable consequence of his developmental work. A child with a collapsed tree such as Fig. 19.3a or 3b would be blocked from positing *rabbit or light bulb* as a candidate word meaning, but not *light bulb or idea*. But children under 8 are prodigious word learners; surely they do not consider such hypotheses. Keil's theory cannot explain the fact that they do not. Whatever alternate account explains why 3-year-olds do not posit *light bulb or idea* as a candidate word meaning could also explain the constraint on adults' word learning as well.

In what follows I argue that the M–W constraint could not play the role Keil claims for it. The first, most important, step in the argument is a demonstration that the M–W constraint is not true. Secondly, I argue that, even if it were largely true, there is positive evidence that it does not constrain hypotheses about word meanings. Finally, I argue that another way of viewing ontological categories, on which the M–W constraint is denied, accounts for the actual constraints on word learning.

The M Constraint—A Counterexample

In a masters thesis at MIT, Davis (1979) presented a class of counterexamples involving predicates of spatial extent (*is long, is tall*) and other inherently comparative adjectives (*is heavy*). In his studies he duplicated Keil's (1979) procedures (with different terms and predicates, of course) and found that subjects' judgments of category mistakes were never consistent with M-constrained predicability trees. This was in marked contrast to Keil's subjects, who virtually never made predicability judgments inconsistent with M-constrained trees. I take this difference to show that Keil chose materials for his studies where the basic ontological types actually were hierarchically related, and where the subsidiary thesis that predicates do not span different ontological types held, but that there is no constraint on human conceptualization to construe language thus.

The example I use differs from Davis'. For purposes of exposition I trust that the reader's intuitions about spanning relations are the same as mine; like Davis, I have checked this with subjects, who all provide patterns of judgments that violate M-constrained trees. The predicates that force an M violation are *is long* and *contains gold*. Figure 19.4 shows the four possible placements of these predicates on an M-constrained tree. They could be conodal (Case 1), as are *is*

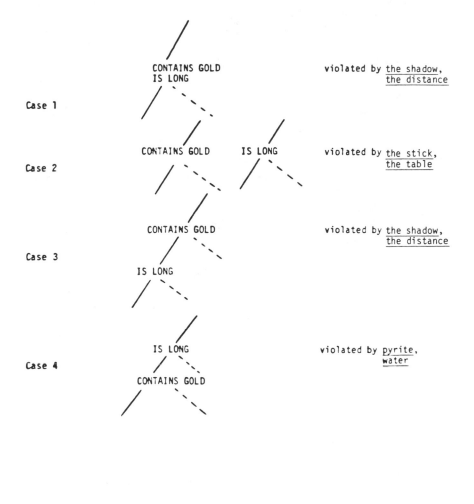

FIG. 19.4   An example of a violation of the M constraint that does not depend on ambiguity.

hungry and *is awake*. They could be on entirely separately parts of the tree (Case 2), as are *is awake* and *is broken*. Finally, they could be hierarchically related, as are *is awake* and *is sorry*. If hierarchically related, *contains gold* could span more terms than *is long* (Case 3) or vice versa (Case 4). To show that the M constraint is not respected, one must find counterexamples to all four possible arrangements. These are provided on Fig. 19.4, as is the M-constraint violation in which these predicates participate.[3]

These are true counterexamples to the M constraint. *Long* is not ambiguous, meaning one thing when it spans *distance* and another when it spans *table*. Things of different ontological types may share a geometry, and terms of spatial extent refer to geometrical properties. Thus, the subsidiary thesis (Thesis 2) about the relation between natural language and ontological types that allows construction of predicability trees is clearly not true. Natural language predicates *may* span different ontological types without implicating ambiguity or metaphor. That holes, surfaces, three-dimensional objects, and types of matter are different ontological types, and that this will be reflected in their different roles in category mistakes, is not here being denied. So far, all that is being denied is that these patterns of category mistakes are M constrained.

Even though Thesis 2 is false, the basic claim that ontological types form a strict hierarchy (Thesis 1) may still be true. However, the preceding counter-example allows us to see that Thesis 1 fails as well. Two ontologically important distinctions—between material and nonmaterial things and between dimension-less and bounded things—cross-classify, as can be seen in Table 19.1. Stuff, as named by prototypical mass nouns, is inherently dimensionless, with the consequence that mass terms such as *water* or *copper* are not spanned by *is big*. Similarly, whereas a region of space can be big or little, space itself cannot be. Conversely, as we saw previously, there are classes of both material and non-material things that are spanned by *is big* and its variants.

Does the M Constraint Constrain Word Learning?

Keil might reply to these counterexamples that they are special, affecting only a small part of the tree, and that the M constraint holds in general in enough cases to be useful as a source of constraint on word learning. This response requires that children would have an inordinate difficulty learning the concepts,

---

[3]In order to establish a counterexample to the Sommers/Keil claims, one must find terms that violate, without ambiguity, each of the four possible placements of the terms on an M-constrained tree. These are provided on Fig. 19.4. For example, *is long* and *contains gold* could not be conodal (Case 1) if a term can be found that only one spans.

TABLE 19.1
Cross-Classification of Two Ontologically Important Distinctions

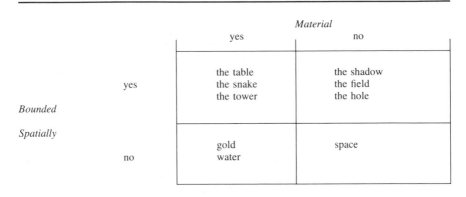

		Material	
		yes	no
Bounded **Spatially**	yes	the table the snake the tower	the shadow the field the hole
	no	gold water	space

terms, and predicates implicated in the violations.[4] However, many other counterexamples can be found, implicating other parts of the tree.

If the M constraint limits hypothesis testing about the meanings of words, languages would be expected to resist systematic and productive violations of it. Rather than showing resistance, languages appear profligate in the ease with which different ontological types are lexicalized with single words. Keil (1979) and Sommers (1963) both discuss a class of apparent counterexamples such as those in Fig. 19.5. *Is sunny* and *is democratic* span any term denoting a country, but *is democratic* spans *senate* but not *isthmus*, whereas the reverse is true for *is sunny*. Keil and Sommers point out that such cases involve ambiguities, as can be seen by a paraphrase test. *Russia* can be paraphrased *the government of Russia* and also *the land Russia*. Governments do not have climates and geographic entities do not have governments, hence the apparent M violation. A similar ambiguity is involved in the second counterexample in Fig. 19.5. *Book* can be paraphrased by *story the author spun* or *material object on which the story is printed*. Physical objects (geographical or literary) are clearly different ontological types than governmental institutions or than abstract entities such as ideas, stories, and arguments. These apparent counterexamples depend on ambiguity, just as did the earlier examples involving *is rational* and *the bat*.

---

[4]It is true that the meanings of these words are worked out late. Spatial adjectives become fully specified only by age 6 or so (see Carey, 1982, for a review), and words for material kinds, like *wood* and *gold*, attain their adult meaning only after age 8 or 9 (Dickinson, 1982). However, the meanings of many words not involved in M violations, such as *alive*, are attained just as late (Carey, in press.) Other explanations for late acquisition can be given that encompass both those that are and those that are not involved in M violations.

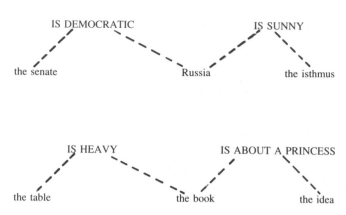

FIG. 19.5 Examples of systematic violations of the M constraint—top of the tree.

As mentioned earlier, Sommers' goal was to provide a criterion for ambiguity. According to him, violation of the M constraint is, in itself, a test for the ambiguity of terms like *the country* and *the story*. These are not counterexamples to Sommers' theory, as long as the two terms are indeed ambiguous, as the theory requires.[5] No, the problem here is for Keil's claim that the M constraint limits hypotheses about the meanings of words. These are not like the accidental and unique ambiguities of *is rational* and *the bat*. There are hundreds of cases like *Russia* and *the book*. Every name for a country, city, or state participates in cases like Fig. 19.5a; every abstract representational entity routinely instantiated by physical tokens participates in cases like Fig. 19.5b. A song can be loud and about a princess, and a sentence can be blurred and about a princess.

It is clear what is going on here. Geographically specified entities have physical properties, such as terrain and climate, and their institutions have nonphysical properties. Whereas there is no ontological necessity to this conjunction (economic and political institutions *could* be defined over kinship networks, for example, irrespective of geography), the conjunction holds and is captured in language by the use of one term *Russia* to refer to both the government and the land. Similarly, given that people express ideas, arguments, stories, etc. in order to communicate them, there is a regular, non-necessary conjunction between the abstract entities and physical tokens that represent them. Many other types of

---

[5]There is, in these waters, a true counterexample to Sommers' claim. *The story* is a term that refers to both types and tokens. The discussion in the text concerns its ambiguity when referring to two different types. However, on standard semantic analyses, a particular token can have both semantic and physical properties, thus actually violating the M constraint. This caveat does not apply to examples such as *the country*, and for the purposes of my present argument I am willing to grant the ambiguity of *the story* as well.

systematic ambiguities that produce M violations could be cited. To give one additional example: the process/product distinction often ignored in our lexicon. *The drawing* refers both to the act of drawing (an event) and to the product that can be framed (an object). Rather than being constrained *against* ambiguities of these types, natural languages opportunistically exploit accidental coincidences of ontological types if it is convenient to do so.

Such systematic ambiguities make dubious the claim that there is any constraint against a single term's referring to two different ontological types. Let me reiterate my argument so far. In the previous section I showed that Sommers' theory is false. Predicates do apply to different ontological types without ambiguity. In the present section I argued that language's ready acceptance of terms that systematically refer (even with ambiguity) to different ontological types militates against Keil's claim that avoiding M violations constrains hypothesis testing during word learning.

A Second True Counterexample

This counterexample, also discussed by Keil (1979), concerns yet another part of the tree (Fig. 19.6). Many people have the intuition that *The man is pregnant* is not merely false, it is a category mistake. *Is pregnant* does not span *man; is impotent* does not span *woman.* This would seem to motivate a branching of the

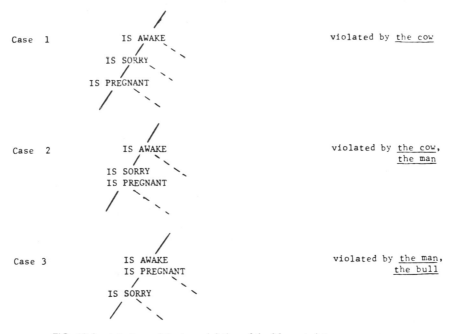

FIG. 19.6   A bottom of the tree violation of the M constraint.

tree below the cluster of predicates that specifies the ontological type *human (is sorry, is wealthy*, Fig. 19.6). But *is pregnant* also spans *cow, ewe, chicken*, etc. This counterexample, like that involving *is long* and *contains gold*, shows that basic ontological types are not hierarchically organized; the ontological distinction male/female cross-classifies the ontological distinction person/animal. *Is pregnant* is not ambiguous; it does not mean something different when it applies to women from when it applies to gerbils.

Keil's response to this and similar counterexamples is to deny that *The man is pregnant* is a category error. It is simply false, just as *The man is not pregnant* is true. So too for *The woman is impotent*; this is merely false. The distinction male/female is not at the ontological level. What are we to do when an important point hangs on a clash of intuitions? As Keil rightly points out, a well-confirmed theory may decide the unclear cases. Unfortunately, the other classes of counterexamples discussed earlier show that we are not in such a situation. We may not appeal to the well-confirmed M constraint and the well-confirmed hierarchy of ontological types to overrule our intuitions that *The man is pregnant* is a category error and to decide in favor of Case 3 on Fig. 19.6

An Alternative View of the Ontological Level

If, as I have argued, both of Sommers' theses are false, are we left with nothing to say about the ontological level, other than that there is one and it is implicated in category errors? Happily, there is another way of thinking about ontologically important concepts on which the denial of the Sommers–Keil claims is expected.

In explicating the ontological commitments of a language, we specify the basic types of entities presupposed by that language. Ontology, we have said, is the study of the basic categories of what exists. What can we do to find out about these basic categories? We have no *choice* other than to use our theories of the world. Ontology rides on the back of scientific theory.

A theory consists of three interrelated components: a set of phenomena that are in its domain, the causal laws and other explanatory mechanisms in terms of which the phenomena are accounted for, and the concepts in terms of which the phenomena and explanatory apparatus are expressed. Some concepts within theories are extraordinarily important, those that figure in the important laws of the theory and those that are involved in the explanatory work of the theory. As theories develop, changes in these central concepts have ramifications for the whole theory. For example, the change from the Newtonian to the Einsteinian conception of mass dictated that kinetic energy is *not* $\frac{1}{2} mv^2$. Such core concepts participate in what empiricists and logical positivists held to be the analytic truths in that theory (see Quine, 1953, and Putnam, 1966, for arguments that there are no analytic truths of the sort sought by empiricists).

If there is an ontological level of concepts, the set of core concepts in our theories is the best candidate. On this view, the clearest cases of category mistakes occur when predicates from one theoretical domain are applied to terms from another. *The sun ate a banana* is a category error because eating is in the domain of biological theory, and the sun is not a biological entity like an animal or a plant. There will also be within-theory category mistakes, as *The man is pregnant* may be. Category errors within a theory occur when predicates are applied across subdomains of fundamentally different types. *Has positive charge* spans *the electron*, but not *the temperature*, even though both terms and the predicates come from the domain of physics. Subatomic particles and average kinetic energy of a collection of molecules, in current physical theory, are fundamentally different kinds of things. Only the former can have electrical charges.

If ontological commitments are to be explicated relative to theories, the conceptual structures that have the status of theories must be distinguished from those that do not. All concepts are embedded in several relatively organized conceptual structures, called in the psychological and AI literatures *schemas, scripts, frames*, etc. If all these conceptual structures can play a role in determining a person's fundamental ontological commitments, that is, if all conceptual structures act like theories in this regard, then making the move of collapsing the study of ontology with the study of theories has not bought us much.

It is possible to distinguish our naive physics, in terms of which our concepts of objects, space, time, and physical causality are constrained, and our restaurant script, even if this script plays some role in explicating our conceptions of waitresses. A central component of theories is their explanatory apparatus. If one queries the events in the restaurant script (Why does one order the food before it comes? Why does one pay for the food? etc.), the explanations given lie outside the script itself. The answer to why one pays for food lies in the theoretical domain of economics, where questions of exchange of goods and services sit. The answer to why one must order first lies partly in the domain of physics, where questions of time and physical causality sit, and also in the domain of psychology, where questions of communication and action sit. There is reason to hope that there are relatively few theoretical domains organizing our causal knowledge, and it is to these we should turn to explicate our basic ontological commitments.

Viewing category mistakes (and the ontological level of concepts) this way accomodates the insights of the Sommers–Keil theory and also its failures. The hierarchical relations person–animal–living thing–physical object follow from the fact that the very same object participates in different theories by virtue of different properties. People are physical objects, so the laws of physics apply to them; they are also biological entities of two ontologically important, nested types—animals and humans. Different theoretical domains are not always hierarchically related. Mathematics, for example, crosscuts many other theoretical domains. Thus, that basic ontological categories do not form a strict hierarchy is no surprise. A final consequence of this view is that the distinction between category errors and falsehoods will not be clear-cut. The distinction between the core concepts of a theory and the peripheral ones is a matter of degree, as is the distinction between conceptual structures that play major explanatory roles and those that do not. Whereas the distinction between male and female is well entrenched in biological theory, it is probably less so than that between animal and plant. Such considerations predict unclear cases, such as whether *The man is pregnant* is a category mistake or merely false.

Implications for Semantic Development

Although I heartily endorse the project of infusing questions of ontology into psychological research, we have made little progress on the question of constraints on semantic development. The Keil–Sommers proposal for a structural constraint on ontological categories fails. We are left with the present state constraint. Theories held at the moment of induction constrain inductive practices. If we had thought about the lessons of another example from the philosophical literature, Goodman's (1955) *grue* example, we might have expected this outcome. To psychologize Goodman's discussion, the problem is what makes *green* a natural concept, whereas *grue* is not. (*Grue* means *green if examined before the year 2000 A.D., otherwise blue*.) Goodman considered at length the possibility of stating a structural constraint on concepts that makes *green* natural and *grue* unnatural. A first suggestion that comes to mind is that *grue* is more complex than *green*; perhaps there are simplicity constraints. A second immediate suggestion is that *grue* contains a proper name in its definition (2000 A.D.); perhaps there is a constraint against property concepts being defined in terms of specific individuals (call this the deictic constraint). Goodman constructed the *grue* example precisely to rule out structural constraints of these sorts. There is no way of specifying complexity on which *grue* comes out more complex than *green*; further, *green* is as much a deictic property as is *grue*. For a flavor of Goodman's argument, consider the obvious fact that *grue* and *green* are symmetric with respect to complexity and having 2000 A.D. in their definitions, depending on the primitives in terms of which the definitions are stated; that is, *green* can be defined as *grue if examined before the year 2000 A.D.—otherwise bleen*, where *bleen* is a concept analogous to *grue*. Of course, we want to say why *green* and *blue* are candidates for being primitives, whereas *grue* and *bleen* are not, but we cannot appeal again to complexity or the deictic constraint. Goodman concluded that there are no structural constraints on conceptual naturalness that would do the required work. Rather, what makes *green* more natural than *grue* is that it is more entrenched in our conceptual systems; that is, it plays an important role in the theories we hold to be true, whereas *grue* does not.

I pointed out before the obvious point that the M constraint alone can do no work, only in conjunction with the present state of the conceptual system. In fact, there are still other ways in which Keil fails to acknowledge the role of

nonstructural constraints on induction. He gives the child the semantically interpreted concept *object* out of which other ontological categories become differentiated. Where does this come from? Further, Fig. 19.1 represents, I believe,
Keil's best guess as to the ontological tree underlying all languages. But if the
M constraint were the only source of constraint on ontological categories, infinitely many M-constrained hierarchies should be possible. Keil must allow that
there are theory-specific constraints on ontological categories, as well as the
structural M constraint; I am arguing here that most probably these are the only
constraints on ontological categories.

If the only constraints on the learner's hypotheses about word meanings are
the concepts held at the time of encounter, the search for an account of word
meaning leads inexorably to an account of the initial state. And because word
learning begins in earnest in the second year of life, studies of infants will be
necessary in order to specify that initial state.

Quine (1960) used the phrase *innate feature space* to denote the features in
terms of which the young child sees his world and in terms of which he forms
hypotheses about its nature. One problem with Quine's *innate feature space*,
like the behaviorist's set of discriminative stimuli, like the empiricist's sense
data, is that no structure in this space is posited that might provide constraints
on hypothesis formation. The line of argument presented here has one clear
implication: If interested in constraints on the child's inductive practices, look
for theories the child is born with. And if I may hazard a guess, there are exactly
two—a naive physics embodying a physical causality and a naive psychology
embodying an intentional causality. Central to the former is the concept *object*,
to the latter, the concept *person*.

Spelke's contribution to the present volume underlies two points about the
infant's conception of objects. First, empirical research on infants is necessary;
some aspects of the adult's concept are present very early on, guiding further
knowledge acquisition; others, like many of the Gestalt principles, are not evident
at all, so far, in the first year of life. Second, and more important to us here,
the infant's concept of *object* cannot be specified apart from related concepts
such as *space, number,* and *physical causality*. Spelke shows that bounded
entities that occupy a unique position in space, or maintain a single trajectory
through space, are seen as single objects. The 4-month-old infant knows that
objects out of sight persist, and that a solid object cannot pass through the space
occupied by another solid object. Spelke shows that we cannot diagnose the
infant's concept of object without examining the expectations the child has about
the behavior of objects. More crucially, she shows that the child's concept cannot
be explicated except relative to other concepts that articulate a set of physical
beliefs.

Although there are claims in the infancy literature that young babies have
very different expectations about the behavior of people than about the behavior

of inanimate objects (Tronick, Adamson, Wise, Als, & Brazelton, 1975), much less-systematic work has been done on the infant's naive psychology than on his naive physics. There is evidence that biological knowledge differentiates out of knowledge of human activities and does not become a separate theoretical domain from psychology until after age 6 (Carey, in press), but we do not know just when the initial psychological theory becomes available as an inductive base, nor its nature.

Conclusions

Considerations of constraints on word learning, on concept acquisition, and on induction in general suggest a research program organized around ontological issues. The view of ontology defended here requires that theory-like conceptual structures be few in number and distinguishable from nontheory-like structures. We must ask whether very young children represent theory-like structures, we must find out which ones are represented early, and we must characterize the ontological commitments of these first theories. We must also spell out just *how* these early theories constrain inductive projection. A host of empirical issues are raised; the work is yet to be done.

REFERENCES

Carey, S. Semantic development, state of the art. In E. Wanner & L. Gleitman (Eds.), *Language acquisition: State of the art*. London: Cambridge University Press, 1982.

Carey, S. *Conceptual change in childhood*. Cambridge, MA: Bradford Books, in press.

Davis, S. *Of ontology and mental representation*. Unpublished masters thesis, MIT, 1979.

Dickinson, D. *The child's concept of material kind*. Unpublished doctoral dissertation, Harvard University, 1982.

Goodman, N. *Fact, fiction and forecast*. Indianapolis: Bobbs–Merrill, 1955.

Keil, F. C. *Semantic and conceptual development: An ontological perspective*. Cambridge, Mass.: Harvard University Press, 1979.

Piaget, J., & Inhelder, B. *Le développement des quantités chez l'enfant*. Paris: Delachaux & Niestlé, 1941.

Putnam, H. The analytic and the synthetic. In *Minnesota Studies in the Philosophy of Science* (Vol. III). Minneapolis: University of Minnesota Press, 1966.

Quine, W. V. O. Two dogmas of empiricism. In W. V. O. Quine (Ed.), *From a logical point of view*. Cambridge, Mass.: Harvard University Press, 1953.

Quine, W. V. O. *Word and object*. Cambridge, Mass.: MIT Press, 1960.

Sommers, F. Types and ontology. *Philosophical Review*, 1963, 72, 327–363.

Tronick, E., Adamson, L., Wise, S., Als, H., & Brazelton, T. B. *The infants' entrapment between contradictory messages in face to face interaction*. Paper presented at the Meeting of the Society for Research in Child Development, Denver, April, 1975.

20 Learning Theory and Neural Reduction: A Comment

Daniel N. Osherson
Massachusetts Institute of Technology

Scott Weinstein
University of Pennsylvania

To understand how a system works it helps to know what it can do. One thing that the human nervous system does is learn. Thus, a perspicuous characterization of human learning might provide useful constraints on neurophysiological theory, in the familiar way that molar phenomena place conditions on molecular theories.

There is ample room for pessimism about such a research strategy. For one thing, a nontrivial theory of learning might never become available; in our view, this is depressingly likely. For another thing, the connection between neurophysiological mechanism and detectable learning might be so complex as to render even an interesting theory of the latter of no use in understanding the former. These misgivings in full view, we nonetheless suggest one theoretical approach to human learning that may provide neurophysiological questions of potential interest. This approach is embodied in the cluster of mathematical results known as *Formal Learning Theory*.

Formal Learning Theory is the study of systems that convert finite amounts of experience into theories about the total environment from which that experience is drawn. A child learning a language is an example of a such a system. At any moment in her development the child has been exposed to only a finite fragment of the ambient language. She projects such finite fragments into theories of the entire language; such theories are known as "grammars."

Of principle interest within Formal Learning Theory is the characterization of conditions under which such systems stabilize to accurate theories of a given environment. In the case of normal language acquisition, such stabilization is thought to amount to the eventual conjecture by the child of the target language, a conjecture from which she never deviates thereafter. Within Learning Theory, the informal notions of "experience," "theory," "stabilization," "accuracy," and

399

"environment" give way to precise definitions. Alternative formulations of these concepts yield distinct models within the theory. The vigorous development of Learning Theory began with a celebrated paper by Gold (1967). An overview of results and concepts in the theory may be found in Osherson and Weinstein (1983).

Some of the issues treated within Learning Theory have neurophysiological bearing. We illustrate by considering again the development of a cognitive competence like language. At each stage of language acquisition the child's projected grammar is neurally represented; for simplicity, imagine that different neural configurations amount to different grammars. After a while, the language conjectured by the child stabilizes, in the sense that further experience with sentences of the target language no longer alters in a fundamental way the language available to the speaker. How is this cognitive stability achieved? There are two possibilities.

Possibility 1.   The conjectured language stabilizes because the neural configuration underlying the child's linguistic competence has stabilized; that is, after stabilization, new sentences affect only word familiarity, idioms, and other systems ancillary to basic grammatical organization. The neural structure of the competence itself remains invariant through continued experience with the language.

Possibility 2.   The neural configurations themselves never stabilize, even though the language they underlie becomes invariant. This possibility rests on the following fundamental fact about grammars and languages. If a language is generated by any grammar at all, it is generated by an indefinite number of distinct grammars (analogously, there are always infinitely many distinct computer programs to compute any given computable function). Thus, it is possible that the child's neural organization for language continues to shift throughout her life even though the conjectured language has permanently stabilized. This will happen if after some point the succession of distinct neural configurations all encode grammars for the same language.

A sequence of equivalent but ever-shifting conjectures need not betray perversity. Such shifting might arise as the result of continual refinements for the sake of efficiency. For example, the learner might discover how to lower the processing time of a subset of sentences already handled, albeit inefficiently, by her latest conjecture; the new processing strategy might require modification of her grammar without change to the language generated. Alternatively, the learner may, from time to time, happen upon an unfamiliar figure of speech from a grammatically reliable source; rather than check whether her current conjecture already generates the new locution, she might incorporate within her current grammar a special purpose modification to encompass it. If her current grammar already generates the locution, the modified grammar will be equivalent to its predecessor. This situation could arise repeatedly for a sufficiently cautious learner.

It is not possible now to decide between possibilities 1 and 2. Indeed, considerable specification would be needed to formulate them as manageable biological questions. It would be surprising, however, if such questions lay outside the pale of current physiological concern or experimental technique. And any progress at the physiological level on these issues would be of considerable interest to the learning theorist., For, it has been proved rigorously that the two possibilities make a difference to the class of natural languages in principle acquirable by human infants—granting the reasonable assumption that neural computation in this regard is a species of machine computation.

To clarify this point, call a language *child-learnable* if it can be acquired by normal human infants on the basis of the usual sort of linguistic input provided to the young. A condition of adequacy on theories of natural language is that they specify a child-learnable collection of languages. Now if possibility 1 obtains, it can be proved that there are collections of languages that cannot be acquired by any learning system, and hence not by children either; these collections of languages, moreover, would be acquirable if possibility 2 obtained. Thus, possibility 1 places nontrivial constraints on what can be learned, constraints strictly greater than those imposed by possibility 2. In this sense, it would be of interest to the learning theorist to know which possibility (if either) is true of human children learning natural language. Conversely, information about the character of children's learning might suffice to rule out possibility 1, since the learning might be shown to embrace a range of languages that cannot be acquired if neural representations stabilize. The mathematical details of the foregoing argument are presented in Osherson and Weinstein (1982). Wexler (1982) provides commentary.

Many other questions of similar character arise within the context of Learning Theory. For example, the extent to which an immature competence can be modified by a single input places additional constraints on the class of mature competencies available, this time assuming that the developing organism operates under memory limitations that can be formalized in various ways (see Osherson, Stob, & Weinstein, 1983). Is it too much to hope that such learning theoretic issues provide research questions of interest and accessibility to students of development at both the neural and cognitive levels?

REFERENCES

Gold, E. M. Language identification in the limit. *Information and Control*, 1967, *10*, 447–474.

Osherson, D., Stob, M., & Weinstein, S. Learning strategies. *Information and Control*, to appear.

Osherson, D., & Weinstein, S. A note on formal learning theory. *Cognition*, 1982, *11*, 77–88.

Osherson, D. & Weinstein, S. Formal learning theory. In G. Miller & M. Gazzaniga, *Handbook of cognitive neurology*. New York: Plenum Press, 1983.

Wexler, K. On extensional learnability. *Cognition*, 1983, *11*, 89–96.

21 Plasticity and Invariance in Cognitive Development

Zenon W. Pylyshyn
The University of Western Ontario

INTRODUCTION: CONSTANTS, VARIABLES, AND LEVELS OF ANALYSIS

Most of the chapters in this volume have provided persuasive and elegant demonstrations of high-level perceptual and cognitive competence in infants. Indeed, it often seems as though the infant's cognitive system is so richly endowed that if experimental psychologists were only more ingenious in their methods they would be able to show that no cognitive skills are learned at all—and that the only ability that developes after 6 weeks is the one involving the motor system! Whatever the eventual outcome of such an inquiry, it seems that there is much more initial structure in infant cognition and many more *fixed* cognitive mechanisms than had been hitherto suspected.

But there is also the other side of this story. In addition to the discovery of certain invariant capacities, or certain very specific properties of what might be called the *initial state* of the cognitive system, developmentalists have also found equally impressive evidence of the amazing plasticity of the infant neural system (see, for example, the contributions by Imbert, Goldman–Rakic, Changeux, and Amiel–Tison). The dual themes of a rich innately given cognitive capacity or initial structure and of malleability or potential for systematic change have always been the central concerns of developmental psychology. This is no accident: The only way we can understand the dynamics of change is in terms of what might be viewed as the constants of the system. In science variation and invariants go hand in hand. Indeed, it is not too much of a caricature to say that the main job of science is to carve some domain of phenomena at its natural joints, as Plato put it, so as to most perspicuously reveal its universal constants and its forms of moment-to-moment variation.

These dual themes recur in one way or another in most of the chapters of this book. Several people have been quite explicit in their concern over the question of what must be the constants or the "fixed points" of the process of development. Clearly not everything can be seen as free to vary, otherwise our theories would have arbitrarily many degrees of freedom and no explanatory value. For example, Eimas notes that the most important task for the psychologist is to discover *mechanisms* underlying various cognitive skills. Such mechanisms would constitute the constants of the cognitive system. One would appeal to the existence of these mechanisms in providing an account of cognitive capacities, including the capacity to learn and hence to change in certain ways. Similarly Aslin, in his filter metaphor, takes the approach that properties of the filter must be viewed as fixed, because if they could change freely we would have succeeded only in moving the problem of development further into the organism: The principles by which the organism changes would then be in the hands of the homunculus who adjusted the filters.

I agree completely with those who take the problem of identifying the constants (or the invariants) of the system as central. But what I want to add to these concerns, in my capacity as commentator and official generalist for this volume, is the suggestion that we are not likely to reconcile the demands of locating the constants with the demands of stating the generalizations governing change unless we are prepared to first make a number of crucial distinctions. To anticipate my main point, I argue for a principled notion of level of description of a biological system and suggest that the constancy we seek must be relativized to each level in this hierarchy. In particular there is a level of description that corresponds to what we generally refer to as the cognitive level, and here our constants are certain fixed mechanisms—where "fixed" refers only to their immunity from a certain class of influences, namely "cognitive" ones (they must be "cognitively impenetrable"). Such mechanisms can, and do, nonetheless vary according to principles at another level (presumably the biological level). These proposals require that we examine the notion of level more closely, because what I have in mind is not simply some convenient level of abstraction or generality—it is a level in the sense of an autonomous set of principles, or of a separate empirically adequate science.

CONSTRAINTS AS ARISING FROM INTRINSIC MECHANISMS OR FROM REPRESENTATIONS

The idea that various aspects of the behavior of the human organism can be described using quite different taxonomies and quite different explanatory principles is well entrenched in psychology. For example, whereas one might believe that there is a neural and chemical explanation for at least certain aspects of the psychophysical principles of color perception, people would be surprised indeed if the explanation of how we decide that the italicised pronoun in the sentence "The doctor did not help the nurse because *she* needed the practice" is that there are certain neural or chemical regularities in our brains. Rather, the explanation would refer to one's knowledge of sex-role stereotypes, usual employer–employee relations, and the effect of helping someone to get something done on the amount of practice they receive. Similarly, we do not find neurophysiologicl explanations for why people assent to certain sentences, or why they make certain sounds when asked where they live, or which style of clothes they prefer, and so on. The way we invariably explain such *interpreted* or meaningful behavior is in terms of processes that depend on the knowledge that subjects have and the way they use this knowledge to further some goals.

Of course many people do believe that this is just a matter of convenience— that it is just easier and more practical for certain purposes to give the answers in terms of people's reasons and the decisions they make, and that in principle a more detailed neural explanation could be given if we only knew all the relevant facts. But this is a misunderstanding of the nature of explanation. An answer to a *why* question presupposes a certain taxonomy under which the puzzling event is viewed. An explanation of a particular piece of emitted behavior viewed as a member of the category "generates a waveform with certain spectral properties" need not qualify as an explanation of *the very same event* viewed as a member of a category, such as "claims that he is a liberal." The reason is quite simple: Other members of the latter category can vary to an arbitrary degree in their acoustical properties. To explain the event under the latter taxonomy is to provide an account that applies to *all* members of that equivalence class. An arbitrarily large disjunction of neural or acoustical explanations (one for each different way that a subject might have of making the claim—including implying it by deed as well as word) does not qualify, but an account that refers to the subject's beliefs about politics, or about the people in whose presence the behavior was emitted, and which refers to the subject's goals and intentions, could (if the antecedent constructs were independently motivated, etc.) do exactly that.

This is not the place to attempt a thorough justification of the autonomy of what might be called the cognitive or "goals and knowledge" level of explanation. Suffice it to point out that: (1) no attempt to dispense with talk about knowledge and goals in favor of talk about operants, neural pathways, or the like has given even a hint of being on the track of an account of cognitive phenomena; (2) the phenomenal success of everyday "folk psychology" in predicting behavior and in permitting us to navigate our way around our social environment depends on the use of notions like goals and knowledge; (3) the modest success of cognitivist accounts based on the assumption that what subjects are doing in typical psychological experiments is making rational decisions based on their beliefs, the information available to them, their goals and utilities, and so on, in contrast with attempts to account for cognitive activities in terms of reinforcement contingencies (Brewer, 1974).

The important point for our present purpose is that there seems to be reasonable grounds for the assumption that what some people have called the "cognitive level" or the "intentional level," or what Newell (1981) calls the "knowledge level," represents a genuine level at which explanations of behavior can be cast. It appears to define a natural class of phenomena and a natural domain of types of causal connections. What I mean by the latter is that there seems to be a set of phenomena that can be systematically altered by the content of information provided to subjects, rather than by physical influences. Of course every case of information provision is also a case of energy transference. But a fundamental discovery of the last half century is that in certain cases the regularities of a system can be captured by talking only about information available to it, or by referring to what certain states of the system represent and ignoring the physics or biology of the particular case at issue. Furthermore, ignoring the physics or biology may even be necessary because the categories over which the system's behavior is regular may include such things as the *meaning* of certain signals, and because the entire equivalence class of signals having the same meaning need not have a description that is finitely statable in a physical vocabulary (as is clearly the case for an infinite set of English sentences that mean the same thing). This has turned out to be true of communication systems, computers, language, and many other aspects of human performance, and it is a discovery of no small importance.

A couple of very simple examples help to illustrate what I mean by an informational or representational level of description. Suppose I showed you a black box into which I had poked an electrode. This box exhibits the following regularity. As we observe it go about its usual function, we discover that either individual short pulses or pairs of such short pulses frequently occur at the electrode, and that when there are both pairs and single pulses (as sometimes happens) the pair appears to regularly precede the single pulse. After observing this pattern for some time, we discover that there are occasional exceptions to this order—but only when the whole pattern is preceded by a pair of long and short sequences. Now suppose we wish to give an explanation of this regularity. What kind of explanation is most appropriate?

The answer, I maintain, depends on what sort of device the black box is—and in particular on what its capacity is beyond the particular behavior we have just been observing (i.e., not on what it is doing, or what it typically does, but on what it *could* be doing in certain counterfactual situations). In this particular example, chosen deliberately to make a pedagogical point, we would not find the explanation of its behavior in its internal structure for the simple reason that the black box exhibits the observed regularity only because it is a box for transmitting International Morse Code, and the regularity we have discovered is attributable entirely to a spelling rule in English (*i* before *e* except after *c*) together with the code convention. The reason that providing a detailed description of the component structure and the operation of the box would not explain this regularity is that the structure is capable of exhibiting a much greater range of behaviors—*the observed constraints on its behavior is not due to its intrinsic capability but to what its states represent.*

Consider now another more relevant psychological example. Take the regularities of color mixing (e.g., perceived yellow light and perceived red light mix to produced perceive orange light—or the color judgment and color memory regularities discussed by Bornstein). What sort of account might we expect as an explanation for these regularities: One that appeals to intrinsic properties of the system, to certain internal biological mechanisms, or one that (as in the Morse Code example) appeals to properties of *what is represented* rather than of the system itself? The question is an empirical one and I wish simply to point out what is at issue and on what kinds of empirical considerations the answer depends. In this case all the evidence points to there being a biological or biochemical mechanism responsible for the regularity. One of the reasons for expecting such an account (apart from the fact that we have quite a large fragment of the account already in hand) is the fact that the regularities appear to be largely insensitive to what subjects think they are looking at, to what they believe about the color of these objects and the principles of color mixing, and to what they think the purpose of the experiment is (within limits because they might, for example, refuse to answer the questions or even lie about what they saw if they believed that the experiment was, say, of a subversive nature). The regularities might still be plastic in certain respects (e.g., they could be influenced by taking drugs, by changes in level of arousal, by disease).

Contrast this with the case in which an investigator seeks to discover the principles of what he calls "imaginal color mixing" (or the "internal psychophysics of color"). He asks subjects to imagine certain colors and to superimpose them in their mental image. Suppose that he is successful in setting up the appropriate clever experiments, with all the necessary controls, and discovers a set of reliable principles relating imagined colors. What sort of explanatory account is likely to be the correct one in this case: an account based on appeal to biological or biochemical principles, or one based on what is being represented in the mind of the subject—including what the subject tacitly knows about the principles of color mixing? Again it is an empirical question, though this time it seems much more likely that the "tacit knowledge" explanation will be the correct one. The reason for this is that it seems likely that the way colors mix in one's image will depend on what one knows about the regularities of perceptual color mixing. And the test for this is whether changing what the subject believes *by providing information* (possibly false information) will change the regularity in a logically explicable way.

This is very close to the principle we invoked in the Morse Code example. We ask whether some observed regularity provides evidence for the structure of a biological mechanism or for the exercise of decisions, inferences, and so on, based on tacic knowledge, by inquiring by what means the regularity can be systematically induced to change. If it changes when we provide the organism with relevant (logically connected) information, we say that the regularity is "cognitively penetrable" and conclude that no account based on intrinsic properties of a mechanism will by itself be adequate to explain the regularity and the way it can be altered. We draw this conclusion (as the reader will verify by considering the preceding examples), not because of an adherence to any dualist doctrine, but because we wish to acknowledge that the evidence does not reveal a cognitively fixed *capacity* inasmuch as the underlying mechanism is compatible with a wider range of behaviors than embodied in the empirically observed regularity. What the biological mechanism provides is a way of *encoding* the relevant knowledge, inference rules, and decision procedures—not the observed regularity itself.

There is much more to be said about the distinction between the two forms of explanation—the one based on intrinsic mechanisms and the one based on inferences from internally represented knowledge and goals—but the previous sketch suffices for the present purpose (for further discussion see Pylyshyn, 1980, 1981a, b, 1984). For brevity we call these two types of explanation the "knowledge-based" and the "mechanism-based" forms or levels of explanation. Clearly there are different principles operating at these two levels. The knowledge-based explanations generally involve inferences and decisions and adhere to some principle of rationality, whereas the mechanism-based explanation may require further explication in terms of biological or biochemical properties of organisms. The constraints on knowledge-based processes rest primarily on questions of what the organism knows (i.e., on what it has inferred from its experiences, on what it has been told). Of course what an organism is capable of finding out (what knowledge it is capable of possessing) *does* depend on what mechanisms, it has—but those it cannot alter by finding out new things. By assumption, the mechanism is the part of the process that itself is not knowledge dependent (it is "cognitively impenetrable"), hence it does not change according to rational principles based on decisions, inferences, and the like, but on other sorts of principles—ones that depend on *intrinsic* properties, which are presumably properties governed by biological laws.

Again it must be emphasized that the preceding is but a sketch of a position whose underlying assumptions are defended at greater length elsewhere (e.g., the references by the author cited previously). Nonetheless, it is a position that is implicit in much of contemporary cognitive science and that is given credence by the relative successes of that approach compared with other approaches. Despite the familiarity of the basic thesis, the implications of this view are far-reaching.

LEARNING VERSUS OTHER KINDS OF CHANGE CAUSED BY THE ENVIRONMENT

The view we have been sketching suggests that it is a mistake to take a monolithic view of developmental change, inasmuch as ontogenetic change can be of two very different kinds. One type of change arises as a rational consequence of certain information-bearing events that the organism experiences. The organism forms a cognitive *representation* of such events and this allows it to infer certain beliefs about the world—to draw nondemonstrative inferences or to induce plausible hypotheses. This type of change is what has always been known in the vernacular as "learning," although this word has been seriously distorted under the influence of behaviorism to include all types of change caused by external events. It is important to distinguish this type of effect from other ways of producing changes in an organism—including changes due to variations in nourishment or noninformative aspects of stimulation, changes due to growth and maturation of glands and organs (including the brain), changes due to injury or trauma, and perhaps even changes due to noninformative aspects of reinforcement and practice (if there is such a thing—see Brewer, 1974). The reason we must distinguish two different kinds of relations between organisms and environments is the same as the reason that we had to distinguish two different kinds of processes in our earlier discussion—namely, that the two follow quite different principles. For example, rational fixation of belief arising from environmental stimulation, unlike just any arbitrary changes in biological state caused by the environment, can proceed in radically different ways depending on how the organism *interprets* the stimulation, which in turn depends on what prior beliefs and utilities it has. This issue is discussed at length by Fodor and Pylyshyn (1981), in relation to alternative proposals for how percpetion might be directly caused by properties of the environment. (Incidentally, those who are puzzled by the claim that two different kinds of principles govern events depending on how we describe them, or with respect to what event categories we view them, should consider that the movement of baseball players simultaneously follows the rules of baseball and the laws of physics, or that the movement of currency simultaneously follows the rules of commerce, the laws of economics and the laws of physics, and that these are independent nonintertranslatable laws.)

Now it is the knowledge-acquisition type of explanation of certain observed change that has increasingly come under question in recent years. More and more frequently it has been argued that the information in an organism's environment is too impoverished to allow it to logically *induce* certain of the beliefs and other representations that form part of its mature state. This argument has been made with particular force in the case of language by Chomsky and others (Chomsky, 1975; Matthews, 1981; Wexler & Cullicover, 1980), as well as in the case of concept attainment by Fodor (1981). It is also implicit in some of the demonstrations (reported in this volume) that a child does not need to *learn* to perceive the world as three dimensional or to perceive speech as consisting of discrete equivalence-classes corresponding to phones.

Such critiques of the learning view have frequently been misunderstood (perhaps in some cases even by their authors) as implying that the final cognitive competence (say for language or conceptualization) is already present at birth, or that no influence of the environment is necessary for its development. But that need not be the case. It is only if we tacitly assume that all change directly attributable to an environmental effect is a case of learning, and if we further assume that all such effects follow the same sort of regularities (i.e., are governed by similar principles) that we find ourselves in what seems like the age-old dilemma of pitting learning against genetic endowment. But what is really under attack is the view that a competence such as that involved in knowing a language, or in seeing the world as three dimensional, or having a concept such as "dog," is constructed from other knowledge by rules operating on representations (i.e., rules that would count as some species of "reasoning"—as might be involved in inference, hypothesis formation and evaluation, decision making, and problem solving). The issue is whether the attainment of certain specific competences occurs by *this* kind of process.

Environmental stimulation, sometimes of a very specific sort (as Aslin's examples show), is undeniably necessary for the achievement of most cognitive competences. Exactly how specific the stimulation must be, in relation to the degree of specificity of the competence, is an open empirical question that is frequently and hotly debated (for example, see the discussions in Piatelli–Palmarini, 1980). Nonetheless, that is not the issue that concerns some of the arguments about learning. The stimulation required to produce in me the belief that this building is on fire is extremely specific to that belief. Stimulations in that category have virtually no chance of causing me to have the belief that the sky is falling, or any other logically unrelated belief. Yet the set of events that have my belief that the building is on fire as their consequence are only specific in an informational sense—they need have nothing in common from the point of view of their physical form (I could hear a shout, be handed a note, see flames, smell smoke, hear a bell that I *interpret* as a fire alarm, etc.). This kind of specificity is precisely the kind that enters into what I have referred to as rational or knowledge-dependent relations. It is what most nonbehaviorists have in mind when they talk about the sort of relation with the environment that one has when one *learns* from it. And that, in turn, is the kind of relation that appears to be absent, at least in the required amount, in cases of the acquisition of linguistic, conceptual, or some perceptual competences—or so people have argued (in my view with considerable persuasiveness).

But of course noninferential (or noncontent-specific) effects of the environment appear to be needed, even for the establishment or maintenance of the most elementary perceptual subskills, such as the detection of horizontal edges. The environment has to provide certain causal antecedents, and sometimes quite specific ones at that, in order to release, maintain, or *tune* (to use Aslin's term) the capacity. We view these influences as making changes to the cognitive mechanisms that consititute the resources out of which cognitive processes are composed. The principles by which such changes are affected are not those of inference—they are not principles of rationality or decision making or other knowledge-dependent processes. Rather the mechanisms are causally affected by the environment according to the laws of biology, chemistry, physics, and so on, inasmuch as the change in their operation is explainable in terms of their intrinsic properties and the physical properties of the environment (unlike the Morse Code and imagined color-mixing examples discussed earlier).

We thus come again to my main theme, which concerns the relativity of the variable-constant distinction in psychology. Cognitive psychology and biology are both what Fodor (1975) has called *special sciences*, which means that, unlike physics, they apply only to some restricted segment of the universe. Though the exact boundaries of the segment always remain to be discovered, we may presume that the domain of biology concerns certain properties of living things and that of cognitive psychology concerns perhaps certain classes of behaviors (e.g., not including such things as accelerating when dropped) exhibited by complex organisms (and perhaps also by certain kinds of machines—the boundaries of cognition are much more poorly understood at the present than those of biology). What counts as a universal or fixed property within such a special science need not be absolutely fixed. The only kind of constancy that can be claimed by a special science is constancy relative to its domain (immunity from influences governed by the principles of that science).

As an organism develops, some of the changes it undergoes wil be attributable to cognitive principles of learning, induction, inference to the best hypothesis, etc., whereas others will be attributable to noncognitive factors, including non-informational (nonrepresentational) properties of its internal and external environment and its genetic structure. It is axiomatic that we are in no position to pronounce on which changes fall into these different categories in the absence of the right kind of empirical evidence. In particular we need to consider evidence collected with some sensitivity to the sorts of distinctions discussed earlier (e.g., we need to examine the "cognitive penetrability" of proposed mechanisms, as I argued in Pylyshyn, 1980, 1981a). It is important to recognize that there is no a priori reason to expect that a child's repertoire of concepts, reasoning skills, linguistic skills, phonological skills, or perceptual skills must have been learned just because they are not exhibited until a certain age or until certain environmental conditions have occurred (regardless of how narrow the range of required conditions is). One must first inquire about the nature of the skill-environment relations and, as in the examples mentioned earlier, about what alternative skills are compatible with the given biological constraints.

The upshot of all this is the suggestion that the only thing that makes many of the results reported in this volume surprising is the background of existing prejudice concerning the nature of learning. We find ourselves wondering how a child could have learned to recognize which of two surfaces is further away when it hasn't had time to find out about the three-dimensional structure of the world. But perhaps the answer is: In the same way as it learns what a circle or a dog is after seeing only one exemplar, or the way it learns to walk or cry, or the way it learns which facial gesture goes with which emotion, or the way it learns that the relation expressed by the word "bigger" is transitive. And perhaps the answer to all these is that the process has nothing to do with that representation-governed process called learning, but with the way tissues grow, dendrites arborate, glands mature, protein molecules combine and transform, and so on. If it is not learning, however, then it is constant with respect to the principles of cognitive psychology, insofar as the latter constitute an independent set of principles (i.e, to the extent that cognitive science is in fact an autonomous science, as many of us believe it to be).

A useful, though not completely accurate, analogy might be to liken such noncognitive alterations of cognitive states to what might occur when the behavior of a computer is changed through some physically induced alteration to its hardware. In such a case it is possible for the physical disturbance to put the computer into a new computational state. Yet the change of state could not be treated as having been produced by symbolic means, such as would occur if new data had been read in by the program. Though both kinds of change are physical, their regularities are governed by quite different principles and they must be explained in different ways. For example, the latter kind of physically induced change cannot be understood in terms of the kind of algorithmic process that governs the behavior of the machine when the latter is executing a program, whereas the physical cause story cannot explain the program-executing form of behavioral regularity in general, because that form of regularity can arise from quite different physical causes each time it occurs.

RELEVANCE TO THE NATURE–NURTURE CONTROVERSY

The distinction we have been discussing previously also helps to cast light on the ancient nature–nurture controversy. There are really two different kinds of issues conflated in this debate. One has to do simply with the sorts of questions outlined by Aslin, such as whether particular environmental properties serve to maintain, facilitate, tune or induce certain skills, how narrowly selective the environmental properties are, and at what age the organism is most susceptible to such effects. The second has to do with the question of *how* the environment contributes to the attained competence, and in particular whether it does so by the special kind of process we call learning.

Notice that any of the questions in the first set can be asked of noncognitive states. For example, they can be asked of the growth, size, shape, and strength of various anatomical structures. One can, for example, investigate whether there are any environmental conditions that affect the growth, color, or texture of hair and skin, and if so at what ages and within what range of variation. Yet despite the wide variety of answers that one is bound to find for different properties, there is no nature–nurture controversy here. These are simply viewed as open empirical questions that may tell us a lot about how narrow the biological constraints on growth and form are, and which aspects of the final anatomical state are inexorably fixed by genetic as opposed to contingent environmental factors.

Although there may be room for considerable disagreement here, the issues have not been fraught with fundamental controversy. By contrast there are extremely strong feelings and doctrinaire positions evoked by the question of whether such cognitive states as having certain concepts, beliefs, or skills (perceptual or intellectual) could possibly be attained without learning—that is, without logical or cognitive construction from new knowledge gained from experience. But this question differs from the one in which we inquired about the role of environmental factors in the development of anatomical structures in just the following respect. It is a question of whether the environment induces the cognitive state in a *particular way,* namely by providing information that enters into cognitive processes such as inferences and that eventuates in the organism's possessing certain rules and certain beliefs.

Of course, if the organism's cognitive state is invariant over any possible environment (compatible with its survival), or if it is present at birth, we have reasonable grounds for believing that it probably isn't learned (because relevant information has either never been provided or differences in information has had no effect). But what if, as in the case of most higher order skills like linguistic or conceptual ones, certain particular environmental conditions are required for the skill to emerge. Can we conclude that such skills are *learned*?

The answer must surely be "no." The mere fact of specific environmental cause is no more reason to believe that the attained cognitive state is learned than is the fact of the influence of sunlight on skin color reason to believe that suntans are learned. Something more is required for learning. What is needed is a demonstration that the cognitive state is arrived at because the environmental conditions provided the organism with certain information about things in the world—information from which the organism was able to infer certain beliefs (or in the case of language, from which it was able to infer the rules that characterize the structure of the linguistic code).

Now if that is what is needed it should be straightforward, at least in principle, to inquire whether the specific environmental conditions that do lead to the cognitive state in question provide sufficient information (or adequate premises) for the logical construction of that state. If the answer is "yes," then learning is certainly a plausible hypothesis. If, on the other hand, the answer is something like "yes, but only if the organism makes the following additional assumptions, or if for some reason it is prohibited from considering the following alternative hypotheses,[1]," then we know at least that the state is not attained solely by learning. Something—such as the "assumptions" or the constraint that prohibits certain hypotheses—must have been achieved by methods other than learning. It must, in other words, be part of what we referred to as the mechanism. Consequently, it must either be part of the initial state or have developed from the initial state (with or without environmental influence), by noncognitive means (where by noncognitive I mean by processes that do not operate on the basis of rules and representations—are not inferential or otherwise knowledge dependent).

It is this independence from logical construction that people usually refer to when they say that some cognitive state or property is *innate*: not that it is immune from environmental influence, but that it is immune from cognitive construction out of the relevant environmentally provided information. It could involve recombinations of arbitrary complexity, but of a sort that is logically independent of the representational content of the cognitive state in question. It might even develop through the sort of "mental chemistry" that J. S. Mill alludes to in a passage discussed at length by Fodor (1981), or perhaps even through something that would qualify as an instance of the process that Piaget calls "equilibration"—but not by cognitive knowledge-dependent logical construction.

From this point of view, it is very likely that many cognitive competences are not learned and hence are innate. Such a possibility must be seriously considered once one accepts the kind of distinction I raised earlier and sheds the prejudices of behaviorism, as the participants in this volume appear to have succeeded in doing. All that remains now is the real work: to discover the nature of the competences at various stages, the nature of the regularities governing their changes (whether intrinsic or representational), and the universal (cognitively fixed) principles that constrain the form that both the competences and the developmental sequences can take.

ACKNOWLEDGMENTS

This chapter is based on informal comments presented at the end of a conference on "Neonate and Infant Cognition," sponsored by the Harry Frank Guggenheim Foundation and held at Rockefeller University, New York, November 3–6, 1981.

---

[1]This is precisely the form of some of the claims made by Wexler and Cullicover (1980).

REFERENCES

Brewer, W. F. There is no convincing evidence for operant or classical conditioning in adult humans. In W. B. Weimer & D. S. Palermo (Eds.), *Cognition and the symoblic processes*. Hillsdale, N.J.: Lawrence Erlbaum Associates, 1974.

Chomsky, N. *Reflections on language*. New York: Pantheon, 1975.

Fodor, J. A. *The language of thought*. New York: Thomas Y. Crowell, 1975.

Fodor, J. A. *Representations*. Cambridge, Mass.: Bradford Books/MIT Press, 1981.

Fodor, J. A., & Pylyshyn, Z. W. How direct is visual perception: Some reflections on Gibson's 'Ecological Approach.' *Cognition*, 1981, *9*, 139–196.

Matthews, R. J *The plausibility of rationalism*. Unpublished manuscript, 1981.

Newell, A. The knowledge level. *A.J. Magazine*, 1981, *2*, 1–20.

Piatelli–Palmarini, M. *Language and learning: The debate between Jean Piaget and Noam Chomsky*. Cambridge, Mass.: Harvard University Perss, 1980.

Pylyshyn, Z. W. Computation and cognition: Issues in the foundations of cognitive science. *The Behavioral and Brain Sciences*, 1980, *3*, 111–169.

Pylyshyn, Z. W. The imagery debate: Analog media versus tacit knowledge. *Psychological Review*, 1981, *88*, 16–45.(a)

Pylyshyn, Z. W. Psychological explanations and knowledge-dependent processes. *Cognition*, 1981, *10*, 267–274.(b)

Pylyshyn, Z. W. *Computation and cognition*. Cambridge, Mass.: Bradford Books/MIT Press, 1984.

Wexler, K., & Cullicover, P. W. *Formal principles of langauge acquisition*. Cambridge, Mass.: Bradford Books/MIT Press, 1980.

Developmental Plasticity: An Approach from Evolutionary Biology

James S. Chisholm
Department of Anthropology
University of New Mexico

Advances in major theoretical paradigms that guide productive new research in any field often follow a dialectical developmental pattern. With what I hope is taken for heuristic oversimplification only, I think it can be said, for example, that the major theoretical paradigms that have guided cognitive developmental and developmental neurobiological research over the past several decades fall on either side of the familiar nature–nurture controversy. In cognitive development, for example, we have the Piagetian constructivists on one side and the Chomskian anticonstructivists on the other. In developmental neurobiology, we have the localizationalists versus the antilocalizationalists, the preformationists versus the epigeneticists, and those who argue for specificity of neural functions versus those who argue for neural equipotentiality. Stein and Dawson (1981) have recently presented an elegantly clear general statement of the specific problem; they say:

> To give the two extreme examples, neurogenesis . . . can be viewed as the unfolding of a preprogrammed genetic plan, unaffected by the environment and not modifiable. Alternatively, neurogenesis might be conceived of as the proliferation of neural elements that make random connections among one another, with the environment supplying the information about which of the connections are adaptively significant. The capacity for sustaining adaptively significant connections would give such a nervous system great flexibility [p. 163].

Without question we must have a synthesis. As Løvtrup (1974) pointed out, if these theses and their antitheses are the only alternatives, then logically they must also be sufficient, and the solution has to lie in their synthesis. For reasons that develop as I proceed, I believe that such a synthesis of "nature" and "nurture"

417

will depend in part on an appreciation of the nature and determinants of flexibility or plasticity during behavioral development.

Any really significant breakthrough in our growing appreciation of the nature and determinants of developmental plasticity will require the identification and complete analysis of the specific causes of such plasticity of the developing organisms. At first glance, because it is not ordinarily immediately concerned with such things as "partial deafferentation of the granule cells of the hippocampal dentate gyrus," evolutionary biology would not appear to have much to say about the causes of developmental plasticity. My purpose today, however, is to suggest on the contrary that, whereas an evolutionary approach may be poorly equipped to identify the specific neural mechanisms that are the proximate causes of behavioral plasticity during development, it is well equipped to illuminate questions about the *ultimate* causes of such plasticity—or why there should be natural selection for such specific neural mechanisms in the first place. An understanding of the ultimate, evolutionary causes of developmental plasticity is not the same thing as an understanding of the neural mechanisms (the *proximate* causes) of developmental plasticity, but an understanding of the ultimate causes might begin to shed some light on why some species seem to exhibit more developmental plasticity in general. In turn, I hope, a better understanding of these evolutionary issues might provide some new insights for future research on the proximate causes of behavioral plasticity during development. I touch on many of these points in this chapter, but my focus is on the evolutionary mechanisms relating to the process of development and developmental plasticity, and my main argument is that there are good evolutionary biological reasons to expect a high degree of plasticity during human behavioral development especially.

Although it has been long recognized that the major features of species-typical patterns of development have a genetic component, are the product of natural selection, and evolve over time, more recent advances in evolutionary biology will undoubtedly have even greater implicaitons for the developmental sciences. I think the most far-reaching of these implications will turn out to have been the relatively recent identification of a continuum of important differences in species' patterns of development that includes a dimension of developmental plasticity, and a new appreciation of how and why particular broad categories of species have developed developmental patterns at one end of this continuum, whereas others have evolved developmental patterns at the opposite end. Before I can adequately describe the two ends of this continuum, however, and suggest why more developmental plasticity is found at one end than the other, I must first outline the selective forces that, over time, would be expected to increase behavioral-developmental plasticity.

At the highest level of abstraction, the concept that provides the best evolutionary theoretical rationale for the evolution of increasingly plastic behavioral development is that of environmental tracking. Put simply, environmental tracking is the evolutionary mechanism whereby natural selection produces the ubiquitous "good fit" between organism and environment. The ultimate evolutionary value of environmental tracking is that it allows populations to "follow" or "track" large-scale and long-term environmental changes with appropriate morphological and behavioral adaptations, whereas at the same time ignoring small-scale, short-term fluctuations in the environment. In the concept of environmental tracking, especially as it has been discussed by Slobodkin and Rapoport (1974), organisms are seen as possessing genetically determined "strategies" for responding to environmental perturbations that match their actual response to the various dimensions of the environmental change (i.e., its magnitude or force of impact, speed of onset, relative novelty, frequency, and duration). This matching is made possible by virtue of the fact that organisms possess a large number of response capabilities organized in an interconnected hierarchy, begining with biochemical and electrochemical responses at the level of the individual cell, proceeding through the range of reflexive and instinctive responses, on to slower but more pervasive and/or long-lasting hormonal responses, then learning responses, and on ultimately, when large numbers of a population are involved in the same environmental perturbation, to population responses in demographic and gene pool characteristics. The most immediate responses, when called into play frequently or for long periods of time, serve to trigger the slower responses. These slower responses may reset the response thresholds of the quicker responses (thus helping them to alleviate the stress associated with the environmental perturbation), or they may serve to trigger still slower and deeper responses. The very slowest responses are the most costly to the organism, because they have such extensive effects on the potential flexibility of all the faster responses above them in the response hierarchy, and because these slowest responses reduce potential flexibility by reducing variability in the gene pool. Figure 22.1 is a schematic representation of a hierarchy of responses to environmental perturbations.

Behavior in general, and perhaps especially social behavior, are good examples of environmental tracking devices. There has been an evolutionary trend toward more complex behavioral organization, because behavioral responses to environmental perturbations tend to provide a high degree of response flexibility that protects the slower, deeper, and only potentially flexible response capacities latent in the gene pool. An appreciation of the reasons for natural selection for behavioral plasticity can be gained from a brief look at the game theory analog of the process of adaptation by natural selection envisioned by Slobodkin and Rapoport. The game is called Gambler's Ruin, and it may be likened to a unique game of poker in which all players have a fixed number of poker chips, each promises to stay in the game indefinitely, and each promises to wager something, no matter how little, on each hand (which corresponds to each environmental perturbation). The strangest rule of this game is that when a player loses all his chips, he is dead. Clearly, there is only one strategy for playing this ultimately losing game: Players should minimize their bets in order to maximize their chances of simply staying in the game. Phrased in evolutionary terms, this means that species that evolved the means of minimizing their bets—more sophisticated

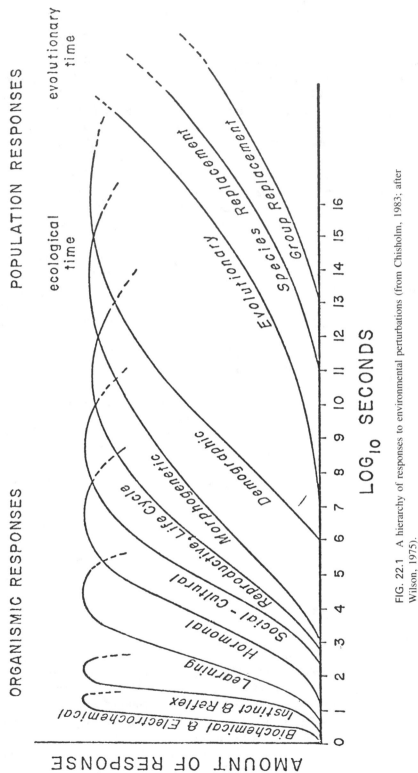

FIG. 22.1 A hierarchy of responses to environmental perturbations (from Chisholm, 1983; after Wilson, 1975).

and finely turned environmental tracking systems—have been able to stay in the game longer.

Slobodkin and Rapoport envisage a *scala naturae*, in which there has been a broad evolutionary trend toward increasingly sophisticated and fine-tuned environmental tracking systems that seem to have reached their most perfect form in H. sapiens. The essence of this response strategy is the same as that of the mimimax strategy in Gambler's Ruin: The least costly, lowest stake, and quickest responses are made first. If the environmental perturbation to which these responses are made is short or unique, and/or if the responses are successful, then stress associated with the perturbation has been alleviated with little cost to the organism's capacity to respond successfully to future perturbations. If the initial perturbation, however, is more severe, lasting, or repeated, these quick and only minimally costly responses may not suffice to remove the stress of the perturbation, and they may be called into play more often or for longer periods of time. They may themselves thus become a set of perturbations that serve to trigger slower, deeper, more costly, and less-flexible response capacities. For example, moving to high altitude constitutes an environmental perturbation because of the lower concentration of atmospheric oxygen. Simple panting constitutes a successful response to this perturbation for a short time, but, if one remains at high altitude for long periods, this panting becomes stressful to the heart and lungs. The new perturbation of panting for long periods thus serves to trigger deeper and slower response capacities that increase lung volume and heart pumping capacity and alter blood chemistry. These physiological responses are slower than the panting reflex and are most costly in the way they actually reduce adaptive potential and response flexibility because they are such slow and long-lasting responses.

Thus, Slobodkin and Rapoport argue that in the evolutionary long run plasticity in immediate behavioral responses to the environment will be selected, because this behavioral plasticity tends to protect and conserve the adaptative potential of the slower, deeper, and more costly physiological, demographic, and population genetic response capacities. These latter responses are ultimately the least flexible and most costly ways of responding to the environment, for responses at the level of the gene pool will use up genetic variability and may depend on just the right mutation occurring or on there already existing in the gene pool just the right set of alleles for recombination to bring into play. In this view of the evolution of progressively more complex environmental tracking systems, there will be directional selection for what Waddington (1968) has called an "essential indeterminancy" (p. 364) in the ontogenetic effect of the genotype on the phenotype, because the genotype will be altered more and more often only when the phenotypical responses (especially the most immediate ones) made at each higher level in the response hierarchy have been at least partially effective in removing the stress of an environmental perturbation. This is because in hierarchically interconnected environmental tracking systems stress is information that the slower and deeper response systems can "use" to alter their values. In sum, the concept of environmental tracking advanced by Slobodkin and Rapoport holds that natural selection will tend to favor increased behavioral plasticity, because the sufficient and most proximate causes of behavior are generally to be found in the organism's environment, whereas only the necessary and most ultimate causes (i.e., the general capacity for the behavior) are found in the organism's genotype. Thus, natural selection will tend to favor phenotypes that are less strictly determined by the nature of the genotype.

Having briefly introduced the abstract theoretical concept of environmental tracking, it is now possible to move on to a more concrete discussion of the evolution of developmental patterns in general, and the evolution of developmental plasticity among hominids in particular. The major impetus for evolutionary biology's recently renewed interest in the relationship between phylogeny and ontogeny comes from an appreciation of the adaptive significance of different patterns of organisms' life histories in different environments. For example, Dobzhansky (1950) noted 30 years ago that the survival and reproductive success of some organisms depended more on essentially random environment events, whereas that of other organisms was more directly a function of the qualities of their phenotypes. The reason for this continuum of relative differences is that there is a broad dimension of differences in organisms' environments that causes natural selection to operate in two general modes where effects also vary along a continuum. At one end of the continuum, in environments where there are periodic catastrophic rates of selection and large numbers of a species are killed for essentially random reasons, natural selection tends to select for characteristics of the organism that allow it to rapidly recover from severe population depressions. This mode of natural selection is termed *r-selection*, because it tends to maximize the organism's natural *rate* of increase. At the other end of the continuum, in environments where selection pressures are more constant and less random, natural selection tends to select for characteristics of the organism that improve its efficiency in exploiting resources in that environment. This mode of natural selection is termed *K-selection*, for populations in relatively constant environments are typically at, or near, the inherent *carrying capacity* of that environment. Species are said to be r- or K-selected or r- or K-strategists, but no species is ever completely one or the other; there is always some compromise between the two selection modes, and the difference between any r-selected and K-selected species is always relative.

Because of major environmental differences and corresponding differences in the mode of natural selection, a conspicuous set of differences between r- and K-selected species lies in their reproductive strategies. The essence of the r-strategy is to quickly transmit as many copies of parental genes as soon as possible into the next generation. This is an adaptation to periodic "boom and bust" cycles in population size, and the evolutionary advantage of this strategy is obvious: Individuals able to reproduce themselves more rapidly and/or in greater numbers are disproportionately represented in the next generation by virtue of their head start in filling available niche space. On the other hand, as an adaptation to the higher levels of intraspecific competition that are usually characteristic of populations at or near carrying capacity, the essence of the K-strategy is to ensure that at least *some* copies of parental genes are represented in the next generation. In populations at or near carrying capacity, because there is no evolutionary advantage in having large numbers of offspring (for this would increase already high rates of intraspacific competition and endanger the survival of any offspring at all), selection pressures work for increased efficiency in the exploitation of scarce resources in relatively crowded econiches. Most weeds, fishes, insects, and rodents are examples of relatively r-selected species, whereas large birds, elephants, the higher primates, and especially humans are examples of relatively K-selected species. Some of the more salient distinguishing features of r- and K-selected species are listed in Table 22.1.

At least in a general way, the essence of K-selection can be said to be "fewer and better offspring." Most accounts of r- and K-selection interpret "better" as meaning increased efficiency in the exploitation of resources, but another interpretation is that one aspect of "better" includes more sophisticated and finely tuned environmental tracking mechanisms and a higher degree of behavioral plasticity. This is because with a more constant and predictable environment, high intraspecific competition, and more density-dependent and directed mortality, natural selection is simply less random, and K-selected organisms are more likely to be selected against because of some real inefficiency in the way they respond to particular environmental perturbations. Pianka (1970), for example, has noted that the large body size and long-life characteristic of K-selected organisms are but two K-selected traits that by themselves tend to increase the

TABLE 22.1
General Characteristics of r- and K-Selected Species

r-Selected	(← Relative →)	K-Selected
Variable or uncertain environment		More constant or predictable environment
Recolonization of empty niches		Constant occupation of same niche
Mortality rates often catastrophic, nondirected		Mortality rates steadier, more directed
Variability in population size		Stability in population size
Intraspecific competition nil		Intraspecific competition keen
Many offspring		Few offspring
Low parental investment		High parental investment
Small body size		Large body size
Short birth interval		Long birth interval
Rapid development		Slow development
Early reproduction		Delayed reproduction
Short life		Long life
Social behavior often simple or weak		Social behavior often complex

Note: From Chisholm, in 1983 (after Pianka, 1970; Wilson, 1975).

organism's adaptability by "buffering" it from environmental perturbations. Having longer lives, K-selected organisms have been selected to develop successful responses to a wider temporal range of environmental cycles and vicissitudes; being larger, they tend to have fewer predators and are (Pianka, 1970): "better buffered from changes in the physical environment [p. 49]." This sort of "buffering" is precisely what is selected for in more sophisticated, complex, and finely tuned environmental tracking systems.

The most significant way that K-selection has operated to produce "fewer and better offspring," however, has probably been through specific selection for individual ontogenetic patterns that are retarded relative to ancestral species. The natural selective basis for more efficient life-history strategies or developmental patterns is well established in evolutionary theory (Cutler, 1976; Gadgil & Bossert, 1970; Stearns, 1976), and the endocrine bases of rates of physical growth and development and sexual maturation are known to have a genetic component (Tanner, 1978). Generally, retarded development is a distinguishing characteristic of K-selected species and represents a major dimension of their more complex and finely tuned mechanisms for tracking environmental changes through behavior. One important reason for natural selection for retarded development in populations at or near carrying capacity is that, with a relatively long period of infant or juvenile dependency and delayed sexual maturity, individuals become more efficient in exploiting resources and responding to environmental changes, because they have more protected time for learning about their environments before they become independent adults.

Simultaneously, there is also a complex interaction between selection for more efficient life-history strategies (i.e., retarded development) and selection for the other hallmark of K-selection, increased levels of parental investment. The interaction of these selection pressures is such that selection for retarded development would be a concomitant of selection for increased parental investment, and vice versa. The reason for this is that because there is a strong correlation between total life-span and such developmental components of total life-span as length of gestation, age at sexual maturity, birth spacing, and period of infant dependency (Cutler, 1976), direct selection for prolonged periods of infant dependency or delayed sexual maturity will tend to be associated with increased life-span. Prolonged periods of infant dependency and delayed sexual maturity will then themselves exert selection pressure for increased parental investment, because parents must be vigilant for longer periods and may have to play a greater teaching role. Selection for longer life per se would also, by itself, give parents more time to invest in their offspring even well after the last one was born.

Another reason for natural selection for retarded development in some K-selected mammals stems directly from the adapative effects of selection for increased parental investment. Goodman (1963), for example, notes that the evolution of the more efficient higher mammalian hemochorial placenta was a prerequisite for the development of the large hominid brain, for the neocortex is especially easily damaged by fetal hypoxia, and a rich supply of both nutrients and oxygen is required for neural differentiation. He argues thus that the appearance of the more efficient hemochorial placenta could have engendered specific selection for delayed development in higher mammalian young. The reason for this is that the primitive mammalian epitheliochorial placenta is less efficient than the higher mammalian hemochorial placenta, in that the former maintains a greater separation between the maternal and fetal circulations, whereas the latter permits more effective placental transfer by bringing the maternal and fetal circulations into more intimate contact. This constitutes greater parental investment in higher mammals with the more efficient hemochorial placenta. Goodman notes too, however, that the close contact between higher mammal maternal and fetal circulations could well bring the maternal immune system into play as a significant prenatal environmental factor to which the higher mammalian fetus would have to adapt, because any new genetic material, from whatever source, would create new fetal proteins that would more easily cross the hemochorial placenta and would thus more easily stimulate the maternal immune system to produce antibodies against the new protein. When this occurred the survival and normal development of the fetus would be increasingly problematical. Goodman suggests that under these conditions there would be selection for a shortened period of gestation and/or for the postponement of the expression of new genetic material until after birth. New genetic material that was expressed only postnatally would have the selective advantage of not provoking the maternal immunological system, but postponing the expression of new genetic material until after birth would also have the effect of postponing the development of the hominid child, making him even more helpless at birth and requiring even more postnatal parental investment.

The selection pressures for retarded development and for increased parental investment interact in another way as well, one that is especially relevant to any consideration of hominid phylogeny. On a *scala naturae* the K-selective trend toward increased parental investment is clearly evident in such major evolutionary steps as internal fertilization, internal gestation, lactation, and the development of close maternal–offspring bonding. With each of these steps there was an increase in the probability of survival of zygotes, fetuses, newborns, and infants, but there was at the same time a corresponding decrease in the total number of offspring any female could bear in her lifetime, because increased parental investment, by observation and definition (Trivers, 1972), lowers the parent's ability to invest in *other* offspring. What one gains in "quality" (increased survivorship), one loses in "quantity." For example, consider increased parental investment through the evolution of longer gestation. By investing in a fetus for several months, a mammalian female reduces the total number of offspring she might bear in her entire life if she invested in a fetus for only a few weeks. One aspect of K-selection for increased parental investment then is a corresponding selection pressure for a longer life, during which parents may increase their reproductive potential simply by bearing and rearing more offspring.

Lovejoy (1981) has recently argued that this interplay between the K-selective pressures for retarded development-prolonged life and increased parental investment had a determining role in early hominid evolution. His argument is that:

> the total reproductive rate of a primate species can remain constant with progressive increases in longevity only if the mortality rate is correspondingly reduced. Actual mortality rate is dependent on both maximum life potential, a genetic factor, and environmental interaction. Deaths caused by predation, accident, parasitism, infection, failure of food supply, and so forth, are at least partially stochastic events beyond the complete control of the organism. Only if mechanisms are developed to increase an organism's resistance to such factors can the effects of increased longevity be reproductively accommodated. Strong social bonds, high levels of intelligence, intense parenting, and long periods of learning are among the factors used by higher primates to depress environmenally induced mortality. It is of some interest that such factors also require greater longevity (for brain development, learning, acquisition of social and parenting skills) and that they constitute reciprocal links leading to greater longevity [p. 343].

In other words, Lovejoy is suggesting that straightforward demographic pressures were important selective forces behind the emergence of the hominid line, because as longevity increased, as a direct result of K-selection, so too did length of gestation, age at sexual maturity, birth spacing, and period of infant dependency, and the reproductive rate of the early hominids decreased to the point where, for there to be any reproductive success at all, there had to be even greater parental investment. In Lovejoy's model of early hominid evolution, it is the reciprocal feedback between retarded development-prolonged life and increased parental investment that sets up the selection pressures for the later hominid evolution of bipedalism, the separation of roles by sex, human sexual morphology and behavior, the home base, the nuclear family and the development and elaboration of male parental investment. Lovejoy (1981) notes that many alternate models of human origins have emphasized: "singular, extraordinary traits of later human evolution [p. 348]," and one of the attractions of his model is that it derives these later, uniquely human traits from a well-established base line of K-selection in the higher primates.

Gould (1977) has also recently outlined a model of human evolution that stresses the unique role of K-selection and retarded development. The crux of his argument is that the most important determinant of human evolution is the increasing K-selective trend toward neoteny. Neoteny is defined as the retention of juvenile characteristics of ancestors by their adult descendants, and it is brought about by natural selection for retarded rates of somatic development. Gould does not in any way suggest that ontogeny recapitulates phylogeny. Ontogeny does not recapitulate phylogeny. Because evolution is opportunistic, building on what it has already produced, the earliest embryological and developmental stages tend to be conserved, whereas evolution adds later stages on to them. Therefore, ontogeny does not recapitulate phylogeny, but ontogeny tends to recapitulate the earlier ontogenetic stages of ancestors. The effect is that the early developmental forms of ancestors and the early developmental forms of descendants tend to resemble each other more than the later, adult stages do.

The centerpiece of Gould's model of hominid evolution is that there was natural selection for retarded somatic development because individuals possessing the morphological and behavioral effects of retarded development (i.e., neoteny) had a greater reproductive success and were more adapative and efficient in the highly K-selective regime that characterized early hominid environments. The crucial adaptive significance of neoteny in K-selective environments stems from two related effects of retarded development. First, by postponing sexual maturity (by slowing the rate of somatic growth and/or by prolonging the period of somatic growth), any given aspect of morphology or behavior is simply given more time to grow. With more time to grow, neotenous, K-selected organisms thus also tend to have longer lives and larger body sizes, two features that by themselves tend to "buffer" the animal against environmental perturbations (as Pianka, 1970, pointed out earlier). Second, and especially important in hominid evolution, by slowing the rate of somatic growth and/or by extending its period, any given aspect of morphology or behavior is also given more time to differentiate. Growth is not simply a unidimensional increase in size but obviously also includes development, differentiation, and an increase in organizational complexity. Because neotenous organisms develop for relatively longer periods, neurological organization can proceed further than it did in ancestral forms. This increase in organizational complexity by itself tends to increase adaptability, because it makes possible more varied responses to environmental changes— which is the essense and function of more sophisticated and finely tuned environmental tracking mechanisms (see also Doering, 1980; Vermeij, 1973).

Gould enumerates many aspects of human morphology and behavior that qualify as examples of neoteny, but one aspect of retarded development that is most significant in this context of increased differentiation and organizational complexity is the extension of the period of growth of the human brain. A good way to see this extended development is to look at neonatal cranial capacity as a percentage of adult cranial capacity in a number of species: In many mammals it is virtually 100%, in rhesus monkeys it is 60%, in chimpanzees it is about 40%, and in humans it drops to only 23% (Gould, 1977, pp. 371–372). It has also been estimated that neonatal australopithecines had a cranial capacity somewhere between 24 and 37% of the adult—showing a degree of retardation in development intermediate between the Pongids and Homo (Leutenegger, 1972; in Gould, 1977; p. 372). Similarly, Holt, Cheek, Mellits, and Hill (1975) plotted brain weight against body weight from early in prenatal development to adult weights in four primate species, including humans. Interestingly, all four species showed the same rate of prenatal growth. However, in the three monkey and ape species, the prenatal growth rate fell off dramatically at around the time of birth, whereas in humans the high rate of prenatal brain growth was extended a full 2 years after birth. Some part of this greatly extended period of growth in humans is due to the general K-selective pressure for retarded development, but a large part of it is also due to the unique selection pressure in hominids for "premature" birth, so that the increasingly large head of the newborn may pass through the mother's pelvic girdle. The pelvis, of course, is under a selection pressure for narrowing as an adaptation for bipedal locomotion.

This extension of the period of hominid brain growth has a number of interesting implications. One that Gould suggests is that the extension of the period of brain growth might be related to the marked and sudden increase in hominid cranial capacity from an australopithecine average of only about 500cc. to a modern *H. sapiens* average of over 1,300cc. in perhaps less than 2 million years. His neoteny hypotheses is not incompatible with any of the several other hypotheses that have been put forth to account for this dramatic increase, but it is an attractive candidate for primacy because, as in Lovejoy's model, brain enlargement through prolonged development is a phenomenon that would follow quite automatically from the already well-established base line of fairly intensive K-selection in the higher nonhuman primates. Evidence that the australopithecines had already achieved a relatively retarded period of development comes from Leutenegger's data on neonatal cranial capacity already mentioned and from Mann's (1975) data on australopithecine dental wear gradients. His analyses of australopithecine dental remains revealed a strong positive correlation between order of molar eruption and degree of dental wear—a correlation that does not obtain with the earlier late pongid fossil forms. This correlation indicates that the period of australopithecine development was now sufficiently long for significant wearing of each molar to occur before the next one erupted.

Although it is necessarily only speculation, one of the most far-reaching implications of the K-selection for greatly extended periods of hominid brain growth, in combination with the selection for relatively shortened periods of gestation, lies in their effects on the epigenetic patterns of the early hominids and the reciprocal selection pressures that this neoteny itself would begin to exert. For at least 2 million years, newborn hominids were presented to their social and physical environments for as long as 2 years with brains that were less mature, less developed, and less differentiated than were those of their immediate ancestors, the pongids and transitional hominids. Accordingly, for these 2 million years, natural selection had 2 years in each individual's life to operate on hominid phenotypes that were more flexible, more sensitive, and more responsive to their social and physical environments than had earlier been the case. Common to all developmental sciences is the generalization that earlier developmental stages tend to be more plastic, more responsive, more open to environmental influences than later ones; Lynch and Gall (1979), for example, in a recent review of neurobiological concepts of developmental plasticity, conclude that the available evidence indicates that: "the most dramatic examples of nervous system flexibility have been found in immature animals [p. 138]." Jacobson (1969) suggests that a neurological basis for this earlier flexibility lies in the greater capacity of immature neurons to establish new connections:

> During ontogeny, there is evidence of a progressive reduction of the capacity to form new neuronal connections and to modify existing ones. This reduction occurs at different times in different classes of neurons, so that those which are generated late in ontogeny and those which mature slowly have the greatest modifiablity in the mature animal. According to this theory, the modifiability of neuronal connections in the adult is regarded as a continuation of developmental processes that are much more pronounced in embryos [p. 547].

Thus, prolonging the period and reducing the rate of early hominid development also prolonged the flexibility characteristic of early developmental stages into later developmental stages, and, perhaps, to a lesser degree, even into adulthood.

In addition to increasing and prolonging developmental flexibility, however, K-selection for retarded and prolonged development would at the same time have set up reciprocal selection pressures affecting the developmental environment of young hominids in some most fundamental ways. With the initial K-selected prolongation of development and consequent increase in the period of infant dependency, perhaps the only avenue to parental reproductive success would have been through increased parental investment. With the marked secondary increase in the early helplessness of the hominid infant as a result of restructuring the pelvis for bipedal locomotion, there would have been even greater selection for increased levels of parental investment. According to most models of human origins and according to the most recent formulations of behavioral ecology, the only remaining avenue to increased parental investment was through increasing male parental investment specifically. Mammalian morphology and physiology ensured that the bulk of parental investment (e.g., gestation and lactation) would remain the province of hominid females, but high levels of intelligence and sociability and complex patterns of social organization (e.g., elaborate dominance relations, matrilineal kin groups, some sharing, and the capacity for at least transient pair bonding) among the higher primates made it possible for males to invest significantly in offspring through investment in females. As Lovejoy (and others) have suggested, this is a likely basis for such uniquely hominid (or human) features as the loss of estrus, the home base, sharing and the sexual division of labor, and the nuclear family. All these secondary adaptations to prolonged development altered the environment of hominid infancy by making it more intensely and constantly social. It is also likely that the environment of hominid infancy would be made more widely social as well: With prolonged development younger siblings of both sexes would more frequently be born before older siblings had acquired much independence, and with prolonged life-spans grandparents and other older adults would more frequently still be alive before children had acquired much independence. Prolonged periods of development in such groups, along with neotenous early flexibility and sensitivity to social-environmental learning and the pre-existing higher primate capacity to form close maternal-infant bonds, may have set the stage, some 2 million years ago, for the extension of these emotional bonds to others within the group. If one takes a behavioral ecological approach to the evolution of extreme sociality rather than a strictly phylogenetic approach, the social carnivores provide here an instructive parallel: Not only are they among the most intensely social of all nonprimate mammals, they are also relatively retarded in their development. Thus, according to Versluys and Lorenz (1939) (in Gould, 1977), it is more than simply a figure of speech to say: "Retardation is the biological basis for societal life [p. 403]."

There are, then, good evolutionary biological reasons for viewing *Homo sapiens* as an animal unique by virtue of its phylogenetic history of natural selection for increased behavioral plasticity. The abstract theoretical concept of environmental tracking suggests that in the long run adaptability or plasticity in immediate behavioral responses to environmental perturbations should be selected for, because this immediate sensitivity or responsiveness to the environment tends to protect and conserve the adapative potential of the slower, deeper, and more costly response capacities latent in the gene pool. The phenomenon of K-selection provides a specific evolutionary mechanism, whereby natural selection could achieve an increase in the adaptability or plasticity of response capacities, because under K-selection, mortality depends less on random factors and more on the efficiency of the organism in a specific environment. At least in a general sense, the phylogenetic history of K-selection in the human line is very deep: Mammals are usually more K-selected than other orders, and the fossil hominids seem to have been more K-selected than other classes, primates are usually more K-selected than other orders, and the fossil hominids seem to have been more K-selected than modern primate families are today. Certainly, modern humans are among the most K-selected of all species. Perhaps the most widespread and significant mechanism whereby K-selection tends to increase adaptability and plasticity is that of retarded development. With K-selected, neotenous retardation of somatic development, hominid infants were not only given more protected time for learning, they were also better able to learn, being presented to their environments for longer periods in a state that was less final, less differentiated and at the same time more sensitive, more reponsive, and more flexible. Under these developmental conditions (for a minimum of 2, and as many as 10 or 15 million years), the survival of the hominid infant depended more and more on steadily increasing and complex forms of female and male parental investment. At the same time, because the hominid infant was in such a relatively unfinished, sensitive, responsive, and flexible developmental condition for longer periods, natural selection on hominid infants and juveniles (which must have been intense) would have been increasingly on the epigenetic effects of their early sensitivity, responsivity, and flexibility. Being more sensitive or responsive to the early environments, and living in increasingly complex, intense, and permanent social (and cultural) environments, the survival of hominid infants would depend more and more on their capacity to be socialized. This growing developmental plasticity would provide a quantum increase in their adaptability and the sophistication of early hominid environmental tracking mechanisms by making it possible to preserve adaptive responses to environmental perturbations in the individual's social-cultural environment.

To conclude, I suggest in broad outline some of the ways that the evolutionary approach to developmental plasticity I have discussed here might contribute to future research in cognitive and neurobiological development. First, at the most abstract level, this approach provides a powerful evolutionary biological rationale for models of development that emphasize flexibility or plasticity of behavior in the developing organism. This is because such an approach predicts increasing degrees of developmental plasticity as one ascends the *scala naturae* and because it describes *ultimate* causal mechanisms whereby this plasticity would be selected for. Such support for models of development that emphasize plasticity, however, obviously does not constitute support for any extreme environmentalist position, for in the evolutionary approach I have presented, developmental plasticity is itself an evolved trait with adaptive significance and is heritable.

Second, an evolutionary approach to questions about developmental plasticity might contribute in a more immediate way to the search for the proximal neural mechanisms that underlie the expression of behavioral plasticity during development. Evolutionary biology is not itself equipped to describe these proximal mechanisms, but by explicitly treating developmental plasticity as an evolved trait with adaptive significance, an evolutionary approach might suggest new research strategies. One such strategy would involve application of the classic comparative method of evolutionary biology to questions about the differences in degree of developmental plasticity within and across various taxa. The classical comparative method of evolutionary biology might, for example, help developmental neurobiologists narrow their search for the specific neural structures and processes serving developmental plasticity: Because species can be at least roughly arranged on a continuum of r- and K-selection, and because developmental plasticity is a major dimension of differences on this continuum, then those specific neural structures and processes serving developmental plasticity should also arrange themselves in a similar way along the same continuum. Likewise, because the continuum of differences in developmental plasticity shown by r- and K-selected species seems to be generally correlated with a similar continuum of differences in rates and periods of growth and development, it should also be possible to at least roughly determine whether or not the specific mechanisms producing developmental plasticity cluster according to these differences in species' rates and periods of growth. Any neural mechanism, for example, that was a candidate for a proximal cause of developmental plasticity should be more commonly found, or found in a more complex or developed state, in species with relatively retarded or prolonged development. Further, because the continuum of differences in developmental plasticity shown by r- and K-selected species is ultimately determined by differences in the mode of natural selection according to large-scale environmental factors, it should be possible also to establish whether or not the proximal mechanisms of developmental plasticity cluster in some way according to these large-scale environmental differences. For example, because behavioral plasticity is more characteristic of K-selected species and because K-selection is strongest in populations at or near the carrying capacity of their environment, then the proximal mechanisms of developmental plasticity should be found more often or in more developed form in species with a long history of being at or near carrying capacity. Similarly, because mortality is more directed and density dependent in K-selected species, the proximal mechanisms of developmental plasticity should be found more often in species where there has been a long history of density-dependent mortality. To my knowledge no one has ever attempted to determine whether or not r- or K-selected species differ in any physiological or neurobiological way, even within broad taxa, but evolutionary theory would predict systematic differences in any neural structures or processes that served the observed and adaptive systematic differences in reproductive strategy, body size, life-span, sociability, patterns of development, and especially in developmental plasticity. I need not belabor the point that demonstrating any systematic differences in cognitive or neurobiological development along the r–K continuum would have immense implications for evolutionary biology.

REFERENCES

Chisholm, J. S. *Navajo infancy: An ethological study of child development.* New York: Aldine, 1983.

Cutler, R. G. Evolution of longevity in primates. *Journal of Human Evolution*, 1976, *5*, 169–202.

Dobzhansky, T. Evolution in the tropics. *American Scientist*, 1950, *38*, 209–21.

Doering, C. H. The endocrine system. In Orville G. Brim & Jerome Kagan (Eds.), *Constancy and change in human development.* Cambridge, Mass: Harvard University Press, 1980.

Gadgil, M., & Bossert, W. H. Life historical consequences of natural selection. *American Naturalist*, 1970, *104*, 1–24.

Goodman, M. Man's place in the phylogeny of the primates as reflected in serum proteins. In S. L. Washburn (Ed.), *Classification and human evolution.* Chicago: Aldine, 1963.

Gould, S. J. *Ontogeny and phylogeny.* Cambridge, Mass.: Harvard University Press, 1977.

Holt, A. B., Cheek, D. B., Mellits, E. D., & Hill, D. E. Brain size and the relation of the primate to the nonprimate. In D. B. Cheek (Ed.), *Fetal and postnatal cellular growth: Hormones and nutrition.* New York: Wiley, 1975.

Jacobson, M. Development of specific neuronal connections. *Science,* 1969, *163,* 543–547.

Leutenegger, W. Newborn size and pelvic dimensions of Australopithecus. *Nature,* 1972, *240,* 568–69.

Lovejoy, C. O. The origin of man. *Science,* 1981, *211,* 341–350.

Løvtrup, S. *Epigenetics: A treatise on theoretical biology.* New York: Wiley, 1974.

Lynch, G. & Gall, C. Organization and reorganization in the central nervous system: evolving concepts of brain plasticity. In F. Falkner & J. M. Tanner (Eds.), *Human growth, Vol. 3. Neurobiology and nutrition.* New York: Plenum, 1979.

Mann, A. E. Paleodemographic aspects of the South African australopithecines. University of Pennsylvania Publications in Anthropology, 1975, *1,* 171.

Pianka, E. R. On r- and K-selection. *American Naturalist,* 1980, *104,* 592–597.

Slobodkin, L., & Rapoport, A. An optimal strategy of evolution. *Quarterly Review of Biology,* 1974, *49,* 181–200.

Stein, D. G., & Dawson, R. G. The dynamics of growth, organization, and adaptability in the central nervous system. In Orville G. Brim & Jerome Kagan (Eds.), *Constancy and change in human development.* Cambridge, Mass.: Harvard University Press, 1980.

Tanner, J. M. *Fetus into man: Physical growth from conception to maturity.* Cambridge, Mass.: Harvard University Press, 1978.

Trivers, R. L. Parental investment and sexual selection. In B. Campbell (Ed.), *Sexual selection and the descent of man.* Chicago: Aldine, 1972.

Vermeij, G. J. Adaptation, versatility, and evolution. *Syst. Zool.,* 1973, *22,* 466–477.

Wilson, E. O. *Sociobiology, the new synthesis.* Cambridge: Harvard University Press, 1975.

Author Index

Subject Index

A

Accommodation, linkage to convergence, 176–178

Accuracy, 399

Acetylcholine
binding of, 268
response of xenopus oocytes to, 276

Acoustic characteristics of speech, variation in, 186

Acoustic cues, 277
"trading relations" between, 247

Acoustic events, organization of, 11

Acoustic features, rearrangements of, 193

Acoustic information
perception of, 189
processing of, 189
language environment and, 213–14, 214n
weighting of, 221–22

Acoustic invariants, 187

Acoustic stimulation, in anencephalic infants, 368

Acoustic stimuli
multiple, habituation to vowel categorization and, 243–45
sorting of, 6, 7, 11, 254, 255f

Acoustic units, processing of, 191–92

"Action withholding," 297

Activations, states of, 6

Active intermodal matching (AIM), in imitation, 153–54
social development and, 154–55

Acuity. *See* Visual acuity

Adaptation, by natural selection, 419, 420

Adenosine triphosphatase (ATPase), 268

Adult(s)
aphasia in, 334
evidence for speech modes in, 210–12
phonological rule systems, 256
speech perception in, 217, 217n

Adult dextrals
crossed aphasia in, 336
right hemisphere lesions in, 338–42

Aggression, cognitive apparatus and, 29

Agronomy, 33

Alertness
of infant, 369
level, in newborn, role of posture in, 370

Ambidexterity, 316

Ambiguity(ies)
criteria for, 392
systematic M violation and, 393

Amblyopia (lazy eye), 40, 41
develoment of, 173
onset of, 41

American Sign Language (ASL), 354, 358

Ames trapezoidal window. *See* Trapezoidal window studies

Amnestic aphasia, 337

Amplification, oligogenic mechanism of, 275–76

Amytal testing, 332, 338

Gene(s), 265
  -environment interactions, experiential influence on, 157
Gene expression, 272
Gene mutation, 274
Genetic constraints, experiential influences on, 161, 162–67, 170
Genetic control, brain symmetry and deviation, 319f, 320
Genetic determinism, 272
  of nervous system organization, limits of, 273–74
Genetic envelope, 83, 274, 278
  genes composing, 279
Genetic factors, for defining of speech area, 333
Genetic transmission, evolution mediated by, 139
Genetics, 34. *See also* Nongenetic information behavior, 34
Genome, complexity of, nervous system complexity and, 272–73
"Genuine imitation," 142
Gestalt principles, 397
  of temporal proximity, 12
Gestalt psychologists, 90
Gestalt psychology, 11
Gestation
  internal, 425
  length of, 426
Glial cells
  cell categories of, 266
  migration of, 314
  proliferation of, 313
Glucose, 302
Grammar(s), 1–2, 16
  acquisition of, 358
  universal, 3
Grammatical behavior, 21
Grammatical functions, brain areas for, 15
Grasping reflex, 369
Grating acuity, 38
Gray matter, 313

H

Habituation procedure, for experiments on perception of partly-occluded objects, 90–91
Handedness, 15
  genetic control over, 319
HAS paradigm, 240

Head control, 369
Head movement. *See* Backward head movement
Head turn
  operant. *See* Operant head turn responses
  in consonant categorization, 250–51, 252f
  in vowel categorization, data on, 245, 246f
  technique, for speech categorization, 235
Hemidecortication, effect on language behavior, 15, 16
Hemiplegia, 342
Hemispherectomy, language ability following, 311
Hemorrhage, 376
Heterotopia, 312, 312n
High-amplitude sucking, for study of categorization of auditory stimuli, 236–37
Histology of nervous system, 265
Home base, 426, 430
Homer and the Homeric Age (Gladstone), 120
Hominid brain growth, extension of period, 428–29
Hominid evolution, 426, 427
Hominid infant, survival of, 431
Hue, maintenance and attunement applied to, 132–33
Hue categories, 117, 118
  animal studies on, 125, 127f
  perception and, 136
  visual, 123
Hue foci, 117
Human development. *See* Development
"Human nature," doctrines of, 31
Humanism versus religious dogma, 30–31
Hydroanencephalic newborn, integrative behavior in, 368
Hypothesis testing, M constraint and, 391
Hypotonia, in brain damage of perinatal origin, 375–76

I

Identity of objects, perception of, 89, 104–108
Illinois Test of Psycholinguistic Abilities (ITPA), 311
Illiterates, aphasia in, 342–44
Image(s)
  alignment on retina, 37–38
  formation of, constraints in, 64
Imagery, 5
Imitation, 5, 139–56
  basic questions in, 142–43